EXISTENTIALISM

Father Charles E. Miller, C.M. has
been Professor of Homiletics at St.
John's Seminary, Camarillo, California
(the major seminary for the arch-
diocese of Los Angeles) since 1956.
He is the author of several books and
many articles.

EXISTENTIALISM

WITH OR WITHOUT GOD

by Francis J. Lescoe

ALBA · HOUSE NEW · YORK

SOCIETY OF ST. PAUL, 2187 VICTORY BLVD., STATEN ISLAND, NEW YORK 10314

Library of Congress Cataloging in Publication Data

Lescoe, Francis J.
    Existentialism: with or without God.

    Bibliography: p.
    1. Existentialism. I. Title.
B819.L466   142'.7   74-1427

ISBN: 0-8189-0340-6

*Designed, printed and bound in the United States of
America by the Fathers and Brothers of the Society of St. Paul,
2187 Victory Boulevard, Staten Island, New York, 10314,
as part of their communications apostolate.*

4 5 6 7 8 9 (Current Printing: first digit).

Patri matrique qui Dominum mihi dederunt

Author's Preface

The aim of this small volume is both modest and unpretentious. While there are many excellent and in-depth studies of individual existentialists, as well as of existentialism itself, there seems to be a real need for a work which could serve as a text-book for a beginners' course in contemporary existentialism. Thus arose the idea of writing *Existentialism: With or Without God*, which would introduce the student to some of the more important existentialist themes.

Clearly, it was an absolute impossibility to include all of the existentialist thinkers in such an introductory volume. The author was, therefore, faced with two options: either (1) he could treat most of the better-known existentialists in a necessarily cursory and superficial manner or (2) he could limit his introductory remarks to a select group of representative thinkers.

The latter option was made and six thinkers were singled out as affording the beginner an opportunity of studying some of the most characteristic existentialist postures. The writers who were selected include three theistic existentialists: namely, Søren Kierkegaard (generally considered to be the father of contemporary existentialism), Gabriel Marcel and Martin Buber. Jean Paul Sartre and Albert Camus were chosen to represent the atheistic existentialist stance and finally, Martin Heidegger, the sage of Todtnauberg, who at the present writing qualifies as neither atheist nor theist, was selected because of his deep impact on the existentialist movement in general.

Obviously, the choice of such a limited number of men as being truly representative of the entire movement can be challenged on various grounds. Some readers may consider the addition of at least two or more thinkers absolutely essential for even an introductory text. The author of *Existentialism: With or Without God* is preparing a companion volume, which will examine the postures of Friedrich Nietzsche, Karl Jaspers, Nikolai Berdyaev, Maurice Merleau-Ponty, Jose Ortega y Gasset, and Miguel Unamuno. Together, the two small volumes should provide an adequate rudimentary outline of existentialist thought.

The present volume consists of seven chapters, of which the first is devoted to a brief consideration of the better-known existentialist themes. The remaining six chapters examine each of the selected representative thinkers. The plan of presentation is the same for all, i.e., there is given first a brief sketch of the man's life, followed by a list of his writings. The major portion of each chapter is then devoted to an examination of the man's thought. Whenever possible direct quotations from the thinker's writings are given, on the premise that the *verba ipsa auctoris* are still the most authoritative and most reliable means of presenting an author's thought. Finally, explanations and evaluations from current leading secondary sources are included in each chapter. Since the volume is intended for beginners, references are almost exclusively to works in the English language. Paginations are given, whenever possible, to paper-back editions on the premise that the book's chief readers will be impecunious students.

In conclusion, the author wishes to express his gratitude to the Most Reverend John F. Whealon, D.D., S.T.L., S.S.L., Archbishop of Hartford, for writing the *Foreword*, which synthesizes so admirably the chief themes of this volume. To M. Gabriel Marcel is due a special note of thanks for his illuminating letters concerning the role of drama in his thought, as well as for the permission to translate and publish all his plays in English. To two recent McAuley Lecturers at Saint Joseph College, the Reverend Frederick Copleston of Oxford, who spoke on the general subject of *Existentialism* and Professor Will Herberg, whose printed address, *Martin Buber: Personalist Philosopher in an Age of Depersonalization*, has been made available by the Publications Department of Saint Joseph College, the author acknowledges his gratitude for encouragement and advice.

Further expressions of appreciation are due Sister

Mary Consolata, Ph.D., Sister M. Leo Joseph, Ph.D., and Reverend Charles Shaw, Ph.D. Cand., President and Deans respectively of Saint Joseph College. To my colleagues, Reverend William Hart, M.S., Ph.D., and Dr. William M. Walton; to the graciously accommodating Head Librarian, Sister Muriel Adams and her staff of the Pius XII Library of Saint Joseph College; to the staff of the Sterling Library in Yale University; to John Thompson for supplying pertinent material on Hasidism; to Reverend John T. Shugrue, M.A., S.T.L., Reverend Robert E. Shea, Reverend Brian A. Shaw, M.A., and Adele Frances Logwin for assistance in proofreading and typing; and especially to the author's brother and sister, Drs. Edmund A. Lescoe and Marie E. Lescoe are due the deepest thanks and gratitude. To the Priests and Brothers of the Society of St. Paul at Alba House, the author acknowledges his debt of gratitude for advice, patience and forbearance.

Finally, to the many students who, over the years, have borne patiently with the author and, by their many insightful queries, have aided him more than they realize in making this volume a reality, the author expresses his most sincere appreciation.

F. J. L.

Acknowledgments

The author wishes to acknowledge his gratitude to the following publishers for permission to quote from copyrighted material: Martin Heidegger, *Being and Time*. Translated by John Macquarrie and Edward Robinson. Copyright © by SCM Press Ltd. By permission of Harper and Row, Publishers Inc.; Jean Paul Sartre, *Being and Nothingness: An Essay of Phenomenological Ontology*. Translated by Hazel Barnes. Copyright © 1956 by The Philosophical Library; Maurice Friedman, *Martin Buber: The Life of Dialogue*. Copyright © by The University of Chicago Press.

Contents

List of Abbreviations

BH —Marcel, Gabriel. *Being and Having*. Translated by Katherine Farrer. Torchbook. New York: Harper and Row, 1965.

BMM —Buber, Martin. *Between Man and Man*. Translated by Ronald Gregor Smith. New York: Macmillan Co., 1968.

BN —Sartre, Jean Paul. *Being and Nothingness: An Essay of Phenomenological Ontology*. Translated by Hazel Barnes. New York: Philosophical Library, 1956.

BT —Heidegger, Martin. *Being and Time*. Translated by John Macquarrie and Edward Robinson. New York and Evanston: Harper and Row, 1962.

CF —Marcel, Gabriel. *Creative Fidelity*. Translated by Robert Rosthal. New York: Farrar and Straus, 1964.

CUP —Kierkegaard, Søren. *Concluding Unscientific Postscript*. Translated by David Swenson and Walter Lowrie. Princeton: University Press, 1960.

HV —Marcel, Gabriel. *Homo Viator*. Translated by Emma Craufurd. Torchbook. New York: Harper and Bros., 1962.

IPQ —*International Philosophical Quarterly*. New York and Heverlee-Louvain.

MAMS—Marcel, Gabriel. *Man Against Mass Society*. Translated by G. S. Fraser. Gateway. Chicago: Henry Regnery Co., 1962.

MB —Marcel, Gabriel. *The Mystery of Being*. Gateway. 2 vols. Chicago: Henry Regnery Co., 1960.

MS —*The Modern Schoolman*. St. Louis.

NS —*The New Scholasticism*. Washington.

PE —Marcel, Gabriel. *The Philosophy of Existentialism*. Translated by Manya Harari. New York: Citadel Press, 1966.

PT —*Philosophy Today*. Celina, Ohio.

WIM —Heidegger, Martin. "What Is Metaphysics?" *Existence and Being*. Edited by Werner Brock. Chicago: Henry Regnery Co., 1949.

EXISTENTIALISM

CHAPTER I

DEFINITION

I. PRELIMINARY REMARKS

Existentialism is one of the most difficult and elusive concepts to define. The term itself is surrounded by a certain amount of confusion, ambiguity and lack of precision. Part of the difficulty is due to the fact that the word "existentialism" is applied to the postures of a number of widely disparate philosophers, whose thought ranges the full spectrum from Søren Kierkegaard's intensely theistic commitment to Christianity, all the way to Jean Paul Sartre's categorical denial of the existence of God and of all spiritual reality. As a result, the same term is used to describe both theistic and atheistic stances which are absolutely contradictory and diametrically opposed to each other.

In addition, most contemporary existentialists have even rejected the term "existentialism" as descriptive of their philosophical postures. In the first place, Søren Kierkegaard, the father of contemporary existentialism, never spoke of himself as an "existentialist." ("I am only a poet.")[1] Martin Heidegger has vehemently repudiated Jean Paul Sartre's description of his thought as an atheistic existentialism. Heidegger had categorically denied that he is an atheist and he has equally emphatically rejected the label "existentialist." He states succinctly that his philosophy is an ontology and that his chief preoccupation is with being and not with existence.[2] Gabriel Marcel, who for some time allowed himself to be called a "Christian existentialist," finally opted for the term "Neo-Socratic" or "Christian Socratic" as more accurately descriptive of his work.[3]

Albert Camus, at the time of his celebrated controversy with Jean Paul Sartre, (with whom he had been intimately associated during the French Resistance days), publicly rejected the term "existentialist" and further proclaimed that he considered existentialism's (i.e., Sartre's brand) conclusions to be completely false and unacceptable.[4] Karl Jaspers, who for some twenty years spoke of his thought as a "philosophy of existence," rejected the term "existence" in favor of "reason" and, until his death in 1969, maintained that the label "philosophy of reason" was more truly representative of his intellectual endeavors. He insisted on the change because he became increasingly convinced that existentialism, in the most popular form, was ignoring the role and importance of reason in philosophy. It is for this reason, Jaspers wrote, that it seemed urgent "to stress the original characteristics of philosophy. Once reason gets lost, everything is lost."[5]

II. TWO TYPES OF EXISTENTIALISM

To add further to the general confusion over terminology, there are historically two completely different philosophical stances which have been designated as "existentialism." The first of these dates back to the thirteenth century and its author is St. Thomas Aquinas. This medieval thinker insisted invariably on the primacy of the *esse* or the act of "to be" in his metaphysics, and hence, made existence the pivotal point of his entire philosophy. At the same time, he also affirmed the stability of essences or natures and defended the role of the intellect and the possibility of intelligibility. Such modern Thomists as Jacques Maritain, Étienne Gilson, Anton Pegis and Frederick Copleston, repeatedly point to what they term the only authentic existentialism rooted in the act of "to be" or existence.[6]

The second type of existentialism, which is the better known of the two and to which we shall refer as "contemporary existentialism," is the subject of our inquiry. Chronologically, it is a phenomenon of the nineteenth and twentieth centuries and it looks to Søren Kierkegaard, the Melancholy Dane, as its founder. It numbers German, French, Jewish, Russian and Spanish thinkers as its exponents.

III. CONTEMPORARY EXISTENTIALISM:
PRELIMINARY DIVISION

Some historians of philosophy have described Blaise Pascal (seventeenth century) as the first authentic existentialist and others have even asserted that the great fourth century Christian thinker, St. Augustine of Hippo, is the founder of the existentialist movement. In spite of these claims, there is general agreement, however, that contemporary existentialism first received articulation of its fundamental postures in the writings of Søren Kierkegaard in the nineteenth century.

A great number of thinkers are usually associated with this movement. Some may properly be called existentialists (despite their most vigorous protests to the contrary). Others, on the other hand, have exerted a most decisive influence on this movement of thought, even though they cannot be classified as contemporary existentialists.

The most obvious names which are associated with the existentialist movement are the following: Søren Kierkegaard, Friedrich Nietzsche and Edmund Husserl (neither of the latter two qualifies as an existentialist), Martin Heidegger, Gabriel Marcel, Martin Buber, Nikolai Berdyaev, Jean Paul Sartre and Simone de Beauvoir, Jose Ortega y Gasset, Miguel Unamuno, Albert Camus, Karl Jaspers, Maurice Merleau-Ponty. This list is by no means exhaustive; its only merit is that it does include the more prominent and better known exponents of the existentialist movement.

Although rigid classifications are always dangerous in philosophy because they tend to impose artificial molds and categories on human thought, we shall, nevertheless, attempt to arrive at some groupings for purely pedagogical reasons. The most logical division of the existentialists, whom we shall study, is into (1) those who admit the existence of God (theists) and (2) those who deny the existence of a personal Transcendent Being (atheists).

Among the theistic existentialists (Group I), we can categorically place the following: Søren Kierkegaard, Gab-

riel Marcel, and Martin Buber. In the atheistic category
(Group II), we place the most articulate and best known
of the atheists, Jean Paul Sartre, his companion Simone de
Beauvoir, and Albert Camus. Martin Heidegger, it would
seem, must be placed in a class all his own. While he
emphatically rejected Sartre's description of his thought
as atheistic (*Existentialism is a Humanism*), Heidegger,
nevertheless, failed to establish any kind of theism in his
thought.[7] The former gods, according to Heidegger, have
died and the new ones have not arrived as yet. This is
the time of waiting for the appearance of the new ones.
Whether Heidegger's thought will ultimately eventuate
in a theism or an atheism seems to be, at this stage, an
open question.

A.   Theistic and Atheistic Existentialism

It is a somewhat ironic twist of history that, although
existentialism traces its origins to the strongly theistic
Christian polemics of Søren Kierkegaard ("How to be a
Christian in Christendom"), most lay people identify
existentialism with the uncompromisingly atheistic stance
of Jean Paul Sartre and Albert Camus. It is no overstate-
ment to say, without any qualification whatsoever, that
the best known existentialist today is Jean Paul Sartre. As
a consequence, Sartre's brand of postulatory atheism has
become identified in the minds of most people with contemporary existentialism.

The reason for this curious inversion is not difficult
to establish. Jean Paul Sartre and Albert Camus rank
among the most highly gifted literary artists of the twentieth century. Both have written outstanding literature
in the form of the play, novel, diary and autobiography.
Albert Camus received the Nobel Prize for Literature in
1957 and Sartre, in 1964, was likewise named for the
same prize, which he spurned. Literally hundreds of
thousands of people have read Jean Paul Sartre's *No Exit*
or *Nausea* and Albert Camus' *The Stranger, The Plague*
or *The Fall*, without devoting a single hour of study to

the formal philosophical analysis of existentialist themes. Hence readers, who would never attempt such technical existentialist works like Heidegger's *Being and Time*, Kierkegaard's *Concluding Unscientific Postscript*, Sartre's *Being and Nothingness* or even Gabriel Marcel's *Being and Having*, to name only several, have been exposed to existentialism in a most "painless" manner.

The theistic existentialists, on the other hand, have resorted almost exclusively to the traditionally technical philosophical tracts as the means of presenting their thought. One notable exception is Gabriel Marcel, who has stated that he attaches more importance to the almost thirty plays which he has written than to the entire corpus of his formal philosophical writings. In spite of the author's contention that it is his plays and not the technically philosophical works that best express his thought and preference, it is truly a regrettable fact that, to date, only four of Marcel's plays, namely, *Ariadne, A Man of God, The Votive Candle* and *The Lantern* have been translated into the English language. Scholars of Marcel's works will be interested to learn that a project is under way to make the remainder of Marcel's plays available in English translation. (*Le Monde Cassé, Le Coeur des Autres,* and *L'Iconoclaste,* with a special Introduction written by Gabriel Marcel, are due to appear this year.)[8]

The inevitable result is that the theistic existentialists who, after all, represent the original and genuine existentialism, have been overshadowed by their more flamboyant and strident counterparts. Sartre's Bohemian life-style, his long-lasting "marriageless marriage" to Simone de Beauvoir (with built-in allowances for "contingent" love affairs on both sides), his recent adoption of a "daughter" in her late twenties, his preoccupation with sex in his writings, his active participation in the underground movement during the Nazi occupation of France, his skirmishes with Marxism, have all conspired to make him a colorful and aggressive standard-bearer for the avant-garde. To some extent these Sartrean preferences and peculiarities have tended to interfere with and obfuscate the image of the strictly professional philosopher's philosopher that Sartre would like to be.

IV. DEFINITIONS

Because of the fundamental insistence on the radically singular and the individual, the term "existentialism" properly interpreted, is not capable of being defined. Definitions always deal with abstractions and universals; existentialism, on the other hand, eschews the universal and the abstract. By its very nature, it is anti-systemic; the basic postures which Kierkegaard enunciated were all in defiance of the system. True to its nature, existentialism refuses to be classified as a system of philosophy and, therefore, logically speaking, no definition of existentialism is possible.

On the other hand, many writers have attempted to formulate definitions of the term. Some of these are incomplete and one-sided, while others are intolerably lengthy and involved, attesting to the fact that no clear-cut and succinct definition of existentialism is possible.

Let us review several of these definitions. The first of these has the virtue of brevity and generality, if not of clarity. It reads, "Existentialism is a way of life which involves one's total self in an attitude of complete seriousness about himself."[9] Admittedly, while the definition is not incorrect, it does not convey too much meaning to the uninitiated.

The second definition prefers to tell us in rather negative terms what existentialism is not. It reads, "Existentialism is not a philosophy but a label for several widely different revolts against traditional philosophy. Existentialism is not a school of thought nor is it reducible to any set of tenets."[10]

The third definition gives us at least one basic insight into existentialism. It reads as follows: "Existentialism is a type of philosophy which endeavors to analyze the basic structures of human existence and to call individuals to an awareness of their existence in its essential freedom."[11]

The fourth definition emphasizes the freedom which man possesses in the existential choices which he makes. It reads, "Existentialism is a philosophy of subjectivity or selfhood, whose fundamental doctrine proclaims man's freedom in the accomplishment of his destiny, and whose principal method is consequently that of description or phenomenology."[12]

The fifth definition emphasizes the atheistic type of existentialism to the exclusion of the theistic posture, "Existentialism is an irrationalistic, humanistic philosophy of crisis, in which uprooted modern man seeks to find certainty in his own existence, which he has elevated to an idol."[13]

In a similar vein, another definition totally disregards theistic existentialism. This is especially curious in view of the fact that the very founder of the movement, Søren Kierkegaard, is automatically excluded. The definition is as follows: "Existentialism is a literary-philosophic cult of nihilism and pessimism popularized in France after World War II, chiefly by Jean Paul Sartre: it holds that each man exists as an individual in a purposeless universe and that he must oppose his hostile environment through the exercise of his free will."[14]

The seventh definition also excludes the theistic stance. We are told, "Existentialism is a recent movement which claims to represent a middle way between traditional materialism and idealism and stresses personal decision in the face of a universe without a purpose."[15] (Needless to say, the definition totally eliminates the postures of such men like Søren Kierkegaard, Gabriel Marcel, Martin Buber, Nikolai Berdyaev, to name a few.)

Another more lengthy definition also restricts itself to the atheistic type of existentialism. We read, "Existentialism is a philosophy born of Christian despair, a way of thinking that has retained Christian metapsychology, while abandoning Christian metaphysics. The feeling of anxiety and loss that is the mark of this philosophy is rooted in the fear of the secularized Christian of never being released from his subjectivity. Thus arises the alternative between a heroic nihilism, which affirms this fate and a sentimental positivism, which flees from it."[16]

The following two definitions, although somewhat diffuse, seem to be more accurate, in that they describe both kinds of existentialism, i.e., theistic and atheistic. The first one reads as follows: "Existentialism is not a philosophy but a mood embracing a number of disparate philosophies. The differences among them are more basic than the temper which unites them. Their temper can best be described as a reaction against the static, the abstract, the purely rational, in favor of the dynamic and the concrete, personal involvement and *engagement,* action, choice and commitment, the distinction between 'authentic' and 'inauthentic' existence, and the actual situation of the existential subject as the starting point of thought."[17]

The second of these definitions speaks of existentialism in the following terms: "Existentialism is chiefly a twentieth century philosophy that is centered upon the analysis of existence, specifically of being, that regards human existence as not exhaustively describable or understandable in idealistic or scientific terms and that stresses the freedom and responsibility of the individual, the irreducible uniqueness of an ethical or religious situation and usually the isolation and subjective experiences (as of anxiety, guilt, dread, anguish) of an individual therein."[18]

Finally, we have a pithy, facetious definition which tries to make up in cleverness what it lacks in completeness: "Existentialism is a clandestine wedding of Nordic melancholy and Parisian pornography."[19]

V. THEMES OF EXISTENTIALISM

Since a clear-cut and concise definition of existentialism is well-nigh impossible, we prefer to examine briefly a number of themes that are common to the six existentialist thinkers we shall study. And since it is generally agreed by most proponents of this movement that existentialism is not a philosophical system, we shall prefer to speak of existentialist "postures" or "stances," as being more accurately descriptive of this type of thought. The themes which we shall examine will include the following: (1) Existence and the individual (2) Authentic and inauthentic existence (3) Community, I-Thou, Co-esse (4) Estrangement, alienation and absurdity (5) Dehumanization, objectification, depersonalization (6) Phenomenology and existentialism.

A. Existence and the Individual

Existentialism insists on a return to the singular, to the individual real-life human being. Gabriel Marcel emphasizes this basic tenet of existentialism, when he observes, "For my part, I should be inclined to deny the properly philosophic quality to all works in which there is no trace of what I can only call the sting of the real."[20]

Whereas previous philosophical systems tended to study the essences and natures of things, namely, that complexity of knowable notes which an intellect could grasp and understand, existentialism adopts a fundamentally anti-intellectualist attitude. This new stance eschews abstract and universal essences. It insists, rather, that the flesh-and-blood individual man and not some Platonic Form or even a moment in a Hegelian dialectical process is the proper object of study for philosophy.

Historically, Kierkegaard's rebellion against Hegel's "dissolute pantheistic contempt for the individual" was the *point de départ* for contemporary existentialism.[21] As a consequence, this philosophical posture insists on studying man in his radical singularity and individuality, a man who is constantly faced with making momentous decisions that spell the difference between authentic and inauthentic existence. A philosophy of existence always considers the individual lived experience in its unrepeatable uniqueness. It abhors any attempt at objectification or universalization of that which is preeminently singular and individual.

In a word, existentialism deals with the here-and-now world of concrete, vibrantly living, individual human beings.

B. Authentic and Inauthentic Existence

All existentialists, whether they are theists or atheists, are constantly preoccupied with the question of authenticity and inauthenticity of existence. The *magnum desiderabile* of every existentialist is an authentic and meaningful existence. For Kierkegaard, authentic existence is achieved by making the leap of faith and by becoming totally committed to a life of subjectivity and truth. Heidegger's man is also urged to live authentically by means of the existential choices he makes in dread and in the shadow of death. Heidegger has even coined a word, *das Man,* to denote the faceless, anonymous individual who is guilty of inauthentic existence.

For Buber, Marcel and Berdyaev, authentic existence is always grounded in communion and intersubjectivity. Every I-Thou relationship between two human beings bestows authenticity of existence upon them because they both reach out to the Absolute and Eternal Thou, Who is the very ground and foundation of their being.

Jean Paul Sartre likewise speaks of the need for a truly authentic existence, even though his intellectual climate is that of an avowed atheist. Sartre's man, who is "to freedom condemned," must choose resolutely, despite the fact that he has absolutely no basis for his choices. One who refuses to choose is guilty of bad faith, which is always associated with an inauthentic existence.

For the early Camus, the Camus of *The Myth of Sisyphus, Cross Purpose* and *The Stranger,* authentic existence is a life amidst the absurd. Authenticity of existence demands a rejection of both physical and philosophical suicide. Sisyphus, who defiantly scorns the gods who have condemned him to roll his stone endlessly, is the personification of authentic existence. For the later

Camus, authentic existence has moved from an ethics of sheer quantity to an ethics of quality. A common brotherhood of man, an insistence that there must be a difference between stoking the Nazi crematory fires and devoting one's life to the care of lepers, the emphasis on limits and on stable essences or natures in the context of early Greek philosophy—these postures characterize an authenticity of existence in the later Camus.[22]

C. Community, I-Thou, Co-esse, Intersubjectivity

Th themes of togetherness, I-Thou, and "being-with" are fundamental to the postures of Marcel, Buber, Berdyaev and the later Camus. Man is not an island and in order to lead a meaningful and authentic existence, he must establish a loving and mutually reciprocal relationship with other human beings. Basic to this posture is the unqualified treatment of a fellow human being as a genuine "Thou," an individual who has personal rights and a sacredness and dignity that I must respect. The meaningfulness and authenticity of my existence as an "I" is totally conditioned by the generosity with which I make myself available in mutual love, fidelity, faith and disponibility to the Thou. In a word, the authenticity of my existence is completely dependent on my genuineness toward the other; the other is the unique means of enriching my own existence. In Buber, the recurrent theme is that of the I-Thou in genuine community (versus collectivism and individualism). Berdyaev speaks of that untranslatable *sobornost* as denoting real community. Marcel finds the I-Thou as pivotal for intersubjectivity and *co-esse*. Although Heidegger does speak very briefly of a *Mit-Sein* in his *Being and Time*, the Heideggerian DASEIN is a solitary and isolated individual in his world of thrownness, homelessness and *Angst*.

The later Camus, as seen in *Letters to a German Friend*, *The Plague* and *The Rebel*, likewise opts for a human solidarity. Contrary to the proud isolation of the defiant Sisyphus, the hero of the absurd, who personified the early Camus, we are now urged to exercise a human compassion, a loving solicitude for our fellow man. A sense of togetherness and community becomes the dominant theme. Camus still finds no hope or rationality in the universe but minimally, he does admit an ethics of quality. There are certain stable essences and natures and there are limits on men's actions. The quantitative ethics of nihilism must be rejected. Man must aid his fellow man. He must extend a helping hand in combatting the evils of the plague.[23]

D.   Estrangement, Absurdity, Homelessness, Alienation

Heidegger, Sartre, and the early Camus dwell on several cognate themes of estrangement and alienation, which are typical of the atheistic existentialist posture. Martin Heidegger describes in detail the estrangement which DASEIN (man) experiences in the world. DASEIN has been thrown into existence (he merely begins to be), without knowing whence he came or whither he is going. As a result of this thrownness (*Geworfenheit*), man experiences an uncanny homelessness and forlornness. He has no specific essence or nature. His life is an on-going process of creating his essence by means of the existential choices he makes. This entire operation, however, will be abruptly terminated by death, which is the total extinction of DASEIN. Man never truly and completely is until he is no longer.[24]

The Sartrean man is best described by Antoine Roquentin, the hero of *Nausea*, when he argues, "Every existing thing is born without reason, prolongs itself out of weakness and dies by chance."[25] Sartre denies the existence of God (he considers this gratuitously assumed stance as a presupposition for all his thought), and because there is no divine Creator, Sartre contends that we must deny to man a specifically human essence or nature. Like Heidegger's DASEIN, man, for Sartre, is something which has been meaninglessly placed into existence. At best, man is a consciousness which, like a mirror, has no essence or content of its own, except the things that it reflects. Accordingly, man is a nothingness, a Being-for-itself, to freedom condemned in a world of absurdity. As a consciousness, For-itself is what it is not and is not what it is. For-itself is constantly outside itself, reaching out to the projects and possibilities which, as yet, it is not. For this reason, For-itself lacks the permanence and stability which are found in the world of objects, i.e., in nonconscious beings. In addition, For-itself feels itself threatened by the massive, opaque, mute solidity of the world of In-itself. Man is in constant fear of being overwhelmed and engulfed by the meaningless, viscous and glutinous world of the In-itself. Estrangement, alienation and forlornness are the inevitable lot of For-itself.

This, however, is not all. Every For-itself is further threatened by every other For-itself. It is Sartre's cardinal principle that every human being is the natural enemy of the other. He tells us emphatically that conflict is the basis for all human relationships. Each human being is attempting to make an object or *en-soi* of the other. In the case of human love, for example, while I plot to appropriate your freedom and to make an object out of you, you, my beloved, are attempting to do the same to me. We are locked in a death-struggle for mutual self-appropriation which, Sartre reminds us, is an a priori impossibility. Even if some kind of viable relationship, however temporary, could be effected between us, it is immediately shattered and pulverized by the look of the third. Sartre graphically describes the resulting alienation and estrangement in his best known work, *No Exit,* where we are told that "Hell is other people."[26]

Albert Camus, in the early period of his writing, also portrayed a world of alienation and absurdity. In *The Myth of Sisyphus* and *The Stranger,* Sisyphus and Jean Meursault exemplify the dark, brooding Camusian world of absurdity and estrangement. It is to Camus' credit, however, that this posture of nihilism and quantitative ethics gave way, as we shall see below, to an ethics of quality and a notion of human solidarity and brotherhood of man.[27]

Such brooding estrangement, alienation and absurdity are hallmarks of atheistic existentialism. Little wonder that Sartre recently observed that atheistic existentialism is "a cruel and grim affair." Gabriel Marcel, the great philosopher of hope, was unerringly on the mark when he stated that alienation and frustration are inevitable consequences of a denial of God's existence and of a future life for man. A world wherein man finds himself leading a meaningless existence and where he is told that there is absolutely no hope (Camus, in fact, called hope "philosophical suicide")—such a world can hardly beget an optimism and a joy of living. Further, when the same man, who is bereft of all hope and optimism, is likewise informed that he is condemned to freedom, i.e., that he has absolutely no basis on which to make his choices, there is little wonder that a sense of overwhelming fatalism, cynicism and deep-rooted pessimism marks the attitude of the atheistic existentialist.

Theistic existentialism, on the other hand—whether it be Jewish or Christian—brings with it a fundamental optimism because man is believed to be neither estranged nor abandoned. In the world of Marcel, Buber and Berdyaev, for example, God, the Eternal and Absolute Thou, the Father and Creator of all men, gives meaning and dignity to human life. It is only in and through the Fatherhood of God that we find genuine brotherhood of man.

While it is true that no eternal paradise can be promised man on this earth, only because this present life is but a preparation for the next, the theistic existentialist, nevertheless, experiences the most unalloyed kind of happiness imaginable. In spite of the fact that he is truly a *Homo Viator*, a traveller, a wayfarer, a pilgrim seeking a permanent home, the theistic man does not suffer the alienation, absurdity and abandonment of the Heideggerian and Sartrean and Camusian man. The man who believes in God as his heavenly Father is full of love and faith. With St. Augustine of Hippo, he agrees that man can never have complete peace and satisfaction on this earth, only because he has been created for the Infinite and Eternal Good in a future life. His present life is, therefore, a loving and hopeful preparation for an eternal existence of indescribable joy and happiness. "Our minds will never rest, until they rest in Thee, O Lord."

E. Depersonalization, Dehumanization, Objectification

Another constantly recurring theme among most existentialists is that of depersonalization, dehumanization and thingification of man. Marcel, Buber, Jaspers and Berdyaev are especially concerned with the frightening erosion of human values and human personality, which they unequivocally attribute to the disproportionate influence of twentieth century technology.

The method of technology is, of necessity, highly impersonal, abstract and objective. Marcel refers to it as the level of the problem and object. The method of the laboratory is always "scientific." It is impersonal and dispassionate; it can never allow the humane factor to interfere with the strict objectivity of its activity.[28]

When this perfectly valid and, in fact, absolutely necessary method of technology is applied to our dealings with men, we are faced with disaster. The technological method can never deal with man as a human being. It can never include in its captivity such human factors as man's dignity and his fundamental rights and aspirations. The technological method can deal with man in one way only: it must treat him as an object—a dehumanized and depersonalized entity. As Marcel repeatedly argues, modern technology regards man's intrinsic worth strictly in terms of the function which he performs. The callous appraisal of a human being's value in such a technocratic society totally ignores man's dignity and inalienable rights. Functionalization of man depersonalizes and dehumanizes him. It stifles, degrades and oppresses him. He is no longer a person but a commodity to be used and exploited by some mass movement, whether social, industrial or political.

Buber, Marcel and Berdyaev argue that such a cynical

disregard for the dignity of man is rooted in a rejection of the only valid mode of interpersonal relationship, namely the I-Thou relationship. When man ceases to regard his fellow man as a genuine Thou, when he calculatingly views him in a highly impersonal manner as an "It," an object to be used or manipulated, then we are faced with a technomania and technolatry.

There are two inevitable consequences of such a dehumanization and depersonalization of man. The first makes man an easy ploy for the tyrant, the dictator and the totalitarian state. Because the average common man is treated as an object, a unit or a statistic, a function or a means to an end, he gradually loses all personal initiative, responsibility and creativity. He inexorably becomes a faceless, anonymous mass man, who seeks refuge from involvement by becoming submerged in collectivism and mass groups. Mediocrity, non-commitment and non-involvement best characterize such a faceless individual. Gabriel Marcel contends that such an erosion of personal individuality begets the most favorable climate for an easy and almost effortless take-over by the totalitarian state. Men are regimented, armed and packed together as so many automatons in the service of the all-powerful State. (Buber)[29]

The second consequence of the depersonalization and dehumanization of man is a brutal fact of history. Because Nazi socialism arrogantly looked upon human beings not as other "Thous," possessing intrinsic rights and dignity but as objects or "Its" to be exploited as means to an end, the twentieth century had witnessed one of the most revolting and demonic phenomena ever recorded in the annals of man. Once atheistic nihilists convinced themselves that other human beings, whether Jews or Christians, were only objects to serve their diabolical ends, then Buchenwald, Dachau and Auschwitz became gruesome realities. The bestialization of man was complete, for Nazi socialism murdered over six million innocent human beings with an abandon and ruthless efficiency which, even today, staggers the imagination.

F. Phenomenology and Existentialism

A number of existentialists, chiefly Heidegger, Sartre, Marcel and Merleau-Ponty, employ the phenomenological method in their philosophizing and hence, they are frequently referred to as "phenomenological existentialists." (Sartre, in fact, subtitles his *opus magnum, Being and Time,* "An Essay on Phenomenological Ontology.")

The particular manner in which contemporary existentialists use the phenomenological method stands in open contradiction and opposition to that of phenomenology's discoverer, Edmund Husserl. Now Husserl, the founder of phenomenology, was interested in arriving at an objective, analytic description of phenomena of any kind. This means that we begin with the facts of our personal consciousness, i.e., with anything which can be the object of either knowledge or feeling. Then we try to describe carefully what is given in consciousness. The object of consciousness is termed a phenomenon, i.e., that which appears or which shows itself (*phainayn*). The science that would study these objects or appearances is thus called phenomenology.

Husserl was especially intent on grasping the essences or *eidoi* of these objects and appearances; he therefore called phenomenology an "eidetic" science. Because the grasping of these all-important *eidoi* or essences was no easy task, Husserl elaborated the *epokay* or bracketing. This meant that, in order to focus our attention more effectively on the essence, we must "bracket" or place in suspension (in brackets) a number of factors which might tend to distract us from grasping this eidos. Husserl in fact spoke of three kinds of *epokay*. The first was the *historical bracketing,* which deliberately disregarded all philosophical systems of thought because phenomenology is interested in the things themselves and not in other people's opinions. The second *epokay,* which Husserl called the *eidetic reduction,* involved the bracketing of the individual existence of the object, in order that the essence or *eidos* might be grasped more effectively. This reduction called for the bracketing of all sciences of nature and of spirit and even of God as the ground of being. All sources of information were to be ignored in order to make the pure essence more accessible to the phenomenologist. The third and final bracketing, which Husserl termed *transcendental reduction,* involved the putting into suspension not only of existence but of everything which could not qualify as a "correlate of pure consciousness." Hence we were left with the following two elements: (1) pure consciousness which is merely a reference point for the intentional object and (2) the object as intentionally given to the subject. Phenomenology, therefore, became the science of essences or *eidoi* in pure experience.

Martin Heidegger, who initially gave all the appearances of being a faithful disciple of Husserl's brand of phenomenology, in actuality, developed a phenomenology which was a direct antithesis to that of Husserl. Whereas Husserl's chief preoccupation was a quest for essences or *eidoi,* as we have seen, and this he hoped to achieve by bracketing existence, Heidegger rejected all notion of essences and made, instead, *existence* his over-all interest. Heidegger made the examination of the various ways in which DASEIN manifests itself, the object of his new ontology, i.e., the search after the Being of beings, (*das Sein des Seiendes*).[30]

Marcel's phenomenology, unlike that of Husserl's search for essences, appears to be a kind of propaedeutic for his ontology. Marcel's phenomenology is concerned with individual, concrete, lived experiences, as for example of hope, love, fidelity, availability and fraternity. From these, we then rise to the level of second reflection and of mystery, which is the level of Marcellian metaphysics. As Herbert Spiegelberg points out, "Marcel's phenomenology is to him only a step in his metaphysical reflection— and not even an essential one—a useful introduction to his metaphysics."[31]

The emphasis, which phenomenological existentialists place on singular, lived experiences, explains why certain literary forms like the novel, play, diary and autobiography have become so popular among the exponents of these postures. The argument is made that the best means of attaining the truly universal is by describing my own individual experiences, since in every spiritual experience, a concrete 'I,' analogous to mine, is involved. I am less unfaithful to reality in describing my own experience in its subjectivity than in trying to universalize an experience which is supposedly 'common to all men.' "[32]

On the other hand, it does not seem that phenomenology can furnish the necessary basis for a universal metaphysics. In order to avoid the dangers and pitfalls of a subjectivism, a certain objectivity and universality are needed for the science of ontology. For that reason, it seems extremely doubtful that phenomenological existentialism can ever become a genuine science of metaphysics.

Soren Kierkegaard

CHAPTER II

SØREN KIERKEGAARD
LIFE

I. EARLY YEARS

Søren Kierkegaard (Kĕr-kĕ-gōr), the "Melancholy Dane," was born on May 5, 1813 in Copenhagen, the youngest of seven children.[1] His father, Mikael Pedersen Kierkegaard, was fifty-six at the time of Søren's birth. Mikael's first wife died giving birth to a still-born child and the elder Kierkegaard married Anne Sørensdatter Lund, a servant in his home, whom he either seduced or raped while his wife was pregnant. The oldest of his seven children was born five months after the wedding and Mikael never forgave himself for his adulterous act.[2]

As a youth of twelve, Søren's father, Mikael, was brought to Copenhagen by his maternal uncle, who employed him in the business of selling the wool of the Jutland heath. The venture was so successful that Mikael was able to retire at the early age of forty, a wealthy man.

Two events in Mikael's life were the causes of an obsessive and morbid melancholy, which Søren would inherit from his father. As a boy of about eleven, who tended the sheep on the Jutland heath, Mikael secretly, in rebellion, cursed God. We read Søren's entry in his *Journals* about the incident concerning his father. He writes, "The dreadful case of a man who, when he was a little boy, suffered such hardship, was hungry, benumbed with cold, stood upon a hillock and cursed God—and the man was not able to forget this when he was eighty-two years old."[3] The second cause for this extreme melancholia was the already mentioned conjugal infidelity.

Retired at forty, Mikael, a deeply religious man, had much free time to brood over his misdeeds and to be constantly tormented by a deep sense of guilt. When his second wife and five of the seven children died in rapid succession (one child died in 1819, another in 1822 and between 1832 to 1835 three more children and their mother died), the father became convinced that God was punishing him through his loved ones. This deep sense of morbidity and melancholia was apparently transmitted to young Søren, who writes of his childhood as follows: "It is terrible when for a single instant, I come to think of the dark background of my life, from the very earliest time. The anxious dread with which my father filled my soul, his own frightful melancholy, the many things in that connection which I cannot record—I got such a dread of Christianity, and yet I felt myself so strongly drawn to it."[4]

In another place Kierkegaard speaks of that overwhelming legacy of melancholy which the old father bequeathed to the little boy. He says, "Such a primitive melancholy, such a prodigious dowry of care, and that, in the deepest sense tragical, to be brought up as a child by a melancholy old man—and at the same time with an innate talent for deceiving everybody, as though I were sheer life and movement—and then that God has helped me so."[5]

In 1830, when Søren was a little over seventeen, he entered the University of Copenhagen and registered in the faculty of theology (no doubt to please his father, although we have no positive indications that it was against his own personal preference). It was during this period (1830-1831), that he speaks of "the great earthquake" that took place. He writes, "Then it was that the great earthquake occurred, the terrible revolution which suddenly forced upon me a new and infallible law of interpretation of all the facts. Then I suspected that my father's great age was not a divine blessing but rather a curse; that the outstanding intellectual gifts of our family were only given to us in order that we should rend each other to pieces; then I felt stillness of death grow around me when I saw in my father an unhappy man who was to outlive us all, a cross on the tomb of his hopes.

There must be guilt upon the whole family, the punishment of God, obliterated like an unsuccessful at-

tempt, and only at times did I find a little alleviation in
the thought that my father had been allotted the heavy
task of calming us with the consolation of religion, minis-
tering to us so that a better world would be open to us,
even though we were overtaken by the punishment which
the Jews always called down upon their enemies: that all
recollection of us should be utterly wiped out, that we
should no longer be found."[6]

Søren thus became convinced that the entire family
was singled out by God to be the special object of divine
punishment. He records this conclusion when he writes,
"Guilt must rest upon the whole family, a punishment
of God must be impending over it and so my life should
properly be employed in doing penance."[7]

But six years later, the young student rebelled against
such a life of penance for his father's misdeeds and, in
1836, he defiantly entered upon the first of the three stages
of his life, i.e., the aesthetic stage or "the path of perdition." Next came the ethical stage, followed by his
awakening and conversion in the religious stage in 1838.
These three stages of the so-called "existentialist dialectic"
will be fully described and examined below.[8]

II. REGINA OLSEN

The most important single event in Søren Kierkegaard's life was his engagement to Regina Olsen, the
youngest daughter of State Councillor Olsen, a superior
official in the Ministry of Finance in Copenhagen. Kierkegaard first met Regina when she was only fourteen
years old. He immediately fell in love with her and dutifully though impatiently, waited four years before he
became engaged to her. Kierkegaard was now twenty-
seven and Regina had turned eighteen.[9] Everyone in
Copenhagen considered them "the perfect couple" and
Kierkegaard recorded in Quidam's Diary his engagement
as follows: "The first kiss—what bliss! A girl joyful in
mood, happy in youth! And she is mine. What are all
the gloomy thoughts and imaginations but a mere spider-
web, and melancholy only a mist which flees before her
reality, a sickness which is healed and is being healed

by this abundant health, this health which indeed is
mine since it is hers, who is my life and my future."[10]

And yet, in a very short time, Kierkegaard convinced
himself that he could never marry Regina and, for the next
eleven months, he tried desperately to get her to break
the engagement. He sent her a note and "sent back her
ring." Regina regarded the note as a symptom of his
melancholy and refused to take him at his word. She
adjured him "in the name of Christ and by the memory
of his deceased father" not to desert her. Regina's father
tried to prevail upon Søren to reconsider. Regina protested that she could never survive this broken engagement; she was sure that if it did not literally cause her
death, she would renounce the world and shut herself
off from society.

Kierkegaard reports in his own words the trying
situation, "From time to time, I said to her bluntly, 'Yield
now, let me go, you can't stand it.' To this she replied
passionately that she had rather stand anything than let
me go. I tried also to so turn the matter that it was she
who broke off the engagement, so as to spare mortification.
. . . For the first time in my life I scolded. It was the only
thing to do. . . . To get out of the situation as a scoundrel,
a scoundrel of the first water if possible, was the only
thing there was to be done in order to work her loose and
get her under way for marriage. So we separated. . . . I
wrote a letter to the Councillor which was returned un-
opened. I passed the night weeping in my bed. But in
the daytime I was, as usual, more flippant and witty than
usual—that was necessary. . . . I journeyed to Berlin. I
suffered a great deal. I remembered her in my prayer
every day."[11]

Finally, the engagement was broken and everyone in
Copenhagen considered Kierkegaard to be a real scoundrel. Regina got over this unhappy experience and after
a comparatively short time, married Fritz Schlegel and
lived a happy life. She died in 1904, having survived
both Kierkegaard and her husband. (Kierkegaard died in
1855.) Of Søren she said in the later years of her life,
"His motive in this breach was the conception he had

of his religious task: he did not dare bind himself to anything upon earth, lest it might check him in his calling; he must offer the best thing he possessed in order to work as God required him. The pain he was obliged to inflict upon himself and me was unspeakably heavy and grievous and indeed left its mark for life; easy my life has not been but happy."[12]

Martin Buber in his *Between Man and Man*, chastises Kierkegaard for rejecting Regina, a creature, so that he might more effectively and unreservedly love God his Creator. Buber writes, "Kierkegaard, the Christian concerned with the 'contemporaneity' with Jesus, contradicts his master. . . . 'In order to come to love,' says Kierkegaard about his renunciation of Regina Olsen, 'I had to remove the object.' That is sublimely to misunderstand God. Creation is not a hurdle on the road to God; it is the road itself. We are created along with one another and directed to a life with one another. Creatures are placed in my way so that I, their fellow-creature, by means of them and with them find the way to God. A God reached by their exclusion would not be the God of all lives in whom all life is fulfilled. A God in whom only the parallel lines of single approaches intersect is more akin to the God of the philosophers' than to the God of Abraham and Isaac and Jacob.' God wants us to come to him by means of the Reginas he has created and not by renunciation of them. If we remove the object, then—we have removed the object altogether. Without an object, artificially producing the object from the abundance of the human spirit and calling it God, this love has its being in the void."[13]

Although Kierkegaard gave up Regina, he never forgot her until his death and in his writings he conferred upon her a fame and immortality which she never would have attained had she become his wife. Just as one speaks of Dante and Beatrice, Abelard and Heloise, so the mention of Søren Kierkegaard immediately calls forth the name, Regina Olsen. Kierkegaard himself was aware of the immortality which he would confer upon his loved one. In his *Journals* he writes, "My existence shall unconditionally accentuate her life, my work as an author can also be regarded as a monument to her honor and praises. I take her with me to history. And I who with all my melancholy had only one wish, to enchant her—*there* it is not denied me: there I walk beside her; like a master of ceremonies I lead her in triumph and say, A little place, please for her, for 'our own dear little Regina.' "[14]

Perhaps some composite explanation for Kierkegaard's breaking of the engagement can be gathered from an entry in the *Journals* of 1843. Evidently Kierkegaard felt that if he married, he would then be duty-bound to speak out to Regina on the matter of his melancholy and his errors and excesses. And although his reason told him that his fears had no rational ground, he nevertheless could not overcome the dread which filled him. He writes, "But if I had explained myself, I must have initiated her into terrible things, my relationship to my father, his melancholy, the eternal night that broods within me, my desperation, lusts and excesses, which yet perhaps in God's eyes are not so atrocious; for indeed it was dread which caused me to go astray, and how could I seek refuge and support when I knew or surmised that the only man I had admired for his force and strength was himself tottering."[15]

III.   INCIDENT OF THE *CORSAIR*

The *Corsair* was the comic newspaper of Copenhagen. Its founder and editor, Meir Aron Goldschmitt, liked to think of it as the Danish counterpart of the London *Punch*. In reality, the newspaper specialized in caricature and ridicule of prominent Danes, published spicy stories and scandals from their private lives. Everyone in Copenhagen considered the paper a "scandal sheet" and while it was read with relish and secret enjoyment, no one had the fortitude to protest openly.

The *Corsair* had lavishly praised Kierkegaard's literary works and, in fact, had predicted immortality for Kierkegaard's name.[16] Kierkegaard, in his pride, wrote an open letter to the editor of the *Corsair*, rejecting, what he called, this preferential treatment of not being criticized by the paper. He invited attack upon himself by asking the editors not to single him out. He wrote in the following bombastic terms: "O cruel and bloodthirsty Corsair, omnipotent Sultan, who holdest the lives of men as a jest in thy mighty hand, and as a whim in the wrath of thy nostrils, oh, be thou touched with compassion, cut short these sufferings—slay me but render me not immortal . . . Consider what it means to become immortal, and especially to become such by the attestation of the Corsair! Oh, what cruel favor and leniency!—to be forever singled out as inhuman because the Corsair inhumanly had designed to spare him! But above all, let it be not this—not this, that I shall never die. Would only I might now shortly get into the Corsair. It is really hard on a poor author to be thus singled out in Danish literature as the only one who is not abused here."[17]

Another hitherto anonymous editor of the *Corsair*, L. P. Møller, had written an adverse review of Kierkegaard's *Stages on Life's Way*. Kierkegaard wrote a scathing attack and disclosed publicly that Møller was in fact, an editor of the disreputable *Corsair*. As a result of this disclosure, Møller, who was hoping to succeed the poet Oehlenschläger to the chair of aesthetics in the University of Copenhagen, was automatically disqualified and his academic ambitions completely shattered.

Goldschmidt and Møller now began their attack upon Kierkegaard in the *Corsair*. For more than a half year, each weekly issue of the paper carried as many as three or four articles and caricatures of Kierkegaard. His ungainly walk (due to a spine injury sustained in childhood), his awkward appearance and dress, and even his unhappy love affair with Regina Olsen were made the object of public ridicule. Other papers in the country joined the *Corsair* in making sport of the best known literary figure of Denmark, with the result that bands of jeering urchins would follow Søren in the streets and ridicule him.[18]

How much this shabby treatment hurt the Melancholy Dane, we can gather from the following entries of

1848 in the *Journals*: "They have treated me scurrily, disgustingly, a national crime has been committed against me, a treachery by the contemporary generation. . . . And so I am wasted upon Denmark. . . . My Christian name exists as a nickname for me which every school boy knows. Ever more frequently the same name is now used by authors in comedies; it appears regularly and everybody knows that it is I."[19]

Kierkegaard now turned more and more to religion but not to the established Lutheran Church of Denmark, for which he had only the deepest contempt. To him, the state supported Church was the embodiment of *Christendom*, which represented a corruption of a living, viable and vibrant Christianity. He even attacked the recently deceased Bishop Jacob Mynster (his father's deeply revered pastor), who had been eulogized by Professor Hans Martensen as a paragon of Christian virtue. Kierkegaard wrote a bitter article, claiming that the late bishop was not even a true Christian, when he wrote in *The Fatherland* issue of Thursday, December 30, 1854, "To represent from the pulpit Bishop Mynster as a witness to the truth, one of the genuine witnesses to the truth, to assign him a place in the holy chain (which stretches through the ages from the days of the Apostles)—against this a protest must be raised."[20]

On October 2, 1855, as Kierkegaard was carrying from the bank the last slim installment of the sizable fortune which he had inherited, he fell unconscious on the street, paralyzed from the waist down. He died at the Frederick's Hospital on November 11, 1855 at the age of forty-two.[21]

KIERKEGAARD'S PRINCIPAL WORKS
(Listed Chronologically)

The Concept of Irony. (1841). Tr. Lee Capel. New York: Harper, 1966.

Either/Or. (1843). Tr. Walter Lowrie. 2 vols. Garden City: Doubleday, 1959.

Johannes Climacus or De Omnibus Dubitandum Est. (1843). Tr. T. H. Croxall. Stanford: Stanford University Press, 1958.

Fear and Trembling. (1843). Tr. Walter Lowrie. Garden City: Doubleday, 1954.

Repetition. An Essay in Experimental Psychology. (1843). Tr. Walter Lowrie. Princeton: University Press, 1941.

Edifying Discourses. (1843-1844). Tr. David and Lillian Swenson. 4 vols. Minneapolis: Augsburg, 1943-1946.

Philosophical Fragments or A Fragment of Philosophy. (1844). Tr. David Swenson. Revised Tr. H. V. Hong. Princeton: University Press, 1962.

The Concept of Dread. (1844). Tr. Walter Lowrie. Princeton: University Press, 1944.

Stages on Life's Way. (1845). Tr. Walter Lowrie. New York: Schocken Books, 1967.

Thoughts on Crucial Situations in Human Life. Three Discourses on Imagined Situations. (1845). Tr. David and Lillian Swenson. Minneapolis: Augsburg, 1941.

Concluding Unscientific Postscript to the Philosophical Fragments. Tr. David Swenson and Walter Lowrie. Princeton: University Press, 1960.

On Authority and Revelation: The Book on Adler. (1846). Tr. Walter Lowrie. Princeton: University Press, 1955.

The Present Age and Two Ethico-Religious Discourses. (1846-1859). Tr. Alexander Dru and Walter Lowrie. London: Oxford University Press, 1940.

Works of Love. (1847). Tr. Howard and Edna Hong. New York: Harper, 1962.

Purity of Heart is to Will One Thing. (1847). Tr. Douglas Steere. New York: Harper, 1938.

The Gospel of Suffering and The Lilies of the Field. (1847). Tr. David and Lillian Swenson. Minneapolis: Augsburg, 1948.

Christian Discourses. (1848). Also included: *The Lilies of the Field and The Birds of the Air.* (1849). *The High Priest; The Publican; The Woman that was a Sinner.* (1849). Tr. Walter Lowrie. New York: Oxford University Press, 1939.

The Sickness unto Death. (1849). Tr. Walter Lowrie. Princeton: University Press, 1941.

Armed Neutrality and An Open Letter. (1849). Tr. Howard and Edna Hong. Bloomington: Indiana University Press, 1968.

Training in Christianity. (1850). Also included: *An Edifying Discourse.* (1850). Tr. Walter Lowrie. New York: Oxford University Press, 1941.

For Self-Examination and Judge for Yourselves! (1851 and 1852). Also included: *Two Discourses at the Communion on Fridays.* (1851). *The Unchangeableness of God.* (1855). Tr. Walter Lowrie. New York: Oxford University Press, 1941.

Attack Upon "Christendom." (1854-1855). Tr. Walter Lowrie. Boston: Beacon Press, 1966.

Crisis in the Life of an Actress (1855) and *Other Essays on the Drama.* Tr. Stephen Crites. New York: Harper, 1967.

The Point of View for My Work as an Author. (1859). Also included: "The Individual," Two "Notes" concerning My Work as an Author. *On My Work as an Author.* (1851). Tr. Walter Lowrie. New York: Oxford University Press, 1939.

THOUGHT

I. THE THREE STAGES

Kierkegaard's life is divided into three well-defined stages or modes of existence which, according to him, represent the so-called existentialist dialectic. They are (1) aesthetic stage (2) ethical or moral stage (3) religious stage. The first two stages (aesthetic and ethical) exemplify the inadequacy and futility of philosophy. Only the third mode of existence which relies on faith and transcends reason is the key to a genuinely authentic existence.[22]

A. Aesthetic Stage

Kierkegaard describes the aesthetic stage versus the ethical stage in *The Diary of a Seducer* (*Either/Or*, volume II) and in *In Vino Veritas* (*Stages* I) and the ethical stage in relation to the religious in *Fear and Trembling* and *Guilty-Not Guilty* (Stage III).[23]

The word *aesthetic* comes from the Greek, meaning "to sense" or "to perceive." The aesthetic individual leads a life of the senses and his motto is "the pleasure of the moment." The future is of no concern to him and the past serves only to heighten the present pleasure. The aesthetic individual is not so much a victim of gross passions as he is a refined and sophisticated hedonist.

The aesthete is strictly an observer, a non-participant. His life is one of cynical non-involvement. He refuses to commit himself to anything which might suggest fixed or observed standards of morality. He rejects anything which might give direction and purpose to his life.

"The aesthetic individual has no fixed principle except that he means not to be bound to anything or anybody. He has but one desire which is to enjoy the sweets of life—whether its purely sensual pleasures or the more refined Epicureanism of the finer things in life and art, and the ironic enjoyment of one's own superiority over the rest of humanity; and he has no fear except that he may succumb to boredom."[24]

Johannes the Seducer, (*Diary*) who lives the aesthetic life, outwardly appears gay, carefree and happy. Inwardly, however, he is full of loneliness, frustration, and despair. He is constantly grasping the will-o-the-wisp moment of sensual gratification. But as soon as he attains his lustful moment, it becomes shallow and empty, dissolving into nothingness and leaving only ashes in his mouth.

Kierkegaard selects three famous characters in Western literature to exemplify the aesthetic mode of existence: Don Juan, Faust and Ahasuerus.

1. Don Juan

Don Juan, the hero of Mozart's opera, is the personification of living for the moment. There is no continuity, no reflection, no pattern to his life. He merely exists in the aggregate of the moments of pleasure which he experiences. As one author describes Juan, "He is an idea, a force, an energy, the very potentiation of the sensuous. He never gains form or substance. He is being constantly formed but never finished. . . . By reason of his nature, it is impossible for him ever to be compacted and finished permanently as an Individual, for he exists in the moment, even as his existence is only the sum of the moments. . . . Within his own concept of himself he is never sinful. Sinfulness is the product of no small degree of reflection which, of course, Don Juan does not possess, for he is innocent of any critical attitude toward himself or towards his pleasures. He knows only that he enjoys them, and that he must consequently have them."[25]

Because the aesthetic man has one aim in life, namely the search for the pleasurable moment—when that moment is gone, so too is his being, since he is nothing more than the repetition of these moments. Inevitably this constant thirst for yet another pleasurable moment gives way to doubt, boredom and despair. Don Juan, therefore, yields to Goethe's Faust.[26]

2. Faust

For Kierkegaard, Faust is the example par excellence of boredom itself. Gone is Faust's former buoyant and easy-going confidence that he will attain permanent and endless pleasure. He begins to suspect that his goal will never be achieved. He becomes doubtful about himself and gives in to boredom. At the same time, he relentlessly continues experimenting and trying different avenues and approaches, while his scepticism about reaching the "truly happy moment" increases with each attempt. James Collins characterizes Faust as "a rebirth of Don Juan, a second phase in the existentialist dialectic. Anyone who reflects upon the futility of trying to satisfy the human spirit in the sheer flow of immediate feeling and pleasure is liable to become sceptical about every supposed certainty, resting place and moment of joy."[27]

3. Ahasuerus

The third and final phase of the aesthetic existence is despair. Just as Don Juan was the embodiment of erotic exaltation and Faust was the personification of doubt and boredom, so Ahasuerus the Wandering Jew is the exemplification of aesthetic despair. Because Ahasuerus believes in nothing and no one—he believes in neither God nor man—he is the true hero of despair. Wandering about aimlessly in the world, totally bereft of any hope, Ahasuerus can find no peace or rest. There is only the dull, numbing pain of indifference, which is the ultimate residue of despair.

Hence "the end of the aesthetic man is despair. . . . Despair over himself, because he no longer believes in himself. . . . Despair over his human nature, because he no longer believes that any sort of self is possible for him. . . . Despair over life, because all his tomorrows will be the same as today." It was at this time in his life that Kierkegaard evidently thought seriously of committing suicide.[28]

As Kierkegaard himself concludes in Either/Or, "So it appears that every aesthetic view of life is despair and that everyone who lives aesthetically is in despair, whether he knows it or not. But when one knows it (and you indeed know it), a higher form of existence is an imperative requirement."[29]

But despair, if it is freely chosen by the aesthetic man, can be a prelude to a genuine emancipation. It is only when the aesthete sees his sickness of spirit, and the shipwreck of his life, that he can break away from all the illusion of the aesthetic stage and really choose his own self. To choose despair is thus to turn away from all the distractions of the outside world and to go within oneself. This choice of oneself is of crucial consequence, since it

launches man on a completely new mode of existence—
the ethical stage.[30]

B. Ethical Stage

The futility and emptiness of the aesthetic mode of
existence give rise to the ethical or moral stage. The disillusioned man now frees himself from the transitory and
fleeting aesthetic pleasures and he chooses a world of
permanent values. It is this choice, freely made, that
bestows upon the individual a unique dignity and purposefulness of life. The ethical man turns towards the
inwardness of his own self and thus "confirms a decision
towards a future which is rich with new existence; for
a life that is nothing, through the act of choosing comes
to have meaning and true being."[31] Like Socrates, whom
Kierkegaard considers to be the best and most famous
example of the ethical mode of existence, the former
aesthete now truly learns "to know himself."

The ethical man has thus achieved both self-under-
standing and self-mastery because he now conforms his
actions to a moral standard. Previously, each pleasurable
moment was the aesthete's norm. Now, the ethical man
has achieved a freedom by his authentic choice. He
knows himself and he is the master of his actions.

Kierkegaard describes this second stage of the existentialist dialectic in Part II of *Either/Or*, as well as in
the *Concluding Unscientific Postscript*.[32] The ethical life
is called by Judge William, the pseudonymous advocate
of the second stage, "the universal and as such divine."
While the aesthetic life could look to no more than single,
isolated and fleeting moments of pleasure, the ethical
life has continuity; it possesses universality. The man who
lives ethically becomes aware of the fact that he is related
to the rational and social order of things. He begins to
realize that he is a human being and hence he can be
himself.

In Kierkegaard's words, "He who chooses himself
ethically chooses himself concretely as this definite individual and he attains this concretion by the fact that
this act of choice is identical with this act of repentance

which sanctions the choice. The individual thus becomes conscious of himself as this definite individual, with these talents, these dispositions, these instincts, these passions, influenced by these definite surroundings, as this definite product of a definite environment. He has his place in the world, with freedom he chooses his place, that is, he chooses this very place. He is a definite individual in the choice; he makes himself a definite individual, for he chooses himself."[33] Now a man who chooses himself acknowledges that there *is* a real and positive distinction between good and evil.

While the ethical stage represents a profound improvement on the aesthetic, it is, nevertheless, sadly incomplete and inadequate. In reaching out toward the universal, the ethical man is still restricted to his own selfhood. Man must search deeper within his own selfhood and by doing so, he will discover his own sinfulness and faith. These will enable him to make that leap or *saltus* to divine Transcendence, which ushers in the religious stage.

The ethical stage, as Sieste Zuidema explains, ". . . does not recognize the Absolute Paradox. It does not even recognize one's own infinite self and does not engage in an abundant striving to attain one's own highest individual salvation. . . . It is purely 'humanistic' and immanent. It knows nothing of an encounter with the Absolute Paradox."[34]

The ethical man, by probing deeper and deeper within himself, discovers his sinfulness and his faith, which are the means whereby he can meet the Absolute Paradox and the divine Transcendence. Kierkegaard cautions us, "An ethics which disregards sin is a perfectly idle science: but if it affirms sin, it is *eo ipso* well beyond itself."[35]

When the ethical man, with sorrow in his heart for his sins, chooses himself as guilty and asks divine forgiveness, he moves at this instant from the ethical to the religious stage.

C. Religious Stage

In the *Journals* (entry of May 19, 1838), Kierkegaard

writes of his religious conversion or the leap of faith, "There is an indescribable joy which glows through us unaccountably as the Apostle's outburst is unexpected: 'Rejoice' and again I say, 'Rejoice'—not a joy over this or that, but full jubilation, 'with hearts and souls and voices.' I rejoice over my joy, of, in, by, at, on, through, with my joy—a heavenly refrain, which cuts short, as it were, our ordinary song: a joy which cools and refreshes like a breeze, a gust of the tradewind which blows from the Grove of Mamre to the eternal mansions."[36]

This religious stage is achieved by acknowledging God, openly confessing one's sinfulness, choosing oneself as guilty and hoping for divine forgiveness. Each individual must make this personal commitment, which involves a passionate, non-rational "leap of faith." There is an Either/Or which makes man greater than the angels. By making this choice for God, man transcends the finiteness and temporality of his own existence and establishes a personal relationship with his Creator. His life is hereafter God-oriented and he is ever living before God.

Kierkegaard cites the example of Abraham, who was torn between the ethical and the religious stage. The act of killing his own son Isaac was demanded of him as a test of his faith. God was requesting Abraham to act contrary to the clearest ethical judgment which any human could make. He was asking Abraham to commit one of the most revolting actions a human being can perform, namely to destroy his own flesh and blood. Abraham loved Isaac beyond anyone else in the world and certainly no conceivable good could come from such a heinous act. Yet God demanded an unqualified faith, whose very nature is contrary to the ethical norms to which men subscribe. As Kierkegaard expresses it, "By his act, he [Abraham] overstepped the ethical entirely and possessed a higher *telos* outside of it, in relation to which he suspended the former . . . why then did Abraham do it? For God's sake and (in complete identity with this) for his own sake. He did it for God's sake because God required this proof of his faith; for his own sake he did it in order that he might furnish the proof. . . . But now when the ethical is thus teleologically suspended, how does the individual exist in whom it is suspended?. . . . How then did Abraham exist? He believed. This is the paradox which keeps him upon the sheer edge and which cannot make clear to any other man, for the paradox is that he as the individual puts himself in an absolute relation to the absolute."[37]

Abraham was thus a perfect knight of faith, ever ready to obey God, even in fear and trembling. He readily gave up the ethical for the religious, the finite for the infinite. "This is . . . clear to the knight of faith, so the only thing that can save him is the absurd, and he grasps by faith."[38] And because of his unwavering faith in God, Abraham received Isaac once again and he was rewarded a hundred fold.

Having entered into a life of faith, man gains his selfhood and he begins to exist authentically. He leaps into nothingness in which the abyss of sin becomes the abyss of faith. As Kierkegaard states, "By faith, I make renunciation of nothing; on the contrary, by faith I acquire everything, precisely in the sense in which it is said that he who has faith like a grain of mustard can remove mountains."[39]

In faith, man risks everything but he receives in return infinitely more than he has been able to give. He has abandoned the ethical and the universal. He has now chosen the religious and, in faith, he has transcended the finite, thereby effecting a union and communion with the infinite God. He is now leading a truly authentic existence.

1. *Religiousness "A" and Religiousness "B"*

In connection with the notion of the consciousness of sin as an absolute necessity for the leap of faith and hence, a truly genuine Christianity, Kierkegaard distinguishes between what he calls Religiousness "A" and Religiousness "B."

Religiousness-A is a definitely inferior state, not because it is a religion of the pagans. As a matter of fact, many baptized Christians frequently subscribe to it. The chief characteristic of this type of religiousness is its immanence. Basing itself on Hegelian pantheism, it holds that the individual human being is but a momentary, yet necessary, manifestation of the Absolute Mind or Idea. In order to achieve eternal happiness, an individual who subscribes to Religiousness-A, must turn toward himself. Here he hopes to discover the Eternal God within himself. Religiousness-A is, therefore, an inward, immanent movement. Sieste Zuidema argues that Religiousness-A, ". . . knows nothing of a concrete revelation of God in history, concentrated in the man Jesus. It does not seek the eternal in a place, in a concrete individual man, but seeks the eternal everywhere and nowhere in particular. It is thus compatible with an idealistic general historical philosophy of religion, such as that of Hegel. Moreover, it does go beyond the standpoint of immanence, even when it seeks the immanence in a different way than does the Hegelian thought, that is, in existential self-reflection and intensification of its passionate or pathetic didactic, rather than in objective speculative thought."[40]

Religiousness-B, on the other hand is the exact opposite. In his quest for happiness, man seeks an entity that is transcendent, a being which is outside man. He begins by acknowledging his guilt and sinfulness before his Creator. Man thus relates himself not with something immanent and within himself, but with a God who is transcendent.

As Kierkegaard explains, "In Religiousness-B, the edifying is a something outside the individual, the individual does not find edification by finding the God-relationship within himself. . . . The paradoxical edification corresponds, therefore, to the determination of God in time as the individual man; for if such be the case, the individual is related to something outside himself."[41]

Hence by the awareness of his sinfulness, man is able to turn to God in repentance and faith. Kierkegaard maintains "All ways come together at one point, the consciousness of sin—through that passes 'the way,' by which

He draws a man, the repentant sinner to Himself."[42]

II. HEGELIAN ABSTRACTIONISM

One of Kierkegaard's greatest complaints was the secularization of Christianity in his native Denmark. Since Lutheranism was the official Danish religion and the church and the bishops and ministers were supported by the State, everyone in Denmark considered himself to be automatically a Christian. To accuse a Dane of not being a Christian would be tantamount to voicing the highest insult possible. In the *Postscript*, Kierkegaard observes, "Christianity is assumed as given. . . . How strange is the way of the world! Once it was at the risk of his life that a man dared to profess himself a Christian; now it's to make oneself suspect, to venture to doubt that one is a Christian."[43]

And yet, complained Kierkegaard, while everyone called himself a Christian, no one thought seriously of God. No one was interested in carrying the cross of Christ. No one was willing to make sacrifices and to live a life of holiness. No one wanted to be a true and committed follower of Christ. The Danes, according to Kierkegaard, had become completely mundane, this-worldly, seeking the comforts and pleasures of the flesh and ignoring completely the life of the spirit. They had succumbed to the siren call; their standards of living had become completely hedonistic and materialistic. Everyone glibly talked of Christianity but no one lived it. As Kierkegaard bitterly concluded, "All are Christians as a matter of course."[44]

Kierkegaard was firmly convinced that the chief reason for this sad state of Christianity in Denmark was the pernicious and all-pervasive influence of the philosophy of Georg Wilhelm Hegel (1770-1831). Hegelianism was THE system of philosophy which was taught in all German universities, as well as in those European universities that were influenced by German scholarship. Just as all Danes were automatically Christians, so all the educated élite of the middle nineteenth century were Hegelians. Simply put, all philosophy was Hegelianism and Hegelianism was the only recognized philosophy.

Fundamentally, Hegel's philosophy was a reaction to the transcendental idealism of Immanuel Kant, who denied the possibility of a speculative metaphysics. In his *Critique of Pure Reason*, Kant concluded that Reason deals with empty concepts (Ideas) and that man can never know the noumenon or the thing-in-itself (*Ding-an-sich*); he knows only the phenomenon. Now Hegel strenuously objects to this dichotomy between what is and the given (noumenon and phenomenon respectively), between reality and knowledge. Hegel, therefore, will insist that Reason must supply its own intuition and knowledge, as well as its forms. In this way, Hegel hoped to bridge the gap which Kant had introduced between thought and reality.

According to Hegel, everything is Mind; God, Nature, Will, Reason, art and philosophy are all Mind. On the other hand, everything is one. The Absolute is Mind. The basis of Hegelianism is System. Hegel's System is unity—which embraces unity of thought and unity of reality and therefore constitutes a complete whole. This system or whole is all in motion. Unlike Spinoza's static pantheism, Hegel holds that there is no static state of being. Reality is motion and becoming. The motion is that of a circular movement, where what is last is also first and what is first is also last. The whole of the System is variously referred to as the Absolute, Spirit, Mind, Intelligence, Idea, which is self-purposive and constantly in the process of becoming.[45]

The rhythm of this becoming or motion has three distinguishable periods: thesis, antithesis, and synthesis. The movement which is always present in this triadic form, Hegel calls the dialectical movement. The motive force of this dialectic is the opposition between thesis and antithesis, which Hegel terms "the creative unrest of the Absolute." Hegel further asserts that the dialectic is the only true method. This is already evident from the fact that the method is in no way different from its object and content. For it is the content in itself, the Dialectic which it has in itself that moves it.[46]

According to Hegel's dialectic, a thesis or "position" which is posited, immediately and necessarily generates an antithesis or op-position. To avoid a contradiction, a broader base or synthesis is needed, which will contain elements of both thesis and antithesis. This becomes the synthesis or "composition." Much like a polysyllogism in logic, wherein the conclusion of the first syllogism becomes the first or major premise of the second syllogism, the synthesis in the Hegelian triad becomes a new thesis, which in turn generates another antithesis or negation and so on.

We therefore have one reality, the Mind or Spirit or God, which is constantly mediating and sublimating itself according to the dialectical triadic process. Little wonder that Hegel insisted on calling this pantheistic idealism a speculative or metaphysical Logic, for he tells us that Logic coincides with metaphysics, the science of things set and held in thought.[47]

In such a pantheism, all concrete individuals are necessary and inevitable manifestations in the universe, known a priori and all coming from the single reality, i.e., the Absolute Mind or Spirit. Man's position in this constantly mediating System is extremely negligible. For each human being is not a separate and independent entity, possessing essence and existence, a free agent who chooses and who is master of his own destiny. No, each individual person is nothing more than one *moment* in the dialectical unfolding of the Absolute. As this fleeting moment in the process, man is absorbed by the System and his actions are not his own; they are the necessary unfolding of the Absolute. Obviously, Hegel left no room for any personal individuality, let alone any personal immortality.

It is this flagrant demeaning of the individual which Kierkegaard found so irritating in Hegel's philosophy. If man was nothing more than a passing moment of a highly complicated System, then how could he expect to live a truly personal and individual Christian life? How could he make genuinely existential choices and lead a meaningful existence? Hegelianism was guilty of the grossest abstractionism: it abstracted from the actually existing reality of things and dealt, not with flesh and blood individuals, but with abstract ideas.

As a result, in his *Point of View, Attack Upon Christendom*, as well as in the *Concluding Unscientific Postscript*, Kierkegaard considers Hegelian philosophy the greatest enemy of Danish Christianity. Hegel's system of abstract thought which ignores the worth and dignity of the individual human being is, in essence, anti-Christian and anti-religious.

In the *Postscript*, Kierkegaard writes, "The more the collective idea comes to dominate even ordinary consciousness, the more forbidding seems the transition to becoming a particular existing human being instead of losing oneself in the race, and saying 'we,' 'our age,' 'the nineteenth century.' . . . For what does a mere individual count for? . . . Each age has its own characteristic depravity. Ours is perhaps not pleasure or indulgence of sensuality, but rather *a dissolute pantheistic contempt for the individual man*. In the midst of all our exultation over the achievements of the age and the nineteenth century, there sounds a note of poorly conceived contempt for the individual man: in the midst of the self-importance of the contemporary generation there is revealed a sense of despair over being human. Everything must attach itself so as to be part of some movement; men are determined to lose themselves in the totality of things, in world-history, fascinated and deceived by a magic witchery; no one wants to be an individual human being."[48]

In another place, Kierkegaard points to the dangers of abstract thinking which ignores the existing individual. He says, "The thinker who can forget in all his thinking also to think that he is an existing individual, will never explain life. He merely makes an attempt to cease to be a human being in order to become a book or an objective something."[49]

In his *Journals*, Kierkegaard openly accuses Hegel of de-Christianizing the Danes by making the individual less important than the human race. In fact, Hegel has resorted to the animal world where the race is always more important than the individual for his inspiration. Kierkegaard writes, "How often have I shown that fundamentally Hegel makes men into heathens, into a race of animals gifted with reason. For in the animal world, 'the individual' is always less important than the race. But it is the peculiarity of the human race that just because the individual is created in the image of God, 'the individual' is above the race. This can be wrongly understood and terribly misused: *concedo*. But that is Christianity. And *that* is where the battle must be fought."[50]

Kierkegaard complained violently and uncompromisingly against the "obliteration" of the individual which Hegel's pantheism advocated. It was this levelling, this anonymity of the individual man which was, according to him, responsible for the lack of commitment on the part of Danish Christians. This basic notion of anonymity and non-involvement will be explored again and again by subsequent existentialists: Martin Heidegger will war against the complacently faceless *das Man*; Martin Buber will denounce the levelling influence of a collectivism, and Gabriel Marcel, in his *Man Against Mass Society*, will warn against the techniques of degradation, depersonalization and functionalization of man, who loses his dignity and individuality by becoming a victim of mass movements.

In *The Point of View*, Kierkegaard asserts, "A crowd —not this crowd or that, the crowd now living or the crowd long deceased, a crowd of humble people or of superior people, or rich or of poor etc.—a crowd in its very concept is the untruth, by reason of the fact that it renders the individual completely impenitent and irresponsible, or at least weakens his sense of responsibility by reducing it to a fraction."[51]

For the Melancholy Dane, the individual who must establish a personal relationship with God, is of paramount importance. Hegelianism, on the contrary, regards man as but a fleeting moment in the dialectical process. Kierkegaard explains, "I have endeavored to express the thought that to employ the category 'race' to indicate what it is to be a man, and especially as an indication of the highest attainment, is a misunderstanding and mere paganism, because the race, mankind, differs from an animal race not merely by its general superiority as a race, but by the *human* characteristic that every single individual within the race (not merely distinguished individuals but every individual) is more than the race. For to relate oneself to God is a far higher thing than to be related to the race and through the race to God."[52]

Kierkegaard, therefore, saw his entire life's work directed to the attainment of one over-riding goal, namely the rehabilitation of the dignity of the individual. This objective he was satisfied to identify with his mission on this earth, namely the overthrow of Hegelian pantheism and the return of the individual to his proper place of honor. With characteristic fervor he wrote, "If I were to desire an inscription for my tombstone, I should desire none other than 'THAT INDIVIDUAL.' "[53]

III. SUBJECTIVITY VERSUS OBJECTIVITY

Kierkegaard's answer to Hegel's abstractionism which denigrates the individual is *subjectivity*. By subjectivity, Kierkegaard means a total, personal assimilation of Christianity as a unique mode of life. Subjectivity is the very antithesis of philosophy which deals with abstract ideas. A speculative philosopher examines the object of his thought in a totally impersonal and uninvolved manner. As Gabriel Marcel would write much later on, the object of thought is something completely separated from the thinker. An object or problem (etymologically from *objicio* and *prosballo* προσβαλλῶ), is something thrown or hurled in front of me. It is distinct and separate from me. In fact, the more completely a thinker can set aside his personal feelings and concerns, the more "philosophical" is the inquiry. "To speculate" means "to look at," "to gaze at," "to examine." It always indicates a fundamental separation between thinker and object.[54] Such philosophical speculation which deals with the radically distinct object, Kierkegaard calls *objectivity*. And because Hegel's philosophy deals with abstract objects of thought, Kierkegaard identifies Hegelian abstractionism with objectivity.

Subjectivity, on the other hand, is diametrically opposed to the abstract speculations of the philosopher. Subjectivity, for Kierkegaard means the *practising* and *living* of Christianity. A man does not stand back and study Christianity as an abstract object, says Kierkegaard. He does not "speculate about Christianity. A genuine Christian LIVES Christianity. To lead an authentic existence, a man must be totally and completely immersed in the practice of Christianity. His Christianity must be one of total involvement and not abstract speculation.

Kierkegaard lashes out against Hegel's system and universal history when he writes, "Christianity protests every form of objectivity; it desires that the subject should be infinitely concerned about himself. It is subjectivity that Christianity is concerned with, and it is only in subjectivity that truth exists, if it exists at all; objectively, Christianity has absolutely no existence. If its truth happens to be in only a single subject, it exists in him alone: and there is greater Christian joy in heaven over this one individual than over universal history and the System, which as objective entities are incommensurable for that which is Christian."[55]

In contrasting subjectivity with objectivity, Kierkegaard points to the inevitable consequences of objective thinking, which ignores the subject who, after all, is more important than anything in the world. He says, "The way of objective reflection makes the subject accidental, and thereby transforms existence into something indifferent, something vanishing. . . . The way of objective reflection leads to abstract thought, to mathematics, to historical knowledge of different kinds; and always it leads away from the subject, whose existence or non-existence, and from the objective point of view rightly, becomes entirely indifferent."[56]

Again, Kierkegaard points to the deficiencies of abstract and objective thought which never reaches the actually existing individual human being. He declares, "The difficulty that inheres in existence, with which the existing individual is confronted, is one that never really comes to expression in the language of abstract thought, much less receives an explanation. Because abstract thought is *sub specie aeterni*, it ignores the concrete and the temporal, the existential process, the predicament of the existing individual arising from his being a synthesis of the temporal and the eternal situated in existence. Now if we assume that abstract thought is the highest manifestation of human activity, it follows that philosophy and the philosophers proudly desert existence, leaving the rest of us to face the worst."[57]

Another succinct condemnation of Hegelian abstract thought follows: "While abstract thought seeks to understand the concrete abstractly, the subjective thinker has conversely to understand the abstract concretely. Abstract thought turns from concrete men to consider man in general; the subjective thinker seeks to understand the abstract determination of being human in terms of this particular existing human being."[58]

IV. THE ETHICAL

While objectivity deals with abstract thought, subjectivity implies human action and therefore ethics. By its nature, ethics always denotes putting something into practice. The sole reason for knowing moral teaching is to implement that knowledge by putting it into practice. This is so because ethics always implies that some particular action should be done or avoided. It involves choice under existential conditions. Christianity, in this sense, demands the ethical, since it is not a body of theoretical knowledge. It is much more—it denotes a way of life, a manner and pattern of action. Moral precepts are not merely to be known and assented to theoretically. Of their very nature, they are to be lived. Subjectivity and Christianity, therefore, are equated with the ethical, since they eminently deal with action. In several places in the *Postscript*, Kierkegaard states his conviction on this point. He says, "It is necessary to be thus careful in dealing with an abstract thinker who not only desires for himself to remain in the pure being of abstract thought, but insists that this is the highest goal for human life and that a type of thought which leads to the ignoring of the ethical and a misunderstanding of the religious is the highest human thinking." Again, "It is on this point about existence, and the demand which the ethical makes upon each existing individual, that one must insist when an abstract philosophy and a pure thought assume to explain everything by explaining away what is decisive. . . . I shall be equally proud, insistent, fearless, and even defiant in standing by my thesis: that the Hegelian philosophy, by failing to define its relation to the existing individual, and by ignoring the ethical, confounds existence."[59]

Hence ethics, like subjectivity, does not deal with abstract universals. Its preoccupation is with individuals, with particulars, with this specific human being. Kierkegaard argues, "Ethics closes immediately about the individual and demands that he exist ethically; it does not make a parade of millions, or of generations of men; it does not take humanity in the lump at large. The ethical is concerned with particular human beings, and with each and every one of them by himself. . . . The ethical requirement is imposed upon each individual, and when it judges, it judges each individual by himself."[60]

The Dane is adamant in stating that without ethics, no individual finds a secure foundation for his individual existence. It is the ethical choice which gives value and worth to his actions, no matter how outstanding and impressive they may be. He says, "Ethics and the ethical, as constituting the essential anchorage for all individual existence, have an indefeasible claim upon every existing individual; so indefeasible a claim, that whatever a man may accomplish in the world, even the most astonishing of achievements, it is none the less quite dubious in its significance unless the individual has been ethically clear when he made his choice, has ethically clarified his choice to himself. . . . Demoralized by too assiduous an absorption in world-historical considerations, people no longer have any will for anything except what is world-historically significant, no concern for anything but the accident, world-historical outcome, instead of concerning themselves solely with the essential, the inner spirit, the ethical, freedom."[61]

In summary, then, Hegel's philosophy, which is a pantheistic idealism, is guilty of abstractionism. Because it considers the System to be the unique reality and because it abstracts from actually existing things, Hegelianism can never accord the individual his proper place in reality. Such an abstract system of thought has no place for action, for the realm of the practical. Kierkegaard, therefore, maintains that only by emphasizing subjectivity and the ethical, can he hope to present Christianity as a practical way of life, an essential involvement and not a mere set of formalistic principles, whereby everyone professes to be a Christian but no one lives the Christian life.

V. PHILOSOPHY VERSUS RELIGION

Hegel's position, which reduced the individual man to a fleeting moment in the dialectical evolutionary process of the Absolute was, according to Kierkegaard's way of thinking, bad enough. But Hegel compounded this error by his most unacceptable attitude toward religion and philosophy. According to the Hegelian dialectic, the self-purposive Mind or Spirit, after having mediated and unfolded itself via a host of triads, would finally return upon itself by way of an ultimate triad. This final triad, wherein the synthesis could not become a new thesis, would be composed of art (thesis), religion (antithesis) and philosophy (synthesis). Note well that it was philosophy and not religion which occupied the highest and ultimate moment in the Hegelian dialectic. In other words, to Kierkegaard's consternation, Hegel was subordinating religion to philosophy and faith to reason.

Although Hegel did insist that the teachings of Christianity were true, yet it was philosophy and not religion which contained the ultimate truths. For religion, according to Hegel, which is the interior manifestation of the Absolute, gives only a *pictorial or figurative* representation of the rational truths which philosophy alone can understand completely and essentially. True, religion is the knowledge of God but it grasps the Absolute merely through representations. Philosophy, on the other hand, grasps the Absolute as it really exists,—essentially and

completely. The philosopher, therefore, removes the obstacle or the pictorial content of religion and gives the
truths an infinitely superior, pure, rational articulation.

For example, continues Hegel, the theological or
religious doctrine of creation of all things by God is but
a pictorial representation of the logically dialectical manifestation or evolution of the Absolute Spirit in nature. In
the case of the Incarnation, (another Christian religious
truth), the philosopher's mind goes beyond the pictorial
form in which this truth is made known to religious
consciousness. The philosopher sees the Incarnation in
its rational essence, namely as a moment in the life of
the Absolute Mind or Spirit. The Incarnation thus represents a kind of fusion of the human and the divine in
process history.

Robert Bretall describes Hegel's position as follows:
"Not only may people accept the Gospel (or what they
think to be the Gospel) because it is made easy and
attractive for them; but they accept it because it is made
to appeal to their intellects as logical or reasonable—*as
sanctioned by human reason.* . . . Abhorrent to Søren
Kierkegaard above all else was the condescending attitude
of the Hegelian philosophers of his day, who were continually 'going further' than Christianity—i.e., from a
supposed higher vantage point looking down upon such
doctrines as the Incarnation and the Atonement and showing that they were indeed true—if one understood them in
a certain sense."[62]

Kurt Reinhardt comments on the Hegelian attitude
toward Christianity when he writes, "Step by step, he
[Hegel] had transformed the Christian dogmatics into a
gnostic theory of knowledge: Redemption was interpreted
as the redeeming force of love; the Holy Trinity became
the 'dialectic of the Absolute Mind'; the God-Man was
transformed into a man who had experienced his identity
with the Absolute; and the Holy Spirit appeared as a
communal spirit of social life. Was Kierkegaard's view
then unduly gloomy when he saw in Hegel the most in-
genious and therefore the most dangerous modern enemy
of Christianity?"[63]

In opting for the superiority of philosophy over religion and faith, Hegel in reality deified reason. While the Christian theologian had traditionally maintained that God cannot be known fully and completely by any finite mind, Hegel was now claiming that through his pantheism, the philosopher uniquely can grasp and fully understand the essential nature of God. This knowledge of the Infinite takes place in the ultimate synthesis, which is philosophy, where we find a final and full reconciling on the part of Mind or Spirit. We have here a Totality in which each part is distinct as only a moment of the evolutionary process but all parts disappear by identifying themselves with the Absolute which absorbs them all. The philosopher, therefore, no longer considers God to be a Transcendent Being because, unlike the theologian or man of faith, he can know God completely through his unaided reason. To this levelling of God with man, Kierkegaard objects most emphatically. He accuses Hegel or having destroyed "the radical otherness" of God.

Kierkegaard emphasizes the absolute difference which exists between God and man. He categorically asserts that any attempt to introduce a similarity or likeness between Creator and creature is to be rejected. He writes, "If God were in the immediate sense the ideal of human beings, it would be right to endeavor to express a direct likeness. Thus when a distinguished man is an ideal for me, it is quite proper for me to attempt to express a direct resemblance to him, since we were both human beings and both within the same sphere. But as between God and a human being (for let speculative philosophy keep *humanity* to play tricks with), there is an absolute difference. In man's absolute relationship to God, this absolute difference must therefore come to expression, and any attempt to express an immediate likeness becomes impertinence, frivolity, effrontery and the like. . . . Precisely because there is an absolute difference between God and man, man will express his own nature most adequately when he expresses this difference absolutely."[64]

In an entry for 1847 in the *Journals*, Kierkegaard succinctly asserts, "All the confusion of modern thought springs from attempting to abolish the qualitative abyss that separates God from man."[65]

Hegelianism has, therefore, insidiously and meretriciously undermined Danish Christianity. The Danish Lutheran ministers, who were educated in the German universities and in the Scandinavian centers of learning, secretly, if not openly, espoused Hegelianism. By subscribing to this pantheistic philosophy of Hegel, the ministers were responsible for the following inexcusable errors: (1) obliteration of the individual human being who is nothing more than a moment in the evolutionary process of the System (2) glorification of the abstract and the belittling of the concrete singular (3) the rendering of reason as superior to faith and of philosophy as more excellent than religion.

Kierkegaard, accordingly, accuses the ministers of betraying Christianity. They have compromised the traditional truths of religion by making them palatable to the sceptics. The ministers have agreed with the latter that religion and faith are for "hoi polloi," for the common ordinary run of mankind, endowed with a pedestrian type of mind. Philosophy, on the other hand, was reserved for the intellectually élite, for those who possessed superior intellects. Only they have the truth because they alone understand all Christian mysteries fully: they see them as momentary yet necessary manifestations of the evolution of the System. The Danish ministers, contends Kierkegaard, have become traitors to Christ; they have sold their noble inheritance for a mess of pottage. They have betrayed their calling.

Kierkegaard indignantly proclaims, "The realm of faith is thus not a class for *minus habentes*, numbskulls, in the sphere of the intellectual, or an asylum for the feebleminded. Faith constitutes a sphere all by itself, and every misunderstanding of Christianity may at once be recognized by its transforming it into a doctrine, transforming it to the sphere of the intellectual."[66]

VI. FAITH VERSUS REASON

Kierkegaard maintains that the only hope for returning to a living, practical and truly viable Christianity is by establishing a complete disjunction between faith and reason, between religion and philosophy. Faith needs no proofs from philosophy. On the contrary, a faith unencumbered by rational proofs is much more firm and genuine than one which looks to the demonstrations of reason for corroboration. In the *Postscript*, Kierkegaard writes, "Here is the crux of the matter and I come back to the case of the learned theology. For whose sake is it that the proof is sought? Faith does not need it; aye, it must even regard the proof as its enemy. But when faith begins to feel embarrassed and ashamed, like a young woman for whom her love is no longer sufficient, but who secretly feels ashamed of her lover and must therefore have it established that there is something remarkable about him —when faith thus begins to lose its passion, when faith begins to cease to be faith, then a proof becomes necessary so as to command respect from the side of unbelief."[67]

It would seem therefore, that there is no place in Kierkegaard's thought for a traditional theodicy or philosophy of God, as the highest branch of metaphysics, which would undertake to demonstrate the existence of a Supreme Being or even to adduce the reasonableness of His existence. Whether philosophy calls this Being a First Cause, or Unmoved Mover or Necessary Being, its conclusions are of absolutely no value. This is so because these conclusions add nothing to the firmness of faith. In fact, according to Kierkegaard, they detract from it. Hence, it is the grossest of presumptions, bordering on arrogance, for man to undertake a proof for the existence of God. Kierkegaard sees the most blatant contradiction in attempting to prove the existence of someone who, according to him, is present before our very eyes. Hence the existence of God can be proved in only one way, namely by *Worship* and not by any proof.

For Kierkegaard, then, rational arguments are absolutely useless in the face of faith. Faith which would find it necessary to look to rational arguments for corroboration ceases to perform its vital function. In the *Concluding Unscientific Postscript*, Kierkegaard speaks of the *absurd* as the proper object of faith and he argues that any attempt to make this object plausible, probable or knowable is a destruction of faith itself. Even a seemingly laudable motive, as for example, "making faith clear to oneself" will inevitably result in the destruction of faith. In a rather extended passage Kierkegaard describes the antithetical position between faith and understanding. It is a case of Either/Or.

The Dane writes, "The absurd is precisely by its objective repulsion the measure of the intensity of faith: let the comedy begin. He wishes to have faith, but he wishes also to safeguard himself by means of an objective inquiry and its approximation—process. What happens? With the help of the approximation—process, the absurd becomes something different: it becomes probable, it becomes increasingly probable, it becomes extremely and emphatically probable. Now he is ready to believe it and he ventures to claim for himself that he does not believe as shoemakers and tailors and simple folk believe, but only after long deliberation. Now he is ready to believe it; and lo, now it has become precisely impossible to believe it. Anything that is almost probable, or probable or extremely and emphatically probable, is something he can almost know, or as good as know, or extremely and emphatically almost know—*but it is impossible to believe. For the absurd is the object of faith and the only object that can be believed.*

Or suppose a man who says he has faith but desires to make his faith clear to himself, so as to understand himself in his faith. Now the comedy begins again. The object of faith becomes almost probable, as good as probable, extremely and emphatically probable. He has contemplated his investigations and he ventures to claim for himself that he does not believe as shoemakers and tailors and other simple folk believe, but that he has also understood himself in his believing. Strange understanding! On the contrary, he has in fact learned something else about faith than when he believed; and he has learned that he no longer believes, since he almost knows, or as good as knows or extremely and emphatically knows."[68]

VII. THE ABSURD AS OBJECT OF FAITH

Kierkegaard never tires of pointing to the irrational and paradoxical character of faith. By definition, the *absurd* is the object of faith, which means that faith deals with that which is absolutely incomprehensible and unintelligible. Now Hegel had maintained that in the ultimate synthesis, i.e., in philosophy, human reason was capable of understanding all the mysteries of the Christian faith, i.e., Trinity, Incarnation, the nature of God and so on. Kierkegaard considers this a kind of blasphemy because Hegel was investing human reason with a power to understand the infinite and the incomprehensible. For Kierkegaard, the greatest mystery, the non-intelligible, that is, the absurd, is the proper object of faith. An excellent example of the absurd is Christ, the God-Man. Kierkegaard tries to express this ineffable mystery when he writes, "The absurd is—that the eternal truth has come into being, in time, that God has come into being precisely like any other individual human being, quite indistinguishable from other individuals . . . that God has come into being, that God's eternal being is bounded by the dialectical determination of existence—this is a contradiction. . . . The absurd is precisely by its objective repulsion, the measure of the intensity of faith by inwardness. . . . The absurd is the proper object of faith and the *only* object that can be believed."[69]

Again, in speaking of faith, Kierkegaard holds that this "paradox-religious sphere" transcends the level of understanding. Anyone who pretends to understand the paradox, in reality, misunderstands it. He says, "This is the paradox-religious sphere, the sphere of faith. It can be believed altogether—against the understanding. If anyone imagines that he understands it, he can be sure that he misunderstands it. He who understands it plainly will confound Christianity with one or another pagan analogy . . . and will forget the qualitative distinction which accentuates the absolutely different point of departure: what comes from God and what comes from man."[70]

Christianity, therefore, is the eternal truth which has come into being in time. It has presented itself as the Paradox supreme, and hence it has demanded an inwardness of faith on the part of each individual. For that reason, it is an absurdity to the understanding and, as Kierkegaard points out, it would be very strange indeed for Christianity, if it came into the world merely to receive an explanation as if it were somewhat bewildered about itself and "hence entered the world to consult the wise man, the speculative philosopher who can come to its assistance by furnishing the explanation."[71]

Christianity, therefore, deals with the paradox of the Incarnation, the paradox of the cross, the paradox of sin. But above all, Christianity stands for the greatest of all paradoxes, namely the divinity of Christ in the Incarnation.

It was Kierkegaard's conviction that only by means of the paradox could God's transcendence and the personal quality of the object of faith be saved. As Henri Bouillard expresses it, "As to God's transcendence, the paradox is the expression of the infinite distance between man and God—and the only way in which it can be bridged."[72] Because Hegel had transformed Christianity into a divinizing of humanity, he had succeeded in changing it into the very opposite. Kierkegaard warns us that all such confusion in modern thought is due to an attempt to eradicate "the qualitative abyss" that separates God from man. The paradox is the means of re-establishing the infinite distance between creature and Creator.

The paradox also saves the personal quality of the object of faith. "If the appearance of the Eternal in time is essentially paradox, it is impossible to treat Christianity as a collection of propositions, a petty system, a philosophy. The object of faith is not a doctrine, it is a person; it is the reality of God in existence: it is Christ as the God-man."[73]

Now traditional Christianity has always held that

faith carries with it a far greater certitude than does human reason. Faith is based on God's authority, whereas human reason is only man's unaided intellect with all its limitations and deficiencies. (In fact, this is what the great medieval thinker, St. Thomas Aquinas, pointed out, when he underscored the many disagreements among philosophers on the most basic issues of philosophy, e.g., the existence of God, man's ultimate end, and so on. Revelation, on the other hand, always carries with it a certitude, e.g., on the question of the immortal soul of man, Christianity gave man a certitude which no philosophical system could even remotely approach.) This is why, too, Aquinas considered it eminently fitting that matters concerning man's salvation should have been revealed to man by God. In matters of such importance, man should not be left to the mercy of the philosophers' uncertainties, whims and vagaries.[74]

Traditional Christianity has always maintained that the great mysteries of the Trinity, Incarnation and the like can never be fully understood by the human intellect. The Christian accepts them on faith, without comprehending them rationally. Kierkegaard, it would seem, is not satisfied with this time-honored distinction between faith and reason. He would go much further. From the texts we have just examined, it is quite apparent that reason is of absolutely *no* value in preparing the believer. The Dane appears to be denying here the very possibility of metaphysics and, more specifically, of natural theology. We might point out, however, that contrary to these allegations, men for centuries have arrived at the notion of order, finality, and purpose in the universe. By means of their unaided intellect, they have argued to the reasonableness of the existence of a Supreme Being, Who is a personal God, Creator of all, since He is the Primary Efficient Cause. Granted that man's knowledge of this Being did not, in any way, pretend to be exhaustive or even satisfactory, due to the inadequacy of limited human knowing powers, the absolutely Transcendent Being could, nevertheless, be known in a partial and analogical manner.

Minimally, countless men have, over the centuries, come to a notion of the existence of God, whether they considered Him in terms of a Necessary Being, an Uncaused Cause or an Unmoved Mover.[75]

The criticism which a contemporary theologian, Robert McAfee Brown, levels against Karl Barth, who similarly denied the possibility of a theodicy or philosophy of God, is especially applicable here. Brown writes, "There is a real problem in the area of Christian communication. To what degree can Barth's approach make contact with the person who does not accept all the presuppositions on which it is based? Must not one already believe before he can hear what Barth has to say? Is there not a danger that his theology will be a source of truth only to those already committed and that others who have to be won to the faith by apologetic tools less pure, perhaps even by the use of natural theology? Until one stands within the circle of faith Barth has circumscribed, can he really hear?"[76]

Concerning Kierkegaard's notion of Christianity as a paradox, two points must be made. First, Kierkegaard rendered a great service by calling attention to the fact that Christianity can never be reduced to the level of human speculation, as if it dealt merely with human thought and human action. Second, Kierkegaard's definition of Christianity as paradox is too exclusively negative. Henri Bouillard summarizes this second point when he says, "Christianity would mean nothing to us if it did not offer something for the mind to hold on to. We would prefer to think of it as a mystery rather than a paradox. The difference lies in the fact that, if the mystery itself is obscure, it lets light through to us. As a statement of scientific truth, we should find it incomprehensible, but it helps us to understand ourselves; it reveals us to ourselves and gives us a guiding principle for our actions. If Christianity is not purely speculative thought, nevertheless thought is an essential element in it. Faith is more than a decision in a paradoxical situation; it is free adherence of the spirit to the divine word who communicates himself through the medium of meaningful human words."[77]

Another commentator finds an inherent contradiction in Kierkegaard's contention that subjectivity involves an outright denial of objectivity. As a matter of fact, this writer holds that subjectivity must presuppose the very objective truths which it claims to repudiate. Faith involves an affirmation on our part of the truth of what we believe. It involves an assertion on the part of the believer that what he holds is, indeed, true and worthy of belief. Specifically, faith demands that what is believed about God and man have objective truth and validity. If this is not true, then faith stands in great danger of losing its transcendent reference and also its transcendent object. We cite the passage, "The point I wish to make is that while it ostensibly turns away from the issue of objective truth, Kierkegaard's procedure presupposes such truth at every step in its retreat into recessive inwardness. His subjectivity is parasitic for its 'existential significance' on the assumed *objective truth of a doctrine about man and God,* whose right to claim such truth it strives at every point to discredit. Not only does it bite the hand that feeds it, but it calls this questionable procedure 'faith'. . . . Of course faith is not knowledge and a man cannot fairly be asked to demonstrate the truth of that which, in the circumstances of his creaturely existence, he must accept on faith or not at all. But faith is at least an affirmation of the objective truth of what is believed and objectively, as a human attitude, is the concern that what is thus affirmed, *shall in fact be true and credible as such* by such standards as are humanly available. It is unreasonable to limit such standards to the procedures of mathematics and the empirical sciences, since these would be inappropriate to the relation between God and man, if such a relation did in fact exist. But to reject not merely a too narrow objectivity but a concern for the objective truth itself, and to make an existential virtue of the inflexible determination to retain a preconceived opinion at all costs is a danger not so much to reason as to faith it-

self. *For when faith loses its concern for objective truth,
it loses its transcendent references* and that means it also
loses its transcendent object."[78]

VIII.   REASON AS AID TO FAITH

Having thus seemingly condemned the legitimacy
and usefulness of reason and philosophy in furnishing
"preambles" of faith, Kierkegaard appears to refute his
own untenable position. In *Sickness Unto Death,* he studies
in detail the "dialectic of despair." Kierkegaard concludes
his examination by saying that the concept of "finiteness"
or "finitude" cannot be grasped except in terms of the
concept of infiniteness or infinitude.[79] Evidently without
realizing it, Kierkegaard seems unwittingly to be enlist-
ing the service of philosophy and reason and especially of
theodicy which he had so roundly condemned. Any undergraduate student in philosophy will recognize Kierkegaard's development as an appeal to the traditional and
classical arguments for the reasonableness of the existence
of God. The notion of finite-infinite; contingent-necessary;
limited-unlimited have a strangely familiar philosophical
ring.

Again, in the same *Sickness Unto Death,* the author
writes, "A self must either have constituted itself or have
been constituted by another."[80] Now this is another traditional philosophical concept which has been used in
theodicy by Christian thinkers in establishing rationally
the existence of a First Principle or God.

Finally, in the *Concluding Unscientific Postscript,*
Kierkegaard notes, "Dialectics is in truth a benevolent
helper which discovers and assists in finding where the
absolute object of faith and worship is. . . . Dialectics itself does not see the Absolute, but it leads, as it were,
the individual up to it and says, 'Here it must be, that I
guarantee; when you worship here, you worship God.'
But worship itself is not dialectics."[81]

These are strange words indeed for a man who has
seemed to repudiate so categorically the role of reason
and philosophy in preparing the way for faith.

Régis Jolivet, in the work, *Introduction to Kierke-*

gaard, attempts to explain this apparent contradiction in the writings of the Dane, by insisting that we have here a very fundamental confusion between two entirely different intellectual activities. Jolivet is convinced that Kierkegaard erroneously identified "the rational demonstration of the truth of something which transcends reason, and the rational demonstration of the reasons *for the belief in something that transcends reason.*" Jolivet asserts that this confusion "is well revealed in the texts where Kierkegaard objects to every attempt 'to prove Christianity' and unremittingly condemns apologetics. . . . But apologetics does not assume the senseless task of proving mysteries; it applies itself solely to assembling and establishing the proofs of credibility. The motives of credibility do not produce faith, but they influence the soul and justify it in admitting the gift of faith."[82]

Cornelio Fabro, the author of the monumental work, *God in Exile,* sets forth his own interpretation of Kierkegaard in a book entitled, *From Existence to the Existent.* In the chapter, "Faith and Reason in Kierkegaard's Dialectic," Fabro points to the complete disjunction between faith and reason, the absurd quality of the object of faith and suffering and persecution which are the hallmarks of a genuine Christianity. He says, "From the beginning to the end of his work, Kierkegaard never ceases to declare 'that truth is subjectivity.' Reason and philosophy have done nothing and do nothing but eliminate God from the human consciousness, since they lower him to their level. The object of faith is the absurd, the hatred of the world, the paradoxical, the irrational. The essence of the Christian life is differing, persecution, martyrdom. Finally . . . Christianity, as demanded by this 'terrible book' which is the New Testament, has never existed and has not yet been realized."[83]

Fabro goes on to show how Kierkegaard contrasts an act of faith with a rational judgment. The activity of the intellect in a judgment always takes place in accordance with a certain intelligible pattern inherent in the object known and hence there is an ability on the part of the intellect to grasp and to understand the object. In other words, the object is "intelligible" and capable of being known.

The act of faith, on the other hand, deals with the irrational and the absolutely unintelligible and incomprehensible. Its object is the absurd, the paradox. In order to believe, man must, therefore, forsake all modes of intellectual inquiry and activity. He must transcend the level of the finite and by a "leap" of faith involving the will rather than the intellect, grasp the "Wholly Other," namely God.

Fabro goes on to say, "The difficulty inherent in the act of faith is of an order completely different from that inherent in a judgment on some doctrine which is to be either followed or rejected. In the case of a doctrine, man finds a structure already present in the object, and in his understanding he has a power, proportionate to his intellectual level, to penetrate and explain this doctrine. . . . The act of faith, on the other hand, implies a total break with the rationality of the immediate and requires the passage into a sphere which is absolutely incommensurable with that of the natural man, even though he be the most gifted genius. The act of faith requires, therefore, a 'leap' (*Spring*) which carries man into a sphere where the criteria of the finite would lose all value—nay, where these criteria are rejected. For the object of faith, the revelation of God to man, is for human reason, the absurd, the paradoxical, the incomprehensible. Thus if a man decides to embrace the faith, this will not happen because of evidence intrinsic in the demonstrations but because of a 'Thou must' presented to the will, which it alone is able to realize."[84]

Fabro contends, however, that in spite of the apparent opposition between faith and reason, Kierkegaard is genuinely located in the tradition of such defenders of Christianity as St. Augustine of Hippo, St. Bernard of Clairvaux, Blaise Pascal, and the medieval Franciscan mystics, who had seen in reason and in its intricate artifices, an actual danger to faith. Fabro expresses it in this manner, "In order that man may arrive at faith and remain in it, there is no need of science or the complicated mechanisms of

КKIERKEGAARD 65

ratiocination; furthermore, if they were needed, faith would be a privilege of the speculative aristocracy and not—as Christianity teaches—the universal vocation of all humanity."[85]

Kierkegaard's own brother Peter, who was first a pastor and then bishop of Aalborg, in a monthly pastoral conference at Roskilde on October 30, 1849, himself accused Søren of a complete denigration of the value and dignity of human reason in relation to faith. It seemed to Peter that Søren categorically rejected the use of reason in support of faith and denied the validity of all apologetics and theological reflection. A contemporary pamphlet, issued by a certain Magnus Eiriksson, likewise interpreted Søren's position as being anti-rationalist. Kierkegaard intended to reply to Eiriksson in print. The work never appeared, although fragments of his reply have been published in the collection of his works, *Papirer*.

Fabro maintains that on the basis of this cumulative evidence, Kierkegaard very definitely subscribed to a position dictated by traditional theology. Søren's chief intent was to defend the absolute transcendence of Christianity against the invasion of an illuministic and idealistic reason, and to destroy the misunderstanding created by the theology of the Hegelian right.

To substantiate this claim, Fabro considers the following points: (1) the possibility of apologetics (*ratio ante fidem, ad fidem*) (2) the possibility of theology (*ratio post fidem, pro fide*).

A. Possibility of Apologetics

Traditionally, Christianity has maintained that reason is *incapable* of supplying the intrinsic ground of revealed truth. Hegel's contention that philosophy gives us the truth of faith is, in reality, a destruction of faith. Kierkegaard points out that faith does not depend on knowledge but on authority. This authority, he hastens to point out, must be firmly grounded. Kierkegaard continues, "When someone says that faith rests on authority and thereby believes himself to have excluded dialectics, he is mistaken; for dialectics begins by asking how it is that one submits to this authority, whether one does not himself understand why he chose it, whether it was only by chance. For in that case, the authority is not authority, not even for the believer if he knows that it was a question of pure chance."[86]

Reason, therefore, has an important function in that it points to authority; it designates the person who has the authority which is required by faith. Kierkegaard appeals by name to St. Augustine, who held that the most perfect expression of the truth of Christianity is to be found in authority, so much so, that were it possible for one to have the same truth without authority, it would be less perfect. He writes, "Alas, even Augustine had learned what men need most: authority, precisely what the human race, wearied by the doubts of philosophers and the wretchedness of the world at the time of the introduction of Christianity, had learned. In our days, things have changed. A self-styled philosophical Christianity finds that authority is something imperfect, at best something for plebeians, and that perfection consists in getting rid of it—in order to get back to the times prior to the introduction of Christianity into the world."[87]

B. Possibility of Theology: Reason and Faith

While reason's function is not to explain faith, it nevertheless does perform the valuable service of preparing and inviting man in a certain way to accept it. Besides, reason can perform the additional service of establishing that the object of faith "transcends reason and cannot depend on it." In Kierkegaard's own words, reason enables us "to understand that it is impossible to understand." Kierkegaard further expands this notion when he writes, "If there is to be a science of Christianity, it must be erected not on the basis of the necessity of comprehending that faith cannot be comprehended. What has been here expounded is what I now understand: in the beginning of my literary activity, I did not understand this as clearly as I do now."[88]

Fabro goes on to state that on the basis of Kierkegaard's unpublished answers to Theophilus Nicolaus

(Eiriksson), the Melancholy Dane believed that the object of faith was the absurd and the paradox only to those who are lacking in faith, i.e., the non-believers. For the believer, for the man of faith, such an object is neither a paradox nor the absurd, precisely because God is the measure of things and to Him, all things without exception are possible. Such an object is eminently the truth that saves. Fabro writes, "The object of faith is the absurd, the paradox, which is the inevitable cause of scandal, but only for whoever sees this object from the outside, i.e., *for him who has no faith*. It is an absurdity which has an existential, not an essential origin. For the believer, for the man of faith, his criterion is God, for whom all things are possible; in the light of faith, he sees that this is absurd, far from being a contradiction, is one truth which saves—the supreme example being the Incarnation."[89]

In his intended answer to Eiriksson, Kierkegaard asserts that the Absurd is a very special kind of category It is not to be identified with absurdities. When it is the object of faith on the part of the believer, the Absurd becomes transformed into a negative criterion which far excels the level of human understanding. All that human reason can do is to recognize the Absurd—its belief is a matter of faith.

Kierkegaard explains, "The Absurd is not indiscriminately absurd or absurdities. . . . The Absurd is a category and accurately and with conceptual precision to define the Christian Absurd requires the most involved thinking. The Absurd is a category, it is the negative criterion for God or for the relationship to God. When the believer believes, the Absurd is not the Absurd—faith transforms it; but in every weak moment, to him it is again more or less the Absurd. The passion of faith is the only thing capable of mastering the Absurd. If this were not so, faith would not be faith in the strictest sense, but would be a kind of knowledge. The Absurd provides a negative demarcation of the sphere of faith, making it a sphere in itself. . . . The Absurd is a negative criterion for that which is higher than human understanding and human knowing. The function of the understanding is to recognize the Absurd as such—and then leave it up to each and every man whether or not he will believe it."[90]

The Paradox does violate, as it were, the laws of reason. By this very fact, however, reason is made aware of its limitations. The Paradox, even though found to be irrational by reason is, nevertheless, not impossible. This is so because reason deals with the question of rationality and irrationality and not with the question of the existential conditions of the Paradox. To that extent, faith shows reason that reason has extended itself to its very limits. At the same time, faith maintains that there *is* a reality, namely, the Paradox which transcends the boundaries of reason. To that extent, while the Paradox is irrational, it is not impossible existentially speaking.

As Herbert Garelick writes in *The Anti-Christianity of Kierkegaard*, "The laws of identity, contradiction, and excluded middle constitute the essence of reason. They are denied in the affirmation of the Absolute Paradox. Thus faith is against reason. But in confronting the Paradox, reason becomes conscious of its own limits. . . . However, having discovered its limits, we must admit that, since reason cannot determine existential facts, it cannot say that the Paradox cannot be. . . . When reason realizes its limits, we can say that reason is 'against' faith and yet faith is 'above' reason . . . faith against reason indicating reason's recognition of the impossibility of judging the reality of that which denies reason."[91]

Fabro points out that between the years 1842 and 1843, when Kierkegaard was reading Leibnitz's *Theodicy*, the Dane recognized along with Leibnitz "the possibility of an agreement between faith and reason." In his commentary on the *Theodicy*, Kierkegaard wrote in big capital letters in the manner of a headline, the following: "INTRODUCTION TO THE THEODICÉE DEALS WITH THE CONFORMITY BETWEEN FAITH AND REASON." Then Kierkegaard wrote the following observation, "When I am accustomed to express by saying that Christianity lies in paradox, philosophy in mediation, Leibnitz expresses by making a distinction between that which is above reason and that which is against reason. Faith is *above* reason. By reason, he understands, as he several times remarks, a linking together of truths, an *enchainement*, a conclusion from causes. Faith can therefore not be proved, grounded, or comprehended, for the link is missing which would make a joining together possible and, what is this but to say that it is a paradox; for this is precisely the desultory feature of the paradox, which lacks continuity; that is to say, which does not originally appear as continuity. In my opinion, it must be said of Christianity's paradoxicality and improbability that they are the first form, both in the history of the world and in individual consciousness[92]

It is Fabro's contention that all critics of Kierkegaard's position who stop at pure negativity are grossly naïve. Further, in distinguishing between the two forms of Religiousness, i.e., "A" and "B," Fabro holds that Kierkegaard "expressly admits a true form of religiousness independent of revelation proper to man in the state of nature, which he calls "Religiousness-A." The Religiousness based on revelation, on the other hand, he calls "Religiousness-B." The first, which is the zenith (apogee) of human wisdom before Christ and was achieved by Socrates—has God, the ontological absolute, as its object. The second has the Word-Incarnate, the "essential paradox" as its center. "For Kierkegaard, then, Religiousness-A is true religiousness and in the spirit structure of man, it has the same positive value that it had in the course of history. Still better, it has a propaedeutic value, which Kierkegaard considers indispensable in relation to Religiousness-B. . . . Religiousness-A must already be present, therefore, before any attention can be given to the dialectic of the other."[93]

Finally, Fabro presents a quotation from Kierkegaard on the relation between "Speculation and Faith," where we find delineated specific contributions which reason can make vis-à-vis faith. The Dane's position on this point seems to be strikingly in harmony with traditional Christianity. Kierkegaard writes, "Speculation can present the problems. It knows that each particular problem is compounded in such wise that it exists for faith and is marked out for faith—and then it puts the question: Will you believe or not?

Furthermore, Speculation can check faith, i.e., check that which in a given moment is believed or is the content of faith, to make certain that no determinations foreign to faith—determinations which are not properly the objects of faith but e.g., of Speculation—have, through somebody's bumbling and babbling, been mixed with it. All of this is extremely involved work. Speculation is gifted with sight —yet only to the point of its being able to say 'Here it is'; then it is blind. After that comes faith which believes that it has the gift of sight in relation to the object of faith."[94]

In concluding this section on "Faith and Reason; Religion and Philosophy," perhaps Kierkegaard's own words best summarize the role of the corrective which he had assigned himself to play. He writes, "The corrective makes himself understood, in a certain measure, at the expense of what is corrected. If that is so, an apparently penetrating mind can reproach the corrective by pointing out that he sees only one side of things and he can easily persuade the public that this is so. Good God! What is easier than for one who has first given the corrective to go on and add the complementary aspect?"[95]

It would seem from the above quotation, that by assuming the role of the corrective, Kierkegaard deliberately and consciously overstated his case. He intentionally and purposely overemphasized the role of faith, in order to compensate for Hegel's overemphasis of the function and importance of reason. By resorting to such an extreme method of presentation, the Dane hoped to restore the proper balance that should obtain between faith and reason, between revelation and philosophy.

IX. CHRISTIANITY VERSUS CHRISTENDOM

The last years of Kierkegaard's life were devoted to a relentless attack upon the state-supported Danish Church, which he described as "Christendom." To Kierkegaard's mind, Christendom exemplified the dry formalism and legalism, the emptiness and hollowness of a once viable and vibrant way of life. This "mediocrity," as Kierkegaard termed it, stood for apathy, non-involvement and complete ennui on the part of so many Danish Christians.

In *The Point of View*, Kierkegaard describes his mission which is to make known to all men, the pretensions of this spurious kind of Christianity. He explains, "The whole of my work as an author is related to Christianity, to the problem of 'becoming a Christian,' with direct or indirect polemic against the monstrous illusion we call *Christendom* or against the illusion that in such a land as ours all are Christians."[96]

In spite of the fact that Denmark calls itself a "Christian nation," it is only masquerading as a counterfeit, a giant hoax. In an article which appeared in *The Fatherland*, on Monday, March 26, 1855, Kierkegaard tries to prod the collective conscience of his fellow Danes. He admonishes, "We are what is called a 'Christian nation'— but in such a sense that not a single one of us is in character of the Christianity of the New Testament, any more than I am, who again and again have repeated and do now repeat, that I am only a poet. The illusion of a Christian nation is due doubtless to the power which number exercises over the imagination. . . . We have what one might call a complete inventory of churches, bells, organs, benches, alms-boxes, foot-warmers, tables, hearses etc. But when Christianity does not exist, the existence of this inventory, so far from being Christianly considered, an advantage, is far rather a peril because it is so infinitely likely to give rise to a false impression and the false inference that when we have such a complete Christian inventory, we must of course have Christianity."[97]

Kierkegaard adamantly maintains that the root cause of this monstrous pretension, i.e., Christendom, is the fact that Danish Christianity is protected by the State. By allowing itself to be supported by the government, Christianity has become despoiled. It has succumbed to the siren call of the courtesan; it has sold its soul for a few pieces of silver. As "the official Church of Denmark," it has ceased to be a living, viable, dynamic Christianity. We witness today, says Kierkegaard, a stagnant Christendom, a degenerate form of the authentic original. Yes, the Church of Denmark owns a complete inventory of the accoutrements of Christianity (they are supported *gratis* by the state), but the soul has departed from the body. In its place, we have a fast decaying corpse.

This is the reason why Kierkegaard asks the question whether such a fallen Christendom is what men really need. In point of fact, he vehemently argues that a fallen Christendom, openly or more hiddenly, now by attack, now by defense, has abolished Christianity.

Ernst Breisach describes the inherent dangers of such a Christendom in the following words: "The central danger posed by Christendom is that man never has the chance truly to search, since what looks like satisfaction is offered to him even before any real religious quest can arise. This means to forget that the cross and what it symbolizes represents a challenge to the total person and should never be the fountainhead of doctrines. The Church is at its worst when it identifies the acceptance of a pre-digested message with becoming a Christian. This complex of dogmas, rituals and administrators of faith which Kierkegaard calls objective Christianity (or Christendom), is nothing but the religious counterpart of secular, philosophical system."[98]

Kierkegaard maintained to the very end that a genuinely Christian Church can never be state-supported because the state, by its very nature, is secular, mundane and "this-worldly." The Church, in order to preserve its identity, must be spiritual, holy and "other-worldly." A state protected Christianity is an absolute contradiction. When Christianity first came into the world, it neither sought nor received state protection. In fact, the state persecuted the Church, and the greater the opposition by Caesar, the more vigorous was its growth. Truly its seed was the blood of its martyrs. In its early days, Christianity represented a great risk. To become a Christian meant very frequently to forfeit one's total earthly possessions—yes, even one's life. Christianity demanded a "total commitment"; it had no place for the weak and the fearful, for whom religion was true only up to a certain point. Today, Danish Christianity represents no risk, no sacrifice, no total involvement, says Kierkegaard. The state, by "protecting" Christianity and by making it the official religion has, in fact, enfeebled and emasculated the originally vibrant and pulsating Christianity. Truly, the state has destroyed the Christianity of the Gospels. Apathy, complaisance and absolute indifference are the hallmarks of Danish Lutheranism.

In *The Instant*, Kierkegaard contrasts what he calls "The Christianity of the New Testament" and "The Christianity of Christendom." He writes, "The result of the Christianity of 'Christendom' is that everything, absolutely everything has remained as it was, only everything has assumed the name of 'Christian' . . . we live a life of paganism."[99]

In another place he charges, "Christendom is not the Church of Christ . . . not by any means. No, I say that 'Christendom' is twaddle which has clung to Christianity like a cobweb to a fruit and now is so polite as to want to be mistaken for Christianity, just as if the cobweb were to think that it was the fruit because it is a thing not nearly so nice which hangs on the fruit. . . . The sort of existence which the millions of 'Christendom' give evidence of, has absolutely no relation to the New Testament. . . . 'Christendom' is the disgusting foolery of willing to remain wholly in finiteness and then . . . allege the promises of Christ."[100]

Finally, in a striking passage in the first issue of *The Instant*, Kierkegaard asks the question, "Is it justifiable on the part of the State—the Christian State!—to make, if possible, Christianity impossible?" His complaint is that Danish Christianity, by making itself subservient to the State, cannot be a real Christianity. To put it more bluntly, the Christianity of the New Testament is not only nonexistent; the State makes it absolutely impossible for it to exist in a so-called "Christian" country. Kierkegaard explains, "For the factual situation in our land is, that Christianity, the Christianity of the New Testament, not merely does not exist, but, if possible, is made impossible. Suppose that the State employed 1,000 officials who with their families lived by opposing and hindering Christianity, and so were pecuniarly interested in doing it—that indeed would be an attempt in the direction of making Christianity, if possible, impossible.

And yet this attempt (which after all has the advantage of openness, that it openly proposes to hinder Christianity) would not be nearly so dangerous as what actually occurs, that the state employs 1,000 officials, who, under the name of preaching Christianity (here precisely lies the great danger, in comparison with wishing quite openly to hinder Christianity) are pecuniarly interested in: (a) having men call themselves Christians (the bigger the flock of sheep the better), assume the name of being Christians and (b) in having it stop there, so that they do not learn to know what Christianity truly is.

The existence of these 1,000 officials amounts to this, that when you hold up alongside of them the New Testament, it is easily seen that their whole existence is an impropriety. . . . And this, this consequence, does not come about in the name of hindering Christianity, it is not with this in view the 1,000 officials with family are paid. No, it comes about under the name of preaching Christianity, spreading Christianity, laboring for Christianity."[101]

X. CONCLUSION

By his public defiance of Hegel's pantheism and idealism, Kierkegaard gave utterance to the fundamental themes and preoccupations of subsequent existentialists. He laid the groundwork for thinkers who would state and restate these themes, albeit in contexts which, at times, would be completely antithetical to those which he had initially articulated. (Witness, for example, the existentialist themes of such atheists as Jean Paul Sartre, Simone de Beauvoir and Albert Camus).

Such familiar themes as authentic existence versus the anonymity of inauthentic existence, involvement, *engagement*, commitment, the dignity of the individual as contrasted with the anonymity imposed by the system— whether it be the totalitarian state or the social pressures of mass society, the necessity of existential choices which rise above mere conformism and a drifting along with the crowd—these and many others look to the Melancholy Dane for their inspiration and initial articulation.

Certainly Kierkegaard has a loud and clear message for all of us today. In fact, Kierkegaard's admonition is just as vital and urgent today as it was in nineteenth century Copenhagen, perhaps even more so. The message sounds like a clarion call: it is an unequivocal emphasis on LIVING a Christian life. Kierkegaard's charges against Danish Christianity, where every one *claimed* to be a Christian but few really lived the life of Christianity, inevitably invites comparisons in our own twentieth century. Cannot perhaps the same be said of many so-called Christian countries today? How faithfully do they reflect in their actions the fundamentally Christian system of values on which they had been founded? Have expediency and opportunism, personal aggrandizement and basic dishonesty become the accepted way of life in today's twentieth century society? Has a cynicism along with a ruthless pragmatism corroded the once shining ideals bequeathed by the founding fathers of these countries?

It is true that in his anxiety to rouse men from their apathy, the Dane seems to resort to the "shock technique"; he seems to go to extremes. His opposition to Hegelianism which denied man his individuality and absorbed him as a cipher in the overpowering System, was well taken. But in the process, Kierkegaard seemed to find it necessary to oppose *all* philosophy. If this judgment is correct, then it is hardly fair to condemn all the efforts of man's unaided intellect, as these efforts have been transmitted through the various philosophies over the centuries, because of one defective and unsatisfactory system. Certainly philosophy has had many more qualified and more representative spokesmen than Georg Wilhelm Hegel. Can Hegelianism be considered as the only valid representative of some twenty-five centuries of philosophy in the Western world? Perhaps Kierkegaard's role of the corrective is the answer to this problem.

On the other hand, Kierkegaard has a most meaningful and relevant message for us today. This obviously is the reason for his steadily growing popularity. The number of new books on Kierkegaard attests to the relevance and eloquence of his message. So, too, the increasing popularity of college and university courses on *Kierkegaardiana* bespeaks the timeliness and appropriateness of this nineteenth century thinker's message.[102] Many so-called "cradle Christians" can profit immensely by studying this great Danish scholar. Most of us have "inherited" our Christianity from our parents. This Christianity is a legacy which represents no personal sacrifice, or even minimal inconvenience on our part. We have never been called upon to make agonizing and soul-searching choices as, for example, people under totalitarian atheistic regimes do every day.

The public confession of our faith involves little or no risk, socially, politically or financially. Few of us are faced with a genuine Either/Or. As a matter of fact, being a Christian is, for most of us, the expected, the respectable thing today, much as it was in the time of Kierkegaard. Being a Christian involves no crucial decisions, no genuinely meaningful commitment. Actually, it is easier for many to become involved in and more concerned about their political affiliations or ecology (which, of course, do have their importance in the proper balance of things), than it is to be mindful about living a truly existential Christian life. In these days of "Madison Avenue image-consciousness," of the inauthentic existence of the uninvolved, uncommitted and faceless members of twentieth century society, Kierkegaard offers a much needed corrective. The message, indeed, is not new; perhaps its phrasing is somewhat different but it echoes a very familiar counsel: "Be you *doers* of the word and not hearers only. . . . Not everyone who says 'Lord, Lord' will enter the kingdom of heaven but he who *does* the will of my Father in heaven, he will enter into the kingdom of heaven."[103]

Gabriel Marcel

CHAPTER III

GABRIEL MARCEL
LIFE

I. EARLY YEARS

Gabriel Marcel was born in Paris on December 7, 1889. His father was Privy Councillor and French Ambassador to Sweden, as well as Director of Beaux-Arts of the Bibliothèque Nationale and Musées Nationaux. His mother died when Gabriel was four years old and he was brought up by a Jewish aunt who had become a liberal Protestant. (His aunt later married Gabriel's father, thus becoming the boy's stepmother.)

Of his father, Gabriel gives us the following word portrait in his *Essay in Autobiography*: "My father, who had been brought up as a Catholic, had ceased practising his religion at an early age; imbued with the ideas of Taine, Spencer, and Renan, his position was that of the late nineteenth century agnostics; acutely and gratefully aware of all that which art owes to Catholicism, he regarded Catholic thought itself as obsolete and tainted with absurd superstitions."[1]

Of his aunt and stepmother, Marcel writes, "My aunt, who brought me up and to whose admirable example I owe that need of rigorous truth to which I have tried to do justice in my writings, was of a very different cast of mind. Of Jewish stock, but coming of a family which was wholly indifferent to religion, she was converted to Protestantism, yet showed by her choice of a pastor that her reason rejected its dogmatic beliefs and that she could accept it only in its most liberal form."[2]

And so Marcel evaluates his father and aunt in the following words: "The same invincible agnosticism was common to the outlook of my father and of my aunt, though they gave it different expressions: the one aesthetic, the other ethical; it created around me an unstable and arid climate in which, as I now realize, I found it difficult to breathe."[3]

As a child who was shy and sensitive by nature and unusually frail and delicate in health, Gabriel endured a most unhappy and lonely home life. In spite of the number of literary and political personalities who frequented the Marcel home, and of travel abroad, Gabriel had no friends his own age in whom he could confide. The thoroughly areligious and agnostic home atmosphere was unbearably stifling. The young boy was literally starved for friendship, companionship and other spiritual values. (As we shall see, this emphasis on "the other" and the desire and need of love, friendship and fidelity became a life-long quest in Marcel's life.) Roger Troisfontaines recounts how Marcel had observed to him, "Nothing is lost for a man—I am convinced of this and I firmly believe it—if he experiences a great love or a true friendship, but everything is lost for the one who is alone."[4]

During these early years, Marcel became an avid reader and began to study the piano, eventually attaining the proficiency of a first class concert pianist. The theatre, too, held great attraction for him and he was recognized among the best dramatists and literary critics of our time.

After completing his secondary education at the Lycée Carnot, Marcel enrolled at the Sorbonne where, at the age of twenty, he was awarded a fellowship in philosophy in recognition of his outstanding performance in a competitive examination. After completing his studies, he taught philosophy at lycées in Vendôme, Sens and Paris.

He volunteered for military service during the First World War but was rejected because of his delicate health. He then offered his services to the Red Cross and it was in this connection that Marcel was to experience some of his most memorable and soul-searing encounters of his life.

As a Red Cross official, Marcel had to act as liaison officer for the families of soldiers who were missing in action. Besieged by distraught relatives—wives, parents, family and lovers—Marcel spent endless days and nights

trying to obtain some jot of information about a missing
soldier, to offer some faint glimmer of hope to the appre-
hensive family.[5] And then, only too often, it was he who
was dispatched on that most difficult of all missions,
namely, to announce to the next of kin, the death of a
dearly beloved one. These missions, these soul-shaking
experiences, Marcel could never obliterate from his memory.

It was during this period of his life that he developed
his great regard for the human being, for "the other." He
saw how completely useless and empty were abstractions
and impersonal generalities. He was not dealing here with
anonymous entities, a so-called "number" or "case." No,
he was in communion with human beings, individuals who
were undergoing one of the most traumatic experiences
allotted to man. That is how Marcel learned "to embrace
the other's cause."

He insists that to be genuine in our interpersonal
relationships, we must be totally and unreservedly available to the other. We must so sympathize with the afflicted,
that we become the afflicted ones ourselves.

II. CONVERSION

Marcel tells us that although his mother had died
when he was but four, he always felt her presence in the
home.[6] The father and aunt refused adamantly to discuss
the mother's death with the boy and so he grew up
wondering about the phenomenon of death and the possibility of immortality. The areligious attitude of the
parents precluded any discussion of such topics; they were
absolutely forbidden. As Gabriel grew into young manhood, the question of immortality haunted him ceaselessly; it became almost an obsession. His Red Cross
experiences, again, brought him face to face with the
phenomenon of death. Marcel keenly felt the spiritual
vacuum in his life and he began to study the conversions
of other men to religion. He felt somewhat attracted to
Protestantism and he even participated for a while in
spiritualist seances. Little by little, he came closer to the
Roman Catholic faith. Finally, at the invitation of Francois

Mauriac, the French Catholic intellectual, who wrote in an open letter, "Come, Marcel, why are you not one of us?"[7] Marcel tells us, "With the brilliance that comes from a lightning flash I knew immediately that through and beyond this letter of my correspondent, God was extending me a direct and personal invitation."[8] Marcel prayed for the strength to make his commitment. His prayer was answered, for he made the following entry in his *Journal* several days later (March 5, 1929):

"I have no more doubts. This morning's happiness is miraculous. For the first time I have clearly experienced *grace*. A terrible thing to say, but it is so. I am hemmed in at last by Christianity—in, fathoms deep. Happy to be so! But I will write no more. And yet, I feel a kind of need to write. Feel I am stammering childishly. . . . This is indeed a birth. Everything is different. Now, too, I can see my way through my improvisations. A new metaphor, the inverse of the other—a world which was there, entirely present, and at last I can touch it."[9]

As a result, Gabriel Marcel made his irrevocable commitment to God. The long search for answers to fundamental questions which had haunted him since his childhood culminated in his Baptism into the Roman Catholic Church on March 23, 1929 at the age of 39. Once again were verified the words of another searcher after truth, who some sixteen centuries ago cried out, "Our minds never rest until they have rested in Thee, O Lord."[10]

Since then, in some forty years, Marcel had never wavered for a moment in his loyalty to the Catholic faith. He had unceasingly championed spiritual and religious values. As a matter of fact, he had made religion, revelation and spirituality the very basis of his philosophical inquiries. He is convinced that secularism and materialism, which consider man as hemmed in by himself with no transcendent values and realities to which he can reach out, inevitably lead to a fracturing of his nature. They depersonalize and dehumanize him. They render him enclosed with himself, leading a life of frustration and meaningless existence. Marcel held, on the other hand, what Etienne Gilson has maintained for years, namely, how can a Christian philosophize as anything BUT a Christian. Philosophizing in a vacuum is a travesty, a monstrosity. Marcel thus held that a concrete philosophy "cannot fail to be magnetically attracted to the data of Christianity. . . . For the Christian, there is an essential agreement between Christianity and human nature. Hence the more deeply one penetrates into human nature, the more one finds oneself situated on the axes of the great truths of Christianity. An objection will be raised: You affirm this as a Christian, not as a philosopher. Here, I can only repeat what I said at the beginning: the philosopher who compels himself to think only as a philosopher, places himself on the hither side of experience in an infrahuman realm; but philosophy implies an exaltation of experience, not a castration of it."[11]

III. DRAMA

We have mentioned Marcel's interest in drama from his earliest years. Author of over twenty plays (unfortunately only four of them have been translated into English), Marcel uses drama as a means of presenting man in real-life situations. In his essay, *On the Ontological Mystery,* he tells us, "I am convinced that it is in drama and through drama that metaphysical thought grasps and defines itself *in concreto.*"[12] And again he states at greater length, "But what is particularly clear to me now is that the dogmatic mode of thought, dealing as it does with subjects as such—that is to say, with their reality as subjects—illustrated and confirmed in advance all that I was later to write on the purely philosophical plane concerning knowledge in its capacity to transcend objectivity."[13]

Marcel describes the manner in which, uniquely, the dramatist can immerse himself in the very heart of reality. He writes, "What, in such a situation, is the function of the dramatist? It is certainly not to mount the pulpit; indeed, each time he tries to preach he betrays his mission. His task is rather to place himself at the very heart of human reality, in all its poignancy and intimacy. He must,

it seems to me, link himself magnetically to the strands of
our most secret agonies and our most secret hopes; and
the accent with which he expresses feelings we hardly dare
admit even to ourselves, must be strong enough and
magical enough to transfigure our interior landscape and
illuminate it in a flash with a light that seems to come
from beyond."[14]

Marcel thus studies man *in situ*, as he finds himself
in reality. He studies him in his loneliness ("There is only
one suffering: to be alone," says Rose in *Le Coeur des
Autres*.)[15] He examines man frustrated, alienated, bewildered and rootless, when he cuts himself off from his
fellow man and from God. He underscored man's deepest
longing for friendship, fidelity, interpersonal relationship
and communion with others. Frequently, Marcel's dramas
conclude without ending in any kind of definite solution,
somewhat reminiscent of the Socratic probings in the
Platonic dialogues. Marcel was convinced that through
drama, one can attempt more successfully to overcome
the level of the problem and of the objective, and thus
rise to the only level on which metaphysics can be con-
ducted, namely, that of the mystery and the metaproblematical.[16]

In spite of Marcel's repeated emphasis on his dramatic
works as being more truly representative of his thought
than his philosophical essays, his plays are largely unnoticed and ignored. He complained of this rather ironic
twist when he wrote, "If I should now be asked to which
of the various aspects of my activity I should give priority,
I would reply without hesitation that my preference goes
to my plays, rather than to my philosophical writings;
this despite the fact that the latter have obtained more
widespread acceptance than my plays. These have undeniably suffered from the fact that without having been
understood or even simply read, they have been judged
by the axiom that, being the work of a philosopher, they
could not be 'good theatre.'"[17]

IV. MUSIC

Music had always played a very influential part in

Marcel's life and he even conjectured that perhaps it was his real vocation in life. As one biographer has expressed it, "In music, Marcel finds a foretaste of a harmony and unity which is given neither in life nor in drama. In this sense, music is the most complete art because it points to a communion and fulfillment which is only imperfectly realised in life."[18] Marcel himself in "The Reintegrating of Honor" points to the profound effect which music can have in restoring to man the dignity that he has lost in a highly technological and depersonalized age. He tells us, "Coming home the other evening from an excellent Bach concert, I thought to myself, 'Here is something that restores to one a feeling that one might have thought lost, or perhaps something more than a feeling, an assurance: the assurance that *it is an honor to be a man.*'"[19]

In the words of Seymour Cain, "In Marcel's life-work, there are three paths: first, the way of music, of spontaneous improvisation, pointing to a realm where communion is fully achieved; second, the way of metaphysical meditation and phenomenological analysis, locating in thought the beacons and reefs on man's spiritual journey; and third, the way of dramatic presentation, acting out in concrete characters and situations, what is explored independently in the metaphysical meditations."[20]

Marcel received numerous prestigious awards and citations. In 1948 he won the Grand Prix de Litterature de l'Academie Francaise; in 1956 he was the recipient of the Goethe Prize and two years later, of the Grand Prix National des Lettres. University of Aberdeen selected him to deliver its world-renowned Gifford Lectures in 1949-1950 and Harvard University honored him in 1961 by inviting him to be its William James Lecturer. (The Gifford Lectures appear in two volumes under the title, *The Mystery of Being* and the William James Lectures as *Existential Background of Human Dignity.*) Marcel was also a member of the Institut de France and Officer of Legion d'Honneur.

On October 8, 1973, Gabriel Marcel, world-renowned philosopher, musician and playwright died at the age of eighty-three.

86   EXISTENTIALISM

MARCEL'S PRINCIPAL WORKS
(Listed Chronologically)

Metaphysical Journal. Tr. Bernard Wall. Chicago: Henry Regnery, 1952.

Being and Having. Tr. Katherine Farrer. New York and Evanston: Harper and Row, 1965.

Creative Fidelity. Tr. Robert Rosthal. New York: Farrar, Straus and Giroux, 1964.

Homo Viator: An Introduction to a Metaphysic of Hope. Tr. Emma Crauford. New York: Harper and Bros. 1962.

Royce's Metaphysics. Tr. Virginia and Gordon Ringer. Chicago: Henry Regnery, 1956.

"An Essay in Autobiography," *The Philosophy of Existentialism.* Tr. Manya Harari. New York: Citadel Press, 1966.

"On the Ontological Mystery," in *The Philosophy of Existentialism.*

The Mystery of Being. Vol. I: Tr. G. Fraser; Vol. II: Tr. R. Hague. Chicago: Henry Regnery, 1951.

Man Against Mass Society. Tr. G. Fraser. Chicago: Henry Regnery, 1952.

The Decline of Wisdom. Tr. Manya Harari. New York: Philosophical Library, 1955.

Problematic Man. Tr. B. Thompson. New York: Herder and Herder, 1967.

Presence and Immortality. Tr. M. A. Machado. Pittsburgh: Duquesne University Press, 1967.

Philosophical Fragments 1909-1914. Tr. Lionel Blain. Notre Dame: University of Notre Dame Press, 1965.

The Existential Background of Human Dignity. Cambridge: Harvard University Press, 1963.

Searchings. Tr. Anonymous. New York: Newman Press, 1967.

PLAYS
(Listed Chronologically)

Le Seuil Invisible—contains two plays, *La Grâce* and *Le Palais de Sable.* Paris: Grasset, 1914.

Le Quatuor en Fa Dièse (1919). Paris: Plon, 1929.

Trois Pièces—contains *Le Regard Neuf, Le Mort de Demain, La Chapelle Ardente* (1919-1921). Paris: Plon, 1931.

L'Iconoclaste (1920). Paris: Stock, 1923.

Le Coeur des Autres (1920). Paris: Grasset, 1921.

Un Homme de Dieu (1921). Paris: Grasset, 1925.

L'Horizon (1928). Aux Étudiants de France, 1945.

Le Monde Cassé, Paris: Desclée de Brouwer, 1933.

Le Fanal, Paris: Stock, 1936.

Le Chemin de Crête, Paris: Grasset, 1936.

Le Dard, Paris: Plon, 1936.

Le Soif, Paris: Desclée de Brouwer, 1938, Republished under the title of *Les Coeurs Avides,* Paris: Le Table Ronde.

Vers un Autre Royaume—contains two plays, *L'Emissaire* and *Le Signe de la Croix,* Paris: Plon, 1949.

La Fin des Temps, Paris: Realities, 1950.

Rome n'est plus dans Rome, Paris: Le Table Ronde, 1951.

Mon Temps n'est pas le Vôtre, Paris: Plon, 1955.

Croissiez et Multipliez, Paris: Plon, 1955.

La Dimension Florestan, Paris: Plon, 1958.

Theatre Comique—contains four plays, *Colombyre* or *Le Brasier de la Paix* (1937); *Le Double Expertise* (1936); *Les Points sur les I* (1936); *Le Divertissement Posthume* (1923), Paris: Albin Michel, 1947.

Théâtre et Religion, Lyon: Vitte, 1959.

L'Heure Théâtrale: de Giraudoux à Jean Paul Sartre, Paris: Plon, 1959.

Only four of the above plays have been translated into English.

Three Plays. New York: Hill and Wang, 1958, contains *A Man of God* (*Un Homme de Dieu*), *Ariadne* (*Le Chemin de Crête*) and *The Funeral Pyre* (*La Chapelle Ardente*). The fourth play, *Le Fanal,* has been translated under the title of *The Lantern* in *Cross Currents,* VIII, 2 (Spring 1958).

THOUGHT

I. REPUDIATION OF IDEALISM

In his early student days, Marcel subscribed to an idealism which was popular during the first decade of the twentieth century. In terms strongly suggestive of Hegelianism, Marcel tells how he believed at that time "the most truly real, under all circumstances, could not be what is most immediate but rather on the contrary, the most truly real is the fruit of a dialectic which is the apogee of an edifice of thought."[21] Marcel also indicated that both the idealism of Francis Bradley and Josiah Royce, as well as the intuitionism of Henri Bergson, influenced his thought considerably at this time.

Marcel soon perceived, however, that an abstract system, which equates being with thought, is a traitor to reality. In his assiduous search for God, he was completely dissatisfied with an Idea or an Absolute which was represented as a synthesis of a logical process. Such a totally impersonal, dessicated and artificial abstraction as presented by Idealism, offers man no hope, no meaning or purpose in the world. At best, it engulfs him; it swallows him up in a system.

Marcel was looking not for an abstraction or a synthesis. He was searching for a real, personal God: a God in Whom he could hope, Whom he could love and with Whom he could enter into a meaningful communion.[22] Certainly *this* is the God of the Bible, the God of Abraham, Isaac and Jacob. And because God is not some impersonal force or fruit of the dialectic, but rather a *person,* I can thus talk to Him, invoke Him and try to work out my salvation with His help. As Étienne Gilson says in a tribute to Marcel, "Through an initial procedure, which he has never since betrayed, this philosopher has written nothing which has not been reaped from the depths of being or directly tested by his own experience. There is scarcely anyone—even among the greatest to whom we can attribute that praise. . . . In philosophy as elsewhere, only the authentic endures, and that is why, like Montaigne, like Maine de Biran, Gabriel Marcel is assured of always having readers. In his work, man speaks directly to man; he will always have readers because he will never cease to make new friends."[23]

It was this basic dissatisfaction with abstractionism that led Marcel to begin a highly personal and individualised type of philosophical investigation. This particular method of philosophizing which begins with the concrete, individual experience is generally referred to as *phenomenology*. And while Edmund Husserl is considered to be its founder, different existentialists have forsaken the Husserlian method in order to develop their own particular brands of phenomenology, in order to suit their own specific purposes.[24] Martin Heidegger, as we shall see below,[25] Jean Paul Sartre and Karl Jaspers are the best examples of this method.

Essentially, phenomenology deals with the description of individual lived experiences. Gabriel Marcel followed the method (which he seems to have developed quite independently) and by beginning with such ordinary experiences as hope, love, fidelity and loyalty, he then ascends to a genuine encounter with the Absolute Thou by way of the I-Thou relationship. As such, then, the method of phenomenology is always restricted to the singular, to the lived experience, to the subjective and spontaneous. For this reason, it seems to be questionable whether any posture which uses phenomenology as a point of departure, can ever end up as an ontology or philosophy. This is why Roger Troisfontaines and Michele Sciacca, as we shall see later on, hold that no phenomenology can provide a basis for a universal metaphysics and

Henri Bouillard pronounces incisively, "Marcel's is a philosophy on the confines of philosophy."[26]

It is interesting to observe that Gabriel Marcel rebelled against the abstractionism of idealism and set down the basic existentialist postures the same way as did Kierkegaard, the father of contemporary existentialism. It was this same "dissolute pantheistic contempt for the individual" which Kierkegaard found so repulsive in Hegelian idealism.[27] And yet Marcel tells us that he can honestly say he arrived at this opposition to Hegelianism by himself, for it was before he had read Kierkegaard, in whom he might so easily have found it. In his *Philosophy of Existentialism*, he observes, "I believe that it is in my essay entitled *Existence et Objectivité*, published in the *Revue de Metaphysique et de Morale* in 1925, that the main lines of this new development (contemporary existentialism) were first formulated in France. I had not then read Kierkegaard, who was still unknown in France, nor had Heidegger or Jaspers as yet published their own works."[28] In this connection, when Jean Paul Sartre granted somewhat condescendingly and with a show of magnanimity that there could also be a "Christian" existential (in addition to the *real* existentialism which is atheistic), Marcel remarked pointedly, "Some of my most significant writings such as *The Metaphysical Journal* of *Being and Having* were published before anybody had even heard of Jean Paul Sartre. There is a fateful error according to which, existentialism in its original form, ought to be regarded as intrinsically atheistic. This implies, of course, a real blind spot since Kierkegaard, who was undoubtedly the founder of what is called existentialism nowadays, was in the deepest sense religious, a Christian thinker."[29]

Both Marcel and Kierkegaard agree on the insufficiency of idealistic abstractionism and they restore to man his rightful and meaningful place in reality, insuring, thereby, his contact with a personal God. In spite of their common theistic orientation, at least one writer sees a difference between them vis-à-vis the fundamental relation between faith and reason, revelation and philosophy.

James Collins states this difference in the following manner: "Kierkegaard regarded Christianity as a means of displacing philosophy and his standpoint is that of a Christian existence versus the prevailing philosophy. Marcel, on the contrary, admits not only the bare possibility of a legitimate rational discipline but the need for a renewal of philosophy itself in an existential direction. . . . His concrete philosophy is centered upon the mystery of being, although he grants that it is both compatible with Christianity and naturally disposes the individual toward receiving such a revelation from God."[30]

By rebelling against the "system" and its inevitable abstractionism, Marcel says, "I suspect that my grievance against transcendental idealism stimulated my inquiry into the metaphysical implications of sense experience as such, and that my general tendency to bring out difficulties instead of concealing them helped to develop my distrust of systems of philosophy of whatever kind; for there is no system that does not involve the temptation to declare a priori that this or that difficulty is to be judged unimportant and consequently set aside. I believe now, more than ever, that it is the first duty of a philosopher to resist this temptation which seems somehow to form part of his very calling."[31]

In another place, he tells us, "The dynamic element in my philosophy, taken as a whole, can be seen as an obstinate and untiring battle against the spirit of abstraction. Since the years 1911 and 1912, the time of my first researches and my still unpublished earliest philosophical writings, I have played the part of a prosecuting counsel against every philosophy that seemed to me to remain the prisoner of abstractions."[32]

II. NEO-SOCRATISM

As a consequence, Marcel tended to reject the label "Christian existentialist" which had been associated with his name and he prefered to be called a "neo-Socratic." This latter characterization Marcel considered more truly representative of his manner of philosophizing. Philosophy, argued Marcel, is never a closed system. It is rather a constant probing, questioning, testing and revising. Concerning his particular manner of philosophizing he stated "It is in this spirit of opposition to those who have artificially attempted to integrate me into what they call existentialism, that I have declared that the term neo-Socratic seemed to be much more appropriate for the at-time-stumbling gait which has been mine since I began to think by myself. Interrogative thought (the calling into question of man by himself) is opposed in the last analysis to everything which presents itself a character of finality."[33]

Marcel's neo-Socratism obviously renders almost impossible any kind of systematic presentation of his philosophy.[34] We shall, therefore, satisfy ourselves with the listing of characteristic Marcellian themes and postures. These we shall proceed to describe and explain. Typically Marcellian are the following: problem versus mystery, first and second reflection, objectification, the metaproblematical, incarnation, ontological participation, presence, encounter, I-Thou, Absolute Thou, being versus having, intersubjectivity, disponibility and indisponibility, fidelity, hope, love, broken world, technocracy, dehumanization, depersonalization and functionalization of man, techniques of degradation, *homo viator* (man the wayfarer).

III.   PROBLEM VERSUS MYSTERY:
FIRST AND SECOND REFLECTION

One of the most fundamental notions in Gabriel Marcel's thought is his well-known distinction between problem and mystery. By *problem* Marcel understands something which can be considered completely objectively, without involving in any manner the person of the one studying it. Systematic philosophies, according to Marcel, always tend to deal with *problems* or *objects*. The very etymology of the word *problem* denotes something which is "thrown in front of us" (from the Greek *pros ballo*), something which is completely separate and distinct from us. The Latin *objectum*, likewise, means "something thrown in front of us." Marcel says, "I am here taking the word 'object,' as I shall always be taking it, in its strictly etymological sense, which is also the sense of the German word *Gegenstand,* of something flung in my way, something placed before me, facing me in my path."[35] Hence *problem* or *object* implies an absolute non-involvement on the part of the individual who examines or studies the question. The knowledge that is obtained is universal, abstract and verifiable. A purely mathematical problem, e.g., in algebra is a case in point.

This is, of course, the technique of the sciences. The investigator studies objectively and impersonally under controlled laboratory conditions the object of his research. There is present here a complete objectivity which science demands. This experiment may be repeated a thousand times, in a thousand different places without involving and accounting for the various personalities of the individuals studying this problem. Marcel does not quarrel with the *modus operandi* of the physical or empirical scientist. He readily agrees that such a procedure is absolutely necessary for science and that its findings and contributions are of inestimable benefit to mankind.[36]

The physical sciences, by following this rigid and impersonal mode of investigation, have made it possible for man to control and use the world of objects. Hence it is of necessity that the scientist should abstract and objectify. What Marcel does fault is the arrogant claim that this rigid mode of investigation, which deals with only one aspect of reality, is all-inclusive and all-exhaustive. Philosophical systems, especially idealisms which deal only with abstractions, are also guilty of this charge. When this happens, persons are "reduced to mere objects, the world to a collection of things, science to scientism."[37]

Marcel contends that this level of first reflection must of necessity yield to a higher one, namely that of mystery, where true metaphysical thought takes place. Mystery is thus at the opposite pole of the problematic. For Marcel, the word *mystery* is pregnant with the notion of involvement, of encounter and of a deep personal relationship between the subject who is conducting the inquiry and that which he is studying. Mystery involves the very being of the questioner, in such a way, that he cannot possibly disregard or bracket his own self. By mystery, Marcel does not mean either a truth revealed by God nor something unknown in the sense that we do not have the means at our disposal of dealing with the particular object of our study. He means something quite different.

In explaining his choice of the word *mystery*, Marcel says, "It will perhaps be objected that there is a danger that the word 'mystery' might confuse this very issue. I would reply that there is no question of confusing those mysteries which are enveloped in human experience, as such, with those mysteries which are revealed, such as Incarnation or Redemption and to which no effort of thought bearing on experience can enable us to attain. It will be asked: Why then do you use the same word for two such distinct notions? But I would point out that no revelation is, after all, conceivable unless it is addressed to a being who participates in a reality which is non-problematical and which provides him with his foundation as subject."[38]

For Marcel, then, the level of mystery, which always involves my person, includes the notion of second reflection; whereas *problem*, which calls for an abstracting of myself from that which I am studying, is to be found in connection with the first reflection.

In his Existentialist Diary, *Being and Having*, Marcel made the often-quoted entry under the date of October 22, 1932. He distinguishes between problem and mystery: "The phrase 'mystery of being, ontological mystery' as against 'problem of being, ontological problem' has suddenly come to me in these last few days. It has enlightened me. Metaphysical thought—reflection trained on mystery. But it is an essential part of a mystery that it should be acknowledged; metaphysical reflection presupposes this acknowledgement which is outside its own sphere. Distinguish between the mysterious and the Problematic. A problem is something met with, which bars my passage. It is before me in its entirety. A mystery, on the other hand, is something in which I find myself caught up, and whose essence is, therefore, not to be before me in its entirety. It is as though in this province the distinction between *in me* and *before me* loses its meaning."[39]

Frederick Copleston in speaking of the contrasting notions of problem and mystery, of first and second reflection, gives us an excellent example in the concrete illustration of *love*. He begins by telling us that we first have the level of immediate experience, namely, the existential level. John and Mary love one another. We have present here a concrete unity. Each certainly thinks about the other but neither John nor Mary reflects about love in general. "Loving and reflecting are indistinguishable activities."

But let us suppose now that John, who loves Mary, begins to reflect specifically about the *nature* of love. In order to do this, John stands back, as it were, from the activity of loving, so that he may examine it, analyze it from the outside. Doing this, John "objectifies" love. He looks at it as a kind of "public property *out there* apart from himself." He now no longer acts as a lover but as a scientist. He might even analyze and describe loving in physiological or psychological terms. John is no longer "John-loving-Mary." He is an example of a scientific mind which is studying and analyzing an object.

Mary is no longer "the unique beloved"; she is but one possible object of an activity which itself has been made an object and is now being scrutinized in a highly impersonal and scientific way. Hence "the magic of love fades away in the cold of impersonal objective science."[40]

This kind of reflection Marcel calls a *first reflection*. The question "What is love?" is treated as a problem, in an objective manner without involving John in any personal way. Marcel maintains that this first reflection breaks up the concrete unity of the pre-reflective immediate experience.

The second reflection, on the other hand, attempts to avoid this fracturing; it tries to combine the immediate experience with reflection.[41] Now it is possible, according to Marcel, to have a reflection which, at the same time, maintains the concrete unity "founded on the personal communion of love." John reflects but while he reflects, he does it from *within* the experience of loving; he does

not reflect "from the outside." John considers "the metaphysical significance of love as a communion or togetherness of persons, as a participation in Being."

But in doing so, he does not consider the significance
of love completely from the outside. Rather, John asks
himself "What does this experience reveal to me of myself
as a human person in common with another and with Being
in general?" In this case, John is no longer dealing with
problem or object; he is unequivocally *involved*. He is
now on the level of mystery and of second reflection.[42]
And as Marcel points out, "Where primary (or first) reflection tends to dissolve the unity of experience which
is at first put before it, the function of secondary reflection is essentially recuperative; it reconquers unity."[43]

IV. INCARNATION

Marcel strongly objects, therefore, to any type of
philosophy which tends to objectify man, a philosophy
which would "abstract" him from the real, concrete, lived
experience. The place of the problematic only perpetuates
the dichotomy that idealistic systems perpetrate. Invariably, idealisms "split man in two"; they view him as a
"spirit," an intellect which is his real self. The body is a
kind of useless appendage, a constant embarrassment to
the pure mind or pure reason.

One of the most notorious examples of an idealist
dichotomy of man was the celebrated *"je pense donc je
suis"* (I think therefore I am) of René Descartes, who
established his own existence as "a thinking being." His
body was an everpresent unassimilated element in the
make-up of man. Marcel rebels against such tenets of
modern idealism, when he insists, ". . . the *Cogito,* as
later in Kant 'thought in general,' is free of every anthropological mark. According to this impersonal thought, the
human situation or condition is only an object of consideration as is an other . . . A fictitious suppression: an
abstraction by which thought is denied access to being."[44]

Alphonse de Waelhens describes Marcel's objection
to the dishonesty of idealism in the following manner:
"Gabriel Marcel has always held that attempts at passing

from thought to existence are conjury or trickery. 'If experience is not at the origin, it will be nowhere.' Thus he condemns in a single phrase the untiring ambition of all idealistic dialectics and, particularly, that one which Hegel assigned to his *Logic*."[45]

The level of the primary or first reflection which deals with abstractions and problems is thus strikingly exemplified in the Cartesian dualism of mind and body. As a result of this dualism, Marcel warns us, "We shall be led either to consider the body and soul as two distinct things between which some determinate relationship must exist, some relationship of abstract formulation, or to think of the body as something of which the soul, as we improperly call it, is the predicate, or on the other hand, of the soul as something of which the body, as we improperly call it is the predicate . . . But in both cases, body and soul at least, are treated as *things*, for the purpose of logical discourse become *terms*, which one imagines as strictly defined, and as linked to each other by some determinable relation."[46]

In rejecting the dualism of mind and body, Marcel offers in its place his doctrine of *incarnation*. Now Incarnation is understood here in a non-theological sense, namely, that I, a person, am not a self-enclosed ego but I am "in the world"; I am "present in a situation." The only way in which I can be present in the world is through incarnation, through my body. For this reason, Marcel holds "Incarnation is the eternal 'given' of metaphysics. Incarnation is the situation of a being who appears to himself to be, as it were, *bound* to a body. This 'given' is opaque to itself: opposition to the *cogito* (the I think). Of this body, I can neither say that it is I, nor that it is not I, nor that it is *for* me (object). The opposition of subject and object is found to be transcended from the start."[47]

In his insistence on incarnation, Marcel tries to overcome the Cartesian dualism, the separation between mind and body. At the same time, he is rebelling against that which is abstract and out of touch with the actually and really existing in the spatio-temporal world. He insists that through his body, man is immersed in a situation. He is *in* the world. As one writer says, "When Marcel insists that we are incarnate beings, he is not suggesting, as the materialist does, that we are merely the chemical and material components of our bodies. Man is neither a mind accidentally residing in a body as the idealists claim, nor a body accidentally housing a mind, as the materialist suggests. He is, rather, essentially incarnate. The only way we can think about the world is through our bodily insertion in it. My incarnation in this particular body is an irreducible condition of my thought."[48]

Marcel then goes on to ask himself whether *my body* is a kind of instrument, "an apparatus which permits me to act upon and even to intrude myself into the world." But an apparatus is always considered by us "from the outside." And so he concludes, "My body is *my* body just insofar as I do *not* consider it in this detached fashion, do not put a gap between myself and it. To put this point in another way, my body is mine insofar as for me, my body is not an object but rather I *am* my body. . . . I *am* my body insofar as I succeed in recognizing that this body of mine *cannot* be brought down to the level of being this object, an object, a something or other."[49]

In another place, Marcel explains, "My body does not reveal itself as a tool which I could do without because I can find another for it, or because I can exercise some other activities for which I have no need of it. It is given to me as the absolute condition of all possible instrumentality—and also of all possible enjoyment; in this sense, it is given to me as being my all, with this reserve, however, that it retains—or rather that I retain, by means of it—the possibility of sacrificing myself."[50]

Marcel gives us a definition of incarnation when he writes, "It goes without saying that the term 'incarnation,' of which I shall have to make a frequent use from now on, applies solely and exclusively in our present context to the situation of being who appears to himself to be linked fundamentally and not accidentally to *his* or *her* body . . . In a former work of mine, my *Metaphysical Diary*, I used the phrase 'sympathetic mediation' to convey

98 EXISTENTIALISM

the notion of our non-instrumental communion with our bodies."[51]

And so, through my incarnation, I am in the world. "The 'I' of the 'I exist' is not an ego isolated from the world, but a self in the world, a self whose incarnation is not completed within its own limits but by the being-together with the whole world . . . All this is not demonstrated—the very attempt would be absurd—but simply is there in the immediacy of exclamatory awareness."[52]

V. I-THOU

Through my incarnation in the world, I am enabled to participate in Being. How is this accomplished? As a human being, I can act in one of two ways: First I can exist and act inauthentically as a faceless individual (Heidegger's *das Man*) who is best described as a monotonous anonymity. In *Homo Viator*, Marcel says, "Nowadays, the individual allows himself, legitimately enough, to be likened to an atom caught up in a whirlwind, if you wish, a mere statistical unit, because most of the time, he is simply a specimen among an infinity of others, since the opinions which he thinks are his own, are merely reflections of the ideas accepted in the circles he frequents and handed round in the press which he reads daily. Thus he is only . . . an anonymous unit of that anonymous entity 'one.'"[53]

Such an individual who shares in this faceless anonymity lives a self-enclosed existence. He regards his fellowman, not as a genuine person but as another "atom" another statistical unit. "From the very fact that I treat the other person as a means of resonance or an amplifier (in my act of posing), in my attitude, I tend to consider him as a sort of apparatus which I can, or think I can, dispose of at will . . . or again I consider the other person as a sort of mechanism, exterior to my own ego, a mechanism of which I must discover the spring or manner of working."[54] This first way of existing and acting treats another human being as a thing, an object or function. He is nothing more than a means or instrument for the in-

flation of my own ego or the gratification of my pleasures.
This is the level of the first reflection; it is the plane of
radical impersonality and of the problematic.

Marcel tells us that there is another way in which I
can exist and act. The second way is the level of authentic
existence. It is the plane of the well-known I-Thou relationship. (Incidentally, it would seem that Gabriel
Marcel is the originator of this now world-famous phrase,
"I-Thou." As early as 1915, Marcel was already studying
the metaphysical nuances of the different kinds of relationships, i.e., between an I and a he, she or it and between
I and Thou. Martin Buber's volume *Ich und Du* did not
appear until 1923. Today this notion is one of the best
known of existentialist themes and while it is absolutely
true that Buber's small volume made the notion known
to millions of people, it would seem that Marcel is the
original author of this very important notion.)[55]

Whenever I consider my neighbor as a thing, as an
object or function, he is nothing more than a he or she or
it for me. When, on the other hand, I look upon him or
her as a *Thou*, I begin to see him as a person. (The *Thou*
is used to express the intimate and familiar form of the
Du, as against *Sie* in German; and the *tu* in French as
against the highly impersonal and polite "vous." Unfortunately, the English language has only one word,
i.e., "you" for both the intimate versus the polite and
impersonal forms.) In the I-Thou relationship, I become
present to the other in a mutual openness and self-giving
We are no longer two isolated entities, two strangers,
two *pour-sois* plotting to plunder each other's freedom
and to possess the other, as John Paul Sartre would have
it. No, Gabriel Marcel speaks here of an encounter, a
genuine meeting in love, friendship and spiritual availability. This meeting involves an invitaton, an appeal to
become involved in a loving encounter.

When I opt to regard the other as a *Thou*, instead of
a he or she or it, I no longer look upon him as an object
to be exploited, as a freedom to be possessed and appropriated. And paradoxically, in the generous giving of myself without any reservation or qualification, in my spirit-

ual openness and availability to the other, I actually discover my own freedom. Marcel points this out when he
says, "For me, the being I love is a third person (he, she,
it) in the least possible degree. Moreover, that being discovers me to myself, since the efficacy of his or her
presence is such that I am less and less him for myself—
my interior defences fall at the same time as the barriers
that separate me from somebody else."[56]

The reciprocal nature of this encounter is viewed
from the other side: "If in fact I treat the Thou as a He,
I reduce the other to being only nature; an animated object which works in some ways and not in others. If I
treat another person as a Thou, I treat him and apprehend him *qua* freedom. I apprehend him *qua* freedom because he is also freedom and not only nature. What is
more, I help him, in a sense, to be freed. I collaborate
with his freedom. The formula sometimes sounds paradoxical and contradictory but love is always proving it
true."[57]

Marcel also speaks of freedom in terms of *fraternity*,
for he says, "The freest man is also the most fraternal." By
this statement he again underscores the notion that man
is most "unfree" when he is enclosed within himself,
egocentric and his own prisoner. The fraternal man is
linked to his neighbor in such a way that this tie of
fraternity "not only does not fetter him, but frees him
from himself." Marcel maintains that freedom is of primary importance, "for each one of us tends to become a
prisoner of himself, not only in respect to his material
interests, his passions, or simply his prejudices but, still
more essentially, in the predisposition which inclines him
to be centered on himself, and to view everything from his
own perspective. The fraternal man, on the contrary, is
somehow enriched by everything which enriches his
brother, in that communion which exists between his
brother and himself."[58]

As one commentator expresses it, "This ambiguity
results from freedom that is the essence of the act of
existing, for it depends on ourselves to be more or less,
to love or to hole ourselves up in our own egotistic selves.

We thus discover the mysterious tangle of being and freedom. If the root of our existence is identified with the possibility of extending our power of communion or of love, the knot of freedom and of being is also fusion of time and eternity. Insofar as we refuse to participate, or at least insofar as we are inclined to cut down our participation to a minimum, to this extent we objectivize the world—the world appears to us as a collection of objects different from ourselves, but capable of being desired and possessed."[59]

Both I and the other discover our freedom in becoming available to each other. I thereby become an I in the most unqualified manner, only, when I meet the Thou. "Two human beings open themselves up for one another, appeal to one another in a free, inner movement of love, by which they break through their narrow individuality and thus become themselves. A new subject originates, a 'we' . . . It is in my relationship with the other that the process of my becoming a person takes place. I do not want to 'comprehend' the other methodically but rather to re-enter into myself in the concrete experience of being with the other."[60]

VI. PRESENCE, ENCOUNTER, INTERSUBJECTIVITY

The I-Thou relationship, which can take place only on the plane of secondary reflection and of mystery, includes the concepts of presence, encounter, and intersubjectivity. Marcel furnishes us with an example: "Let us think, if you like, of a conductor whom we have habitually to deal with in the train or bus ride to our work—to our office. At the start, this man has for us only the functional reality bound up with the fact of punching the tickets or of driving the bus. But let us imagine that something unusual draws our attention to him. For instance, a sign of physical suffering, or perhaps some moral distress. The link between us ceases to be purely functional. This man really becomes a human being for us—a *presence*! And this will perhaps extend itself through the question which I shall perhaps ask him if I succeed in mastering my discretion or my natural shyness.

Let us suppose I ask him 'What is the matter?' and he answers me, perhaps moved to see that he has aroused my interest. In this way, we become really present to one another, at least for a brief moment. It is the dawn of what I have called intersubjectivity, that is to say, mutual openness. It would be useful to show that this cannot be conveyed in strictly relational language; for from the moment we become *presentially* aware of one another, we can no longer be considered as two terms external to one another. We are on the verge of becoming interior to one another. But of course this interiority is only fully realized, that is to say, effected in LOVE or more precisely AGAPE."[61]

Presence for Marcel implies much more than a mere "being there alongside others." It is a state or quality which contains "certain overtones of conscious participation" which can be predicated uniquely of human persons and never of things. "Presence denotes something rather different and more comprehensive than the fact of just being there; to be quite exact, one should not actually say that an object is present. We might say that presence is always dependent on an experience which is at the same time irreducible and vague, the sense of existing, of being in the world."[62] Again, we are told, "Presence can only be—not grasped, for that would be contradictory—but evoked through the aid of direct and unchallengeable experiences which do not rise from the conceptual apparatus which we make use of in order to reach objects."[63]

In Marcel's *Presence and Immortality*, an entry dated May 3, 1943, develops the notion of intersubjectivity in the following manner: *"Presence is intersubjective.* It cannot be interpreted as the expression of a will which seeks to reveal itself to me; but this revelation supposes that I do not put an obstacle in its way. In short, the subject is treated not like an object, but as the magnetic center of presence. At the root of presence, there is a being who takes me into consideration, who is regarded by me as taking me into account. Now, by definition, an object does not take me into account. I do not exist for it . . . Presence as response to the act by which the subject opens himself to receive; in this sense, it is the gift of oneself. Presence belongs only to the being who is capable of giving himself."[64]

In another place, Marcel furnishes us with this additional insight: "We must recognize that each one of us, in order to 'grow,' must open out to other and different beings and must be capable of meeting them without allowing himself to be dominated or neutralized. This is what I have called 'inter-subjectivity.' It cannot be considered a mere given fact, or rather, it only assumes value where it is more than a given fact, where it appears as a gradual victory over all that incites us to become withdrawn and self-centered."[65]

The encounter or meeting, along with its cognate notion of intersubjectivity, is not something accidental; it is not something which takes place by chance. Marcel contends that the encounter or meeting has a deep metaphysical implication: it is something that involves, as it were, a mingling of two presences. There is present an unconditioned mutuality which affects the very being of the individuals. He writes, "To encounter someone is not merely to cross his path but to be, for the moment at least, near *to* or *with* him. To use a term I have often used before, it means being a *co-presence*."[66] In such a situation, we have a real subject-object relationship. Contrary to the menacing threat by the Sartrean "other," Marcel's "other" is a loving, co-present Thou. The "I" is never viewed in isolation, enclosed within its own self-centeredness. Rather, we find here a genuine, meaningful dialogue which takes place between a gracious I and Thou. This meeting or encounter is not a mere interaction, Marcel warns us. Instead, it is "a reciprocal intercourse of I and Thou, who get to know one another as persons."[67] Thus I become aware of persons who are centers not merely of functional interest but of a non-functional, loving interest, and this is in virtue of their being centers of conscious participation, responsible and responsive. As such, they are capable of a like awareness and appropriation of our common ontological participation and, thus, of entering

into a conscious communion in which our common
exigency for Being can find increasing fulfillment."[68]

VII. DISPONIBILITY AND INDISPONIBILITY

The reciprocal intercourse so necessary for the meeting or encounter also suggests another typically Marcellian
theme, namely that of *disponibilité and indisponibilité*.
This is an exceedingly difficult notion to convey in English.
Let us listen, then, as Marcel presents his case: "We
come up against a notion here which seems to me of
central importance but of which, it is difficult to find an
idiomatic English equivalent—at least neither I nor the
English translator of my previous work, *Being and Having*, managed to do so. The French terms I used are
disponibilité and *indisponibilité*. Literally in English, one
would render these as availability and unavailability; but
it might sound more natural, if one spoke of handiness
and unhandiness, the basic idea being that of having and
not having, in a given contingency, one's resources to
hand or at hand.

The self-centered person in this sense, is unhandy:
I mean that he remains incapable of responding to calls
made upon him by life and I am not thinking merely of
the appeals for help that may be made to him by the unfortunate. I mean rather that, over a much wider field,
he will be incapable of sympathizing with other people,
or even of imagining their situation. He remains shut up
in himself, in his petty circle of his private experience,
which forms a kind of hard shell round him that he is
incapable of breaking through. He is unhandy from this
point of view and unavailable from the point of view of
others. . . . The theory of the second person (the Thou),
the presence of two persons to each other, their being with
each other and belonging to each other, their cultivating in
fidelity the "we" which thou and I create, implies the
notion of disposability (*disponibilité*)."[69]

It may be questioned whether "handiness" and "unhandiness" are truly felicitous terms, whether they are
much of an improvement on the original versions of *dis-*

ponibilité. One writer has suggested the unqualified and unreserved availability of a mother for her child as the best example of disponibility. The notion carries with it a stance which is characterized by a readiness to respond, an openness, a kind of being at hand, or being at the service of others, a welcoming. A person who possesses this quality makes himself available to another for instant communion because he is "uncluttered by a sense of his own importance."[70] (Marcel, himself, seemed to be the very personification of this quality of disponibility; he could communicate this openness to total strangers almost instantaneously.)

Seymour Cain, who prefers to use the terms "disposable" and "indisposable," appeals to Gabriel Marcel's play, *The Broken World,* and its characters, Laurent Chesnay and Antonov, as personifications of "indisposability," which he equates with a "self-encumbrance." He explains, "Whereas the disposable (available) person opens freely and gives himself unreservedly to a 'witness' of being and a mutuality of presence, the indisposable person is self-preoccupied, self-encumbered, self-enclosed, incapable of giving himself, of opening up, of giving out.

Indisposability is marked by having, the tendency to identify oneself with what one has, to be possessed by one's possessions. This is not so much a material having as a preoccupation with one's own life, talents, qualities and status. Indisposability means 'self-preoccupation,' which is occupation in a *certain way* and not with a certain object.

Laurent Chesnay in *The Broken World* is a man self-encumbered, beset with *amour-propre,* unable to get in touch with others; and Antonov in the same play, who throws himself at others, encumbers others with himself, is in no better state. Neither intends the other as other. . . . As the personal being is stifled through a 'closed-in-ness' and self-encumbrance, a boundless anxiety ensues that is not evoked by any particular object. The disquietude is, for Marcel, the anxiety of temporality, of being prey to time, of being consumed and macerated by existence. It calls forth 'un-hope' (after Thomas Hardy) which becomes despair when it is related to a determinate object."[71]

Kenneth Gallagher, in his excellent study on Marcel, is of the opinion that *disponibilité* is untranslatable and he prefers to adopt the anglicized form "disponibility." He writes, "The English word (disposability and availability) manage to convey the idea of 'being at the service' of the other, which would not be bad if correctly understood, but which is not self-explanatory. It would undoubtedly be better to anglicize the French form, while realizing what it connotes: openness, release, abandonment, welcoming, surrender, readiness to respond. . . . The disponible person is hospitable to others; the doors of his soul are ajar. . . . Disponibility will be proclaimed in acts like love, sympathy, admiration."[72]

VIII. ABSOLUTE THOU AND FIDELITY

Marcel believes that it is on the level of the mystery, of the metaproblematical and of secondary reflection that man can discover his authentic personhood. And so it is only in a genuine I-Thou relationship, in that encounter or meeting on the plane of intersubjectivity that I can engage in such personal relationships as disponibility, fidelity and love.

When I enter into communion with another, I thereby transcend the level of having, i.e., the level of object, and I rise to the sphere of Being. By nature I am so constituted that I clamor for the Absolute and Unconditioned Being or God. I constantly desire Him and reach out for Him in all my activities. And so, in my desire for the Absolute Thou, I enter into communion with "the other." Through my spiritual availability, my love and fidelity to the other and reciprocally, his to me, we both begin to participate in the Unconditioned Being Himself.

Marcel explains, "I would be prepared to say dogmatically that every relation of being to being is personal and that the relation between me and God is nothing if it is not a relation of being with being, or strictly, of being with itself. . . . While an empirical *thou* can be converted

into a *him*, God is the absolute *Thou* who can never become a *him*."[73]

In these total commitments to each other, we reach
out for an absolute and complete fidelity, love and disponibility. By beginning on the plane of the human, the
finite and the conditioned, we mutually assist each other
in our ascent to the Unqualified, to the Infinite. "Reflection shows me that this (partial fidelity and disponibility)
involves the invocation of the Absolute Thou, Who is the
ground of all being and value and Who alone makes
eternal fidelity possible. Thus in the exploration of the
relationships which arise on the plane of intersubjectivity, I 'discover' God as the personal transcendent Absolute."[74]

As Marcel records in his *Metaphysical Journal*, "Perhaps my soul would only be the *ego* of the psychologists,
which is really only a *him*, were I not to converse about
it with God, were it not involved and vitally interested
in this conversation. . . . My soul is always a *thou* for God;
for God it is always confounded with the subject who
invokes Him. . . . And of course, the more God is for me,
the more I *am*; in that way we can see the intimate relation that unites us."[75]

In fidelity, I find that I become absolute and totally
committed, without any reservations whatsoever. Marcel
explains, "I cannot really confuse this attachment of the
soul to its own glory—the most arid, strained and irritable
of all forms of self-love with that which I have all my life
called Fidelity—I cannot base my argument on the effort
of my own will. I must admit, then that something un-
alterable is implied in the relation itself. I must start from
Being itself—from commitment to God."[76] This act of
genuine commitment is something transcendent in its
very nature because it is *beyond* my own limited powers.
It is made possible only because of my complete and
unquestioning faith in God. Like Abraham, the Knight
of faith, I place my complete trust in God or the Absolute
Thou. I am fully conscious of my own insufficiency. I call
upon God Himself to serve as a ground for the fidelity
which I exhibit toward my neighbor. "Hence this ground

of fidelity which necessarily seems precarious to use as soon as we commit ourselves to one another who is unknown, seems unshakable when it is based not, to be sure, on a distinct apprehension of God as some one or other, but on a certain appeal delivered from the depths of my own insufficiency *ad summam altitudinem*: I have sometimes called this the absolute resort. This appeal presupposes a radical humility in the subject; a humility which is polarized by the very transcendence of the one it invokes. Here we are, as it were, at the juncture of the most stringent commitment and the most desperate expectation. It cannot be a matter of counting on oneself, on one's own resources, to cope with this unbounded commitment; but in the act in which I commit myself, I at the same time extend an infinite credit to Him to Whom I did so; Hope seems nothing more than this."[77]

And because God Himself is present to me in faith, my fidelity becomes possible toward my fellowman. Because of this Absolute and Unconditioned Fidelity, the other "partial fidelities are made possible." My own fidelity is rooted in this Absolute Fidelity, which is the infinite Being of God Himself. "To display real fidelity toward my fellows, I must give myself completely to God Who is the Faithful One. For this reason fidelity can only rest upon faith in God, and this faith is the highest existential relation which I transcend myself."[78]

And since it is in constant communion with the very source of all fidelity, it itself is constantly revitalized and becomes a "creative fidelity." We read, "It is because fidelity is creative that, like liberty itself, it infinitely transcends the limits of what can be prescribed. Creative when it is genuine, it is so fundamentally and in every way, for it possesses the mysterious power of renewing not only the person who practices it but the recipient. ... It is in this way, too, that a code of ethics centered on fidelity is irresistibly led to become attached to what is more than human, to a desire for the unconditioned, which is the requirement and the very mark of the Absolute in us."[79]

Such a fidelity is augmented by those rare qualities

of humility and patience." Fidelity is at her most unmistakable, where her face shines with clearest light, she goes hand in hand with a character so opposed to Pride or anything we can imagine. Patience and humility—virtues whose very names today are forgotten and whose true nature is further darkened to our sight with every step forward in man's technical and impersonal equipment, his logical and dialectical equipment with the rest."[80]

IX.   FAITH, HOPE, LOVE
A.   Faith

Fidelity, for Marcel, always implies an unconditioned vow to another person, a commitment to the other. But such fidelity is manifestly impossible without a *faith* in the other, for faith is the highest expression of fidelity. Marcel writes, "Faith, the force of invisible truths. I say this illuminating sentence over and over to myself—but it only illuminates *after* the event. Also, I become conscious more and more of the part played in faith by will. The thing is to keep myself in a certain state analogous, on the human level, to the state of grace. In this sense, faith is essentially fidelity, and in the highest possible form."[81]

Faith, however, can be understood in two different ways: (1) as conviction (2) as commitment. Understood as conviction, faith is still on the level of the problematic and that of having, rather than on the level of mystery and being. Marcel explains faith as conviction, "Let us express ourselves once more clearly. When I believe in God and when one asks me questions about this faith or I question myself about it, I would of necessity, have to declare that I am convinced of the existence of God. But on the other hand, it seems this translation ('believing as being convinced'), which in reality is unavoidable, lets escape that which is original, and this is precisely its existential character."[82] Far more enriching and productive on the ontological plane is the faith understood as commitment because it carries with it the richness of a binding obligation. "When I believe *in*, that means I place myself at the disposal of or rather, that I conclude a formal obligation not only with regard to what I *have* but also to

what I *am*. . . . If I believe *in*, I attach myself to, with
a certain kind of gathering-together that this act carries
with it. Seen thus, one might say that the strongest faith,
or more exactly the liveliest faith is that faith which
most completely bundles together all the forces of your
'being.' "[83]

Through faith as genuine commitment, I engage in a
mystical encounter with the other. Such an encounter
which implies a binding obligation, since it carries with
it a complete bundling together of all the forces of being,
adds a new dimension both to me and the other or the
Thou. By becoming spiritually available to my neighbor,
I immediately transcend the narrow limits of my own
being. I overcome the restrictions of my egocentricity and
discover at this moment the Absolute Thou. I find that
God is the very ground of my faith and fidelity. I invoke
Him and enter into loving communion with Him.

C. Love

Whenever there are faith and fidelity, there will also
be love: love of God by man, love of man by God, and
love of man by his fellowman. The mutuality of this
reciprocal love gives meaning and authenticity to man's
existence in the world. As one commentator phrases it,
"Where Sartre sees in the initial situation which makes
us men, nothing but an absurd and incomprehensible
accident, Marcel sees the gracious gift of a Transcendent
Lover, who invites us to collaborate with Him in the
perfecting of our own being. The great and unique task
of men here below is to pass from existence to being:
that is from initial participation in which he is immersed
independently of his own will to a new participation, this
time conscious and freely willed, with the world, himself,
other men and God."[84]

All true love of the other must ultimately be based
on the love of God. It is this love which gives value to
man's actions. And so, really to love a creature, Marcel
would agree, "is to love him in God. Only in the Absolute
does the promise of eternity, with which all love is redo-
lent, attain to unconditionality. This is not a matter of

inference or argumentation: it simply means that our experience of presence is truncated and our assurance sapped unless they arise within an enveloping Absolute."[85]

B. Hope

Genuine love always carries with it a necessary concomitant, namely, hope. For it is hope which gives a meaningfulness to man's existence. Marcel argues very convincingly when he states, "Once again we are led to draw attention to the indissoluble connection which binds together love and hope. The more egoistical love is, the more, the alluringly prophetic declaration it inspires, should be regarded with a caution as likely to be literally contradicted by experience; on the other hand, the nearer it approaches to true charity, the more the meaning of its declaration is inflected and tends to become full of an unconditional quality which is the very sign of presence. This presence is incarnated in the 'us' for whom 'I hope in Thee,' that is to say in a communion of which I proclaim the indestructibility."[86]

Marcel next presents a striking analogy in speaking of the absolute necessity of hope for the soul. Without hope, there can be no life whatsoever. He writes, "Hope is for the soul what breathing is for the living organism. Where hope is lacking, the soul dries up and withers. . . . We might say that hope is the availability of a soul which has entered intimately enough into the experience of communion to accomplish in the teeth of will and knowledge, the transcendent act—the act of establishing the vital regeneration of which this experience affords the pledge and first fruits."[87]

Marcel engages in a lengthy phenomenological analysis of this important quality of hope. In fact, his entire work, *Homo Viator*, bears the subtitle, *Introduction to a Metaphysic of Hope*. He underscores the close relationship between love and hope: "Hope, in this sense, is not only a protestation inspired by love, but a sort of call, too, a desperate appeal to an ally who is Himself also Love. The supernatural element which is the foundation of Hope is as clear here as its transcendent nature, for nature, unilluminated by hope, can only appear to us the scene of a sort of immense and inexorable book-keeping."[88]

Hence it is preeminently through Hope that I discover my relationship to the Absolute Thou. Because I realize my complete dependence on this Infinite Being, I am forever protected from despair. I am not tortured by a Heideggerian dread and homelessness; neither am I overwhelmed by Sartre's absurdity or nausea. I am, in truth, a *homo viator*, a pilgrim, a wayfarer but not a wanderer of endless and confusing "forest trails." I experience a nostalgia for Being and, therefore, I direct my gaze to another life where I shall experience the complete fulfillment.

Marcel says, "This is what determines the ontological position of hope—absolute hope, inseparable from a faith which is likewise absolute, transcending all laying down of conditions, and for this reason every kind of representation whatever it might be. The only possible source from which this absolute hope springs must be stressed once more. It appears as a response of the creature to the Infinite Being to Whom it is conscious of owing everything that it has and upon Whom it cannot impose any condition whatsoever without scandal. From the moment that I abase myself in some sense before the Absolute Thou, Who in His infinite condescension has brought me forth out of nothingness, it seems as though I forbid myself ever again to despair, or, more exactly, that I implicitly accept the possibility of despair as an indication of treason, so that I could not give way to it without pronouncing my own condemnation. Indeed, even in this perspective, what is the meaning of despair if not a declaration that God has withdrawn Himself from me? In addition to the fact that such an accusation is incompatible with the nature of the Absolute Thou, it is to be observed that in advancing it, I am unwarrantably attributing to myself a distinct reality which I do not possess."[89]

Marcel, therefore, will refuse to accept Albert Camus' thesis that man is condemned to live hopelessly in a world of absurdity. In *The Myth of Sisyphus*,[90] Camus maintains that his absurd hero, Sisyphus, can be happy without a shred of hope in his life. Condemned for all eternity to roll a huge stone uphill and knowing that every time he reaches the top, the stone will roll down again, Sisyphus refuses to resign himself to this hopeless situation. Deprived of all hope, he knows that he is doomed to failure before he starts each trip. Yet Camus (at least in this earlier period of his life), holds that his hero saves himself by acting resolutely, scornfully and defiantly in the face of his fate. Such is the lot of every man in the face of the absurd.

Marcel first challenges Camus' right to speak of an absurd world: "We must ask whether any philosopher is really qualified to pass on the universe, namely, that the universe is absurd. . . . There is no point in saying that the universe is absurd, unless I can compare the universe with some idea of order of rationality to which I observe that it does not conform."[91]

Secondly, Marcel allows that while Camus is hard put to justify his position metaphysically, nevertheless, it does contain some moral validity. He says, "For a sensitive conscience like that of Albert Camus, the existence of undeserved sufferings (the suffering of children, for instance, and that due to accidents considered as things that happen gratuitously), forbids an honorable thinker to allow either that the world can be the work of God or can even, in the fullest sense of the word, be an intelligible world. . . . A stand like that of Camus, whatever we may think of it at a metaphysical level has undoubtedly a certain moral validity: it is honest and honorable, the stand of a man who does not want to let himself be imposed on, and who refuses from the very depths of his being, to confuse what he desires with what actually exists. But at the same time, I should add that this attitude of Camus is also extremely simple-minded (naïve). It is that of a man who has never reached the stage of what I have often called secondary reflection."[92]

Camus' naïveté with respect to the meta-implications is somewhat redeemed by his "fate-despising courage" on the ethical level. But while we find that his courage is moving "by its sympathy with the nameless misery in the world," we nevertheless find it "unattractive and repelling by its hopelessness."[93]

Marcel's answer to Camus (as well as to Sartre, de Beauvoir and Heidegger), is that there *is* hope in the world. And it is the presence of this hope that denies the absurdity, the thrownness, and the despair and anguish of the atheistic existentialists. It is hope that gives meaning, rationality and genuine authenticity to man's existence here on earth.

Marcel further contends that hope receives its being from something which "according to the order of nature does not depend on us . . . it is perhaps characteristic of Hope to be unable either to make direct use of any technique or to call it to her aid. Hope is proper to the unarmed: it is the weapon of the unarmed or (more exactly) it is the very opposite of a weapon and in that mysteriously enough, its power lies. Present-day scepticism about hope is due to the essential inability to conceive that anything can be efficacious when it is no sort of a power in the ordinary sense of the word. . . . To hope is to put one's trust in reality, to assert that it contains the means of triumphing over this danger."[94] In another place Marcel describes how with "insolent ingenuity," hope always tends to disregard the pompous pronouncements of a dogmatism, which calls upon the muchly-vaunted present-day techniques to bring about results. Contrary to techniques, "Hope is not interested in the *how*; and this fact shows how fundamentally untechnical it is, for technical thought, by definition, never separates the consideration of ends and means. An end does not exist for the technician if he does not see approximately how to achieve it."[95]

For Gabriel Marcel, hope is inextricably bound up with the "other-worldly." Repeatedly he tells us that hope is only possible "in a world where there is room for miracles." For him, hope always carries with it "an affirmation of eternity and of eternal goods." Consequently, the efficacy of hope is realized in its fullest when there is an admission of complete "inadequacy on the phenomenal level, of an absolute powerlessness in the empirical realm."

And so it should be obvious to us that the "estuaries of
Hope do not lie entirely within the bounds of the visible
world." And so Hope has "the unusual virtue of somehow
putting in a false predicament the powers over which it
claims to triumph, not by fighting them, far from it, but
by transcending them." This is why Marcel says that
the supernatural element "which is the foundation of
Hope is as clear as its transcendent nature."[96]

The Marcellian man is not condemned to freedom
as a foundationless base; neither does he live a purposeless and meaningless life. The I-Thou relationship, which
he establishes through hope, can best be described as
"I hope in thee for us." The vital link which makes such
a hope possible, the vital link which makes "In thee for
us" a reality is none other than the Absolute Thou or God
Himself. Not only is this Transcendent Thou a guarantee
which "holds us together, myself to myself or the one to
the other, but it secures and confirms this union." More
than that, it is Marcel's contention that the Absolute Thou
is "the very cement that binds the whole into one." And if
this is true, then "to despair of myself or to despair of us
is essentially to despair of the Thou."[97]

Marcel's world, in contrast to the brooding darkness
of the Heideggerian *Unheimlichkeit* and *Geworfenheit*,
is one of optimism because the Marcellian man can and
does find intelligibility in the universe. That there are
many imperfections and injustices in it, Marcel is the first
to admit. Nevertheless man is not condemned to despair;
neither is he asked to clench his fist and grit his teeth in
the face of absurdity. Fortified with faith, fidelity, love
and hope, the Marcellian man enters into intersubjective
relationships of disponibility with his fellowman. He lives
in a genuine communion, a togetherness, a co-esse, which
takes place on the level of being and not on the level of
having and objectification. In his spiritual availability and
responsiveness to the thou, he discovers a transcendent,
Absolute Thou—God Himself.

Life, therefore, has meaning for the Marcellian man.
He can find happiness in this life precisely because he
has hope. As one author puts it, "Because I trust Being,

I come to trust myself and my fellow-men. I am filled with hope, knowing that I am worthwhile and that life is good. Hope enables me to see that I have a purpose and a mission, that the substance of my life will benefit my fellow-man and please God. In hope, I enter into deep communion with those about me. In hope, I find Being and rely upon God."[98]

X. BROKEN WORLD, FUNCTIONALIZATION, DEHUMANIZATION

"Don't you feel sometimes that we are living . . . if you can call it living . . . in a broken world? Yes, broken like a broken watch. The mainspring has stopped working. Just look at it, nothing has changed. Everything is in place. But put the watch to your ear, and you don't hear any ticking. You know what I am talking about, the world, what we call the world, the world of human creatures. . . . It seems to me it must have had a heart at one time, but today you would say the heart has stopped beating."[99]

The speech by Christiane, the heroine of Marcel's play, *The Broken World* is a fitting introduction to one of his chief preoccupations today, namely, the ills of the present day world. In describing his heroine, who is but a personification of the mass "dis-ease" and anguish so prevalent today, Marcel says, "The young woman who makes this speech is not intended to rank among what we usually call intellectuals. She is a fashionable lady, smart, witty, flattered by her friends, but the busy, rushing life that she seems so much at home in obviously masks an inner grief, an anguish and it is that anguish which breaks through to the surface in the speech which I have just quoted."[100]

The twentieth century man has become a stranger to himself. He has denied the existence of God and by doing so, he has lost his moorings, his own identity. Without any fixed purpose in life, without any roots or foundation to which he might anchor himself, contemporary man experiences a Heideggerian *Geworfenheit*, a thrownness into the world and a gnawing homelessness. He feels an overwhelming estrangement and alienation. A nausea is about to overcome him because of the uselessness of it all. The absurdity of reality is best epitomized in the observation that man is a useless passion.[101] Increasingly pressed on all sides, man senses a relentless erosion of his own individuality and personality. Like sand slipping through the fingers of his hands, his personhood is being lost to him. Inevitably, against his own inner better judgment, he finds himself succumbing to mass movements and collectivities, whether they be political, social or industrial.

The state, society and highly organized groups conspire each moment to make man just a little less human. Human society, according to Marcel, seems to be on the verge of becoming a sort of ant hill. He warns us, "It is by starting from the fact of growingly complex and unified social organization of human life today, that one can see most clearly what lies behind the loss, for individuals, of life's old intimate quality. In what does this growingly complex organization—this socialization of life, as we may call it—really consist? Primarily in the fact that each one of us is being treated today more and more as an *agent*, whose behavior ought to contribute towards the progress of a certain social whole—something rather distant, rather oppressive, let us frankly say, rather tyrannical. . . . There are sectors of human life in the present world where the process of automatization applies not only, for instance, to certain definite techniques, but to what one would have formerly called the inner life, a life which today, on the contrary, is becoming as outer as possible."[102]

As a result of this condition, we are witnessing a "devaluation of life" in the same sense, says Marcel, that one might speak of a currency devaluation. The inevitable consequence of such a cheapening of human life and of the loss of the dignity of the human being, has been a gnawing alienation and estrangement in the human breast. This alienation, Marcel maintains, is due to the fact that "in a world increasingly under the hegemony of technology, the human life is undergoing what might be called an enucleation. . . . In such a world, the life of each of us tends to lose its existential weight because circumstances which formerly would have been taken in their intrinsic seriousness, now tend to be interpreted in terms of adjustment or maladjustment."[103] And consequently, we can recognize that "in a world where technology enjoys absolute primacy, a desacralizing process inevitably sets in, that is directed against life and its manifestations and particularly against the family and everything connected with it."[104]

As Gibson Winter observes in his penetrating analysis, *Being Free*, "Technology achieves power through domination and control, but even as technology makes life more interdependent, it estranges by objectifying and controlling the relationship of man to nature, to other men and to his world. Objective and impersonal, technology is the rational ordering of processes for deliberate aims, bringing each relevant relationship into its purposeful design, subjecting that relationship to pre-determined control. Every unit—whether man or thing—has to be reduced to a calculable quantity so that it can be brought within the logic of technology. . . . The alienating character of technology is precisely this reduction of the world to the calculable. Yet men and cultures resist being reduced to calculable entities. Thus in creating interdependence, the techno-society also alienates and estranges."[105]

The intrinsic dignity and sacredness of the human being have now been replaced by his functional value. No longer is man considered in terms of his humaneness. No longer is man's dignity accorded its place among entities. Today man's worth is cynically calculated and computed in terms of the function he performs. Almost unconsciously man himself begins to evaluate himself and his every action solely from the point of view of the functions he performs in society. And "as the capacity to love, to admire and to hope dries up, the functional man loses the ability, even the desire, to transcend his situation of alienation and captivity. . . . Life in a functionalized world becomes a process without a purpose, a utilization of means with no clearly defined end, a journey without a goal. When the sense of dignity and purposefulness in life is lost, nothing ultimately matters."[106]

In his essay, *On The Ontological Mystery,* Marcel complains that man appears more and more, both to others and to himself, as an "agglomeration of functions." He gives a concrete example of what he means by describing the well-known ticket-puncher in the Métro in Paris. He says, "Traveling on the Underground, I often wonder with a kind of dread what can be the inward reality of the life of this or that man employed on the railway—the man who opens doors, for instance, of the one who punches the tickets. Surely everything within him and outside him conspires to identify this man with his functions—meaning not only with his functions as a worker, a trade union member or as a voter, but with his vital functions as well. The rather horrible expression 'time table' perfectly describes his life. So many hours for each function. Sleep, too, is a function which must be discharged so that the other functions may be exercised in their turn. The same with pleasure, relaxation; it is logical that the weekly allowance of recreation should be determined by an expert on hygiene; recreation is a psycho-organic function which must not be neglected any more than, for instance, the function of sex. . . . It is true that certain disorderly elements—sickness, accidents of every sort—will break in on the smooth working of the system. It is therefore natural that the individual should be overhauled at regular intervals like a watch. . . . As for death, it becomes objectively and functionally the scrapping of what has ceased to be of use and must be written off as a total loss."[107]

Such a condition produces a stifling impression of sadness produced by this functionalized world. The resulting uneasiness is enough to show that there is in all this "some appalling mistake, some ghastly misinterpretation, implanted in defenceless minds by an increasingly inhuman social order and an equally inhuman philosophy."[108] The product of such a condition is the creation of "submen, beings who tend more and more to be reduced to their own strict function in a mechanized society."

Marcel is realistic enough to admit the place of technology in modern day life. Technology, as such, is necessary and valuable. There is no point in thinking of technical progress as "being in itself an expression of sin." What Marcel does object to most emphatically and relentlessly is technocracy, technolatry and technomania. This is an attitude of worshipping technical progress and its method to the degree that it is allowed to arrogate to itself the traditional position reserved for speculation or philosophical contemplation. This is, as Marcel insists, *misosophy*—a hatred of wisdom.[109]

William Luijpen graphically describes the condition of modern man who has been overpowered by technocracy. Man experiences a "choking sadness." He lives in an empty and hollow world of mathematical calculations. He has lost his selfhood and has become a mere function.

Luijpen writes, "In our technocratic society, finding oneself not to be well has fully overpowered finding oneself to be well. As Marcel expresses it, our society is characterized by a 'choking sadness.' Man does not feel at home in a technocratic society, because in it integrally being human, authentically being a person, is mutilated. The world raised by technology in which man has to live is wholly a world of mathematical calculation; it is empty and sounds hollow. In the world of technology, there is practically no longer any difference between day and night, nor are there any seasons left. The rhythm of life becomes more and more the rhythm of a machine. Within it man is a 'function' and his fellow-man is 'another function' calculated by the psycho-technician. Technocracy has deprived man of his *selfhood*. Nowhere so much as here is he reduced to anonymity."[110]

XI. TOTALITARIAN STATE

In such a climate where modern man is regarded less and less as an individual and more and more as a mere function, it becomes comparatively easy for the totalitarian state "to take over." Like a giant octopus with its tentacles reaching out in all directions, the state arrogantly invades the previously sacred precincts of individual human rights. The "functional man," who has been demeaned and de-humanized, is quickly engulfed by the Leviathan. With efficiency and ruthlessness, everything is organized, systematized and categorized. The value and intrinsic worth of each individual is coldly and impersonally calculated by the State in terms of the services and functions he performs. In the name of maximum efficiency and output, rigid controls are imposed on all of man's activities: nothing escapes the State's scrutiny. Art, music, literature, religion and science are constantly under the surveillance of the all-powerful State and any deviation from the arbitrary regulations of state bureaucracy is subject to swift punishment, sometimes even death. The twentieth century totalitarianisms in Russia, China and Cuba are the most immediate examples which come to mind. The Almighty State has power over everything, even life itself. It decrees not only who shall live but even who shall be born. As Vincent Miceli observes, "Even the activity of parenthood is interpreted as an activity of the State and is rewarded according to State laws. The father is just an instrument and the mother is a channel through which the State gets the manpower it needs and will drain for its own prolongation in economic, political and martial supremacy."[111]

XII. EXISTENCE OF GOD

In terms strongly reminiscent of Kierkegaard's condemnation of theodicy and the function of human reason vis-à-vis the existence of God, Marcel categorically denies the very possibility of theodicy.[112] In his *Metaphysical Journal,* we read the following entry: "God cannot and must not be judged. For judgment is only possible regarding essence. That explains why every kind of theodicy must be condemned, because a theodicy necessarily implies a judgment, it is a judgment, a justification. Now God cannot be justified. The thought that justifies is the thought that has not yet been elevated to love and to the faith that claims to transcend the mind (belief). Theodicy is atheism."[113]

Marcel points out that, inasmuch as the proofs for

God's existence have not always seemed to be too effective, "it might well be that the idea of a proof in the
traditional sense of the word, of the existence of God
implied a paralogism or a vicious circle. . . . One fact,
however, remains: the proofs that have been given of the
existence of God have not always seemed convincing—far
from it—even to the historians of philosophy who expounded them most minutely. . . . So we stumble on this
paradox: the proofs are ineffectual precisely when they
would be most necessary, when, that is, it is a question
of convincing an unbeliever; conversely when belief is
already present and when, accordingly, there is the minimum of agreement, then they seem to serve no useful
purpose."

"If a man has experienced the presence of God, not
only has he no need of proofs, he may even go so far as
to consider the idea of a demonstration as a slur on what
is, for him, a sacred evidence. Now from the point of
view of a philosophy of existence, it is this sort of testimony which is the central and irreducible datum."[114]

The reasons why arguments for the existence of God
are useless and hence of no value, continues Marcel, is
because they do not do what they claim.[115] In actuality,
they are deceptions. He writes, "The arguments [for God's
existence] presuppose that we have already grounded
ourselves on God and what they are really doing is to
bring to the level of discursive thought, an act of a wholly
different kind. These, I believe, are not ways but blind
ways, as one can have blind windows." The so-called
proofs, Marcel contends, in reality already presuppose a
prior datum. "All proof refers to a certain datum which
is here the belief of God, whether in myself or another.
The proof can only consist in a secondary type of reflection—a reconstructive reflection grafted on a *critical reflection*: a reflection which is a recovery but only insofar
as it remains the tributary of what I have called blindfold
intuition. It is clear that the apprehension of the ontological mystery as a metaproblematic is the motive force of
this recovery through reflection. . . . The proof can only
confirm for us what has really been given to us in another

way. . . . Anyhow, there can only be a solution, where
there is a problem and the phrase 'problem of God' is
certainly contradictory and even sacrilegious."[116]

In his work, *Problematic Man*, Marcel specifically
denies the viability of the arguments for God's existence
from causality. Let us listen to his pronouncements: "I
think we should have done with the idea of a God as
cause, of a God concentrating in himself all the causality,
or even, in more rigorous terms, with all theological usage
of the notion of causality. It is precisely here that Kant
has shown us the way, perhaps without himself proceeding
to the final consequences of his discovery. It could be, I
will say in order to resume the thread of my argumentation, that the God whose death Nietzsche truthfully announced, was the god of the Aristotelian-Thomistic tradition, god the prime mover. . . . It would seem that if we
claim to make of the idea of cause a transcendent use,
we arrive at a dead-end, or, which amounts to the same
thing, we get lost in a labyrinth. The words 'transcendent
use' have here an extremely precise meaning: they mean
a use which extends beyond the domain of instrumentality
strictly speaking—that is, that in which man exercises his
mastery—or even any other domain conceived arbitrarily
or not, as analogous to the first . . . it is to be feared, indeed, that the idea of causality, whatever effort modern
philosophers have made to spiritualize it, to unfetter it,
to detach it from its primitive anchors, is inseparable
from the existence of a being provided with instrumental
powers; it is in short, bio-teleological."[117]

Many people disagree with Marcel's contention that
theodicy is dead; on the contrary, they maintain that as
the crowning point of metaphysics, theodicy will long
outlive Marcel's Neo-Socratism. They point out that
Marcel's antipathy to theodicy is actually due to a misunderstanding of the traditional arguments for the existence of God. James Collins, for example, maintains that
Marcel's difficulty with these proofs for God's existence
is due to the latter's peculiar "rationalistic notion" of what
it means to prove something. For Marcel, proof involves
the "pointing out of the logical implications of certain

admitted definitions and propositions." And so, for him, demonstration is a purely logical deduction, which moves exclusively "in the realm of essences and conceptual constructs."[118]

And it is for this reason, says Collins, that Marcel can never have a truly existential demonstration. In the existential position of Thomas Aquinas, for example, Collins points out that proof "may sometimes bear upon the implications of a given existent and thus may move from an *existential datum* to an *existential conclusion* (italics added). If the starting point of inference lies in some apprehension of an existent, then reasoning may proceed in an *a posteriori* way to certainty about some other existent, whose actuality is required in order to account for the original point of departure. Hence Aquinas regards his proofs of God's existence as giving demonstrative certainty about the actually existing first cause of the sensible world. In order to join issue with Aquinas, Marcel would first have to subject the rationalistic notion of proof to critical scrutiny and then compare this view with other theories of demonstration. Apparently the existential foundation of the Thomistic theory of *a posteriori* demonstration was not sufficiently stressed in the textbooks consulted by Marcel. But to omit this aspect is to pass over the distinctive procedures in Thomistic metaphysics."[119]

Collins further maintains that Marcel interprets causality in a very narrow and therefore inadequate manner. Causality for Marcel is strictly limited to the sphere of *instrumental* causality. Within that narrow context, if the only way in which I understand *cause* is in the nature of a power which man exercises as a wielder of instruments, then obviously I can never transcend this level of human instrumentality. I will never be able to arrive at a being which is outside this narrow, limited conception of causality. Collins explains this point as follows: "Marcel takes causality in the primary sense to mean an instrumental use of power on the part of man, a human exercise of mastery. This cause refers properly to man as the principle of instruments, as dealing with things and shaping his own organism in view of his needs. Every other usage is only a variant of this central meaning and hence, there can be no causal meaning which genuinely transcends the domain of human instrumentality. From this it follows, for Marcel, that causal inference belongs entirely within the field of relations between man and things, or organic parts under his mastery. To treat God as a cause, would then mean reducing Him to a wielder of instruments or a producer in the non-creative sense. And it would also mean reducing us to the status of tools and objects, which would destroy the personal relationships upon which religious life feeds."[120]

For Gabriel Marcel, then, to regard God as a cause is to demean Him and to reduce Him to the level of a maker and user of tools. This is the inevitable consequence of understanding Him in the restricted way of instrumental causality. But Collins goes on to say that Marcel is not exactly consistent, since he frequently speaks of God as a cause in a much wider sense than that of instrumentality. For aside from his initial definitional framework, Marcel's God is "not an instrumental producer but He is the Center of all things. He is the infinite Person who communicates being to us and we are participants in being from Him. We also seek His personal presence as the goal of our desire, as the only way of bringing our inquietude to its proper fulfillment."[121] And so the basic difficulty seems to be that Marcel thinks "the causal explanation is ir-remediably bound down to a materializing, reifying, em-pirico-technical treatment of the related beings; whereas the religious relationship is found in the communion of spirit with spirit."[122]

Frederick Copleston believes that Marcel's position concerning the indemonstrability of the existence of God is "a version of the old distinction between the God of philosophy and the God of Abraham, Isaac and Jacob." He goes on to observe that Marcel's point of view is not adequate, since it does not give us the complete picture.[123]

Now it is perfectly true that some philosophers have tended to treat God as a problem. They have considered Him as some sort of depersonalized abstraction, a conclusion of a syllogism in the realm of pure ideas. This criticism is certainly valid in the case of men like Descartes, Spinoza, Leibnitz and Hegel. But this does not constitute an argument for the repudiation of a realist metaphysics, any more than Kierkegaard's rejection of Hegelian pantheistic idealism could be accepted as a valid denigration of all philosophy. Unlike the idealists, the realist metaphysician begins with actually existing singulars in reality. By examining the condition of "participated beings on the scale of ascending perfections," the realist then arrives at the source of all analogous being, namely, the Unconditioned, Transcendent, eminently existing Being. This God of a realist metaphysics is not the same logical abstraction or problem as Marcel seems to indicate. On the contrary, a realist metaphysics begins with actual, real existents, finite and contingent, and it ends with the real personal Existent, God Himself. This is, indeed, the same personal God of the Bible but He is arrived at in another manner.[124]

Copleston, perceptive historian of philosophy that he is, sees a striking parallel between men like Marcel and Jaspers on the one hand, and medieval thinkers like Ockham on the other, who relegated to faith what was formerly regarded as demonstrable by reason. In considering the existence of God, Marcel is always inclined to speak of "faith" rather than of philosophic proof. Copleston concludes that in this respect, "Marcel seems to resemble those medieval thinkers who, dissatisfied with the aridity of logical studies, turned to mysticism in a speculative form (as distinguished from the actual mystical life) and sought an answer to man's deeper questionings and desires in a metalogical sphere. Such a rejection of metaphysics is in reality a flight from reason." Those existentialists who are theistic and hence accept the existence of God do so apparently "on faith." But in such a case, Copleston contends, "subjectivism and emotion tend to take the place of reason. Emotion certainly has its place in life; it may even have a place in philosophy; but it cannot take the place of argument. My wishes are not the criterion of truth."[125]

Here the criticism of Frederick Patka seems to be especially apposite. After pointing out that, for Marcel, God reveals Himself in his mystical experience, Patka says, "While accepting the legitimate value of mysticism on its own ground, we may question its validity in the field of philosophy. What criteria can we use, for instance, to validate the emotional and volitive efforts of the existentialists to achieve the region of Absolute Being? These experiences being basically a-logical and meta-problematic, any logical insight into their objective validity is made a priori impossible. The strain of subjectivism cannot be removed in any way."[126]

At the same time, a philosophical position that bases itself upon an existential demonstration (such as that of Thomas Aquinas), should be able to explain why its proofs for God's existence are frequently unable to convince many honest and inquiring minds. Surely an explanation of such a phenomenon should be forthcoming, even though it is held that there *is* an essential distinction between "the intrinsic force of an argument and its ability to convince this or that person under particular circumstances."[127] It would seem that it is especially in such an instance, that Marcel's descriptive method makes an invaluable contribution. Not unlike Pascal's and Newman's psychological observations on the causes of scepticism, Marcel's insights are of inestimable value. As Collins concludes, "Marcel discloses a prephilosophical drama, in which the individual either acknowledges the participated and contingent nature of his hold upon existence or closes all thought of an absolute source of his being. The whole of Marcel's philosophical reflection is centered upon this unavoidable alternative and upon the consequences of this primary choice. A denial of our creaturely openness and sharing in being results in a radical infidelity to the human condition. What Thomas Hardy called man's unhope is the outcome of refusing to extend credit to the universe in the direction of its transcendent source. And the fruit of unhope is despair."[128] It is hardly necessary to point to the appropriateness of the last observation in the case of such atheistic existentialists as Jean Paul Sartre, Albert Camus and Simone de Beauvoir.

XIII.   CONCLUSION

After having examined some of the salient features of Marcel's existentialist postures, we shall now attempt to locate him in some philosophical perspective, as well as to arrive at some sort of evaluation of his contributions. This we shall do by studying a number of penetrating critiques offered us by well-qualified Marcellian scholars.

F. H. Heinemann feels that one of the greatest contributions which Marcel has made to contemporary thought is the bringing to the fore a genuine philosophy of HOPE. In answer to Jean Paul Sartre's atheistic existentialism of godlessness, nausea and despair, Gabriel Marcel shows that there is a more genuine form of existentialism, namely, a *theistic* Christian existentialism. Marcel challenges Sartre's contention that man is doomed to live out his life in an absurd world, endlessly plotting to make an object of another *l'être pour-soi*, at the same time running the risk of becoming himself entrapped and pulverized by the menacing other. Heinemann observes, however, that Marcel's philosophy is but one specific possibility in the domain of metaphysics. The partial truth that "being is mystery" is used as the very "cornerstone of a new metaphysics." Heinemann warns, however, that from this attempt, "interesting reflections result, which elucidate certain phenomena of the human scene, but that a new ontology can be based on it, still has to be proved. It would not be difficult to point to contradictions implied in this enterprise. Either there is the 'ontological mystery,' then no science of ontology is possible; or there is ontology, then 'being' becomes a problem and within the precincts of this science, the mystery disappears. . . . Marcel has a pertinent feeling of the human situation . . . he points the way, but he remains a *homo viator*, a Moses, who himself is not allowed to enter the promised land."[129]

Joseph Mihalich praises Marcel for preserving the dignity of man by emphasizing the close connection between the human being and God, the Absolute Thou.

Whereas Sartre and Camus consider man's existence as absolutely meaningless and futile, Marcel holds that human life has dignity, content and purpose. Rather than subscribing to Heidegger's emphasis on "stark finitude," Marcel shows that the properly oriented human being can negate death "through an invocation of an infinite source of Truth and value." At the same time, Mihalich finds Marcel's philosophy essentially limited by its reliance on the phenomenological method. This specialized technique (which can be highly desirable in psychology), is limited to the objects and states of consciousness, as they present themselves to the apprehending subject. In such a method of procedure, argues Mihalich, both deduction and a priori reasoning are excluded. The inevitable consequence of this particular method is that the only type of analysis possible is "the subjective description of phenomena as they manifest themselves in the concrete situation. This necessarily limits the observer to his own personal experiences and there is no justification for the extension of his experiences into the universal experience of all mankind."[130]

Kurt Reinhardt, in his highly sympathetic evaluation of Marcel's contributions, praises the French existentialist for criticizing so incisively not only idealism but also rationalism and positivism. But he tempers his praise with the following qualifications: "This critique [by Marcel] could be even more convincing, if it were implemented by a more positive acknowledgement of the legitimacy of certain indispensable objective and rational requisites and categories of any strictly philosophic and metaphysical reflection which refuses to be led into the blind alleys of either fideism or agnosticism." Reinhardt corroborates this evaluation with the following pertinent observation, when he says, "Marcel himself seems to feel the need for such an implementation when, in the final pages of *Être et Avoir*, he states emphatically 'it would be foolish indeed to believe that the speculative work of the intellect is a luxury. I repeat it is a necessity and not only from the point of view of the intellect, but from the point of view of love (*charité*). . . . To say it matters little what you *think* as long as you *live* like a Christian is, I believe, to make oneself guilty of the most serious offense against Him who said 'I am the Way, the Truth and the Life.' The Truth. It is above all on this territory of Truth that the religious battle must be fought; it is on this territory that it will be won or lost."[131]

Michele Sciacca pays Marcel the highest tribute when he says, "Of all the forms of existentialism, Marcel's is the only one that does not refuse but, rather, fulfills the experience of a Christian existence."[132] Sciacca does find disconcerting, however, Marcel's notion of metaphysics as something which cannot be rendered objective and hence is restricted to a live experience. He says, "It seems that Marcel's position is as follows: everything becomes insoluble and wrapped up in doubt if it slips to the level of objective thought and this is true of *everything* (the problem of the relationship between body and soul, of the existent and the others, of the existent and God and so on); everything, on the other hand, is clear, certain and infallible, provided that it is within primary indistinctness, beyond thought and within the zone of mystery or of the metaproblematical. . . . We are face to face with a pure phenomenology unable to justify itself or all the 'mysteries' on which it is founded."[133]

Sciacca goes on to say that, on such a basis, it becomes absolutely impossible for Marcel to oppose the atheistic existentialism of Jean Paul Sartre. Much as he would wish, Marcel's stance has no fundamentally different foundation on which he could formulate a meaningful refutation. As a matter of fact, it is only a question of different existential experiences. Sciacca says, "We cannot tell him (J. P. Sartre) that he is wrong or in *error* because we would have to demonstrate it, that is, we would have to *objectivate,* to 'discourse' and to mediate the original immediateness. Hence, Marcel's criticism against the objective and the problem can be assumed only as a polemical position, that is, as a corrective of the opposite rationalistic tendency by which everything is to be transcribed in terms of rational clearness, wherein existence is made abstract and null. . . . The problem is not to oppose the two worlds of 'being' and 'having,' or to condemn science, technology, reason, society, and so on; the problem is instead, to see how the two worlds meet each other, and how it is possible to attain an authentic objectivation (and not that of idealism, positivism and the like), which is not abstraction, possession, slavery and impoverishment of the immediate. This is possible only through objectivation itself, through reason and *not* through condemnation of reason."[134]

Henri Bouillard, author of the monumental three volume work on Karl Barth,[135] offers us the following insights: "Marcel justly criticizes the degraded forms of intelligence and objective knowledge that have given birth to the various kinds of positivism. This criticism would be still more convincing, if it were accompanied by a positive appreciation of objective and impersonal thought at its different levels, which would bring out, at the same time, by immanent reflection its essential role and its limitations. Metaphysical thought itself, which ceases to have any hold on reality the moment it ceases to be related to existence and to participate in being, has recourse, however, to universal categories. Now 'secondary reflection' is sound, only, when dialectic and the experience of presence there, encounter one another. Can a metaphysic of essence be worked out without recovering the structure of this dialectic? We should like to have details of an epistemology of 'ungraded' intelligence. We should then see that worship can and ought to have a mainstay for reflection and, moreover, that the movement that leads man to worship has an intelligible structure. . . . Marcel's is a philosophy on the confines of philosophy."[136]

Finally, Roger Troisfontaines, to whom Marcel confided the task of putting into organized form the main tenets of his philosophy, gives us a very penetrating resumé of the shortcomings of a phenomenology as a basis for metaphysics. It would seem that these delineations underscore best what the authorities, whom we have cited, have tried to say. Troisfontaines writes, "In regard to phenomenology itself, several points of view are possible. While it constitutes an excellent method of explanation and illustration, it does not provide the basis for a universal metaphysics. Each one claims to be right from his own viewpoint. Who will decide? Who will determine the hierarchy of these perspectives? Who will show where truth and goodness lie, or where, on the contrary, there is perversion? Under pain of falling into subjectivism, subjectivity has to base itself on an objective foundation, and it must do so according to criteria and norms which, far from crushing freedom, will be the sole means of enabling it not to degrade itself. Subjectivity and objectivity have complementary roles to play, and it would be equally harmful to abandon the one as to reject the other."[137]

Martin Buber

CHAPTER IV

MARTIN BUBER
LIFE

I. EARLY YEARS

Martin Buber, Jewish theologian, author, journalist, translator, educator and social philosopher was born
in Vienna in 1878 of a famous Galician rabbinical family.
When he was three, his parents divorced and Martin was
sent to live with his grandparents in Lemberg in Galicia.
His grandfather, Salomon Buber, was a brilliant scholar
and a leader of the central European Haskalah or Enlightenment. The young grandson was given a rich education by his learned grandfather. In particular, Martin
learned to speak and write classical Hebrew; he was
introduced to the wisdom of the Bible and educated in
the rich spiritual traditions and deep piety of Judaism.
During the summer months, the Buber family stayed in
the little villages of Sadagora and Czortkov, where Martin
first came into contact with the Hasidim.[1] There he observed first hand, as he tells us, the life and practices of
the Galician Jewish Hasidic communities, which would
have such an enormous influence on his own life and his
writings. Martin stayed in the richly cultural home of his
grandfather until he was fourteen years old. His father
remarried and Martin went to live with him and attended
the grammar school in Lemberg.[2]

At the age of eighteen, he entered the University of
Vienna, where he studied philosophy, literature and history of art. He then moved on to the University of Berlin,
where he was deeply influenced by the famous philosophers Wilhelm Dilthey and Georg Simmel. Buber received
his doctorate from the University of Berlin in 1904. He
married a brilliant German student, Paula Winkler, a
native of Munich, who later wrote under the nom de
plume of Georg Munk.

During his student days, when he was in his early twenties, Buber joined the Zionist movement which was just becoming organized under the leadership of Theodor Herzl and Achad Ha'am. In 1901 he became editor of the Zionist paper, *Der Welt*, in Vienna. This position was of short duration because of his sharp disagreement with the almost rabid political Zionism of Herzl and the moralism of Achad Ha'am. Buber was primarily interested in a cultural type of Zionism which aimed at a spiritual and aesthetic renascence of Jewish life and ideals.[3] In 1902, Buber helped found in Berlin a Jewish publishing company, *Judische Verlag*, which made its publications available to Jewry throughout central Europe.

II. STUDY OF HASIDISM

From 1904 to 1909, as he tells us in his *Roads to Hasidism*, Buber retreated from the active life of Zionism and publishing and devoted five full years to the study of Hasidic texts and traditions. He tells us how it was the chance reading of Baal Shem Tov's (the founder of Hasidism) small work, *Zevaat Ribesh*, that impelled him to this dedication of love and study of the Hasidic texts. He writes, "The words flashed toward me, 'He takes unto himself the quality of fervor. He arises from sleep with fervor, for he is hallowed and become another man and is worthy to create and is become like the Holy One, blessed be he when He created the world.'

It was then that overpowered in an instant, I experienced the Hasidic soul. The primally Jewish opened to me, flowering to newly conscious expression in the darkness of exile; man's being created in the image of God I grasped as deed, as becoming, as task. And the Primally Jewish reality was a primal human reality, the content of human religiousness. Judaism as religiousness, as 'piety' as *Hasidut*, opened to me there. The image out of my childhood, the memory of the zaddik and his community, rose upward and illuminated me; I recognized the idea of the perfected man. At the same time, I became aware of the summons to proclaim it to the world.

But first came the time of study. At twenty-six, I withdrew myself for five years from activity in the Zionist party, from writing articles and giving speeches, and retiring into the stillness; I gathered not without difficulty, the scattered, partly missing literature and I immersed myself in it, discovering mysterious lands."[4]

III. INTELLECTUAL PURSUITS

Buber's first public appearance after these years of retirement from public life, was a lecture on Judaism delivered to the Jewish Student Society of Bardocha at Prague University in 1901.[5] In 1916 Buber founded and edited a periodical entitled *Der Jude* which, for the next eight years, became the leading organ of German speaking Jews in their quest for a spiritual and cultural basis for Zionism. From 1926 to 1930, in partnership with the Catholic theologian Joseph Wittig and the Protestant physician and psychotherapist, Viktor von Weizsächer, Buber published the journal, *Die Kreatur*, which was devoted to pedagogical and social problems as they relate to religion.

In 1920, in company with Franz Rosenzweig, a brilliant Jewish scholar and author of the famous work, *The Star of Redemption*, Buber established the Free Jewish Academy (*Freies Judisches Lehrhaus*) in Frankfurt. For the next ten years the Academy, which at its height numbered well over 1,000 students, became a world-renowned center of studies, specializing in Jewish history, theology, Biblical studies and literature. In order to make available to the students of the Academy their rich spiritual heritage in the only language they knew, Buber undertook in the company of Rosenzweig, the translation of the Jewish Bible into modern German. This work was brought to its completion by Buber after Rosenzweig's death in 1929.[6] From 1923 to 1933 Buber held the chair of philosophy of religion and history of religions at the University of Frankfurt. When the Nazis rose to power, Buber was removed from his professorship but he staunchly remained in Germany for the next five years, giving spiritual leadership and inspiration to his hard pressed people in those gruesome days of Auswitzsch and Buchenwald.

In 1938, at the age of sixty, he departed for Palestine to become professor of social philosophy at the Hebrew University in Jerusalem. He constantly strove for a genuine cultural Zionism, often in the face of an extreme and militant nationalism on the part of his fellow-refugees in Palestine.[7] As Buber himself observes, "I would simply say this: that the idea of a Jewish State, with flag and cannon and so forth, I will have nothing to do with—not even in my dreams. How things turn out will depend on what people make of them; therefore those who are concerned about the person and about humanity must give themselves to the task—here, now that once again, it lies with men to build a community, a fellowship."[8] Buber was firmly convinced that a peaceful Arab-Jewish co-existence was the only solution to the Palestine question.[9]

In 1949 Buber founded an Institute for Adult Education which trained teachers who would go to the immigration camps of the newly arrived refugees and aid them in becoming integrated into the new Jewish community.

At the age of seventy-three, Martin Buber retired from his position at the Hebrew University and then left on an extended lecture tour of the United States. Everywhere he went, he drew admiring audiences: Protestant, Catholic and Jewish scholars and students alike flocked to hear his words of love, dialogic discourse and community. On June 13, 1965, the author of the world-famous *I and Thou* died at the age of eighty-seven.[10]

BUBER's PRINCIPAL WORKS
IN ENGLISH TRANSLATION

(Compiled by Maurice S. Friedman)

"Adult Education." *Torah* (Magazine of National Federation of Jewish Men's Clubs of United Synagogue of America), June 1952.

Arab-Jewish Unity. Testimony before the Anglo-American Inquiry Commission for the Ihud (Union) Association by Judah Magnes and Martin Buber. London: Victor Gollancz Ltd. 1947.

At the Turning. Three Addresses on Judaism. New York: Farrar, Straus and Young. 1952.

"The Beginning of the National Idea." *Review of Religion,* X (1945-1946), 254-65.

Between Man and Man. Tr. Ronald Gregor Smith. London: Kegan Paul, 1947. (Includes 'Dialogue,' 'The Question to the Single One,' 'Education of Character' and 'What is Man?') Boston: Beacin Paperbacks, 1955.

"Distance and Relation." Tr. Ronald Gregor Smith. *Psychiatry,* XX, no. 2 (May 1957), 97-114.

Eclipse of God. Studies in the Relation between Religion and Philosophy. Tr. Maurice S. Friedman et al. New York: Harper and Bros., 1952. Torchbook, 1957.

For the Sake of Heaven. Tr. Ludwig Lewisohn. Philadelphia: The Jewish Publication Society, 1945. Second edition with new Foreword—New York: Harper and Bros., 1953. Meridian-Jewish Publication Society Paperback, 1958.

Good and Evil. Two Interpretations. (Includes *Right and Wrong* and *Images of Good and Evil*). New York: Charles Scribner's Sons, 1953.

Hasidism. New York: The Philosophical Library, 1949.

"Hope for This Hour." Tr. Maurice S. Friedman. Address given in English at Carnegie Hall, New York City, April 6, 1952. *World Review,* December 1952; *Pointing the Way,* pp. 220-29.

I and Thou, 2nd edition with Postscript by Author. Tr. Ronald Gregor Smith. New York: Charles Scribner's Sons, 1959.

I and Thou. Tr. Walter Kaufmann. New York: Charles Scribner's Sons, 1970.

Images of Good and Evil. Tr. Michael Bullock. London: Routledge and Kegan Paul, 1952.

Israel and Palestine. The History of an Idea. Tr. Stanley Godman. London: East and West Library; New York: Farrar, Straus and Young, 1952.

Israel and the World. Essays in a Time of Crisis. New York: Schocken Books, 1948.

The Legend of Baal-Shem. Tr. Maurice S. Friedman. New York: Harper and Bros., London: East and West Library, 1953.

"Letters to Franz Rosenzweig on the Law" in Franz Rosenzweig, *On Jewish Education.* Ed. N. N. Glatzer. New York: The Noonday Press, 1954.

Mamre. Essays in Religion. Tr. Greta Hort. Melbourne and London: Melbourne University Press and Oxford University Press, 1946.

"Myth in Judaism." Tr. Ralph Manheim. *Commentary,* IX (June 1950), 562-66.

Moses. Oxford: East and West Library, 1946. Harper Torchbook, 1958.

"A New Venture in Adult Education." *The Hebrew University of Jerusalem.* Semi-Jubilee volume published by the Hebrew University, Jerusalem, April 1950, 116-20.

"On the Suspension of the Ethical." Tr. Maurice S. Friedman. *Moral Principles of Action.* Ed. Ruth Nanda Anshen. Vol. VI of Science of Culture Series. New York: Harper and Bros., 1952.

"Our Reply." *Towards Union in Palestine, Essays on Zionism and Jewish-Arab Cooperation.* Ed. Martin Buber, Judas Magnes and Ernst Simon. Jerusalem: Ihud Association, 1945, 33-36.

Paths in Utopia. Tr. R. F. D. Hull. London: Routledge and Kegan Paul, 1949. Boston: Beacon Paperback, 1958.

Pointing the Way: Collected Essays. Tr. Maurice S. Friedman. New York: Harper and Bros., London: Routledge and Kegan Paul, 1957.

"Remarks on Goethe's Concept of Humanity." *Goethe and the Modern Age.* Ed. Arnold Bergstraesser. Chicago: Henry Regnery, 1950, 227-33.

Right and Wrong, An Interpretation of Some Psalms. Tr. Ronald Gregor Smith. London: SCM Press Ltd., 1952.

"Society and the State." *World Review*, New Series 27 (May 1951), 5-12. *Pointing the Way*, pp. 161-76.

Tales of the Hasidim. The Later Masters. Tr. Olga Marx. New York: Schocken Books, 1948.

Ten Rungs. Hasidic Sayings. Tr. Olga Marx. New York: Schocken Books, 1947.

Two Letters to Ghandi. With Judah Magnes and including public letters by Buber and Magnes and the original text of Ghandi's statement about the Jews in *Harijan*, November 26, 1938. Pamphlets of *The Bond*. Jerusalem: Rubin Mass, April, 1939.

Two Types of Faith. Tr. Norman Goldhawk. London: Routledge and Kegan Paul, 1951; New York: Macmillan Co., 1952.

The Way of Man, According to the Teachings of Hasidism. London: Routledge and Kegan Paul, 1950; Hasidism and Modern Man, Bk. IV.

THOUGHT

I. HASIDISM

Without a doubt, Hasidism was the single greatest influence in the formation of Buber's fundamentally personalist and existentialist postures.

Hasidism was a popular revivalist and mystical movement which burst upon East European Jewry in the eighteenth and nineteenth centuries.[11] The Hebrew word *hasid* means "pious" and "benevolent"; the adjective *hasid* comes from the noun *hesed* meaning "mercy," "lovingkindness" or "grace." Hasidism was a rebellion on the part of the common people of the European ghettos and small rural communities against the artificial, legalistic and foramlistic Rabbinical interpretation of the Talmud or Law. It was a kind of uprising of the masses against "the establishment," which was represented by the official teaching authority of the rabbis. Hasidism was a revolt against the stuffy, suffocating artificialities, the almost obsessive preoccupation with the minutiae and details which were concerned with the *letter* rather than with the *spirit* of the Law. Thus Hasidism held that the meticulous and scrupulous obedience to the 613 laws of the *Taruag Mitzvoth* was an empty and hollow formalism. Man could never hope to find God and to live a genuine existence in the performance of such an empty and meaningless ritual.[12]

Hasidism sought to establish a common bond of community among its followers. It emphasized charity, kindness, the performance of good works, generosity to one's neighbor, a fervor and joy in the service of God and one's fellow man. It downgraded the traditional rabbinical exaltation of asceticism and self-mortification.[13] The Hasidim or "the pious ones" or "those loyal to the covenant" preached that the world was not something basically evil from which man must flee in order to lead a good life and save his soul. Rather, as St. Bonaventure had preached so convincingly in the thirteenth century, the world was an open book in which we can read the glory of God. On the pages of this book, we can discern shining examples of God's boundless goodness and beneficence. We can read the *vestigia* or imprints of divine goodness, for all nature proclaims God's goodness and generosity to man.[14]

The Hasidim thus held that man should not shun or avoid this world as something basically evil or undesirable. Neither should he try to die to this world or matter as the Neoplatonic man was counselled to do, in order to rise above evil and return to the One. No, man was altogether capable of living within the world and he was also capable of living a life of holiness, purity and deep spiritual joy in the service of God and his fellow man.[15] Zalman Hilsenrad in the work, *The Baal Shem Tov: His Birth and Early Manhood*, writes, "Here is a gem of a thought that has come down to us in the name of the Baal Shem Tov. Since all of our people are God's children, He wants us to be good to each other; to live in peace with each other; to do deeds of lovingkindness to each other at every possible moment. At times, a Jew may fulfill his whole life's purpose by doing not more than one thing for a fellow-Jew. For this reason, God may take a soul from under His Heavenly Throne, and send it down to earth to inhabit a body for seventy or eighty years, with the sole objective of performing a singular act of lovingkindness, either material or spiritual."[16]

Paul Pfuetze describes the life of the Hasidic communities in the following words: "Devotion to God and personal union with Him, the cultivation of mystical personal religion; belief in the presence of the holy spirit; the blending of order with liberty, individualism with community; a strong spirit of brotherhood; a joyous spiritual fervor which found expression in singing and loving deeds; these were the common elements of the piety in both the Hasidic and Brethren communities."[17]

Aubrey Hodes in his recent work, *Martin Buber: An Intimate Portrait*, develops two key concepts which Buber held to be most characteristic of Hasidism. He writes, "There is a divine spark in every human being, the Hasidim taught. But these sparks are isolated by shells—the *klippot*—which enclose each person as armor would. Only by living an authentic life and hallowing the world can a man cast off these shells and break their confining embrace.

The way of doing this is through *kavannah* and *hitlahavut*—two key Hasidic concepts. I know no better definitions of them than those Buber himself gave me when I asked him how I should explain them to some non-Jewish friends.

'*Kavannah*,' he said, 'is the direction of the heart. It is the concentration of your will, focused toward the highest Thou, toward God, if you wish. *Hitlahavut* is fervor, enthusiasm, responding with all one's heart and soul. It is a total commitment to the particular *kavannah* you wish to hallow at that time."[18]

A.   Baal-Shem-Tov

The founder of Hasidism was Rabbi ben Eliezer (1700-1760), who was better known as Baal-Shem-Tov (Master of the Good Name) or simply as the "besht." He was born in the little town of Okup, in the Carpathian Mountains in the province of Podolia in Poland. His father Eliezer died when Israel was only five years old. The young orphan was a ward of the Jewish community. At the age of fourteen, Israel joined a group of itinerant mystics (Nistarim), who were followers of Rabbi Adam Baal Shem of Ropshitz. They wandered from town to town and tried to bring cheer to the Jewish people and help them to lead good lives. When Israel acquired the manuscripts which belonged to Rabbi Adam Baal Shem, he studied them in secret and committed them to his

memory. Upon the death of Rabbi Adam, Israel became
the undisputed leader of the Nistarim. From the age of
twenty-six to thirty-six, Israel spent ten full years in study
and seclusion. At the end of this time, he "revealed" himself as the founder and leader of the new Hasidic movement. He now became known as "Baal-Shem-Tov"; many
people flocked to hear him in Mezibush, where he made
his home.[19]

Martin Buber describes Rabbi ben Eliezer as a rare
charismatic leader who firmly held "a realistic and active
mysticism for which the world is not an illusion from
which man must turn away in order to reach true being,
but the reality between God and him in which reciprocity manifests itself, the subject of his unanswering service
of creation, destined to be redeemed through the meeting
of divine and human need; a mysticism, hence, without
the intermixture of principles and without the weakening
of the lived multiplicity of all for the sake of a unity of
all that is to be experienced."[20]

In his remarkable study, *Martin Buber: Jewish Existentialist*, Malcolm Diamond describes the message of
Baal-Shem-Tov as follows: "By the time of Baal-Shem-
Tov they [the rabbis] had converted the discipline of
Torah into a complex logical activity that had much in
common with chess; it was utterly divorced from everyday
life, and only the most brilliant could play well enough
to make it worthwhile. Furthermore, the prestige of the
scholars became so great that they constituted a social
and religious, as well as an intellectual, aristocracy. The
Baal Shem challenged this abuse of the Rabbinic tradition
by teaching that the inequalities which existed in the
outer realm of human affairs could not penetrate to the
core of man's relation to God. The simple man of genuine
piety stood higher than those whose learning led them
to undue pride."[21]

Nissan Mindel, in *Rabbi Schneuer Zalman of Liadi*,
develops the point at greater length. He writes, "In the
tradition of the Kabbala, the Besht taught that at the
end of Divine worship is attachment to G-d (*devekuth*),
which is essentially a service of the heart rather than the

mind. For ultimately, G-d cannot be apprehended rationally, and it is by means of emotional commitment and obedience to the Divine Will, rather than by intellectual speculation, that the human being can come closest to his Creator. . . . To attain *devekuth,* the Besht preached, it is not even necessary to know the meaning of the prayers and psalms, or the significance of the religious precepts; the sincere recitation of the holy words and the simple performance of the precepts are in themselves sufficient to establish contact with G-d, provided this desire for communion was the object of worship. This was a concession to the most illiterate, the *am ha-aretz,* as the Besht taught that none is excluded from Divine service."[22]

But Mindel holds that the Besht went even further than that because he taught that in some respects, "The simple, unlearned worshipper, unaware of the esoteric or even elementary functions of the precepts, has a two-fold advantage over the scholar. In the first place, the unlearned Jew possesses a greater measure of natural humility and, in the second place, it is possible for him to attain the very heights of passionate worship, often beyond the reach of the cool, intellectual, and sophisticated scholar. For, whereas the scholar finds an outlet for his religious feelings through his prayers and the study of the Torah which he is able to understand, the non-scholar continues to be consumed by the fire of his passionate yearning to cleave to G-d, like a 'burning bush which is not consumed.' "[23]

B. The Zaddik

The spiritual leader of a Hasidic community was the zaddik (tsaddik) or the "holy or righteous one." It was this "saint-mystic" who replaced the learned rabbi and the Torah. As a leader of his community, the zaddik was charged with the guidance and direction of the souls entrusted to his care. His direction of the souls under him did not, in any way, relieve his charges of their own personal responsibilities. At the same time, while the zaddik was the teacher of his pupils, yet in times of need, the teacher did depend on his pupils for help and inspiration. This accounted for an intimate interpersonal relationship between master and students, between zaddik and Hasidim in each community. Buber explains the relationship in the following graphic way, 'The zaddik helps everyone, but he does not relieve anyone of what he must do for himself. . . . The teacher helps his disciples find themselves and in hours of desolation, the disciples help their teacher find himself again. The teacher kindles the souls of his disciples and they surround him and light his life with the flame he has kindled."[24]

Although the zaddik was the undisputed leader of his particular community, he nevertheless was the personification of humility. At no time and in no way did he consider himself superior to his flock; their trials were his trials; their temptations were his temptations. Beek and Weiland describe the zaddiks in the following way, "They did not come along with any specific creed or with an infallible authority. Although each zaddik was accepted among his people as though he were the messiah, it was held to be idolatry for anyone to regard his rabbi as the only true one. The secret of their influence is to be sought first and foremost in the humble spirit in which they shared the life of their fellows, participating in their confusion and their sorrows, their ignorance and sin. They never set themselves up on a pedestal, but lived and moved among the people, all of whom, as they believed, carried within them a spark of divine fire. . . . Humility in Hebrew is *shiphlut*. It is the mark of a true mystic in his relationship toward other men. *Shiphlut* ensures that he never sets himself over against some one else in a hostile or competitive spirit, but rather sees himself as the other and sees the other in himself."[25]

Because Hasidism emphasizes this strong interpersonal relationship, it cannot condone a private mysticism, which would turn man away from this world and from other individuals who constitute his community. As a member of a Hasidic community, each individual has a determinate duty with respect to his fellow-man. He cannot engage in an empty and fruitless solipsism. He cannot practice a solitary extreme mysticism which would separate him from others. He has an obligation to make himself available to other members of the community, ever willing to give them strength and encouragement in time of need.

Buber tells us a very moving story how in earlier days, he had failed a young man in need, only because he did not make himself completely available to him. In *Between Man and Man*, he recounts how one forenoon, after he himself had experienced a morning of religious enthusiasm and mystical experience, a young man came to visit him. Buber was still enjoying the exhilaration of his experience and, as a result, he did not give the unknown young man his complete and undivided attention. He was certainly friendly and as cordial as one might have expected him to be during such a meeting. He talked attentively and openly with the young man but, because of his preoccupation with the mystical, Buber tells us that he failed to guess the question which the young man himself did not ask. The young man left, seemingly satisfied with the encounter.

But later, not long after, Buber confesses that he learned from one of the young man's friends—because he himself was no longer alive—the essential content of these questions. He learned that the young man had come to him "not casually but borne by destiny, not for a chat but for a decision." The young man was in despair. He had come to Buber, seeking to be told that nevertheless there is meaning. He went away without the help he had sought.[26]

Aubrey Hodes tells us that after having read the passage in Buber's *Between Man and Man* describing the incident of the young man, something was still not clear to him. He recounts that at his next meeting with Buber, he asked him the following question, "What happened to the young man?" Buber's reply was, "He went and shortly afterward he took his own life." Hodes then describes Buber's commentary on the incident. "Buber closed his eyes for a moment, as if in pain. Then he said quietly, 'Do you see what that means? He came to consult me in the hour of his deepest need. He came to ask me whether he should choose life or death. I talked to him openly. I was sympathetic. I tried to answer his questions. But I answered only the questions he had asked. And so I failed to see through to the man behind the questions. And why did I fail? Because that morning, before his visit, I had been filled with religious enthusiasm, a mystical ecstasy, in which I felt myself in tune with eternity, and the life beyond. Then this young man came to see me. It was an everyday event, an event of judgment. And it 'converted' me because it showed me that there could be no division between the life here and the life beyond."[27]

Since that time, Buber points out that he had given up the extreme form of mysticism. He had given up the "religious" which is nothing but the "exception, extraction, exaltation, ecstasy." As a result of this experience, Buber concludes, "I possess nothing but the everyday out of which I am never taken. The mystery is no longer disclosed, it has escaped or it has made its dwelling here where everything happens or as it happens. I know no fullness but each mortal hour's fullness of claim and responsibility. Though far from being equal to it, yet I know that in the claim I am claimed and may respond in responsibility, and know who speaks and demands a response."[28]

Buber's mysticism can thus be characterized as a moderate, practical type, which avoids the excesses that render a man unavailable to other members of a community. In Paul Pfuetze's words, "Buber turned his back upon all mysticism of the monistic, pantheistic type. That kind of mysticism is silent and man's spirit withers in the air of soliloquy. Buber wants to say *Thou* to God, to *address* God as a real Other. . . . [He advocates] a mysticism of the practical ethical type—mild rather than extreme, pervasive of daily living, into which moral discernment and discipline enter, not as a means to induce the ecstatic vision but as a condition of the practice of the presence of God."[29]

Hasidism further holds that every man can achieve a fulfillment of his existence in the very community in which he finds himself. There is no need to travel to distant lands, to dream of herculean tasks to be accomplished. Man can live a fullness and richness of life, as Buber says, in the very hearth of his home. "For there is no rung of being on which we cannot find the holiness of God everywhere and at all times."[30] The place where man's treasure of meaningful existence can be found is in the very place where he stands.[31]

Buber brings out this point very effectively by recounting the following Hasidic tale: "Rabbi Bunam used to tell young men who came to him for the first time, the story of Rabbi Eizik, son of Rabbi Yekel of Cracow. After many years of great poverty which had shaken his faith in God, he dreamed someone bade him look for a treasure in Prague, under the bridge which leads to the king's palace. When the dream recurred a third time, Rabbi Eizik prepared for the journey and set out for Prague. But the bridge was guarded day and night and he did not dare to start digging. Nevertheless he went to the bridge every morning and kept walking around it until evening. Finally the captain of the guards, who had been watching him, asked in a kindly way whether he was looking for something or waiting for somebody. Rabbi Eizik told him of the dream which had brought him here from a faraway country.

The captain laughed: 'And so to please the dream, you poor fellow wore out your shoes to come here! As for having faith in dreams, if I had had it, I should have had to get going when a dream once told me to go to Cracow and dig for treasure under the stove in the room of a Jew—Eizik, son of Yekel, that was the name! Eizik, son of Yekel! I can just imagine what it would be like, how I should have to try every house over there, where one half of the Jews are named Eizik and the other Yekel!' And he laughed again. Rabbi Eizik bowed, travelled home, dug up the treasure from under the stove, and built the House of Prayer which is called 'Reb Eizik Reb Yekel Shul.'

'Take this story to heart', Rabbi Bunam used to add, 'and make what it says your own: There is something you cannot find anywhere in the world, not even at the zaddik's, and there is nevertheless, a place where you can find it. . . . There is something that can only be found in one place. It is a great treasure, which may be called the fulfillment of existence. The place where this treasure can be found is the place on which one stands. . . . If we had the power over the ends of the earth, it would not give us that fulfillment of existence which a quiet devoted relationship to nearby life can give us. If we knew the secrets of the upper worlds, they would not allow us so much actual participation in true existence as we can achieve by performing with holy intent, a task belonging to our daily lives. Our treasure is hidden beneath the hearth of our own home."[32]

In summary, Maurice Friedman writes, "The real essence of Hasidism is revealed not so much in its concept as in the three central virtues which derive from these concepts, love, joy, and humility. For Hasidism, the world was created out of *love* and is brought to perfection through love. Love is central in God's relation to man and is more important than fear of God, justice or righteousness. . . . The Hasidic emphasis on *joy* comes from the knowledge of the presence of God in all things. This joy has a double character. It is at once a joyous affirmation of the external world and a joyous penetration into the hidden world behind the externals. . . . *Humility*, for Hasidism, means a denial of self but not self-negation. Man is to overcome the pride and his desire to compare himself with others. . . . Thus Hasidic humility is a putting off of man's false self in order that he may affirm his true self—the self which finds its meaning in being a part of the whole."[33]

Martin Buber himself gives us the following description of Hasidism: "The teachings of Hasidism can be summed up in a single sentence: God can be beheld in each thing and reached through each pure deed. But this insight is by no means to be equated with the pantheistic world view, as some have taught. In the Hasidic teaching, the whole world is only a word out of the mouth of God. Nevertheless, the least thing in the world is worthy that through it, God should reveal Himself to the man who truly seeks Him; for no thing can exist without a divine spark, and each person can uncover and redeem this spark at each time and through each action, even the most ordinary, if only he performs it in purity, wholly directed to God and concentrated in Him. Therefore, it will not do to serve God only in isolated hours and with set words and gestures. One must serve God with one's whole life, with the whole of everyday, with the whole of reality. The salvation of man does not lie in his holding himself far removed from the worldly, but in consecrating his life to holy, to divine meaning; his work and his food, his rest and his wandering, the structure of the family and the structure of society. It lies in his preserving the great love of God for all creatures, yes, for all things. . . . Here is no separation between faith and work, between truth and verification, or, in the language of today, between morality and politics: here all is one kingdom, one spirit, one reality."[34]

Buber thus found in Hasidism a number of themes which he was to incorporate in his own system of thought. First among these was the great emphasis which Hasidism placed on the value and dignity of individual personal existence. This individual existence, however, is not lived out in isolation; rather, it can be lived authentically only in a genuine community, where a loving dialogue flows between man and man. At the same time, such a dialogue is possible only if man acts in the wider context of a dialogic relationship with God. Hasidism held that religion was by no means a set of dessicated laws and empty precepts, whose letter should be obeyed blindly and slavishly. On the contrary, it meant a joyous and loving meeting with a personal God, by serving Him and bringing happiness into the lives of others. It meant a true sense of community, of togetherness and of lovingkindness. Hasidism also held that each individual could live a genuine and meaningful and authentic existence, not in "extraordinary exploits, not by asceticism, not by theurgy but by the hallowing of the deeds of everyday."[35] These are the basic notions which Buber culled from the Hasidic

literature and made them the touchstone of his famous
world of the I and Thou.

II. INDIVIDUALISM, COLLECTIVISM
AND COMMUNITY

In his essay *What Is Man?* Buber criticizes the two
prevalent errors of our age, namely, individualism and
collectivism. "As life erroneously supposes that it has to
choose between individualism and collectivism, so thought
erroneously supposes that it has to choose between an
individualistic anthropology and a collectivist sociology.
Individualism understands only a part of man, collectivism
understands man only as a part; neither advances to the
wholeness of man, to man as a whole. Individualism sees
man only in relation to himself, but collectivism does not
see man at all; it sees only 'society.' "[36] Buber goes on to
state that however antithetical they may seem to be,
individualism and collectivism are, in actuality, different
expressions of the same condition. He says, "This condition is characterized by the union of cosmic and social
homelessness, dread of the universe and dread of life,
resulting in an existential constitution of solitude such
as has probably never existed before to the same extent.
The human person feels himself to be a man exposed
to nature—as an unwanted child is exposed—and at the
same time a person isolated in the midst of the tumul-
tuous human world. The first reaction of the spirit to the
awareness of this new and uncanny position is modern
individualism, the second is modern collectivism."[37]

An individualistic anthropology which concerns itself only with the relations of man to himself, according
to Buber, cannot give us a knowledge of man's being.
"Just because man is exposed by nature, he is an individual
in this specially radical way in which no other being in
the world is an individual; and he accepts his exposure
because it means that he is an individual. In the same
way, he accepts his isolation as a person, for only a monad
which is not bound to others can know and glorify itself
as an individual to the utmost. To save himself from the
despair with which his solitary state threatens him, man

resorts to the expedient of glorifying it. Modern individualism has essentially an imaginary basis."[38]

Buber maintains that in an individualism "the person in consequence of his merely imaginary mastery of his basic situation, is attacked by the ravages of the fictitious, however much he thinks or strives to think, that he is asserting himself as a person in being."[39] While modern individualism fails completely because it understands only a part of man, collectivism does no better. In actuality, man is just as solitary a being in a collectivism as he is in an individualism. This is so because while man tries to free himself from the haunting feeling of having been abandoned and of being alone in an individualism, he becomes "completely embedded in one of the massive modern group formations. The more massive, unbroken and powerful in its achievements this is, the more man is able to feel that he is saved from both forms of homelessness, the social and the cosmic. There is obviously no further reason for dread of life, since one needs only to fit oneself into the general will and let one's own responsibility for an existence which has become all too complicated, be absorbed in collective responsibility, which proves itself able to meet all complications."[40]

Buber asserts with vehemence that in a collectivity, man is *not* a man. The collective promises to give him security in the "whole." It promises to take care of his every need, but in doing so, it prevents him from being a man. It does not allow him to commune with other human beings. The solitariness which man sought to escape in an individualism, becomes magnified in a collectivity. Man learns that the security which is offered him is largely an illusion. The result is that by claiming the wholeness of man, a collectivity only succeeds in "neutralizing, devaluating, reducing and desecrating every bond with living beings." Further, the natural desire in every man for contact with other human beings is deadened, desensitized and ultimately, completely eroded. As a result, instead of overcoming man's isolation, a collectivity "overwhelms and numbs it."[41]

Buber significantly asks, "But who in all these massed,

mingled marching collectivities still perceives what that is for which he supposes he is striving—what *community* is? They have all surrendered to its counterpart. *Collectivity is not a binding but a bundling together; individuals packed together, armed and equipped in common, with only as much life from man to man as will inflame the marching step.* But community, growing community, is the being no longer side by side but *with* one another of a multitude of persons. And this multitude, though it also moves towards one goal, yet experiences everywhere a turning to, a dynamic facing of, the other, a flowing from I to Thou. Community is where community happens. Collectivity is based on an organized atrophy of personal existence, community on its increase and confirmation in life lived towards one another. The modern zeal for collectivity is a flight from community's testing and consecration of the person, a flight from the vital dialogic, demanding the staking of the self, which is the heart of the world."[42]

As a consequence, Buber insists that we must "smash the false alternative" to which our age subscribes, i.e., either individualism or collectivism. For there is "a genuine third alternative," one which is not an outcome or partial reconciliation of the other two.[43] This third alternative which represents the true human condition is COMMUNITY or the existence of man with man. "Only when the individual knows the other in all his otherness as himself, as man, and from there breaks through to the other, has he broken through his solitude in a strict and transforming meeting."[44]

Maurice Friedman describes community in terms of a common goal, namely the Eternal Thou. He says, "True community arises through people taking their stand in living in mutual relation with a living Centre and only then through being in living mutual relation with each other. Community cannot be set up as a goal and directly attained, but can only result from a group of people being united around a common goal, their relation to the Eternal Thou."[45]

Ernst Breisach comments as follows: "Buber's new

community grows out of the free decision of authentic persons. The new community must be established without destroying the personal independence which man has achieved by centuries of struggle. Community must be based on the mutual recognition of the dignity of the individual person which in turn demands free persons working together in voluntary co-operation."[46]

III. THE BETWEEN

Genuine community, which is the only valid alternative between collectivism and individualism, is impossible without the sphere of "the between." Buber insists that "the between" is not phantasy or fiction. The between is a reality that needs constant working out anew. It is not something inert, permanent and changeless. Rather, it is ever re-created whenever two human beings meet. One turns to the other and in order to communicate with each other, each must reach out to a sphere beyond his own, namely the sphere of the between. Buber describes this reality in his own words, "The fundamental fact of human existence is man with man. What is peculiarly characteristic of the human world is, above all, that something takes place between one being and another, the like of which can be found nowhere in nature. . . . It is rooted in one being turning to another as another, as this particular other being, in order to communicate with it in a sphere which is common to them but which reaches out beyond the special sphere of each. I call this sphere which is established with the existence of man as man but which is conceptually still uncomprehended, the sphere of 'between.' " Buber goes on to say, "The view which establishes the concept of 'between' is to be acquired by no longer localizing the relation between human beings, as is customary, whether within individual souls or in a general world which embraces and determines them, but in actual fact *between* them. 'Between' is not an auxiliary construction but the real place and bearer of what happens between men."[47]

With his customary clarity, Maurice Friedman explains the between as he understands it: "When two in-

dividuals 'happen' to each other, then there is an essential
remainder which is common to them, but which reaches
out beyond the special sphere of each. The remainder
is the basic reality, the 'sphere of the between' (*das
Zwischenmenschliche*)."[48]

Martin Buber gives us a number of examples of "the
between" that takes place between individuals who genuinely transcend their own private spheres. He cites the
following: (1) A genuine conversation which is absolutely spontaneous and in which each speaks directly to
the other and elicits thereby his unpredictable reply. (2)
A real lesson which is neither a routine repetition nor a
lesson whose findings the teacher knows before he starts
but one which develops in mutual surprise. (3) A real
embrace and not one of habit. (4) A real duel and not
a mere game (5) "In the daily crush of an air-raid shelter,
the glances of two strangers suddenly meet for a second
in astonishing and unrelated mutuality. (6) In the darkened opera house, there can be established between two
of the audience, who do not know one another and who
are listening in the same purity and with the same intensity to the music of Mozart, a relation which is scarcely perceptible and yet is one of elemental dialogue."
Finally, Buber contends, "No factory or no office is so
abandoned by creation that a creative glance could not fly
up from one working-place to another, from desk to
desk, a sober and brotherly happening—*quantus satis*.
And nothing is so valuable a service of dialogue between
God and man as such an unsentimental and unreserved
exchange of glances between two men in an alien place."[49]

In one of his most lyrical passages, Buber paints a
picture of fragile beauty as he describes the realm of the
between, "In the most powerful moments of dialogic,
where in truth 'deep calls unto deep,' it becomes unmis-
takably clear that it is not the *wand* of the individual or
of the social, but of a third that draws the circle round
the happening. On the far side of the subjective, on the
side of the objective, on the narrow ridge, where the I
and Thou meet, there is the realm of the 'between.' "[50]

Will Herberg in his *Martin Buber: Personalist Phil-*

osopher in an Age of Depersonalization, sees the between as the only locus where the fulness of being can be found. He writes, "Buber's existential ontology is an ontology that proceeds from personal being outward to being as such. . . . It is Buber's basic ontological contention that being—and not merely *human* being—is rooted in the 'between': the fulness of being is in the 'between.' In apprehending being, we apprehend it, for some purposes, objectively; for others, subjectively. But these are abstractions—necessary abstractions, but abstractions nevertheless—from the reality of the 'between.' Only in the 'between' of the I-Thou, where such relation is possible, is being truly grasped."[51]

IV. I AND THOU

In 1923, there appeared a small volume by Martin Buber, entitled *Ich und Du,* which has been described as "one of the epoch-making books of our generation"[52] and of which Joseph Oldham in *Real Life is Meeting,* said, "I question whether any book has been published in the present century, the message of which, if it were understood and heeded, would have such far-reaching consequences for the life of our times."[53]

As Gabriel Marcel had initially expressed it, the use of the second person singular "DU" (in French "TU") is especially significant, since it denotes a loving familiarity, a togetherness and unreserved intimacy, which cannot be conveyed by the pronoun "YOU" in the English language. (In English, the same pronoun "YOU" is used to translate both the impersonal and formal forms of "VOUS" or "SIE," as well as the highly personal and intimate forms of 'TU" and "DU.")

The English translator of *Ich und Du,* Ronald Gregor Smith, tells us that he tried to convey this special nuance of the "DU" by using the rather archaic English pronoun "THOU." He did this, fully conscious of the possible misunderstanding the particular choice of word might occasion in the minds of his readers. He states, "It was indeed with some misgivings, yet it seemed to me unavoidable, that I gave the book in English the title which

I did. 'THOU' has through the very fact of its survival as
an uncommon usage, reserved for prayer, tended to
heighten the danger of sacralisation. But there is in
Buber's whole thought no suggestion of a return to a
metaphysic which sees a double order of being, the immanent and the transcendent, in which the transcendent
is understood as being somehow imposed upon the 'natural'
or immanent order."⁵⁴

More recently, Walter Kaufmann has issued a new
translation of Buber's *Ich und Du*. In the Prologue of the
book, he tells us that he rejects Ronald Gregor Smith's
use of "THOU" and he insists that "YOU" is a more desirable
English rendition of the German "DU." Kaufmann writes,
"German lovers say *du* to one another and so do friends.
Du is spontaneous and unpretentious, remote from for-
mality, pomp, and dignity. What lovers or friends say
THOU to one another? THOU is scarcely ever said spontaneously. THOU immediately brings to mind God; DU does
not. And the God of whom it makes us think is not the
God to whom one might cry out in gratitude, despair,
or agony, not the God to whom one complains, or prays
spontaneously; it is the God of the pulpits, the God of the
holy tone. . . . THOU is a preacher's word but also dear to
anticlerical poets. THOU is found in Shakespeare and at
home in the English Bible. . . . THOU can mean many
things, but it has no place whatsoever in the language of
direct, nonliterary, spontaneous human relationships."⁵⁵

In spite of Kaufmann's observations, it would seem
that, thanks to Smith, the word THOU has by now acquired
the additional nuanced meaning of DU and TU. Kaufmann
himself would seem to acknowledge this fact, since he
still retains the THOU in the title of his new translation
of the work.⁵⁶

Buber's chief insight in the *I and Thou* is that there
are two fundamental attitudes or postures to be found
in all human experience. These may be conveniently
called the *personal* and the *functional,* or the world of
the "I-Thou" and the "I-It" relations. Buber points out
that the "I" in these two worlds is not the same because
"the primary I-Thou can only be spoken with the whole

being. The primary I-It can never be spoken with the whole being."[57] The fundamental difference between these two attitudes is not determined by the object with which the "I" relates, but rather, by the *manner* in which the "I" relates himself to the object.

The two postures are described as follows: "The essence of man arises from this twofold relation to the existent. These are not two external phenomena but the the two basic modes of existing with being. The child that calls to his mother and the child that watches his mother—or to give a more exact example, the child that silently speaks to his mother through nothing other than looking into her eyes and the same child that looks at something on the mother as at any other object—show the twofoldness in which man stands and remains standing. Something of the sort is sometimes even to be noticed in those near death. What is here apparent is the double structure of human existence itself. Because there are two basic modes of our existence with being, they are the two basic modes of our existence in general—I-Thou and I-It."[58]

Will Herberg contrasts the two stances in these words: "The primary word I-Thou points to a relation of person to person, of subject to subject, a relation of reciprocity involving 'meeting' or 'encounter,' while the 'primary word' I-It points to a relation of person to thing, of subject to object, involving some form of utilization, domination, or control, even if it is only so-called 'objective' knowing."[59]

Maurice, Friedman speaks of the two-fold relationship in the following terms; "*I-Thou* is the primary word of relation. It is characterized by mutuality, directness, presentness, intensity and ineffability. Although it is only within this relation that personality and the personal really exist, the 'Thou' of the 'I-Thou' is not limited to men but may include animals, trees, objects of nature and God. *I-It* is the primary word of experiencing and using. It takes place *within* a man and not between him and the world. Hence it is entirely subjective and lacking in mutuality. . . . The 'I' of 'I-It' may equally be a he, a she, an animal, a thing or spirit. . . . Thus *I-Thou* and *I-It* cut across the lives of our ordinary distinctions to focus our attention not upon individual objects and their causal connections but upon the relations between things, the *dazwischen* (there-in-between)."[60]

Will Herberg has suggested the term "transjective mode" as more accurately descriptive of the I Thou relationship. If the "objective mode" indicates that which is "outside of you" and the "subjective mode" points to that which is "inside you", then the "transjective mode" refers to what you have relation with, which is there *across*, the one with whom, as person, you establish a "dialogue." Herberg explains, "The transjective mode is precisely the mode in which the I-Thou, and all truly existential thinking takes place; it is what Buber calls the 'dialogic life.' Buber never uses the term, but since he rejects both the objective and the subjective as inappropriate to the I-Thou, some other term is needed to break the vicious subject/object dichotomy and *transjective* would seem to fill the requirement."[61]

Buber therefore believes that the only way in which I can exercise a genuine existence is by engaging myself in a truly interpersonal relationship with the other. It is only by concentrating my total being on the interests and needs of the other that I can effect that perfect mutual relationship which results in my genuinely existential living. In fact, my "I" is affected to the extent and in proportion as I affect the "Thou." For Buber, life is *between* persons and not *in* them. He tells us that Spirit is not in the I but between the I and the Thou. Spirit is not like the blood that circulates within man but it is like the air which man breathes. Hence man lives in the Spirit only to the extent that he is responsive to the Thou. There can never be an I in itself and in isolation. It is always an I which faces a Thou in a truly personal relationship. *"Through the Thou man becomes I."*[62] As Paul Pfuetze states, "The man who stands in lonely and proud isolation is doomed to loss of life, futility and unreality. . . . Buber is here not merely expressing a pretty moral sentiment; he insists that he is stating a law of human nature and existence—namely, that we cannot become selves as selves except in relationship."[63]

The world of I-Thou always establishes relations, whereas the I-It world is one of experience. In the I-It world, man regards living things, works of art and other persons as objects of experience, something which he judges, uses, classifies. But in the world of the I-Thou, another person, a living thing or a work of art can speak to us and we thereby establish a relation with it. Paul Pfuetze gives us the following example à propos of the distinction between the two worlds: "How does the biologist look at a flower? And how does the artist or poet respond to the same flower? The biologist may take a very objective, dispassionate, scientific pose; he may dissect the plant, analyze it, classify, study its histology, anatomy, ecology etc. And that is important and supplies a certain kind of data. The artist or lover, on the other hand, does not think of its usefulness, its biological form or function. He regards it concretely as a living and beautiful whole, he responds to it as a unique totality; he sings his rapture. He enters into it with empathy. It says something to him, it stirs his being and he answers. It is not merely an It, a thing to be perceived, an object to be studied or used. It becomes a Thou, to be enjoyed, to be loved; and the artist or lover mingles his soul, as it were, with the soul of the flower. He is filled by its presence and he may desire to recreate its beauty."[64]

In summary we are given six qualities or characteristics of the "I-Thou" world. (1) In the "I-Thou" world, there is a "wholeness," whereby in contrast with the "I-It" world, the whole of one's being is involved and one is conscious of meeting the whole. All partial actions (characteristic of the "I-It" world, are suspended; the whole being becomes a unity as he goes out to the meeting. (2) Meeting a Thou conceived as a whole, involves an exclusiveness, a sacrificing of other possibilities to the demands of this particular relation. There must be no abstractions, diversions, no irrelevancies. The Thou is not just a thing among other things. "He is 'Thou' and fills the heavens. This does not mean that nothing exists except himself.

But all else lives in his light."[65] (3) The "I-Thou" relation
is direct. The Thou is an end in itself and no mediation of
sense, idea or fancy is necessary. In the "I-Thou" relation,
every means is an obstacle, everything indirect, irrelevant.
The real is apprehended as personal, as a Thou. (4) In
temporal terms, the quality of presentness belongs only
to the "Thou-world." While the "I-It" world is only of the
past, the "I-Thou" world deals with the present. "The
real, filled present exists only insofar as actual presentness,
meeting, and relations exist. The present arises only in
virtue of the fact that the 'Thou' becomes present."[66] (5)
Not *Eros*, not subjective feeling. Buber has in mind an
ethical principle, akin to what the Bible calls *agape*.
(6) The "I-Thou" relation involves genuine response and
responsibility. There is mutual obligation, pledge, and
promise, binding and loyal bonds. The I of the "I-Thou"
world is a loyal self, "pledged to the other in bonds of
covenant, one who has exchanged vows of fidelity, one
who has claims upon the other and, at the same time, puts
himself under claim."[67]

The world of the I-Thou relation thus involves an
openness, a wholeness and directness. All its relations
presuppose an authentic love with an accompanying
responsibility and presentness.

V. I-IT WORLD

Unfortunately, such is the condition of the world, that
it is impossible for man to live continuously and without
interruption in the world of the I-Thou relation. As
Buber explains, "This is the exalted melancholy of our
fate, that every 'Thou' in our world must become an 'It.'
It does not matter how exclusively present the Thou was
in the direct relation. As soon as the relation has been
worked out or has been permeated with a means, the 'Thou'
becomes an object among objects—perhaps the chief, but
still one of them, fixed in its size and its limits . . . the
human being who was even now single and unconditioned,
not something lying to hand, only present, not able to
be experienced, only able to be fulfilled, has now become
a 'He' or 'She,' a sum of qualities, a given quantity with

a certain shape. . . . Every 'Thou' in the world is by its nature fated to become a thing, or continually re-enter into the condition of things."[68]

Hence it is impossible for man to remain permanently in the "I-Thou" relation. Precisely because he must live in the world, man finds it necessary to use and to control things, and sometimes even men. As a matter of fact, the world of the "I-It," according to Buber, is not intrinsically evil, but it does contain a great danger and temptation for man. It is so easy and so seductively inviting for man to order his life *exclusively* according to the world of the "I-It." This world offers man a sense of security and stability; everything conspires to make him a captive. And so man is moved "to look on the world of the 'It' as the world in which it is comfortable to live, as the world, indeed, which offers him all manner of incitements and excitements, activity and knowledge. . . . *Without 'It,' man cannot live. But he who lives with 'It' alone is not a man.*"[69] Eugene Borowitz explains the threat of the exclusiveness of the "I-It" relation. He warns, "The difficulty arises when the 'I-It' relation becomes imperialistic and claims to be the only legitimate form of knowledge. Because it is distinguished by the precision and control it bestows, it seeks to become the exclusive means by which man relates to his surroundings. Place behind this natural inclination, the tremendous social and economic power of an industrial, technological age, and the drive toward the dominance of 'I-It' becomes irresistible."[70]

In reality, the "I-It" relation, which can be equated with Gabriel Marcel's notion of the problem or the level of the first reflection, is not evil in itself. The domain of impersonality and objectivity is an absolutely valid and essential category in science and technology. The "I-It" relation becomes a threat to man, however, when it arrogates to itself an exclusiveness; it alone claims to possess all the answers to the problem of reality. The consequent depersonalization and dehumanization of man are the result of a *mis-use* of the "I-It" relation.

As Malcolm Diamond states the case, "The 'I-It' posture is not evil any more than power or any other basic element of existence is in itself evil. Power becomes evil when it is abused. . . . In the realm of thought, the 'It' posture becomes evil when it oversteps its limits and claims to encompass the totality of truth, thereby choking off the possibility of response to the deeper levels of meaning that may emerge from 'I-Thou' encounters."[71]

In the *Eclipse of God*, Buber warns, "In our age, the 'I-It' relation, gigantically swollen, has usurped, practically uncontested, the mastery and the rule. The 'I' of this relation, an 'I' that possesses all, makes all, succeeds with all, this 'I' that is unable to meet a being essentially, is the lord of the hour. The selfhood that has become omnipotent, with all the 'It' around it, can naturally acknowledge neither God nor any genuine absolute which manifests itself to men as of non-human origin. It steps in between and shuts off from us the light of heaven."[72]

According to Buber, the present twentieth century civilization threatens to destroy completely the world of the I-Thou. Increasingly, the "I-It" world is smothering and, in some instances, even obliterating completely the "I-Thou" relationships. The root cause of this situation can be described in Gabriel Marcel's words as "the depersonalization and degradation of man"[73] and in Nikolai Berdyaev's expression "the objectification of man."[74]

With the spectacular advances of modern science and with the application of the principles of modern technology on an almost universal scale, there is growing an alarming tendency to consider man less and less a human being or genuine Thou. More and more, he is viewed in an absolutely impersonal way as a number, a statistic, an anonymous unit in the highly organized and complicated system. There is less and less attention paid to him as a *person*, who has his own individuating qualities and preferences. In Will Herberg's words, the cultural climate of the Western world has been increasingly "dominated by the technological spirit which tends to depersonalize men and turn them into faceless units of a mass society, into interchangeable cogs in a vast impersonal mechanism held together by a proliferating bureaucracy."[75]

As a result, the sociologist, the psychologist, the pollster and the politician look upon man and his actions as a set of predictable curves on a graph or chart. Increasingly, man has become a commodity which is to be exploited by modern industry, politics and technology. To achieve what is euphemistically called "success," man must mold himself in conformity with a pre-computerized "image." There is absolutely no place for personal initiative and creativity; there is no regard for man as a human being. There is only a vulgar mediocrity, unanimity and facelessness of Heidegger's *das Man*. And so, in the name of progress, the individual has become an It, a kind of automaton, a cog, blindly serving the Moloch of twentieth century technology.

And this is not all. Because his dignity as a human being has been totally disregarded, modern technology does not feel that it has any more responsibility to man than it has to a tool or a machine. After man's dignity and initiative have been ravished and despoiled, after he has been sapped of all his strength and energy, man is tossed upon the scrap heap of human discards. The once proud and dignified creative human being is now cast aside—worn out, disconsolate and broken. Once more, man has been victimized by modern progress.[76]

Buber adamantly maintains that when man is treated in this highly impersonal and undignified manner by modern technology, he cannot but fail to treat his fellow man in the same shameful way. The more he is treated as a *thing* by modern civilization, the more he considers his fellow man as a thing to be used and exploited at will. With such a monstrous disregard for the dignity of man, the groundwork was laid for the ultimate degradation of the human being which we witnessed some twenty years ago. The bestial, yes, demoniacal, slaughter of millions of innocent people by the Nazis at Buchenwald, Dachau and Auswitzsch was possible only because long before, men had already convinced themselves that the world of I-It is the only legitimate one. Man, for these individuals, was made only for *use*. He was only a *thing*, an instrument to serve the physically stronger overlord. Human rights and human dignity were empty words. Little wonder, then, that in this context, the stoking of crematory fires, in the words of Albert Camus, was no different from service to the lepers.

Buber concludes, therefore, that the more the "I-It" world supplants the world of the I-Thou, the easier it will be for man to debase himself, to bestialize himself in the wanton mass murder of his fellow man as the Nazi Socialists had done. The more we regard our fellow man as an It, an object or thing to serve our pride, vanity or sensual gratification, the more bestial and dehumanized we ourselves become. Conversely, the more we allow the "I-Thou" world to condition and influence man's thinking and relationships, the more human and humane, the more noble and understanding we ourselves become. A despotism, a totalitarianism, a police state cannot thrive in the world of the I-Thou. When each person respects the inalienable rights and dignity of the human being, there can never be any misuse of the human being for selfish and evil ends. "A self-giving love of genuine relation does not in any way imply a suppression of the self."[77] As Buber develops this point, "It is not the 'I' that is given up but the false, self-asserting instinct. . . . There is no self love that is not self-deceit . . . but without being and re-maining oneself, there is no love."[78]

It is Buber's belief, therefore, that peace and harmony among nations can be achieved only when initially and fundamentally a genuine "I-Thou" relationship has been established between man and man. Only then, can we hope to have nations living in mutual respect and consideration of each other.

Joseph Oldham considers Buber's warning especially timely in our days. He says, "The realization of the crucial significance of relations between persons, and of the fundamentally *social natures of reality is the necessary,* saving corrective of the dominance of our age by the scientific way of thinking, the result of which, as we know, may involve us in universal destruction, and by the technical mastery of things, which threatens man with the no less serious fate of dehumanization."[79]

VI. THE ETERNAL THOU

We have seen that the only authentic existence for man is in the "I-Thou" relation. Man becomes an I through the Thou that he meets in loving relation. By establishing a genuine dialogue with a Thou, man truly becomes man. And yet, paradoxically, in doing so, he transcends, as it were, his own personality, his own limits, for it is in such a dialogue relation that "human life touches upon absoluteness" and it acquires a dignity and value rooted in the Infinite. "Every particular 'Thou,'" Buber tells us, "is a glimpse through to the Eternal Thou: by means of every particular 'Thou', the primary word addresses the Eternal Thou."[80]

Buber emphasizes the point that it is only in our partial and limited dialogues with one another that we can encounter the Eternal Thou or God. He tells us the following story to illustrate what he means, "There is a tale that a man inspired by God once went out from the creaturely realms into the vast waste. There he wandered until he came to the gates of the mystery. He knocked. From within came the cry: 'What do you want here?' He said, 'I have proclaimed your praise in the ears of mortals, but they were deaf to me. So I came to you that you yourself may hear and reply.' 'Turn back,' came the cry from within. 'Here is no ear for you. I have sunk my hearing in the deafness of mortals.' True address from God directs man into the place of lived speech, where the voices of the creatures grope past one another, and in their very missing of one another succeed in reaching the eternal partner."[81] This is why Will Herberg states emphatically, "The *Zwischenmenschliche*, the 'between man and man,' is the paradigm for the between man and God. 'The relation (of man) with man,' Buber emphasizes, is the real simile of the relation with God, in it true address receives true response.'"[82]

God is thus the indispensable foundation and basis for every genuine "I-Thou" relationship. In fact, without the Eternal Thou, man's relationships are doomed to become sterile and impotent on the "I-It" level. God is then the absolute guarantor, the absolute person who makes possible every "I-Thou" relationship.

And while it is "the exalted melancholy of our fate that every 'Thou' in our world must become an 'It,'" Buber holds that the Eternal Thou alone is above this fate. For he says, "The Eternal Thou can by its nature never become 'It'; for by its nature, it cannot be established in measure and bounds, not even in the measure of the immeasurable, or the bounds of the boundless being; for by its nature it cannot be understood as a sum of qualities, not even as an infinite sum of qualities raised to a transcendental level; for it can be found neither in nor out of the world; for it cannot be experienced or thought; for we miss Him, Him who is, if we say 'I believe that He is'—'He' is also a metaphor, but 'Thou' is not. . . . He who speaks the word 'God' has 'Thou' in mind . . . (and) addresses the true 'Thou' of his life, which cannot be limited by another 'Thou', and to which he stands in a relation that gathers up and includes all others."[83]

In this connection Buber goes on to say, "The description of God as Person in indispensable for everyone who like myself means by 'God' not a principle (although mystics like Eckhart sometimes identify him with 'Being') and like myself means by 'God' not an idea (although philosophers like Plato at times hold that he was this); but rather means by 'God' as I do, him who—whatever else he may be—enters into a direct relation with us men in creative, revealing and redeeming acts, and thus makes possible for us to enter into a direct relation with him. This ground and meaning of our existence constitutes a mutuality, arising again and again, such as can subsist only betwen persons. The concept of personal being is indeed completely incapable of declaring what God's essential being is, but it is both permitted and necessary to say that God is *also* a Person."[84]

Paul Roubiczek characterizes the Eternal Thou as the absolutely indispensable foundation for every genuine "I-Thou" encounter. He says, "The fact that, in a personal meeting, the other addresses me and that I am addressed, that I see in him also the person who I am, indicates that we meet on common ground. This common ground cannot be our human nature alone, for it is experienced as an 'inescapable claim'—that is, it reveals something absolute which addresses every man. We are, according to Buber, addressed by what he calls the 'final Thou'—a 'Thou' which cannot become an 'It,' because it transcends immensely all our knowledge; we know it only through being addressed. This final 'Thou' is the basis of every human 'Thou'. . . . In other words: God, by addressing us, sets us free to experience the 'I-Thou' relationship. A relationship which we actually experience becomes possible because there is a God."[85]

And while God is a Person, the Person of the Bible, Buber hastens to point out that in no way does this description limit His infinity and His absoluteness: "It is indeed legitimate to speak of the person of God within religious relation and in its language; but in so doing we are making no statement about the Absolute which reduces it to the personal. We are rather saying that it enters into the relationship as the Absolute Person whom we call God. One may understand the personality of God as His act. It is, indeed, even permissible for the believer to believe that God became a person for love of him, because in our human mode of existence, the only reciprocal relation with us that exists is a personal one."[86]

VII. CONCLUSION

Martin Buber's unique contribution to the present century has been his unrelented emphasis on the dignity of the human being. By steeping himself in the rich fund of Hasidic literature, Buber was able to appropriate the most salient Hasidic ideals of spiritual fervor, loving-kindness, holiness and joy in the service of God and fellow man and make of them the very foundation of his own philosophical personalist position. Buber's theistic posture is an invaluable antidote to the dark and despairing atheistic existentialism of a Jean Paul Sartre and Simone de Beauvoir. (Perhaps even Martin Heidegger and the earlier Albert Camus might be included here.) Where Sartre proclaims the death of God as a "valid statement of fact," Buber proclaims an Eternal Thou, ever-present in every genuine human interpersonal relationship. This Eternal Thou is the Center, the Bond, the foundation for the between, so absolutely indispensable for every true community, every valid "I-Thou" relationship. While Sartre holds that mankind "must take courage, it must give up once and for all the search for God, it must forget God," Buber counters by asserting that the only way in which man can find a meaningful and authentic existence is against the background of the Eternal Thou of God, who alone gives purpose and rationality to life.[87]

We may aptly close our remarks with the following two tributes penned by Buber scholars. The first was written by Eugen Biser two years before Buber's death. Biser wrote, "Martin Buber stands out as one of the few great minds among us, unbroken by the distress of his people or the burden of a long life, standing upright under the light of true wisdom as one who wants light even while he speaks of darkness, a man who has increased knowledge and therefore suffering also. He awakens confidence in victory, and he reaches out a brother's hand to everyone who is willing."[88]

Will Herberg evaluates Buber's contribution to twentieth century thought in the following words: "There can be no doubt as to the greatness and originality of Buber's thought. Not since Maimonides in the Middle Ages has there been a Jewish philosopher who has had such a profound impact upon the religious and humanistic thinking of his time as Martin Buber has had upon the thinking of our generation. . . . What is the secret of this man? In what does the unique power and relevance of his thought consist? I should say that the significance of his thinking consists primarily in this—that he, more than any man of his time, has succeeded in developing a philosophy that does full justice to the unique reality and value of the individual human being over against the mass man. Martin Buber has shown us what it really means to be a human being—in the inwardness of the self, in community with others, in fellowship with God. Herein lies his message for our time and for all time."[89]

Martin Heidegger

CHAPTER FIVE

MARTIN HEIDEGGER
LIFE

I. EARLY EDUCATION

Martin Heidegger was born in Messkirch, Baden in the southern part of Germany on September 26, 1889. Both his father, who was a sexton of St. Martin's Catholic Church and his mother, Johanna Kempf Heidegger, were devout Catholics.[1] Martin attended the public school of his home town and then the Gymnasium of Constance from 1903 to 1906. (The most likely reason for his attending the Constance Gymnasium was his desire to study for the priesthood.) After the third year, he was accepted by the Jesuits at the Bertholds-Gymnasium in Freiburg-im-Breisgau, where he received his diploma in 1909. He then studied one full semester of theology as a Jesuit novice at the University of Freiburg. Herbert Spiegelberg relates that he has it on Heidegger's own testimony that the first philosophical book which he ever read was given him casually by one of his seminary professors. The book was a doctoral thesis examining the multiple meanings of being in Aristotle, (*Von der mannigfachen Bedeutung des Seienden nach Aristoteles*) and it evidently was a strongly determining factor in establishing Heidegger's life-time pre-occupation.[2]

After the first semester, for reasons known only to himself, Heidegger gave up his theological studies for the priesthood. He remained at the University of Freiburg, however, devoting his complete time to the study of philosophy. His first publication in 1912 was a short article on epistemology entitled, *The Problem of Reality in Modern Philosophy*, which revealed no influence of such men as Kierkegaard, Dilthey and Nietzsche. His doctrinal dissertation, *The Theory of Judgment in Psychologism,*

7

was written under the direction of a Catholic philosopher, A. Schneider, in 1913.[3]

Because of his frail health, Heidegger was exempted from military service during World War I. As a result, he was able to continue his studies at the University of Freiburg during the war years. In 1916, he published his *Habilitationsschrift*, a special thesis or dissertation, which entitled him to teach philosophy at Freiburg as a *Privat-dozent*. This work was entitled *Duns Scotus' Doctrine of Categories and Meanings*, although Martin Grabmann, the great medieval scholar, had established in 1926, that the *Grammatica speculativa*, on which Heidegger's study was based, was not authored by Scotus but by Thomas of Ehrfurt.[4]

Herbert Spiegelberg holds that this study "shows Heidegger in full transition not only from scholastic philosophy but even from Rickert's (under whose direction Heidegger had prepared his thesis) transcendental philosophy to Husserl, in fact not the Husserl of the *Logische Untersuchungen* but of the *Ideen*. This is all the more remarkable since at that time, Heidegger was not yet in personal contact with Husserl, although the concluding chapter may have been written after Husserl's arrival in Freiburg. . . . Thus the basic themes of Heidegger's phenomenology, Being, time and history were already formulated when Heidegger came in personal contact with Husserl."[5]

II. HUSSERL AND PHENOMENOLOGY

With the arrival of Edmund Husserl at the University of Freiburg in 1916, we now come to the so-called "phenomenological period" in Heidegger's life. Although Martin Heidegger had never been a student under Husserl, there fast developed a very intimate friendship between the full Professor and the young *Privatdozent*. (Husserl was fifty-seven and Heidegger was twenty-seven at this time.) It is very likely that Husserl was hoping to imbue Heidegger (who was an extremely promising young scholar) with a real sense of dedication to the cause of phenomenology, so that the young Heidegger might eventually succeed Husserl as phenomenology's standard bearer. Heidegger's actions gave Husserl good reason to believe that he was succeeding. From 1919 until his transfer to Marburg as full professor in 1923, Heidegger identified himself with the cause of phenomenology. All his lecture courses and seminars were, without exception, devoted to an exploration of the various facets of phenomenology. But what Husserl never suspected was that, in spite of the apparent lip service, Heidegger was in actuality moving *away* from Husserl's conception of phenomenology and the transcendental reduction.

When Husserl was asked to write an article on Phenomenology for the 13th edition of the *Encyclopedia Britannica,* he invited Heidegger (as a future standard bearer) to collaborate with him in this writing. Heidegger's draft of the article was a stunning revelation to Husserl. For the first time, the elderly Husserl realized how completely at odds was Heidegger's interpretation of phenomenology with that of his own. In a letter of December 26, 1927 to Roman Ingarden, Husserl states with amazement, "Heidegger has not grasped the whole meaning of the phenomenological reduction."[6] Nevertheless, Husserl still hoped that he could win Heidegger back to his cause. Evidently, it was for this reason that he recommended Heidegger as the *only* qualified successor to his chair of philosophy at the University of Freiburg. After his five years' stay at the University of Marburg, Heidegger was now called to succeed Husserl at Freiburg. Once Heidegger had obtained this highly coveted chair of philosophy, the two scholars saw less and less of each other.

Heidegger's *opus magnum, Sein und Zeit (Being and Time),* was published in 1927 and Husserl now began an exhaustive study of the work which Heidegger had dedicated to him. One can readily gather Husserl's consternation from his marginal notes in the text, when he discovered not only fundamental differences between his own position and Heidegger's but even hidden attacks upon his own position.[7]

Husserl now became totally convinced that not only

was Heidegger beyond all hope as a possible successor to the leadership of the phenomenological movement, but that by substituting DASEIN for the pure ego, Heidegger had actually become a traitor to phenomenology itself. In point of fact, argued Husserl, Heidegger was attempting to reinstate that very same anthropology (a species of psychologism) which Husserl had tried to overthrow by means of his phenomenology. It was most obvious to Husserl that Heidegger had not succeeded in rising above the level of the naïve.

In the *Nachwort* to the *Ideen* on the last page of the terminal volume of the *Jahrbuch für Philosophie und phänomenologische Forschung* (XI, 1930), Husserl roundly criticizes Heidegger's position when he says that certain objections were "based on misunderstandings and fundamentally upon the fact that one misinterprets my phenomenology backwards, from a level which it was its very purpose to overcome, in other words, that one has failed to understand the fundamental novelty of the phenomenological reduction and hence the progress from mundane subjectivity to transcendental subjectivity; consequently that one has remained stuck in an anthropology, whether empirical or a priori, which according to my doctrine has not yet reached the genuine philosophical level, and whose interpretation as philosophy means a lapse into 'transcendental anthropologism'; or psychologism.'"[8]

As a result of these public denunciations, Heidegger abandoned all references to phenomenology, not only in his lectures and seminars, but also in his writings. More and more the two scholars drifted apart. Heidegger's critics censure him most severely for his desertion of Husserl in the latter's hour of need. During the Nazi takeover, Husserl was subjected to unspeakable humiliations because of his Jewish origins. Heidegger, who was now a favorite of the Nazis, made absolutely no effort to come to the aid of his benefactor, who had so generously bequeathed him the Freiburg chair of philosophy.[9]

III. POLITICAL ACTIVITY

During the period between 1930 and 1935, Heidegger

published very little but he devoted much of his time and energy to the cause of Nazi Socialism. This political activity and allegiance have been the object of attack by many of his critics. In 1933, Martin Heidegger accepted the presidency (post of *Rector Magnificus*) of the University of Freiburg. In his inaugural address of May 27, 1933, entitled *The Self-Preservation of the German University*, Heidegger unequivocally endorsed the Nazi Socialism of Adolf Hitler.[10] As a card-carrying Nazi, he argued that up until the present time, the educational aims of the university were without any definite end or purpose. Nazi Socialism now gave the university students a definite goal, namely an active participation in the fashioning of the destiny of the German nation. They would share in the establishing of freedom and self-determination of the German people by the conquest of other nations. The Jews, in particular, as the enemies of the state were to be subdued.[11]

Some of Heidegger's pupils who heard the address listened with incredulity. One of them records the following reaction: "In comparison to the numerous . . . speeches which professors of equal rank have given since the take-over of power, this philosophical and forceful speech is a little masterpiece. Service in the labor forces and in the armed forces merge with service in the realm of learning in such a way that, at the end of this speech, one no longer knows whether to study Diel's *Presocratics* or to march in the ranks of the Storm Troopers."[12]

Heidegger's official entry into Hitler's party was proclaimed in the paper, *Der Alemanne* of May 3, 1933, which editorialized as follows: "On the day of German Labor, on the day of the Community of People, the Rector of the Freiburg University, Dr. Martin Heidegger, made his official entry into the National Socialist Party. We Freiburg Nazis see in this act more than a superficial acknowledgment of the revolution that has been accomplished. . . . We know, too, that he [Heidegger] has never made any secret of his German character, that for years he has supported the party of Adolf Hitler in its difficult struggle for existence and power to the utmost of his strength, that he was always ready to bring a sacrifice to Germany's holy altar, and that no National Socialist ever knocked in vain at his door."[13]

The following short excerpts from messages to university students leave little doubt as to Heidegger's sympathies: "A sharp battle is to be fought in the spirit of National Socialism which must not stifle on account of humanistic Christian notions that hold us down by their imprecision. . . . You are pledged to know and to act, cooperating in the shaping of the New School of the German spirit. . . . Doctrine and 'idea' shall no longer govern your existence. The FUHRER himself, and only he, is the current and future reality of Germany and his word is your law. Heil Hitler! (Signed) Martin Heidegger."[14]

Whether Martin Heidegger found Nazi Socialism too uncongenial and unyielding in matters of university administration or whether he had become disillusioned with it almost overnight, we shall never know. At any rate, he resigned his rectorship after only one year's tenure, ostensibly to devote his time to teaching. The following year, i.e., 1935, the Nazis offered Heidegger the presidency of the University of Berlin, which he refused. Heidegger has never attempted to defend or justify his Nazi affiliations. The only public reference to his political activity is to be found in a postscript to his *Unterwegs zur Sprache* where he does try to answer his critics' charges concerning his treatment of Husserl. Heidegger was accused of suppressing in the 1942 edition of his *Being and Time*, a dedication to Edmund Husserl because of the latter's Jewish nationality. Heidegger argues in his own defence by stating that he removed the dedication only under pressure of his editor but he maintains that he still retained his acknowledgment of gratitude to Husserl on page thirty-eight of the text itself.[15]

IV. POST-WAR EXILE

With the defeat of Hitler's Third Reich and the collapse of the Nazi regime, Martin Heidegger, the one-time collaborator, now became a *persona non grata*. The

French, who occupied the southern part of Baden, forbade him to teach at the university. Heidegger thus retired to his small ski hut at Todtnauberg in the Black Forest. There he still lives in seclusion, pondering the meaning of being, and writing his increasingly cryptic and esoteric works. Periodically, he has come out of seclusion to deliver a series of lectures or to hold an infrequent seminar. The reactions to his philosophical efforts range all the way from absolute adulation on the part of his dedicated admirers to charges of deliberate obfuscation on the part of his critics.[16]

One of Heidegger's former pupils, Stefan Schimanski, gives us the following first-hand account of his visit to the famous philosopher: "I had to drive for an hour to the small town of Todtnau in the Black Forest Mountains, then to climb still farther until the road became a path and all human habitation scattered and invisible. There on the top of a mountain, with the valley deep down below, with nothing but space and wilderness all around, in that ski hut, I spoke to the philosopher. . . . His living conditions were primitive; his books were few, and his only relationship to the world was a stack of writing paper. His whole life revolved within those white sheets and it seemed to me that he wanted nothing else but to be left in peace to cover those white sheets with his writing. The atmosphere of silence all around provided a faithful setting for Heidegger's philosophy. . . . The external world faithfully reflected the world of the mind. . . . In Heidegger's case it was the spirit of overwhelming solitude."[17]

HEIDEGGER'S MAJOR WORKS AVAILABLE IN TRANSLATION
(Listed Chronologically)

Being and Time. (1927). Tr. J. Macquarrie and E. Robinson. New York: Harper, 1962.

Kant and the Problem of Metaphysics. (1929). Tr. J. Churchill. Bloomington: Indiana University Press, 1962.

The Essence of Reasons. (1929). Tr. Terrence Malick. Evanston: Northwestern University Press, 1969.

What Is Metaphysics? (1929). Tr. R. Hull and A. Crick in *Existence and Being.* Ed. Werner Brock. Chicago: Henry Regnery, 1949.

Hölderlin and the Essence of Poetry. (1937). Tr. Douglas Scott in *Existence and Being.*

On the Essence of Truth. (1943). Tr. R. Hull and A. Crick in *Existence and Being.*

"Plato's Doctrine of Truth." Tr. J. Barlow. "Letter on Humanism." Tr. E. Lohner in *Philosophy in the Twentieth Century.* (1947). Eds. W. Barrett and H. Aiken. 4 vols. New York: Random House, 1962. Vol. 3.

"The Way Back into the Ground of Metaphysics." Tr. Walter Kaufmann in *Existentialism from Dostoevsky to Sartre.* (1947). Ed. W. Kaufmann. New York: Meridian, 1956.

Hegel's Concept of Experience. (1953). Ed. J. Glenn Gray. New York: Harper, 1970. An Essay from *Holzwege.*

Introduction to Metaphysics. (1953). Tr. Ralph Manheim. New Haven: Yale University Press, 1958.

What Is Called Thinking? (1954). Tr. J. Glenn Grey. New York: Harper, 1968.

What Is Philosophy? (1956). Tr. W. Kluback and J. T. Wilde. New York: Twayne, 1958.

The Question of Being. (1956). Tr. W. Kluback and J. T. Wilde. New York: Twayne, 1958.

Essays in Metaphysics: Identity and Difference. (1957). Tr. K. Leidecker. New York: Philosophical Library, 1960.

Discourse on Thinking. (1959). Tr. J. Anderson and H. Freund. New York: Harper, 1966.

What Is a Thing? (1962). Tr. W. Barton / V. Deutsch. Chicago: Henry Regnery, 1967.

Poetry, Language, Thought. Tr. Albert Hofstadter. New York: Harper, 1971.

THOUGHT

I. NEOLOGISMS AND LINGUISTIC PECULIARITIES

Before we begin an attempt to understand some of the chief notions of Heidegger's philosophy, we must first point to the linguistic difficulties present in his writings. Heidegger has taken it upon himself to remold and remake many words in the German language, in order better to convey the nuances of his thought. To this end, he has created a number of totally new words; he has resurrected a number of archaic terms and imposed upon them completely new meanings. He has appealed to shadings and nuances which are indigenous to the German word alone and which are totally lost in translation to another language. He has even seen fit to coin verbs from nouns, as for example, *"dingen"* = to thing (from *Ding*); *menschen"* = to man (*Mensch*) and *"nichten"* = to nothing (*Nichts*). Rudolf Carnap, the logical positivist, has made great sport of Heidegger's *Das Nichts nichtet* ("The nothing nothings").[18]

The following warning by Spiegelberg à propos of

the inherent obscurities and difficulties of language, is to the point. He says, "The most formidable hurdle for any attempt to understand Heidegger, particularly the Heidegger of the decisive middle period, is no doubt linguistic. No reader without an exceptional command of German can expect to fathom the sense and the full connotations of Heidegger's language. . . . But even the native German finds himself all too often stymied by Heidegger's way of writing which would almost call for a translation into ordinary German. For Heidegger has a way of not only forming new terms based on obsolete root meanings, but of using existing words for new and un-heard of purposes, without providing a glossary as a key or introducing his new uses by explicit definitions."[19]

II. EXISTENTIALIST OR ONTOLOGIST

"I am not primarily concerned with existence", Heidegger told Stefan Schimanski during the interview described above. "My book bears the title *Being and Time* and not *Existence and Time*. For me, the haunting ques-tion is and has been, not man's existence, but 'being-in-totality' and 'being as such.' "[20] In another place, Heideg-ger had expressly refused to be grouped with the exis-tentialists. In a communication sent to a colloquium of the French Society of Philosophy, Heidegger rejected the label of "existentialist." He wrote, "I must . . . say again that my philosophical tendencies . . . cannot be classified as a philosophy of existence. . . . The question which preoccupies me is not the question of human existence, but it is the question of being as a whole and as such."[21]

In spite of these protestations, Heidegger is reckoned among the leading and most influential existentialists to-day. His themes and postures, his preoccupations and even method of investigation are patently existentialistic. As one author indicates, "Martin Heidegger as a man and as a philosopher has always been somewhat of an enigma, yet his thought lies at the center of contemporary Euro-pean philosophy and is itself undeniably modern. The existentialists, anthropological psychologists and pheno-menologists have all grown up under the influence of his work and have often acknowledged this debt."[22]

H. J. Blackham says of Heidegger, "He is inescapably put amongst the existentialists because he is one of them in the themes and ideas and in his treatment of them and in the language he uses, as well as in his debt to Kierkegaard and in his influence upon the others, especially upon Sartre."[23]

Paul Tillich openly acknowledges the influence of Heideggerian thought on his own existentialist theology. He tells us, "In Marburg in 1925, I began on my *Systematic Theology*, the first volume of which appeared in 1951. At the same time that Heidegger was in Marburg as professor of philosophy, influencing some of the best students, existentialism in its twentieth century form, crossed my path. It was years before I became fully aware of the impact of this encounter on my own thinking."[24] Heidegger's existential analytic has also served as an indispensable basis for Rudolf Bultmann's well-known demythologizing of the New Testament. By using Heidegger's notion of existence, Bultmann holds that "the *kerygma* or the divine word addressed to men must be disengaged from its mythical framework" and thus it will be set free "to address the men of the post-mythical age." In such a new orientation, "Pauline terms like 'sin,' 'faith,' 'flesh,' 'spirit' are interpreted in the light of Heideggerian *existentialia*" and thus "the New Testament becomes thoroughly relevant and contemporary."[25]

Finally, in spite of Heidegger's vigorous repudiation of any direct continuity between his own philosophy and that of Jean Paul Sartre, it is nevertheless true that the *enfant terrible* of French atheistic existentialism looks to the hermit of Todtnauberg for much of his inspiration.[26]

III.   ANALYSIS OF *BEING AND TIME*

It is no exaggeration to say that Heidegger's claim to the philosophical fame he enjoys today is due almost exclusively to his major work, *Sein und Zeit (Being and Time)*.[27] This work, which was published in 1927, when Heidegger was still at the University of Marburg, established him as one of the most influential thinkers of the century. One might choose either to agree or disagree with this *opus magnum* of Martin Heidegger (and many thinkers have reacted almost violently both ways), but one cannot possibly afford to ignore *Sein und Zeit*. According to Heidegger's initial intent, the work was to contain two parts, the first of which would be composed of three sections, i.e., (1) an examination and description of human existence (2) a study of the temporality of human existence and (3) an approach of being as such from the horizon of time. The second part of the work was to contain a description of Heidegger's *new ontology*, after he had shown the inadequacy of such classic ontologies as those of Aristotle, Descartes and Kant. To date (forty years later), only the first two sections of Part I have been published. Many of Heidegger's readers believe that the remainder of the book will never be written because the initial position adopted in *Being and Time* made it absolutely impossible for Heidegger to finish the work. (We shall have more to say about this point later on.)[28]

Let us proceed to examine briefly some of the chief themes of Heidegger's philosophy as developed in his *Being and Time*. (Incidentally, Heidegger has warned us that to date, very few of his readers have grasped the true meaning of this work.)[29] Heidegger begins his work with this opening quotation, taken from Plato's *Sophistes*, "For manifestly you have long been aware of what you mean when you use the expression 'being.' We, however, who used to think we understood it, have now become perplexed."[30] Heidegger then asks, "Do we in our time have an answer to the question of what we really mean by the word 'being'?"[31] His own answer is a categorical "NO" and hence he feels that we must once more reexamine his most crucial question of the meaning of Being. He continues, "This question has today been forgotten . . . not only that. On the basis of the Greeks' initial contributions towards the interpretation of Being, a dogma has been developed which not only declares the question about the meaning of Being to be superfluous but sanctions its complete neglect. It is said that 'Being' is the most universal and emptiest of concepts. As such, it resists every attempt at definition. Nor does this most universal and indefinable concept require any definition, for everyone uses it constantly and already understands what he means by it. In this way, that which the ancient philosophers found continually disturbing as something obscure and hidden has taken on a clarity and self-evidence, such that if anyone continues to ask about it, he is charged with an error of method."[32]

A. The Being of Beings

Heidegger next announces that he is the first thinker in the entire history of philosophy who has raised the question of the sense of Being.[33] For centuries, according to Heidegger, man has lived in a complete oblivion of the question of being and it is this forgetfulness on the part of man, that is responsible for "the decline and crisis of man's history on this planet." Western philosophy and even Western civilization have been completely distracted from a contemplation of Being as such which, incidentally, is the very *raison d'être* of any philosophical system. Heidegger concedes that at the very dawn of philosophy, Greek thinkers like Anaximander, Heraclitus and Parmenides did pose the question of Being correctly. In their wonder, which is the beginning of all philosophy, they sought to explain the "Being of beings." But with the coming of Plato and Aristotle on the scene and ever since then to the present time, philosophy has diverted its attention from the Being of beings and has concentrated its efforts on *this* or *that* being.[34]

In Heidegger's eyes, his task now is to effect a total destruction of the entire history of ontology, such as it has been studied for the last twenty-five centuries. Heidegger states this explicitly, "We understand this task as one in which by taking *the question of Being as our clue,* we are *to destroy* the traditional content of ancient ontology until we arrive at those primordial experiences in which we achieved our first ways of determining the nature of Being. . . . The destruction of the history of ontology is essentially bound up with the way the question of Being is formulated, and it is possible only within such a formulation."[35]

Let us pause for a moment here to see what Heidegger means by this all-important "Being of beings" (*das Sein des Seiendes*). In the first place, the word "being" in the English language is an ambivalent term; as such, it can have more than one meaning. One of its meanings is that of a noun or substantive. For example, I can say that I am a "being"; a dog is a being; a tree or a stone is a being. While we normally apply the term "being" to man alone and not to inanimate or even irrational entities, nevertheless, we can use it interchangeably with the word "entity" or "something-which-is."

Another meaning of the term "being" refers to its "ising" or to the "to be" of a thing. When I say "To be or not to be—that is the question," I can substitute the word "being" for the "to be" and say "Being or not being—that is the question." In this second use of the word, I am referring not to *a* being but to the "ising" of a thing.

Now other languages have two different words for these two different notions. Whereas the English language is forced to use the word "being" in both instances, the Greek language uses *to on* to refer to *a* being or to "that which is" and it uses *to einai* to refer to the "ising" or the "to be" of a thing. Again, Latin uses *ens* to designate the noun or substantive (*a* being) and it employs the infinitive form *esse* to denote the "to be" of a thing. In German, *das Seiende* is the equivalent of the *to on* and the *ens*, i.e., *a* being, while *das Sein* is equated with the Greek *to einai* and the Latin *esse*.

As John Macquarrie says, "'Being' may mean 'that which is,' 'entities,' *ta onta, das Seiende*. It may also mean 'ishood,' the character in virtue of which entities 'are', *to einai, das Sein*. If we use 'entity' for the first of these two senses, and reserve 'being' for the second sense, then we must admit that traditional theology has wobbled between them, sometimes speaking of him as if he were an entity, sometimes speaking of him as if he were pure being. Clearly, however, he cannot be both. . . . To say

God is being rather than that he is an entity is not to detract from his reality, but rather to assert for him a 'reality' beyond that of any possible entity."[36]

While Macquarrie's statement about the "wobbling" of traditional theology is historically accurate, there has been at least one theologian in the history of Christian thought who cannot be charged in this manner. Thomas Aquinas, in the thirteenth century, never wavered for even a moment in asserting that the "Ego sum qui sum" (I am Who am) for the Bible categorically denoted God as the Highest Being and as Being itself. In virtue of the *Ipsum esse,* His act of to-be, God, for Aquinas, is Being itself. He is the fulness of being. In fact, God uniquely is. At the same time, as the Creator of all things, He is the Cause of the being of all things. In Him alone, the act of "to be" (His *esse*) is identical with His essence. All beings below Him, merely share or participate in being in a limited or restricted manner. Their limitation is determined by their essence or nature.[37] Macquarrie's observation that God "cannot be both a Being and the Being of beings" obviously would be invalid vis-à-vis such a position.

It is Heidegger's contention, then, that philosophy has allowed itself to become diverted from its chief pre-occupation, namely the study of the Being of beings (*das Sein des Siendes*). From the moment that Plato instituted the distinction between that which is really real and that which is only a shadow on the wall, and next when Aristotle made the study of being as *substance* or subject of action the work of philosophy, Western thought betrayed its noble calling.[38] Instead of searching for the Being of beings, as did the early Pre-Socratics, Heidegger claims that philosophy was now firmly committed to the exclusive consideration of the "to on" or "ens" of "that-which-is," namely "das Seiende." As James Collins points out, it is Heidegger's contention that metaphysicians "declare themselves to be investigating the nature of being, whereas their statements really bear upon *this* being, *a* being, beings or the totality of 'that-which-is.' That, in virtue of which each being is what it is—an instance of being, a manifestation of being-ness —has been obscured in the effort to explore and universalize some particular region of being."[39] As a result, philosophy which is supposed to be a study of being, has in reality become an "ontology," namely a study of "that-which-is," when it actually should have been an "einai-logy," i.e., a study of the "to be" of Being, as opposed to beings.[40] As William Barrett observes, "What it means is nothing less than this: that from the beginning, the thought of Western man has been bound to things, to objects."[41]

Heidegger next points to the ambiguous nature of the science of metaphysics as it has been studied by the Greek philosophers. According to these thinkers, says Heidegger, metaphysics has meant two different things. On the one hand, it pretends to be a study of the widest notes and attributes common to all beings. On the other hand, metaphysics considers itself to be a study of the highest being, i.e., God. This ambivalent interpretation of the role of metaphysics which, incidentally is synonymous with the development of Western thought itself, is extremely misleading, since it involves a movement from one interpretation of metaphysics to another.[42] As Cornelio Fabro points out, Heidegger holds that classical metaphysics "began with 'to on' as its object and so it inevitably moved within the realm of *ens in quantum ens* (being as being) in its totality. . . . Subsequently, this totality came to be considered in the sense of the supreme and therefore divine Being. In this way Aristotelian metaphysics perpetrated the supreme equivocation of posing at once as an ontology and a theology. . . . By its ambiguous and double-faced approach, metaphysics confines itself within being and renders itself incapable of any experience of Being which hides in being."[43]

Heidegger next gives us his famous definition of the Being of beings. According to him, "(It) is not God, nor (some) ground of the world. Being is broader than all beings—and yet it is nearer to man than all beings, whether they be rocks, animals, works of art, angels or God. Being is what is nearest (to man). Yet (this) nearness remains farthest removed from him."[44]

Heidegger, therefore, refuses categorically to identify the Being of beings with God and he excludes the notion of God from his own interpretation of metaphysics. He rejects as absolutely unsatisfactory the traditional scholastic approaches to God because he maintains that Christian thinkers accepted uncritically and indiscriminately the faulty Greek approach to metaphysics. Heidegger further argues that to call God the *first cause*, the *highest good*, or the *ultimate end*, for example, is but to understand God as merely the highest among beings. In such a context, God is *not* the *Being of beings*. He is merely the superlative in the category or "to on" "the things that are." To apply the categories of the objective world to the Supreme Being is, according to Heidegger, tantamount to regarding God as but another being in the world.[45]

Many scholars emphatically disagree with Heidegger's definition of the Being of beings and with his notion of God. They find his oracular pronouncements neither original nor satisfactory. They refuse to agree with Heidegger's sweeping condemnation of twenty-five centuries of metaphysical thought as being completely useless. In fact, some thinkers point to definite shortcomings and inadequacies on Heidegger's part rather than on the side of ontology. They maintain that some of the philosopher's observations are not so original as he would like to have us believe. A better knowledge of the history of philosophy on Heidegger's part would have saved him from making such extravagant claims. Further, they find Heidegger guilty of a definite misunderstanding of certain fundamental philosophical notions. While readily admitting the value of a number of original Heideggerian insights, these thinkers feel that Heidegger's unorthodox interpretations of the Being of beings and of the nature of God have shed more darkness than philosophical light. Let us now examine some specific evaluations on these points.

F. H. Heinemann observes, "It is Heidegger's am-

bition to become the Aristotle of our time, i.e., to transcend
the old definition of metaphysics as the science of being
as being, in this sense to overcome the old metaphysics
and to redefine it as the science of "being" or *Sein*, as
opposed to *Seiendem*, or the "truth of being". . . . Is the
distinction between *Sein* (to be) and *Seiendem* (being)
really of that basic importance which is here attributed
to it? . . . Is it not perhaps based on a naïve realism (in
the Platonic sense of the word) i.e., on a standpoint which
on grounds that are linguistically and logically untenable,
maintains that objects have 'being' through participation
in *Sein* or in 'being as such' or in the 'essence of beings'?"[46]

Walter Kaufmann offers us an interesting and original
insight when he writes, "Many of Heidegger's statements
about Being that are puzzling at first glance become clear-
er when we realize that Heidegger substitutes 'Being'
where the theologians say 'God'. . . . At the end of the
Introduction (to *What Is Metaphysics*), Heidegger sums
up what Being is as opposed to Becoming, Appearance,
Thinking, and Ought; it is that which abides, that which
is always the same, that which is there, that which is
extant. And Heidegger concludes that all four of these
characterizations of Being 'at the bottom say the same;
constant presence: ὄν as *ōusía*' (p. 154). It is interesting
to note that this may be the meaning of the Hebrew name
of God, which according to Buber's interpretation of
Exodus, 3:14, might be translated HE IS PRESENT. Heidegger's Being is to use a Nietzschean phrase, the shadow of
God. Those who feel that they have known God himself,
either through a living religious tradition or Scripture
or through personal experience, will hardly settle for his
shadow; and those who have not, will hardly understand
Heidegger's attitude. . . . Heidegger's metaphysics of
Being is a development of Christianity or, as some Catholic
interpreters might say, a Christian heresy."[47]

Michele Sciacca speaks of a basic sophism which
makes all ontology an impossibility for Heidegger. He
says, " 'Being' (for Heidegger) is *not* the 'object' of investigation, something that is before me. I, who am
positing the problem of being, *am*. Therefore I partake

of being which makes me be: and I am a phenomenon of being. . . . My question concerning being is a question concerning me, as I am. It is here that Heidegger introduces the sophism (on which all his philosophy is founded) which destroys being, ontology and metaphysics. . . . The participation of the ego in being merely means this: *being is only a moment of abstraction from the concrete* DASEIN, *the being-in, the being-here.* . . . Being reaches its nadir in the DASEIN. The starting point of this inquiry is not being, but DASEIN, within whose limits being has been constructed and immured. . . . Heidegger's discourse on ontology was ended—before it has begun, because it begins by denying being and continues with an analysis of the moments of DASEIN."[48]

H. J. Blackham seems to betray a certain sense of frustration when he writes, "How does Heidegger justify his proposal to restore the primacy and rule of the question of Being? . . . When it is said that the word Being speaks of the treasure which has been preserved and transmitted in the philosophical tradition and those who will hear the word are the elect, one seems no longer to be listening to the lucid and persuasive language of that tradition and to have turned back to the oracular obscurity of the Pre-Socratics."[49]

Étienne Gilson, the great historian of medieval philosophy, says "Heidegger wants us to go beyond being in order to reach the act in virtue of which being is; beyond *das Seiende* up to *das Sein.* Of *das Sein,* Heidegger says that it had been the question asked by Western speculation right at the beginning and forgotten at once . . . a better historian of philosophy could show that many philosophers have looked beyond the bare fact that being is, in the hope of finding there the reason for its actual existence. Were I asked to quote one of them, I would unhesitatingly answer, Thomas Aquinas. There is in every being (*ens*), Thomas says, an act in virtue of which that being is. That act is its *esse,* its *Sein.*"[50]

James Collins holds in his work, *The Existentialists,* that Heidegger's position concerning the place of God in metaphysics is due to his inability to understand properly the doctrine of analogy. He writes, "Heidegger never discusses the scholastic theory of analogical predication of transcategorical concepts like cause and the good. . . . He fails to see the connection established by Aquinas between the meaning of being and the need for analogical predication. Furthermore, he does not observe that the distinction between the primary and secondary analogates in such predication is intended as a safeguard against merely patterning the meaning of being as such after the being of the material world."[51]

Finally Reynold Borzaga observes, "Heidegger wants to know what it is that makes it possible for each being to exist in the world, to assert its presence, both as an individual being that exists open to others and yet always remaining itself. . . . The problem, of course, is not new in the history of philosophy. . . . Thomas Aquinas in *De ente et essentia* faced the problem and called existence the element actualizing the form to the perfection of its being. Substance, existence, act of being are not separate entities somehow entering a being, but only necessary metaphysical structures of *one* being. . . . If being is a conglomeration of opaque Parmenidean individual existents, how do we explain knowledge and communication? . . . Heidegger forgets that at least one philosopher discussed the same problem long before him. Thomas Aquinas, still an inexperienced youth of twenty years of age, in his *De ente et essentia* understood that being cannot be an indeterminate genus, though it is universal; he understood that being cannot be added to each particular thing as another being or as a superimposed existence. Thomas Aquinas saw that being for each existent is nothing other than the completion of essence, the 'act' of an essence. Therefore being does not exist indeterminately. On the contrary, it *acts* from within all particular existents as the principle that makes them possible in their own individual presence."[52]

The same author closes with these remarks, "Heidegger is unfair to Christian theology when he labels God the highest of the existents, as a man-made entity in contrast to the absoluteness of his 'Being as such.' Christian theology deals with the Supreme Being who is the foundation of himself and of all existents. But Heidegger . . . looks down with scorn on a God trapped by Aristotelian language into the immobility of a *causa sui*. 'Man may neither pray to this God, nor may he sacrifice to him. Confronted by *Causa sui* man may neither fall to his knees nor sing and dance.' And we could agree with him in his judgment of the God of the Christians, if we were not aware that the Aristotelian-Thomistic philosophy is just one effort, limited in time and space, to represent with concepts, inadequate as they are, a transcendent God. But every Christian knows with absolute certainty that only faith allows us to recognize the identity between the *causa sui* and the living, loving God of Abraham, of Jacob, of David, of the God of Augustine and Pascal, the living God who did not disdain to be a man and to walk the streets of Galilee."[53]

B. DASEIN as Starting Point

Heidegger next searches for the best possible way in which he can conduct his quest for the Being of beings. Obviously, he is in need of a starting point; he needs some kind of actually existing being, which he can use as a kind of base from which he can launch his philosophical investigation. By analyzing minutely this particular being which will serve as a *point de départ*, Heidegger hopes to be able to arrive at the object of his new ontology, i.e., the Being of beings.

After examining the various beings in the world, Heidegger comes to the conclusion that there is only one being uniquely qualified to serve in this privileged capacity. This being is none other than the being of the questioner himself. In other words, man is peculiarly suited to serve as a starting point in the inquiry precisely because the question of the Being of beings is of special importance to him. Man differs ontologically from all other existents. The human being alone can make an ontology possible because he alone can ask the question, "What is the Being of beings?" By asking this all-important question, man can thus transcend his own being and

that of every other concrete entity. In this way, he is able
to approach Being as such, which is the ultimate object
of our inquiry.[54]

Heidegger describes his choice of a starting point as
follows: "Insofar as Being constitutes what is asked
about, and Being means the Being of entities (i.e., Being
of beings), then entities themselves turn out to be what
is interrogated. . . . Thus to work out the question of
Being adequately, we must make an entity—the inquirer—
transparent in his own being. . . . This entity which each
one of us is himself and which includes inquiring as one
of the possibilities of its Being, we shall denote by the
term DASEIN. . . . DASEIN is an entity which does not just
occur among other entities. Rather, it is ontically distinguished by the fact that, in its very Being, that Being
is an issue for it. . . . It is peculiar to this entity that with
and through its Being, this Being is disclosed to it. *Understanding of Being is itself a definite characteristic of
DASEIN's Being.*"[55]

From the above quotation, we observe that Heidegger
uses the word DASEIN to designate "man." In fact, he
refuses to use the ordinary word "man" to describe "human beings" or "human existence" and this, for two special
reasons. As William Barrett points out, "One of the most
remarkable things about Heidegger's description of human
existence is that it is made without his using the term
"man" at all. He thereby avoids the assumption that we
are dealing with a definite object with a fixed nature—that
we already know, in short, what man is. His analysis of
existence also takes place without the use of the word
'consciousness,' for this word threatens to bring us back
into the Cartesian dualism. That Heidegger can say
everything he wants to say about human existence without using either 'man' or 'consciousness' means that the
gulf between subject and object, or between mind and
body, that has been dug by modern philosophy need
not exist if we do not make it."[56]

Heidegger thus rejects the notion of a permanent
essence or nature for man. In speaking of the human
being, he refers to him as DASEIN, a term traditionally

meaning "existence" in German philosophy. Heidegger
here reserves this word to signify uniquely "human existence." Now literally, DASEIN means There-Being," but
as usual, Heidegger reads much more into the term than
might appear at first sight. "DA," which translates literally
into "there," signifies infinitely more than a mere spatial
relationship, says Heidegger. Through the "DA," man is
understood as being capable of having a number of encounters with other beings in the world. The "DA" immerses
man in the world of objects and hence enables him "to
begin to comprehend the Being of beings."[57]

Accordingly, while other entities merely are—for example, a stone *is*; a hammer is merely a tool, a something
to be handled—man as DASEIN is infinitely more than all of
these things. DASEIN owns his own being. He has a responsibility to his own being, without being responsible for
being here. Hence, while other entities merely *are*, man
exists. DASEIN, according to Heidegger, is synonymous with
Existenz but *Existenz* is not some fixed quality. On the
contrary, it is a constant possibility.[58]

As Heidegger explains, "The essence of DASEIN lies
in its existence. Accordingly, those characteristics which
can be exhibited in this entity are not 'properties' present-
at-hand of some entity which 'looks' so and so and is itself
present-at-hand; they are in each case possible ways for
it to be; and no more than that. All the Being-as-it-is
(*So-Sein*) which this entity possesses is primarily Being.
So when we designate this entity with the term 'DASEIN,'
we are expressing not its 'what' (as if it were a table,
house or tree) but its Being. . . . Thus DASEIN is never
to be taken ontologically as an instance or special case
of some genus of entities as things that are present-at-
hand. . . . In each case, DASEIN is its possibility, but not
just as a property (*eigenschaftlich*) as something present-
at-hand would. And because DASEIN is in each case essentially its own possibility, it *can* in its very Being, 'choose'
itself and win itself; or only 'seem' to do so. . . . In determining itself as an entity, DASEIN always does so in the
light of a possibility which it *is* itself and which, in its
very Being, it somehow understands. This is the formal

meaning of DASEIN's existential constitution."[59]

Heidegger would, therefore, have us hold that DASEIN is his own possibility. We can never speak of him as something completed, something stable or fixed. DASEIN never quite is. He is constantly realizing his possibilities. He is forming and fashioning himself through his existential choices. John Macquarrie describes the process as follows: "DASEIN stands out (ex-sists) in the sense that he is not just another item in the world but a being open to himself and to this world so that, within limits, he has responsibility for both of these and can shape them to some extent. . . . DASEIN never is complete in his Being. To exist is always to be on the way, so that one can never, as it were, pin down the existent at any precise moment and give an exhaustive description. He is constituted by possibilities rather than properties. . . . DASEIN has no fixed essence. . . . So far as we can talk about his 'essence' at all, we would have to say that he makes it as he goes along, fulfilling his possibilities or letting them slip, but always on the move from one situation to the next. This is what is meant by saying 'The essence of DASEIN lies in its existence.' "[60]

There have been various unsuccessful attempts to translate the term DASEIN into readable English. Such renditions as "There-Being," "Being-There," "human-being," "man," "Human existence" and "thing-in-being-called-man" appear to us to be most unsatisfactory, unwieldy and inaccurate. We have, therefore, decided to retain the German word DASEIN, as originally introduced by Heidegger and thus we hope to avoid further proliferation of English barbarisms.[61]

C. Ontology and Phenomenology

Heidegger maintains that traditional ontology has failed because it deals with vague ideas: it speaks of some kind of entity which is supposed to be infinite, eternal and perfect; it speaks of the "other-worldly" and of the "beyond." It is Heidegger's contention that a truly genuine ontology, on the other hand, must be "this-worldly." Such an ontology cannot deal with abstractions. It must concern itself, rather, with the concrete, individual things of this world. Hence, a radically new ontology will be needed which will be totally different from the inadequate traditional ontology. This new ontology will be an existential analysis of man's being and its method will be none other than that of the new science of phenomenology.

The advantage of the phenomenological method, according to Heidegger, is obvious, for we are guided by the very things themselves as they immediately appear to us. "Back to the things themselves" was the favorite saying of Edmund Husserl, phenomenology's founder.[62] Heidegger embarks on an extended explanation of the meaning of phenomenology as he understands it. By analyzing the two Greek words *phainomenon* and *logos,* he gives us the following insights: the word *phainomenon* implies "to appear," "to show" or "to manifest itself." A phenomenon, therefore, will be something which shows or manifests itself. It is anything that can be brought to light. *Phos* is the Greek word for "light," having the same root as *phainesthai.* Now the Greek word *logos,* continues Heidegger, has had many meanings in the history of Philosophy. It has meant reason, concept, ground, definition, thought, discourse, to name only a few. Heidegger understands *logos* as *discourse,* whose function is to expose, to uncover or to make manifest to the speaker that about which he speaks.

If therefore *phenomenon* is "that which is made manifest" and *logos* is "that which discloses or makes itself manifest," then, Heidegger concludes that *phenomenology* is the disclosing or making manifest that which shows itself on its own, as it shows itself on its own. Phenomenology is consequently a method which "demands a direct approach and an unbiased openness toward that which may reveal itself in the investigation. It is pristine disclosure or unprejudiced description."[63] Phenomenology will thus concern itself with everything that manifests itself to us. It will deal not only with "that which merely appears to the senses; a feeling, a work of art, a political institution, a philosophical idea—all these show themselves just as real to us as color or sound, though in quite a different way. Moreover that which shows itself does not have to appear to everyone; even my states of consciousness show themselves to me, so that they, too, can be objects of phenomenological analysis and description."[64]

Phenomenology, for its founder, Edmund Husserl, meant a methodic attempt to arrive at the pure *eidos* or essence of a thing. This Husserl hoped to accomplish by means of his famous phenomenological reduction or *epokay*. By a progressive bracketing of all extraneous and peripheral knowledge, Husserl sought to grasp the pure essence or *eidos*. Now the *epokay* even called for a bracketing or placing in suspension any judgment concerning the real existence of things. For Husserl, then, the question of the *eidos* was of paramount importance because it constituted the very basis of his science of phenomenology. The question of existence or of being was bracketed or placed in suspension.[65]

Heidegger, on the other hand, had proclaimed his task as the creation of a new ontology which would supplant the past twenty-five centuries of metaphysical thinking. This new ontology would have as its object, the study of the Being of beings.[66] The particular method that Heidegger would follow would be that of phenomenology but it would be a phenomenology quite *unlike* that of its founder, Husserl. While the latter had bracketed existence in favor of arriving at the pure forms of essence, Heidegger categorically rejected the bracketing of existence. The *epokay* of Husserl was directly discarded as being absolutely unnecessary and, in fact, destructive of the new ontology. Hence, while Husserl acknowledged that the phenomenological method with its analyses and descriptions was an authentic mode of arriving at being, it was still only a method. Phenomenology for Heidegger was only a means or way of establishing a new ontology.

For Husserl, phenomenology was the only valid science which was absolutely independent of any other science and the method of science. As Joseph Kockelmans expresses it, "For this reason, phenomenology is for Husserl *the* philosophy and, if it makes sense to speak of metaphysics or ontology, then this metaphysics or on-

tology is either phenomenology itself or only a system of
conclusions which of necessity results from phenomenology. According to Husserl, therefore, ontology derives
its object, problems and everything that is needed to
solve them from phenomenology, while phenomenology
constitutes itself independently from an ontology or a
metaphysics."[67]

For Heidegger, then, phenomenology is merely a
method whereby through analysis and description, we
shall be able to describe those phenomena which are
capable of giving us knowledge concerning the Being of
beings. "Phenomenology is fundamentally a stripping
of that which shows itself, a stripping away of conceal-
ments and distortions, such as will let us see that which
lets itself be seen for what it is."[68] And since the Being
of beings does give meaning and foundation to that which
appears immediately, this Being itself remains concealed
and hidden. Phenomenology will thus lead us to this
Being of beings, which is the proper object of the new
ontology. According to Heidegger, that which phenomenology is to "let us see" is the phenomenon itself, which
"proximally and for the most part does show itself; but
at the same time, it is something that belongs to it so
essentially as to constitute its meaning and its ground
. . . that which remains *hidden* in an egregious sense, or
which relapses and gets *covered up* again, or which
shows itself only 'in disguise' is not just this entity or
that, but rather the *Being of beings* . . . in the phenomenological conception of 'phenomenon' what one has in
mind as that which shows itself is the *Being of entities*
(beings), its meaning, its modifications and derivatives."[69]

D.   Dasein as Being-in-the-World

The most basic and constitutive state of DASEIN is
being-in-the-world (*in-der-Welt-sein*). By this particular
characterization, Heidegger means to show that DASEIN
is not some disembodied Cartesian thinking substance.
Rather, the human existent is most really and tangibly
immersed in the world of actually existing concrete individuals. Man cannot even be thought of in isolation from

the world. At the same time, the world is unthinkable without DASEIN. The world is inextricably bound up with DASEIN in a most intimate manner. "Both are what they are only in being related to one another."[70]

Although this basic state of being-in-the-world, which is the fundamental existential constitution of DASEIN is a unitary phenomenon that must be viewed as a whole, Heidegger nevertheless observes, "This does not prevent it from having several constitutive items in its structure. Indeed, the phenomenal datum which our expression indicates, is one which may, in fact, be looked at in three different ways."[71] Heidegger then devotes some 130 pages of his *Being and Time* to an analysis of the three components within this unitary relationship. They are (1) the notion of "being-in" (2) the concept of "the world" in which existence is located (3) that which is in the world, namely "the who" or "the self."[72] Let us now examine briefly the above three notions.

1. *Being-in*

The notion of "being-in" carries, much like the "DA" of DASEIN, a much wider connotation than that of a mere spatial relationship. Heidegger warns us that "Being-in is distinct from the present-at-hand insideness of something present-at-hand 'in' something else that is present-at-hand; Being-in is not a characteristic that effected or even just elicited, in a present-at-hand subject by the 'world's' Being-present-at-hand; Being-in is rather an essential kind of Being of this entity itself."[73]

Heidegger further maintains that "Being-present-at-hand 'in' something is likewise present-at-hand, and Being-present-along-with (*Mitvorhandensein*) in the sense of a definite location-relationship with something else which has the same kind of Being, are ontological characteristics which . . . are of such a sort as to belong to entities whose kind of Being is *not* of the character of DASEIN. . . . One cannot think of Being-in as the Being-present-at-hand of some corporeal thing (such as a human body) in an entity which is present-at-hand. Nor does the term 'Being-in' mean a spatial 'in-one-another-ness' of things present-at-hand, any more than the word 'in' primordially sig-nifies a spatial relationship of this kind."[74]

In simpler language, we may say that Heidegger re-fuses to understand "Being-in" as something "being-at-hand" or "being-along-with", as for example when we say "the water is in the glass or the clothes are in the ward-robe." Man cannot be in space as some kind of extended object which is in an extended spatial container. As William Richardson says, "It [DASEIN] is to be immersed somehow in the World (*Sein bei*) into which There-Being [i.e., DASEIN] has entered and with which it has intercourse. This immersion in the World is obviously more than mere juxtaposition of There-being and the World, as if they were two entities placed alongside of each other but mutually inaccessible."[75] Heidegger thus speaks of DASEIN's "Being-in" more in the sense in which we say "a man moves in the artistic world" or that "he is at home in the society world." To use the example given by one commentator, When we say a woman lives IN her domestic world, we mean "one specific concretiza-tion of being-in-the-world in Heidegger's sense: the pos-sibilities of this woman's existence, we imply are gathered up in family and home, on which she habitually spends herself . . . a woman does not live in her domestic world by occupying space in it but by keeping herself to these familiar possibilities of her existence . . . 'being-' is con-cretely experienced by us as 'living-in' or 'moving-in' or 'being-at-home-in.' All these phrases express the same meaning: staying-close-to . . . being-familiar-with . . . inhabiting (both in the sense of habituation and dwelling) . . . a world of this or that specific character."[76]

The different ways in which Being-in can manifest it-self are described by Heidegger as *concern*. Some examples of this concern are as follows: ". . . having to do with something, producing something, attending to something and looking after it, making use of something, giving something up and letting it go, undertaking, accomplish-ing, evincing, interrogating, considering, discussing, deter-mining. . . . All these ways of Being-in have *concern* as their kind of Being. . . . Leaving undone, neglecting, renouncing, taking a rest—these are also ways of concern; but these are all *deficient* modes, in which the possibilities of concern are kept to a bare minimum."[77]

2. *The World*

Traditional ontology has failed miserably in giving an authentic notion of the world, says Heidegger. He complains, "When it comes to the problem of analyzing the world's worldhood ontologically, traditional ontology operates in a blind alley, if, indeed, it sees this problem at all."[78] Heidegger goes on to say that "the world" is not some separate and independent thing which has its own independent existence. Neither can the world be described as an entity composed of an aggregate of individuals. The reality of the world, therefore, cannot be described as consisting in the connection or assemblage of real things.

The world, according to Heidegger, is but a characteristic of DASEIN, for the world actually represents the different ways in which man can understand his own being in the totality of his possibilities. The external world is nothing more than the means for the realization of human existence. In this context, one can never speak of a dualism between man and the world, between man and nature. Man and the world can never be separated, for they are essentially relational in their very constitution. The world, far from representing some distinct and separately existing reality, actually stands for the totality of DASEIN's relationship. Now totality "does not refer to the sum total of things in themselves invested with a substantial existence in an abstract and theoretical universe; it expresses the unity of DASEIN's world as a *continuous whole of interconnected relationships*."[79]

3. *The* Who *or* Self

The last component of the Being-in-the-world relationship is "the who" or "the self" which exists in the world. Obviously we are speaking here of man, the human existent. But as we have seen above,[80] Heidegger insists on

speaking of man as DASEIN, with the concomitant denial
of anything stable like a human essence or nature. We
do not speak here of a human nature which possesses
fundamental properties and qualities. We speak only of
"being," simply given and of the different ways in which
it is possible for him to be. DASEIN is never a completed
being. He is always "on the way." He is constantly forging
his nature, by means of the existential choices which he
makes. That is why it is more accurate to say that man
as a being is "constituted by possibilities rather than
properties. While other beings like inanimate objects,
a stone or chair, have a fixed nature, containing certain
observable properties, such as color, hardness etc., DASEIN
has no such fixed nature. Man constitutes himself as he
goes along, engaging in his various existential projects.
Heidegger sums up his position by stating succinctly,
"The person is no Thinglike or substantial Being."[81]

Heidegger's insistence above[82] that *Existenz* is the
essence of DASEIN needs clarification. By *Existenz*, Heidegger does not mean what traditional ontology understands
by *esse* or "to be," which is the correlative of *non-esse* or
"non-being." (When Heidegger wants to indicate this
latter notion as opposed to "non-being," he always uses
the Latin word *existentia*.) Hence he reserves the German
word *Existenz* to indicate the essence of Person or the
human existent. In using the word *Existenz*, he once again
appeals to the etymology of the term. *Existenz* comes
from the Latin word *existere* which means "to stand forth,"
"to stand out" or "to arise." Hence the human DASEIN "ex-
sists" rather than "insists." Man does not "insist," i.e.,
"stand-in-itself" in the manner of stones, plants or brutes
but he "stands out," transcending himself into the realm of
Being, from which he derives his own meaning as well
as bestowing meaning on his own self and the being of
every other existent. As Calvin Schrag summarizes it,
"Heidegger uses the terms *Ek-sistenz, Ecstasis* and
Entwurf (project), to denote the distinctive character of
human existence. Human existence is ecstatic and pro-
jective. To exist means 'to stand out' from non-being and
to be projected into one's possibilities of actualization."[83]

E. *Mit-Sein* or *Co-Dasein*

In *Being and Time*, Heidegger tells us that there can never be an isolated DASEIN; rather, we always deal with a CO-DASEIN. As soon as DASEIN discovers the world, he also discovers other DASEINS that co-exist with him. And just as there can be no DASEIN without the world, so too, there can be no DASEIN apart from other existents. Being-in-the-world thus implies a sharing of this world with other DASEINS and entering into a mutual relationship with them. Like Gabriel Marcel's *co-esse* (being-with), so, Martin Heidegger's *Mit-Sein* or *Mit-Welt* would seem to call for a "togetherness" with others. Heidegger seems to emphasize this point in the following words: "The kind of Being which belongs to the DASEIN of others, as we encounter it within-the-world, differs from the readiness-to-hand and presence-at-hand. Thus DASEIN's world frees entities which not only are quite distinct from equipment and Things, but which also—in accordance with their kind of Being as DASEIN themselves—are 'in' the world in which they are at the same time encountered within-the-world, and are 'in' it by way of Being-in-the-world. These entities are neither present-at-hand nor ready-at-hand; on the contrary, they are *like* the very DASEIN which frees them, in that *they are there too and there with it*. . . . By reason of this *with-like* (*mithaften*), Being-in-the-world, the world is always the one that I share with others. Their Being-in-themselves within-the-world is DASEIN WITH (*Mit-dasein*)."[84]

H. J. Blackham sees this relationship as follows: "My being-in-the-world, in this sense of being constituted by my projects and by my relations with the objects which I make use of and develop as tools for realizing them, involves my being-with-others who are also in the world in the same sense. Here again, the existence of others is not merely accidental, nor a problem for thought, but is a necessity of thought, is constitutive of my being and implied in it. . . . The nature of DASEIN is being-in-common, human existence is a shared existence and the social interdependence of our everyday experience is primordial and constitutive. My full self-consciousness and self-affirmation derive from my consciousness of others: it is not that I begin with myself as given and indubitable and somehow deduce the existence of others like myself. Thus I am constituted both by my preoccupation in which I make use of objects as tools and by my solicitude for persons."[85]

Another author, Vincent Vycinas observes, "DASEIN never reveals itself in isolation, however, but rather in togetherness with others. DASEIN is always taking care of things, and in this care or at its work, it meets other DASEINS—not as things, but to-be-together-in-the-world, i.e., as CO-DASEINS . . . togetherness with others belongs to our existential structure as one of our existentials. . . . Our very existence has the character of togetherness, and only because of this character can we reveal the others and have their understanding."[86]

And yet, another scholar, Thomas Langan, in his extremely sympathetic work, *The Meaning of Heidegger,* finds the sketchy and inadequate treatment of "the other" or the CO-DASEIN to be one of the major weaknesses in Heidegger's thought. He says, "The absence of the other kind of 'otherness' from any consideration in Heidegger's *Denken,* namely the extraordinary 'otherness' of another person, is even more startling. The reader can almost exhaust Heidegger's sustained analysis of the experience and reality of persons other than myself by reading the paragraph on *Mitsein* in *Being and Time.* The vast and significant phenomena of human contact, love, hate, responsibility toward others, of justice and civism and war as revelations of the fundamental situation of exis-tents, simply cannot be reduced to the suggestion that human affairs incorporate themselves in language, in which form they pass into history. That this is in part true is unimportant, and the *Mitsein* treatment and the discussions of *Sprache* in the other works never touch the essential point. It is in this rich intrinsic reality of our contacts with the other, that we need to look for indica-tions of what we are and what he is. What is more funda-mental to the question of Being of the things-that-are than insight into what I am, sought in understanding how the other person is both like me and inexorably other?"[87]

Marjorie Grene points to a similar deficiency when she writes, "Heidegger's man of resolve is wanting in all sense of community with his fellow beings. *Mitdasein*, being-together, occurs only on the level of forfeiture. The authentic individual knows no friend or fellow. He alone for the sake of his own integrity, faces his own death, alone. Yet surely authenticity involves not only the winning of my freedom, but the respect for freedom, not only the achievement of dignity in the individual but the acceptance of the Kantian maxim of the dignity of all individuals. . . . [Heidegger's philosophy] is a doubly-centered philosophy; a philosophy of the individual centered in his own responsibility to become himself, of man in his own unique relation to his own Being. It is a philosophy in which the concept of the person is all-important, yet it can give us no account of any reaching out from one to another. It is a philosophy for which birth and life and death are all-important; yet it admits no kinship between man and any of the other things that are born and live and die."[88]

Renée Weber, another perceptive commentator, finds Heidegger's definition of "co-being" so vague and indeterminate that it fails to provide for an interpersonal ethic, which thus leaves the door wide open for all kinds of subjective perversions of ethics. She says, "The reality of 'co-being,' after all is said, is nothing more substantial than Heidegger's verbal stipulation of it, for he does not present a single instance of an *intrinsically authentic* benevolent interaction (the kind, for example, Buber presents in his I-Thou relationship), and thus exiles his entity 'DASEIN' to an inhuman, egoistic vacuum, where it is condemned forever to turn in upon itself.

Heidegger's failure to provide for an interpersonal ethic is more pernicious than it might be in a less troubled time in history. For his ontological system advocates and widens the gap between man and man that he himself deplores. His notion of conscience confuses the ethical issue by its 'indeterminateness,' which Heidegger cites as 'necessarily as part of resoluteness.' But this very indeterminateness opens the door not to those 'laws and rules' that should presumably issue from the voice of Being, but to the most rampant subjective perversions of ethics. . . . Heidegger's system, for all its complexities and ingenuities, is so vague and generalized that it yields no ethical theory, but rather a climate of permissiveness that allowed Heidegger himself to lend his thought to totalitarianism, the epitome of herd being in its most diabolically destructive possibility."[89]

F. Modes of DASEIN

While Being-in-the-world is the most basic state of DASEIN, Heidegger also speaks of two basic modes in which this state manifests itself. These modes are (1) Self-awareness (*Befindlichkeit*), along with its cognate notion of Thrownness (*Geworfenheit*) and (2) Understanding or comprehension (*Verstehen*). Let us now briefly examine Heidegger's definitions of these modes.

1. *Self-awareness*

The word *Befindlichkeit* comes from the German verb *befinden,* which means "to find," "to judge" or "to deem." The reflexive *sich befinden* means "to become aware of" or "to notice." Hence the closest English translation of *Befindlichkeit* would seem to be "self-awareness," "finding oneself," "realization of one's situation." The English translators of *Sein und Zeit* use the expression "state of mind."

According to Heidegger, DASEIN "finds himself in the world," i.e., "becomes aware of himself" in the world. Such an encountering of oneself is also spoken of as "mood" or "moodness." When we say that DASEIN has found himself, Heidegger admonishes us that DASEIN has found himself "not in the sense of coming across himself by perceiving himself. To be disclosed does not mean 'to be known' as this sort of thing. . . . The pure 'that is' shows itself but the 'whence' and the 'whither' remain in darkness."[90] Heidegger then proceeds to introduce his famous notion of Thrownness (*Geworfenheit*).

a. THROWNNESS

Heidegger himself explains the notion of Thrownness in the following words: "This characteristic of DASEIN's Being, 'that it is'—is veiled in its 'whence' and 'whither,' yet disclosed in itself all the more unveiledly; we call it the 'thrownness' of this entity into its 'there'; indeed it is thrown in such a way that, as Being-in-the-world, it is 'there.' The expression 'thrownness' is meant to suggest the *facticity of its being delivered over.* The 'that it is and has to be' which is disclosed in DASEIN's state-of-mind (self-awareness) is not the same 'that-it-is' which expresses ontologico-categorically the factuality belonging to presence-at-hand. . . . The 'that-it-is' which is disclosed in DASEIN's state-of-mind (self-awareness), must rather be conceived as an existential attribute of the entity which has Being-in-the-world as its way of Being."[91]

DASEIN, therefore, is a being always already in the world. DASEIN never had anything to say about his having been put there. He knows nothing of his "whence and whither." At best, DASEIN can only find himself already here—having been thrown and flung or cast into being. Further, DASEIN never originated his own being; more precisely, he was "delivered over" to himself. And now DASEIN must take over this being as his own.[92] As John Macquarrie expresses it, "[Thrownness] is that outside our control which enters into the structure of our existence to circumscribe and narrow down our possibilities. I am responsible for my existence and I can choose between my possibilities but already with my existence and its possibilities, there is given my facticity, for which I am not responsible and which I have not chosen—namely, that I have to be myself in the world."[93]

b. FACTICITY

"Thrownness," according to Heidegger "suggests the *facticity* of DASEIN's being delivered over."[94] By "facticity" (*Faktizität*), Heidegger wishes to convey the notion that DASEIN understands his "own-most" being, in the sense of a certain factual "Being-present-at-hand." And yet, the factuality of DASEIN's being is quite different ontologically from the factual occurrence of a mineral or a stone. Hence, "Whenever DASEIN *is*, it is a fact; and the factuality of such a fact is what we shall call DASEIN's *facticity*."[95] For Martin Heidegger, then, facticity is a very special and definite way of being on the part of DASEIN. It is peculiar to DASEIN and to no other entity. Heidegger says, "The concept of 'facticity' implies that an entity 'within-the-world' has Being-in-the-world in such a way that it can understand itself as bound up in its 'destiny' with the Being of those entities which it encounters within the world."[96] In another passage, Heidegger emphasizes, "Facticity is not the factuality of the *factum brutum* of something present-at-hand, but a characteristic of DASEIN's Being—one which has been taken up into existence, even if proximally it has been thrust aside. The 'that-it-is' of facticity never becomes something that we can come across by beholding it."[97]

DASEIN, therefore, is not just another object in the world; neither can he be viewed as just another fact in the world. DASEIN has an existence which is peculiarly his own. When he finds himself thrown into the world, he already discovers a great number of "givens" which condition his "being-in-the-world". DASEIN thus is never an absolutely "pure and unconditioned" possibility. His projects and possibilities, on the other hand, will be essentially controlled and conditioned by his own past choices, as well as by factors determined by "his race, sex, intelligence, heredity, emotional stability and all the 'raw material,' so to speak, out of which I have either to attain myself or fail to be myself."[98]

2. *Understanding*

The second mode of authentic existence is Understanding. Traditionally, the word "understanding" or "comprehension" has denoted an intellectual or rational grasping of an object. Heidegger gives the word *Verstehen* (understanding) a completely different interpretation. Appealing to the etymology of *Verstehen*, (*Stehen* = to stand), he holds that understanding refers to DASEIN's ability to stand his thrownness and thus enables him actively to develop his possibilities and projects. DASEIN is not merely "thrown into existence as is a stone but it is thrown in the manner of possibility." Hence Understanding, for Heidegger, is "the existential Being of DASEIN's own potentiality-for-Being; and it is so in such a way that this Being discloses itself what its Being is capable of."[99]

Now "understanding" always has the existential structure called "projection" (*Entwurf*). By projecting himself, DASEIN does not act in accordance with some plan that has been thought out and in accordance with which DASEIN "arranges" his Being. The opposite is true, for Heidegger tells us, "The character of understanding as projection is such that the understanding does not grasp thematically that upon which it projects—that is to say, possibilities. To grasp it in such a way would be to take away from what is projected, its very character as a possibility and would reduce it to the given contents which we have in mind; whereas projecting in throwing, throws before itself the possibility and lets it be as such. As *projecting*, understanding is the kind of Being of DASEIN in which it *is* its possibilities as possibilities."[100]

According to Heidegger, then, because I see myself as the author of possible actions and self-determinations, I thereby have, in a way, seized upon the future, inasmuch as I am "a being-which-is-not"—*yet-can-be*, as an as yet unrealized possibility."[101] Hence by projecting my possibilities in the future, I also project these possibilities on the things that I discover in the world, thus seeing them in their structural unity. And so as I discover these things "in their serviceability and usability," they are "incorporated into the significant world and are understood."[102]

As Magda King points out, "Understanding thus throws a world over beings as a whole, among them man himself as he already is. . . . Understanding opens up a distance between the factual self man already is and the utmost limit of his possibilities. Only from this distance to himself can man become fully illuminated *as* a self; that he can be himself only and always as the thrown self he already is, referred to beings he has not made and cannot master, but with this essential difference: he can be this self in the mode of flights and covering over, or he can take over his finite possibilities as fully and wholly as his own."[103]

3. *Discourse*

Heidegger holds that self-awareness and understanding are impossible without discourse. ("State-of-mind and understanding are characterized equiprimordially by discourse.")[104] Now discourse is not language but the very foundation of language. By means of discourse, interpretation or the granting of meanings to things is made possible. Heidegger tells us, "The intelligibility of something has always been articulated even before there is any appropriative interpretation of it. Discourse is articulation of intelligibility. That which gets articulated as such in discursive articulation, we call the 'totality-of-significations'. . . . Discoursing or talking is the way in which we articulate 'significantly' the intelligibility of Being-in-the-world. . . . The intelligibility of Being-in-the-world—an intelligibility which goes with a state-of-mind—*expresses itself as Discourse.*"[105] Discourse then expresses the intelligibility of the world, and language is the concrete expression in words and sentences of this very intelligibility.

G. Inauthentic and Authentic Existence

Heidegger maintains that there are two basic ways in which DASEIN can exist in the world, namely (1) authentically and (2) inauthentically. As we have already seen, DASEIN knows nothing concerning his "whence or whither."[106] He finds himself thrown into the world. He had nothing to say about his coming into being. (Perhaps if he had, he would not have wished to be.) At any rate, his existence is a brute fact and he must now face it. What will he do? The choice that confronts him is as follows: Either (1) he will turn away from his being and thus not permit his being to reveal itself fully. As a result,

he will fall victim to the endless distractions of the world
—this is INAUTHENTIC EXISTENCE. Or, (2) He will choose
to take over his being as his own responsibility. He will
face it squarely and unequivocally and allow it to disclose itself fully and uniquely as his own. This is AUTHENTIC
EXISTENCE.

H. Inauthenticity and *Das Man*

A DASEIN who refuses to face his being fully and to
assume personal responsibility for it, is guilty of *inauthenticity* of existence (*Uneigentlichkeit*). Inauthentic existence, says Heidegger, is best exemplified by a monotonous
"everydayness" and banality (*Altäglichkeit*). A DASEIN who
leads such a banal, colorless type of existence, fails to live
as a genuine, *bona fide* individual. He fails to exploit his
truly existential possibilities. As a result, such an inauthentic individual lives as a faceless, featureless ego, an
anonymous entity whom Heidegger calls *das Man*. Such a
DASEIN is never referred to as someone definite or determinate. *Das Man* is always spoken of as "one" or as the
indefinite "they" (cf. the French *"l'on"*). Heidegger describes the impersonality of the "they" or the "one" as
follows: "The 'others' whom one thus designates in order
to cover up the fact of one's belonging to them essentially
oneself, are those who proximally and for the most part
'are there' in everyday Being-with-one-another. The 'who'
is not this one, not that one, not oneself (*man selbst*) not
some people (*einige*), and not the sum of them all. The
'who' is the neuter, the 'they' (*das Man*)." Heidegger goes
on to say "It was always the 'they' who did it, and yet it
can be said that it has been 'no one.' In DASEIN's everydayness, the agency through which most things come
about is one of which we must say 'it was one'. . . .
Everyone is the other and no one is himself. This 'they'
which supplies the answer to the question of the 'who'
of everyday DASEIN has already surrendered itself in
Being-among-one-other."[107]

In such a state of "everydayness," we find that
DASEIN's individuality has been completely obliterated.
Mired deep in a levelling mediocrity and shirking his

personal responsibility, DASEIN leads a numbed type of existence. His every action is controlled and determined by the all-pervasive impersonality of *das Man*. Heidegger observes, "We take pleasure and enjoy ourselves as they (*das Man*) take pleasure; we read, see and judge about literature and art as *they* see and judge; likewise we shrink back from the 'great mass' as *they* shrink back; we find 'shocking' what *they* find shocking. The 'they' which is nothing definite, and which all are, though not as the sum, prescribes the kind of Being of everyday-ness."[108]

The result of such domination by the *das Man* mentality is an overwhelming "averageness" and levelling-down of all individuals. It is a naked and unabashed dictatorship which controls each and every being, stifling thereby all originality, excellence and superiority. Thus, "Everyday supremacy is silently suppressed, every original thought is glossed over as well known, every triumph is vulgarized; every mystery loses its power."[109] By applying the same yardstick to all, *das Man* controls every DASEIN, not allowing him to deviate in the slightest degree from the rigid and unbending norm of "averageness" which it imposes. In exchange, *das Man* offers a guarantee of security and tranquility, born of complete apathy and non-involvement. As Bocheński so excellently phrases it, "[Such a situation] relieves human existence of the necessity for decision and for the acknowledgement of responsibility; 'one' (*Man*) does this or that. *Das Man* is a seduction, a narcotic, an estrangement; it externalizes itself in talk, in being-said, where the mere dictum passes for appropriateness of discourse, in restless curiosity, in distraction, haste, and finally, ambiguity. It becomes impossible to decide what has been disclosed and what has not. These form the characteristics of day-to-day being, which is termed the 'falling away' of human existence, because in this case, human existence falls away from itself and falls into the world."[110]

I. Fallenness

Inauthentic existence, which shows itself in the

"everydayness" of DASEIN, can also be called a "fallenness." Instead of searching for truly existential projects which will give him a meaningful and authentic existence, DASEIN allows himself to be distracted by intraworldly beings. He, therefore, falls away from himself and falls into the world. By "fallenness" (*Verfallenheit*), Heidegger does not understand something negative, as for example, a total loss of Being. Fallenness, rather, indicates something positive, a definite condition or distinctive type of being, which is "completely fascinated by the 'world' and by the DASEIN of others in the 'they' (*das Man*)."[111]

Heidegger explains, "Fallenness does not express any negative evaluation but is used to signify that DASEIN is proximally and for the most part alongside (*bei*) the 'world' of its concern. This 'absorption in' . . . has mostly the character of Being-lost in the publicness of the 'they.' DASEIN has, in the first instance, fallen away (*abgefallen*) from itself as an authentic potentiality for Being its self and has fallen into the world."[112]

As a result of the above analysis, Heidegger is now ready to define with greater precision, the meaning of inauthenticity in the world. He writes, "Through the interpretation of falling, what we called 'inauthenticity' of DASEIN may now be defined more precisely. On no account, however, do the terms 'inauthentic' and 'non-authentic' signify 'really not,' as if in this mode of Being, DASEIN were altogether to lose its Being. . . . 'In-authenticity' does not mean anything like Being-no-longer-in-the-world, but amounts rather to a quite distinctive kind of Being-in-the-world. . . . Not-Being-its-self (*Das Nicht-es-selbst-sein*) functions as a positive possibility of that entity which, in its essential concern, is absorbed in a world."[113] Heidegger goes on to explain, "This kind of *not-Being* has to be conceived as that kind of Being which is closest to DASEIN and in which DASEIN maintains itself 'for the most part. . . . Neither must we take the fallenness of DASEIN as a 'fall' from a purer and higher moral primal status. . . . We would also misunderstand the ontologico-existential structure of falling, if we were to ascribe to it the sense of a bad or deplorable property."[114]

Robert Olsen has the following interesting observations to make concerning Heidegger's description of fallenness: "The choice of this term [fallenness] is a bit curious, since Heidegger regards this condition as the one in which all of us find ourselves upon the dawning of consciousness. There is no primitive paradise or original condition of being from which we have fallen; there is only a superior mode of being to which we must rise. Be that as it may, fallenness, being-in-the-midst-of-the-world, and inauthenticity are three names for the same thing."[115] Fallenness is also a kind of "scattering" because DASEIN has allowed himself to be diverted by various factors outside himself. These extraneous elements destroy the unity and cohesion which are necessary for an authentic existence.

There are three chief ways in which inauthentic existence on the part of DASEIN makes itself known. They are the following: (1) Idle talk or Chatter (2) Curiosity (3) Ambiguity. The first mode, idle talk or chatter (Gerede) is a kind of "useless talk which usurps the place of meaningful communication and thoughtful silence." The second way is a type of curiosity (Neugier), which is a distracting preoccupation with information about life, rather than with the fundamental question in search of the Being of beings. The final mode of inauthenticity is described as ambiguity (Zweideutigkeit), which is a "giving-in or surrendering to the practical necessities of life, rendering a true search after Being impossible."[116]

Fallenness, then, far from expressing a negative quality, actually designates a very positive way of Being. True, this mode of Being is inauthentic because DASEIN does not follow the proper road in its search for the Being of beings. The "I" is no longer itself and its possibilities are no longer its own.[117] And yet, inauthenticity seems to be a kind of necessary pre-requisite for achieving genuine authenticity. Somewhat reminiscent of Kierkegaard's existential dialectic of the three stages, each DASEIN arrives at authenticity only by way of a previously inauthentic state.[118]

J. Authentic Existence

Since inauthenticity is viewed as a necessary pre-requisite for the attainment of a genuinely authentic existence, Heidegger next considers the way in which DASEIN can accomplish this "leap" or transition to authenticity. He tells us that it is only through the phenomenon of dread or anxiety (*Angst*) that DASEIN can become authentically existential.[119] Heidegger sharply distinguishes between *fear* and *dread*. He says that too often fear (*Furcht*) is designated as dread (*Angst*), while the character of dread is attributed to fear. It is, therefore, necessary for us to make a clear-cut distinction between these two states.

K. Fear

We experience fear, when we come up against some other entity in the world. This entity may be some definite person or thing. There is always present, at least, some partial knowledge of that of which I am afraid, whether it is another DASEIN or situation. The object of my fear is thus "an entity within-the-world, with the character of threatening." It is always something imminent and "fear-some."

L. Dread

Dread or anxiety, on the other hand, is altogether different. Whereas fear always involves some known object, dread knows no such entity. Heidegger states, "That in the face of which one is anxious (i.e., has dread) is completely indefinite. Not only does this indefiniteness leave factically undecided which entity within-the-world is threatening us but it also tells us that entities within-the-world are not relevant at all. Anxiety (*Angst*) does not 'know' what is in the face of which it is anxious. Therefore, that which threatens cannot bring itself close from a definite direction within what is close by; it is already 'there' and yet somewhere; it is so close that it is oppressive and stifles one's breath and yet it is nowhere. . . . When anxiety has subsided, then in our everyday way of talking, we are accustomed to say 'it was really nothing.' "[120]

Hence that which DASEIN dreads is something completely indeterminate. There is no way of identifying it or pointing it out. There is a kind of uncanniness about the whole situation.

As William Richardson describes it, "This is how it differs from fear because fear is always in view of something, as a child is afraid of a dog. But in the uncanny emptiness of anxiety [i.e., dread], things about us seem to dissolve—or at least, their meaningfulness dissolves. We become ill-at-ease, disoriented, alienated from the world-about. But precisely what are we anxious about? That's the trouble—we can't say. About nothing! Yet not *absolutely* nothing. About 'something' quite real but which is no 'thing' like any other 'thing,' nor is it situated here nor there nor anywhere. It is no thing and nowhere. We call it the No-thing, i.e., Non-being (*Nichts*)."[121] (We shall examine in greater detail later on Heidegger's analysis of Being vis-à-vis nothingness.)[122]

M.   Death, Being-to-Death

The word *dread* or *anxiety* might suggest to some readers that we are speaking here of a basic deficiency or weakness on the part of DASEIN. Actually, the contrary is true. Dread, according to Heidegger, demands a great deal of fortitude and strength on DASEIN's part. Instead of trying to overcome this dread, man must learn to face it bravely and resolutely. Now it is the peculiar service of dread that it reveals to man his fundamental finitude. Dread shows man that his existence is finite because it is always lived in the shadow of death. And death is the one fact through which man can grasp himself as a whole.

As long as DASEIN lives, he is always incomplete, still projecting his many possibilities. In one sense, we can say that it is impossible to grasp DASEIN in his completeness and totality. But when death does come, DASEIN has disappeared completely and cannot be grasped at all. According to John Macquarrie, death has a special function in Heideggerian thinking for "Death sets a boundary. It marks off DASEIN as Being-in-the-world from nothing into which he disappears, when he ceases to be in the world; and to be marked off from nothing in this way is precisely to stand out from it, that is to say 'ex-sist.' Moreover, it is to exist authentically, for when one has become aware of the boundary of existence, then one has become aware of one's *own* existence."[123]

We have seen above the distinction between fear and dread. While fear always discloses its object (we are afraid of this or that particular thing), dread can point to absolutely nothing. Hence it is *nothingness* that DASEIN dreads. I am filled with dread when I regard my whole world which is my life. When I view my life as a complete entity, I see standing menacingly at its end, DEATH. This fact has prompted Heidegger to define DASEIN as a Being-to-death (*Sein zum Tode*). Man's whole life is but a life facing death.

Heidegger explains, "Just as DASEIN *is* already its 'not-yet,' and is its 'not-yet' constantly as long as it is, it *is* already its end too. The 'ending' which we have in view when we speak of death, does not signify DASEIN's Being-towards-the-end (*Sein zum Ende*) of this entity. Death is a way to be, which DASEIN takes over as soon as it is. 'As soon as man comes to life, he is at once old enough to die.' "[124]

Dread and death, then, restore man to his authentic existence. They are the scaffolding which DASEIN uses in order to emancipate himself from inauthenticity. When DASEIN previously existed under the domination of *das Man*, he was prevented from exercising his proper and full freedom. Dread and the realization of death have now rescued DASEIN from this control. They have freed DASEIN and have set him apart, so that he can engage in his freely chosen possibilities. We are told, "Anxiety [dread] makes manifest in DASEIN its *Being-towards* its ownmost potentiality-for-Being—that is *Being-free* for the freedom of choosing itself and taking hold of itself. Anxiety [dread] brings DASEIN face to face with its *Being-free-for* (*propensio in*) the authenticity as a possibility which it always is."[125]

Thomas Langan expresses this point with characteristic clarity, "Because he knows he will die, DASEIN takes

possession like no other thing does, of the course of his
personal destiny, even before it is in fact realized. Consequently, when Heidegger speaks of DASEIN as Being-
toward-death (*Sein zum Tode*), he signals the finite self-
possession which characterizes the free being who in
projecting himself unfolds the reality of his own destiny."[126] Joseph Kockelmans points to the relationship
which exists between death and authentic existence. He
says, "At the moment that DASEIN understands death as
its ultimate possibility, i.e., as a possibility which makes
its being impossible, and at the moment when it accepts
and recognizes this final possibility as its very own, DASEIN
becomes transparent to itself as a personal be-ing, i.e.,
in its self. . . . By really understanding death and by
accepting it as its own death, DASEIN breaks away from
inauthentic being and throws itself into its *authentic
being*."[127]

N.   Conscience and Authentic Existence

An indispensable aid in the restoring of DASEIN to
authenticity is *conscience*. For Heidegger, conscience is
not "the voice of some alien power (God)" but it is a
call or summons of the authentic self to the self which has
become bogged down in the everydayness and averageness
of *das Man*. As William Luijpen expresses it, "Man calls
himself from his inauthenticity to his most proper potential being."[128] Conscience calls upon DASEIN to shake off
the mesmerizing influence of mediocrity and inauthenticity. Man is thus called upon to commit himself spontaneously to the possibilities of his being. Coupled with
death, which is DASEIN's "ownmost possibility," conscience
enables me to be confronted with my true self. In choosing
to take upon myself the being which I received in thrownness and which is now handed over to death, I begin to
understand fully my "Being-to-death." I now restore my
selfhood to myself, rising above the trivialities of everyday
life which characterized my previously inauthentic existence. As Heidegger explains it, "When the call of conscience is understood, lostness in the 'they' (*das Man*) is
revealed. Resoluteness brings DASEIN back to its ownmost

potentiality-for-Being-its-Self. When one has an understanding Being-towards-death—towards death as one's
ownmost possibility—one's potentiality-for-Being becomes
authentic and wholly transparent."[129]

And so I now face death resolutely and with determination (*mit Entschlossenheit*). Whereas previously my
existence was scattered and dispersed amidst the trivial
and insignificant preoccupations of everydayness, I now
achieve a wholeness and completeness of life. I have dis-
pelled all illusions of a false security in a faceless anonymity and I have restored to myself, a genuinely free existence in the exercise of my possibilities. I now possess an
"authentic existence."[130]

O. Care

Heidegger now concludes the first part of his *Being
and Time* by grouping under one comprehensive concept,
all the insights gathered from his existential analysis of
DASEIN. This over-all and general concept he calls *Care*
(*Sorge*). Under the general term *Care*, he sets forth a
three-fold structure of being, namely, (1) Possibility
(2) Facticity (3) Fallenness. Heidegger tells us, "The
formally existential totality of DASEIN's structural whole
must therefore be grasped in the following structure: the
Being of DASEIN means ahead-of-itself-Being-already-in-
(the-world) as Being-alongside (entities encountered
within-the-world). This Being fills in the signification of
the term 'care' (*Sorge*) which is used in a purely ontologico-existential manner. . . . Care does not characterize
just existentiality, let us say, as detached from facticity
and *falling*: on the contrary, it embraces the unity of
these ways in which Being may be characterized."[131]
And while these three aspects of possibility, facticity and
fallenness compose one structural whole, it is nevertheless
possible to consider them separately for a deeper understanding of their function.[132]

P. Possibility

DASEIN is the kind of being who is concerned about
his own being. Further, he is always free for his potential-

ity of being is either for authenticity or inauthenticity. Hence in his being, DASEIN is always ahead of himself or in advance of himself. This state involves also understanding and projecting. Heidegger states, "DASEIN is an entity for which, in its Being, that Being is an issue. . . . The phrase 'is an issue' has been made plain in the state-of-being of understanding—of understanding as self-projective Being towards its ownmost potentiality-for-being. . . . Being towards one's ownmost potentiality-for-Being means that in each case, DASEIN is already *ahead* of itself (*ihm selbst . . . vorweg*) in its Being. DASEIN is always 'beyond itself' (*über sich hinaus*) not as a way of behaving towards other entities which it is *not,* but as Being towards the potentiality-for-Being which it is itself. This structure of Being, which belongs to the essential is an issue, 'we shall denote as DASEIN's 'Being-ahead-of-itself.' "[133]

John Macquarrie summarizes this point in the following manner: "Man's being gets projected ahead of itself. The entities which are encountered are transformed from being merely 'present-at-hand' to being 'ready-at-hand' to man in their serviceability, and out of them man constructs an instrumental world which is articulated on the basis of his concerns."[134]

Q. Facticity

While DASEIN is Being-ahead-of-himself, he is not to be understood as an entity in isolation from the world. Instead, DASEIN has been thrown into the world and has been left to his own responsibility and resources. Hence, he is a factical being. Heidegger explains, "Being-ahead-of-itself does not signify anything like an isolated tendency in a worldless 'subject' but characterizes Being-in-the-world. To Being-in-the-world, however, belongs the fact that it has been delivered over to itself—that it has in each case already been thrown *into a world.* . . . 'Being-ahead-of-itself' means, if we grasp it more fully 'ahead-of itself-in-already-being-in-a-world'. . . . To put it otherwise, existing is always factical. Existentiality is essentially determined by facticity."[135]

While DASEIN is a "being-ahead-of-himself" in "al-ready-in-a-world," he also exhibits the character of fallen-ness. DASEIN, as a being-in-the-world, involves himself with and spends himself in the world. Because of this in-volvement, he becomes absorbed in the cares and concerns of things that are at hand. This, as we have already seen above,[136] is a condition of DASEIN's in-authenticity which hopefully will yield to a genuinely authentic exis-tence. Heidegger explains, "DASEIN's factical existing is not only generally and without further differentiation a thrown potentiality-for-Being-in-the-world; it is always also absorbed in the world of its concern. In this falling Being-alongside . . . fleeing in the face of uncanniness, announces itself, whether it does so explicitly or not, and whether it is understood or not. Ahead-of-itself-Being-already-in-a-world essentially includes one's falling and one's Being-alongside those things ready-to-hand-within-the-world with which one concerns oneself."[137]

Heidegger concludes this examination of the three-fold structure of existence under the general concepts of *Care* with these words, "Care, as a primordial structural totality, lies before (*vor*) every factical 'attitude' and 'situation' of DASEIN, and it does so existentially a priori; this means that it always lies *in* them."[138]

R. Summary

Let us now pause briefly and take stock of the pro-gress which Heidegger has made. Heidegger's initial quarrel with all metaphysics was that, ever since the days of the early Greek thinkers, philosophy has forgotten its very *raison d'être*. Instead of trying to arrive at a knowl-edge of the Being of beings, metaphysics has frittered away its time in the study of this or that particular being. Hence, a "destruction of ontology" is necessary, in order that we may concern ourselves with the real problem of philosophy. This Heidegger proposes to do.

In his search for a *point de départ*, Heidegger comes to the conclusion that the only valid one is the being of the questioner himself. It is man, alone, who is genuinely concerned about the question of the Being of beings. To him, alone, is the question of Being meaningful. Heidegger concludes that by studying man, we shall be able to arrive at important insights into the Being of beings which, after all, is the proper aim of all metaphysics.[139]

In beginning his study of man, Heidegger refuses to attribute to him the traditional essence or nature "rational animal." As a matter of fact, he will not allow that man is a substance or subject of action or a *suppositum* of a rational nature. Instead, Heidegger appropriates the German word DASEIN, which means "existence" and reserves this term for the entity, which traditional philosophy has designated by the phrase *animal rationale*. Literally, DASEIN means "There-Being" or "Being-There" and it has received a number of barbaric renditions in English. Heidegger proposes to engage in a number of analyses of DASEIN, in order to arrive at certain basic notions which will ultimately, he hopes, shed light on the Being of beings.

First of all, Heidegger characterizes DASEIN as "Being-in-the-world." Man can never be thought of in isolation from the world and neither is the world meaningful without DASEIN. Heidegger then proceeds to analyze separately the notions of "Being-in," "the world" and the "who" or the "self" who is the being in the world.

By "being-in", Heidegger understands a much wider connotation than a purely spatial relationship. Being-in does indicate spatiality but it also includes the notion of "staying close to" or "being familiar with." This aspect of DASEIN is best evidenced in the quality of *concern* on the part of man.

"The world," according to Heidegger, is not some separate and independent entity, nor is it an agglomerate of individual things, as if we added up all the things that are and then called them "the world." In reality, argues Heidegger, the world represents the different ways in which DASEIN can understand his world in the totality of his existential possibilities. The world can perhaps be best defined as a "continuous whole of interconnected relationships."

Thirdly, the "who" or the "self" is not some "thinglike or substantial being." Heidegger refuses to speak of man as a stable permanent subject. He prefers to define person as *Existenz*, meaning by it, not an entity which is (as against one which is not), but rather as one which "ex-sists," i.e., stands out or stands forth. In this way, DASEIN transcends himself into the realm of Being and thus both derives his own meaning and bestows meaning upon all other existents. DASEIN as being-in-the-world must, therefore, be understood in this special Heideggerian sense.[140]

But DASEIN, in Heidegger's *Being and Time,* is also referred to as *Mit-Sein* or CO-DASEIN. Heidegger speaks here, albeit briefly, of a "togetherness with others." I meet other DASEINS and I share the world with them as a *Mit-Sein*. It is significant, however, that aside from the very brief treatment of *Mit-Sein* in *Being and Time,* we are hard pressed to find any other development of this important notion in Heidegger's other writings. Whereas Gabriel Marcel's *co-esse* and "I-Thou" relationship are basic to all his thought, Heidegger's *Mit-Sein* receives only a passing and most incomplete consideration. And while Heidegger does hold the concept of "person" to be an extremely important one in his thought, the fact remains that there is no genuine reaching out on the part of man to other DASEINS as, for example, in the notion of "The Between" in the thought of Martin Buber. Each human being in the Heideggerian world must work out his authenticity alone and in solitude. He must likewise face death alone and in isolation from others. (Heidegger has been severely criticized by some writers for this position.)[141]

There are three different ways or modes in which DASEIN as a "being-in-the-world" can exist authentically. Heidegger designates these ways as (1) self-awareness or moodness (2) understanding and (3) discourse. Self-awareness or moodness points to an initial "encountering of oneself in the world." Apropos of this mood, Heidegger introduces the notion of "thrownness," whereby DASEIN does not know his whence or his whither but finds himself "flung" or "cast" into existence, without ever having

anything to say about it. Thrownness, in turn, suggests a
"facticity," which means that when DASEIN discovers himself already in the world, he has a number of "givens."
Such factors as race, sex, intelligence, heredity, emotional
stability or lack of it and the like, are the "already present
endowments," with which each DASEIN begins his existence.
In other words, DASEIN is at no time an absolutely pure
and unconditioned possibility.

The second mode of DASEIN, i.e., understanding, has
no reference to an intellectual grasping of a concept. With
its accompanying structure of "projection," understanding
indicates man's ability to stand his "thrownness" and to
develop his possibilities and his potentialities for being.
In this way, DASEIN seizes upon his future. He projects
his own possibilities and in doing so, he also discovers
the things in the world with their serviceability and usability.

The third mode, discourse, is not language but the
very foundation of language. By discourse, Heidegger
understands the "significant articulation of the intelligibility of Being-in-the-world" even before there has been any
interpretation of it. Language is but the concrete expression in word and sentences of this intelligibility.[142]

Heidegger next considers the two basic ways in which
DASEIN can exist in the world, namely, (1) inauthentically
and (2) authentically.

(1) When DASEIN refuses to face his being fully and
to assume personal responsibility for it, he is guilty of
inauthentic existence. Such an existence is characterized
by a banality and monotonous "everydayness." An individual who fails to exploit his truly existential possibilities and fails to assume his responsibilities is living the
life of a faceless, anonymous *das Man* (the indefinite
"one"). Such an inauthentic existence inevitably results
in a stifling of originality, a levelling down of all individuals and a complete apathy and non-involvement. Inauthentic existence also manifests itself as fallenness. By
falling away from himself and from his genuinely existential possibilities, DASEIN is completely fascinated by the

world and by the DASEIN of others in *das Man*. At the same time, fallenness and inauthenticity seem to be a kind of necessary pre-requisite for the attainment of genuinely authentic existence. And just as self-awareness, understanding and discourse are modes of authentic existence, so, curiosity, ambiguity and idle talk (chatter) are modes of an inauthentic existence.[143]

(2) Heidegger now sets out to show that it is only through dread or anxiety that DASEIN can hope to attain authenticity of existence. He sharply distinguishes between fear and dread. The object of fear is always some definite and known entity; the object of dread, on the other hand, is absolutely unknown and indeterminate. Dread or anxiety (*Angst*) is, however, not a weakness or deficiency on the part of DASEIN which the latter must seek to overcome. Rather, dread requires fortitude and perseverance. It must be lived with, bravely and resolutely. The special function of dread is that it discloses to man his fundamental finitude through death. Once DASEIN grasps the reality of his own death, which is a boundary of existence, he then becomes authentically aware of his own existence. Heidegger thus defines DASEIN's life as "Being-to-death." As soon as man comes to life, he is old enough to die. Hence dread and death are the means whereby DASEIN gains his authenticity of existence. Conscience, which is a summons of the authentic self to the self bogged down in the everydayness of *das Man*, also helps DASEIN to rise to the call of authenticity. As a result, I now face death resolutely and with determination. I have shaken the mesmerizing illusion of a false security in the anonymity of *das Man*. I am free to exercise my possibilities. I now possess authentic existence.[144]

Heidegger concludes the first part of *Being and Time* by grouping under the one term, "care," all the various insights gathered from his existential analysis of DASEIN. Under the general heading of care, he sets down the three-fold structure of existence: (1) possibility, understanding and projecting (2) facticity and thrownness (3) fallenness.[145]

S.   Temporality

We have seen above[146] that in *Division I* of his *Being and Time,* Heidegger had arrived at the general notion of "care" as representing the basic constitution of DASEIN's existence. In the second half of the book, i.e., *Division II,* entitled *Dasein and Temporality,* Heidegger advances his novel interpretation of the nature of time. And while "care" did serve as a kind of general heading for all the constituent elements making up DASEIN, nevertheless, it is *Time,* Heideggerian time, which is the primordial foundation making DASEIN's unity possible.[147]

We have already observed Heidegger's refusal to consider the human being as a substance, a permanent subject of action, possessing a determinate nature, i.e., that of a rational animal. Heidegger preferred to speak of "care," rather than of the substantial soul as the basis for DASEIN. As John Macquarrie observes, the result of this position is that genuine selfhood is not "something ready-made (like a substantial soul that is there from the beginning) but rather a *condition,* that may be either gained or lost in the concrete acts and decisions of existence."[148] In seeking this most basic foundation of DASEIN's unity, Heidegger concludes that it is "temporality, with its three *ecstases* of what is to come, the present, and what has been" that is the ultimate ground. Time, then, can explain more satisfactorily "the complex and dynamic character of personal life than the traditional model of the substantial soul."[149] As William Richardson comments, "DASEIN is not a mere entity but 'essentially an anticipatory drive-towards-Being' by reason of which it is its own potentiality, sc., it already is what it can be."[150]

Temporality (*Zeitlichkeit*) holds a very privileged and unique position in the analysis of DASEIN. The reason for it is that time is the very means whereby the human being is rendered whole and entire. Whereas care considered the various aspects of DASEIN's existence under the three headings of possibility, facticity, and fallenness, it is temporality, with its parallel trio of future, has been and the present, that melds them altogether and renders them as one unified whole. In Heidegger's words, "Temporality makes possible the unity of existence, facticity and falling, and in this way, constitutes primordially the totality of the structure of Care."[151] Heidegger reminds us that in defining the totality of DASEIN as Care, he spoke of it as "ahead-of-itself-already-being-in (a world) as Being-alongside (entities encountered within the world)." Now this authentic potentiality-for-Being-a-whole of anticipatory resoluteness "is possible only through the unifying activity of temporality" precisely because *the primordial unity of Care lies in temporality.*"[152]

But Heidegger goes on to caution us that the items of Care "have not been pieced together cumulatively any more than temporality itself has been put together 'in the course of time' out of the future, the having been and the present. Temporality 'is' not an *entity* at all. It is not but it *temporalizes* itself. . . . Temporality temporalizes, and indeed it temporalizes possible ways of itself. These make possible the multiplicity of DASEIN's modes of being, and especially the basic possibility of authentic or inauthentic existence."[153] One commentator renders Heidegger's position as follows; "The temporality of man designates his possibility of attaining to the full authenticity of his being or of missing it, if he remains tied to the past. Temporality is an ontological affirmation and designates a structure of being: it does not designate the Real cycle of past-present-future."[154]

In proceeding to elaborate his understanding of the nature of temporality, Heidegger categorically rejects the traditional and accepted definition of time. Now the ordinary man in the street normally thinks of time as "proceeding out of an indefinitely stretching past into an indefinitely stretching future." Whether you consider Newtonian time or Leibnitzian time, the basic concept is that such happenings "go on forever in an unending chain, from past to future." For the ordinary man who never stops to consider what conditions make time possible, time is "an obscure power which continuously makes

short moments of 'now' reach the present from the future,
thereby making them real, and the driving them at once
into the past by constantly bringing forward new moments of 'now.' "[155] To put it in very simple terms, the ordinary man generally thinks of time as a succession of
"nows" which he designates as present, past and future.

Such a notion of time, Heidegger labels completely
unacceptable and inauthentic because it is "abstract and
derivative." It is for this reason, therefore, that we must
"hold ourselves aloof from all those significations of
'future, past, and present' which thrust themselves upon
us from the ordinary conception of time. This holds also
for conceptions of a "time" which is "subjective" or "objective," "immanent" or "transcendent." Inasmuch as
DASEIN understands himself in a way which proximally
and for the most part is inauthentic, we may suppose
that 'time' as ordinarily understood does indeed represent a genuine phenomenon, but one which is
derivative. It arises from inauthentic temporality which
has a source of its own. The conception of 'future,' 'past'
and 'present' have first arisen in terms of the inauthentic
way of understanding time."[156] According to Heidegger,
therefore, inauthentic time which is "accessible to the
ordinary understanding consists, among other things,
precisely in the fact that it is a pure sequence of 'nows,'
without beginning and without end."[157]

T.   Heideggerian Time

After rejecting the commonly accepted notion of
time as inadequate because it is abstract and derivative,
Heidegger proceeds to develop his own theory of temporality. First of all, Heidegger holds that time is not
something external to DASEIN, as if DASEIN were moving
from one "now" to another. Time, says Heidegger, is
actually the span of DASEIN's life. Man is not *in* time; he *is*
time. By anticipating his own death as something which is
intensely personal ("it is MY death and not some else's"),
DASEIN receives his own foundation, i.e., he *returns* to his
foundation. Now "to come to be himself," i.e., *Zu-Kunft*,
is also the word for *future*. Heidegger points out, "This

letting oneself come toward itself in that distinctive possibility which (DASEIN) puts up with, is the primordial phenomenon of the future (*Zu-Kunft*) $=$ (coming toward)."[158]

Furthermore, time is ecstatic. Now this characterization has nothing to do with the traditional meaning of a mystic's ecstasy. Once again, Heidegger is appealing to the etymology of the word. "Ecstasis" means literally "standing besides itself" (*ausser sich*) in the sense that DASEIN is always "reaching out beyond itself, that it is beyond itself, i.e., in the future which 'comes toward' it, that it goes back to its past facticity and that it meets its present."[159] Now these are not disparate and unrelated phases. Rather, they form a "dynamic system of references in which one form implies the other."[160]

1. *The Future*

Heideggerian existential time is thus primarily futural. But by "future," Heidegger does not mean a "before," which would mean "in advance of something" in the sense of "not yet now-but later." The "before" and "after" indicate rather a future as of "a sort which would make it possible for DASEIN to be such that its potentiality-for-Being is an issue. Self-projection upon the 'for-the-sake-of-oneself' is grounded in the future and is an essential characteristic of existentiality. *The primary meaning of existentiality is the future.*"[161]

Heidegger goes on to say, "In enumerating the *ecstases,* we have always mentioned the future first. We have done this to indicate that the future has a priority in the ecstatical unity of primordial and authentic temporality. . . . Primordial and authentic temporality temporalizes itself in terms of the authentic future and in such a way that in having been futurally, it first of all awakens the present. *The primary phenomenon of primordial and authentic temporality is the future.*"[162]

2. *The "Having Been"*

DASEIN's projection towards his own death involves not only the future but also the past, or more precisely the "having been." This latter ecstasis is necessary because it is possible for me to project myself toward death (the future) only on the condition that I already am. Hence in order "to-be-toward-death," I must accept my thrownness, i.e., what I already am. In this way, there exists an absolute interdependence between the future and the past. Just as the future necessarily implies a "having been," so the past cannot make itself evident unless there is a future. Heidegger says, "Taking over thrownness is possible only in such a way that the futural DASEIN can be its ownmost 'as-it-already-was'—that is to say, its been. Only insofar as DASEIN is an 'I-am-as-having,' can DASEIN come towards itself futurally in such a way that it comes back. As authentically futural, DASEIN is authentically as 'having been'. . . . The character of 'having been' arises in a certain way from the future."[163]

By speaking of time as "having been" (*Gewesenheit*), rather than as "past" (*Vergangenheit*), Heidegger once again rejects the description of past time as being merely the sequence of past "nows" which no longer exist. By speaking of "having been," he wishes to emphasize that DASEIN is not something distinct and separate from time. DASEIN itself *is* time. To predicate "having been" of DASEIN is to underscore the fact that DASEIN has been and still *is* in a certain way. As Joseph Kockelmans expresses it, "The 'having been' is that which, having been, is still present, that which is present *as* having been."[164]

3. *The Present*

The final ecstasis of temporality is "the present," which DASEIN achieves by his projection into the future and then his turning back to assimilate the thrownness of "the past." According to Heidegger's definition, "The character of 'having been' arises from the future which 'has been' (or better, which is in the process of having been), releases from itself the present. The phenomenon has the unity of a future which makes present in the process of having been; we designate it *temporality*."[165]

Temporality is, therefore, the primordial foundation making the unity of DASEIN possible. As the "ontological basis," time is a structural whole; it is not a morsellation or a "parcelling out." It is a unity which manifests itself through the three ecstases of future, having been and the present. Heidegger concludes that it is only when DASEIN is unified via these three ecstases of temporality, that he can hope to achieve what is of paramount importance, namely an authentic existence.

U. Historicity

Heidegger's notion of historicity is closely connected with his novel and unusual interpretation of the nature of temporality. He tells us, "Analysis of the historicity of DASEIN tries to show that this entity is not 'temporal' it gives us information concerning DASEIN's possibilities, which are essentially futural." The future is, therefore, the basis for DASEIN's historicity. We read, "But if fate constitutes the primordial historicality of DASEIN, then history projects. History is thus directed to the future because it 'stands in history,' but that, on the contrary, if it exists and can exist historically, it is because it is temporal in the very basis of its being."[166] Now the word "history" has an ambiguous meaning because it can be understood in two different ways. Heidegger says, "The most obvious ambiguity of the term 'history' is one that has often been noticed, and there is nothing 'fuzzy' about it. It evinces itself in that this term may mean the 'historical' actuality as well as the possible science of it."[167]

Heidegger next proceeds to assign the word *Geschichte* to denote the "historical actuality" or the "historical process" and he uses the word *Historie,* to indicate the science or study of the process itself. He admonishes us that far too many people think of history as being concerned with the past. The truth of the matter is that history is something which pertains to the future. Heidegger supports this rather startling conclusion by means of the following argument: we had seen above that DASEIN is temporality and temporality is chiefly oriented towards the future because human existence is always interpreted in terms of man's possibilities, i.e., in terms of his future projects. History is thus directed to the future because it gives us information concerning DASEIN's possibilities, which are essentially futural. The future is, therefore, the basis for DASEIN's historicity. We read, "But if fate constitutes the primordial historicality of DASEIN, then history has its essential importance neither in what is past, nor in the 'today' and its connection with what is past, but in that authentic historizing of existence which arises from DASEIN's future. As a way of Being for DASEIN then, history has its roots so essentially in the future that death, as that possibility of DASEIN which we have already characterized, throws anticipatory existence back upon its factical thrownness, and so for the first time, imparts to *having been,* its peculiarly privileged position in the historical."[168]

Helmut Peukert expresses the above relationship between temporality and historicity in the following manner: "For Heidegger, existence's relationship to history can be seen only through the structure of the more basic temporality. If human existence exists in time, then in its basis, existence is historical. For inasmuch as existence finds itself in the present as already having been (and finds this by drawing on its future), the possibility of history consists in the possibilities of its own existence. . . . The *moment* of authentic temporality is the origin of the relationship to history."[169]

John Wild, in his work, *The Challenge of Existentialism,* explains, "Men are neither *in* history, like things and artifacts, nor can they free themselves from history and become detached from it. They *are* their history. Their being in the world is historical. Thus the world is not a number of things that were once all there in a certain form, but which have had a history so that our things are now quite different. The world itself is historical. But the world itself was never all there. It was always temporalizing itself as a past, a present and a future. The future is still ahead of us now in the world of today, our future as well as that of the past."[170]

History, therefore, is primarily concerned with DASEIN's possibilities and for this reason, it is directed toward the future and not to the past. History is to be understood existentially and not in terms of categories which apply only to things. And yet, the historian does concern himself with things, i.e., with facts or happenings, with what Heidegger calls "equipment or antiquities preserved in museums"—tools, works of art and artifacts of the past. But such equipment and antiquities become "historiological objects" only in a secondary sense. The historian studies these objects only because of their past association with DASEIN. After all, it is DASEIN who is primarily historical; it is *he* who is the primary concern of history.

Heidegger says apropos of this point, "We contend that what is primarily historical is DASEIN. That which is secondarily historical, however, is what we encounter within-the-world—not only equipment ready-to-hand, in the widest sense, but also in the environment NATURE as the 'very soil of history.' Entities other than DASEIN which are historical by reason of belonging to the world, are what we call 'world-historical.' "[171]

History is thus primarily concerned with DASEIN and only secondarily with objects or equipment, insofar as the latter are in any way related to or associated with human beings. Of its very essence, history is interested in the examination and investigation of the authentic possibilities of existence. John Macquarrie summarizes Heidegger's position in the following words: ". . . history cannot be an objective connection of events. Objects only enter into history so far as they have been of concern to man and man himself, the primary historical, is never an object. Man exists, he stands before possibilities. The stuff of history—if we may so speak—is, therefore, existence and that means possibility."[172]

In this connection, Heidegger introduces the term *wiederholbar*, which can perhaps be best translated as "repeatable" or "retrievable." Macquarrie describes it aptly, "Repetition is not just a mechanical reproducing, but rather a going into the past in such a way that one fetches back the possibility which it contains and makes present this possibility in our existence now. . . . The past has to be seized and broken open as it were. It becomes significant for the future, and might also be said to get integrated with the future in the moment of vision and decision."[173]

The retrievability of past events and their incorporation into the future is described by Heidegger as follows: "The theme of historical study is neither that which has happened just once for all nor something universal that floats above it, but the possibility which has been factically existent. This possibility does not get repeated as such—that is to say, understood in an authentically historical way—if it becomes perverted into the colorlessness of a supratemporal model. Only by historicality which is factical and authentic can the history of what has-been-there, as a resolute fate, be disclosed in such a manner that in repetition the 'force' of the possible gets stuck home into one's factical existence—in other words, that it comes toward that existence in its futural character."[174]

Hence the chief characteristic of history is the possible or the futural. By studying history, man can understand the authentic possibilities which were once open to DASEIN and which can still be retrieved and repeated in the future. Heidegger applies this notion of history to his own method of writing philosophy. It is his contention that the primordial insights of the Pre-Socratics, the early Physicists and Naturalists in the quest for being were eminently valid and especially promising. But the successive encrustations of metaphysical systems have caused man to be diverted from his original quest, i.e., the search for the Being of beings. Instead of seeking to discover the Being which makes all beings possible, philosophers have wantonly pursued this or that being and have become traitors to the cause of wisdom. Heidegger now hopes to retrieve and to repeat the original and primordial Greek insights, in order to arrive at a new metaphysics which will be faithful to the object of philosophy, namely the Being of beings.[175]

At least one commentator has found Heidegger's efforts in this direction a dismal and unqualified failure. In her evaluation of the effectiveness of historicity in his philosophy, Marjorie Grene says, "Heidegger was acclaimed as a prophet of *'Geschichtlichkeit,'* as one who

carried on the message of Dilthey concerning the unique
and living nature of history. In fact, he declares that his
whole purpose in *Sein und Zeit* was to support the doctrines of Dilthey and Yorck on this subject. . . . He did
not do this effectively; for he failed to show how the
historical character of the individual's life bears on the
broader problems of the history of nations. His *'Geschichtlichkeit'* remains that of the individual; the *'Geschick,'*
the destiny of peoples, is tied to it by a mere pun, not by
any solid argument. . . . For it is certainly important for
the philosophical interpretation of history to consider
how the sense of individual life is related to the understanding of more general issues."[176]

V. Nothingness

One of the best known and most widely discussed
Heideggerian themes is that of "Nothingness" or "naught"
(*das Nichts*). The first suggestion of the privileged
position which nothingness would occupy in Heidegger's
ontology was indicated in his examination of Dread
(*Angst*) in *Being and Time*, which appeared in 1927.
("When Dread has subsided, then in our everyday way
of talking, we are accustomed to say 'it was really nothing.'")[177]

Two years after the publication of *Being and Time*,
Heidegger made nothingness the principal theme of his
inaugural lecture as professor at the University of Freiburg. Under the title of *What Is Metaphysics?*, the philosopher addressed the entire academic community upon
the most unlikely subject of nothingness. Let us examine
the main points of this now world-famous lecture.[178]

Heidegger opened his address by mentioning the
great variety of subjects or sciences (in the wide sense of
bodies of organized knowledge) taught in a university.
While "their methodologies are fundamentally different
and their disrupted multiplicity is held together only
by the technical organization of the universities and
their faculties . . . they are nevertheless all related insofar
as they study 'what-is'. . . . The world-relationship which
runs through all the sciences as such constrains them to

seek what-is *in itself*, with a view of rendering it, according to its quiddity (*Wasgehalt*) and its modality (*Seinsart*), an object of investigation and basic definition."[179]

Man is one being (*Seiendes*) among others, who is involved in the pursuit of science. Now such a pursuit puts him squarely into the midst of that which is. Heidegger explains, "In this 'pursuit' what is happening is nothing less than the irruption of a particular entity called 'Man' into the whole of what-is, in such a way that in and through this irruption, what-is manifests itself *as* and *how* it is. . . . This triple process of world-relationship, attitude, and irruption—a radical unity—introduces something of the inspiring simplicity and intensity of DASEIN into the scientific existence."[180]

Man as DASEIN thus attempts to understand both *what* the world of being *is* and *how* it is (quiddity and modality). Now that to which "the world-relationship refers is what-is—and nothing else. That by which every attitude is moulded is what-is and nothing more. That with which scientific exposition effects its 'irruption is what-is—and beyond that, nothing."[181]

At this point, Heidegger observes that most paradoxically, while science asserts that it deals with "what-is," it must underscore the existence of its surest possession by an appeal to something else. For we have just read, "What is investigated is what-is and *nothing else*: only what-is—and *nothing more*; simply and solely what-is—and beyond that, nothing."[182] Heidegger thus asks, "What is this 'nothing else'?" Is it merely a manner of speaking or is there something more to it? Suppose we reject this *nothing* as being something absolutely null and void. But Heidegger then asks, "But if we abandon Nothing in this way, are we not, by that act, really admitting it?"[183]

Of one thing, we are unconditionally certain: science deals with what-is. It has no interest in anything except what is. Science wishes to know "nothing of nothing." And yet, observes Heidegger, "Even so the fact remains that at the very point where science tries to put its own essence in words, it invokes the aid of Nothing. It has recourse to the very thing it rejects."[184]

From this preliminary observation, Heidegger concludes that while science puts aside the question of this "nothing else," it does so correctly because in reality, the question belongs to metaphysics. Hence nothingness, according to Heidegger, is intimately bound up with the study of being, namely metaphysics. Heidegger now proceeds to elaborate. When we normally speak of "Being," we fail to consider the real heart of the matter. We fail to see that "Being" cannot be identified with any particular kind of being, as for example, a stone, plant, an animal or man. Being is in everything that is. As we have already seen above,[185] Heidegger claims that we have always erroneously concerned ourselves with Tó ὄν (ens), i.e., with some particular, determinate being, rather than with Tó Εἶναι (esse), i.e., that in virtue of which beings are. This, of course, is the transcendent notion of *das Sein* or the Being of beings. As Werner Brock aptly points out, "Heidegger suggests that the problem of 'nothingness,' really understood is intimately and inseparably connected with the problem of 'Being,' only if we have faced the problem of 'nothingness.' In discussing the problem of 'nothingness,' he thus shows how rare it is that we truly meditate upon 'Being.' "[186]

Heidegger now proceeds to examine the nature of nothingness. He tells us that when we ask the question, "What is nothing?", we already postulate nothing as "something that somehow or other is." But the question as to the *what* and *wherefore* of Nothing turns the thing questioned into its opposite. The question deprives itself of its own object."[187] It would seem, therefore, that every answer to this question is impossible from the very start because it necessarily implies that nothingness "is" this, that or the other.

The reason for this situation is that we are now face to face with the most fundamental principle of non-contradiction and the basic law of common logic. Now thinking is always, of its very nature, "thinking about something." But if thinking were to be of nothingness, then thinking would be forced to act against its own nature. Heidegger, therefore, concludes that his inquiry concerning the nature of nothingness already seems to be doomed to failure. But he does detect one faint ray of hope. His inquiry is doomed to failure ONLY if we assume that logic is "the highest court of appeal, that reason is the means and thinking the way to an original comprehension of nothing and its possible revelation."[188]

Heidegger now boldly asks whether perhaps the very laws of logic might not be challenged. Men have always held that nothingness is derived from the general idea of negation. Suppose we now effect a Copernican revolution, muses Heidegger, and put things the other way around. Suppose we hold that nothingness is really the very ground or foundation which makes our negations possible. Heidegger expresses this insight as follows: ". . . is reason so sure just what we are postulating? Does the Not (*das Nichts*), the state of being negated (*die Verneinheit*), in fact represent that higher category under which Nothing takes its place as a special kind of thing negated? Does Nothing 'exist' only because the Not, i.e., negation exists? . . . Or is it the other way about? Does negation and the Not exist only because Nothing exists? . . . *We assert: 'Nothing' is more original than the not and negation.* If this thesis is correct, then the very possibility of negation as an act of reason, and consequently the reason itself, are somehow dependent."[189]

It is obvious from the above quotation, that Heidegger is here positing a priority of nothingness over negation. Negation is possible only because nothingness is first given. As Werner Brock comments, "Heidegger insists that, as long as the 'nothing' is sought for in this field of purely intellectual and abstract thought (i.e., in the realm of formal 'Logic'), it cannot be encountered in its genuine and primary nature. In his view, the 'nothing' is not a derivative of logical negation, but, on the contrary, the logical form of negation and the various kinds of 'not' that may be found and cognised are the outcome and relatively remote derivatives of the 'nothing' given in an actual, if rare, fundamental experience."[190]

James Collins expresses Heidegger's understanding of the priority of nothingness in the following way: "[Nothingness] is more original and primary than our negations. We encounter rather than constitute it, and we are able to encounter it because it is first given to us for acceptance. Hence the naught (nothingness) cannot be demonstrated from a prior premise. It is not an a posteriori explanation but the anterior principle for both our logical acts of negation and our understanding of particular instances of being."[191]

1. *Unitariness of the Whole*

Heidegger accepts as a fact that the totality of all that is can never be grasped by man in the absolute sense. And yet, we do have the phenomenon where we as individual human beings are placed in the midst of a great multitude of beings "within the whole." And while many men subscribe to the actuality of man's being placed amid a great multitude of beings, they fail to admit that this takes place "within the whole." What Heidegger is underscoring here is what he terms the "unitariness" of the *whole,* which we experience in our everyday life. Heidegger says, "As certainly as we shall comprehend absolutely the totality of what-is, it is equally certain that we find ourselves placed in totality. Ultimately there is an essential difference between comprehending the totality of what-is and finding ourselves in the midst of what-is-in-totality. The former is absolutely impossible. The latter is going on in existence all the time."[192]

Werner Brock refers to this "unitariness of the whole" when he says, "No experience, be it of a landscape or of friends or of our own professional activity, is without this width of horizon within which the special persons or things are met and activities performed, to which, from an early time onwards, the name of the 'world' or the 'universe' was attached and which produces a familiar though usually unnoticed atmosphere of unitariness. The mood, the specific *'Gestimmtsein,'* as we know from earlier discussions, evoked in the individual, is the outcome of his being placed concretely amidst the variety of things within the whole."[193]

Nothingness, therefore, has the special function of serving as a kind of structure and intelligibility of Being. Vycinas describes it as follows: "Just as death is that which gives life (in the sense of existence) its fulness and makes it stand out as an organized whole, so nothingness is presupposed to give Being its framework and graspability. DASEIN is related to death, just as BEING is to nothingness. Death and nothingness help to reveal DASEIN and BEING."[194]

Egon Vietta speaks of nothingness as a gap, which being the absolute opposite of being, puts a limit on being, by isolating it and making of it a united whole. He writes, "Without a gap we never would have an insight into that which is. Only where the rocks move apart, does an abyss open. If there were not something (the gap), which contrasts beings in their totality, but only being, if there were no outlets into the totally opposite, being as being could not appear or 'sojourn' for us."[195]

William Richardson describes this particular service which Nothingness renders when he states, "Non-being repels attention from itself and directs There-being's [DASEIN's] gaze, so to speak, to being in their totality, which are thereby discovered again with a fresh appreciation for the fact that they are beings and not Non-being. It is Non-being, then, that renders possible the manifestation of beings as beings. This, however, is precisely the function of *Being* itself. . . . In the Being of beings comes to pass Non-being in its very essence . . . Non-being . . . reveals itself as belonging to the Being of beings."[196]

2. Mood versus Reason

Logic and human reason are, therefore, powerless in proving the existence of nothingness. But if reason fails, man's feelings can help him. Even if we cannot prove nothingness logically, we are capable of experiencing it existentially. And since reason cannot give us this fundamental experience of nothingness, Sciacca points out that, for Heidegger, "The nought making up being is revealed to us by the feeling of anguish, as well as by that of weariness. Being-Nought is not a condition 'mirrored' by the intellect, but a truth (a fundamental truth) that is felt and suffered, an understanding that everything is 'destined' to be lost, a reaching for the primary root of existence . . . the being of beings is Nothingness and anguish is the emotional transparency of existence to itself—that is, the transparency of nothingness which constitutes existence itself. . . . Nothingness does not confront Being, but it is Being itself. 'In the state of anguish, nothingnesss exhibits itself to us simultaneously with the totality of being.' Nought is not a logical category but an ontological category."[197]

The mood wherein nothingness is given to us is always situated within the broad context of the "unity of the whole." An example of this "wholeness" which comes over us, says Heidegger, is to be found in the experience of boredom. When I am bored, this "profound boredom, drifting hither and thither in the abysses of existence like a mute fog, draws all things, all men and oneself along with them, together in a queer kind of indifference. This boredom reveals what-is in totality."[198] Such moods as boredom and joy bring us face to face with "what-is-in-totality" but they do hide the nothingness for which we are searching.

3.   Dread and Nothingness

Heidegger next asks whether there ever exists a mood wherein we are brought to face with nothingness itself. His answer is, "This may and actually does occur albeit rather seldom and for moments only, in the key-mood of dread (Angst)."[199] Heidegger here makes the same distinction which we have already seen between fear and dread in Being and Time.[200] Fear is always of something definite—of an object, a person or some entity, whereas dread involves something completely indefinite. When we experience dread we say that we feel something unknown, indistinct and uncanny. Now this "something" that gives us the uncanny feeling is really nothing definite. We merely "feel" it generally. Heidegger describes it as follows: "All things and we with them, sink into a sort of indifference. But not in the sense that everything simply disappears; rather in the very act of drawing away from us, everything turns towards us. This withdrawal is what oppresses us. There is nothing to hold on to. The only thing that remains and overwhelms us whilst what-is slips away, is this 'nothing.' Dread reveals nothing."[201]

Nothingness, therefore, is revealed in dread but does not reveal itself as something that "is." In other words, nothingness cannot be considered an object, even though its presence is revealed through dread. While nothingness repels in the mood of dread, we ourselves are withdrawing. In our withdrawal, we point to the totality-that-is which is "slipping away" from us. This pointing at, this designation by us, gives a certain "solidification to this totality." It shows that the totality is what it is and at the same time, that it is different from nothingness.[202]

As Werner Brock expresses it so aptly, "The 'nothing' is said essentially not to attract, but to repel, thereby bringing about the withdrawal or retreat on the part of the individual. But while the repelling force is thought to emanate from 'nothing,' experienced in the state of dread, the attention of the individual is drawn and fixed to the things in the world, as they slide away and sink; it is as if the 'nothing' in repelling the individual was pointing to them, inducing him to get a proper hold of them, impossible as this is in the very state of dread. . . . It is the essence of nothingness to press, through dread, upon the DASEIN of the individual, by repelling and enforcing a withdrawal, by making the things in the world slide away out of reach and yet by directing and fixing the attention of the powerless man on them. (Heidegger here coins the word *nichten* to designate nothingness at work, i.e., as it nothings or is nothinging.) . . . Against the background of 'nothingness,' a background of horror and awe, the things in the world begin to stand out as what they actually are. And with this experience of the 'nothing' behind him, man is endowed with the power and made ready to grasp reality itself."[203] Heidegger sums it up in a few words: "The essence of Nothing

as original nihilation lies in this: that it alone brings
DASEIN face to face with what-is as such."[204]

Heidegger now proceeds to answer the question,
"What about Nothing?", which he posed at the beginning
of the lecture. He says, "Nothing is neither an object nor
anything that 'is' at all. Nothing occurs neither by itself
nor 'apart from' what-is, as a sort of adjunct. Nothing is
that which makes the revelation of what-is as such
possible for our human existence. Nothing not merely
provides the conceptual opposite of what-is but it also
is an original part of essence (*Wesen*). It is in the Being
(*Sein*) of what-is that the nihilation of Nothing (*das
Nichten des Nichts*) occurs."[205]

William Richardson describes nothingness as given
in dread. He says, "It is no thing and nowhere. We call
it No-thing, i.e., Non-being (*Nichts*). But even as these
things seem to slip away, they light up for him with a
startling strangeness that leaves him struck with wonder
at the simple fact that they 'are.' Thus in the '. . . effulgent
night of Non-being (disclosed by) anxiety, there occurs
for the first time the original open-ness of beings as such;
that they are beings and not non-being.' Much has been
said of Heidegger's so-called nihilism in meditating on
Non-being (*Nichts*), but the sense of it is clear. It is
simply an attempt to bring the scientist to an experience
of Being as he understands it, but if one approaches it in
the context of beings as the scientist must, the most that
can be said about it, initially at least, is that it is not-a-
being."[206]

Twenty years later, Heidegger had this to say concerning the nature of nothingness or no-thing: "From
the viewpoint of scientific (thinking) that knows only
beings, what is wholly and completely not a being (namely
Being) offers itself as Non-being. That is why the lecture
asks about *this* Non-being. . . . It asks: What about that
which is wholly other than each and every being, that
which is not a being?"[207]

Thomas Langan with his customary incisiveness
describes for us DASEIN's experience of nothingness and
the particular service which this experience renders to

man. The clarity with which DASEIN perceives his position with respect to the rest of beings in reality is presented as follows: "The metaphysician never discovered that the fundamental experience of the basis of this relation is that anguish before my death in which I am afforded a compelling grip on the reality of my contingency. In the vision of the last moment, I see literally everything slipping away together, dissolving in the gloom of an all-pervading Nothing. It is thus that I come to see that the presence of anything and everything before me is a united whole, as I also see that it is due to nothing other than my own finite horizon-projection. I see for the first time clearly, that the *Seienden als Ganzen* (the totality of the things-that-are) could not 'be' without my DASEIN, and at the same time I realize that the apparent solidity of that 'world' of things offers no lasting thing upon which I can depend as a protection from the dissolution of the world in death."[208]

Heidegger now concludes that his inquiry into the nature of nothingness will lead us directly to metaphysics itself. Inasmuch as metaphysics studies being, nothingness will thus enable us to understand being. He states, "Non-being (nothingness) is that which makes the revelation of what-is (being) as such possible for our human existence (i.e., for DASEIN)."[209]

IV. HEIDEGGER II (THE LATER HEIDEGGER)

The sum of Heidegger's efforts in *Being and Time* can be described as one sustained analysis, by means of the phenomenological method, of the metaphysical structure of DASEIN. As we have already seen above,[210] it is precisely because DASEIN is "that being who in his being is concerned with Being itself," that Heidegger hoped to arrive at a knowledge of the Being of beings, through an in-depth existential analysis of man himself. That is why many writers have characterized *Being and Time* as an anthropology in the service of ontology. The dominant theme during this period of Heidegger's life was DASEIN, i.e., man as "being-in-the-world." Man was Heidegger's starting point and man was his total preoccupation. This

"DASEIN Period" is frequently referred to as the period of *Heidegger I*.[211]

We now come to the *Kehre* or *turning*, to the period of "poetic thought." This period began with Heidegger's writing, *The Essence of the Ground* in 1929 and it is the so-called period of *Heidegger II*. The second period makes a very sharp and definite shift from the thought of the Heidegger of *Being and Time*, for we find that Being rather than DASEIN is the starting point. As John Macquarrie expresses it, "The earlier phase of Heidegger's thinking was dominated by the inquiry into human existence, though this inquiry was undertaken not for its own sake, but as the most promising way into the question of Being. The later phase is concerned directly with being and man himself is now understood in the light of Being."[212]

Herbert Spiegelberg describes the shift in emphasis. He says, "Perhaps the most startling change in the content of Heidegger's later thought is that Being, the distant goal of *Sein und Zeit*, suddenly appears to be so close and manifest that hardly any special approach or method seems to be needed to discover it. After the 438 pages of *Sein und Zeit*, which constantly stressed our utter ignorance of the meaning of Being, in fact our unawareness of the question, and which made Being seem the darkest possible mystery, to be approached via *human being* and even via the experience of nothingness, it now appears that Being is essentially open and unconcealed all the time and that we have direct access to it, provided we do not forget it."[213]

Not only does Heidegger shift his focus of attention from DASEIN to DA-SEIN (from man to Being) but he does much more. He has definitely postponed and now, it would seem completely abandoned, the notion of writing the remaining parts of *Being and Time*. As originally planned, the third section of the first half of *Being and Time* was to be entitled *Time and Being* and it was this portion of the work which would give us the final and definitive answer concerning the meaning of the Being of beings. But in his *Letter on Humanism*, Heidegger tells us that this section was "held back because thinking failed in the attempt to express adequately the turning (*Kehre*) from *Zeit und Sein*—and did not reach its goal by using the language of metaphysics."[214]

Heidegger's concern in this *post-Being and Time* period is with the discovery of a totally new type of thought which would best express the meaning of Being in human language. And so we detect an increasing hostility on Heidegger's part towards the traditional language of metaphysics. Gradually we find a total rejection of the conventional precise terminology of metaphysics and in its place, we are offered a completely new kind of "poetic" or "originative" thought.[215] J. Glenn Gray tells us, "Heidegger is convinced that poets can come to the aid of thinkers now, when the latter are so out of touch with the sources of being. The importance of poetry has steadily grown in his estimation to the point where it appears to overshadow systematic philosophic analysis. . . . Heidegger's interest in poets is in their ontological significance, the truths they can teach us about man's way of dwelling on earth."[216]

And because DASEIN is essentially limited by time and death, Heidegger concludes that this finitude on man's part, makes it impossible for him to act as a kind of threshold to the house of Being. Once again, Heidegger concludes that this deficiency on the part of both traditional metaphysics and DASEIN, can be righted only by seeking some less rigid and more pliant type of thought that will render Being unconcealed.[217]

A. . Failure of Metaphysics

As we have already seen, Heidegger contends that the whole of Western metaphysics has been guilty of the "forgetting of Being." Since the time of Plato, men have allowed Being to fall into oblivion because in their philosophical investigations, they have failed to rise above the level of *ontic* knowledge. Such knowledge on the ontic level deals only with this or that particular being instead of concerning itself with the Being of beings, which is the only valid object of metaphysics. The level of *ontolo-*

gical knowledge dealing with the Being of beings has completely escaped traditional metaphysics.[218]

Heidegger deplores the present state of philosophical bankruptcy in which modern man finds himself. And because Western thought has failed to distinguish between beings and Being, metaphysics has been completely helpless in dealing with the question of GOD, BEING and the HOLY. In reality, metaphysics has become an *onto-theo-logy.* As Heidegger asserts, "Metaphysics is *onto-theo-logy.* (It fails to distinguish between Being and beings.) Anyone who has, through his own development, experienced theology, whether that of Christian faith or that of philosophy, nowadays prefers to be silent about God, so far as thinking is concerned. . . . For the onto-theo-logical character of metaphysics has become questionable to thinking people, not because of some kind of atheism, but because of an experience of thinking in which the still unthought unity of the essence of metaphysics revealed itself in onto-theo-logy."[219]

Heidegger's complaint is that metaphysics, which has degenerated into an onto-theo-logy, employs concepts no longer acceptable to man. The forms of representative thinking which traditional metaphysics uses cannot give us any valid information about the true Being or the true God. Heidegger insists that Western metaphysics has never been able to arrive at the notion of a true God. He steadfastly maintains that it is absolutely impossible for the human intellect to move from beings, finite and contingent, to a Being, who is necessary and infinite. As long as man starts with be-ings, he will always end in a be-ing, even though he calls it a Supreme be-ing. Now such a be-ing can never be the true God. And so, Heidegger argues, traditional metaphysics, considered from this point of view, is actually atheistic. Parenthetically, we might point out that just as Kierkegaard and Marcel, Heidegger rejects here categorically the possibility of a natural theology, whereby the human intellect could move from the contingent to the necessary, from the finite to the infinite.[220]

At best, traditional metaphysics can arrive only at a

God who is "the Cause as *causa sui* and this is the appropriate name for God in philosophy. To this God, man
cannot pray or bring a sacrifice," complains Heidegger.
"Before the *causa sui*, man cannot fall on his knees in
awe, nor can he play music, or dance for Him. In this
sense, godless thinking, which must give up the God of
philosophy, God as *causa sui*, is perhaps closer to the
'godly' God. In this context that means that God-less
thinking is freer for Him than onto-theo-logic would be
willing to admit."[221]

From the above quotation, it becomes quite apparent
that Heidegger finds no hope for metaphysical thinking
in the traditional sense. Joseph Kockelmans describes
Heidegger's quarrel with metaphysics as follows: "All
philosophical terms which have been standardized by
metaphysics become insufficient and misleading as soon
as one penetrates into the dimension of Being itself. How
could one still speak here about substance, unity, act,
subject, foundation, ground, principle, spirit, or God,
since all these terms have already been appropriated by
a philosophy that has forgotten Being itself but continues
to speak about the being of beings? Lack of words makes
a thinker now practically helpless before Being. One
must even admit that it remains open to question whether
'the Western languages have been stamped exclusively
with that of onto-theo-logic' or whether these languages
offer other possibilities of speaking as well as of saying
nothing while speaking."[222]

B.   Hölderlin and Poetic Thought

Having convinced himself of the utter failure of
twenty-five centuries of metaphysical thought, Heidegger
now turns to poetry as offering us some hope for the future.
The new modes of thinking which poetry utilizes are in
the strict sense "originative." These new poetical modes
of thinking reject the "representative" forms of traditional philosophy. Poetry will have nothing to do with
such static and rigid notions as essence or be-ing, which
metaphysics has canonized and enshrined on its altars.
Poetry must be free of all logical terms and expressions; it

cannot be hemmed in and circumscribed by the rigidity of representative thinking.[223]

Heidegger speaks glowingly of the special office of the poet in establishing rapport with the Being of beings. He says, "The poet names the gods and names all things in that which they are. This naming does not consist merely in something already known, being supplied with a name; it is, rather, that when the poet speaks the essential word, the existent is by this naming nominated as what it is. So it becomes known *as* existent. Poetry is the establishing of being by means of the word. . . . Being is never an existent. But because being and essence of things can never be calculated and derived from what is present, they must be freely created, laid down and given. Such a free act is establishment. . . . If we conceive the essence of poetry as the establishing of being by means of the word, then we can have some inkling of the truth of that saying which Hölderlin spoke long after he had been received into the protection of the night of lunacy."[224] For Martin Heidegger, then, the poetry of Friedrich Hölderlin is the best exemplification of the service that the poet can render to man in his search for God, the holy and the Being of beings.

C. Friedrich Hölderlin

Let us now take a closer look at Friedrich Hölderlin, the man. Hölderlin (1770-1843, like Heidegger, was a native of Swabia. He studied theology at the University of Tübingen and while there, the poet met and associated with Schelling, Hegel, Fichte, Goethe and Schiller. And while his friends Fichte, Schelling and Hegel achieved fame and were held in high esteem as scholars, Hölderlin always lived on the brink of poverty and obscurity. He became involved in an unhappy love affair with the wife of a wealthy Frankfurt banker. The result of this experience clouded his entire life. He became bitter and disillusioned. Rejected and dejected, he lived like a "loner" (not unlike the hero of his novel, *Hyperion*), brooding over his inability to become an accepted member of society. He tried to find consolation in the writing of poetry which sought to find in nature, art and love, a kind of fusion of the divine. Hölderlin had an unsurpassed love and admiration for the Greek poets, in whom he found (as Nietzsche would later), the well-known opposition and tension between the orgiastic Dionysian exuberance, on the one hand, and the calm, rational Apollonian composure and serenity, on the other. Somewhat anticipatory of Nietzsche's tragic finale, Hölderlin spent the last thirty-seven years of his life, suffering from a mental derangement.[225]

D.   Poetry and Waiting for God

While the poet is incalculably better equipped than the metaphysician to speak of God and the holy, we must not raise our hopes prematurely. Heidegger cautions us that we are living in "the night of the world" in which the gods in whom men should believe are no longer—yet a new god has not arrived. The present time must, therefore, be understood as a "time of waiting for the holy and for the gods." We must not become impatient, during this time of expectancy.

As Kurt Reinhardt describes this period, "The age in which Hölderlin lived and wrote is, with only minor modifications, also the age and cultural environment of Kierkegaard, Nietzsche and Heidegger; an age in which 'the old gods' have sunk into oblivion and the 'new God' has not yet appeared. God 'withholds his presence' and 'holy names are lacking.' In the modern age, 'the God remains afar,' no matter how hard man labors to fill the void by the invention of substitute 'gods.' In such an age, the one necessary thing is, according to Heidegger, to preserve and be ready for the time when the word that could reverently and convincingly 'name' the High One will be granted again."[226]

F. H. Heinemann looks somewhat unsympathetically on Heidegger's claim that he is offering something more satisfactory than the metaphysics he claims to dislodge. Heinemann believes, "Heidegger destroys the basis of the preceding metaphysics without being able to lay the foundations for a new one. . . . [As a result] Heidegger's latest nihilistic ontology . . . bears witness to the 'night of Europe' (A. Camus) which he, following Hölderlin, prefers to call *Weltnacht* (world-night). *Weltnacht* designates an age, in which the old gods are dead and the new gods are not yet born. God is absent; He withholds Himself: there is no god who visibly and univocally could unite men, fill the world with splendour and give meaning to it. The time is barren for it does not even notice God's absence. Nothingness has replaced God. . . . Yet this extreme nihilism is counterbalanced by positive tendencies. The 'deputy of Nothingness' (*Platzhalter des Nichts*) is simultaneously the 'shepherd of Being' (*Hirte des Seins*). He knows that only the Christian God, but not God Himself, is dead. Like Nietzsche, he remains in search of God and it is in this search that he turns to poets such as Hölderlin and Rilke, because he holds that the poets name gods and that it is they who discover their traces."[227]

H. J. Blackham sees Heidegger as viewing our present age as "post-theological and post-metaphysical." He says, "As Heidegger characteristically puts it in his interpretation of the poet Hölderlin, the time is a time of need because it lies under a double negation, the no-more of the gods that have fled and the not-yet of the god that is coming. . . . The present phase is post-theological and post-metaphysical: it is with the recognition that God is dead and that man has no standpoint outside the totality of things that man must approach again in this age, the problem of Being."[228]

Rudolph Gerber characterizes Heidegger's efforts as follows: "Poetic thought replaces analysis, calculative endeavors yield to originative thinking, truth as correctness of proposition gives way to truth as unconcealment, and conceptualization (*Denken*) becomes a combined emotional-intellectual activity (*Danken*) literally 'thanking' . . . such a notion of metaphysical thought reflects a quasi-idealistic immanentism, whereby Being appears purely immanent to DASEIN. Being is 'humanized,' man is 'instrumentalized' and philosophy, for Heidegger, becomes paradoxically realized when it abdicates to a non-categorical expression which affirms, in its poetical passivity, the reality and nature of Being which is separable from the being of man."[229]

Laszlo Versenyi is of the opinion that Heidegger's attempt to transcend metaphysics inevitably leads him to obscurity and contradiction. He writes, "Heidegger's going beyond metaphysics would require a corresponding going beyond language, a complete relinquishing of the use of words that have meaning within, and only within, the disclosure of a world and in reference to the beings in the world thus disclosed. . . . Heidegger's real trouble is that any language *qua* language is metaphysical—a finite disclosure of Being within finite horizons of disclosure—and Heidegger's attempts to ignore this, only result in straining language beyond its limits, and producing a welter of ambiguity, obscurity, contradiction and paradox rather than meaningful disclosure."[230]

Pierre Thévenaz charges Heidegger with a deliberate forgetfulness or rejection of the history of philosophy. He writes, "If the first going-beyond established a metaphysics and the second excludes it, we cannot, in spite of the protests of the author, interpret the first approach in function of the second and refuse the second precisely in the name of the first. It is rather improbable that the later Heidegger will be called upon to fecundate philosophical thought to the extent that the early Heidegger did. And if the distinction of Being from beings should lead finally to the discrediting of metaphysics, it is because Heidegger did not succeed in incorporating in it the substance of the Western metaphysical tradition. Rejected or forgotten history takes its revenge as much, if not more than, the forgetfulness of Being. In reality, neither the meta-metaphysics, nor the metaphysics of interiority, nor of the act, nor the metaphysics of the *cogito*, nor that of Kant was oriented towards beings. Unfortunately, Heidegger has not rendered justice to all these attempts. He has chosen to dismiss them as concerned only with beings—in which he sees an ancient illusion as well as an obstacle that is all too present."[231]

Finally, Paul Roubiczek is convinced that literature cannot do the work of philosophy and Heidegger's efforts to define "being" leave much to be desired. He says, "The absolute existentialist in general, and Heidegger in particular, try to make philosophy do what literature could do. The unity of existence can be experienced when a work of art or the evocative language of poetry appeal to our feelings, but it cannot be expressed in philosophical or abstract terms. When Heidegger finally tries to define 'being' directly, he fails, for he defines it as 'constant presentness' and varies this definition in several ways. He therefore concludes by quoting a few lines from Hölderlin which, by their beauty, awaken a strong feeling and thus cover up the emptiness of the actual definition and the wrongness of the attempt to make experience provide us with ultimate knowledge."[232]

E. Theism or Atheism

One of the most enigmatic aspects of Heidegger's entire philosophical career has been his persistent refusal to be categorized either as a theist or an atheist. The famous Heideggerian notion of man as DASEIN, whereby it is impossible to speak of a definite human nature or essence, the thrownness of DASEIN, the refusal to subscribe to the Principle of Sufficient Reason, the position that existence precedes essence, that man is temporality and Being nothingness, that the Being of beings whereby beings are, cannot be identified with God—all these philosophical stances led men to classify Heidegger as an atheist.

As a matter of fact, the discerning Jean Paul Sartre wrote in his *Existentialism is a Humanism* the following words: "The question (of definition) is only complicated because there are two kinds of existentialism. There are, on the one hand, the Christians, amongst whom I shall name Jaspers and Gabriel Marcel, both professed Catholics; and on the other, the existential atheists, *amongst whom we must place Heidegger as well as the French existentialists and myself*. What they have in common is simply the fact that they believe that existence comes before essence—or, if you will, that we must begin from the subjective."[233]

Heidegger vehemently rejected Sartre's description of his philosophy as atheistic. As a matter of fact, he contended that his philosophy was neither theistic nor atheistic. In a letter to Jean Beaufret, *Letter on Humanism,* 1946, Heidegger maintained that his thinking is neither anti-God nor theistic. He writes, "This philosophy distinguishes itself neither for nor against the DASEIN of God. It remains ensconced in indifference. Thus the religious question is to it 'all the same.' Nihilism does not achieve such an indifferentism."[234]

And so while Heidegger did repudiate the label "atheist," he nevertheless would not allow himself to be described as a theistic thinker. As James Collins observes, "It is significant that the German thinker rejected the atheistic variety of existentialism in such a way that he did not at the same time, reinstate either theism or the theory of religion as topics within his own philosophy."[235]

Thomas Langan, in commenting on Heidegger's letter to Jean Beaufret, tells us that Heidegger's "indifference" to which he refers, is not an end in itself but it is rather preparatory for a more positive goal or purpose. Specifically, Heidegger wants to get beyond the religious position of the 19th century atheism "not by opening the door to a new theism, but by getting completely beyond the God-murdering time of Nietzsche into a time when God is as irrelevant as the gods, in the way of Camus' Meursault is beyond Ivan Karamazov."[236] Secondly, Heidegger seeks to preserve the mystery of the dimension of the Holy. Now the question of God cannot even be brought up "until the dimension of the Holy, which as a dimension remains closed to us, is reopened and the illumination of Being is rediscovered."[237]

Langan goes on to elaborate his position when he says, "The notion of the *Heilige* is bound to remain perfectly incomprehensible to Heidegger's readers, and is destined therefore to continue to receive personal interpretations, as long as it is not understood in the context of

Heidegger's active *Denken*. It is only when we admit that Heidegger is seeking to restore the full richness of all human existence in every department of its historical manifestation, from religion to art and politics, *without God*, locating the center of the mystery of the inexhaustible richness of existence not in a transcendent God but in Being conceived as the finite relation of DASEIN to the things that are, that we can hope to understand what the *Heilige* represents. One should never forget that Heidegger wanders the 'forest trails' already worked out by Zarathustra."[238]

Langan concludes the above analysis with the following remarks: ". . . a Christian will never find in the Heideggerian *Denken* the intellectual footing a life of faith requires. The Christian who would be at the same time a Heideggerian, will have difficulty compartmentalizing his life. For the Heideggerian philosophy is, in my opinion, not just neutral to the notion of the transcendent; it sets out to explain *without* the transcendent everything that has up to now needed a transcendent for its explanation.[239]

A large number of scholars tend to agree that, in spite of Heidegger's eloquent protestations of neutrality, Heideggerianism is an atheism. We shall submit a number of excerpts for the reader's consideration and judgment.

Helmut Kuhn, in his *Encounter With Nothingness* has the following to say: "Heidegger has repeatedly repudiated the imputation of atheism in *Vom Vesen des Grundes* (p. 28, note), and more recently in an interview where he said that, while not denying God, he stated his absence: 'My philosophy is a waiting for God' (*Partisan Review*, April, 1948, p. 511). We need not quarrel with this assertion. But we must note that it is difficult to imagine a more effective exclusion of God from human vision than is achieved in *Sein und Zeit*. The idea of transcendence, ancient bridge connecting this world with God, is so twisted as to become the basis of finitism. The circuit of power that is to proceed from God to His creatures is enclosed within the walls of human finitude.

In Kierkegaard's terms, this is a philosophical expression of the demonic, the language of passion, locked up in the chamber of inwardness."[240]

Michele Sciacca examines in detail a number of Heideggerian themes and concludes with these words, "Heidegger's latest writings contain, according to some interpreters, the cues, cautiously stated or hardly hinted at, of a new orientation toward the positivity of Being. In our opinion, the so-called last Heidegger is still the first Heidegger, the one found in *Sein und Zeit* and in the other minor works. It is true that Heidegger in his *Letter on Humanism* rejects the atheistic interpretation of his thought; yet all that can be read in it is still a confirmation of his absolute dogmatic and preconceived atheism. To say that 'through the existential determination of man nothing has been decided concerning the *existence of God* or his *non-being*' and that consequently, theological Transcendence is a 'possibility' toward which existence is still 'open,' amounts to saying nothing, because, as long as Being is Nothingness, such a possibility can only signify the identification of God with the Nought; it amounts to repeating the old position maintained by the 'first Heidegger,' wherein Being is Nothingness. As long as Heidegger does not abandon this position (that is, his 'metaphysics'), though he speaks about something divine revealed to men by poetry (*Hölderlin and the Essence of Poetry*) and about truth as a 'revelation' (*Unverborgenheit*) of being to the existent, or as an overture (*Offenheit*) of the existent toward being, he still repeats the same identical things with equivocal words which, perhaps, signify that he himself is aware of the insurmountable difficulties of his philosophy."[241]

Karl Löwith, in his *Nature, History and Existentialism*, has this to say of his former professor's philosophical position, "Heidegger's entanglement of death, guilt, and conscience in a DASEIN responsible to itself alone, uproots these concepts from their Christian source, but for that very reason, they are dependent upon that origin. . . . All of them originated in the *Christian tradition*, however much death, conscience, guilt, care, anxiety and corruption are formalized ontologically and neutralized as concepts of the DASEIN. . . . The Heidegger of *Being and Time,* however, is no sceptic but a godless 'Christian theologian.' Therefore suicide for Heidegger is neither sin nor freedom, but an act of 'despair.' Suicide is not a case of dying at the proper time, as Nietzsche taught, in accordance with the classical model, but in the style of an anti-Christian sermon."[242]

Laszlo Versenyi makes this perceptive observation in his work, *Heidegger, Being and Truth,* "In spite of Heidegger's claim that his thinking is neither theistic nor atheistic (*Hum.* 37), he has overcome humanistic metaphysics—as well as philosophy—only by becoming a mystic poet and godless theologian. To be sure, his faith has no articulate creed (but this is not necessary for mysticism either) and no God or gods (as some religions do not either). But for all that, the relationship between resemblance to the God-man relationship that is the subject of theology; the language he now uses is most analogous in its structure to theological language; and his ambiguous passion for Being is most like faith's passion for God."[243]

For Cornelio Fabro, atheism is the only position which Heidegger can logically espouse. He writes, "Heidegger's own thought, both in the earlier and in the later Heidegger, is in the tradition of Kant; pure reflective thought cannot attain to the assertion of God and is powerless to decide the God-problem; God is at best solely the object of religious experience, not of philosophy.

Perspicacious theologians allege that reason and faith are irreconcilably opposed in the Heideggerian conception: what Heidegger styles 'openness' to *Sein* (Being), a Being which is intrinsically finite, necessarily involves and imposes its own ontologico-metaphysical 'closedness' to all transcendence and revelation in the sense of religion as a doctrine of salvation (*Heilslehre*) for the world in thrall to the radically lethal powers of error and death. The Heideggerian stand, contending that the human *logos* is intrinsically atheistic constitutes the most radical inherent atheism."[244]

Martin Buber complains that Heidegger's existence is monological; there is no genuine *mit-sein* and hence there is no room for the Absolute Thou. In his *Between Man and Man*, he says, "Heidegger turns away not merely from a relation to a divine unconditioned being, but also from a relation in which man experiences another than himself in the unconditioned, and so experiences the unconditioned. Heidegger's 'existence' is monological. And monologue may certainly disguise itself ingeniously for a while as dialogue, one unknown layer after the other of the human self may certainly answer the inner address, so that man makes ever fresh discoveries and can suppose that he is really experiencing a 'calling' and a 'hearing'; but the hour of stark, final solitude comes when the dumbness of being becomes insuperable and the ontological categories no longer want to be applied to reality. When the man who has become solitary can no longer say 'Thou' to the 'dead' known God, everything depends on whether he can still say it to the living unknown God by saying 'thou' with all his being to another living and known man. If he can no longer do this either, then there certainly remains for him the sublime illusion of detached thought that he is a self-contained self; as man he is lost. . . . Heidegger isolates from the wholeness of life, the realm in which man is related to himself, since he absolutizes the temporally conditioned situation of the radically solitary man and wants to derive the essence of human existence from the experience of a nightmare."[245]

In a somewhat similar vein, William Luijpen complains in his *Existential Phenomenology* that the Heideggerian man is condemned to isolation and dread. He has been deprived of the love of his fellow man. To that extent, Heidegger's man is "a mutilated man." Luijpen writes, "Is it a mere coincidence that love finds no place in Heidegger's works? In dread, man's most proper possibility reveals itself, for in dread man stands *alone, isolated*, before the extreme possibility of his potential being, in dread man is eminently an "I." This revelation calls upon man to make the only proper reply—namely 'resolve,' a radical 'no' to the world. His authentic being

himself is not the lonely, isolated, doomed-to-death being-in-the-world, but being-together with his fellow man
in love. In love, the world shows man a face that is
entirely different from the one described by Heidegger.
What Heidegger says may be true of the unloved
'Barracks-type of man' (Marcel), but one who loves cannot speak in this way. Man cannot live without being
loved but, on the other hand, neither can he die without
love. Whoever faces death alone, isolated, will curse the
world-as-world and being-in-the-world-as-such. But such
a man is a mutilated human being."[246]

Dietrich Bonhoeffer, in his *Akt und Sein*, states apodic-
tically, "Heidegger's philosophy is a *consciously and deliberately atheistic philosophy of finitude*. In this philosophy, everything is biassed by the instrumentality of There-
being (DASEIN) to the 'closedness' of finitude as such. The
closed conception of finitude is crucial for the existential
analysis of There-being. The solidary 'closedness' here
involved can no longer be separated from finitude. The
existential being-potential, like all other existential features of There-being is revealed, not as a generic existential
feature of finite There-being, but rather as essentially
conditioned by the 'closedness' of finitude. The philosophical concept of finitude is in its very essence a concept
of closed finitude. *There is therefore no room left for the
notion of revelation*: and all concepts of being must
therefore be recast in the light of the recognition imposed
by revelation that finitude as creatureliness is open for
God. And so, despite its powerful broadening influence
due to its disclosure of the existential sphere, the Heideggerian concept of being must be said to be unusable for
theology."[247]

Gabriel Marcel, on the other hand, does not feel that
Heidegger should be classified with the atheists. At the
same time, he finds the inherent ambiguity in Heidegger's
thought as vitiating any possible basis for a meaningful
theology. He writes, "I will observe in passing, moreover,
that by the avowal of Heidegger himself . . . it is not fitting
to classify him among the atheists, or to regard his doctrine
as atheism. His thought, he said, is in suspense on the

problem of the existence of God.... It must be repeated that Heidegger refuses to be classified among the atheists, that in certain respects his thought presents more and more as oriented towards a certain resacralization. And this helps to reinforce the feeling of profound ambiguity which one experiences in reading this difficult philosopher, no doubt the most profound of our time, but the *least capable of formulating anything resembling clear directives, of effectively orienting the young people who turn to him as a guide.*"[248]

In addition to the vexing question of theism-atheism in Heideggerian thought, there are other troublesome aspects of Heidegger's ontology that demand closer scrutiny. Thomas Langan, for example, finds Heidegger's notion of DASEIN extremely frustrating and unsatisfying. He says, "The DASEIN comes from we know not where, destined to an end that makes little sense, impelled by a need that cannot be fulfilled, and energized by an originativeness of freedom which draws its newness from the Nothing. The DASEIN is 'thrown' into the world, the origins of his having the peculiar impulses he possesses unknown. Whatever their origin (and therefore their sense) may be, these impulses are destined to obliteration in death, except for a lingering trace of historical influence that can survive the personal annihilation. . . . Who is this DASEIN that wanders in the service of a partial and always dissimulating revelation of Being toward a death that ends, not fulfills, his quest for whatever it is he seeks? That is the worst part about the Heideggerian existent: that he has not personal reality. The servant of Being making present the past in the light of a projection toward the future, has no proper reality of his own, nothing that does not slip through the fingers like the sands of time, nothing that can *confront* the other as other because it itself is a definite someone."[249]

According to Laszlo Versenyi, Heidegger's search for the Being of beings ends in complete emptiness and negativity. He states, "In his overcoming of metaphysics, Heidegger overextended reason's demand for continued form-giving, defining, de-limiting, and disclosing into a demand for the ultimate and absolute completeness of all definition and disclosure, and thus he ended up with a negative, limiting concept, an empty transcendental idea (of absolutely transcendent Being). In his overcoming of humanistic ethics, he overextends the existential, onto-teleological demand of human nature (for continued self-transcendence) and thus ends up with an empty, totally negative notion of a transcendent existence."[250]

Rudolph Gerber states succinctly, "Scholastic-oriented critics cannot fail to see, in the first place, that Being is not identical with God and, in the second, that Heidegger's ontological distinction allows no analogical or causal ascent to Being from an inductive analysis of the beings of the experiential world. Apart from several notions of *phusis*, Being remains indefinable. Any resulting Heideggerian metaphysics could hardly expect to escape this ineffable agnosticism which hangs like midnight darkness around its most central focus."[251]

James Collins finds that Heidegger's notion of the Being of beings is not sufficient because it is too limited and restricted. He explains, "It remains an open question whether the predication of 'to be' may not be extended also to the reality of God. The concept of being, as resident in our minds, is certainly finite. Some intrinsic adjustment is required, so that Heidegger can say of both being it-self and that-which-is that they *are*. Moreover, he recognizes that it may be applied more properly in the former case than in the latter. The way is open for extending the meaning of being beyond the act whereby finite things receive finite being."[252]

Michael Wyschogrod is of the opinion that Heidegger's attempt to create a new ontology is a dismal failure. He argues, "It does not seem possible for Heidegger to take the experiences that lie at the basis of human existence and to view them from a point of view other than in-volvement in the experiences themselves. To do so would be analogous to converting existence into essence, thereby making possible an intelligible discussion of the subject, but at the same time, losing that element which makes existence, personal or otherwise, not essence. The destruction of the factuality of existence which results from such a procedure is analogous to the detached objectivity of Heidegger's ontology which, on the human level, destroys the existential element of involvement and subjective appropriation, the characteristics of existence."[253]

Michele Sciacca finds Heidegger's rejection of the doctrine of creation as vitiating his entire metaphysics. He states, "First of all, we deny that a DASEIN, an ego, a subject, can emerge from Nothingness. From Nothing comes nothing and least of all, as Heidegger claims, an *ens*, that is ego. The *ens* can come out ex nihilo only through the creative act of God. In other words, a metaphysics that makes the world rise from Nothingness is a creative one by implication; if it excludes God's creative act, it also excludes the birth of the world from Nothingness and so it must follow another way out (the world exists *ab æterno;* it springs forth from a primary principle—air, fire or whatever it may be—that is, from an original and living matter and so on). Ancient metaphysics was right on this point. Heidegger rejects creation (naturally, he denies the existence of a creative God) and yet, he has *omne ens* be born *ex nihilo,* thus gratuitously affirming an absurd hypothesis: the *ens* comes from Nothing, without a God creating *ex nihilo.*"[254]

Finally, F. H. Heinemann sees Heidegger as the personification of *heroic defiance*. He tells us, "Heidegger represents a specific form of alienation, i.e., the despair of an individual who desperately wants to be himself, inaugurating a new world era of philosophic thought. His attitude, the only one considered adequate to the encounter with Nothingness, is one of *heroic defiance*. He writes in *defiance* of traditional terminology, grammar, thought, metaphysics, logic and ethics; and in so doing he introduces an unbearable jargon and ungrammatical usage of verbs. He bids defiance to the traditional understanding of 'truth,' to all interpreters of his philosophy and to all existentialists, to humanism, and even to God; for 'the It' (*das Es*) or 'the Being' is claimed to be higher than God. He defies eternity for the sake of time. It is exactly as Kierkegaard said: 'Whereas the weak despairer will not hear about the comfort eternity has for him, so neither will such a despairer hear about it, but for a different reason, namely because this comfort would be the destruction of him as an objection against the whole of existence.' This is Heidegger's case, through defiance to absurdity."[255]

Jean Paul Sartre

CHAPTER SIX

JEAN PAUL SARTRE
LIFE

I. EARLY YEARS

Jean Paul Sartre was born in Paris on June 21, 1905, the son of Jean-Baptiste and Anne Marie Sartre. On his mother's side of the family, Sartre is a Schweitzer. His maternal grandfather was Charles Schweitzer, author and professor of German and inventor of the "direct method" of teaching foreign languages.[1] Through this relation, Jean Paul is a second cousin of the world-famous missionary and doctor, Albert Schweitzer.

Jean Paul's father, Jean-Baptiste, a marine engineer, died from a fever contracted in Indo-China, shortly after Jean Paul's birth. Like Marcel and Camus, Jean Paul Sartre was orphaned in his earliest years. After his father's untimely death, Sartre and his mother, Anne Marie, moved into the home of Charles Schweitzer, his maternal grandfather. In order to support his daughter and grandson, Professor Schweitzer, who had recently retired from teaching, now founded the Modern Language Institute, which "taught French by the direct method to foreigners who were in Paris."[2] Charles Schweitzer was a hard working and dedicated scholar, but a doting grandfather who regarded his little grandson, in the words of Jean Paul, as a "favor of fate, as a gratuitous and always revocable gift . . . whose mere presence filled him to overflowing."[3] He would call Jean Paul "his tiny little one in a voice quavering with tenderness and his cold eyes would dim with tears."[4]

The grandfather who was the undisputed head of the household, wore a large flowing beard and became for Jean Paul a personification of authority, almost a "God-figure." Of him, Jean Paul recalls in his autobiography, "There remained the patriarch. He so resembled God the

Father that he was often taken for him . . . beard flowing in the wind, body erect, feet at right angles, chest out, arms wide open."[5]

The spiritual poverty in the Schweitzer home was ultimately responsible for the atheism which became Sartre's way of life. His grandfather, a Protestant, "who never missed the opportunity," as Jean Paul tells us, "to ridicule Catholicism . . . was too much of an actor not to need a Great Spectator, though he hardly thought of God except in his good moments. As he was sure of finding Him in the hour of his death, he kept him out of his life."[6]

The grandmother and Sartre's mother, who were non-practising, nominal Catholics, could provide Jean Paul with no example of authentic Christian living. Of them, Sartre writes, "On Sunday, the two ladies sometimes go to Mass, to hear good music, a well-known organist. Neither of them is a practising Catholic, but the faith of others inclines them to musical ecstasy. They believe in God long enough to enjoy a toccata. . . . I was led to dis-believe not by a conflict of dogmas but by my grandparents' indifference."[7]

Strongly reminiscent of the early years of Søren Kierkegaard, who never really had a childhood because of his aged father's morbidity and guilt-ridden preaching, Sartre likewise grew up without having a normal childhood. In his case, however, it was Professor Schweitzer's inordinate zeal to get the grandson's educational process under way, that robbed Jean Paul of the care-free "growing-up" years of normal children. In his autobiography, *The Words*, Sartre complains of having been deprived of all the ordinary, normal childhood experiences. He says, "In vain would I seek within me the prickly memories and sweet unreason of a country childhood. I never tilled the soil or hunted for nests. I did not gather herbs or throw stones at birds. But books were my birds and my nests, my household pets, my barn and my countryside. The library was the world caught in a mirror."[8]

And so, amidst the major French and German classics of his grandfather's library, the lonely, anemic boy, with no playmates his own age, taught himself to read. Books were his whole world, the only world he knew. From the age of seven, he became a writer, filling notebooks with all kinds of tales, grim and pleasant, which presaged his life vocation.

When Sartre was eleven, his mother married again, this time a supervisor of the dockyards of La Rochelle. The mother and son came to live with Jean Paul's step-father in La Rochelle and the boy attended the local lycée between the ages of twelve and fourteen. Because of the "dissipated atmosphere of the youth of La Rochelle," as one biographer tells us, Sartre was sent back to Paris to continue his studies.[9]

In 1924 at the age of nineteen, Sartre enrolled at the École Normale Supérieure. He received his *baca-lauréat en philosophie* with only a "fairly good" (*assez bien*, the equivalent of our C^+) rating. When he presented himself for his *agrégation de philosophie* in 1929, he failed the examination. A year later, he took the examination over again and this time, placed first.[10]

Upon his qualifying as a teacher, Sartre accepted a position on the faculty of the Le Havre Lycée and afterwards at the Lycée of Laon. (Le Havre later became the town of *Bouville* in his first successful work, *Nausea*.) Sartre satisfied the required military service with the army at Tours but he was excused from active combatant duty because of poor eyesight.

Although Sartre had been writing and composing ever since he was a child of seven or eight, his first pub-lished piece appeared in *Revue sans titre*, when he was eighteen. In a kind of premonitional way, his first work was entitled, *The Angel of Morbidity*. Sartre next tried to obtain a publisher for his *Essais* which, however, neither Aubier nor Gallimard found interesting enough to warrant publication. His book, *L'Imagination*, did find a publisher and it appeared in 1936. Gaston Gallimard, the most influential publisher in France, accepted Sartre's first novel, after having persuaded the latter to change its title from *Melancholia* to *Nausea*.[11] Much to the astonishment of Gallimard, the book became a best seller.

The existentialist themes introduced in this novel later received a speculative and analytical treatment in his philosophical *opus magnum* entitled *Being and Nothingness: An Essay of Phenomenological Ontology*, which was published by Gallimard in 1943.[12]

II. WORLD WAR II

With the outbreak of World War II, Sartre was recalled into the military service. He was stationed at the Maginot Line as a meteorological observer, where he faithfully took readings day by day, without knowing whether anyone ever bothered to use them. Sartre records a sense of ennui and uselessness in connection with his "pacific" operation, when he writes to a friend, Jean Paulhan: "My work here consists of launching balloons into the air and following them with binoculars; this is called 'taking a meteorological reading.' When I've done this, I telephone the wind-direction to the artillery officers, who do with it what they please. The younger school files the information; the old school throws it in the waste-paper basket. Both methods are equally valid, as they never fire. This extremely pacific work (I feel that only carrier-pigeon-keepers, if the army still has any, can have a more gentle and poetic employment) leaves me many hours of spare time, which I am making use of to finish my novel."[13]

In the summer of 1940, Sartre was taken prisoner by the Nazis and he was interned for approximately a year. By a clever hoax, he succeeded in having himself repatriated as a civilian "for health reasons."

As soon as he returned to Paris (he had obtained a teaching position at the Lycée Pasteur just prior to the outbreak of the war), Sartre became active in the underground movement of the French Resistance. It was here that he came to know the young Algerian, Albert Camus, as another fiercely patriotic worker, seeking the overthrow of the Nazi invaders.[14] The Communists also labored with them in the underground, in the common effort of obtaining the liberation of France. Camus and

Sartre clashed bitterly concerning their attitude toward these Communists. Camus, who had joined the Communist Party in Algiers and then broke away from it because of his disenchantment, maintained adamantly that the Communists were not primarily interested in the liberation of France. Camus contended that their fellow-workers merely wanted to drive out the Nazis so that France could then be taken over by the Communist Party. Sartre, on the other hand, maintained that the Communists were dedicated and genuine patriots, interested in freeing France. These differences between Sartre and Camus were never resolved and they finally erupted in that celebrated open debate between the two most famous literary figures in France. (We shall examine this event and its repercussions when we study Camus' life.)[15]

In the summer of 1943 under the watchful eyes of the Nazi censors in Occupied France, Sartre scored a triumph in producing his famous play *Les Mouches*. It is almost inconceivable that such a patently defiant production could have escaped the German censors. A partial explanation may be the fact that Sartre's lengthy *Being and Nothingness*, which appeared the same year as *Les Mouches*, was regarded as a scholarly exposition of German phenomenology and existentialism. Sartre, to all appearances, was a champion of German *Wissenschaft* and was, therefore, above reproach. After several performances, however, the German masters abruptly suppressed the play.

Since 1944, due to the great popularity of his writing, Sartre has given up teaching altogether in order to allow him full time for writing.

III. SIMONE DE BEAUVOIR

While Sartre was still studying at the university, he met a fellow-student, three years his junior, a young woman named Simone de Beauvoir. In the *agrégation* examination (the second one for Sartre), only one person ranked higher than Simone; it was Jean Paul Sartre.

Simone would write later of him, "It was the first time in my life that I had felt intellectually inferior to anyone else."[16]

Simone decided to cast her lot with Sartre and to enter into a union with him. Because of their total disdain for "stifling bourgeois values and conventions" (Simone had been brought up a Catholic but ceased to believe in God when she had turned fifteen), Sartre and Simone refused to go through a marriage ceremony. And so their "marriageless marriage" became a partnership which would allow for what they euphemistically called "contingent loves" but, at the same time, made no provision for divorce. Some of these affairs Simone later describes in her books under the guise of fiction, e.g., the affair between Sartre and a white Russian girl Olga (Xavière in *She Came to Stay*) and the contingent love between Simone and the American novelist, Nelson Algren, in *The Mandarins* and again in *Force of Circumstance*. (Algren in his review of the latter work wrote rather plaintively, "Will she ever quit talking?")

Simone has never made any home for Sartre. In *Force of Age*, the second volume of her autobiography, Simone writes at length of the long hours she and Sartre spent at café tables and in bleak desolate hotel rooms. Their vacations consisted of tramping with packs on their backs through much of Europe. Frequently, they slept "on decks, in mountain huts or in the open air."[17] For years, Sartre has done most of his writing in cafés, especially *Le Flore* in St-Germain-des-Près. For a period of time, Sartre was subject to hallucinations. Simone recounts how she spent one whole night with Sartre walking in the city of Venice throughout the night. Ironically, the Sartre-Beauvoir pact made some forty years ago, has turned out to be one of the most permanent marriageless marriages of recent times and as one observer has put it, "It has become more binding than a stack of marriage licenses."

Today at sixty-five (1973), Simone de Beauvoir

seems to be obsessed with the idea of mortality. Even as far back as seventeen years ago, she had begun to worry about the fact that she was growing old. When she was fifty-seven, Simone wrote in *Force of Circumstance,* "Since 1944, the most important, the most irreparable thing that has happened to me is that I have grown old. How is it that time which has no form or substance, can crush me with so huge a weight that I can no longer breathe?" Simone goes on to say that she finds herself "hostile to the society in which I belonged, banished by my age from the future, stripped fiber by fiber from my past."[18]

In appraising her life, she judges herself to have been a dismal failure and she feels today overwhelmed by a complete sense of frustration. She writes, "If it (my life) had at least enriched the earth. If it had given birth to . . . what? A hill? A rocket? The promises have all been kept. And yet, turning an incredulous gaze toward that young and credulous girl, I realize how much I have been gypped."[19] And so the world-famous author of *The Second Sex,* the classic which expounded woman's discontented state in modern society, now finds herself empty, useless and unfulfilled.

Perhaps a recent action on the part of her long-trusted and solicitous Jean Paul has contributed somewhat to her disillusionment and discontent. In its characteristically terse and pungent style, *Time* magazine recorded the incident in the following words, "Ever since they met as students at the Sorbonne, existentialist Jean Paul Sartre, fifty-nine, and novelist Simone de Beauvoir, fifty-seven, have been constant companions, though they deliberately refrained from becoming enmeshed in the bourgeois snares of matrimony. But now a little one is on the way—sort of. Sartre is adopting a daughter—Algerian-born Arlette Elkaim, twenty-eight, a movie critic on his magazine *Les Temps Modernes.* Simone remains his good *amie,* but unless he leaves a will to the contrary, Arlette will be his legal heir. And while he spurned $53,000 worth of 1964 Nobel Prize money, his novels, plays, and current autobiography all sell at a distractingly bourgeois rate."[20]

SARTRE'S PRINCIPAL WORKS
(Listed Chronologically)

Imagination: A Psychological Critique. (1936). Tr. Forrest Williams. Ann Arbor: University of Michigan Press, 1962.

Nausea. (1938). Tr. Lloyd Alexander. New York: New Directions, 1964.

The Wall and Other Stories. (1939), i.e. *La Chambre, Érestrate, Intimité, L'Enfance d'un chef.* Tr. Lloyd Alexander. New York: New Directions, 1948.

Emotions: Outline of a Theory. (1940). Tr. Bernard Frechtman. New York: The Philosophical Library, 1948.

The Flies. (1943). Tr. Stuart Gilbert. New York: Alfred Knopf, 1947.

Being and Nothingness: An Essay of Phenomenological Ontology. (1943). Tr. Hazel Barnes. New York: Citadel Press, 1964.

Roads to Freedom. I. Age of Reason. II. The Reprieve. (1945). Tr. Eric Sutton. New York: Alfred Knopf, 1947. *III. Troubled Sleep.* (1949). Tr. Gerard Hopkins. New York: Alfred Knopf, 1951.

No Exit. (1945). Tr. Stuart Gilbert. New York: Alfred Knopf, 1947.

Existentialism and Humanism. (1946). Tr. Philip Mairet. London: Methuen and Co., 1960.

The Respectful Prostitute. (1946). Tr. Stuart Gilbert. New York: Alfred Knopf, 1947.

Anti-Semite and Jew. (1946). Tr. George Beckman. New York: Schocken Books, 1948.

Baudelaire. (1947). Tr. Martin Turnell. New York: New Directions, 1950.

The Chips are Down. (Scénario du film) (1947). Tr. Louise Varèse. New York: Ambassador, 1948.

Situations I. Situations II-IV (1948-1964). *Situations IV.* Tr. Benita Esther. New York: Braziller, 1965.

In the Mesh. (A scenario) (1948). Tr. Mervyn Savill. London: A Dakers, 1954.

Dirty Hands. (1948). Tr. Lionel Abel. New York: Alfred Knopf, 1949.

The Devil and the Good Lord. (1951). Tr. Kitty Black. New York: Alfred Knopf, 1960.

Saint Genet, Actor and Martyr. (1952). Tr. Bernard Frechtman. New York: Braziller, 1963.

The Condemned of Altoona: A Play in Five Acts. (1960). Tr. Sylvia and George Leeson. New York: Alfred Knopf, 1961.

Search for a Method. (1961). Tr. Hazel Barnes. New York: Alfred Knopf, 1963.
The Words. (1964). Tr. Bernard Frechtman. New York: Braziller, 1964.

THOUGHT

I. PHILOSOPHICAL INFLUENCES

Jean Paul Sartre's atheistic existentialism is a melding of a number of notions appropriated from the writings of such thinkers as Friedrich Nietzsche, Martin Heidegger, Georg Wilhelm Hegel and Edmund Husserl (the latter through Heidegger's inverted phenomenological method). Sartre took over these notions either in whole or in an accommodated form. He then combined them into a series of postures which have become the most widely known form of atheistic existentialism today.

In the first place, from contemporary nihilism, Sartre accepts the strident call that "God is dead." Sartre has made the categorical denial of God's existence the very cornerstone of his existential stance. Indeed, his atheism is postulatory, in the sense that it is an absolutely indispensable starting point for all his philosophizing.[21]

Secondly, Sartre made his own, the well-known DASEIN of Martin Heidegger. As we have already seen above,[22] Heidegger's refusal to grant man a stable human nature is the basis for his concept of DASEIN. According to the hermit of Todtnauberg, we can speak of man only as a "There-being (DASEIN), who has been gratuitously thrown or cast into existence. (*Geworfenheit*). Man thus creates his own essence through the existential choices which he makes "in the shadow of death," which, incidentally, is the supreme possibility of man's existence. DASEIN can never be said to be; rather, it is something which is constantly "being made."

Sartre appropriates Heidegger's DASEIN and renames it "being-for-itself" (*l'être pour-soi*) or consciousness, which creates itself through the choices it makes. Death for Sartre, is not the supreme possibility; it is the cancellation of all possibility. There is a further difference betwen the postures of these two thinkers. Heidegger was indeed interested in a minute analysis of DASEIN; the burden of his entire masterpiece, *Being and Time*, was to arrive at the different ways in which DASEIN could be studied and examined. Yet this scrutiny of DASEIN was not an end in itself. Heidegger's primary concern was to arrive at that elusive "Being of beings" (*das Sein des Seiendes*) and he used his analysis of DASEIN as a kind of scaffolding whereby he might approach this all-important question. Jean Paul Sartre, on the other hand, is not interested, even remotely, in any kind of Being of beings. He is perfectly content to devote all his energies to the examination and dissection of the individual Being for-itself.[23]

In the third place, Sartre accepts the opposition or dichotomy represented by "being" and "nothing" and translates it into his celebrated opposition between Being in-itself and Being for-itself. Everything else in nature, i.e., every other being that lacks consciousness is signified by the term Being in-itself.

Again, Sartre institutes a change. While Hegel insisted on a mediation or sublimation, whereby the opposition between thesis and antithesis was always resolved by way of a reconciliation in the synthesis, Jean Paul Sartre unequivocally rejects any such reconciliation. He demands this bipolarity of being with its relentless opposition between Being for-itself and Being in-itself as a pre-requisite for his type of existentialism.[24]

In the fourth place, Sartre adopts the phenomenological method in its Heideggerian version. We have already seen that Edmund Husserl's phenomenology had for its purpose, the arrival at stable *eidoi* or essences by means of the various reductions.[25] Heidegger, on the other hand, turned Husserl's phenomenology upside down, as it were. Whereas Husserl was in search of stable essences, Heidegger rejected the very possibility of any such essences. This was especially true in the case of man, where Heidegger substituted the well known DASEIN for that of a permanent human nature or man. Gratuitously thrown into existence, DASEIN and his various states would be the object of Heidegger's phenomenology.

Sartre appropriated this Heideggerian version of phenomenology and popularized the now very well known expression, "existence precedes essence." For Sartre, man does not begin with a stable and permanent human nature. Instead, he begins with the brute fact of existence which is pure consciousness, i.e., Being for-itself. It is precisely the content of consciousness which Sartre will analyze by means of his phenomenological method.

II. POSTULATORY ATHEISM
AND ITS CONSEQUENCES

We have already observed that Sartre's primary starting point is the outright denial of the existence of God. In spite of the fact that existentialism owes its beginnings to a committed, believing Christian, Søren Kierkegaard, Sartre has worked strenuously to convey the impression that atheistic existentialism is the only accepted and legitimate type of existentialism. (This attempt to equate existentialism with atheism is the basis for Marcel's objection that Jean Paul Sartre ignores the facts of history; such theists like Kierkegaard and Marcel were setting the basis and groundwork for existentialism long before anyone even heard of Jean Paul Sartre.)[26]

In his essay, *Existentialism is a Humanism,* Sartre insists that atheistic existentialism must be recognized as a genuine and valid existentialist posture. He writes, ". . . there are two kinds of existentialists. There are, on the one hand, the Christians, amongst whom I shall name Jaspers and Marcel, both professed Catholics; and on the other, the existential atheists, amongst whom we must place Heidegger as well as the French existentialists and myself."[27] (Incidentally, Heidegger vehemently disavowed any doctrinal connection with Sartre and the other French existentialists.)[28]

After having granted rather magnanimously that there *are* some Christian thinkers, whose stance may be characterized as existential, Sartre proceeds to assert dogmatically that his type of existentialism is the only valid kind. He proclaims, "Existentialism is nothing else but an attempt to draw the full conclusions from a consistently atheistic position. . . . Existentialism is not atheist in the sense that it would exhaust itself in demonstration of the non-existence of God. It declares, rather, that even if God existed, that would make no difference from its point of view. Not that we believe that God does exist, but we think that the real problem is not that of His existence; what man needs is to find himself again and to understand that nothing can save him from himself, not even a valid proof of the existence of God."[29]

From the above quotation excerpted from Sartre's *Existentialism is a Humanism,* it is obvious we are dealing with an avowed atheist. There is no God, says Sartre, and therefore we cannot speak of the creation of human beings. Man merely begins to be. (Heidegger also holds the same position but he refuses to label his thought as atheistic.) Neither is there any plan or idea of what men will be like, before they suddenly begin to exist. In other words, we have a gratuitous positing of existence without any attempt to explain its beginning. It is for this reason that Sartre announces dogmatically that "existence precedes essence." Sartre develops the consequences of his atheistic position when he asserts, "Atheistic existentialism of which I am a representative, declares with greater consistency that if God does not exist, there is at least one being whose existence comes before its essence, a being which exists before it can be defined by any conception of it. That being is man or as Heidegger has it, the human reality."[30]

Sartre next goes on to explain what he means by the expression "existence precedes essence." A book or a paper-knife, for example, is an article of manufacture—it is something which an artisan has made by following a certain pattern, blue-print or formula in his mind. The paper-knife as fashioned by man, is an article which serves a definite purpose and hence it would be quite inconceivable for us to suppose that man could make a paper-knife without knowing its purpose, i.e., what he was going to use it for. To that extent, the essence, viz., "the sum of the formulæ and the qualities making the knife's production possible" *precedes* existence.

Sartre goes on to say that when we speak of God as a Creator, we think of Him as a "supernal artisan." The implication is that just as man fashions the paper-knife in accordance with some intelligible pattern or formula in his mind, so, too, God as the Creator, brings man into existence in accordance with a certain idea or intelligible essence. Hence each individual man is a faithful reflection of the pattern or idea in divine understanding. As a result, "Man possesses a human nature;

that human nature which is the conception of human being found in every man; which means that each man is a particular example of an universal conception."[31]

Since there is no Creator who has the essence of man in His divine understanding prior to the act of creation, man's existence precedes his essence. All we can say is that man merely begins to exist. He encounters himself, comes into being in the world. To begin with, man is actually nothing. It is only later that man will define himself through the choices which he will make. Stated succinctly in Sartre's own words, "There is no human nature because there is no God to have a conception of it."[12]

III. BEING FOR-ITSELF AND BEING IN-ITSELF

The world of Jean Paul Sartre is split into two antithetical modes or ways of being, i.e., Being for-itself (*l'être pour-soi*) and Being in-itself (*l'être en-soi*). The Hegelian influence is very apparent here in that Being for-itself is identified with nothingness and Being in-itself with being or reality (antithesis and thesis respectively of the first Hegelian triad). These two modes, by their very nature, are contradictory and mutually exclusive.[33] Unlike the Hegelian world, however, the world of Jean Paul Sartre admits of no synthesis of contradictories. The opposition is basic and inexorable. Let us examine in detail the nature of Being for-itself and Being in-itself.

A. Being for-itself

We have already seen that, according to Sartre, there is no God and hence there is no stable human nature. Man is characterized as Being for-itself, which Sartre identifies with consciousness. All other entities besides man, which lack human consciousness, belong to the antithetical class of beings, namely "Being in-itself." In our examination of man, i.e., of Being for-itself, we shall first consider Being for-itself as consciousness of an object and secondly, Being for-itself as nothingness.

Being for-itself is essentially consciousness and consciousness is always of something. With Brentano and Husserl, Sartre holds that consciousness *ipso facto* posits an object which necessarily transcends it and is different from consciousness itself. This object he labels the "In-itself" (*en-soi*), which is in opposition to consciousness or the "For-itself (*pour-soi*). In any given case, I can be aware of my consciousness but this awareness will always be an awareness of my being conscious of *something*. This something, the object of my consciousness is obviously other than the conscious subject. It is, of course, the In-itself. And inasmuch as consciousness is a consciousness of something it therefore separates itself from something not itself.[34]

In the preliminary remarks in his *Being and Nothingness*, Sartre describes the fundamental relation between consciousness (For-itself) and object (In-itself). He writes, "All consciousness, as Husserl has shown, is consciousness of something. This means that there is no consciousness which is not a positing of a transcendent object, or if you prefer, that consciousness has 'no content'. . . . All consciousness is consciousness of something . . . this means that consciousness in its inmost nature is a relation to a transcendent being . . . it means that transcendence is the constitutive structure of consciousness, that is, that consciousness is born, supported by a being which is not itself. . . . To say that consciousness is consciousness of something is to say that it must produce itself as a revealed-revelation of a being which is not it and which gives itself as already existing when consciousness reveals it."[35]

Consciousness always presupposes an object of which it is conscious. And because an object is an absolute necessity, since there is no consciousness without it, Sartre states that there is no need to spend time in demonstrating the existence of the object. The latter is an indisputable presupposition.

Consciousness which is always of something can be compared to a mirror. A mirror has content only when objects are reflected in it. Of itself, it is empty. In like manner, consciousness has no content except the objects which it reflects. These objects are always other than consciousness itself.[36]

Sartre readily admits the influence of Heidegger's DASEIN on his notion of Being for-itself, i.e., consciousness. He writes, "Certainly we could apply to consciousness the definition which Heidegger reserves for DASEIN and say that it is a being such that in its being, its being is in question. But it would be necessary to complete the definition and formulate it more like this: consciousness is a being such that in its being, its being is in question insofar as this being implies a being other than itself."[37]

Further, inasmuch as consciousness is always of something and this something is absolutely other than the conscious subject, consciousness always denotes a separation from, a distance from and a negation of its object, namely the In-itself. This is why Sartre identifies nothingness with consciousness or the For-itself. Norman Greene expresses it this way, "Sartre attempts to demonstrate . . . that consciousness is non-substantial, or nothingness. Nothingness not in the sense of not being anything but a 'nihilating' activity. As nothingness, it is separated from the object by not being the object and preserves a distance from it."[38]

Consciousness, therefore, cannot have any essence or content. It is nothing more than existence. What appears to be its content comes, in reality, from its object. For-itself cannot be any definite being, otherwise it could not be consciousness. Things and consciousness are interdependent. Without consciousness, things are but a meaningless chaos. Without things, consciousness does not even exist, since its very life consists in imagining them. Bocheński explains why consciousness cannot be identified with being. He writes, "If consciousness were a given being, it would be dense and full and could not become that other being which it becomes in being known, and this fundamentally is what knowing is. Consciousness is, therefore, a release of a being, a kind of fission of being. Negating is evident in self-consciousness also, for between that of which we are conscious and consciousness itself, there is only a segment of the nothing."[39]

Man, consequently, can be described by Sartre as a being who is not what he is and who is what he is not. Man is not what he is, inasmuch as he is not now what his past has been. At the same time, man is what he is not, since he is not as yet the undetermined future which he will become in terms of the choices he will make. Man's present stands as a kind of nothingness of pure existence, midway between his past accomplishments which are now history, and his future projects which, as such, are still undetermined. The present becomes meaningful only in the light of what has already been achieved and that which still remains to be accomplished. As Norman Greene interprets it, "Human reality, then, is something insofar as it is the series of individual actions which constitute a person's past history, together with those actions which are added to the past by the progressive realization of future projects. But the past and the future are constantly being questioned by the nothingness of the present."[40]

According to this view, man cannot have a stable and permanent human nature. Instead of a common human nature, men possess, in Sartre's words, "a human condition" which is common to all men. By this distinction Sartre means to say that all human beings begin with certain "a priori constraints," i.e., the fact that they are born and will die, that they are finite and live in a world with other men. Men can never be spoken of as having a completed or permanent being. There is a constant element of futurity and negativity. H. J. Blackham describes the condition of man in the following words: ". . . *pour-soi* must be recognized for what it is: perpetual pure separation and denial, embodied in historical existence in the world, yet not identified with that existence as a property of it not as its totality, but perpetually reconstituting itself and having a virtual totality of its own. This pure nothing, which limits and defines being and is not a property of it, not something else set over against it, is not a mere hypothesis to overcome the riddle of philosophy; it falls into place in the description of the only conditions which make our human presence in the world possible."[41]

Maurice Cranston's description is brief and to the point. He writes, "Man cannot be in a fixed and final manner: he has continuously to choose, to make decisions, to reaffirm old purposes and projects or to affirm new ones. He is continuously engaged in the work of self-construction, a task which is never completed but only ended by his death."[42]

B.   Existence preceding Essence

Sartre has always insisted that every theistic position demands the priority of essence over existence. Inasmuch as he has categorically denied the existence of God, as we have already seen, Sartre contends that existence must in all cases precede essence. Upon closer examination, however, it becomes apparent that the question cannot be resolved in such a simplistic manner. Let us now see how Sartre misrepresents the position of theistic thinkers. In the first place, it is true that historically many theists have held that a divine exemplar idea is present in the mind of God prior to the production of the individual being. But the manner in which Sartre understands, or at least presents, this position leaves much to be desired. As James Collins expresses it, "This exemplar notion is not, however, a sort of master die, in accord with which finite individuals are struck off, in assembly-line fashion. It represents the entire being of the creature in its unique existential act and individual traits, as well as in its essential nature."[43]

When we consider the case of any given concrete individual, the question of the priority of essence over existence or vice versa becomes totally meaningless. This is so because, while it is true that the act of existing does enjoy a kind of primacy within being, yet both essence and existence are concomitant principles. With regard to created, finite being, neither its essence nor its existence is prior; both actively constitute a composite being. The essence determines or limits the existence which a particular entity exercises. Since essence and existence are absolutely co-related, acting in the manner of co-principles, there is no way in which one of the principles can rightly be said to exercise a priority over the other.

Concerning this general question of the relation between essence and existence. Sartre is guilty of an obvious ambiguity. As Gabriel Marcel had pointed out in his *Being and Having,* a full ten years before Sartre even began writing, there are two distinct ways in which essence can be understood.[44] In the first place, essence can be understood on the metaphysical plane, as referring to the nature or quiddity of the being. Marcel speaks of it as "my essence *qua* nature." In such a case, there is a simultaneous co-existence of the real individual essence and the act of existence. Albert Stern expresses it in this way, "It seems to me that Sartre's basic existentialist thesis implies a logical difficulty, for it is impossible *to be* without being *something*. . . . Sartre had been warned by Professor Laporte against the kind of abstraction by which we think of certain things as isolated which are not made to exist isolatedly. Existence and essence seem to be such things."[45]

The second way in which essence can be understood is on the moral plane. Here we deal with the free development of the moral character of a person. In one way, it is true that man fashions his nature in the sense that the existential choices which he makes throughout his life will determine the kind of person he will be. But to substitute moral essence for metaphysical essence is somewhat dishonest or obtuse. Sartre himself admits to the necessity of a given essence which is mandatory at the very outset.

He tries to circumvent the difficulty by speaking of a "human condition" instead of a "human nature." But "man," whether he is called DASEIN or Being for-itself, needs to be *something* whereby he is differentiated from a stone, tree or fish, as Frederick Copleston has graphically observed.[46]

Paul Foulquié criticizes Sartre's claim that man makes

or chooses his own essence. He charges, "Not having distinguished between the universal essence, which makes us man, and the individual essence, that makes us this or that particular man—timid or brave, honest or dishonest— M. Sartre arrives at propositions that are paradoxical to the point of absurdity: 'Man first *is*—only afterwards is he this or that . . . man must create for himself his own essence' (*Action: op. cit.*). Obviously, we do not create the universal or specific essence in virtue of which we belong to the human species, but the individual essence which is peculiar to us and which is not to be found in any other human being. This goes without saying, but it would have been better to be precise; we have not to choose between the essence 'green pea' or 'cucumber' or 'toad' or 'vulture' and the essence 'man'; our generic and specific essence—'animal' and 'man'—*is not determined by us;* we are men—only our individual or specific essence presents a certain indetermination. We are men, but what man shall we be? It is only within these limits that a door remains open upon liberty."[47]

Sartre writes, "To be in a certain situation signifies to choose oneself in a certain situation and men differ from one another as their situations differ and also according to the choice they make of their own persons. What men have in common is not a nature, but a condition, i.e., an ensemble of restrictions and coercions: the necessity of dying, or working in order to live, of existing in a world together with other people. And this condition is *the fundamental human situation or if one prefers the ensemble of abstract characters common to all situations.*"[48]

In his essay, *Existentialism is a Humanism,* Sartre again tries to substitute "human condition" for "human essence." He writes, "Furthermore, although it is impossible to find in each and every man a universal essence that can be called human nature, there is, nevertheless, a human universality of *condition.* It is not by chance that thinkers of to-day are so much more ready to speak of the condition than of the nature of man. By his condition, we understand with more or less clarity, all the *limitations* which a priori define man's fundamental situation in the universe. His historical situations are variable: man may be born a slave in a pagan society, or may be a feudal baron, or a proletarian. But what never vary are the necessities of being in the world, or having to labor and to die there. These limitations are neither subjective nor objective, or rather there is both a subjective and an objective aspect of them. Objective because we meet with them everywhere and they are everywhere recognizable: and subjective because they are *lived* and are nothing if man does not live them—if, that is to say, he does not freely determine himself and his existence in relation to them. And, diverse though man's purposes may be, at least none of them is wholly foreign to me, since every human purpose presents itself as an attempt either to surpass these limitations or to widen them, or else to deny or to accommodate to them. Consequently every purpose, however individual it may be, is of universal value."[49]

In both instances, Sartre is guilty of ambivalence. He denies the existence of human essence and substitutes for it "human condition." His "human condition," however, is invested with all the characteristic notes of "human essence." Even a novice in undergraduate philosophy knows that essence is not a thing, but an abstract notion which becomes actualized the moment a human individual begins to exist. As Wilfrid Desan points out, "As an abstract notion, human essence is indeed 'an ensemble of abstract characters' which one finds in each of the existentialistic 'situations.' As such, i.e., as abstract notion, *essence precedes existence,* whatever Sartre may say."[50] And as Régis Jolivet trenchantly remarks, "This precession (i.e., of essence before existence) is purely logical; before it exists, the essence is nothing but an abstract possibility, an ensemble of 'abstract characters.' "[51]

David Roberts in the work, *Existentialism and Religious Belief,* accuses Sartre of outright dishonesty. He argues, "Sartre is cheating when he refuses to talk about essential human nature. He is willing to talk about 'universal human condition' in connection with the fact that all men have to exist in the world of mortals along with other people. But this concession does not meet the most important point. He persists in associating 'essence' (as applied to man) with the idea that selfhood is an eternal entity with which I am endowed by a power beyond myself. The notion, when held in this form, is undeniably objectionable, but it is objectionable because it has been separated gratuitously from freedom."[52]

Wilfrid Desan points to another inherent contradiction in Sartre's position that existence precedes essence. Sartre maintains, as we shall see shortly, that For-itself (*l'être pour-soi*), which he equates with consciousness or human condition, is free from stability and fulness of the In-itself (*l'être en-soi*). For-itself is, in reality, a lack of being and in its seeking after being, it is total and absolute freedom. Sartre goes on to say that human freedom, therefore, has no limits. In accordance with this reasoning, human reality cannot, in any way, be defined or set within limits or bounds. Human reality is only what, in complete freedom, it makes itself to be.

In other words, Sartre refuses to consider human reality as an essence because For-itself is absolute and undefinable freedom. Desan points out, however, "There precisely appears the antinomy. If For-itself is pure freedom, one is, in fact, presented with an essence of human reality. Sartre does not escape the necessity of defining that about which he is talking."[53]

Desan further argues that the very expressions, which Sartre himself uses, contradict his position that existence must precede essence. In *Being and Nothingness*, Sartre states several times that "man is a being condemned to be free,"[54] and that absolutely nothing can prevent him from being completely and unconditionally free. In this context, freedom is understood to have no limits except its own. But Aimé Patri rejoins that to use the expression "condemned to freedom" and "the necessity of freedom" is "simply to return to the philosophy of essences from which Sartre has tried so energetically to escape."[55] Desan then concludes, "In fact each thing is what it is and can only be what it is. If according to Sartre, a human being is free by nature, freedom is its essence—or least, part of it."[56]

Paul Roubiczek likewise criticizes Sartre's rejection of the notion of essence in preference to existence. He writes, "Sartre is claiming, in short, that we are not merely developing our personalities by a growing understanding of the different aspects of our human nature, but are creating ourselves, entirely and arbitrarily. But it is evident that our power of choice with regard to our essence is little greater than that with regard to our existence; we act as human beings, whatever we do. We can develop, strengthen and purify the humanity within us, or degrade and almost destroy it, but by no effort can we become, as French critics often say, strawberries or peas or cats. . . . It is true that concentration on essence alone leads to abstraction and thus estranges philosophy from life. This kind of philosophy is rightly attacked; essence has to be combined with existence if it is to come to life. Nevertheless, essence cannot be omitted, for, if it is, existence is left void of any content. It is, after all, plainly wrong to consider man as a completely undefined being, as material which can be transformed into anything; there are reasons why he is called a *human* being, and his humanness can—and must—be made the basis of his endeavors.

If essence disappears, everything concrete which could guide our understanding of existence disappears with it—the characteristics of man, of freedom, of the transcendental, of external reality and even of his historical situation."[57]

René Lafarge writes, "In man, existence does not precede essence, as Sartre would have it, at least not in the sense that existence would actuate nothing that pre-exists it. I would exist, but I would be nothing; man would exist, but there would be no human nature. It is true that we make ourselves through our choices and this is why we are responsible for ourselves. But we do not make ourselves anything we please. We are men and we remain men. As Amiel said, 'Man is but what he becomes

—this is a profound truth. Man becomes, only what he is—an even more profound truth.' To think otherwise would be to flounder into the un-intelligible."[58]

Finally, Paul Tillich in his study entitled, *Existentialism and Psychotherapy,* in making the following observation concerning Sartre's rejection of a human essence, emphasizes the absolute dependence of existentialism on an essentialist doctrine. He writes, "There are, however, only rare moments in this monumental development in which an almost pure existentialism has been reached. An example is Sartre's doctrine of man. I refer to a sentence in which the whole problem of essentialism and existentialism comes into the open, his famous statement that man's essence is his existence. The meaning of the sentence is that man is a being of whom no essence can be affirmed, for such an essence would introduce a permanent contradictory to man's power of transforming himself indefinitely. According to Sartre, man is what he acts to be.

But if we ask whether his statement has not, against his intention, given assertion about man's essential nature, we must say, certainly, it has. Man's particular nature is his power to create himself. And if the further question is raised of how such a power is possible and how it must be structured, we need a fully developed essentialist doctrine in order to answer; we must know about his body and his mind, in short, about those questions which for millenia have been discussed in essentialist terms.

Only on the basis of an essentialist doctrine of freedom does Sartre's statement have any meaning. Neither in theology nor in philosophy can existentialism live by itself. It can only exist as a contrasting element within an essentialist framework."[59]

In reality, then, Sartre does admit the necessity of an equivalent of essence in the metaphysical sense. We might observe rather pointedly that Sartre's emphasis on the creation of man's moral essence or nature is hardly an original notion in the history of philosophy. Marcel refers to this essence of man as "my essence *qua* freedom —my essence to be able not to be what I am; in plain words to be able to betray myself."[60] All theistic positions have traditionally maintained that by exercising his free will and freedom in making his own decisions, individual man was thereby determining or creating his moral essence. Even before the advent of Christianity, Aristotle spoke of the prudent or ethical man who, through repeated good actions based on right prudential judgments, was living a life of virtue and avoiding vice. Sartre's disjunction between essence and existence seems to be based on an ambiguity in the interpretation of the meaning of "essence."

In summary, then, For-itself is consciousness. Consciousness is necessarily *of* something, for without an object, there can be no consciousness. Like a mirror, its content is only of the reflected objects. There is also a fundamental separation between consciousness and its object. Sartre speaks of For-itself as nothingness, since consciousness cannot have any essence or content of its own. Human reality is a kind of nothingness of the present situated between the past of accomplishments performed and the future of the projects to be embarked upon. Hence man possesses no fixed or permanent nature. He is in the constant process of creating it; this process is always rendered incomplete by the intervention of death. Failing to distinguish properly between metaphysical and moral essence, Sartre insists that existence precedes essence.

C. Being in-itself

In *Being and Nothingness*, Sartre gives us the following description of Being in-itself: ". . . in-itself is expressed by the simple formula: being is what it is. In the in-itself there is not a particle of being which is not wholly within itself without distance. When being is thus conceived, there is not the slightest suspicion of duality in it; this is what we mean when we say that the density of being of the in-itself is infinite. It is a fulness. The principle of identity can be said to be synthetic not only because it limits its scope to a region of definite being, but in particular, because it masses within it the infinity of density. 'A is' means that A exists in infinite compression with an infinite density. . . . The in-itself is full of itself, and no more total plenitude can be imagined, no more perfect equivalence of content to container. There is not the slightest emptiness in being, not the tiniest crack through which nothingness might slip in."[61]

Being in-itself is, according to Sartre's own words, diametrically opposed to Being for-itself. The In-itself is a world of objects that simply are what they are. They obtrude with a solidity and permanence which are the very opposite of the For-itself's lack of stability. These objects are exactly what they are and no more. They are mute, shapeless and possess a density and viscosity which threaten to overpower the Being for-itself. Opaque and identical with themselves, the objects which constitute In-itself, are things which lack consciousness; they are self-identical. They must be accepted as existing quite independently of any conscious spontaneity. Sartre uses the example of a sheet of white paper which presents itself to consciousness. He writes, "One thing is certain and that is that the white sheet I observe cannot be the product of my spontaneity. The inert form, which is beyond all conscious spontaneities and which must be observed and gradually learned, is what is called a 'thing.' "[62]

Being in-itself is the thesis of the Hegelian triad; it is equivalent to the world of things lacking consciousness. This totality of non-conscious beings can best be described as massive inertia. There is absolutely no reason for the existence of all these things which proliferate themselves with an overwhelming obscenity. They are one great tautology. In their mute and meaningless superfluousness, the objects which constitute In-itself, stand menacingly as a threat to the constantly moving, shifting, and changing consciousness of the world of For-itself.[63]

Being in-itself is thus a world of things existing without any reason whatsoever because Sartre's world admits of no God. Since there is no Creator, everything merely is —it exists without purpose or reason. We have no right to inquire where it came from or why it is here. Sartre's postulatory atheism precludes any questions concerning

the origins and beginnings of things. Everything is gratuitously posited. It just exists. Things exist without any
rational meaning or foundation. This meaninglessness and
absurdity of existence is trenchantly described in Sartre's
famous autobiographical diary, *Nausea,* wherein we are
told, "Every existing thing is born without reason, prolongs itself out of weakness, and dies by chance."[64]

Régis Jolivet in *Sartre, The Theology of the Absurd,*
paints a striking picture of the world of In-itself. He
writes, "The In-itself, the specific revelation of nausea,
is being itself: massive, opaque, gloomy and glutinous.
We can say nothing about it, except that *it is,* for it is
devoid of any relationships, either interior or exterior.
It is so listless that it cannot stop itself from being. Where
does the In-itself or being, come from? From no place,
from nothing. It is, without reason, unjustifiable, absurd,
'too much for all eternity.' It is and it proliferates itself
horribly, obscenely. Any attempt to explain it is fruitless.
First of all, God does not exist, being self-contradictory.
Moreover the very idea of creation is meaningless."[65]

IV.   BEING FOR-ITSELF-IN-ITSELF

While the world of In-itself enjoys a permanence and
stability (even though it is completely meaningless), man
as consciousness is the very antithesis of In-itself's stability. For-itself or consciousness, which by its nature is
not what it is, is constantly seeking to transcend itself.
It is contingent and radically unstable. But Being for-
itself envies the rock-like stability of In-itself and it is
continuously engaged in the attempt to overcome its lack
of being and its contingency. It seeks to make the stability
of In-itself its own. Hence, Sartre maintains that there is
present in every For-itself a fundamental drive toward
self-transcendence. While retaining the precariousness and
lack of stability which is essential to his consciousness, man
as Being for-itself relentlessly continues to seek his contradictory condition. He engages in an absolutely impossible task, namely, the unification of For-itself with In-
itself. Sartre warns us that such a project can never be

realized; it is absolutely futile. This is why man is so aptly described as a "futile passion."

Sartre's description of man as a consciousness, fluttering against walls which it can never escape is strikingly rendered by Mathieu Delarue in the trilogy of novels, *The Roads to Freedom*. Mathieu says to Marcelle, his mistress, "And when you bring a child into the world, do you realize what you're going to do? A child: another consciousness, a little centre-point of light that would flutter round and round, dashing against the walls, and never able to escape."[66]

William Barrett in his insightful work, *Irrational Man*, describes the tension which is present in this ceaseless struggle to unify the contradictories of For-itself and In-itself. He writes, "Because we are perpetually flitting beyond ourselves, or falling behind our possibilities, we seek to ground our existence, to make it more secure. In seeking for security we seek to give our existence the self-contained being of a thing. The for-itself struggles to become the In-itself, to attain the rocklike and unshakable solidity of a thing. But this it can never do so long as it is conscious and alive. Man is doomed to the radical insecurity and contingency of his being; for without it he would not be a man but merely a thing and would not have the human capacity for transcendence of his given situation. There is a curious dialectical interplay here: that which constitutes man's power and glory, that which lies at the very heart of his power to be lord over things, namely his capacity to transcend himself and his immediate situation, is at one and the same time, that which causes the fragility, the wavering and flight, the anguish of our human lot."[67]

The impossible task which man sets for himself, namely to rid himself of the instability which consciousness inevitably demands, is clearly a most frustrating undertaking. It is a foregone conclusion that man cannot be both a For-itself and an In-itself. Joseph Mihalich describes this exercise in futility in the following words: "The whole existence of the For-itself is expended in an

impossible effort to become something—to become a thing
in itself. This is an impossible goal because it would mean
a dual contradiction. It is a contradiction to posit the
For-itself as in any way fixed or delineated (as it would
be if it were a thing), and it is equally contradictory
to posit the In-itself as in any way knowledgeable or
conscious. The For-itself must remain wholly translucent;
the slightest measure of permanence—even the permanence of an egological structure—is anathema. The For-
itself is thus completely free and unbounded—it is condemned to be free and nothing else."[68]

V.   FOR-ITSELF-IN-ITSELF AS GOD

After having established the utter futility of the
For-itself-in-itself project, Sartre next proceeds to assert
that when the note of infinity is added to this self-defeat-
ing undertaking, it becomes the idea of God. Man seeks
to acquire the firm foundation of reality by fleeing from
his own emptiness and contingency. But the only way
in which he can transcend his emptiness is by divesting
himself of the only mode in which he can exist, namely,
his consciousness and self-presence. Nevertheless, Sartre
contends that man cannot avoid this drive in his very
nature, which constantly urges him on to attempt the
impossible synthesis of For-itself-in-itself. Further, because man is essentially unhappy with his present state
of mundane consciousness, he tends to project this synthesis into another world. He now invests it with a transcendence and actuality. The illusion of an infinite, transcendent For-itself-in-itself is none other than what religion calls God.

Sartre argues, "Human reality is its own surpassing
toward what it lacks . . . imperfect being surpasses itself
toward perfect being; the being which is the foundation
only of its nothingness surpasses itself toward the being
which is the foundation of its being. But the being toward
which human reality surpasses itself is not a transcendent
God; it is at the heart of human reality; it is only human
reality as a totality. . . . This perpetually absent being
which haunts the For-itself is itself fixed in the In-itself.

It is the impossible synthesis of the For-itself and the In-itself; it would be its own foundation, not as a nothingness but as a being and would preserve within it the necessary translucency of consciousness, along with the coincidence with itself of Being-in-itself. . . . When the being and absolute absence of this totality is hypostasized as transcendence beyond the world, it takes on the name of God."[69]

In another place Sartre writes, "Thus the being of human reality is originally not a substance but a lived relation. . . . Man is neither the one nor the other (In-itself and In-itself-for-itself) of these beings, for strictly speaking, we should never say of him that he is at all. He is what he is not and he is not what he is; he is the nihilation of the contingent In-itself and in so far as the self of this nihilation is its flight ahead toward the In-itself as self-cause. Human realty is the pure effort to become God without there being any given substratum for that effort, without there being anything which so endeavors. Desire expresses this endeavor."[70]

Toward the end of his *Being and Nothingness*, Sartre again describes his notion of God as a contradictory project on the part of man. He writes, "It is as consciousness that it [For-itself] wishes to have the impermeability and infinite density of the In-itself. It is as the nihilation of the In-itself and a perpetual evasion of contingency and facticity that it wishes to be its own foundation. . . . The fundamental value which presides over this project is exactly the In-itself-for-itself; that is, the ideal of consciousness which would be the foundation of its own Being-in-itself by the pure consciousness which it would have of itself. It is this ideal which can be called God. Thus the best way to conceive of the fundamental project of human reality is to say that man is the being whose project is to be God."[71]

Finally, Sartre concludes the more than 600 closely printed pages of his masterpiece with the following manifesto: "Each human reality is at the same time a direct project to metamorphise its own For-itself into an In-itself-for-itself and a project of the appropriation of the world as a totality of Being-in-itself, in the form of a fundamental quality. Every human reality is a passion in that it projects losing itself so as to found being and by the same stroke to constitute the In-itself which escapes contingency by being its own foundation, the *Ens causa sui*, which religions call God. Thus the passion of man is the reverse of that of Christ, for man loses himself as man in order that God may be born. But the idea of God is contradictory and we lose ourselves in vain. Man is a useless passion."[72]

Sartre obviously accepts as his premise, Nicolai Hartmann's dictum that the idea of God is a patent contradiction which is the result of man's wishful thinking. For Sartre, God is not a transcendent personal being; God is but the impersonal goal of man's activity of self-transcendence. Further, Sartre's insistence that the essence of God demands the contradictory notes of For-itself and In-itself, of necessity and contingency is absolutely groundless and completely gratuitous.

As James Collins points out, "The contradiction lies not in God or in the religious conception of God but in the Sartrean theory of the modes of being. He defines Being in-itself in a univocal and material way and then shows that being, as so defined, excludes consciousness and the other attributes usually applied to God. Clearly enough the trouble lies in the doctrine of the In-itself and not in the concept of a purely actual being. This doctrine overlooks the gradual convergence of consciousness and being in the higher forms of living things. Far from being in contrast with every sort of self-identity, consciousness is the means whereby animals and men secure a more perfect self-identity than is possible for material things deprived of consciousness. At these higher levels of existence, self-identity is not equated with limp immobility but displays itself as conscious self-presence."[73]

VI.   BEING FOR-ANOTHER

Perhaps the most notorious aspect of Sartre's existentialism, which has drawn such large reading audiences from non-philosophers, is that of "Being-for-another." It is under this general heading that Sartre explores a number of themes that form the basis for his highly successful plays and notorious works—*No Exit, The Flies, Intimacy, The Reprieve*, to name only a few. These themes include the glance or the look, shame, conflict as the basis for all human relations, possession of the other, seduction, sadism and masochism, love and hate. Alfred Stern writes, "Existentialism in itself had no specific relation to sex until Sartre made it 'sexy' . . . and most of his novels and short stories are almost pornographic. Perhaps this is also one reason for the tremendous success of Sartre's version of Existentialism. In Heidegger's work there is no reference to sex, for he thinks that existence is the same for men and women. And interest in this type of Existentialism is restricted to the professional philosophers."[74]

Let us now examine Sartre's particular brand of existentialism as it is developed under the aspect of "Being-for-another." While Sartre maintains that the first two modes of being (Being for-itself and Being in-itself) divide all reality, he nevertheless devotes much of his writing to a detailed analysis and description of a third category, which he names "Being-for-another," "Being-for-others" or just "The Other."

Just as Sartre had stated that For-itself or consciousness is a given fact, whereby man becomes aware of himself through the *cogito*, so, too, he maintains that the Other is an absolutely essential condition for the very existence of For-itself. Sartre writes, ". . . when we say 'I think,' we are attaining to ourselves in the presence of the Other, and we are just as certain of the Other as we are of ourselves. Thus the man who discovers himself directly in the *cogito* also discovers all the others and discovers them as the condition of his existence. He recognizes that he cannot be anything (in the sense in which one says one is spiritual or that one is wicked or jealous) unless others recognize him as such. . . . The Other is indispensable to my existence, and equally so to any knowledge I can have of myself. Under these conditions, the intimate discovery of myself is at the same time the revelation of the Other as a freedom which confronts mine, and which cannot think or will without doing so either for or against me."[75]

Robert Cumming explains Sartre's position in the following words: "Self-consciousness is consciousness of myself as something of which the Other is conscious but of which I cannot become conscious. His consciousness of me transcends my consciousness, because I have become for him the object that I can never become for myself. When he looks at me I am conscious of his consciousness identifying me as having this or that character; I cannot pass comparable value judgments on myself, except by attempting the impossible—to look at myself with another's eyes."[76]

In *Being and Nothingness*, Sartre devotes some 200 pages to the section entitled "Being-For-Others." He argues that we immediately become aware of other existents who, like ourselves, are consciousness, i.e., Being-for-itself. Obviously, it is of the greatest import to be able to ascertain the exact relationship that exists between two For-itselves or consciousnesses. It is Sartre's contention that the existence of the Other is primarily given in the glance or the look (*le regard*) and its accompanying phenomenon of fear or shame. He cites two examples (which have become rather celebrated) of the way in which Being-for-itself can become Being-for-another.

A.   The Park: Fear

The first example is of a For-itself or consciousness in a park. Suppose I am sitting in a public park. Not far away there is a broad lawn bordered by chestnut trees and along the edge of the lawn there are also some benches. A man slowly passes by the benches. He is reading a book and he is deeply engrossed in it. I see this man and I apprehend him as an object in my world, much as I do the fountain-in-the-park and the statue-in-the-square. He is man-reading-a-book and he fits the same category as the other objects in my world. Sartre explains, "His relation with the other objects would be of the purely additive type; this means that I could have him disappear without the relations of the other objects around him being perceptibly changed. In short, no new relation would

appear through him between those things in my universe;
grouped and synthesized from my point of view into instrumental complexes, they would from his, disintegrate
into multiplicities of indifferent relations."[77]

Let us suppose, however, that this man who has
been reading the book, suddenly raises his head and his
eyes begin to wander, looking now at the lawn, then at
the benches along the edge of the lawn and finally, he
looks at me. Such an action on his part poses an enormous
threat to my existence and security. Up until this moment,
the man-reading-book was one among a number of objects
in a world constituted by my consciousness. He, along
with other things, was integrated in my network of projects. Together, they constituted a world for me and they
depended on me for their organization and grouping.
Now, however, the Other, as another consciousness has
invaded my world. He is responsible for a regrouping of
objects which previously peopled my own world. For
the grass is now something qualified; it is this given green
grass which exists for the Other. "This green turns towards
the Other a face which escapes me. . . . I apprehend the
relation of the green of the Other as an objective relation
but I cannot apprehend the green as it appears to the
Other. Suddenly, an object has appeared which has
stolen the world from me. . . . The appearance of the
Other in the world corresponds to a fixed sliding of the
whole universe, to a decentralization of the world which
undermines the centralization which I am simultaneously
effecting."[78]

Stated bluntly, the Other is stealing my world from
me. From now on, objects are no longer my objects,
distances are no longer my distances. There is a kind of
internal hemorrhage because the world of objects is beginning to bleed toward the stranger, who has disrupted my
well-organized world. This threat of stealing my world
from me is compounded by a yet greater danger. For
the Other's look turns upon me and the stranger is now
threatening to transform me, a consciousness, into
one more object in his own organized world. The glance
of the Other pierces through me. It transfixes and congeals

me so that what was formerly a consciousness is now reduced to the state of an object.

In *The Reprieve*, Sartre speaks of the look which
makes of Daniel an object. He writes, "It clove him like
a scythe, amazing, awful and delightful. . . . *They* saw
me—no, not even that; *it* sees me. He was the *object* of
looking. A look that searched him to the depths, pierced
him like a knife-thrust, and was not his own look; an
impenetrable look the embodiment of night, awaiting him
in his deepest self and condemning him to be himself,
coward, hypocrite, pederast, for all eternity. Himself,
quivering beneath that look and defying it. That look!
That night! As if the night was the look. I am *seen*.
Transparent, transparent, transfixed. But by whom? 'I
am not alone,' said Daniel aloud."[79]

The inevitable reaction to such a threat which the
Other's look begets is one of fear. Far from assisting me
in my projects, far from aiding me in my undertakings,
the Other stands poised to dismember one by one my
world of objects. Worse, not only does he steal my world
from me, he now makes *me* an object in his own world—
an object which will be the means of accomplishing
his own projects.

"Fear implies that I appear to myself as threatened
by virtue of my being a presence in the world, not in my
capacity as a For-itself which causes a world to exist.
. . . Fear is the discovery of my being-as-object on the
occasion of the appearance of another object in my perceptive field. It refers to the origin of all fear, which is
the fearful discovery of my pure and simple object-state
insofar as it is surpassed and transcended by possibles
which are not my possibles."[80]

B.   The Keyhole: Shame

Sartre's second example of Being-for-another is that
of the "keyhole." He describes the situation as follows:
"Let us imagine that moved by jealousy, curiosity, or
vice I have just glued my ear to the door and looked
through a keyhole. I am alone and on the level of a non-
thetic self-consciousness. This means, first of all, that

there is no self to inhabit my consciousness, nothing therefore to which I can refer my acts in order to qualify them.
They are in no way known. I am my acts and hence they
carry in themselves their whole justification. I am pure
consciousness of things, and things, caught up in the
circuit of my selfness, offer to me their potentialities as
the proof of my non-thetic consciousness of my own
possibilities. This means that behind the door a spectacle
is presented 'as to be seen,' a conversation as 'to be heard'.
. . . No transcending view comes to confer upon my acts
the character of a given on which a judgment can be
brought to bear. My consciousness sticks to my acts; it
is my acts. . . . But all of a sudden, I hear footsteps in
the hall. Someone is looking at me! What does that mean?
It means that I am suddenly affected in my being and
that essential modifications appear in my structure—modifications which I can apprehend and fix conceptually
by means of the reflective *cogito*."[81]

The result of this sudden appearance of another
consciousness is that I become ashamed. This means that
I am aware of being looked at by the Other. I am the
object of his gaze. Shame, says Sartre, indicates that I
am ashamed of myself *before* the Other. The Other is
another subject or consciousness which is an absolutely
independent being and which, in no way, depends upon
my thinking. Shame is an open admission that I have
fallen into the degrading condition of being an object
of another's consciousness. I feel degraded, fixed and dependent not only on my freedom, but on the freedom
of the Other. Sartre writes, "Shame is by nature recognition. I recognize that I am as the Other sees me. . . .
Shame is shame of oneself before the Other. . . . Shame is
the recognition of the fact that I am indeed that object
which the Other is looking at and judging. I can be
ashamed only as my freedom escapes me in order to
become a given object."[82]

Sartre further maintains that shame is much wider
than merely a feeling which one has when he has been
discovered doing something awkward or clumsy, as for
example, gluing one's eye to the keyhole. Sartre argues,

"Pure shame is not a feeling of being this or that guilty object, but in general, of being an object; that is, of recognizing myself in this degraded, fixed and dependent being which I am for the Other. Shame is the feeling of an original fall, not because of the fact that I may have committed this or that particular fault but simply that I have 'fallen' into the world in the midst of things and that I need the mediation of the Other in order to be what I am."[83]

The example of the park and the keyhole portray graphically the manner in which the existence of another subject or a For-itself can beget either fear or shame in me. In either case, my existence is in danger. As Roger Mehl describes the situation, "The existence of the Other is my negation. It endangers me. By the attention which it places on me and which reaches me right in my heart, the Other attempts to fix and freeze my destiny for all time. Under the attention of the Other, I am reduced to being only a thing, to being only a means or an obstacle for the realization of the projects of the Other. It would be necessary for me to escape the attention of the Other, but this is impossible."[84]

In *The Reprieve*, Daniel describes his being-for-another. He says, "You must have experienced, in the subway, in the foyer of a theatre, or in a train, the sudden and irksome sense that you were being looked at from behind. . . . Well, that is what I felt for the first time, on September 26, at three o'clock in the afternoon in the hotel garden. I became more compact and concentrated. . . . I existed in the presence of a look. . . . What anguish to discover that look as a universal medium from which I can't escape! But what a relief as well! I know at least what I am. I adapt for my own use . . . your prophet's foolish, wicked words: 'I think therefore I am'. . . . I say 'I am seen, therefore I am.' I need no longer bear the responsibility of my turbid and disintegrating self; he who sees me, causes me to be; I am as he sees me. . . . For one instant you were the heaven-sent mediator, between me and myself, you perceived that compact and solid entity which I was and wanted to be."[85]

C. Conflict as Basis for Being for-others

Every human being in Sartre's world qualifies as a consciousness. Each consciousness is a subject which is a potential threat to every other subject. This means that every human being is the natural and a priori enemy of the other, since he is determined to do everything in his power to make an object of the other. And because this is a mutually interlocked struggle (I try to make an object of you, while you try to make an object of me), Sartre holds that absolute frustration is the inevitable outcome of this endless struggle. Each human being attempts to assert his own subjectivity, while the other is just as assiduously striving to destroy the subjectivity of his opponent by reducing him to the level of an object.

Sartre, unequivocally, contends that all human encounters must be viewed as a form of conflict. He writes, "Everything which may be said of me in relation with the Other applies to him as well. While I attempt to free myself from the hold of the Other, the Other is trying to free himself from mine; while I seek to enslave the Other, the Other seeks to enslave me. We are by no means dealing with unilateral relations with an object-in-itself but with reciprocal and moving relations . . . descriptions of concrete behavior must therefore be envisaged within the perspective of conflict. *Conflict is the original meaning of being-for-others.*"[86]

Needless to say, Sartre's theory of the Other is in direct opposition to the I-Thou relationship, so characteristic of the existentialist postures of Gabriel Marcel, Martin Buber and Nikolai Berdyaev.[87] While the theistic existentialists make intersubjectivity, disponibility, fidelity, fraternity, love and spiritual availability and community the very cornerstone of all interpersonal relationships, Sartre cynically regards each human being as the inevitable and natural enemy of his fellow-man. (Even Martin Heidegger, who treats DASEIN as a solitary being and who most weakly and superficially speaks of a *Mitsein*, does not *ex professo* argue that one DASEIN plots the appropriation and domination of another DASEIN.)[88]

While Buber, Marcel, and Berdyaev urge us to treat

every human being as a genuine Thou, gifted with dignity and spirituality, radiating a fraternity which releases within us our own freedom from an egocentricity, Sartre looks upon the Other as piercing us with a Medusa-like stare, ready to transform pulsating life into stone-like rigidity and inertness. The warmth, spontaneity, lovingkindness and spiritual availability of the theistic thinkers are replaced in Sartrean ontology by a sinister and calculating, mutual plotting, whose aim is to entrap and appropriate the freedom of the Other.·

The relentless struggle which goes on between two human beings in the Sartrean world seeks to make an object of the Other. Sartre hastens to remind us that such a struggle does not hope to eventuate in the physical overpowering of the Other, as for example, in the killing of the Other. Rather, the aim of this conflict is the domination of the Other as freedom, as a free being. Such an enterprise, however, is an inherently contradictory operation. It is impossible for the Other to be simultaneously subject and object. He must remain a subject in order to retain his freedom, since it is his very freedom which makes him desirable. Yet as an object of my subjectivity, (I can dominate him only if I make of him an object) he is devoid of the freedom which I must possess. This endless, self-contradictory, mutual entrapment is Sartre's explanation of all human relations.[89]

D.   Human Love as Conflict

Sartre, next, states that human love is the clearest and most striking example of mutual conflict between two human beings. In love, even more than in any other relationship between two individuals, it is the freedom or liberty of the beloved that the lover wishes to appropriate. If love were only the physical possession of the Other's body, it would be easily satisfied. But love, as we well know, argues Sartre, is much more: it is the freedom of that partner which is desired in love. By the same token, if I do succeed in possessing my beloved, I can possess her only as an object, for possession *ipso facto* destroys freedom and subjectivity. All human love is, therefore, an endless engagement in mutual frustration. As a project, love can never be realized.

In Sartre's opinion, my loving you is nothing more than my trying to make you love me. I try to force you, my beloved, to make me the limit and end-all of your life. At the same time, you, my beloved, try to make me love you and make you the *raison d'être* of my existence. As a result, we are faced here with an infinite regress and total frustration. Sartre explains, "Each one wants the other to love him but does not take into account the fact that to love is to want to be loved and that thus by wanting the other to love him, he only wants the other to want to be loved in turn. Thus love relations are a system of indefinite reference—analogous to pure 'reflection-reflected' of consciousness—under the ideal standard of the value 'love,' that is, in a fusion of consciousness in which each of them would preserve his otherness in order to found the other. . . . I demand that the Other love me and I do everything possible to realize my project; but if the other loves me, he radically deceives me by his very love. I demanded of him that he should found my being as a privileged object by maintaining himself as pure subjectivity confronting me; and as soon as he loves me he experiences me as subject and is swallowed up in his objectivity confronting my subjectivity."[90]

From another point of view, love is an attack upon my freedom and the freedom of the beloved. While I want my beloved to make me the end-all of her existence and I want her to do this freely, nevertheless, I am trying to impose upon her a system of values which will not threaten in any way, my own values.

Vincent Miceli speaks of this project in the following terms: "I can never 'get inside' the other's subjectivity. We are intrusions into each other's lives, without ever being able to control each other's freedom or subjecthood. And love is the project seeking this control. Thus, the interpersonal relationship remains essentially one of isolation, while paradoxically functioning as attack and counterattack to reduce each other into objects through the complete domination of the other's liberty. Unity with the other is, therefore, unrealizable both in theory and in fact. Its realization would necessarily entail, as in Hegel's dialectically evolving Spirit, the annihilation through absorption of the other."[91]

Sartre goes on to state that even if I could maintain for a lifetime such a relationship of perpetual tension with my beloved, the presence of a third person poses a threat to us. The look or the gaze of the third is, according to Sartre, sufficient to cause "the petrification of their relationship in a dead possibility." He writes, "But it suffices that the lovers should be looked at together by a third person in order for each one to experience not only his own objectivation but that of the other as well. Immediately the Other is no longer for me the absolute transcendence which founds me in my being; he is a transcendence-transcended, not by me but by another. My original relation to him—i.e., my relation of being the beloved for my lover, is fixed as a dead possibility. It is no longer the experienced relation between a limiting object of all transcendence and the freedom which founds it; it is a love-as-object which is wholly alienated toward the third. Such is the true reason why lovers seek solitude."[92]

In the play, *No Exit*, we have an excellent example of the frustration which the third person causes in two lovers. Garcin, the coward, discovers Estelle, who drove her lover to suicide by killing their baby, most attractive. He is drawn to her and she arouses a desire in him. Estelle is also desirous of possessing Garcin. But neither Garcin nor Estelle can fulfill this desire because of the constant gaze of the third. Inez, the Lesbian, shatters this relationship by constantly gazing into the eyes of the two frustrated lovers. Truly, Sartre concludes, "Hell is other people."[93]

Sartre thus speaks of "the triple destructibility" of love. He writes, "In the first place, love is, in essence a deception and a reference to infinity since to love is to love to be loved, hence to wish that the Other wish that I love him. A preontological comprehension of this deception is given in the very impulse of love—hence the lover's perpetual dissatisfaction. It does not come, as is so often said, from the unworthiness of being loved but from an implicit comprehension of the fact that the amorous intuition is, as a fundamental-intuition, an ideal out of reach. The more I am loved, the more I lose my being, the more I am thrown back on my own responsibilities, on my own power to be. In the second place, the Other's awakening is always possible; at any moment he can make me appear as an object—hence the lover's perpetual insecurity. In the third place, love is an absolute which is perpetually made relative by others. One would have to be alone in the world with the beloved in order to preserve its character as an absolute axis of reference—hence the lover's perpetual shame (or pride—which here amounts to the same thing.)"[94]

William Barrett summarizes in the *Irrational Man*, Sartre's fundamental posture vis-à-vis the Other and human love. He writes, "This relation to the Other is one of the most sensational and best known aspects of Sartre's psychology. To the other person who looks at me from the outside, I seem an object, a thing; my subjectivity with its inner freedom escapes his gaze. Hence his tendency is always to convert me into the object he sees. The gaze of the Other penetrates to the depths of my existence, freezes and congeals me. It is this, according to Sartre, that turns love and particularly sexual love into a perpetual tension and indeed warfare. The lover wishes to possess the beloved, but the freedom of the beloved (which is his or her human essence) cannot be possessed; hence, the lover tends to reduce the beloved to an object for the sake of possessing it. Love is menaced always by a perpetual oscillation between sadism and masochism. In sadism I reduce the other to a mere lump, to be beaten and manipulated as I choose, while in masochism I offer myself as an object, but in an attempt to entrap the other and undermine his freedom."[95]

Michele Sciacca writes the following: "In its concrete relationship with *le pour-l'autre*, the *per-se* tries to dominate it as object and freedom; this, for Sartre, appears evident in sexual love, which, typically, is a form of *possession* whose extreme behavior consists of masochism and sadism. Love is a proof of force: one body wishes to possess and dominate the other *qua* other, and not only as a body or for pleasure. *Sexual love is a reciprocal plundering on the part of two souls.* Whatever the relationship between two men, it is a conflict. And social life as such is a conflict: 'The others are the Inferno.' "[96]

E. Masochism and Sadism

Since human love as mutual fulfillment is a radical impossibility, two resultant attitudes ´are explored by Sartre. They are masochism and sadism. (*Masochism*— from von Sacher Masoch, 1835-1895, an Austrian novelist who described abnormal sexual passion characterized by pleasure in being tortured and abused by one's loved one. *Sadism*—from Count de Sade, 1740-1814,—a sexual perversion by which the torture of a loved person begets sexual gratification and pleasure.)

Sartre contends that the impossibility of achieving true love inevitably begets one or other of two extreme attitudes: (1) either I try to make of myself a kind of object in the eyes of the Other, an instrument for the pleasure of the Other (masochism) or (2) I try through violence and pain to make the Other an instrument and to pulverize his subjectivity for my own pleasure (desire, sadism, hate).

1. *Masochism*

The masochist, according to Sartre, wants to surrender his freedom and become totally an object for the Other. He demands pain and suffering which he normally would avoid at all costs. The masochist projects himself in such a way that he could be "absorbed" by the Other, losing himself in the subjectivity of the Other, in order to rid himself of his own subjectivity. Sartre explains, "Since the Other is the foundation of my being-for-others, if I relied on the Other to make me exist, I should no longer be anything more than a being-in-itself founded in its being by a freedom. Here it is my subjectivity which is considered as an obstacle to the primordial act by which the Other would found me in my being."[97]

Sartre then explains that it is specifically my own subjectivity which my freedom must deny. As a result, I am totally preoccupied with my being-as-object. I insist on being nothing more than an object. I am dependent on the Other and as I experience this being-as-object in shame, I revel in the shame as an unqualified proclamation of my objectivity.

Masochism begets both shame and guilt. I suffer guilt because of the fact that I am an object and I have consented to my complete alienation. I am also guilty because I have given the Other an opportunity to be guilty, i.e., guilty of radically missing my freedom. Masochism, according to Sartre, is an attempt not to fascinate the Other by means of my own objectivity but rather "to cause myself to be fascinated by my objectivity-for-others; that is to cause myself to be constituted as an object by the Other in such a way that I non-thetically apprehend my subjectivity as a *nothing*, in the presence of the In-itself which I represent in the Other's eyes. Masochism is characterized as a species of vertigo, vertigo not before a precipice of rock and earth but before the abyss of the Other's subjectivity."[98]

But masochism is doomed to failure because the masochist wants to give up his freedom, to become an instrument for the Other and to engage himself totally in his being-as-object. In reality, it is he who uses the Other for his own ends. Hence, "It is useless for the masochist to get down on his knees, to show himself in a ridiculous position, to cause himself to be used as a simple lifeless instrument. It is for the Other that he will be obscene or simply passive, for the Other that he will undergo these postures; for himself he is forever condemned to give them to himself. . . . The more he tries to taste his objectivity, the more he will be submerged by the consciousness of his subjectivity—hence his anguish. Even the masochist who pays a woman to whip him is treating her as an instrument and by this very fact posits himself in transcendence in relation to her."[99]

Maurice Friedman describes this frustrating activity in the following manner; "If one wishes, through masochism, to immerse oneself in pure objectivity before the abyss of the Other's subjectivity, one ends by finding the Other's objectivity which, in spite of oneself, frees one's own subjectivity. If one tries instead to look at the Other's look, attempting to confront the Other's freedom on the ground of one's own freedom, one ends by converting the Other into an object."[100]

The second attitude which Sartre explores involves desire, sadism, and hate.

2. Desire

In desire, a consciousness deliberately makes itself body, so that by making itself flesh, it can incarnate the consciousness of the Other. I try to capture your freedom by making it my thing. Sartre explains, "Desire is an attitude aiming at enchantment. Since I can grasp the Other only in his (her) subjective facticity, the problem is to ensnare his (her) freedom within this facticity. It is necessary that he be caught in it as the cream is caught up by a person skimming milk. So the Other's For-itself must come to play on the surface of the body, and be extended all through his body; and by touching this body I should finally touch the Other's subjectivity. This is the true meaning of the word *possession*. It is certain that I want to *possess* the Other's body, but I want to possess it insofar as it is itself a 'possessed,' that is, insofar as the Other's consciousness is identified with his body."[101]

However, desire likewise is fated to end in failure because in the very satisfaction of desire, pleasure arises. Pleasure is the very death of desire not only because it is the fulfillment of desire but because it is also its limit and end. My desire has now lost its goal. I suffer from this frustration and yet I cannot comprehend it. "I am like a sleepwalker who wakens to find himself in the process of gripping the edge of the bed while he cannot recall the nightmare which provoked his gesture. It is this situation which is at the origin of sadism."[102]

3. *Sadism*

The aim in sadism, according to Sartre, is to seize and make use of the Other as object or instrument in a very special manner, namely, one which is the incarnation of a captured freedom. Sadism differs from desire, inasmuch as desire sought to enchant the Other's freedom by means of a mutual incarnation. Sadism, on the other hand, eschews this mutuality. The sadist refuses to be incarnated and through violence and pain, he attempts to make the Other an instrument, thus appropriating the Other's freedom in his flesh. Sadism attempts to incarnate the Other through brute violence. It is a "passion, barrenness and tenacity." Sartre writes, "The sadist's effort is to ensnare the Other in his flesh by means of violence and pain, by appropriating the Other's body in such a way that he treats it as flesh so as to cause flesh to be born. But this appropriation surpasses the body which it appropriates, for its purpose is to possess the body only insofar as the Other's freedom has been ensnared within it. This is why the sadist will want manifest proofs of his enslavement of the Other's freedom through the flesh. He will aim at making the Other ask for pardon, to deny what he holds most dear."[103]

Nevertheless, sadism will also end in frustration. The sadist has persistently attempted to ensnare the transcendent freedom of his victim. However, we have already seen that a priori freedom cannot possibly be appropriated. Hence the more the sadist attempts to treat the Other as an object or instrument, the more the victim's freedom escapes him. Instead of the freedom which he so intensely desires to own, he has nothing more than a grovelling body before him. He realizes that he cannot possibly act on the Other's freedom even if he forces the Other to humiliate himself and to beg for mercy.

The sadist becomes acutely and painfully aware of failure through the LOOK of the victim, for the look is something which the sadist cannot prevent or kill. The look torments him because he realizes that he has failed to capture his victim's freedom. Further, he himself, who has been a being-in-the-act-of-looking, has now become a being-looked-at, before the look of the victim.[104]

4. Hate

The failure of sadism can result in only one other attitude, namely that of hate. Since I cannot establish any kind of satisfactory relationship with the Other, I make him the object of my most profound and bitter hatred. Complete, unalloyed hatred of the Other has only one logical objective, namely the death of the Other. I desire the death of the other consciousness. I hate absolutely and completely the Other's existence because I cannot endure the thought of any limitation of my own freedom. I see now the futility of my numerous attempts to appropriate the Other's freedom. I abandon my claim to realize any union with the Other. I give up any further attempt to use the Other as a means of recovering my own being in-itself. As a hating-for-itself, I resign myself to being a mere For-itself, fully aware of the fact that I cannot make use of my being-for-others. I no longer project being an object.[105]

As a result of this insight, I desire the death of the Other. Sartre writes, "Hate knows the Other-as-object and attaches itself to this object. It wishes to destroy this object in order, by the same stroke, to overcome the transcendence which hates it . . . it leaves in me the feeling that there is 'something' to be destroyed, if I am to free myself. . . . That is why hate is a black feeling; that is, a feeling which aims at the suppression of an Other and which qua project is consciously projected against the disapproval of others."[106]

Yet even hate cannot beget satisfaction and quiescence. Even if I were to destroy the Other through death, still the memory of the look or gaze of the Other will constantly haunt me throughout my life. Even if I could abolish or annihilate the Other at this moment, I cannot possibly bring it about that the Other had not been. There constantly remains the explicit recognition that the Other had existed as a pre-requisite for my having abolished him. Hence victory itself is wedded to defeat. Sartre argues, "He who has once been for-others is contaminated in his being for the rest of his days even if the Other should be entirely suppressed; he will never cease to apprehend his dimension of being-for-others as a permanent possibility of his being. He can never recapture what he has alienated; he has even lost all hope of acting on this alienation and turning it to his advantage since the destroyed Other has carried the key to this alienation along with him to the grave. What I was for the Other is fixed by the Other's death, and I shall irremediably be it in the past. I shall be it also and in the same way in the present if I persevere in the attitude, the projects and the mode of life which have been judged by the Other. The Other's death constitutes me as an irremediable object exactly as my own death would do."[107]

Marjorie Grene describes in vivid terms the final frustration experienced in this devastatingly hopeless project when she writes, "Not even hate, as a last remedy, can break these bonds; for, as we said, murder itself, impelled by hate as the attempt at total destruction of the other person, fails of its object. He has been and has been free; that encroachment on my total liberty I cannot cancel or forget. The circle, then of conflict on conflict is still unbroken; it is a treadmill from which, in my endeavor to approach another's freedom, I can never escape."[108]

Such is the distorted, short-sighted and myopic view which Sartre gives us of the relationships that obtain between human beings. Friendship, devotion, and filial love are total strangers in the dark, murky and menacing world of Sartre's absurdity. Hatred, manipulation and degradation are the order of the day.[109] As Vincent Miceli comments in *The Gods of Atheism*, "In Sartre we are back again to Hegel's and Nietzsche's Master and Slave relationship and morality. The lover seeks the mastery of the beloved whom he must enslave; he demands 'the beloved's freedom first and foremost.' From the enterprise of seduction, which begins with the look, through language, indifference, desire, to the perversion of hate, masochism, and sadism, Sartre has few peers as an analyst of the techniques used by man to dehumanize his fellow man."[110]

In Sartre's play, *The Devil and the Good Lord*, Heinrich, the traitorous Bishop of Worms, expresses the impossibility of any genuine love or human relationship. He exclaims, "God had made it impossible for man to do good on earth. . . . Completely impossible! Why don't you try and love your neighbor? You can tell me afterward what success you had. . . . If only one man should hate another, it would be sufficient for hatred to spread from one to another and overwhelm mankind. . . . The world itself is iniquity; if you accept the world, you are really iniquitous. If you try and change it, then you become an executioner. The stench of the world rises to the stars."[111]

René Lafarge criticizes Sartre in the following way, "We are beginning to see that despite a certain variety of expressions, the relations between men allow for only two fundamental attitudes: love and hate and that, tossed from one to the other, we never succeed in escaping the threats of the Other on our freedom. We are caught in an infernal circle from which there is no escape."[112]

In his work, *The Unquiet Vision*, Nathan Scott gives us the following evaluation of Sartre's analysis of the human condition: "Despite its sensationalistic profundity, it is, of course a very narrow kind of vision—astonishing, indeed, in its narrowness. For so committed is Sartre to a view of the Other as enemy that whole ranges of experience are brushed aside, the affectionate tenderness in the relation between parents and children, the bonds of love and fidelity between husband and wife, the attachments of fondness and devotion that make up the myriad phenomena of friendship."[113]

Régis Jolivet rejects Sartre's position for the following reasons: "Love, friendship, sympathy, good will, generosity—all appear as sadistic conflicts and inevitably end in failure. It is a strange 'existential' philosophy which

finds in the gift only a 'craze to possess' and in charity
the 'ignoble light' of sadism. Even conflict can never be
an interpersonal relationship. In Sartre's system, there
is really no contact possible among persons as such. They
flee each other and exclude each other with a fatality
which defines them. Under these conditions, how can
we explain the existence of a society of souls or of persons?
If each individual, by the complete gratuitousness of his
existential project, is rigorously alone, if there is not and
cannot be a universal order which guarantees the reciprocity of consciences, then we are forced to retreat into
solipsism."[114]

Finally, Gabriel Marcel, who frequently criticized
Sartre's failure to understand the true nature of man and
of interpersonal relationships writes, "What, in fact, is
Sartre's approach to the theory of the awareness of others?
Its whole tendency is to assert that human communication
is doomed to failure; that the sense of community—the
sense of forming part of a *we*-subject—is only experienced
on such occasions as when a regiment is marching in
step or a gang of workmen is pulling together, circumstances where the rhythm is in fact produced by myself
and happens to coincide with that of the concrete community of which I am a member. But when it comes to
the genuine community, the community of love or
friendship, Sartre's analysis of love in *L'Être et le Néant*
and, still more, the illustrations of the analysis in *L'Age
de Raison*, reveal the fundamental agnosticism and even
nihilism of his view. . . . It is clear that the whole of this
dialectic, with its undeniable power, rests upon the complete denial of we as subject, that is to say upon the
denial of communion. For Sartre, this word has no meaning at any possible level, not to speak of its religious and
mystical sense. This is because in his universe, participation itself is impossible; this philosophically, is the essential
point. There is room only for oppropriation."[115]

VII.   TO FREEDOM CONDEMNED

We have already seen that one consequence of Sartre's
postulatory atheism is the denial of any human essence

or nature. Since there is no God and, therefore, no supra-human consciousness to preconceive man's essence, man, according to Sartre, is fundamentally existence and no-thing else. (This is the basis for Sartre's dictum that exis-tence precedes essence.) As a result, man is completely free because there is no archetypal idea or essence in God's mind to which man must conform. During his entire life on this earth (and there is no other life), man is constantly fashioning himself by means of the existen-tial choices which he makes. He is creating his own essence which will be complete only at the moment of his death, when he will be no more. Hence, man is eminently and unqualifiedly free because he is nothing more than the sum of his actions—there is no other reality than his own acts.

In his famous lecture delivered in Paris in 1945, *Exis-tentialism is a Humanism,* Sartre argues, "Man is con-demned to be free. Condemned because he did not create himself, yet is nevertheless at liberty, and from the moment that he is thrown into this world, he is responsible for everything he does. . . . Everything is indeed permitted if God does not exist, and man is in consequence forlorn, for he cannot find anything to depend upon either within or outside himself. He discovers forthwith, that he is without excuse. For if indeed existence precedes essence, one will never be able to explain one's action by reference to a given and specific human nature; in other words, there is no determinism—man is free, man *is* freedom. Nor, on the other hand, if God does not exist, are we provided with any values or commands that could legiti-mise our behavior. Thus we have neither behind us, nor before us in a luminous realm of values, any means of justification or excuse. We are left alone, without ex-cuse."[116]

In a Godless world, man is, in truth, abandoned and condemned to freedom. Since God is dead, there also disappears the possibility of finding values. Put bluntly, there cannot be any prior good to the choice which I make, since there is no infinite Being to give it ground and foundation. To maintain with atheistic existentialists that nothing besides the individual man exists is to hold the following: (1) there is no God (2) there is no system of objective values (3) there are no permanent essences or natures (4) man *is* freedom

A.   Man as Freedom

Sartre insists that man does not have freedom. He is not an agent who possesses a nature and who can experience his will in freedom. For Sartre, on the contrary, man is freedom. Sartre presents his argument in the following manner; "I am indeed an existent who learns his freedom through his acts, but I am also an existent whose individual and unique existence temporalizes itself as freedom. As such I am necessarily consciousness [of] freedom since nothing exists in consciousness except as the non-thetic consciousness of existing. Thus my freedom is perpetually in question in my being; it is not a quality added on or a property of my nature. It is very exactly the stuff of my being; and, as in my being, my being is in question, I must necessarily possess a certain comprehension of freedom."[117]

In the *Age of Reason*, Mathieu suddenly becomes aware of the implications of his condemnation to freedom. We read, "The brake was suddenly slammed down and the bus stopped. . . . Mathieu thought: 'It is *by my agency* that everything must happen.' Even if he let himself be carried off, in helplessness and in despair, even if he let himself be carried off like an old sack of coal, he would have chosen his own damnation; he was free, free in every way, free to behave like a fool or a machine, free to accept, free to refuse, free to equivocate, free to marry, to give up the game, to drag this dead weight about with him for years to come. He could do what he liked, no one had the right to advise him, there could be for him no Good nor Evil unless he brought them into being. All around him things were gathered in a circle, expectant, impassive and indicative of nothing. He was alone, enveloped in this monstrous silence, free and alone without assistance and without excuse, condemned to decide without support from any quarter, condemned forever to be free."[118]

In a similar vein, the hero of Sartre's play, *The Flies*, speaks to Jupiter of the overwhelming freedom and its implications for him. Orestes says, "Suddenly, out of the blue, freedom crashed down on me and swept me off my feet. . . . And there was nothing left in heaven, no right or wrong, nor anyone to give me orders. . . . I shall not return under your law; I am doomed to have no other law but mine."[119]

B.   Inventor of Values

Accordingly, man is thrown into the world and he is free to act as soon as he has become conscious of himself. Like the Heideggerian DASEIN, he neither knows nor cares whence he came or whither he is going. And because there is no higher being and consequently no permanent essences or natures, there are likewise no norms or values. Man's freedom is a crushing and overwhelming condemnation. He finds himself faced with the appalling necessity of making choices without the help of any norms. Man must *invent* values, since there are no rules of conduct or morality to serve him as guidelines for his actions. There is absolutely no one and no thing that can either condemn man or justify him. He is the supreme maker and inventor of values and with a shudder and great trepidation, he must assume complete responsibility for every act which he performs.

Man is thus free in every respect—free to choose his manner of acting and free to choose the cause for his particular actions. (This is what Albert Camus will later call quantitative ethics and he will reject it in favor of a *mésure* which recognizes stable essences.) The Sartrean man, however, rejects all rules and guidelines which men normally follow in the performance of actions. And whereas it is generally agreed that these guidelines imply certain obligations on the part of man, Sartre categorically refuses to subscribe to this position. For him, value is not a given. Rather, it is an ideal which man's freedom can create and destroy at will[120]

In *Being and Nothingness*, Sartre explains, "Value derives its being from its exigency and not its exigency from its being. It does not deliver itself to a contemplative intuition which would apprehend it as being value and thereby would remove from it its right over my freedom. On the contrary, it can be revealed only to an active freedom which makes it exist as value by the sole fact of recognizing it as such. It follows that my freedom is the unique foundation of values and that nothing, absolutely nothing, justifies me in adopting this or that particular value, this or that particular scale of values. As a being by whom values exist, I am unjustifiable. My freedom is anguished at being the foundation of values while itself, it is without foundation. It is anguished, in addition, because values, due to the fact that they are essentially revealed to a freedom, cannot disclose themselves without being at the same time 'put into question'; for the possibility of overturning the scale of values appears complementarily as my possibility. It is anguish before values which is the recognition of the ideality of values."[121]

As unqualified and ungrounded freedom, man must carry the entire responsibility of the world by himself. He is abandoned in the world in a very positive sense. This abandonment does not involve a passivity on his part. Rather, it is a positive realization that absolutely nothing will permit me to tear myself away from the awesome responsibility. Hence, I must make my own choices without any assistance whatsoever and invent values.

Sartre develops the point, ". . . man being condemned to be free, carries the weight of the whole world on his shoulders, he is responsible for the world and for himself as a way of being. . . . I am responsible for everything, in fact, except for my very responsibility, for I am not the foundation of my being. Therefore, nothing takes place as if I were compelled to be responsible. I am abandoned in the world, not in the sense that I might remain

abandoned and passive in a hostile universe like a board
floating on the water, but rather in the sense that I find
myself suddenly alone and without help, engaged in a
world for which I bear responsibility without being able,
whatever I do, to tear myself away from this responsibility for an instant."[122]

C. Anguish

This absolute and unlimited freedom, which man is,
gives him the power to choose projects and to define the
meaning of situations which constantly confront him in
the world. In this connection, we meet one of the most
ridiculed categories of contemporary existentialism, namely
the category of anguish. While anguish or dread (*Angst*)
for Heidegger represents a means whereby DASEIN encounters nothingness, for Sartre, anguish (*angoisse*) concerns man's freedom as distinguished from the ensemble
of man's past choices which represent his "up-to-now"
provisional and incomplete essence.

Sartre writes, "I emerge alone and in anguish confronting the unique and original project which constitutes my being; all the barriers, all the guard rails collapse,
nihilated by the consciousness of my freedom. I do not
have nor can have recourse to any value against the fact
that it is I who sustain values in being. Nothing can ensure
me against myself, cut off from the world and from my
essence by this nothingness which I am. I have to realize
the meaning of the world and of my essence; I make my
decision concerning them—without justification and without excuse. Anguish, then, is the reflective apprehension
of freedom by itself. . . . In anguish I apprehend myself
at once totally free and as not being able to derive the
meaning of the world except as coming from myself."[123]

Herbert Spiegelberg displays a certain impatience
with Sartre's assertion that all values depend upon our
freedom and that we are subjected to this great anguish
as a result. He accuses Sartre of a number of gratuitously
assumed propositions which are absolutely lacking in
proof. He writes, "Sartre's anguish has nothing to do
with cowardly timidity in the face of real or imaginary

dangers. It expresses man's response to his assumed responsibilities, which in Sartre's case are particularly overwhelming since they embrace no less than the meaning of his world as a whole. On the other hand, this passage [quoted above] includes in its sweep such phenomenologically surprising assertions as the dependence of all values upon our freedom, which Sartre asserts in a number of other places, but without attempting any real demonstration. Suffice it to say that in cases like these Sartre seems to be starting from original and significant observations, only to be carried away to paradoxical formulations bordering on the nonsensical."[124]

D. Bad Faith

While Sartre insists that anguish or dread is a category that accompanies human freedom, he hastens to point out that in most cases, it is conspicuous by its absence. The reason for this condition is the fact that most people are guilty of "bad faith," which is essentially a refusal to become anguished and thereby exercise absolute freedom. Such individuals resort to patterns of flight. But because anguish is a veritable "immediate given" of my freedom, even if I wish to veil this aspect of my being; i.e., "not to see it," I must, nevertheless, indicate this very aspect in order to be able to turn away from it. Still more correctly, I must think of anguish constantly in order to take care not to think of it. Hence, Sartre contends, "I flee in order not to know but I cannot avoid knowing that I am fleeing; and the flight from anguish is only a mode of becoming conscious of anguish."[125]

But to flee anguish and to be anguish are not exactly the same thing. If I am anguish in order that I may flee it, this indicates that I can be anguish by "not being it," that I can rid myself of a "nihilating power at the very heart of anguish itself." This nihilating power renders anguish null, to the degree that I try to escape it and it nihilates itself, insofar as I am anguish, so that I can escape it. This attitude, according to Sartre, is "bad faith."

Hence it is impossible for me to purge myself of anguish in my consciousness; neither can I make it an unconscious psychic phenomenon. I am guilty of bad faith while I apprehend the anguish I am. If I try to flee from this anguish or anxiety, which is somewhat like the vertigo a man experiences on the edge of a precipice, I am attempting to hide my freedom from myself. In other words, I am trying to conceal from myself the "nothing" which separates my essence from my choice. For example, I can ascribe my choice "to my essence, my physico-psychological make-up or to the social environment or to divine predetermination." When I do this, I am guilty of bad faith.

Sartre contends, however, that bad faith is different from lying. When I lie, I say what I know or believe to be false. My reason for lying is the deliberate deception of others. In the case of bad faith, on the other hand, I try to mask the truth from myself. This possibility of bad faith is part of the very structure of consciousness itself. In *Being and Nothingness,* the author promises us in a footnote that he will disclose to us the manner in which we can escape bad faith by a return to authenticity, but to date, he has failed to present us with his promised solution.[126]

E. Ethical Implications of Freedom

We have seen above that Sartre wrote the following words: ". . . my freedom is the unique foundation of values and nothing, absolutely nothing, justifies me in adopting this or that particular value, this or that particular scale of values."[127]

Alfred Stern argues that by adopting this position of Jean Paul Sartre vis-à-vis the nature of freedom, the French followers of Sartre, who labored with him in the underground during the Nazi occupation of France, were no more correct in espousing the values of French democracy, than were the disciples of Martin Heidegger for championing Nazi ideals and fighting for them with the German Storm Troopers. In Sartre's own words, "Every time a man chooses his engagement and projects in all sincerity and lucidity, whatever this choice may be, it is impossible to prefer another to it."[128]

Obviously, to subscribe to such a complete and un-
trammeled freedom is tantamount to championing a quantitative ethics, wherein the genus or kind of action performed is of no consequence whatsoever. The only criterion
is the sincerity with which the action is done. As Albert
Camus pointed out, what matters in such an ethics is
not the kind of living but the "most living." We cannot
say that one action is by its very nature, e.g., the murder of
an innocent human being, intrinsically evil. If it is performed with sincerity and lucidity, such an act, according
to Sartre, must be judged good.

In his argument with Sartre on this very point, Camus
challenged Jean Paul to put his theory into practice.
Specifically, he challenged Sartre to reveal Camus' activity in the French Resistance movement to the Nazis
and thus bring certain death to his co-worker. Sartre refused, thereby repudiating his own theory of absolute and
unqualified freedom.[129]

Continuing his critique of Sartre's notion of freedom,
Stern writes, "Placing the difference between 'good' and
'evil' in an inner criterion—that of sincerity—existentialist
ethics has to admit a kind of moral equivalence of all projects, because a Nazi can be as sincere as a democrat, a
murderer as sincere as a benefactor of mankind. This
is certainly one of the greatest danger spots of existentialism, according to which everybody has his own ethics,
by stating, 'We should ask ourselves: What would happen
if everybody would do the same?' And he adds that only
by a kind of 'bad faith' can a man evade this reflection
when acting. The man who lies and excuses himself by
declaring that not everybody acts the same feels uneasy
because the fact of lying implies a universal value ascribed
to a lie."[130]

VIII. EVALUATION OF SARTREAN ETHICS

A number of commentators have found glaring deficiencies in Sartre's ethical teaching. The consequences
of his interpretation of human freedom beget an area of
confusion and gratuitous assumptions. Let us examine a
few of these evaluations.

Frederick Copleston writes, ". . . the philosopher cannot tell a man how he ought to act, if by telling him how he ought to act means relating a possible particular act to a universally-obligatory moral law and there is no set of absolute values. . . . Ultimately, therefore, every individual human being creates his own values and his own moral law. He is totally responsible, and he can find no justification for his choice from without. For there are no God, no transcendent values, and no universally-obligatory moral law. A man may, of course, make his particular choices as a member of 'the one' and try to throw the responsibility on society. But he is merely masking from himself the fact that he has chosen this way of acting. The individual as free subject is essentially isolated and alone. And it is in this isolation and loneliness that he creates his world and his values."[131]

F. H. Heinemann finds Sartre's interpretation of human freedom inadequate and incomplete. The Sartrean man is completely free of the influence of emotions and passions. Furthermore, man becomes a would-be creator, a *homo-creator,* who becomes only naturally responsible and not morally responsible. This interpretation of course, begets total irresponsibility.

Heinemann writes, "He desires freedom. Wonderful! But he wants too much. He wishes to be completely and absolutely free in all the spheres of his being, in his emotions and passions as well as in his will. He claims total and infinite liberty. Whereas in fact people are dominated by their emotions and passions, he tries to persuade us that we ourselves have chosen to be jealous or sad; that we have chosen our own being and, in a certain sense, even our coming into the world. . . . But if we ask what he means by liberty, he answers 'a spontaneity which determined itself to be' (p. 517). He mistakes natural, or rather naturalistic, spontaneity for moral liberty. . . . This so-called freedom which in reality is not freedom at all, is absurd (p. 559).

But is he not right in connecting liberty with responsibility? Does he not make us responsible for our

being, our actions, for the world in which we live, for the
world war and for the Universe itself? Yes, he does, and he
even reaches the startling conclusion that man, being
condemned, 'carries the load of the whole world on his
shoulders and is responsible for the world and for himself in his specific being' (p. 639). This sounds wonderful,
but what does it amount to? 'Responsibility' here has
a merely naturalistic meaning, namely, 'consciousness of
being the incontestable author of an event or of an object' (*loc. cit.*). It simply means that *homo-creator,* or
rather man, the would-be creator, regards himself as the
author of all things. In this sense, he is 'naturally responsible,' but he is not 'morally responsible'; he is not answer-
able either to God who does not exist, nor to a moral
law nor to values which are denied objective validity and
depend on the individual as their creator. Sartre maintains
that whatever happens is 'mine' and that no happening
is inhuman. . . . 'The most atrocious situations in war,
the worst tortures do not create an inhuman state of
affairs' (p. 639). This statement reveals the confusion,
not only of this writer, but of our time. It seems irresponsible, not worthy of a member of the Resistance, because
it implies a justification of the most cruel actions of the
most inhuman dictators. Torturers are not only inhuman,
they are subhuman, they violate the dignity of the human
person which is and should be an end in itself, but which
is here merely an object of sadistic practice."[132]

James Collins analyzes in his typically methodical
and perlucid manner the implications of Sartre's brand
of freedom. He presents the following points for our
consideration: "Freedom is here reduced to spontaneity.
. . . Condemnation to freedom would then mean not only
that one cannot avoid acting freely and well by the very
fact of initiating any project with resoluteness and afore-
thought. . . . Sartre realizes that an unqualified acceptance of this view will lead to a glorification of power
displayed for its own sake. Hence under cover of the
new existentialist terminology, he is obliged to restore

some common objective standards. He says that one 'ought' to act authentically and 'ought' to respect the liberty of others.

. . . What authenticates an individual's act of choice so that it becomes a humane act? Sartre offers two criteria: that it be done with perfect lucidity, and that it involves an acceptance of responsibility for other men as well. If these conditions are fulfilled, then the act is unconditionally true, value-creative, and authentic and good. Most moralists would grant that a clear understanding of the situation is a requirement of moral behavior, not in the specific sense of good behavior but merely responsible behavior. Freedom has its roots in an intellectual judgment, based upon a calm appraisal of the situation. But this is no guarantee that the choice will be a good one or in conformity with human nature. . . . Malicious action may also be performed on the basis of unblinking honesty about oneself. As Marcel remarked apropos of André Gide's similar celebration of lucid disillusionment as the distinguishing mark of humane conduct, 'there is a diabolical lucidity which can pierce the deepest shadows of the self without removing one bit of the gloom or one degree of the perversion'. . . . The attitude of choosing for other men as well as for oneself is compatible with the most diverse courses of action. There is a sense of social destiny dignifying the policies of dictators and petty tyrants as well as those of liberators and benefactors of humanity. The most ruthless use of power is often exercised by men who have a keen sense of its effect upon the lives of others."[133]

John Wild, in his work, *The Challenge of Existentialism,* complains of Sartre's deficient view of human existence. And in spite of the fact that Sartre has not, as yet, written his ethics, Wild contends that the type of existentialist ethics which Sartre must defend is already clear in outline form. He writes, "We may describe this as an ethics of pure freedom; man has no stable nature; he possesses no constant tendencies. There are no changeless norms, to which he can look for guidance of his conduct. To set up such norms is merely to rationalize choices that have already been made. . . . Whether I decide to die for justice or drink at a bar, the matter is indifferent. . . . Liberty itself is the only stable norm. To maintain this is always good. To stifle it, especially in myself, is always evil. What is this freedom? For Heidegger, with his positive view of human existence, it is a freedom *for* final commitment-unto-death. For Sartre, with his negative view, it is rather a freedom *from* any such commitment, save the principle of having no final commitment at all."[134]

Walter Odajnyk sees the Sartrean man as usurping the prerogative of a God whom Sartre has denied. Man is a deity and it is he who creates values not only for himself but for others as well. He makes his own essence; he puts values upon his actions and upon the life and actions of others. Odajnyk writes, "Sartre claims that this exactly is the starting point of existentialism: everything is permitted. And so it is man who is the creator of all values, for by choosing certain values for himself, by implication, he chooses them for all others also. Man is now God because he creates himself—he makes his own essence, and he also decides what values will be placed upon his life and his actions and even upon the life and actions of all others. It is no wonder that anguish comes to haunt him in his work, for he must make decisions alone without reference to heaven or to any stable norms; and he knows that he alone bears the entire responsibility for his decisions. He is a God, but a God chained; he is condemned to make these decisions. He has not chosen to play God, and yet no matter what he does he cannot escape his role."[135]

In much the same vein, Copleston refers to Sartre's doctrine as a "philosophy of atomic individualism," wherein the individual's choice alone creates values. Even though Sartre proclaims that man must choose and legislate ideally for all men, yet it is the individual who creates a given value. And should another individual refuse in all sincerity to assume this social responsibility (by making capricious choice *his* value), I must admit that his choice is no worse than mine; they are both equally valid.

Copleston argues, "If by 'atomic individualism' we mean the doctrine that there is no universally-obligatory moral law and no values which are not created by the individual's choice, Sartre's philosophy is obviously a philosophy of atomic individualism. Furthermore, it appears to me that the notion of choosing and legislating ideally for all men simply masks, and in no way really diminishes the individualism latent in the system. For if to choose with a sense of social responsibility is a value, it is the individual who creates this value, on Sartre's premises, that is to say. If someone does not regard it as a value and exalts capricious choice without any sense of social responsibility, I can, indeed, disapprove of this attitude from within the set of values which I have chosen; but if I am a follower of Sartre, I must admit that in the long run the other man's set of values is as good as mine."[136]

Jean Paul Sartre has gone to great lengths in order to protect his stance on freedom and ethics from being charged with a reckless libertarianism. Sartre emphasizes that each individual is completely free in making his choices and in no way is he responsible to any authority—divine or human—or to traditional values. At the same time, his admonition is: While you are free, this does not mean that you can do whatever you please. In choosing, man chooses for all men. He is the embodiment of humanity. Hence, in exercising his freedom, no individual can so choose his values that he might violate the freedom of others. In this sense, man does not exercise absolute freedom.

Helmut Kuhn asserts that Sartre at this point is abandoning his existentialist position. In decreeing that the individual man must respect the freedom of others, Sartre is, in reality, appropriating the Kantian principle that man can never be used as a means; he is always an end. But Sartre fails to provide a necessary foundation for this claim. In other words, while the Kantian Imperative has a solid foundation in the concept of Reason, Sartre's position is totally lacking a basis. In fact, it violates the most fundamental tenets of his own exis-

tentialism. Kuhn explains, "In Kant the self-limiting freedom—the principle that no individual should be used
as a means towards an end other than himself—rests on
the solid foundation of a concept of reason. The will as
truly free is for Kant identical with practical reason *in
actu*. In Sartre, the same principle is a gratuitous affirmation. Not only does it lack the supporting idea of
reason, but it contradicts the Existential premises. Developed into its consequences, it would result, just as it
does in Kant, in universal rules of conduct. These rules
as enunciated by Kant in the various formulæ of the
Categorical Imperative are, it is true, very general, and
therefore of uncertain application to concrete cases. But
they have precisely that character which values do not
and should not have according to Sartre: *they exist independently of our consent*. They have a foundation other
than our bottomless freedom. Sartre's ethics clearly defines a position not only beyond crisis but beyond existentialism."[137]

IX. CONCLUSION

We now come to the end of our brief examination
of some of the salient points of Sartre's existentialism. Because of his singular talents as a playwright, novelist, and
essayist, for which he was selected to receive the Nobel
Prize for Literature in 1964 (which, as we have already
seen, he spurned), Sartre has succeeded in becoming the
best known existentialist in the world today. He has a
vast reading audience numbering in the millions, who
would never had even heard of his name if he had restricted himself to the writing of strictly professional
philosophical works like *Being and Nothingness* and
Critique of Dialectical Reason. Because of his highly
successful literary works, Sartre has likewise succeeded
in creating the impression that his atheistic brand of
existentialism is the only existentialism in existence today.
This, of course, is rather ironic in view of the fact that
Exstentialism, as a philosophical stance, was founded by
a most devout Christian, Soren Kierkegaard. This attitude
likewise disregards completely the outstanding work of

such theistic existentialists as Martin Buber, Gabriel Marcel and Nikolai Berdyaev.[138]

Be that as it may, we have seen that Sartre must be credited with a number of totally unproved and gratuitously assumed positions which form the basis of his existentialism. To name only a few: atheism is a postulated a priori starting point. Sartre categorically denies the existence of a Transcendent Being, without even a token attempt at examining the nature of contingent and necessary being. Since God is cavalierly outlawed, Sartre contends that we must likewise deny a human essence to man. The argument for this position is patently specious as we have already seen above.[139]

Sartre further assumes, without any proof whatsoever, that all being must be divided into the In-itself and the For-itself. Man, as For-itself or pure consciousness, is nothingness which is constantly poised midway between its past choices and accomplishments which no longer are, and his future projects which as yet are not. His entire life will consist in this forging ahead and creating his own essence, which will never be completed until the moment that death intervenes and man is no more.

The In-itself which is massive, permanent and stable self identity is the very antithesis of For-itself's nothingness and constant insecurity and changeableness. As such, the In-itself poses a threat to For-itself. At the same time, For-itself strives futilely to acquire the stability and permanence of the In-itself. This contradiction of For-itself-in-itself Sartre blithely and almost roguishly proclaims to be a definition of God. Every human being is a continuous engagement in this self-contradictory, frustrating operation of attempting to become God.

Not only is the In-itself a constant threat to the For-itself but each For-itself is likewise a threat to every other For-itself. In his notorious analyses of the gaze of look (the park, the keyhole), Sartre holds that each human being is the natural enemy of the other. Human love is the clearest example of the incessant struggle that takes place between the lover and the beloved. While

I strive to make of my beloved an object, an In-itself, by possessing her, my beloved is locked in a struggle to make me her object or In-itself. In reality, contends Sartre, each attempts to appropriate the freedom or subjectivity of the other. This, however is a manifest impossibility, since an object or an In-itself intrinsically involves a denial of freedom. But the only attraction which the beloved poses to the lover is the beloved's freedom. In order to appropriate this freedom, the lover would then be forced to make of the beloved an In-itself or object, which is the very antithesis of freedom. Hence all human love is a frustrating, contradictory relationship which has been strikingly defined as "the mutual plundering on the part of two souls." It is superfluous to point out that Sartre's analysis fails to portray accurately the condition of man in the world.

Furthermore, For-itself as consciousness and nothingness is also freedom. Man does not possess or exercise freedom. He IS freedom. This freedom to which man is condemned makes him the creator of all human values. There is absolutely no thing, person or norm to which man can turn for guidance in the choices he must make. Obviously, we have here an ethics of quantity where only intensity or sincerity of the doer is the norm. The *kind* of action involved has absolutely no meaning.

As it has been observed, this norm of intensity or sincerity is a highly subjective and relativistic criterion. The actions of a highly dedicated and altruistic philanthropist and those of a bloodthirsty tyrant or dictator can be equally justified. Sartre sees the weakness of his position and he appeals to the Kantian principle that in a matter of choices, we must never make another human being a means to an end. But by appealing to the Kantian imperative, Sartre accepts a stable and universal norm which is in open contradiction to his existentialist stance.

To be sure, there are some contributions to philosophy to be gleaned from Sartre's existentialism. The emphasis on the importance of the individual and his responsibility in making truly existential choices looms large in Sartre's thought. (But this is also true of every theistic existentialist.) The emphasis on the inevitability of death is certainly a point which twentieth-century man can well ponder. (Sartre's answer, however, is a purely negative and dismal one, since the entire orientation of his thought is atheistic. There *can* be no question of a future life in this context.) Again, perhaps the most positive contribution of Sartre's thought is the underscoring of alienation and forlornness of man when he denies the existence of God and a future life for man. As Sartre himself has confessed in his autobiography, "Atheistic existentialism is a cruel and long-range affair."[140]

We shall now conclude with a number of evaluations of Jean Paul Sartre's thought.

George Novack in speaking of Sartre's existentialism makes the following evaluation: "Existentialism remains fundamentally a creed of frustration in the midst of fulfillment. The most brilliant success turns into failure as coal into ashes. . . . For Sartre the act of transcendence negates itself in the very process of materialization, trickles out and dies. It must be followed by a fresh exertion of creative revolt which, in turn, will not reach its goal. Thus mankind hungers but is never fully fed. We ask for nourishing bread and receive a stone. The most promising road forward winds up in a blind alley. Life is not only a gamble; it is in the end a cheat. We are swindled by the limitations of time, history, and death which nullify our·fondest hopes. 'The sorrows of our proud and angry dust are from eternity and will not fail.' But man always will.

Sartre epitomized this pessimism coiled in the heart of Existentialism in the famous aphorism from *Being and Nothingness*: 'Man is a useless passion.' So grim a humanism in which every venture must turn out to be a lost cause can stimulate spasmodic expenditures of energy in social struggle. But the expectation that defeat lurks in ambush, spreads scepticism and cripples the steadfastness of the inwardly divided individual at every step."[141]

Kurt Reinhardt finds Sartre guilty of a number of unfounded and arbitrarily stated assertions. Particularly in the case of Sartre's *opus magnum,* Reinhardt has the following to say: "A critique of the main tenets of Sartre's philosophy, as set forth in *L'Être et le Néant,* will necessarily have to begin with pointing out the complete arbitrariness of many of the French thinker's assumptions and assertions. Among such postulatory and unproven *points de départ* are the concepts of *en-soi* and *pour-soi;* the reduction of human existence to the sphere of consciousness; the contention of an aboriginal state of hate and strife between man and man; the way the concept of 'nothingness' is used (or abused); the apodictic denial of the existence of God; and the proclamation of the absoluteness of freedom. . . . Sartre's world is, in short, an absurd and impossible universe, populated by contingent and isolated beings, all self-enclosed and merely physically juxtaposed in a metaphysical and moral vacuum. The neighbor is 'the other,' and he is the enemy, and since God (if he existed) would be 'the absolute other,' he would logically be the most formidable and most hated enemy."[142]

Michele Sciacca underlines the scepticism and atheism in Sartre's philosophy; he also calls Jean Paul a moralist in the tradition of French moralism inspired by Jansenism. Sciacca observes, "As a moralist Sartre does not believe in 'good actions,' for he holds that virtues are the alibi for vices, and that men preach them without practising them. His is naturally an absurd moralism, in that he denies not only morality but also the virtues and moral principles; once these are denied, moralism itself ceases, and, everything being negative, it no longer makes any sense to reproach men for failing to practise the virtues.

Sartre's man is neither attractive nor repellent; he just remains there and we do not know what he is; he has no drama, as he is a shapeless mass that wrinkles his skin, moves a limb, curls himself up and stretches . . . his words are meaningless . . . it does not make any difference whatsoever—this thing or that thing makes no difference, since everything is absurd. With Sartre, existentialism ceases to be an existential experience and it destroys itself while it reveals its nothingness of human consistency."[143]

Anthony Manser in his study of Sartre's philosophy complains of the tendency to reduce all moral action to the level of arbitrary decision. Given these premises, it would seem that meaning is given to the action only after the decision is made. He argues, "The whole attack on the notion of human nature, the categorisation of man as the being who is not what he is and is what he is not, is aimed at destroying a belief in values embodied in the structure of the universe, and hence the notion that there is a single moral way of acting. The danger of this attempt to be radical is that it reduces moral action to the level of arbitrary decision. It is even doubtful if we could talk of 'decisions' here, for a decision can only be made in the context of a meaningful way of life. For Sartre it would appear that the meaning is subsequent to the decision, in which case it is impossible to know what is being decided. Similarly, if morality results from a bare project, it is hard to see in what sense it can be called morality."[144]

Fritz Pappenheim in *The Alienation of Modern Man* finds fault with the total lack of standards and values in Sartre's philosophy. The widespread appeal of total involvement he attributes to the fact that twentieth century man is desperately trying to return from his alienated existence. He writes, "Following Heidegger, Sartre has stated that man thrown into a world which has no road signs cannot be told which way to go, which values he ought to choose. He has to choose his own person, and there is no guide-post along the road but the awareness that only total involvement counts. As much as this idea appeals to contemporary man, it does no more than reflect his desire to return from his alienated existence, from a condition in which he has become a mere object."[145]

Paul Foulquié finds the note of absurdity in Sartre's posture especially reprehensible. He writes, "As a reply to all the problems raised by existence, we have regularly been given the oracular reply: it is absurd. The fact of the *en-soi* is absurd; the emergence of the *pour-soi* is likewise absurd; likewise, is the free choice of our essence. . . . 'Being is without reason, without cause and without necessity,' we read towards the end of *L'Être et le Néant* (p. 713); and in *La nausée*: 'All existing beings are born without reason, continue through weakness and die by accident' (p. 170). It is really absurd that, being able, according to his principles, to choose his philosophy, M. Sartre should have chosen the philosophy of the absurd, which is the very negation of philosophy."[146]

Joseph Mihalich finds Sartre's existentialism defective because of its avowed refusal to examine seriously the traditional preoccupations of philosophy. If philosophy is truly wisdom, then we must be able to expect more from a philosopher than a bald statement to the effect that absurdity is the ultimate answer when we are investigating the first principles and causes of things.

Mihalich states his case, "A serious shortcoming to Sartrean existentialism (and in other forms) is its refusal to give ultimate answers to ultimate questions—e.g., questions of origin and destiny. Sartre puts the general problem of origin and destiny in the context of the absurd (*de trop*) in that they cannot be explained or justified. In his words, things just are—they are or come to be without reason and cease to be or die purely by chance. Philosophy in the best sense of the term is wisdom—the disposition of knowledge of ultimate principles and causes and structures of all things. A philosophical system loses something of what it is supposed to be, if it arbitrarily stops its investigation with obvious and important phenomena still to be explained. Granting that not every aspect of reality is equally susceptible of explanation and analysis, a consistent pattern or refusal to offer a realistic answer to critical questions is not in existentialism's favor. A philosophical system is somehow obligated to suggest something more meaningful than 'absurdity' as the ultimate answer to questions of origin and destiny."[147]

Vincent Miceli in his recent work, *The Gods of Atheism,* sees a positive contribution which Sartrean thought has made to the twentieth-century man. He says, "Sartre has rendered mankind some useful service. He has analyzed sin with deep penetration. It is the bitter estrangement from God and from our fellow man. It is the great divine-human schism. He has exploded the secularized myths that guarantee man happiness in and through temporal achievements. No present, no future earthly condition of man will ever make life worth living. He has stressed, once again, in a stark manner, man's personal responsibility for making his own being and world. He has focused the mind and heart of man on his great power of freedom with all its dangerous possibilities. He has ruthlessly unmasked the poses men take to escape hard decisions. He has re-created the confrontation between freedom and grace. He has forced the collectivized atheism of positivism and Marxism to come out from behind their protective wall of science and politics in order to prove to the individual that absurd existence is worth living. He has put their panaceas to a severe test.

But in the last analysis, Sartre's philosophy leads logically and directly to despair and suicide. His doctrine of salvation leads man to the abyss of social atomism. His first and final word on life, liberty and love is that they just happen and are always absurd, contradictory and doomed to frustration. His world of atheism is a kingdom of nothingness plunged into intellectual darkness, convulsed with spiritual hate and peopled by inhabitants who curse God and destroy each other in their vain attempt to seize His vacant throne."[148]

F. H. Heinemann sees in Sartre's position a lack of balance and moderation. According to him, we are constantly presented the extreme interpretation, whether it is a question of responsibility, commitments or negativity. Heinemann writes, "Uncertain of himself [Sartre] overstresses his commitments. He goes too far in his negativity. He is entitled to disclaim that we have any knowledge of God and of the Transcendent, but he is unable to prove their non-existence. He is right in distinguishing logical negation and ontological not-being, and in maintaining that man brings *some* negativity into this world, but he is wrong in claiming that he is the source of *all* negativity. He is right in stressing the responsibility for others even in solitary decisions, but he is wrong in making men responsible for actions they did not do and for situations they did not bring about, and for overloading them with total responsibility. He condemns them to infinite liberty which they are unable to bear."[149]

Mary Warnock sees some unresolved contradictions in Sartre's position that man is committed to a ceaseless struggle with his fellow man and, at the same time, that he has absolute freedom to choose whatever life he wants. She cannot see how an ethics can become viable in a climate where domination of the other person and subordination of his freedom to ours is the overriding factor. She explains her point, "What, then, are the possibilities for ethics? First, we must notice the unresolved contradiction in *Being and Nothingness,* which Sartre does not pay enough attention to. How can we reconcile the belief that we are absolutely free to choose whatever life we want, to be what we want, with the belief that in our dealings with others, we are committed to an unending conflict from which there is no escape? It seems that these two beliefs cannot be wholly reconciled, and that this constitutes at least part of the difficulty with which Sartre is faced in constructing any ethical theory at all. If ethics, as we have supposed, is concerned with the fitting together of the interests and choices of one person with those of another, there is no way into the subject at all if our aim is *necessarily* to dominate the other person and subordinate his freedom to our own."[150]

Alfred Stern objects very emphatically to Sartre's contradictory attitude towards ethical situations. He finds it extremely strange that a philosopher who grants everyone absolute freedom in inventing his own system of values, can utter the most categorical value judgments on the behavior of others. Stern finds the root for this attitude in the irrationalistic stance which existentialism takes with respect to the position and value of reason. He contends that emotional states, such as anxiety, sorrow and nausea are judged superior to reason.

Stern writes, ". . . in discussing Existentialist ethics, Sartre rejects all given, constituted values as limitations of our liberty and grants everybody the freedom to invent his own system of values, without any possibility of having it legitimized by any supra-individual authority. Of one of his characters, Sartre says, 'There would be neither right nor wrong unless he invented them.' It is strange that a philosopher who denies in this way all bases for value judgments that are objectively valid, would utter so frequently the most offensive valued judgments, with the most apodictic certainty, on the moral behavior of other people, and claim universal validity for such 'philosophical categories' as 'coward' and *salaud*. . . . If Sartre's characters find existence unbearable because it does not offer absolute necessity, they show only that they are philosophical absolutists. Their philosophy must be called irrationalist because it considers that the universe is not subjected to rational laws and is, therefore, not logically deducible. Existentialism is irrationalist, also because it ascribes to emotional states such as anxiety, sorrow and nausea a power superior to that of reason, refuting the claim of reason and defeating the efforts of reason."[151]

Martin Buber in his *Eclipse of God* renders the following judgment upon Sartre's rejection of the existence of God. He says, "Sartre has started from the 'silence' of God without asking himself what part our not hearing and our not having heard has played in that silence. From the silence, he has concluded that God does not exist. . . . Now, however, Sartre goes further. One 'must draw the consequences.' God is silent, that is, nothing is said to one that is unconditioned and unconditionally binding. 'There is no sign in the world.' Since, therefore, no universal morality can tell us what to do, since all possibility of discovering absolute values has disappeared with God, and since man, to whom henceforth 'all is permitted,' is at last free, is indeed freedom itself, it is for him to determine values. 'If I have done away with God the father' Sartre says literally, 'someone is needed

to invent values. . . . Life has no meaning a priori . . . it
is up to you to give it meaning, and value is nothing else
than this meaning which you choose.' That is almost
exactly what Nietzsche said, and it has not become any
truer since then. One can believe in and accept a meaning
or value; one can set it as a guiding light over one's life
if one has *discovered* it, not if one has *invented* it. It can
be for me an illuminating meaning, a direction-giving
value only if it has been revealed to me in my meeting
with Being, not if I have freely chosen it for myself
from among the existing possibilities and perhaps have,
in addition, decided with some fellow-creatures; This
shall be valid from now on."[152]

Finally, Iris Murdoch emphasizes the elements of
negativity and hopelessness present in Sartre's writings
which, at the same time, try to assert the importance of
the individual in the inhuman determinism of the modern
world. She writes, "The general impression of Sartre's
work is certainly that of a powerful but abstract model
of a hopeless dilemma, colored by a surreptitious romanticism which embraces the hopelessness. . . . Sartre's
great negatives are not the negatives of cynicism, but of
an obstinate and denuded belief, which clings to certain
values even at the expense of seeming to make them
empty . . . what Sartre wishes to assert is precisely that
the individual has an absolute importance and is not to be
swallowed up in a historical calculation. Sartre's man
is depicted in the moment-to-moment flux of his thoughts
and moods, where no consistent pattern either of purposeful activity or of social condition can easily be discerned;
at this level freedom seems indeed like randomness of indifference.

Sartre wishes at all costs to withdraw his man to a
point at which he is independent of what seems to him
the inhuman determinism of the modern world, the realm
of the economist and the sociologist—even if it means
depicting him as an empty shell."[153]

Perhaps Sartre's own words at the end of his autobiography, *Les Mots*, convey best the futility of his life-
project. We read, "The retrospective illusion has been

smashed to bits; martyrdom, salvation, and immortality are falling to pieces; the edifice is going to rack and ruin; I collared the Holy Ghost in the cellar and threw him out; *atheism is a cruel and long-range affair;* I think I've carried it through. I see clearly, I've lost my illusions. . . . For the last ten years or so I've been a man who's been waking up, cured of a long, bitter-sweet madness, and who can't get over the fact, a man who can't think of his old ways without laughing and *who doesn't know what to do with himself.* I've again become the traveler without a ticket that I was at the age of seven. . . . I've given up the office but not the frock; I still write. What else can I do?"¹⁵⁴

Albert Camus

CHAPTER VII

ALBERT CAMUS
LIFE

I. EARLY YEARS

Albert Camus was born in the small town of
Mondovi, Algeria on November 7, 1913. His father, Lucien
Camus, a poor agricultural worker of French descent,
was killed in the Battle of the Marne during the First
World War, when Albert was hardly a year old. His
mother, née Catherine Sintès, who was of Spanish ancestry,
moved into the crowded Belcourt district of Algiers, upon
her husband's death. The infant Albert, his mother and
his elder brother Lucien, along with his maternal grandmother and uncle, all shared a two room apartment in
this poorest section of the city. Camus' mother, who was
illiterate, worked long hours as a charwoman to support
her family.[1]

The abject poverty and squalor of their living conditions are vividly portrayed by Camus in a passage of
L'Envers et L'Endroit. He writes, "I think of a child
living in a poor district. That neighborhood, that house!
There were only two floors, and the stairs were unlit.
Even now, long years later, he could go back there on
the darkest night. He knows that he could climb the stairs
without stumbling once. His very body is impregnated
with this house. His legs retain the exact height of the
steps; his hand; the instinctive, never-conquered horror
of the banister. Because of the cockroaches."[2]

And yet, Camus never resented those years of poverty
and privation. In his *Notebooks* (entry for May 1935),
he writes, "What I mean is this: that one can, with no
romanticism, feel nostalgia for lost poverty. A certain
number of years lived without money are enough to
create a whole sensibility. . . . When I see things clearly,
I have only one thing to say. It is in this life of poverty,
among these vain or humble people, that I have most

certainly touched what I feel is the true meaning of life."[3]

Again, Camus describes in *L'Envers et l'Endroit*, the true sense of values which the beauty of nature imparted to him, in spite of his poverty. "There is a solitude in poverty, but a solitude that gives everything back its value. At a certain level of wealth, the heavens themselves and the star-filled night are nature's riches. But seen from the very bottom of the ladder, the sky recovers its full meaning: a priceless grace. Summer nights mysterious with crackling stars! Behind the child was a stinking corridor, and his little chair, splitting across the bottom, sank a little beneath his weight. But, eyes raised, he drank in the pure night."[4]

Due to a childhood illness, Camus' mother lost her hearing and suffered a serious speech impediment. And yet, in spite of the fact that communication between mother and son was minimal, Camus had a boundless affection for his mother, whom he remembered and revered all his life. Germaine Brée touchingly describes the rapport between the deaf mother and her child, "In this barrenness, the silent uncomplaining figure of his deaf mother seems to have created in the child an overwhelming sense of compassion; all the harder to bear because of his helplessness. . . . The silence that both separated and united the mother and son, born as much of her endless labor as of her deafness, was later to influence the young writer's thought deeply concerning the problem of communication and expression."[5]

Young Albert, who was a bright student, attended the local primary school, where he attracted the attention of a teacher, Louis Germain. It was because of the additional tutoring and encouragement from his teacher (to whom, incidentally, Camus dedicated his Nobel Prize Speech in 1957), that Albert won a scholarship to the lycée in 1923. Upon graduation nine years later, Camus, at the age of nineteen, entered the University of Algiers, where he studied philosophy with the intention of making a career of teaching. Four years later in 1936, he was awarded a *diplôme d'études supérieures*, upon the completion of a thesis which traced the influence of the Neoplatonism of Plotinus on the philosophy of St. Augustine of Hippo. (His judgment was that Augustinianism represents a successful melding of Neoplatonic essentialism and Christianity.) It was at the University of Algiers that Camus came under the influence of Jean Grenier, a professor of philosophy. Of him, Camus was to say later in an interview in *Les Nouvelles littéraires* of May 10, 1951, "Grenier gave me a taste of philosophical meditation."[6]

In 1959, Camus wrote of the decisive influence exerted on him by Jean Grenier's *Les Iles*. He wrote, "I think I already wanted to write when I read *Les Iles;* but I really decided to become a writer only after reading this book. Other books played a large part in this decision. But then I forgot them. This book, on the other hand, has always remained alive for me although it is now twenty years since I read it."[7] Camus acknowledged the great esteem in which he held his former professor of philosophy by dedicating to him both *L'Envers et L'Endroit* (which has appeared in English both as *Betwixt and Between* and *The Wrong Side and the Right Side*) and *The Rebel.*

II. TUBERCULOSIS

Camus' doctoral studies were brought to a brusque halt by a severe attack of tuberculosis (actually his first seizure occurred when he was only seventeen) and during the next five years, i.e., from 1937 to 1942, Camus spent much of his time in and out of the sanatorium. The author of *The Nuptials* and *The Wrong Side and the Right Side,* who formerly sang paens of joy to the sun and the sea, who spoke of his espousals with nature, now became a bitter protestor against the cruelties of life. Where only recently, he wrote glowing lines of sensual, romantic happiness, Camus now developed a bitter, brooding obsession with the absurd. And while it is true that the notion of the absurd did eventually yield to that of revolt and rebellion, and even to some positive concern for humanity and a solidarity among men in *The Plague,* many scholars attribute Camus' preoccupation with his ill health as a determining factor in this sudden change from carefree happiness and exuberance to a gnawing, relentless absurdity.[8]

Camus' ill health was to plague him the rest of his life. He volunteered for military service and he was rejected. His health interfered with his literary productivity. Tuberculosis was an unwanted companion with whom he had to learn to live the remainder of his life. (And yet ironically, it was a violent automobile accident and not his life-long affliction that was the cause of his death.) Camus records in his *Notebooks* (entry for August 1935) his preoccupation with tuberculosis, "On the way to Paris; this fever beating in my temples. The strange and sudden withdrawal from the world and men. The struggle with one's body. Sitting in the wind, emptied and hollowed out inside, I spent all my time thinking of K. Mansfield, about that long, painful and tender story of a struggle against illness. What awaits me in the Alps is, together with loneliness and the idea that I shall be there to look after myself, the *awareness* of my illness."[9]

Camus' tuberculosis made it impossible for him to pass the mandatory medical examination for the *Doctorat d'Etat*, which renders a man eligible for university teaching. With this avenue closed to him, he tried his hand at such various occupations as clerk for an import-export firm, salesman of automobile accessories, meteorologist, and private tutor. When a left wing paper, the *Alger-Républicain* was established in 1938, with Pascal Pia as its editor, Camus joined the staff and his first article appeared on October 10, 1938. The following year, he was made editor of the left wing *Le Soir-Républicain,* for which he wrote a number of articles under the name of Jean Meursault. (Cf. *The Stranger*).

Emmett Parker maintains that it was during these early days of journalism that Camus formulated many of his attitudes vis-à-vis the great social and political questions of the day. These would remain substantially unchanged the remainder of his life. Parker says, "Although his outlook was naturally to undergo certain changes as his experience and the course of history brought about new developments, the principles that had fostered that outlook were to remain deeply rooted in the early years of his experience in Algeria."[10]

In January-February 1940, both *Le Soir-Républicain* and *Alger-Républicain* were discontinued and because of his undesirable political affiliations (he was both pro-Arab and left wing), Camus found it impossible to find employment as a journalist in Algiers. He then left for Paris where Pascal Pia secured him a position on the *Paris-Soir*. Camus disliked this paper's policies and consequently wrote nothing for it. He worked on it as a typesetter. Just before the German invasion of Paris, he left with the staff of *Paris-Soir* for Clermont-Ferrand. Here he abandoned the paper and moved to Lyons, where he married his second wife, Francine Faure in 1940. (His first marriage to Simone Hie, an Algerian was short-lived and ended in divorce.) Because he found Lyons "a dark depressing city," Camus left with his wife for Oran and Algiers. In 1942 he returned to France alone and because of the Allied landing in Algiers in November of the same year, Camus was separated from his wife for the duration of the war.[11]

III. RESISTANCE

Even though Camus was rejected in 1939 for military service for reasons of health, in 1943 we find him a most active member of the French Resistance movement. He became editor of the famous clandestine underground paper, *Combat*, which exerted such a profound influence in galvanizing French opposition to the Nazi invaders. August 21, 1944 was a momentous day. Not only was it the first day of the Battle of Paris but it was also the day when the admiring French learned for the first time that the highly respected author of *The Stranger* and *The Myth of Sisyphus* and the editor of *Combat* were one and the same person. Overnight, Albert Camus at the age of 31, became an international celebrity and an idol of all Frenchmen.[12] This sudden prominence weighed heavily on him and his private life all but disappeared. On all sides, he was sought out as a kind of oracle: to make pronouncements on all kinds of questions, whether they were national, political, moral or international.

As a university student, Camus had joined the Communist party but he soon became disenchanted with it and left.[13] During the Resistance days when he worked with the Communists in the underground, he had an opportunity to observe, first-hand, their technique of boring from within. As a result of this experience, Camus became convinced that Communism was not interested in a free France; its aim was rather to wrest the country from the Nazis, in order to acquire yet another Russian satellite. As a result of these observations, when the Liberation of France became an actuality, Camus refused to collaborate with the Marxists. He pointed out in *The Rebel* that there can be no justification for the use of violent political means of repression, in order to justify a predetermined Marxist end. He says, "History without a value to transfigure it, is controlled by the law of ex-pediency. Historical materialism, determinism, violence, negation of every form of freedom which does not coincide with expediency and the world of courage and of silence, are the highly legitimate consequences of a pure philoso-phy of history."[14]

Jean Paul Sartre, a former fellow-Resistance worker, criticized Camus severely for this "hard line" towards Communism. Sartre felt that the only way in which the French workingman could be helped was through some sort of "rapprochement" with the Communists. Camus, on the other hand, remained adamant, maintaining that any type of compromise with Communism, meant death to the freedom of France. He pointed to the complete dis-regard for human life in the notorious Russian labor camps as a case in hand.

Their disagreement was finally brought to a head by Francis Jeanson's unfavorable review of Camus' *The Rebel*, which appeared in Sartre's *Les Temps Modernes*. A series of controversial articles between Camus and Sartre in the latter's paper, resulted in the break between the two best known intellectuals of France. (It was in this connection, that Camus is supposed to have repudiated existentialism when he said, "I have little liking for the too famous existential philosophy and, to speak frankly, I think its conclusions false.")[15]

In all objectivity, it would seem that neither Sartre nor Jeanson could answer satisfactorily Camus' charge. ". . . that Communist revolution substitutes future goals for practical activity to alleviate present injustice and suffering."[16] Thomas Hanna, author of the remarkable work, *The Thought and Art of Albert Camus*, says, "In *The Rebel*, the sections dealing with Marxist theory and prophecy constitute one of the most trenchant critiques of Communist thought and action ever written from the viewpoint of moral philosophy."[17]

Two years later, Simone de Beauvoir published a novel, *The Mandarins*, wherein she recounted the Sartre-Camus controversy and presented Camus quite unfairly as "an attractive but undisciplined figure who is willing to sacrifice principles for his personal pleasure."[18] This quarrel, along with disagreements with other critics of his work, affected Camus deeply. He withdrew from political involvements and devoted himself to his writing. *The Fall*, which appeared in 1956, is considered as a reflection of his unhappy, brooding state of mind. His last creative work, *The Exile and Kingdom*, a collection of short stories, seems to represent a more tolerant and optimistic attitude toward life.

IV. THEATRE

Before concluding this brief account of Camus' life, we must mention his deep interest in the theatre. As far back as 1935, Camus was instrumental in organizing and directing *Le Théâtre du travail* (The Workers' Theatre) in conjunction with the Algiers Communist Party. The aim of this group was to bring together students, working-men and *avant-garde* intellectuals in the collective writing and producing of drama, somewhat akin to the concept of a "literature of the masses."[19] When Camus terminated his membership in the Communist Party, he changed the *Théâtre du travail to Théâtre de l'Équipe*, whose announced aim was to present good theatre to the people. As its director, adaptor, actor, and writer, Camus labored with this group up to the outbreak of the World War in 1939, trying to restore the popular appeal which the theatre once enjoyed among the masses.[20]

In 1957, at the age of forty-four, Albert Camus was awarded the Nobel Prize for Literature. For the first time in his life, he became financially independent. With the prize money, he bought a house in the village of Lourmarin, at the foot of the Alps, where he could write in quiet and privacy.

Early in the morning on the fourth day of January, 1960, Camus was riding in a car with his publisher, Michel Gallimard, Mme. Gallimard and their eighteen year old daughter. Near Sens, about seventy-five miles south-east of Paris, the rear tire blew out. The car struck a tree at a speed of eighty to ninety miles. The other three occupants of the car were hurled from the car and lay bruised and injured. Albert Camus was killed. An unused railway ticket was found in his pocket. He had decided at the last minute to return from Lourmarin to Paris by car. As Jean Paul Sartre expressed it in his *Tribute*, "For all those who loved him, there is an unbearable absurdity in that death."[21] François Mauriac wrote that Camus' death "is one of the greatest losses that could have affected French letters at the present time. A whole generation became aware of itself and of its problems through Camus."[22]

CAMUS' PRINCIPAL WORKS
(Listed Chronologically)

The Wrong Side and the Right Side (also *Betwixt and Between*), in *Lyrical and Critical Essays*. (1936). Tr. E. Kennedy. Ed. P. Thody. New York: Alfred Knopf, 1968.

Nuptials in *Lyrical and Critical Essays*. (1938).

The Notebooks, 1935-1942. Tr. P. Thody. New York: Alfred Knopf, 1963.

The Myth of Sisyphus. (1942). Tr. J. O'Brien. New York: Alfred Knopf, 1955.

A Happy Death. (1936-1942?). Tr. R. Howard. New York: Alfred Knopf, 1972.

The Stranger. (1942). Tr. S. Gilbert. New York: Alfred Knopf, 1946.

Caligula and Cross Purpose. (1944). Tr. S. Gilbert. Norfolk: New Directions, 1949; *Caligula and Three Other Plays*. Tr. S. Gilbert. New York: Alfred Knopf, 1958.

Letters to a German Friend, in *Resistance, Rebellion and Death*. (1945). Tr. J. O'Brien. New York: Alfred Knopf, 1961.

The Plague. (1947). Tr. S. Gilbert. New York: Alfred Knopf, 1948.

State of Siege, in *Caligula and Three Other Plays*. (1948).
Actuelles I, II, III. (1950, 1953, 1958). Translated partially in *Resistance, Rebellion and Death*.
The Notebooks, (1942-1951). Tr. P. Thody. New York: Alfred Knopf, 1965.
The Rebel. (1951). Tr. A. Bower. New York: Alfred Knopf, 1954.
The Fall. (1956). Tr. J. O'Brien. New York: Alfred Knopf, 1957.
Exile and Kingdom. Tr. J. O'Brien. New York: Alfred Knopf, 1958.

THOUGHT

I. ALGERIAN NEOPAGANISM AND BEAUTIES OF NATURE

Camus' mediterranean origins are believed by some to be responsible for his "instinctive atheism and neopaganism." In a region of the world where Christianity and Christian values have never made the impact that they did, for example, on European civilization, we still find present today a strong ancient pagan culture. Camus himself frequently referred to this characteristic of his Algerian background. The average Westerner fails to realize the strongly non-Christian attitudes so prevalent in North African culture. This contrast between Algeria and Europe is strikingly presented in a work on the Neopaganism of André Gide. (The observation is eminently applicable, it seems, in the case of Camus.) We read, "In Algeria itself, far more after crossing the Atlas into the desert, the traveller is conscious of having left Europe far behind, not the mere geographical entity, but all the complex edifice of Christianity, social, moral, intellectual, legal organization and custom, the civilization of centuries. In entering a world so different, so remote, to which one has so little place or meaning, one has the sense of being in a vacuum, free—if that be the word—to create *ab ovo*, thought, religion, laws, an ethic for oneself."[23]

As Camus' early works, *The Wrong Side and the Right Side, The Nuptials*, and the most recently printed, *A Happy Death*, indicate, the native Algerian is fully immersed in a sensualism, a deep communing with the beauties and pleasures of nature. There is present in him an instinctive desire for pleasure and gratification of his appetites. Everything round about him—the brilliant Algerian sun, the sea and the sky—beckon alluringly and invite him to enjoy himself as a happy child of nature. Camus writes, "The landscape is drenched by the sun to become a tumult of light and color. The air is heavily perfumed by a vivid profusion of flowers. . . . The sea is laced with silver and white and the sky is a flaxen blue. . . . The senses are quickened, the blood is stirred and he must give the name of imbecile to anyone who is afraid to enjoy himself in such conditions. Shame would be a meaningless word on the Algerian beaches; there can be nothing shameful in being happy."[24]

The typical Algerian, as Camus tells us, is a child of nature. He wants to live his life to the fullest, enjoying his pleasures and satiating his senses with ever-new pleasurable experiences. His total preoccupation is with the present. There is a kind of "earthly naiveté," whereby the Algerian finds absolutely meaningless such notions as sin, hope for a future life, and immortality. As Camus describes it, "Between this Algerian sky and the faces turned toward it, there is nothing on which to hang a mythology, a literature, an ethics or a religion . . . only stones, stars, and those truths which the hand can touch."[25] The Algerian is thus totally immersed in the present and the present alone is uniquely meaningful. Camus continues, "There are some words which I have never quite understood, like that of sin. Yet I do think I know that these men (the Algerians) have ever sinned against life. For if there *is* a sin against life, it lies perhaps less in despairing of it than in hoping for another life and evading the implacable grandeur of the one we have."[26]

The Europeans, on the other hand, strike Camus as being morbidly preoccupied with a future life. Instead of living this present life to the fullest, they idly dream of something, which Camus considers non-existent—an immortality and a future life, which they consider infinitely superior to the present. In words somewhat reminiscent of Nietzsche's condemnation of Christianity and its belief in an after-life, Camus contrasts quite unfairly the European mentality with a typically Algerian philosophy of the present. He writes, "The men of Europe, abandoned to the shadows, have turned their backs upon the fixed and radiant point of the present. They forget the present for the future, the fate of humanity for the delusion of power, the misery of the slums for the mirage of the eternal city, ordinary justice for an empty promised land. They despair of personal freedom and dream of a strange freedom of the species; reject solitary death and give the name of immortality to a vast collective agony. They no longer believe in the things that exist in the world and in living man; the secret of Europe is that it no longer loves life."[27]

Hence, Camus tells us that he refuses to repudiate the joys and the pleasures and the collective beauty of the world about him. He will not be deterred from enjoying all these pleasures by succumbing to the idle prattlings about another life. He is perfectly satisfied with the present. Why should he recklessly cast aside the pleasures and riches of nature which are rightfully his, in exchange for something unattractive, indefinite, in fact, downright morbid. Why should the depressing notion of death and the possibility of some kind of future life interfere with the present. In no uncertain terms, Camus argues, "If I obstinately refuse to accept all the 'later ons' of this world, it is because I have no desire to give up my present wealth. I do not want to believe that death is a gateway to another life. For me it is a closed door. I do not say that it is a step we must all take, but that it is a horrible and dirty adventure. Everything I am offered seeks to deliver man from the weight of his own life. . . . If I am at one with the passive passion, the rest ceases to concern me. I have too much youth in me to be able to speak of death. But it seems to me that if I had to speak of it, I would find the right word here between horror and silence to express the conscious certainty of a death without hope."[28]

II. STAGE I: THE ABSURD

"The pages that follow, deal with an absurd sensitivity that can be found widespread in the age—and not with an absurd philosophy which our time, properly speaking, has not known. . . . But it is useful to note at the same time that the absurd, hitherto taken as a conclusion, is considered in this essay as a starting point. In this sense, it may be said that there is something provisional in my commentary . . . no metaphysics, no belief is involved in it for the moment."[29]

With these opening words in *The Myth of Sisyphus*, Albert Camus began his world-famous inquiries into the nature and notion of the Absurd. And in spite of the above quotation, which specifically indicates that his attitude toward the absurd was a purely provisional one, the majority of his readers have chosen to ignore this clear and unequivocal statement. Further, despite the fact that in his rejection of nihilism, the absurd phase was to yield to the phase of rebellion (i.e., the movement is from an ethic of *quantity* to an ethic of *quality*), Camus is known to most men as the "philosopher of the absurd."[30]

What Camus had to say in *The Myth of Sisyphus*, concerning the absurd, was not particularly original nor did he claim it to be such. In essence, his treatment of the absurd was a modern restatement of a basic scepticism which goes as far back as the Book of Ecclesiastes and Greek Pyrrhonism. But what gave Camus an almost overnight world audience was the fact that he so accurately reflected the mood of his time. His fundamental assumption that there was no hope, that life had no meaning and his adamant refusal to take refuge via "philosophical suicide" in some transcendent entity or God, eloquently articulated the innermost feelings of millions of disconsolate Frenchmen. The setting was ideal. A military defeat which resulted in a most hated occupation of France, the total lack of optimism concerning an early liberation only heightened the dismal feeling of frustration and helplessness. The absurd seemed to epitomize the prevalent climate in France. At the same time, however, Camus insisted that while life could be incomprehensible, it was not thereby meaningless. Life *did* hold some meaning and Camus refused to equate the two notions of the absurd and the meaningless. He tells us, "Hitherto, and it has not been wasted effort, people have played on words and pretended to believe that refusing to grant a meaning to life, necessarily leads to declaring that it is not worth living. In truth, there is no necessary common measure between these two judgments."[31]

A. Contributing Factors

In his lengthy and detailed analysis of the absurd, Camus advances a number of reasons why the absurd reigns supreme in the world today. Men are seeking reasons and explanations but none is forthcoming. The world defies explanation and man is frustrated. Camus now enumerates the reasons for this frightening situation under the following headings: (1) Science (2) Meaninglessness and monotony of life (3) Time (4) The World (5) Inhumanity (6) Death.

1. *Science*

The first reason for the far too prevalent feeling of the absurd is the complete inadequacy of science. In spite of its pretensions and impressive dogmatic claims, says Camus, science inevitably ends in hypotheses. We are given instead, he argues, "an infinite number of shimmering fragments," with the result that "we must despair of ever reconstructing the familiar, calm surface which would give us peace of heart." Camus reproaches science and its pretensions when he says, "All knowledge on earth will give me nothing to assure me that this world is mine. You describe it to me. You teach me to classify it. You enumerate its laws and in my thirst for knowledge, I admit that they are true. You take apart its mechanism and my hope increases. At the final stage, you teach me that this wondrous and multicolored universe can be reduced to the atom and that the atom itself can be reduced to the electron. All this is good and I wait for you to continue. But you tell me of an invisible planetary system in which electrons gravitate around a nucleus. You explain this world to me with an image. I realize that you have been reduced to poetry: I shall never know . . . so that science that was to teach me everything ends up in a hypothesis, that lucidity founders in metaphor, that uncertainty is resolved in a work of art. . . . I have returned to my beginning. I realize that if through science I can seize phenomena and enumerate them, I cannot, for all that, apprehend the world."[32]

The result is that when man seeks answers, he receives hypotheses. When he looks for coherence and understanding, he finds in their stead "the irrationality and opacity of the world." This ineluctably begets the absurd.

2. *Monotony of Life*

The absurd makes itself shockingly evident to any man when a monotonous, habitual chain of daily events is suddenly broken. The man who has been living a meaningless, treadmill existence, performing the same routine acts day by day, is brusquely awakened to a consciousness of it all. He sees the structures and forms, which previously gave meaning to all his actions, fall away and crumble. "It happens that the stage sets collapse. . . . Rising, street-car, four hours in the office or factory, meal, street-car, four hours of work, meal, sleep, and Monday, Tuesday, Wednesday, Thursday, Friday and Saturday, according to the same rhythm—this path is easily followed most of the time. But one day, the 'why' arises and everything begins in that weariness tinged with amazement. 'Begins'—this is important. Weariness comes at the end of the acts of a mechanical life, but at the same time, it inaugurates the impulse of what follows. What follows the gradual return into the chain of it is the definitive awakening. At the end of the awakening comes, in time, the consequence: suicide or recovery."[33]

3. *Time*

We suddenly become aware of the fact that time "is not our helper but our worst enemy." We are being carried along by time and ultimately, it will destroy us. "During every day of an unillustrious life, time carries us. But a moment comes along always, when we have to carry *it* . . . after all, it's a matter of dying. Yet a day comes when a man notices or says he is thirty. Thus he asserts his youth. But simultaneously he situates himself in relation to time. He takes his place in it. He admits he stands at

a certain point on a curve that he acknowledges having
to travel to its end. He belongs to time and by the horror
that seizes him, he recognizes his worst enemy."[34] This
again begets absurdity.

4. *World*

"The primitive hostility of the world rises up to face
us across the millenia. For a second, we cease to understand it because for centuries, we have understood in it
solely the images and designs that we had attributed to it
beforehand . . . that denseness and that strangeness of the
world in the absurd."[35] And so man, as the feeblest reed
in nature, is overwhelmed by the world's denseness and
opacity.

5. *Inhumanity*

Camus goes on to point out "Men, too, secrete the
inhuman. At certain moments of lucidity, the mechanical
aspect of their gestures, their meaningless pantomime
makes silly everything that surrounds them. A man talking on the telephone behind a glass partition; you wonder
why he is alive. This discomfort in the face of man's
own inhumanity, this incalculable tumble before the
image of what we are, this 'nausea'—as a writer of today
calls it, is also the absurd."[36]

6. *Death*

The last, and perhaps most powerful factor in the
begetting of the absurd is the inevitability of death itself.
No matter how ambitious are man's plans; no matter how
noble his desires and ideals—they will all inexorably end
with death. It matters little how many more acts man
plans to perform, how many more projects he hopes to
accomplish—death terminates all. Each human act which
man authors is performed in the shadow of death. As
soon as man is born, he is already on his way to death.
This sinister, threatening, ever-present shadow of death
brings into relief the utter futility of all human endeavors.
It is the absurd, Camus says, "This elementary and definitive aspect of the adventure (of dying) constitutes the

absurd feeling. Under the fatal lighting of that destiny, its uselessness becomes evident. No code of ethics and no effort are justifiable a priori in the face of the cruel mathematics that command our condition."[37]

Hence it is because of this awareness that death will ultimately end all, that Camus' hero Meursault in *The Stranger (The Outsider)* was living out his absurd existence. We are given a clue to Meursault's apathy and indifference, which had so methodically dominated all his actions throughout the entire novel, when he finally refuses the chaplain's prayers and bitterly confesses, "Nothing, nothing had the least importance, and I know quite well why. He, too, knew why. From the dark horizon of my future, a sort of slow, persistent breeze had been blowing toward me, all my life long, from the years that were to come. And on its way, that breeze had levelled out all the ideas that people had tried to foist on me in the equally unreal years I then was living through. What difference could they make to me, the deaths of others, or a mother's love, or his God; or the way a man decides to live, the fate he thinks he chooses, since one and the same fate was bound to 'choose' not only me but thousands of millions of privileged people who, like him, called themselves my brothers. . . . Every man alive was privileged; there was only one class of men, the privileged class. All alike would be condemned to die one day."[38]

B. The Triad: Human Nostalgia, the Irrational, the Absurd

After enumerating the various conditions which awaken us to an awareness of the state of absurdity in the world, Camus next proceeds to investigate the very nature of the absurd itself. According to Camus, the world is neither absurd nor reasonable, when considered by itself. Absurdity is begotten in the relation that exists between the world and the human intellect. Absurdity involves a confrontation between man's reason which seeks "a complete understanding of a world which cannot be understood. Man's mind is yearning for universal truth and the world shows it only fragmentary truths;

man is searching for clarity and the world remains a mystery."[39]

Camus puts it this way, "I said that the world is absurd, but I was too hasty. This world in itself is not reasonable, that is all that can be said. But what is absurd is the confrontation of this irrational and the wild longing for clarity whose call echoes in the human heart. The absurd depends as much on man as on the world. For the moment, it is all that links them together. It binds them one to the other, as only hatred can weld two creatures together."[40] Camus goes on to say that there are three *dramatis personae* involved in this encounter. They are mutually related, with each depending on the other. "At this point of his effort, man stands face to face with the irrational. He feels within him his longing for happiness and for reason. The absurd is born of this confrontation between the human need and the unreasonable silence of the world. This must not be forgotten. This must be clung to because the whole consequence of life can depend on it. The irrational, the human nostalgia, and the absurd, that is born of this encounter—these are the three characters in the drama that must necessarily end with all the logic of which an existence is capable."[41]

As Thomas Hanna expresses it, "In simple terms, the absurd always involves a contradiction between a given state of affairs and reality itself, between one's intentions and the given possibilities, between an action and a world not in accord with that action."[42]

Camus continues his description of the nature of the absurd with the following remarks: "The absurd is essentially a divorce. It lies in neither of the elements compared; it is born of their confrontation. In this particular case and on the plane of intelligence, I can therefore say that the absurd is not in man (if such a metaphor could have a meaning) nor in the world, but in their presence together. If I wish to limit myself to facts, I know what man wants. I know what the world offers him and now I can say that I also know what links them. . . . The odd trinity brought to light in this way is certainly not a startling discovery. . . . Its distinguishing feature in this regard is that it cannot be divided. To destroy one of its terms is to destroy the whole. There can be no absurd outside the human mind. Thus, like every thing else, the absurd ends with death. But there can be no absurd outside the world either. And it is by this elementary criterion that I judge the notion of the absurd to be essential and consider that it can stand as the first of my truths."[43]

David Denton interprets this passage as follows: "The relationship between man and the world is an absurd one, for it prompts certain types of questions from man but makes no provisions for answers. For example, man seeks for order in the universe, but no guarantee of order is found; he has nostalgia for unity, but finds only greater multiplicity; he questions the problem of evil, but no promise of protection is proferred; ultimately, he ponders the mystery of death and there is only silence."[44]

Camus himself gives us a graphic description of absurdity which has been characterized as the exile of man in the era of the "death of God." He writes, "In a universe suddenly divested of illusions and lights, man feels an alien, a stranger. His exile is without remedy since he is deprived of the memory of a lost home or the hope of a promised land. This divorce between man and his life, the actor and his setting is properly the feeling of absurdity."[45]

C. Physical Suicide

What is man to do in the face of this absurdity, of this utter meaninglessness of life? Man is acutely aware of the absence of harmony about him. The world is obstinately unyielding and unsatisfying. The human intellect, on the other hand, is demanding and frustrated. Its desires are utterly thwarted. There is no God. There are no absolutes. There is no future life. Man is living out each day in the relentless shadow of death, which is the common heritage of us all. An identical fate awaits us all —extinction.

Camus' answer to this state of affairs is that man must face squarely the question of suicide, either (1) physical or (2) philosophical suicide. He tells us, "There is but one truly serious philosophical problem and that is suicide. Judging whether life is or is not worth living amounts to answering the fundamental question of philosophy. All the rest—whether or not the world has three dimensions, whether the mind has nine or twelve categories—comes afterwards. These are games; one must first answer."[46] The question of suicide, then, is inextricably bound up with that of the absurd. In a sense, says Camus, suicide is a confession. "It is confessing that life is too much for you or that you do not understand it. . . . It is merely confessing that that is not worth the trouble. . . . Dying voluntarily implies that you have recognized, even instinctively, the ridiculous character of that habit, the absence of any profound reason for living, the insane character of that daily agitation and the uselessness of suffering. . . . One kills oneself because life is not worth living, that is certainly a truth—yet an unfruitful one because it is a truism. But does that insult to existence, that flat denial in which it is plunged come from the fact that it has no meaning? Does its absurdity require one to escape it through hope or suicide?"[47]

Camus answers that the absurdity of existence requires neither suicide nor hope. If man were to take his own life, he would then destroy the absurd. And so man must rather steel himself to live a meaningless life, which "will be lived all the better if it has no meaning whatsoever. Living an experience, a particular fate, is accepting it fully. . . . Negating one of the terms of the opposition on which he lives, amounts to escaping it. To abolish conscious revolt is to elude the problem. . . . Living is keeping the absurd alive. Keeping it alive is, above all, contemplating it. Unlike Eurydice, the absurd dies only when we turn away from it."[48]

Camus, therefore, rejects physical suicide because it is an ineffective means of dealing with absurdity. A suicide is a coward and by his cowardly act, he destroys the absurd. Camus argues, "This is where it is seen to what a degree absurd experience is remote from suicide. It may be thought that suicide follows revolt—but wrongly.

For it does not represent the logical outcome of revolt. It is just the contrary by the consent it presupposes. Suicide, like the leap [philosophical suicide] is acceptance at its extreme. . . . In its way, suicide settles the absurd. It engulfs the absurd in the same death. But I know that in order to keep alive, the absurd cannot be settled. It escapes suicide to the extent that it is simultaneously awareness and rejection of death."[49]

D. Philosophical Suicide

Having rejected physical suicide as a means of resolving the absurdity of existence, Camus next examines the nature of philosophical suicide. According to this position, the individual is perfectly aware of the presence of absurdity and irrationality of existence. Yet, Camus tells us, by a peculiar inversion of principles, certain philosophers denied, destroyed and killed the very elements of irrationality with which they had begun their inquiry. Somehow, in a most illogical manner, he continues, they perform an about-face: they deny the very irrationality that they had just proclaimed and now they declare that the intellect's desire for the reasonable is no longer valid. By a peculiar twist, complains Camus, they take a "leap" which is rationally unjustifiable. They thereby destroy the absurd by taking refuge in what Camus calls "philosophical suicide." He writes, "Through an odd reasoning, starting out from the absurd over the ruins of reason, in a closed universe limited to the human, they deify what crushes them and find reason to hope in what impoverishes them. That hope is religious in all of them."[50]

Camus complains that all the theistic existentialist philosophers, without exception, suggest escape. He specifically names Jaspers, Chestov, Kierkegaard and Husserl as the guilty parties. Jaspers, for example, says that his failure to infer a satisfactory principle reveals not the absence but the very presence of transcendence. Hence for Jaspers, "the absurd becomes God (in the broadest meaning of the word) and that inability to understand becomes the existence that illuminates everything. Nothing logically prepares this reasoning." Camus concludes by saying, "I can call it a leap."[51]

Leo Chestov is also guilty of identifying the absurd with God. According to Chestov, "The only true solution is precisely where human judgment sees no solution. Otherwise, what need would we have of God. We turn toward God only to obtain the impossible. As for the possible, men suffice."[52] Thus Camus argues that Chestov presupposes the absurd but "proves it only to dispel it. . . . Man integrates the absurd and in that communion, causes to disappear its essential character which is opposition, laceration and divorce. This leap is an escape."[53]

Of Soren Kierkegaard, Camus has the following to say, "Thus it is that through a strained subterfuge, he gives the irrational the appearance and God the attributes of the absurd: unjust, incoherent, incomprehensible. Intelligence alone in him strives to stifle the underlying demands of the human heart. Since nothing is proved, everything is proved."[54]

Finally Edmund Husserl is guilty of speaking of "extra-temporal essences" and as a consequence, "thought hurls itself into an abstract polytheism. And paradoxically, while he claims to obey the desire to escape 'the inveterate habit of living and thinking in certain well-known and convenient conditions of existence,' the final leap restores in him the eternal and its comfort."[55] (We might add parenthetically, that while Camus does not seem to mention Gabriel Marcel by name here, he would also reject categorically the Marcellian metaphysics of hope which, according to Camus, would be another illegitimate leap, i.e., philosophical suicide.)[56]

Camus, therefore, finds completely unacceptable the "facile solutions" on the part of the above thinkers. He tells us that he cannot take refuge in a "false hope" because hope has no place in a universe where there is no God (The absence of God is, of course, a gratuitous assumption on Camus' part.) Albert Camus concludes that both philosophical and physical suicide lack a fundamental honesty, since they represent a refusal to face the situation squarely and unflinchingly. Both resort to a subterfuge. Camus refuses to capitulate to what he terms a cowardly compromise. He asserts, "I don't know whether this world has a meaning that transcends it. But I do know that I do not know that meaning and that it is impossible for me just now to know it. What can a meaning outside my condition mean to me? I can understand only in human terms. What I touch—what resists me— that is what I understand. And these two certainties—my appetite for the absolute and for unity and the impossibility of reducing this world to a rational and reasonable principle—I also know that I cannot reconcile them. What other truth can I admit without lying, without bringing in a hope I lack and which means nothing within the limits of my condition?"[58]

Having rejected both physical and philosophical suicide as a way out, Camus now opts to face the absurd squarely and to keep it alive by means of constant confrontation. This consciousness of the absurd on the part of man, gives rise to several new conditions, namely, (1) revolt (2) freedom (3) quantitative ethics and passion.

E.   Revolt

When man refuses to yield to either form of suicide, he defiantly revolts against the absurd. Instead of destroying the absurd through suicide or hope, he elects to engage in an on-going struggle with the absurdist condition. He is keenly aware of the fact that he can never win this struggle but he resolutely refuses to capitulate. Camus writes in *The Myth of Sisyphus*, "One of the only coherent philosophical positions is thus *revolt*. It is a constant confrontation between man and his own obscurity. It is an insistence upon an impossible transparency. It challenges the world anew every second. Just as danger provided man the unique opportunity of seizing awareness, so metaphysical revolt extends awareness to the whole of experience. It is that constant presence of man in his own eyes. It is not aspiration, for it is devoid of hope. That revolt is the certainty of crushing fate, without that resignation which ought to accompany it. . . . This revolt gives life its value. Spread over the whole length of a life, it restores its majesty to that life."[59]

Maurice Friedman states it in this manner, "The revolt is the affirmation which the absurd makes *despite* the absurd, the purely subjective affirmation which enables him to continue living without illusion and without suicide."[60]

Camus goes on to say that there is no finer sight than to observe an intelligence that is constantly struggling and grappling with a reality that transcends it. And so the sight of such a struggle is the finest example of human pride in action. There is a majesty about a man who will so discipline his mind, in order to continue this relentless but entirely hopeless struggle. Hence Camus argues, "It is essential to die unreconciled. The absurd man can only drain everything to the bitter end and deplete himself. The absurd is his extreme tension, which he maintains constantly by solitary effort, for he knows that in that consciousness and in that day-to-day revolt, he gives proof of his only truth which is defiance."[61]

The rebel does not revolt against the human lot because such a revolt would involve foregoing a part of man's humanity. What he does forego is the hope of ever satisfying his nostalgia for eternity and for a total understanding of the world. As Germaine Brée points out, "Camus' *homme absurde* can be said to be without hope only in terms of the two human dreams of eternity and total understanding; he is not without hope in life itself. He is not without faith in the reality of his experience within the prison walls, nor is he without joy. Life offers him inexhaustible possibilities which, within the limits of his mortality, he is free to accept."[62]

F. Freedom

Man's revolt against the absurd, in turn, results in a newly-found freedom. Previously, before he had become aware of the absurd, man imagined that there was a purpose to his life. Mistakenly, he thought that his actions were related to certain goals and he, therefore, adapted himself to the demands of this purpose. He was convinced that something in his life could be directed, that there were certain attainable ends to be achieved. Under these conditions, man falsely believed himself to be free. According to Camus, freedom was impossible in such a situation, for the following reasons: "To the extent to which I hope, to which I worry about a truth that might be individual to me, about a way of being or creating, to the extent to which I arrange my life and prove thereby that I accept its having a meaning, I create for myself barriers between which I confine my life. . . . Thus the absurd man realizes that he was not really free."[62]

Now, however, everything has been changed. The man who revolts against the absurd begins to experience genuine freedom. There are no restraints on his actions. He knows that there is no future. There is no being superior to him. He is his own master. Man is eminently and unqualifiedly free.[64]

G. Quantitative Ethics and Passion

The truly liberated man is completely indifferent to the future. Because he has rejected all belief in the future and in all meaning of life, he also rejects a scale of values. He abides by no preferences, no choices. Logically, therefore, the absurd man rejects an ethics of quality and substitutes for it an ethics of quantity. This means that what counts in the life of the newly-liberated man is not the *best* living but the *most* living. Since man's rule of conduct and his scale of values have no meaning except the quantity of experience he can accumulate, his ultimate goal must be not to live *better* but to live *more*. And because the absurd man is intensely aware of his imminent death, every moment of his life is most precious to him. Hence Camus concludes, "The present and the succession of presents before an ever conscious mind, this is the ideal of the absurd man."[65]

Camus explores at length the implications of the absurd and an ethics of quantity when he writes, "If I convince myself that this life has no other aspect than that of the absurd, if I feel that its whole equilibrium depends on that perpetual opposition between my conscious

revolt and the darkness in which it struggles, if I admit
that my freedom has no meaning except in relation to
its limited fate, then, I must say that what counts is not
the best living but the most living. It is not up to me to
wonder if this is vulgar or revolting, elegant or deplorable.
Once and for all, value judgments are discarded here in
favor of factual judgments. . . . A man's rule of conduct
and his scale of values have no meaning except through
the quantity and variety of experiences he has been in a
position to accumulate."[66] As David Denton succinctly
expresses it, "Since all actions are free and innocent,
there are no qualitative differences between and among
behaviors. One experience is as good as another. Since
God does not exist, and since every man must die, everything is permissible. Man can live with the divine 'irresponsibility' of the condemned criminal who has nothing
else to lose. This ethics which allows for no qualitative
differences among behaviors is a quantitative ethics."[67]

Such an ethics of quantity is also accompanied by an
intense passion. While the absurd initially presented itself
as an invitation to suicide, it has now become a way of
life. By means of his revolt, the absurd man has come to
grips with the absurd itself. He has entered into the very
heart of absurdity. "Having begun with an anguished
awareness of the inhuman, the meditation on the absurd
returns at the end of its itinerary to the very heart of the
passionate flames of human revolt."[68]

According to the above quotation, it is obvious that
Camus holds that *most living* is synonymous with being
aware of one's life, of one's revolt and one's freedom, to
the maximum. The rebel is most conscious of every act
he performs. Hence *most living* involves a succession of
qualitatively *indifferent* acts before a constant consciousness; everything concerns the present only. Revolt is a
continuous struggle against the absurd and it is revolt
that restores greatness to a man's life. Freedom which
is born of absurdity challenges the commonly accepted
goals and the order of life. It itself is based on that which
is uniquely certain, namely, our death, and the absurd.
Finally, passion is the result of the absurd, for by facing

proudly and defiantly a foreign universe, man rediscovers
his human dignity and he also rediscovers a new passion
"at the very heart of the passionate flames of human
revolt."[69]

1. *Sisyphus*

The Myth of Sisyphus very fittingly ends with a
description of Sisyphus himself, "the hero of the absurd."
We are told that "the gods had condemned Sisyphus to
rolling ceaselessly a rock to the top of a mountain, whence
the stone would fall back of its own weight. They had
thought with some reason that there is no more dreadful
punishment than futile and hopeless labor."[70]

According to the legend, after his death, Sisyphus
had obtained permission from Pluto to return to earth in
order to chastise his wife. But when Sisyphus came back
to earth, he was so happy and contented there that he
refused to return to the infernal darkness of the underworld. Threats and warnings by the gods could not persuade him to return. Finally, the gods sent Mercury, who
snatched Sisyphus from this earth and led him forcibly
to the underworld, where his rock was awaiting him.
Camus then explains that Sisyphus is this absurd hero.
"His scorn of the gods, his hatred of death and his
passion for life won him that unspeakable penalty in
which the whole being is exerted toward accomplishing
nothing. . . . One sees merely the whole effort of a body
straining to raise the huge stone, to roll it and push it
up a slope a hundred times over; one sees the face screwed
up, the cheek tight against the stone, the shoulder bracing
the clay-covered mass, the foot wedging it, the fresh start
with arms outstretched, the wholly human security of
the two earth-clotted hands. At the end of his long effort
measured by skyless space and time without depth, the
purpose is achieved. Then Sisyphus watches the stone
rush down in a few moments toward that lower world
whence he will have to push it up again toward the
summit. . . . At each of these moments, when he leaves
the heights, and gradually sinks toward the lair of the
gods, he is superior to his fate. He is stronger than his

rock. . . . Sisyphus, proletarian of the gods, powerless and rebellious, knows the whole extent of his wretched condition; that is what he thinks of during his descent. The lucidity that was to constitute his torture at the same time crowns his victory. There is no fate that cannot be surmounted by scorn."[71]

The happiness that comes to Sisyphus is due to a realization that he will never abdicate the struggle. This refusal to give in is an eloquent proclamation of the superiority of the human spirit. At the same time, it is an incontestable evidence of the loyalty to human dignity. As Nathan Scott expresses it, "In the rugged persistence of his refusal to allow the rock to remain at the bottom of the mount, he remains faithful to the essential *humanum* within himself, loyalty to which will bring a man the only sort of genuine happiness that is possible for humankind-namely the happiness that comes from not betraying the dignity that belongs to one's nature as a man. He therefore *is* and suggests by the example of his passion, that the human spirit may not be utterly exhaustible by the absurd; at least he proves himself to be stronger than his rock, for the rock is still rolling."[72]

Camus concludes *The Myth of Sisyphus* with the following words: "I leave Sisyphus at the foot of the mountain! One always finds one's burden again. But Sisyphus teaches the higher fidelity that negates the gods and raises rocks. He too concludes that all is well. This universe henceforth without a master seems to him neither sterile nor futile. Each atom of that stone, each mineral flake of that night-filled mountain, in itself form as a world. The struggle itself toward the heights is enough to fill a man's heart. One must imagine Sisyphus happy."[73]

2. *Meursault*

It is the same scorn for the absurd that Meursault in *The Stranger* shows in his indifference toward everything. The world is completely indifferent to human beings and Meursault is correspondingly indifferent to all. And in this indifference, he has discovered the real answers to reality. Nothing really matters. He has led a life within himself, perfectly indifferent to all. He was indifferent to his mother's death and to her funeral. He was indifferent to his girl friend, Marie. It was a matter of complete indifference to him whether he married her or not. And now, all of a sudden, he realizes the real truth of life.[74]

Sitting in his prison cell and awaiting execution, Meursault muses, "Actually, I was sure of myself, sure about everything, far surer than he [the chaplain], sure of my present life and of the death that was coming. That, no doubt, was all I had but at least that certainly was something I could get my teeth into, just as it got its teeth into me. . . . It was as if that great rush of anger had washed me clean, emptied me of hope, and gazing up at the dark sky spangled with its signs and stars, for the first time, for the first, I laid my heart open to the benign indifference of the universe. To feel it so like myself, indeed, so brotherly, made me realize that I had been happy, and that I was happy still. For all to be accomplished, for me to feel less lonely, all that remains to hope was that on the day of my execution, there would be a huge crowd of spectators and that they should greet me with howls of execration."[75]

We have now concluded what is generally referred to as the first stage in Camus' thought; namely, the stage of the absurd. In *The Myth of Sisyphus*, Camus began with the notion of the absurd as the confrontation between a mute and silent world and an intellect that sought to discover rationality and purpose within that world. A very serious question was next considered; namely, that of suicide. Camus rejected physical suicide because it would destroy the absurd itself. At the same time, he refused to give in to what he termed "philosophical suicide," i.e., a belief in a transcendent being, namely God—a stance which is characteristic of all theistic existentialists. The only honest solution, as far as Camus could see, was to resort to revolt or rebellion against the absurd. By scorning his inevitable lot, much like the condemned Sisyphus, man would defiantly live out his life of absurdity, fully conscious that with each act performed, he was hastening toward death. And inasmuch as there are no moral standards, ethics is a question of *quantity* rather than of *quality* of actions. It is not a question of the *kind* of action which a man performs—whether an act is good or bad—but rather, the *number* of actions that he performs in an allotted life-span. As Camus summarizes it, "Thus it is that no depth, no emotion, no passion and no sacrifice could render equal in the eyes of the absurd man (even if he wished it so) a conscious life of forty years and a lucidity spread over sixty years . . . there will never be any substitute for twenty years of life and experience."[76]

III. STAGE II: REBELLION AND MODERATION

A. *Letters to a German Friend*

The Myth of Sisyphus was published in 1942. Shortly thereafter, Camus was forced to submit his philosophical conclusions to an acid test. Would they stand up when applied to the hard, cold facts of reality? World War II, with its cataclysmic up-heavals became the crucible wherein Camus' philosophical principles would undergo their purification by fire. The results were most disconcerting. As a member of the French Resistance (Camus had previously volunteered for military service but was rejected because of his health), he now had a first hand opportunity to observe the effects of Nazi nihilism. The shocking atrocities and brutalities were, in effect, but the implementation of the quantitative ethics and unlimited freedom which Camus had so loudly advocated in *The Myth of Sisyphus*.[77] Anyone who agreed with Camus' Sisyphus conclusions, had no right to object to Hitler's nihilism, the concentration camps and gas chambers.

As one author expressed it, "If morality is only man-made, then it is left to each individual to make his own standards; if men are innocent in the meaning of Camus, namely, that there is no right and wrong but only consistency; if men are innocent in the sense that there are only responsible agents but no guilty ones, then one would be forced to admit that Hitler with his concen-

tration camps and his gas chambers was just as right as
anyone else. If one is entirely captivated by the nihilism
of Nietzsche's doctrine, why should one feel outraged
when Hitler makes that nihilism more existential by
putting it into practice?"[78]

With dismay and stunned incredulity, his mind reel-
ing at the enormity of man's bestiality toward his fellow
man, Camus wrote of "the hundreds of thousands of men
assassinated at dawn, the terrible walls of prisons, the soil
of Europe reeking with millions of corpses of its sons."[79]
He now knew that if he wanted to preserve his integrity
and intellectual honesty, he would be forced to abandon
the philosophical principles which he had formulated in
The Myth of Sisyphus. The Nazi atrocities were but the
logical outcome of an ethics of quantity which admits of
no distinction between right and wrong, between good
and evil. Further, how could a purely quantitative ethics
explain "the sacrifice, the nobility, the purpose which he
saw among the men fighting the Nazi terror?"[80]

With that characteristic candor which, to our mind, is
one of the most attractive traits of Albert Camus' thought,
we now find our philosopher admitting the impossibility
of the positions which he had formulated in *The Myth*.
In the celebrated *Letters to a German Friend* (written
between 1943 and 1945 and published in 1945), Camus
openly confesses that he can no longer espouse a nihilism
and its inevitable consequences. He admits that he, too,
once tended to agree with his German friend's scepticism
concerning moral absolutes. He writes, "For a long time
we both thought that this world had no ultimate meaning
and that consequently we were cheated. I still think so in
a way. But I came to different conclusions from the ones
you used to talk about, which, for so many years, you have
been trying to introduce into history. I tell myself now that
if I had really followed your reasoning, I ought to approve
what you are doing. And this is so serious that I must
stop and consider it. . . . You never believed in the meaning of this world, and you therefore deduced that idea
that everything was equivalent and that good and evil
could be defined according to one's wishes. You supposed

that in the absence of any human or divine code, the only values were those of the animal world—in other words, violence and cunning. Hence you concluded that man was negligible and that his soul could be killed, that in the maddest of histories, the only pursuit for the individual was the adventure of power and his only morality, the realm of conquests. And to tell the truth, believing, I thought as you did, I saw no valid argument to answer you except fierce labor of justice which, after all, seemed as unreasonable as the most sudden passion."[81]

But now, Camus says, he sees that the nihilism of Nazi socialism means violence, bestiality and utter contempt for human life; it flaunts openly its arrogant and cynical disregard for justice. It is for this reason, then, that Camus finds it necessary to reject the injustice practised by his Nazi friend. Although unable to believe that this world has an ultimate meaning, Camus is, nevertheless, convinced that there *are* certain values and hence he has chosen to remain on the side of justice. He writes in the *Fourth Letter to a German Friend,* "I chose justice in order to remain faithful to the world. I continue to believe that this world has no ultimate meaning. But I know that something in it has a meaning and that is man, because he is the only creature to insist on having one. The world has at least the truth of man, and our task is to provide its justifications against fate itself. And it has no justification but man; hence we must be saved if we want to save the idea we have of life."[82]

Camus thus dramatically opts for some sort of values in life. He contends that everything cannot be absolutely relative; there must be some fundamental differences between actions. If everything is completely indifferent, if there is no system of values, if one act is absolutely the same as every other act, then nothing matters and we have an unabashed relativism. In such an instance, every act can be simultaneously good and bad, much the same as the Sophists held in the time of Socrates and Plato. As one commentator points out, "If each good is as good or as valueless as another, if all are equally inconse-quential, the question of which goods shall take precedence over others can be answered and solved in practice by the strongest man ending all the arguments by making his value supreme."[83]

Now the only answer—the only rational response—is that there *must* be some system of values, otherwise everything is lost. For indeed if everything is completely indifferent, then what the Nazis were doing to millions of innocent human beings was perfectly acceptable and morally indifferent, DACHAU, AUSCHWITZ and BUCHENWALD could not be condemned by anyone. Atrocity, rape, murder, sadistic tortures were perfectly acceptable because they were morally neutral actions. Camus then graphically expresses the alternatives. He says, "If we believe in nothing, if nothing has any meaning, and if we can affirm no values whatsoever, then everything is possible and nothing has any importance. There is no pro or con: the murderer is neither right nor wrong. *We are free to stoke the crematory fires or devote ourselves to the care of the lepers.* Evil and virtue are mere chance or caprice."[84] Camus, therefore, could not get himself to hold that it was a matter of moral indifference "whether one adds more victims to the gas chambers or devotes one's life to curing lepers . . . or whether the quisling or the informer could be put on a level with the Resistance fighter."[85]

In this connection, a story is told of a memorable conversation that took place one morning in a Parisian café between Camus and Sartre. The meeting occurred during the hated Nazi occupation of the city of lights. Sartre was heatedly maintaining that man has infinite freedom, that there are absolutely no limits on what he does. Camus, on the other hand, just as stubbornly and vehemently defended the opposite position. He argued for limits on the type of action which man can perform. Camus then declared to Sartre, "If freedom is really infinite, if it has no limits, then you can turn me over to the Nazis." (It was Camus who was the anonymous but highly admired writer of the inspiring editorials carried by the French underground paper *Combat*. To expose Camus to the Nazis would have been a fatal blow to the efforts of the Resistance workers.) Sartre, who was also a member of the underground, protested that he could not do something so despicable and treacherous. To this, Camus made his famous reply, "Obviously, then, freedom *must* have certain limits."[86]

B. *The Plague*

The Plague, which appeared in 1947, underscored perhaps even more dramatically than the *Letters to a German Friend*, Camus' move away from a stance of a complete philosophical relativism, unrestricted freedom, and an ethics of quantity. Written as an allegory, *The Plague* is a representation of the irrational brutality of the absurd itself. While Camus rejects most emphatically any traditional theistic or Judaeo-Christian attitude toward suffering, he nevertheless argues that we must at least extend a helping hand to our brothers in combatting the incomprehensible and irrational absurdism of life. True, there is comparatively little that we will be able to accomplish. The inevitable death awaits us all without distinction. But minimally, if we join forces on the side of man rather than *against* him, we shall at least choose to resist the absurd. In this way, we reject the radical pessimism of Sisyphus and proclaim that there *is* something more important than the absurd, namely the human spirit itself.[87]

As Thomas Hanna describes it, "In the common struggle against the oppressive plague, men have discovered their solidarity, and with this discovery, they have learned compassion and sympathy. . . . The plague is unrelenting and never-dying and, consequently, our revolting against it is endless."[88]

We find, therefore, that there is a common human nature in which we all share. It acts as a bond which unites all men. Humanity is a good which must be protected against the plague at all cost. It is common decency that demands that we extend a helping hand to our brother in distress. We all share in an undying obligation to keep this human solidarity alive.

Camus describes the sympathy and love which men

must have for each other while they are engaged in the
life-long struggle. In a conversation between Rieux, the
medical doctor and narrator of the story, and Tarrou
who organized volunteers to fight the plague, we read,
"After a short silence, the doctor raised himself a little
in his chair and asked if Tarrou had an idea of the path
to follow for attaining peace. 'Yes,' he replied, 'The path
of *sympathy.*'"[89]

Contrary to the proud isolation of the absurd hero
in *The Myth of Sisyphus*, Camus emphasizes the need
for love that all men have. He writes, "Rieux thought it
too; that a loveless world is a dead world, and always
there comes an hour when one is weary of prisons, of one's
work, and of devotion to duty, and all one craves for is
a loved face, the warmth and wonder of a loving heart
. . . at this moment he suffered . . . and what filled his
breast was the passionate indignation we feel when
confronted by the anguish all men share."[90]

And yet, we must remember that man's condition is
never one of victory. In spite of the solidarity among
men, in spite of their sympathy and love for each other,
there is still a collective impotence, a grim realization that,
in spite of man's heroic rebellion and struggle against
the absurd, his ultimate end is defeat and death.

Dr. Rieux witnesses Tarrou's dying gasps and he
muses at the inevitability of the common lot of all men.
"This human form, lacerated by the spear-thrusts of the
plague, consumed by searing, superhuman fires, buffeted
by all the raging winds of heaven, was foundering under
his eyes in the dark flood of the pestilence, and he could
do nothing to avert the wreck. He could only stand, un-
availing, on the shore, empty-handed and sick at heart,
unarmed and helpless yet again under the onset of
calamity. And thus, when the end came, the tears that
blinded Rieux's eyes were tears of impotence; and he
did not see Tarrou roll over, face to the wall, and die
with a short hollow groan, as if somewhere within him
an essential cord had snapped . . . this defeat was final,
the last disastrous battle that ends a war and makes peace
itself an ill beyond all remedy. The doctor could not tell

if Tarrou had found peace, now that all was over, but for himself, he had a feeling that no peace was possible to him henceforth, any more than there can be an armistice for a mother bereaved of her son or for a man who buries his friend."[91]

Camus concludes *The Plague* by reminding us that the present victory over the plague is only provisional. It can never be complete and final. Man must constantly struggle with the absurd. He can never master it completely. Dr. Rieux feels compelled to write this account of man's struggle with the plague in order to emphasize the injustices which men must undergo. Yet in their common battle with the plague, men do find a solidarity and community. At times, it may seem as if they had overcome completely their common enemy. In reality, the seeming victory is nothing more than a reprieve. Inevitably, the plague will rear its ugly head and attack man once again.

Dr. Rieux writes, "He resolved to compile this chronicle, so that he should not be one of those who hold their peace but should bear witness in favor of those plague-stricken people; so that some memorial of the injustice and outrage done them might endure.... None the less, he knew that the tale he had to tell could not be one of final victory. It could be only the record of what had had to be done, and what assuredly would have to be done again in the never ending fight against terror and its relentless onslaughts.... And indeed, as he listened to the cries of joy rising from the town, Rieux remembered that such joy is always imperiled. He knew what those jubilant crowds did not know but could have learned from books; that the plague bacillus never dies or disappears for good; that it can lie dormant for years and years in furniture and linen-closets; that it bides its time in bedrooms, cellars, trunks, bookshelves; and that perhaps the day would come when, for the bane and the enlightening of men, it would rouse up its rats again and send them forth to die in a happy city."[92]

In a comparatively short space of time, Camus had made great progress in his thought. From a pessimistic resignation to the utter futility of man's life and a nihilism which advocates the most living by rejecting any value system (*The Myth of Sisyphus*), Camus has now repudiated nihilism, opted for an ethics of quality (*Letters to a German Friend*) and advanced the notion of a human nature and human solidarity (*The Plague*).

C. *The Rebel*

Four years after the publication of *The Plague*, there appeared in 1951, Camus' most penetrating analysis of the nature of rebellion under the title of *The Rebel*. We shall now examine its chief features.

Camus had already warned us in *The Myth of Sisyphus* that the absurdist stage was not meant to be a permanent one. It was, in reality, only a preparation for a second stage, namely that of rebellion, whose outlines Camus had set down in *The Myth*. Now, ten years later, Camus writes in the Introduction to *The Rebel*, "The real nature of the absurd is that it is an experience to be lived through, a point of departure, the equivalent in existence of Descartes' methodical doubt. The absurd is, in itself, a contradiction. . . . Absurdism, like methodic doubt, has wiped the slate clean. It leaves us in a blind alley. But, like methodical doubt, it can, by returning upon itself, open up a new field of investigation, and the process of reasoning then pursues the same course. I proclaim that I believe in nothing and that everything is absurd, but I cannot doubt the validity of my proclamation and I must at least believe in my protest. The first and only evidence that is supplied me, within the terms of the absurdist experience, is rebellion. Deprived of all knowledge, incited to murder or to consent to murder, all I have at my disposal is this single piece of evidence, which is only affirmed by the anguish I suffer. Rebellion is born of the spectacle of irrationality, confronted with an unjust and incomprehensible condition. But its blind impulse is to demand order in the midst of chaos, and unity in the very heart of the ephemeral."[93]

Again, speaking of the tentativeness of the nature of the absurd and of the transition to the state of rebellion, Camus observed in *Les nouvelles littéraires* of May 10, 1951, "When I analyzed the feeling of the absurd in *The Myth of Sisyphus,* I was looking for a method and not a doctrine. I was practising methodical doubt. I was trying to make a *tabula rasa,* on the basis of which it would then be possible to construct something. If we assume that nothing has any meaning, then we must conclude that the world is absurd. But does nothing have a meaning? *I have never believed that we could remain at this point.* Even as I was writing *The Myth of Sisyphus,* I was thinking about the essay on revolt that I would write later on."[94]

In the opening pages of *The Rebel,* Camus has this to say, "The purpose of this essay is once again to face the reality of the present, which is logical crime and to examine meticulously the arguments by which it is justified; it is an attempt to understand the times in which we live. One might think that a period which, in a space of fifty years, uproots, enslaves or kills seventy million human beings should be condemned out of hand. But its culpability must still be understood. In more ingenuous times, when the tyrant razed cities for his own glory, when the slave chained to the conqueror's chariot was dragged through the rejoicing streets, when enemies were thrown to the wild beasts in front of the assembled people, the mind did not reel before such unabashed crimes and judgment remained unclouded. But slave camps under the flag of freedom, massacres justified by philanthropy or by taste for the superhuman, in one sense, crippled judgment. On the day when crime dons the apparel of innocence—through a curious transposition peculiar to our times—it is innocence that is called upon to justify itself. The ambition of this essay is to accept and examine this strange challenge."[95]

In the face of such a strange transvaluation of values, Camus tells us that we shall know nothing until we find out definitely, whether we have the right to kill our fellow-men or the right to let them be killed. If murder does have a rational foundation, then Camus holds "our period and we ourselves are rationally consequent." On the other hand, if murder has no rational foundation, then we are all insane and we must either find some kind of justification for it or we must turn our faces away from what is going on.

Camus then begins his investigation of the nature of rebellion by reiterating his argument against physical suicide. He writes, "The final conclusion of the absurdist reasoning is, in fact, a repudiation of suicide and the acceptance of the disparate encounter between human inquiry and the silence of the universe. Suicide would mean the end of this encounter, and absurdist reasoning considers that it would not consent to this without negating its premises."[96]

The rejection of suicide, which is the conclusion of *The Myth,* is therefore made a foundational principle of *The Rebel.* Camus now argues for certain limitations— for a certain stable human nature. He writes, "But it is obvious that absurdism hereby admits that human life is the only necessary good, since it is precisely life that makes the encounter possible. . . . From the moment that life is recognized as a good, it becomes a good for all men. Murder cannot be made coherent when suicide is not coherent. . . . The absurd is contradictory in its content because in wanting to uphold life, it excludes value judgments, when to live is, itself, a value judgment. To breathe is to judge. Perhaps it is untrue to say that life is a perpetual choice. But it is true that it is impossible to imagine a life deprived of all choice."[97]

The absurdist position thus ineluctably forces man to abandon a stance of absolute relativism and neutrality. Choose he must, if he wishes to live. But in order to choose, man must accept some scale of values.

In the Foreword to *The Rebel,* Herbert Read tells us, "Just as an earlier work (*Le Mythe de Sisyphe*) began with a meditation on living or not living—on the implications of the act of suicide—so this work begins with a meditation on enduring or not enduring—on the implications of the act of rebellion. If we decide to live, it must be because we have decided that our personal existence has some value; if we decide to rebel, it must be because we have decided that a human society has some value."[98]

D. Metaphysical Rebellion

Camus now distinguishes between metaphysical and historical rebellion, which are two different positive reactions to the state of absurdism. We shall first examine the nature and implications of metaphysical rebellion.

When a man rebels, he says "no," but his refusal does not simply mean a renunciation. A slave, for example, who had been dutifully obedient all his life, suddenly says "no" to his master. By this he means that "up to this point, 'yes,' but beyond it 'no.'" Or again, he categorically states, "There is a limit beyond which you shall not go." Camus is trying to assert as positively as he can that rebellion *cannot* exist without the conviction that somewhere, somehow, one is right. The rebel maintains that there are limits and "he demonstrates with obstinacy, that there is something in him, which is worthwhile and which must be taken into consideration."[99] As a result of this stance, he brings into play a "standard of values, so far from being gratuitous, that he is prepared to support it, no matter what the risks . . . and if he prefers the risk of death to the negation of the rights he defends, it is because he considers these rights more important than himself. Therefore he is acting in the name of certain values, which are still indeterminate but which he feels are common to himself and to all men.

. . . When he rebels a man identifies himself with other men and so surpasses himself . . . the first progressive step for a mind overwhelmed by the strangeness of things is to realize that his feeling of strangeness is shared with all men . . . the malady experienced by a single man becomes a mass plague . . . this evidence lures the individual from his solitude. It founds its first value on the whole human race. I rebel—therefore we exist."[100]

Adele King emphasizes this belief in the common dignity of man which Camus advances in *The Rebel* by contrasting it with the position which was adopted in *The Myth of Sisyphus*. While it is true that both essays agree that there are no transcendent values and that man is left completely to his own resources, *The Rebel* decidedly argues for a common humanity. She writes, "If in *Le Mythe de Sisyphe*, Camus examines the implications of 'the absurd' for the individual, in *L'Homme revolté*, he is concerned with the effects of rebellion against the absurd upon society. . . . In *Le Mythe de Sisyphe*, Camus says that the hero of the absurd must preserve his individual consciousness in his rebellion against death. In *L'Homme revolté*, however, Camus claims that the political rebel prefers to die rather than to continue as a slave. Because he chooses to fight for justice rather than for his life, the rebel's action suggests that a man can value something beyond his own existence, something that he wants to share with other men. Revolt is based on a belief in a common human dignity."[101]

The rebel, therefore, acts not in his own name as a private individual who is interested only in his own personal good. Rather, he is acting in the interest of certain values which are common to all men. Hence it is for the sake of everyone in the world, that the slave refuses to obey a command. He is convinced that this command infringes not so much on private and personal right but rather on something far more important, namely on a "common ground where all men—even the man who insults and oppresses him—have a natural community."[102]

As Thomas Hanna says in his work, *The Thought and Art of Albert Camus*, "Revolt affirms the complicity of all men around a common value and against a common oppression. It affirms a value which all men possess, even the oppressor himself. It carries man toward all men, showing that the solidarity of men is metaphysical, or, as Camus puts it, that this value is 'horizontally transcendent' of the individual."[103]

It is at this point, therefore, that Albert Camus disagrees most emphatically with such existentialists like Martin Heidegger, and especially Jean Paul Sartre and Simone de Beauvoir, who maintain that most literally "existence precedes essence," and that man's nature is completed only after man's choices have all been made at the moment of death—when, incidentally, he ceases to exist altogether. In rejecting such a position, Camus argues, "But it is already worth noting that this concept of values as pre-existent to any kind of action contradicts the purely historical philosophies, in which values are acquired (if they are *ever* acquired) after the action has been completed. Analysis of rebellion leads at least to the suspicion that, contrary, to the postulates of contemporary thought, *a human nature does exist,* as the Greeks believed. Why rebel if there is nothing permanent in oneself worth preserving?"[104]

When the slave rebelled against the master and proclaimed himself ready to defend certain values in the name of humanity, he thereby asserted the existence of certain *limits.* (This far you can go but not beyond it.) In other words, a rebel maintains that there are certain limits and the acknowledgement of these limits negates the possibility of absolute freedom. If, for example, I were to exercise unconditional and absolute freedom, I would necessarily encroach on the very rights of my fellow-man for which rights I declared myself ready to die. In fact, by interfering with the rights of another, I now assume the role of an offending master. As Emmett Parker points out, "If the former slave asserts his own superiority at the expense of others, he has merely substituted one master-slave relationship for another."[105] The essence of revolt, therefore, presupposes limits and limits make absolute freedom impossible.

We shall close this examination of metaphysical rebellion with a quotation from *The Rebel.* Camus writes, "If the limit discovered by rebellion transfigures everything, if every thought, every action that goes beyond a certain point negates itself, there is, in fact, a measure by which to judge events and men. In history, as in psychology, rebellion is an irregular pendulum, which swings in an erratic arc because it is looking for its most perfect and profound rhythm. But its irregularity is not total: it functions around a pivot. Rebellion, at the time that it suggests a nature common to all men, brings to light the measure and the limit which are the very principle of this nature."[106]

E. Historical Rebellion

Camus next examines the manner in which a number of literary and historical figures had implemented the principles of revolt in history. He is especially interested in studying the way in which men, who had rejected the limits and restraints imposed by Christian moral precepts, had made use of their freedom. Parker remarks, "Camus, observing that modern man has lost sight of the relativity of all revolt, concludes that, having turned away from religion as a source of values, men have set up a new source of absolute values by deifying either man himself or history. . . . In their zeal to see perfect social order toward which they were certain the march of history was predirected, revolutionary leaders from Saint-Just to Lenin justified the destruction of those human beings who impeded the attainment of perfection within the social order. Thus *murder, conquest and enslavement were accepted as legitimate political weapons* in the attempt to establish the reign of the Superman or a utopia."[107]

Whether we move in the tradition of Rousseau or Saint-Just, Hegel or Bakunin, Marx or Engels, the exponents of historical rebellion are all guilty, without exception, of ignoring the fundamental pre-requisite of rebellion, namely, that of *mésure*, of limits, of moderation, of balance. And ironically, many of these individuals who began as champions of humanity and defenders of human rights, inexorably became the most notorious oppressors of the very humanity they professed to defend. All major historical rebellions since the eighteenth century to the present have been unconditioned failures. In each instance, as history testifies, they enslaved the very men they were claiming to liberate. As Nathan Scott writes, "What is tragic in each case is that, given the desacralization of life in the modern period, a rebellion that was initiated *for* man turns in the end *against* man, its demonized purposes being consecrated in blood. What is lost is the *mésure,* which might make such demonic fanaticism on behalf of any absolute appear impossible, whether it be the dream of the absolute freedom or the dream of absolute justice."[108]

Camus categorically rejects the Marxist doctrine of the end of history. Although the great Revolution arose because of the noble aspirations of revolt, because of the desire to free the oppressed, it has now destroyed every vestige of justice, freedom and truth. Russian Marxism has ruthlessly obliterated the very human solidarity in whose name the Revolution was launched. Men are of no consequence today in the totalitarian state. The state is the only reality that exists and everything else exists for the state. Man is merely a means to an end. He is something to be used and manipulated by the state. Such a condition has resulted in what Camus has called "an infinite plasticity of men." Man has no nature which should be respected. The state molds and fashions man any which way it desires.

Thomas Hanna describes Camus' evaluation of historical revolt in the following words: "The critical study which Albert Camus has made of revolt in history has attempted to show that in usurping God's functions, the rational and irrational empires have ended in terror and slavery and have created submen rather than supermen. Whether the hangman exalts himself, as in Nazism, or is exalted by his victims, as in the communist state, in either case, the motivating spirit is no longer revolt but consent. Revolution has betrayed its origins by seeking the shortest way to earthly immortality: nihilism and terror."[109]

Ernst Breisach describes Camus' critique of historical revolt in these terms: "Camus soon expressed himself more specifically by equating the ideologists of all shades and the utopians of all kinds, in short the extremists and dreamers of the 'last great revolution,' with the *forces of destruction.* Against them he puts the man of revolt who protests against any tyranny, against ideologies which dull men's minds and against all those who want to restrict man because they think it necessary either for the improvement of mankind or just for their own advantage. The revolutionaries and extremists do not know moderation. They are far removed from the Mediterranean spirit of reason and restraint exemplified in the rebel, the man of the revolt without utopian hopes and coercive tendencies."[110]

Camus ends *The Rebel* by observing that notion of *mésure*, of balance and proportion and of positing limits by avoiding the extremes, is characteristic of the "Mediterranean mind." Contrary to the German ideologies, as exemplified in the absolutism of history, the Mediterranean spirit, which has been kept alive in the countries of Spain, Italy, Greece and North Africa, is 'in the tradition of the Greeks.' It speaks of a nature which must be respected. It speaks the language of the Golden Mean, the Mean of Aristotle's *Nicomachean Ethics*. It argues for humanistic ideals which will result in dialogue and compassion. Jean Onimus describes it in the following words: "Between extreme disorder and vicious order stands civilization, and civilization rests upon moderation. To civilize man is to reduce his ambitions and teach him the value of limits. Thus . . . Camus advocates equilibrium, harmony, respect for natural norms, and the overcoming through dialogue of mortal antagonisms."[111]

IV. STAGE III: REPENTANCE?

With the publication of Albert Camus' last two works, *The Fall* (1956) and *Exile and Kingdom* (1957), we seem to be entering upon a third stage in Camus' thought, however inchoate it may be. Tentatively, we shall call this third stage, the *Stage of Repentance* because the new themes set forth in these last two works can hardly be characterized as a continuation of the *Stage of Revolt and Moderation*. The themes which both *The Fall* and *Exile and Kingdom* explore are revelatory of a soul in anguish but which is well along the way of some kind of religious values. Let us examine these works a little more closely. *The Fall*, which appeared five years after *The Rebel* and just four years before Camus' untimely death, is a very disturbing book.[112] Many critics have wrestled with only

modest success in their attempt to interpret Camus'
thought correctly in this enigmatic and ambiguous work.
For one thing, *The Fall* seems to epitomize a complete
reversal in Camus' direction of thought. Whereas *The
Myth of Sisyphus, The Misunderstanding, The Stranger*
and *The Plague* consistently represented man as a helpless victim of some sinister, unknown and external force,
Camus now tends to take a diametrically opposite position.
No longer is man the innocent party in this blind struggle
with the plague—that unjust force in nature. Man's deplorable state is now due to the evil *within* himself. He
himself is the author of his misery. He alone is the guilty
one.

This about-face in Camus' thought is well expressed
by Thomas Hanna when he writes, "*The Fall* constitutes
a reversal of Camus' concerns precisely because he is
no longer dealing with 'I the innocent rebel' but rather
with 'I the guilty other'. . . . The true moral stature of
Albert Camus comes into focus in this moment when he
confesses, 'I am an innocent rebel, but more than this:
I am also an evildoer.' "[113]

A number of critics have pointed to the intensely religious, psychological and introspective nature of *The Fall*.
Some have found the brooding pessimism of Clamence,
"the penitent-judge," a striking portrayal of Camus' own
state of mind. To that extent, *The Fall* has been called a
kind of autobiography, much like Jean Paul Sartre's
Nausea, when the latter recently admitted in *The Words*,
that, in actuality, he himself was Antoine Roquentin.[114]

Commentators point to the indisputably religious
character of this work. The very title, *The Fall*, is religious.
Jean-Baptiste Clamence's name is a clear adaptation of
John the Baptist, "a voice crying in the wilderness" and
preaching penance in order to gain salvation. The canals
of Amsterdam are unmistakable references to the con-
centric circles of Dante's hell. Clamence's cry of despair
and the need to confess his sin seem to point to an
anguished longing for salvation. No longer do we see
here the defiant hero of *The Myth of Sisyphus*, clenching
his fist and proudly warring with the evil in the world.

Jean-Baptiste is rather a penitent voice, proclaiming his guilt and seeking salvation, innocence, and grace. As one writer has observed, "Camus is seeking either a Christ or a God which, as yet, he has not been able to find. And obviously, without God, there can be no salvation, no innocence, no saving grace."[115]

The story of Jean-Baptiste Clamence is a confession of a man who cannot live with his conscience. The young woman whom he failed to save from death because of his cowardice is haunting him ceaselessly. Clamence is looking for a judge who will condemn him and then pardon his sin. But there is neither condemnation nor pardon in sight. It is this desire for repentance latent in Clamence's search which reveals a totally new direction in Camus' thought.

Jean Onimus describes this aspect of *The Fall* when he says, "Clamence's drama consists in his being vainly in search of a judge: 'Who would dare condemn me in a world without a judge where no one is innocent?' No condemnation? Then no pardon either! Man is alone with his sin and no savior is going to deliver him from it. For only a savior, one having power over sin, could in fact cure him. . . . Clamence tried to punish himself by abandoning his job, by withdrawing, like a hermit, into the tumult of Amsterdam, and—especially—by intoning his *mea culpa* before anyone who cared to listen. . . . This is the instinct for confession in its raw state. . . . One can only ask oneself, with the critic Marcel Arland, if in driving man to despair 'this devil's advocate does not serve God's cause.' "[116]

Bernard Murchland sees *The Fall* as possibly expressing "a realization of sin and unworthiness—the dark night of the soul before the coming of grace" and he sees Camus' *Exile and Kingdom* as "stressing new values of penance and expiation."[117]

Philip Thody, in his excellent study of Camus and his work, writes, "*The Fall* . . . seems to be a book which, as Donat O'Donnell argued, might be read and understood in a Christian manner . . . the obsession with man's unworthiness links it closely to the Catholic novels of

Graham Greene or François Mauriac, and it seems to be a deeply felt cry *de profundis* for salvation."[118]

It is our conclusion, therefore, that in spite of Camus' avowedly anti-Christian and atheistic stance over the years, his last works betray a very serious pre-occupation with religious, and even Christian themes. The testimony of Conor Cruise O'Brien in his work, *Albert Camus of Europe and Africa*, is especially significant, inasmuch as it is corroborated by Camus' own agreement with O'Brien's judgment. We quote, "Under the surface of irony and occasional blasphemy, *La Chute* is profoundly Christian in its confessional form, in its imagery, and above all in its pervasive message that it is only through the full recognition of our sinful nature, that we can hope for grace. Grace does not, it is true, arrive, and the novel ends on what is a pessimistic note. Yet the name of the narrator—that of the forerunner—hints, however teasingly, at the possibility of a sequel."[119]

In a footnote, O'Brien adds an insight which we consider very noteworthy in advancing the possibility of the beginning of *Stage III: Repentance*. He writes, "When in a review in *The Spectator* of the English version of *La Chute*, I stressed its Christian tendency, Camus wrote to his English publishers, Hamish Hamilton, *confirming that this approach to the novel was sound*."[120]

V. CONCLUSION

We now come to the sudden and abrupt end of what promised to be one of the most creative and brilliant literary careers of this century. A Nobel Prize winner at forty-four, with at least a good twenty-five years of productivity ahead of him, Albert Camus was struck down by death at the age of forty-seven. (One writer has observed that Camus' sudden death due to an auto accident was the supreme expression of the absurd which so obsessively plagued him most of his life.)

Today, a little over a decade since his death, Albert Camus' influence is far from diminishing because, as the Nobel citation stated, he was the eloquent spokesman of the problems of our age. Camus always rejected the strident and abrasive type of atheism which Sartre and his followers touted. In an interview (*Le Monde*, 1956), Camus stated that he found "in irreligiousness something . . . yes something trite."[121] At the same time he remained an atheist, an unbeliever.[122]

Camus began as an atheist and he died an atheist but his thought, as we have seen, had undergone a dramatic re-direction. He began with a thorough-going nihilism and absurdism, which argued for unlimited freedom and an ethics of quantity. The "most living" best described the hero of the absurd. But Camus was forced to abandon his nihilistic principles when he saw their gruesome implementation by Nazi socialism during World War II. He rejected the quantitative ethics in favor of an ethics of quality. All actions could not be equivalent. There *had* to be a distinction between good and evil, between right and wrong; otherwise, it was the same to stoke the crematory fires of the Nazi gas chambers as it was to devote one's life in the service of lepers.

Rebellion or revolt replaced the absurd. But rebellion always implied the recognition of values and the imposition of limits on man's actions. The rebelling slave proclaimed by his very act that he was defending certain values—a stable human nature, a community, a human solidarity. Camus, therefore, argued for the famous Mediterranean moderation, which recognized the Greek concept of a stable human nature.

His subsequent preoccupation with genuinely religious themes would seem to indicate that had he lived longer, he would have taken, almost inevitably, some definite and positive position vis-à-vis the question of spiritual and religious values. One is not justified to say more.

Cornelio Fabro in his monumental work, *God in Exile,* has this observation to make concerning the notion of HOPE, which Camus had so categorically and unequivocally excluded from his earlier thought. Fabro writes, "Camus proceeded to found a publication series with the over-all title ESPOIR (HOPE), in which there appears a number of philosophical essays, with a decidedly positive bias, much as B. Parain's *L'embarras du choix* and Simone Weil's famous works of Christian inspiration, *L'enracin-ement, La connaissance surnaturelle, Lettre à un religieux,* and *La condition ouvrière.*

The 'foreword' to this Series included a declaration of aims which is worthy of serious study, as indicating something more than a mere change of style. It is a pro-fession of faith in the value of man, despite the abyss of nihilism into which civilization has hurled him: 'We are in nihilism! Is there any way out of nihilism? That is the question with which we are saddled. But we shall not slip out of it by making a show of being oblivious of the malady of the age nor yet by resolving to deny its exis-tence. The only hope lies in calling it by its name and effecting a detailed diagnosis of it, so as to find the cure in the extremity of the disease.' The aim of the Series is, therefore, to arouse and promote this hope: the individual volumes may present a confirmation of nihilism or may, on the contrary, attempt to get beyond it; but the over-all program is clear. 'They will all, however, form a common front, they will all witness to an identical effort to define or surmount the lethal contradiction in which we are living. If the time has come when we must choose, this very compulsion itself represents progress. *Let us then realize that this is the time of hope,* even if it be a hard-won and demanding hope!' The aim of the Series is, there-fore, to aid, albeit in the simplest and most modest way, '. . . to expose the tragedy and to show that tragedy is not a solution nor yet despair a defensible ultimate stand. It depends on us to convert these unavoidable trials into pledges of hope.' "[123]

Fabro then adds, "It is not easy to say whether Camus so tragically struck down at the height of his powers, might have completed his Odyssey in a positive sense; but this declaration we have just cited bears witness to the fact that he was indeed already far along the road."[124]

Albert Camus, the spokesman of an age torn by war and dissension, exhibited a rare and even passionate concern for his fellow-man. In the name of justice and compassion, he urged a solidarity, a confraternity, a community among men. Atheist though he died, his plea had a strikingly familiar resemblance to the theistic urgings of Martin Buber for community, Gabriel Marcel for I-Thou and intersubjectivity, and of Nikolai Berdyaev for *sobornost*. This is why the thought of Albert Camus is so important for the world today.

We shall conclude our study with three evaluations of Camus' importance for twentieth century man. John Hayward sees Camus as an eloquent chronicler of the ravages of nihilism. He writes, "The writings of Albert Camus are uniquely relevant to our inquiry because he embodies and, at the same time, transcends the existentialist pathos. No one has more eloquently expressed the nihilism and lonely individualism of modern European civilization than he. But even as he documents the breakdown of traditional and religious values, he continues to transmit in altered form much that is religiously sustaining in Western culture. It is as though he had learned to appropriate the nourishment of his history while remaining free of it. He points the way beyond nihilism, but he does not advocate a return or explicit recourse to either sectarian liberalism or the Judaeo-Christian tradition. . . . *The Fall* shows the devastating range and effects of nihilism; it confronts the reader with a picture of the personal suffering, moral depravity and utter meaninglessness of a life which is wholly self-centered, unprincipled and unrelated."[125]

Arthur Gibson sees Camus as challenging every theist to love man as mortal. He argues, "Albert Camus, seasoned by many desperate nights and days of clandestine underground combat, tortured and enlightened by the spectacle of irreverence for life on the part of misguided crusaders for ideals, and at the examples of heroism in defense of life, has fashioned a challenge for every theist! Learn to love man as mortal. To your supernaturally motivated charity for the salvation of his eternal immortal soul, learn to add a tormented and heroic natural crusading love for the perishable entity, the existent human being in the here and now, the mortal human being."[126]

Emmett Parker's tribute is succinct and thought-provoking: "Camus sensed that a certain common ground existed between Christians and those unbelievers like himself, who were animated by a strong sense of human justice, and he hoped that they could join forces against the rising tide of oppression he saw threatening whatever vestige of human freedom was left in Western Europe. . . . Camus has much to offer to the world. It is important to both Christians and non-Christians that the· full implications of his thought be understood. It is not too late to establish the kind of dialogue Camus called for—a free and sincere exchange between men with a keen sense of justice and human compassion, willing to break down the ideologically imposed barriers of solitude that may separate us."[127]

Notes

CHAPTER I

1. Cf. below, p. 71.
2. Cf. below, p. 181.
3. Cf. below, pp. 90-91.
4. Cf. below, pp. 348-49, note 15, p. 429.
5. Karl Jaspers, *Reason and Anti-Reason,* trans. Stanley Godman (London: SCM Press, 1952), p. 63. While some writers assert that Jaspers was the first to use the term "Existence Philosophy," F. H. Heinemann writes, "In 1929, I published a book *Neue Wege der Philosophie,* in which I introduced the term *Existenz-philosophie;* and to my knowledge I was the first to describe this phenomenon. I interpreted the whole modern philosophy from Descartes to the present time as being based on the antithetical principle of discursive reason (*ratio*) and life. I understood 'existence' as a new principle which aims at overcoming the onesidedness of the rationalist as well as irrationalist philosophies."—F. H. Heinemann, *Existentialism and the Modern Predicament,* Torchbook (New York: Harper and Row, 1958), p. 1.
6. "There are two fundamentally different ways of interpreting the word 'existentialism.' One is to affirm the primacy of existence, but as implying and preserving essences or natures and as manifesting the supreme victory of the intellect and of intelligibility. This is what I consider authentic existentialism. The other way is to affirm the primacy of existence, but as destroying and abolishing essences or natures, and as manifesting the supreme defeat of the intellect and of intelligibility. This is what I consider apocryphal existentialism, the current kind which no longer signifies anything at all."—Jacques Maritain, *Existence and the Existent.* Image Book (Garden City: Doubleday and Co., 1957), p. 13.
   Cf. Étienne Gilson, *The Christian Philosophy of St. Thomas Aquinas* (New York: Random House, 1956): ———, *History of Christian Philosophy in the Middle Ages* (New York: Random House, 1955), pp. 361-83; ———, "On the Art of Misunderstanding Thomism," in *In Search of St. Thomas Aquinas, McAuley Lectures,* 1966 (West Hartford: Saint Joseph College, 1966), pp. 33-43; Anton Pegis, "Thomism as Philosophy," in *St. Thomas Aquinas and Philosophy, McAuley Lectures* 1960 (West Hartford: Saint Joseph College, 1961), pp. 15-29; ———, "Thomism 1966" in *In Search of St. Thomas Aquinas,* pp. 19-31; ———, *St. Thomas and Philosophy* (Milwaukee: Marquette University Press, 1964); Frederick Copleston, *History of Philosophy,* 8 vols. (Garden City: Doubleday and Co., II, 2; 20-155; ———, *Aquinas* (Baltimore: Penguin Books, 1970).
7. Cf. above, p. 3.
8. Gabriel Marcel, *Three Plays,* trans. Rosalind Heywood, Mermaid Dramabook (New York: Hill and Wang, 1965). A fourth play, *The Lantern* (*Le Fanal*), can be found in *Cross Currents,* VIII, 2 (1958). In letters to the author dated July 19, 1972 and April 3, 1973, Gabriel Marcel writes, "Je considère que mon théâtre est beaucoup trop peu connu aux U.S.A. où au contraire presque tous mes Ecrits Philosophiques sont traduits . . . il est pour moi de la plus grande importance que mes pièces soient enfin connues en Amérique. En Angleterre aussi, elles sont pratiquement inconnues, et le résultat en est qu'on se fait de mon oeuvre et de ma pensée une idée tout a fait fausse. Je ne pourrais jamais assez vous remercier de ce que vous tentez pour reduire cette ignorance."
   The McAuley Institute of Religious Studies, Saint Joseph College, West Hartford, has been granted exclusive rights for the translation and publication of all of Gabriel Marcel's plays. In addition to the three plays which appear in 1974, six additional ones are being readied for publication.
9. Carl Michalson, ed., *Christianity and the Existentialists* (New York: Charles Scribner's Sons, 1956), p. 3.
10. Walter Kaufmann, ed., *Existentialism from Dostoevsky to Sartre,* Meridian Book (Cleveland and New York: World Publishing Co., 1966), p. 11.
11. Fernando Molina, *Existentialism as Philosophy* (Englewood Cliffs: Prentice-Hall, 1962), p. 2.
12. Roger Troisfontaines, *What Is Existentialism?,* Overview Studies (Albany: Magi Books, 1968), p. 5.
13. J. M. Spier, *Christianity and Existentialism* (Philadelphia: Presbyterian and Reformed Publishing Co., 1953), p. 109.
14. *Webster's New World Dictionary,* 1966.
15. *Random House Dictionary,* 1956.
16. Gerard Szczesny, *The Future of Unbelief,* trans. Edward Garside (New York: Braziller, 1961), p. 7.
17. Maurice Friedman, ed., *The Worlds of Existentialism: A Critical Reader* (New York: Random House, 1964), pp. 3-4.
18. *Webster's New Collegiate Dictionary,* 1967.
19. Michalson, *op. cit.,* p. 2. For other definitions, cf. Nino Languilli, *The Existentialist Tradition,* Anchor Book (Garden City: Doubleday and Co., 1971), pp. 4-9; St. Elmo Nauman, *The New Dictionary of Existentialism* (Secaucus, N.J.:

Citadel Press, 1972), pp. 45-53.
    20. Gabriel Marcel, *Du refus à l'invocation* (Paris: Gallimard, 1940), p. 89.
    21. Cf. below, p. 5.
    22. Søren Kierkegaard, pp. 38ff.; Martin Heidegger, pp. 211ff.; Gabriel Marcel, pp. 98ff.; Martin Buber, pp. 156ff.; Jean Paul Sartre, pp. 315ff.; Albert Camus, pp. 371ff.
    23. Cf. Gabriel Marcel, pp. 98ff.; Martin Buber, pp. 151ff.; Martin Heidegger, pp. 203ff.; Albert Camus, pp. 371ff.
    24. Cf. Heidegger, below, pp. 206-21.
    25. Jean Paul Sartre, *Nausea*, trans. Lloyd Alexander (New York: New Directions Publishing Co., 1964), p. 180.
    26. Cf. below, p. 306.
    27. Cf. below, pp. 371-86.
    28. Cf. below, pp. 91-95.
    29. Cf. below, pp. 152-53.
    30. Cf. below, pp. 195-221.
    31. Herbert Spiegelberg, *The Phenomenological Movement*, 2 vols., 2nd ed. (The Hague: Martinus Nijhoff, 1971), II, 442.
    32. Cf. below, pp. 128-32.

CHAPTER II

    1. *Søren* is the Danish rendering of the Latin *Severinus*.
    2. Cf. Walter Lowrie, *Kierkegaard*, Torchbook, 2 vols. (New York: Harper and Bros. 1962), I, 19-23. James Collins, *The Mind of Kierkegaard*, Gateway (Chicago: Henry Regnery, 1965), pp. 2-7; Kenneth Hamilton, *The Promise of Kierkegaard* (Philadelphia and New York: J. B. Lippincott Co., 1969), pp. 13-17; Robert Perkins, *Søren Kierkegaard* (Richmond: John Knox Press, 1969), pp. 1-3.
    3. Søren Kierkegaard, *Journals*, entry for Feb., 1946, #5 quoted in Lowrie *op. cit.*, I, 22. Eight years after Søren's death, his brother Peter, now Bishop of Aalborg, was shown the passage which Søren wrote: "How terrible about a man who once as a little boy cursed God etc." and Bishop Peter broke down and cried and said, "This is my Father's story and ours too."
    4. *Ibid.*, #411 quoted in Lowrie, *op. cit.*, I, 20. "A pietistic, gloomy spirit of religiosity pervaded the household in which the severe father was the undisputed master, and absolute obedience the watchword. Little Søren as he himself tells us, heard more of the Crucified and the martyrs than of the Christ-Child and good angels."—Lee Hollander, *Selections from the Writings of Kierkegaard*, Anchor Book (Garden City: Doubleday and Co., 1960), p. 2; cf. Walter Lowrie, *A Short Life of Kierkegaard* (Princeton: University Press, 1969), p. 13.
    5. *Journals*, #70. "His [Mikael's] vigorous mind was imprisoned in a narrow disfiguring Protestantism, an arid predestinarian theology and meagre pietism that accentuated the personal dependence of man on God at the price of confining it in an almost mechanistic conception of Divine Providence. To him the chain of cause and effect of guilt and punishment reached from his first rebellion of God, down through his sensuality to successive deaths of his children. It was a religion which neither education nor vision touched; it remained morose, intense and sterile."—Alexander Dru, ed., *The Journals of Kierkegaard*, Torchbook (New York and Evanston: Harper and Row, 1959), p. 13.
    Kierkegaard considered his home as one given over to death. He writes, "It seems as though I were a galley slave, chained to death; every time life moves, the chains rattle and death withers everything—and that happens *every minute*."—*Journals*, #66, p. 136.
    "He [Mikael] had a rich imagination and enormous dialectical skill, and yet, as his son said, he was the most melancholy man he had ever known."—Perry LeFevre, *The Prayers of Kierkegaard* (Chicago and London: University of Chicago Press, 1969), p. 138.
    6. *Journals* (Dru) p. 243.
    7. *Ibid.*, Kierkegaard seems to have discovered the reason for his father's "silent despair" some time during the year of 1835, after he had been at the university for five years. In his *Journals* of 1844, he states, "A relationship between father and son, where the son secretly discovers everything after, yet dares not acknowledge it. The father is a respectable man, severe and God-fearing, only once in a state of intoxication, he lets drop a few words which hint at the worst. Otherwise, the son does not discover what it is and never dares ask his father or others."—(Dru) p. 503.
    8. Cf. below, pp. 33-40. "A period of complete upheaval began; everything that had been holy for Kierkegaard collapsed. He had lost all religious and moral orientation. Regularly he came home drunk, and he continuously hovered on the verge of insanity. The inevitable moral fall finally took place in the Spring of 1836; it was to leave its stamp on his whole future life."—Dupré, *Kierkegaard as Theologian* (New York: Sheed and Ward, 1963), p. 10.
    9. Lowrie, *Kierkegaard*, I, 197-98. Hanna Mourier records Regina's account of her first meeting with Kierkegaard as follows: "You remember to have seen S. Kierkegaard for the first time when you were 14-16 years of age. You met him at the home of the widow Rørdam, where you were invited to a party given for a girl your age. . . . Kierkegaard made a call on the family, and the liveliness of his mind made a strong impression upon you, which, however, you did not let any one observe."—quoted in Lowrie, *op. cit.*, I, 197.
    10. Kierkegaard, *Samlede Veerker*, 2nd ed. by A. B. Drachmann, J. L. Heiberg and H. O. Lange. 15 vols. (Copenhagen: Gyldendalske Boghandel, Nordisk Forlag, 1920-1936) VI, 223 quoted in Lowrie, *op. cit.*, I, 209-10.

11. *Journals*, #129 quoted in Lowrie, *op. cit.*, pp. 222-23. In his *Journals* of 1844, Kierkegaard wrote, "You say, what I have lost or rather deprived myself of—ah, how should you know that or understand it. When this subject is mentioned, you would do well to hold your peace. And how should anyone know better than I? . . . What have I lost?—the only thing that I loved."—quoted in Lowrie, *op. cit.*, p. 224; cf. Perkins, *op. cit.*, p. 4.

12. Hanna Mourier, *Appendix* in Hjalmar Helweg, *Søren Kierkegaard* in *Psykiatrist-psykologisk Studie* (1933) quoted in Lowrie, *op. cit.*, I, 195. "The impression remains that at the bottom of his trouble lay his melancholy, aggravated admittedly by an 'insane education' and coupled with an exaggerated sense of misspent youth. That nothing else prevented the union is clear from his own remarks that, with more faith, he would have married her."—Hollander, *op. cit.*, p. 11.

13. Martin Buber, *Between Man and Man,* trans. Ronald Gregor Smith (New York: Macmillan Co., 1965), p. 52; cf. Nathan Rotenstreich, "Buber's Dialogical Philosophy: The Historical Dimension," PT, III, 3 (1959), 173-75.

14. *Journals*, #92; cf. Lowrie, *op. cit.*, I, 191. "Kierkegaard was never able to come to terms with sex. Carnal intercourse always remained sinful in his eyes. His entire education led him to see in women only an object of sinful lust. Nevertheless, owing perhaps to the mother-image, he felt himself drawn to woman as an ideal of pure innocence which might liberate his highest spiritual possibilities."—Dupré, *op. cit.*, p. 14.

15. *Journals*, 1943 quoted in Peter Rohde, *Søren Kierkegaard*, trans. Alan Williams (New York: Humanities Press, 1963), p. 65. "Then once again I was plunged down, almost sympathetically, into the abyss of my melancholy by having to break off my engagement—and why?—simply because I dared not believe that God would lift the elemental misery of my being, take my almost deranged melancholy away, something I now desired with all the passion of my soul for her sake and for mine."—Søren Kierkegaard, *Entries Pertaining to Armed Neutrality,* ed. Howard Hong and Edna Hong, Clarion Book (New York: Simon and Schuster, 1969), p. 64. "Whether it was his deep melancholy, sexual impotence, his inability to reveal himself and the sins of his past life fully, his acute awareness of the incommensurability of personalities so different as his and Regina's, or his continued sense of being an exception may never be known. Suffice it to say that this event became one of the focal experiences through which Kierkegaard came to understand himself and the meaning of personal experience."—LeFevre, *op. cit.*, p. 153; cf. Lowrie, *A Short Life,* pp. 100-01.

16. The issue of November 14, 1845 of the *Corsair* had the following to say: "Lehman [editor of a liberal journal] will die and be forgotten but Victor Eremita [Søren's pseudonym as editor of *Either/Or*] will never die."—quoted in Lowrie, *Kierkegaard,* I, 348; cf. Rohde, *op. cit.*, pp. 113ff.

17. Lowrie, *op. cit.*, II, 349-50. "Kierkegaard's purpose with his letter was to confront Goldschmidt, whose talent he in turn appreciated (and of whom he entertained certain hope), with a choice, an either/or: either to reveal himself as the scoundrel he might be or to think again and abandon his scurrilous journalistic methods instead of continuing an ambiguous 'both/and'; acting like an ethical individual and yet, at the same time, employing disreputable methods."—Peter Rohde, "Søren Kierkegaard: The Father of Existentialism," in *Essay on Kierkegaard,* ed. Jerry Gill (Minneapolis: Burgess Publishing Co., 1969), p. 22.

18. "He had refused to tolerate praise given him by the *Corsair*, a vicious satirical paper published in Copenhagen; it retaliated by making such a fool of him, that for a long time, he was the laughingstock of all the Copenhagen guttersnipes."—Hermann Diem, *Kierkegaard* (Richmond: John Knox Press, 1966), p. 12; cf. Hamilton, *op. cit.*, p. 22.

19. *Journals*, 1848, quoted in Lowrie, *op. cit.*, II, 353-54; cf. ———, *A Short Life,* pp. 176-84.

20. Cf. Lowrie, *Kierkegaard,* II, 504-31. While Bishop Mynster was still alive, Kierkegaard made the following entry in his *Journals* in 1849; "Sometimes I am almost afraid for the man when I think of Bishop Mynster. He is now 72 and soon will go to his judgment. And what has he not done to harm Christianity by conjuring up a lying picture—so that he could sit back and rule. His sermons are quite good—but in eternity, he will not have to preach—but be judged."—(Dru), p. 169. On the other hand, Walter Lowrie describes Bishop Mynster in these words, "Mynster was in all respects one of the most admirable bishops the Protestant churches can boast of, a man of imposing presence and persuasive eloquence, whose sermons were not only heard with acclaim but read with devotion, an orthodox theologian who, at the same time, was well abreast of the highest intellectual culture of his age, a wise ecclesiastical ruler, and withal a man of genuine piety."—Lowrie, *op. cit.*, II, 504-05; cf. Hermann Diem, *Kierkegaard's Dialectic of Existence,* trans. Harold Knight (New York: Frederick Ungar Co., 1965), pp. 149ff.

21. Concerning the size of Kierkegaard's inheritance, cf. Lowrie, *op. cit.*, II, 500-04. On details concerning his death, cf. ———, *A Short Life,* p. 265.

22. Cf. below, pp. 34-40. Kierkegaard himself tells about the tripartite division of the stages. "There are three stages; an aesthetic, an ethical, and a religious. But these are not distinguished abstractly, as the immediate, mediate, and the synthesis of the two, but rather concretely, in existential determinations, as enjoyment-perdition; action-victory; suffering."—*Concluding Unscientific Postscript,* trans. David Swenson and Walter Lowrie (Princeton: University Press, 1960), p. 261. Henceforth CUP. Cf. James Collins, *The Existentialists,* Gateway (Chicago: Henry Regnery, 1964), p. 6; Sieste Zuidema, *Kierkegaard,* trans. David Freeman (Philadelphia: Presbyterian and Reformed Publishing Co., 1960), pp. 25ff. "To

begin with the aesthetic, the ethical and religious stage, these are clearly not exhaustive but are mere projections of what were for Kierkegaard himself live options. When he discusses the religious stage, he speaks of what tempts him, not of Calvinism, Catholicism, or Judaism. When he speaks of the ethical stage, he does not speak of Spinoza or the Stoics but of the possibilities that mean a great deal to himself."—Walter Kaufmann, *From Shakespeare to Existentialism*, Anchor Book (Garden City: Doubleday and Co., 1960) pp. 190-91.

On the other hand, Gregor Malantschuk adopts the position that Kierkegaard found his three stages in the thought of St. Augustine of Hippo. He writes, "Augustine outlines the three positions of man in relation to Christianity: (1) the condition of innocence *'posse non peccare,'* (2) man's slavery under sin *'non posse non peccare,'* (3) man's regeneration through Christianity *'non posse peccare.'* Kierkegaard incorporates this as the central methodological point of view in his work of characterizing the steps and stages in man's spiritual development. . . . Kierkegaard finds in Augustine's 'system' the initial contours of his outline of the stages."—Gregor Malantschuk, *Kierkegaard's Thought*, trans. Howard Hong and Edna Hong (Princeton: University Press, 1971), p. 144.

23. Kierkegaard. *Either/Or*, trans. Walter Lowrie, Anchor Book, 2 vols. (Garden City: Doubleday and Co., 1959); ———, *Stages on Life's Way*, trans. Walter Lowrie (New York: Schocken Books, 1967); ———, *Fear and Trembling*, trans. Walter Lowrie, Anchor Book (Garden City: Doubleday and Co., 1954).

24. Cf. Hollander, *op. cit.*, pp. 12-13. In Part II of *Either/Or*, Judge William, the spokesman for the ethical stage, describes five different ways of aesthetic existence, each mode representing a higher and more refined type of pleasure. These five ways are depicted by the five guests attending the banquet described in *In Vino Veritas*, cf. *Stages*, pp. 27-93; *Either/Or*, I, p. 299ff; II, 195ff. "The aesthete constructs for himself a fictitious world of dreams, lives only in the immediate present, rejected by life's moral realities, as Nietzsche's later tragedy illustrates. It is a dead-end route that leads to boredom and disgust and deprives life of all meaning."—William Hubben, *Dostoevsky, Kierkegaard, Nietzsche and Kafka* (New York: Collier Books, 1962), p. 31; cf. Adi Shmuëli, *Kierkegaard and Consciousness*, trans. Naomi Handelman (Princeton: University Press, 1971), pp. 14-30.

25. Cf. George Price, *The Narrow Pass* (New York and Toronto: McGraw Hill Co., 1963), p. 162. "The aesthetic person knows nothing of any universal moral standards. He has no specific religious belief. His chief motivation is a desire to enjoy the widest variety of pleasures of the senses. His life has no principle of limitation except his own taste; he resents anything that would limit his vast freedom of choice."—Samuel Stumpf, *Philosophy, History and Problems* (New York: and Toronto: McGraw Hill Co., 1971), p. 458.

26. Cf. *Either/Or*, I, 45ff; 203ff; Price, *op. cit.*, pp. 161-70; Reynold Borzaga, *Contemporary Philosophy* (Milwaukee: Bruce, 1966), pp. 9-10.

27. Collins, *Mind of Kierkegaard*, p. 57. In the summer of 1835, Kierkegaard recognized himself as a modern Faustus, a man without any central point, who had innumerable interests but who was possessed of a pervading doubt which accompanied and hampered all his endeavors. This state of dissolution continued after 'the earthquake' (autumn 1835), but the Faustian longing and insatiable desire to embrace everything had then acquired a strong likeness to a defiance of Christianity."—Aage Henriksen, *Methods and Results of Kierkegaard Studies in Scandinavia* (Copenhagen: Ejnar Munksgaard), p. 109. "In protest against his father's upbringing, Kierkegaard was attracted to the figures which he regards as representatives of the negative position toward Christianity—namely Faust, Don Juan, and Ahasuerus."—Malantschuk, *op. cit.*, p. 37.

28. Cf. Price, *op. cit.*, p. 169; Lowrie, *Kierkegaard*, I, 140-45; Kurt Reinhardt, *The Existentialist Revolt* (New York: Frederick Ungar, 1964), p. 55; Copleston, *op. cit.*, VII, 338.

29. *Either/Or, II,* 197. In another place Kierkegaard says, "Occasionally you plunge into pleasure, and every instant you are devoting yourself to it, you make the discovery in your consciousness that it is vanity. So you are constantly beyond yourself; that is, *in despair*. That is the reason why your life lies between two prodigious contradictions; sometimes you have enormous energy, sometimes an indolence just as great."—*Ibid.*, p. 199.

30. *Ibid.*, p. 255; cf. George Thomas, *Religious Philosophies of the West* (New York: Charles Scribner's Sons, 1965), pp. 296ff.

31. Borzaga, *op. cit.*, pp. 9, 11; cf. Diem, *Kierkegaard*, pp. 33ff.

32. *Either/Or*, II, 161ff; "While the upholder of the aesthetical view of life is self-centered in all his behavior, the spokesman of an ethical one is conscious of being part of a totality, a member of a community, and consideration of this totality constitutes the guiding star and principle of his conduct."—Rohde, *op. cit.*, p. 159; cf. George Stack, "The Basis of Kierkegaard's Concept of Essential Possibility," NS, XLIV, 2 (1972), 139-72.

33. *Either/Or*, II, 255-56; cf. Shmuëli, *op. cit.*, pp. 31-48; George Stack, "Kierkegaard and Nihilism," PT, XIV, 4 (1970), 288ff.

34. Zuidema, *op. cit.*, p. 31. "He who turns away from this world in order to seek fulfillment in himself attains to ethical existence, and this time it is Socrates who constitutes the model, for he is the man of the saying, 'Know thyself.' Yet he is only a witness to the truth, and his doctrine was destined to stiffen into system or purely cynical attitudes."—Gabriel Marcel, *Problematic Man*, trans. Brian Thompson (New York: Herder and Herder, 1967), p. 106.

35. Søren Kierkegaard, *Sickness Unto Death*, trans. Walter Lowrie (Princeton: University Press, 1941), pp. 218, 226.

36. *Journals,* 1838 (Dru, 59); cf. Frederick Copleston, *A History of Philosophy,* 8 vols. (Westminster: Newman Press, 953-1963), VII, 343ff. "While the aesthetic and ethical stages express only the immanent and indwelling components of man, the religious stage explores the relationships between these immanent factors and those which are independent of and transcendent to man. It is in this stage that man becomes a 'spirit,' which is, as Kierkegaard says, 'a relationship which relates itself to its own self, and in relating itself to its own self, relates itself to another.' "—Shmuëli, *op. cit.,* p. 49.

37. *Fear and Trembling,* pp. 69-70, 72. "The new category to which Abraham belongs is that of faith; he existed not in the ethical sphere, not as a modern but as believer, a Knight of faith. The Knight of faith becomes such because the individual is in an absolute relation to the absolute, here meaning God."—Thomas Gallagher, "Kierkegaard," in *Existentialist Thinkers and Thought,* ed. Frederick Patka (New York: Citadel Press, 1964), p. 86.

38. *Fear and Trembling,* p. 57. "The truly religious man lives the highest keynote here, without some anguish no one can be a religious person. The 'leap' of faith brings one to an awareness of subjectivity, and of God's inward presence within the subject."—Vernon Bourke, *History of Ethics,* Image Book, 2 vols. (Garden City: Doubleday and Co., 1970), II, 193. "Thus the religious mode of life suspends or absorbs the ethical. By the 'leap of faith' the *homo religiosus* imparts to the finiteness and temporality of his existence an infinite and eternal significance. Every aspect of his life is henceforth determined and permeated by his God-relationship."—Reinhardt, *op. cit.,* pp. 56-57.

39. *Fear and Trembling,* p. 59.
40. Zuidema, *op. cit.,* p. 36. "The first stage or manner of human existence is the aesthetic stage. Its focal point is pleasure; and the result of this pleasure, perdition. The second stage is the ethical stage; its focal point is action, and the result of action is victory. The third and last stage is the religious stage. Its focal point is simply suffering."—Gallagher, *op. cit.,* p. 78.

41. CUP, p. 498; cf. Henry Allison, "Christianity and Nonsense" in Gill, *op. cit.,* pp. 136-37; Dupré, *op. cit.,* p. 78. "In religion A a man presumed to be in a state of spiritual integrity endeavors to assure himself of beatitude by maximizing the 'God-idea' immanent in himself. . . . But religion B posits conditions external to the individual, without which he cannot hope for salvation. To wit: a God who comes into being in time and declares himself the proper object of faith; and a condition of radical non-integrity in the individual (sin), from which he can be saved only through faith by the grace of this same God-in-time."—Louis Mackey, *A Kind of Poet* (Philadelphia: University of Pennsylvania Press, 1971), pp. 204-05; cf. Nauman, *op. cit.,* p. 78; Carl Michalson, ed. *The Witness of Kierkegaard,* Reflection Book (New York: Associated Press, 1960), pp. 120-22.

42. Søren Kierkegaard, *Training in Christianity,* trans. Walter Lowrie (Princeton: University Press, 1944), p. 155; cf. Thomas, *op. cit.,* p. 302. "In general, Kierkegaard's phenomenological analysis of the three distinct attitudes or levels of consciousness which he describes possess a value and a stimulative power which is not destroyed by his characteristic exaggerations."—Copleston, *op. cit.,* VII, 347.

43. CUP, p. 49. "Søren Kierkegaard's great insight was into the fact that a Christian environment, far from helping one to become a Christian, puts special obstacles in the way, and particularly two—the aesthetic obstacle and the speculative obstacle."—Robert Bretall, ed. *A Kierkegaard Anthology* (New York: Modern Library, 1946), p. xxii; Shmuëli, *op. cit.,* pp. 49-50.

44. Søren Kierkegaard, *Point of View,* trans. Walter Lowrie (Oxford: University Press, 1939), p. 22.

45. Cf. Georg Hegel, *Selections,* ed. J. Loewenberg (New York: Charles Scribner's Sons, 1957), pp. 98ff, 281ff, 308ff; Pyama Gaidenko, "Existentialism and the Individual," in *Existentialism versus Marxism,* ed. George Novak (New York: Dell Publishing Co., 1966), pp. 260-62.

46. Cf. *Hegel, op. cit.,* pp. 99ff.
47. *Ibid.,* pp. 103ff.
48. CUP, p. 317, italics added.
49. *Ibid.,* p. 85. "This questionable character of abstract thought becomes especially apparent in connection with all existential problems, where abstract thought gets rid of the difficulty by leaving it out and then proceeds to boast of having explained everything. It explains immortality in general and all goes quite smoothly, in that immortality is identified with eternity, with eternity which is essentially the medium of all thought. But whether an existing human being is immortal, which is the difficulty, abstract thought does not trouble to inquire."—*Ibid.,* pp. 267-68.

50. Cf. *Journals,* #1050. "Unlike the Hegelian, whose thought addresses itself to man in general, Kierkegaard chooses to remind us that we exist as particular men; and in contrast to Hegel's belief that individuals perform their duty because of the controlling immanence of God's will, Kierkegaard maintains that the individual's ethical reality is exclusively his own, realizable only by him."—Molina, *op. cit.,* p. 12. "Christianity is related to truth as to an objective doctrine, which may be assented to as correct without the believer receiving from it any existential impact, with the consequence that the transformation of existence which Christianity requires can no longer take place."—Diem, *Dialectic of Existence,* p. 195.

51. *Point of View,* p. 114.
52. *Ibid.,* pp. 88-89.
53. *Ibid.,* p. 129.
54. Gabriel Marcel, cf. below, pp. 91-95; cf. Valter Lindstrom. "The Problem of Objectivity and Subjectivity in Kierkegaard," in *A Kierkegaard Critique,* ed.

Howard Johnson and Niels Thulstrup, Gateway (Chicago: Henry Regnery, 1967), 228-41.

55. CUP, p. 116; "The believer is passionately solicitous for his eternal salvation and orients all his life towards the attainment of that absolute good. Faith, therefore, is not disinterested knowledge of an object towards which we are quite indifferent; it means the fervor of passion, decision, engagement. In other words, it is subjectivity, existence."—Henri Bouillard, The Logic of the Faith (New York: Sheed and Ward, 1967), p. 62.

56. CUP, p. 173. "The subjective reflection turns its attention inwardly to the subject, and desires in this intensification of inwardness to realize the truth . . . the subjectivity of the subject becomes the final stage and objectivity a vanishing factor. Not a single moment is it forgotten that the subject is an existing individual."—Ibid., pp. 175-76; cf. H. Richard Niebuhr, "Søren Kierkegaard," in Christianity and the Existentialists, ed. Carl Michalson (New York: Charles Scribner's Sons, 1956), pp. 36ff.

57. CUP, p. 267. "This existential thinker should be understood in opposition to the abstract thinker whose thought evolves upon the terrain of pure thought and without worrying about the needs or dispositions of his own being. The type of the abstract thinker is, of course, Hegel."—Marcel, op. cit., p. 102.

58. CUP, p. 315. "Hegel, the metaphysician, and Goethe, the esthete, are so enamored of the notion of a 'pure humanity' that they seem to forget the empirical and quite individual being that each one is."—Collins, Mind of Kierkegaard, p. 129.

59. CUP, pp. 272, 274-75.
60. Ibid., p. 284.
61. Ibid., pp. 119-21.
62. Bretall, op. cit., p. xxiii. "For Hegel whatever is real is intelligible. He thereby allows no qualification which would set the human mind apart from the divine mind. . . . For Kierkegaard, God and man are separated by an eternal abyss. Whatever He communicates to us can, therefore, never be reduced to philosophical categories. The revelation cannot be understood, it must be believed, that is, accepted on authority. This is particularly the case with its primordial data that man is sinful and needs redemption."—Dupré, op. cit., pp. 39-40; cf. Malantschuk, op. cit., pp. 58-59.

63. Reinhardt, op. cit., p. 38.
64. CUP, p. 369; cf. Rhode, op. cit., pp. 105-07.
65. Journals, 1847, #222; cf. Sickness Unto Death where Kierkegaard pointedly states that in the pantheistic idealism of Hegel, "the qualitative distinction between God and man is pantheistically abolished."—p. 192: cf. Edwin Garvey, Process Theology and Secularization (Houston: Lumen Christi Press, 1972), pp. 8-9.

66. CUP, p. 291; cf. Jerome Hamer, Karl Barth, trans. Dominic Maruca (Westminster: Newman Press, 1962), pp. 226-29.

67. CUP, p. 31. "In the concept of God, he wishes to highlight one element; absolute divine transcendence. . . . God is above all sovereign, majestic, omniscient. He has the attributes which render him 'totally other.'"—Hamer, op. cit., p. 234.

68. CUP, p. 189, italics added. "Kierkegaard of course was closer to Luther; anti-philosophical and individualistic. A little more subtly, to be sure, he echoes Luther's dicta: 'Whoever wants to be a Christian, should tear the eyes out of his reason and not know anything of it and even kill it; else one will not get into the kingdom of heaven.'"—Kaufmann, op. cit., p. 18.

69. CUP, pp. 188-89. "He admits that by rational standards, this fact is inconceivable and inconsistent with itself. A being who is eternal and out of time cannot have measured out his life in human years. A being who is omnipotent could not be confined in his movements to a small area in the Eastern Mediterranean. A being who is omniscient cannot grow in knowledge, or a being who is perfect grow in grace. . . . So speaks logic. But faith requires us to put logic aside and accept what Kierkegaard admits to be 'contradictory.'"—Brand Blanshard, "Kierkegaard on Faith," in Gill, op. cit., p. 119.

70. CUP, pp. 513-14.
71. Ibid., p. 191; cf. Blanshard, op. cit., pp. 114ff.
72. Bouillard, op. cit., p. 69. "In the Socratic paradox, eternal truth itself was not paradoxical but only became so by the fact that it entered into relation with a mind existing in time. But the position is otherwise when God Himself appears as a teacher in history by becoming a particular man. This means that eternal truth itself became paradoxical. It then repels the one who wishes to assimilate it, no longer, as in the case of the Socratic paradox, but its objective uncertainty, but by its absurdity and self-contradictory nature."—Diem, Dialectic Existence, p. 60; cf. N. H. Søe. "Kierkegaard's Doctrine of the Paradox," in Johnson and Thustrup, op. cit., pp. 207ff. "The decisive borderline between philosophy and Christianity is reached for the first time when philosophy is confronted with the 'absolute paradox' which for Kierkegaard means Christ as the God-man."—Malantschuk, op. cit., p. 61.

73. Bouillard, op. cit., p. 70. "The Absolute Paradox of the central revealed fact breaks through all immanence, and in the man, Jesus, confronts us as the historical in the first degree; it confronts us as a sign which points beyond itself and places us in the situation of the encounter with the becoming of God. . . . It places man in a situation which is foreign to him, which is created by God and places him thus before the face of God.—Zuidema, Kierkegaard, p. 36.

74. Cf. St. Thomas Aquinas, Summa Contra Gentiles, I, 4; Anton Pegis, ed., St. Thomas Aquinas, On the Truth of the Catholic Faith, Book I (Garden City: Doubleday and Co., 1955), pp. 66-68; Gilson, Spirit of Mediaeval Philosophy, pp.

20-41.

75. Cf. St. Thomas Aquinas, *Summa Theologiae*, I, q. 2, art. 3; Anton Pegis ed., *Basic Writings of St. Thomas Aquinas*, 2 vols. (New York: Random House, 1945), I, 21-24. "Kierkegaard's interest in the absurdity of Christianity lies strongly in the consideration that, if Christianity is absurd, then the truth of Christianity remains objectively uncertain. This uncertainty regarding the objective truth of Christianity makes faith (as contrasted with knowledge) possible, for without the element of risk in believing what is uncertain, there can be no faith."—Molina, *op. cit.*, p. 15.

76. Robert McAfree Brown, "Introduction," in George Casalis, *Portrait of Karl Barth*, Anchor Book (Garden City: Doubleday and Co., 1964), p. xiii; cf. LeFevre, *op. cit.*, pp. 164-66; Hamer, *op. cit.*, p. 248.

77. Bouillard, *op. cit.*, p. 75. "The paradox of the person of Christ, as Kierkegaard understands it, emphasizes the strictly personal character of the act of faith. Christianity is not doctrine, but a Person to Whom I entrust myself without reserve."—Dupré, *op. cit.*, p. 137. "In the writings of the Danish thinker, there is an attempt to reduce this opposition of two natures into an Hegelian synthesis. The two natures, one as true as the other, clash in the person of Christ. For this reason, Jesus is the paradox par excellence."—Hamer, *op. cit.*, p. 240.

78. Arthur Murphy, "On Kierkegaard's Claim that Truth is Subjectivity," in Gill, *op. cit.*, pp. 99-100, also in William May, Marcus Singer and Arthur Murphy eds., *Reason and the Common Good: Selected Essays of Arthur Murphy* (Englewood Cliffs: Prentice-Hall, 1963). "But does not the existential exploration of a subjective question presuppose an answer to an objective question? . . . a person cannot reflect upon what it means for him to be Christian unless he knows what Christianity is. Before a man can become a Christian in the Kierkegaardian sense, he has to know, e.g., that Christianity aims at the greatest intensification of subjectivity. He also has to know the categories of Christianity—such as sin, suffering, and guilt."—Raymond Weiss, "Kierkegaard's 'Return' to Socrates," NS, XLV, 4 (1971), 581.

79. *Sickness Unto Death*, pp. 162-63.
80. *Ibid.*, p. 146.
81. CUP, pp. 438-39.
82. Régis Jolivet, *Introduction to Kierkegaard*, trans. by W. H. Barber (London: Frederick Muller, 1950), pp. 55ff, quoted in Reinhardt, *op. cit.*, p. 32.
83. Cornelio Fabro, "Faith and Reason in Kierkegaard's Dialectic," in Johnson and Thulstrup, *op. cit.*, p. 157.
84. "The distinction between Socratic faith and Christian faith is first of all, for Kierkegaard, a question of object. The object of Christian faith is the 'paradox', and the paradox is an entirely new category, completely foreign to the Greek mind, and in general, to the human mind as such. How can man accept as true that which he cannot understand?"—Fabro, *ibid.*, p. 166.
85. *Ibid.*, p. 174. "Any attempt to defend Christianity only undermines its authority, and Kierkegaard argues that 'he who first invented the notion of defending Christianity is *de facto* Judas No. 2,' he also betrays with a kiss. Kierkegaard exhorts his reader 'to become a believer—*nota bene*! by adoringly humbling himself under the extraordinary.' It is in 'the absurd' that 'Christianity begins—and the offense'; and we must believe without any possibility of comprehension."—Kaufmann, *op. cit.*, p. 177.
Kierkegaard states in his reply to Theophilus Nicolaus, "If a scholar goes so far as to declare that we cannot remain at the level of faith, but must go further—to speculation as something higher—well, in that case, the existential police had better arrive on the scene."—quoted in Fabro, *op. cit.*, p. 178.
86. *Journals*, #482, V, A32, quoted in Fabro, *ibid.*, p. 175.
87. *Ibid.*, XI, A436, quoted in Fabro, *ibid.*, p. 176.
88. *Ibid.*, X6 B114, quoted in Fabro, *ibid.*, p. 179.
89. Fabro, *ibid.*
90. *Ibid.*, p. 182-84. "The absurd of faith in an ontological sense is meta-rational, that is, it is the object of faith, which, however, truly knows the truth of its object and is even able to convince reason itself."—Fabro, *ibid.*, p. 185.
91. Herbert Garelick, *The Anti-Christianity of Kierkegaard*, (The Hague: Martinus Nijhoff, 1965), p. 45.
92. Kierkegaard, *op. cit.*, IV, C, 23, quoted in Fabro, *op. cit.*, p. 187.
93. *Ibid.*, p. 191.
94. *Ibid.*, p. 192.
95. *Journals*, X, 1, A640, quoted in Jacques Colette, ed. *Kierkegaard, The Difficulty of Being Christian*, trans. Ralph McInerney (Notre Dame and London: University of Notre Dame Press, 1968), p. 27. "The fact remains that Kierkegaardian Christianity is imbalanced and excessive. And the decisive fact, still outstanding, is that Kierkegaard knew it and meant it that way. To all such friendly apologetics, as well as to all proper protests of his accusers, Kierkegaard would reply that *Training in Christianity, Fear and Trembling*, the *Fragments*, the *Postscript*, and all the rest were but 'correctives' recommended to the complacent debility of 'the present age.' "—Mackey, *op. cit.*, p. 243.
96. Kierkegaard, *Point of View*, p. 506. "Kierkegaard saw the reintroduction of Christianity into Christendom as his life's work. He was of the opinion that it was impossible in the present secularized state of Christendom to gain any impression whatsoever of the passion of the Christian faith. A wealth of information about Christianity had caused men to forget what it means to *exist* as a Christian."— Diem, *Kierkegaard*, p. 29.
97. Kierkegaard, "The Religious Situation," in *The Fatherland*, Monday,

March 26, 1855 in *Attack Upon Christendom*, trans. Walter Lowrie (Boston: Beacon Press, 1966), p. 30.

98. Ernst Breisach, *Introduction to Modern Existentialism* (New York: Grove Press, 1962), p. 29. "In the early ages of Christianity, to be a Christian meant to separate oneself from the crowd—to do what was not easy to do, humanly speaking. It meant an effort, it meant sacrifice; it *cost* something. Today, says Kierkegaard, the situation is exactly the opposite: one becomes a Christian by the easiest and most natural of processes."—Bretall, *op. cit.*, p. xxii; cf. Kierkegaard, "Cycle of Ethico-Religious Treatises," in *On Authority and Revelation*, trans. Walter Lowrie (New York: Harper and Row, 1966), p. lvi. "In Kierkegaard's opinion, it was hardly possible any longer to gain a decisive impression of the Christian faith from within Christendom as it actually was. Christianity had gained a Pyrrhic victory by entering the 'Christian' world and being absorbed by it. By making Christianity a topic for a speculative, historical, or aesthetic study instead of a concern affecting the existence of every individual, the philosophers swindled the world and robbed it of Christianity."—Diem, *op. cit.*, pp. 15-16.

99. Kierkegaard, *The Instant*, no. 5. "The Christianity of the New Testament/The Christianity of 'Christendom,'" in *Attack Upon Christendom*, p. 164. "The security of a Christian Church meant to him the betrayal of every tenet of Christ's teaching and example. To live 'Christianly' should be identical with the greatest possible insecurity before man and God. Christ's disciples suffered persecution and death; they had no official status and were never recognized in any manner or form. The anonymous early Christian followers were martyred, not honored, paid, and respected for belonging to the Church."—Hubben, *op. cit.*, p. 25.

100. *The Instant*, no. 6, *op. cit.*, p. 192. "A Church whose whole life is corrupted in this way by the help of a State guarantee can no longer fulfill its duty over against the State, i.e., the duty of caring for vitality in opposition to the officialdom of the State."—Diem, *Dialectic of Existence*, p. 128.

101. *The Instant*, no. 1, "Is it Justifiable on the part of the State—the Christian State!—to Make if Possible, Christianity Impossible?" *op. cit.*, p. 83. Elsewhere Kierkegaard complains, "Thus it was established by the state as a kind of eternal principle that every child is naturally born a Christian. As the state obligated itself to furnish eternal bliss for all Christians, so, to make the whole complete, it also took upon itself to produce Christians."—XI2, A112, quoted in Liselotte Richter, "Kierkegaard's Position in his Religio-Sociological Situation," in Johnson and Thulstrup, *op. cit.*, p. 61.

102. Louis Dupré is convinced that Kierkegaard's existential stance can serve as an invaluable aid toward ecumenical dialogue. He writes, "One of the major problems of this dialogue [Catholic-Protestant dialogue] is that the partners do not understand each other, even though they speak the same language. Kierkegaard's writings provide a deeper insight into the religious impact of one of the basic principles sadly lacking among non-Protestants. Even more important is the fact that for Kierkegaard, Christianity is a vital matter of the individual conscience and not a social institution concerned primarily with respectability."—*op. cit.*, p. x.

103. "Unlike the believer of today, living in a naturally a-religious world, Kierkegaard thought and lived in an officially Christian world. But in that condition of Christianity which he combatted so much, he fought for the re-discovery of the specificity of Christian becoming. His effort is still ours, since for him as for us, it is no longer a matter of rediscovering the true sense of hope which is as different from despair as from that faith in progress by which so many of our contemporaries are instinctively animated."—Colette, *op. cit.*, p. 82.

CHAPTER III

1. Gabriel Marcel, *The Philosophy of Existentialism*, trans. Manya Harari (New York: Citadel Press, 1966), p. 109. Henceforth, PE. For an up to date bibliography, cf. François Lapointe, "Bibliography on Gabriel Marcel," MS, XLIX (1971), 23-49.

2. PE, p. 110.

3. *Ibid.*

4. Roger Troisfontaines, *De l'Existence a l'Être*, 2 vols., 2nd edit. (Louvain: Editions Nauwelaerts, 1968), I, 18.

5. "Everyday I received personal visits from the unfortunate relatives who implored us to obtain what information we could; so that in the end every index card was to me a heart-rending personal appeal."—PE, p. 121.

6. *Ibid.*, p. 112.

7. Troisfontaines, *op. cit.*, I, 23.

8. *Ibid.*, pp. 23-24.

9. Gabriel Marcel, *Being and Having*, trans. Katherine Farrer, Torchbook (New York: Harper and Row, 1965), p. 15. Henceforth, BH.

10. St. Augustine, *Confessions*, trans. Edward Pusey (New York: Modern Library, 1949), Bk. I, p. 3.

11. Gabriel Marcel, *Creative Fidelity*, trans. Robert Rosthal (New York: Farrar and Straus, 1965), pp. 79-80. Henceforth, CF. "That every word Marcel has written invites one to look beyond natural grace to the supernatural, and beyond the plane of participation with other persons to the supreme origin of all the gifts which compose our existence is obvious and intended."—Étienne Gilson, Thomas Langan and Armand Maurer, *Recent Philosophy: Hegel to the Present* (New York and Toronto: Random House, 1966), p. 380. Cf. Étienne Gilson, "What is Christian Philosophy?" in Anton Pegis, ed., *A Gilson Reader*, Image Book (Garden City: Doubleday and Co., 1957), pp. 177-91; ———, *Spirit of Mediaeval Philosophy*

(New York: Charles Scribner's Sons, 1940), pp. 1-41.

12. PE, p. 26.

13. *Ibid.*, p. 107; cf. Troisfontaines, *What is Existentialism?*, p. 21.

14. Gabriel Marcel, "The Drama of the Soul in Exile" in *Three Plays*, trans. Rosalind Heywood, Mermaid Dramabook (New York: Hill and Wang, 1965), pp. 32-33.

15. Gabriel Marcel, *Le Coeur des Autres* (Paris: Librairie Grasset, 1921), p. 111.

16. "The role of drama at a certain level, seems to be to place us at a point of vantage at which truth is made concrete to us, far above any level of abstract definitions."—Gabriel Marcel, *The Mystery of Being*, Gateway, 2 vols. (Chicago: Henry Regnery, 1960), I, 71. Henceforth, MB. "Avoiding traditional metaphysical categories and principles, his thought revolves around a number of root ideas which are not so much ideas as modes of concrete experiences: estrangement, nostalgia and homecoming; presence and absence; appeal and response; fidelity and betrayal; availability and unavailability; despair, recollection, courage and hope."— Jean Wilde and William Kimmel, eds., *The Search for Being* (New York: Noonday Press, 1962), p. 419.

17. Gabriel Marcel, "Foreword" in Vincent Miceli, *Ascent to Being* (New York: Desclee, 1965), pp. x-xi.

18. Sam Keen, *Gabriel Marcel* (Richmond: John Knox Press, 1967), p. 4.

19. Gabriel Marcel, *Man Against Mass Society*, trans. by G. S. Fraser, Gateway (Chicago: Henry Regnery, 1962). p. 249. Henceforth, MAMS.

20. Seymour Cain, *Gabriel Marcel* (New York: Hillary House, 1963), p. 17.

21. Troisfontaines, *De l'Existence a l'Être*, I, 41.

22. "[Marcel's] criticism of Roycean metaphysics bear on the monistic tendency of the system to reduce all meaning to the comprehensive and omniscient experience which is the Absolute . . . 'the problem goes beyond even Royce's philosophy and bears on the legitimacy of philosophy which accepts to some extent Hegel's idea of synthesis' (G. Marcel, *Royce's Metaphysics*, p. 153). What troubles Marcel in any philosophy accepting the Hegelian idea of synthesis is that such a philosophy tends to view the finite and individually existing self as ultimately *contained* within the Absolute."—C. V. Pax, "Philosophical Reflection: Gabriel Marcel," NS XXXVIII (1964), 164.

23. Étienne Gilson, "Un Exemple," in *Existentialisme Chrétien*, ed. Étienne Gilson (Paris: 1947), p. 2, quoted in Miceli, *op. cit.*, p. 3; ———, "A Unique Philosopher," PT, IV (1960), 278.

24. Cf. above, pp. 19-21. "Broadly speaking, then, Marcel's method is 'phenomenological,' but there are basic contrasts between his metaphysical position and that of Husserl. . . . Jean Hering, himself a French disciple of Husserl, sees Marcel as 'an independent phenomenologist,' who explored the method long before he encountered the work of Husserl and Scheler; and he ventures the opinion that even if the work of the German phenomenologists had remained unknown in France, a French phenomenology would have arisen independently, largely inspired by Marcel." —Cain, *op. cit.*, p. 99.

25. Cf. below, pp. 195-98.

26. "Marcel's method is often a combination of critical studies and highly metaphorical evocations of personal experience. . . . Marcel comments that what he means by 'phenomenological' is the primacy of experience over pure thought. An essay which he entitles *Outlines of a Phenomenology of Having* is a concretely based exploration into such experiential phenomena as possession, the experience of the body, autonomy and evil. For Marcel, phenomenological analyses seem to be analyses of phenomena as they are directly experienced."—Patricia Sanborn, *Existentialism*, Pegasus Book (New York: Western Publishing Co., 1968), p. 30. "Although there are similarities between the phenomenological methods of Husserl and Marcel, the differences are much greater than the similarities. Whereas Husserl at least in the earlier part of his work conceived of philosophy as a rigorous science leading by way of the *transcendental epoche* to pre-suppositionless science and by way of the *eidetic reduction* to a knowledge of essences, Marcel insists upon the necessity of grounding the study of being on a non-objectifiable experience that can only be pre-supposed. He would prefer, it would seem, to call his analysis the way to an irreducible rather than a reduction to the pre-suppositionless."—Pax, *op. cit.*, p. 169.

27. Cf. above, p. 45.

28. PE, p. 5. "In point of time, Marcel is the first of the contemporary existentialist philosophers. As early as 1914, he enunciated existentialist themes in his article, *Existence et objectivité*."—I. M. Bocheński, *Contemporary European Philosophy*, trans. Donald Nicholl and Karl Aschenbrenner (Berkeley and Los Angeles: University of California Press, 1961), p. 182.

29. Gabriel Marcel, "Some Reflections on Existentialism," PT VIII (1964), 249; cf. ———, PE, p. 91.

30. Collins, *Existentialists*, p. 118; cf. MB, II, 199.

31. PE, p. 118.

32. MAMS, pp. 1-2.

33. Gabriel Marcel, *Problematic Man*, pp. 60-61; cf. William Luijpen, *Existential Phenomenology* (Pittsburgh: Duquesne University Press, 1962) p. 314. "Like Socrates, in Plato's *Gorgias*, Marcel has looked to a community of feelings to assure a communication of impressions and experiences between men. That is one of the reasons why he has preferred to be known as a 'neo-Socratic' or a 'Christian Socratic' rather than an existentialist, finding an affinity with Socrates' interrogative, dialogical stance, his constant address to a concrete *thou*, and his depreciation of 'any kind

of physics' as irrelevant to ultimate human concerns."—Cain, *op. cit.*, p. 114.

34. "The position of Marcel is so expressly anti-systematic that his views are more difficult to put together than those of any other existentialist. In fact, no one has yet succeeded in doing so."—Bocheński, *op. cit.*, p. 181. F. H. Heinemann concurs when he says, "Textbook writers find no other philosophy so difficult to summarize."—*op. cit.*, p. 134.

35. MG, I, 57; J. V. Langmead Casserley, "Gabriel Marcel" in Michalson, *op. cit.*, pp. 86ff. "A *problem* is limited in its scope, it can be approached objectively from the outside, and it may be solved in a way that is susceptible of empirical verification. A mystery, on the other hand, cannot be grasped from the outside. . . . Here we can only understand what is in question through becoming involved in it ourselves."—John Macquarrie, *Twentieth Century Religious Thought* (New York and Evanston: Harper and Row, 1963), p. 360.

36. Cf. Gabriel Marcel, *Metaphysical Journal*, trans. Bernard Wall (Chicago: Henry Regnery, 1952), p. 326. "A problem is before me. I can walk around it, examine it from all possible angles; but, when it trespasses on the domain of my own experiences, that is, when it is likewise within me, and when I cannot legitimately abstract myself from it, then it becomes a mystery."—Troisfontaines, *What is Existentialism?*, p. 13.

37. Keen, *op. cit.*, p. 19. "A problem, then, for Marcel is a mental investigation that is undertaken with respect to an object. A problem bears on something completely outside of the investigator . . . objectified thought is used to solve problems; the person as person is not involved in the solution or make-up of the problem. . . . Scientific knowledge embodies, par excellence, the problematic approach to objects. It is made secure and public by the spectator-investigator approach to objects."—Miceli, *op. cit.*, p. 96.

38. PE, pp. 45-46; cf. ————, *The Existential Background of Human Dignity* (Cambridge: Harvard University Press, 1963), pp. 81ff. "The world of the problematical is the world of fear and desire, which are inseparable; at the same time, it is that world of the functional—of what can be functionalized . . . finally, it is the kingdom of technics of whatever sort." PE, p. 30.

39. BH, p. 100; cf. ————, *Some Reflections on Existentialism*, p. 255. In PE, Marcel explains, "A mystery is a problem which encroaches upon its own data, invading them, as it were, and thereby transcending itself as a simple problem." PE, p. 19. Cf. Spiegelberg, *op. cit.*, II, 432.

40. Frederick Copleston, *Contemporary Philosophy* (Westminster: Newman Press, 1956), p. 167; cf. Rudolph Gerber, "Marcel and the Experiential Road to Metaphysics." PT, XII, 4 (1968), 267-71.

41. "Marcel suggests that the mode of reflection that the philosopher uses is secondary reflection, whereas knowledge on the subject-object level is primary reflection. Primary reflection breaks experience up into its component parts, and leads to Cartesian mind-body dualism. Secondary reflection, however, is recuperative in nature. It reconquers the unity of experience that is shattered by primary reflection. Only secondary reflection can do justice to the immediacy of experience. Primary reflection takes the object reflected upon and categorizes it, whereas secondary reflection permits an understanding of what a thing is in its own right."—Sanborn, *op. cit.*, p. 65.

42. Copleston, *op. cit.*, p. 168; cf. Eugene Borowitz, *A Layman's Introduction to Religious Existentialism* (New York: Dell Publishing Co., 1966) pp. 108-09.

43. MB, I, 85.

44. Gabriel Marcel, *Presence and Immortality* (Pittsburgh: Duquesne University Press, 1967), p. 23.

45. Alphonse de Waelhens, "The Phenomenology of the Body," trans. Mary Ellen and N. Lawrence from *Revue philosophique de Louvain*, XLVIII (1950) 371-97 in Nathaniel Lawrence and Daniel O'Connor, eds., *Readings in Existential Phenomenology* (Englewood Cliffs: Prentice Hall, 1967), p. 150; cf. PE, p. 17.

46. MB, pp. 115-16; cf. Bocheński, *op. cit.*, p. 183.

47. BH, pp. 11-12. "Marcel feels one of the great errors of Cartesianism was to substitute body in the abstract for the older and truer Christian conception of the flesh—the flesh that is the inevitable shortcoming of a fallen creature."—Marjorie Grene. *Introduction to Existentialism*, Phoenix Book (Chicago and London: University of Chicago Press, 1962), p. 128.

48. Keen, *op. cit.*, p. 26 "The point Marcel is making is that my body and myself are not an instrumental duality. 'I *am* my body.' The body which is *mine* is not something I *have*. This is the mistake of Plato and Descartes and the psychophysical parallelists. Whatever man does, he does as an incarnate being. The body participates in the world and it is through this indispensable channel that the mind is able to experience things as contiguous."—Eugene Fitzgerald, "Gabriel Marcel," in Patka, *op. cit.*, p. 142.

49. MB, I, 124; cf. Fitzgerald, *op. cit.*, pp. 143ff; Spiegelberg, *op. cit.*, II, 439. "Accordingly, I neither 'am' my body nor 'have' it. My body is precisely mid-way between two extremes. It constitutes the transition from the conscious self to the worldly object. It is the mysterious reality which grafts me on things, secures my being-in-the-world, involves me in the world, and gives me a standpoint in the world."—Luijpen, *op. cit.*, p. 190.

50. Marcel, *Presence and Immortality*, p. 137.

51. *Ibid.*; cf. Kenneth Gallagher, *The Philosophy of Gabriel Marcel* (New York: Fordham University Press, 1962), pp. 16ff.

52. *Ibid.*, p. 19; cf. Reinhardt, *op. cit.*, p. 209. "I am my body, then, in

the sense that to feel, to be, or to be identified with anything or anyone else, I must first be incarnated in just this body. My body enjoys this absolute priority. It follows that my body cannot, without distortion, be made the independent object of thought. Rather, it is the condition of my thinking of other things."—Edward Ballard, "Gabriel Marcel: The Mystery of Being," in *Existential Philosophers: Kierkegaard to Merleau-Ponty*, ed. George Schrader (New York: McGraw Hill Inc., 1967) pp. 218-19.

53. Gabriel Marcel, *Homo Viator: An Introduction to a Metaphysic of Hope*, trans. Emma Craufurd, Torchbook (New York: Harper and Bros., 1962), pp. 20-21. Henceforth HV.

54. *Ibid.*, pp. 17, 23.

55. Keen, *op. cit.*, p. 29.

56. Cf. Marcel, *Metaphysical Journal*, p. 148: Borzaga, *op. cit.*, p. 257; Ferdinand Ebner, "Word and Personality," PT, XI (1967), 233-37.

57. BH, pp. 106-07.

58. Marcel, *Existential Background*, p. 147.

59. Jeanne Parain-Vial, "Notes on the Ontology of Gabriel Marcel," PT, IV (1960), 275.

60. Thomas van Ewijk, *Gabriel Marcel*, trans. Matthew van Velzen, Deus Book (Glen Rock: Paulist Press, 1965), pp. 68-69.

61. Marcel, *Some Reflections*, pp. 254-55; cf. Luijpen, *op. cit.*, pp. 213-14; F. J. Smith, "Phenomenology of Encounter," PT, VII (1963), 200, 205.

62. HV, p. 15; cf. John O'Malley, *The Fellowship of Being* (The Hague: Martinus Nijhoff, 1966), p. 85.

63. Marcel, *Existential Background*, p. 67.

64. Marcel, *Presence and Immortality*, p. 157.

65. Gabriel Marcel, "Authentic Humanness and its Existential Primordial Assumptions," in Balduin Schwarz, *The Human Person and the World of Values* (New York: Fordham University Press, 1960), p. 90; cf. H. J. Blackham, ed., *Reality, Man and Existence: Essential Works of Existentialism*, Bantam Book (New York, 1965), p. 160.

66. CF, p. 12; cf. Luijpen, *op. cit.*, pp. 176-80.

67. van Ewijk, *op. cit.*, p. 73; cf. Colin Smith, *Contemporary French Philosophy* (New York: Barnes and Noble, 1964), pp. 73-74, note 1; William Luijpen and Henry Koren, *A First Introduction to Existential Phenomenology* (Pittsburgh: Duquesne University Press, 1969), pp. 171-73.

68. O'Malley, *op. cit.*, p. 83; cf. Thomas Higgins, *Ethical Theories in Conflict* (Milwaukee: Bruce, 1967), p. 131.

69. BH, I, 201. "To be indisposable is to be self-absorbed, that is, fixed in the realm of having and to be restless, gloomy and anxious by condition, to be possessed by a vague unquiet which in relation to particular objects on which interest fixes hardens into despair, for I tend to identify myself with what I have and to reflect that when I no longer have anything, I shall no longer be anything."— H. J. Blackham, *Six Existentialist Thinkers*, Torchbook (New York and Evanston: Harper and Row, 1959), p. 80.

70. CF, pp. 38-39; cf. Keen, *op. cit.*, p. 5; Gallagher, *op. cit.*, p. 26; Miceli, *op. cit.*, pp. 106ff.

71. Cain, *op. cit.*, pp. 66-67.

72. Gallagher, *op. cit.*, p. 26.

73. Marcel, *Metaphysical Journal*, p. 137; cf. Breisach, *op. cit.*, pp. 158-59.

74. Copleston, *op. cit.*, pp. 170-71. Marcel writes in *Metaphysical Journal*, "Without a doubt, I am to the extent that God is more for me."—p. 206; cf. Donald McCarthy, "Marcel's Absolute Thou," PT, X, 3 (1966), 175-81.

75. Marcel, *Metaphysical Journal*, pp. 156, 200, 210; cf. J. M. Spier, *op. cit.*, p. 48. "Fidelity is not an arid dedication to the preservation of one's title to self-esteem; its axis is not the self at all, but another. It is the spontaneous and unimposed presence of an I to a Thou. . . . The creation of the self is actually accomplished *via* an emergence to a *thou* of reality. I created myself in response to an invocation which can only come from a thou."—Gallagher, *op. cit.*, p. 70.

76. BH, pp. 53-54. "The central virtue of the community is fidelity. . . . But fidelity itself has its ontological foundations and points beyond the human community to the being of God. Thus when once the limits of a narrowly egocentric existence are transcended, we do not halt until we come to God."— Macquarrie, *op. cit.*, p. 370; cf. Pedro Adams, "Marcel: Metaphysician or Moralist," PT, X, 3 (1966), 188.

77. CF, p. 167; cf. Keen, *op. cit.*, pp. 34ff. "Fidelity is not a mere act of the will; it is faith in the presence of an other-than-me, to which I respond and to which I shall continue to respond. It is this continuous response in the bond of fidelity which is my life and my permanence, and more fully represents and reveals the structure of Being than does conformity to a law. Fidelity is a response to a person and can never be rightly practiced towards an idea or an ideal, which is idolatry, for a principle can make no demands upon me, because it owes the whole of its reality to the act whereby I sanction it."—Blackham, *op. cit.*, p. 76.

78. Spier, *op. cit.*, p. 48; cf. Albert Dondeyne, *Contemporary European Thought and Christian Faith*, trans. Ernan McMullin and John Burnheim (Pittsburgh: Duquesne University Press, 1958), p. 63.

79. HV, pp. 133-34; PE, p. 36; cf. Smith, *op. cit.*, p. 73.

80. BH, p. 56; cf. Macquarrie, *op. cit.*, p. 361.

81. BH, p. 22.

82. *Ibid.*, p. 89.

83. *Ibid.*, pp. 78-79.
84. Troisfontaines, *What is Existentialism?*, p. 530. "Like hatred and indifference, love is a mode of being-companions, of *co-existing* in mutual presence and subjects."—Luijpen and Koren, *op. cit.*, p. 173; Leonard Marsak, *French Philosophers from Descartes to Sartre* (Cleveland and New York: World Publishing Co., 1961) p. 439.
85. Gallagher, *op. cit.*, p. 80; cf. Luijpen and Koren, *op. cit.*, pp. 174-84. "Essentially, love is the act of a free mind affirming another free self and which is free only by this very affirmation. There is, at the root of love, the belief in the inexhaustible richness and the unpredictable spontaneity of the being who is loved."—Gabriel Marcel, *Philosophical Fragments*, 1909-1914 *and the Philosopher and Peace* (Notre Dame: University Press, 1965), pp. 109-10
86. HV, pp. 66-67; cf. MB, II, 191.
87. HV, pp. 10-11. "As far as I am concerned, I will not hesitate to say that in my eyes it is in the notion of the mystical body, of *the all in all*, that the philosophy of Hope culminates, but it would be very unjust to doubt that Hope can exist for unbelievers and fulfill itself at least partially with some approximation or surrogate."—Gabriel Marcel, "Desire and Hope" in Lawrence and O'Connor, *op. cit.*, p. 285.
88. BH, p. 79. "But because Hope is directed towards Eternity, it ignores the repetition and the repugnance which are attached to it; one could say that it locates itself in a dimension which is that of perpetual novelty, and it is just for that reason that it does not know fatigue."—Marcel, *Desire and Hope*, p. 278.
89. HV, pp. 46-47. In *Philosophy of Existentialism*, Marcel says, "The only genuine hope is hope in what does not depend on ourselves, hope springing from humility and not from pride."—p. 32.
90. Albert Camus, *The Myth of Sisyphus*, trans. Justin O'Brien, Vintage Book (New York: Random House, 1959), pp. 88-91.
91. MAMS, pp. 116, 118.
92. *Ibid.*, p. 117; cf. Gabriel Marcel, "Contemporary Atheism and the Religious Mind," PT, IV (1960), 260.
93. van Ewijk, *op. cit.*, pp. 52-53.
94. *Ibid.*, pp. 74-75.
95. HV, p. 51.
96. BH, pp. 76-79. In MB, Marcel asks, "But would it not be possible for hope to be another name for the exigence of transcendence or for it to be that exigence itself, inasmuch as it is the driving force behind man the wayfarer?"—II, 182.
97. HV, pp. 60-61.
98. Anthony Padovano, *The Estranged God* (New York: Sheed and Ward, 1966), p. 54; cf. David Roberts, *Existentialism and Religious Belief* (New York: Oxford University Press, 1957), pp. 327-28.
99. Gabriel Marcel, *Le Monde Cassé* (Paris: Desclée de Brouwer, 1933), p. 44; cf. James Collins, *Crossroads in Philosophy*, Gateway (Chicago: Henry Regnery, 1969), p. 14. "The chatter of idle talk is an impossible attempt to avoid the past and future by incessant activity in the present. Marcel's play *The Broken World* presents a heroine who experiences such irresponsibility. She finds that her world has run down, much like a clock that needs repair. She goes through a ritual of meaningless performances in the social world that she has chosen. The image that she has tried to fit becomes increasingly empty."—Sanborn, *op. cit.*, p. 106.
100. MB, I, p. 27. "When Marcel calls ours a broken world, he means one in which the social tendencies obstruct the lucidity about the basic question for men (i.e. either to accept or to refuse to acknowledge their participation in being), until some shock or crisis permits the question of theism to be posed."—Collins, *op. cit.*, p. 16.
101. Cf. Jean Paul Sartre, *Being and Nothingness: An Essay of Phenomenological Ontology*, trans. Hazel Barnes (New York: Philosophical Library, 1956), p. 615.
102. MB, I, pp. 34-35; 30-31. "Men are not only regarded as physical complexes reducible to their objective functions, subject to external manipulation and control; they are now being actually treated in this way."—John Wild, *The Challenge of Existentialism* (Bloomington: Indiana University Press, 1959), p. 173; cf. Luijpen, *op. cit.*, pp. 47-52.
103. Marcel, *Existential Background*, pp. 163-64; cf. Roger Shinn, *The Existentialist Posture* (New York: Association Press, 1959), pp. 32-37. "The function of each person is reduced even in his own eyes, to that of an instrument of production. The man's unity with his body is broken and his body comes to be regarded as a handy instrument. When ill or idle, he is regarded as deficient, an unprofitable burden to society. When dead, he is a broken machine, a useless tool ready for the scrap heap."—Ballard, *op. cit.*, p. 226.
104. Gabriel Marcel, *Searchings* (New York and Westminster: Newman Press, 1967), p. 51. "The physical sciences are good and technology is a benefit to mankind, but the absolutism of the spirit of technology gave rise to what is nowadays often called *technocracy*. As early as 1933 Marcel pronounced his terrible indictment of this technocracy. . . . In a technocratic society the spirit of technology has become absolute."—Luijpen, *op. cit.*, p. 48.
105. Gibson Winter, *Being Free: Reflections on America's Cultural Revolution* (New York: Macmillan Co., 1970), p. 38; cf. Gerber, *op. cit.*, pp. 265-66.
106. Keen, *op. cit.*, p. 10; cf. BH, p. 208; HV, p. 80. "A dehumanized society is one in which the primacy of being over having is reversed, and hence in which the person is reduced in significance to the function he performs in the world of goods

and services. Since another individual can do the same service, the given man has no
distinctive worth. Within the technical universe, he cannot claim to be unique and
irreplaceable, with the tragic result that he may accept this abstract view of himself
as final."—Collins, *op. cit.*, p. 16.
    107.   PE, pp. 11-12; cf. Camus, *op. cit.*, pp. 10-12; cf. Sieste Zuidema,
"Gabriel Marcel: A Critique," PT, IV, 4 (1960), 283.
    108.   PE, p. 12. "I am not sure that every kind of technical progress may not
entail, for the individual who takes advantage of it *without having had any share*
in the efforts of overcoming difficulties of which such a progress is the culmination,
the payment of a heavy price, of which a certain degradation at the spiritual level
is the natural expression."—MAMS, p. 55; cf. Parain-Vial, *op. cit.*, p. 275.
    109.   MAMS, p. 62; cf. Miceli, *op. cit.*, pp. 77ff; Pax, *op. cit.*, pp. 159-77.
    110.   Luijpen, *op. cit.*, p. 61. "Technology dominates its objects—whether
things, men, women, peoples, worlds—reducing the object to the predictable, powerless function in order to control it. The response to the object—its movements or
answers—become feedback within the system; then allowances can be made and
control sustained. The object is reduced to its *meaning* for the system. . . . Technology reduces its objects to elements in its project, reduces men to functions for its
operations, reduces the world to a field for its exploitative drive."—Winter, *op. cit.*,
pp. 38-39.
    111.   Miceli, *op. cit.*, p. 79. "Just as Marcel is resolutely opposed to all those
social and political forces which tend to 'objectify' completely the human person,
turning him into an 'it,' a mere member of a collectivity, or reducing him simply to
his social function, so in philosophy he is opposed, not only to positivism, but also
to absolute idealism (to which in its Anglo-Saxon form, he was once attracted) and
to all forms of philosophy which appear to him to surrender to the spirit of 'objectification' and, in particular, to slur over, disregard or mutilate the concrete experience
of the human person as person."—Copleston, *Contemporary Philosophy*, p. 169; cf.
Ballard, *op. cit.*, p. 227.
    112.   Cf. above, pp. 54-57. Marcel does, however, part company with Kierke-
gaard by maintaining "the intelligible aspect of faith" and that "faith and the spirit
of truth" are ultimately bound together.—MB, II, p. 199.
    113.   *Metaphysical Journal*, p. 64.
    114.   MB, II, pp. 197-198.
    115.   BH, p. 98; cf. Luijpen, *op. cit.*, pp. 66ff.
    116.   BH, *ibid.*, p. 121.
    117.   Marcel, *The Problematic Man*, pp. 54-55.
    118.   Collins, *The Existentialists*, p. 165.
    119.   *Ibid.*, p. 166.
    120.   James Collins, *Religious Themes in Existentialism* (Detroit: Sacred
Heart Seminary, 1961), p. 36, also in ————, *Three Paths in Philosophy* (Chicago:
Henry Regnery Co., 1962), pp. 45-73.
    121.   *Ibid.*, p. 39; cf. Lionel Blain, "Marcel's Logic of Freedom in Proving the
Existence of God," IPQ, IX, 2 (1969), 177-204.
    122.   *Ibid.*
    123.   Copleston, *op. cit.*, p. 172.
    124.   Étienne Gilson, "Can the Existence of God Still be Demonstrated?" in
St. Thomas Aquinas and Philosophy, McAuley Lectures 1960 (West Hartford: Saint
Joseph College, 1960), pp. 1ff; ————, *Elements of Christian Philosophy*, Mentor-
Omega Book (New York: New American Library, 1963), pp. 11ff; Leo Sweeney,
"Marcel's Position on God," NS, XLIV, 1 (1970), 101-24.
    125.   Frederick Copleston, *Existentialism and Modern Man* (Oxford: Black-
friars, 1948), pp. 22-24.
    126.   Frederick Patka, "Five Existentialist Themes" in Patka, *op. cit.*, pp.
70-71; cf. above, p. 60 for Robert McAfee Brown's comments on Karl Barth.
    127.   Collins, *The Existentialists*, p. 116.
    128.   *Ibid.*, pp. 166-167; cf. Étienne Gilson, "On Behalf of the Handmaid,"
in *Renewal of Religious Thought*, ed. Lawrence Shook, 2 vols., (Montreal: Palm
Publishers, 1968), I, 236-49.
    129.   Heinemann, *op. cit.*, p. 148.
    130.   Joseph Mihalich, *Existentialism and Thomism* (New York: Philosophical
Library, 1960), p. 34.
    131.   Reinhardt, *op. cit.*, p. 225; cf. Blackham, *Six Existentialist Thinkers*,
pp. 84-85.
    132.   Michele Sciacca, *Philosophical Trends in the Contemporary World*, trans.
Attilio Salerno (Notre Dame: University Press, 1964), p. 306.
    133.   *Ibid.*, pp. 306-307.
    134.   *Ibid.*, pp. 307-08. J. M. Spier says that Marcel's view of reality is both
irrationalistic and subjectivistic in character.—*op. cit.*, pp. 50-51; cf. Cornelio Fabro,
God in Exile: Modern Atheism, trans. Arthur Gibson (New York and Westminster:
Newman Press, 1968), p. 867.
    135.   This work presented by Fr. Henri Bouillard to the Sorbonne as a doctoral
dissertation is composed of two theses. The secondary thesis, *Karl Barth, Genesis and
Evolution of Dialectical Theology*, comprises Vol. I. The principal thesis, *Karl Barth,
Word of God and Human Existence*, is found in Vols. II and III. These were printed
in Paris in 1957 in the series *Théologie* and appear as Vols. 38 and 39.
    136.   Bouillard, *Logic of the Faith*, pp. 158-59.
    137.   Troisfontaines, *What is Existentialism?* p. 26; cf. Spiegelberg, *op. cit.*,
II, 434-43; Copleston, *Existentialism and Modern Man*, p. 24

CHAPTER IV

1. "In my childhood (at a very early age, I came from Vienna, where I was born, to Galicia and grew up there with my grandparents) I spent every summer on an estate in Bukovina. There my father took me with him at times to the nearby village of Sadagora. Sadagora is the seat of a dynasty of 'zaddikim' (zaddik means righteous, proven, completed), that is, of Hasidic rabbis."—Martin Buber, *Hasidism and Modern Man*, trans. Maurice Friedman, Torchbook (New York: Harper and Bros., 1966), pp. 50-51.

2. *Ibid.*, p. 55; cf. Paul Pfuetze, *Self, Society, Existence*, Torchbook (New York: Harper and Bros., 1961), pp. 117-19.

3. Apropos of the Zionist movement and the question of the Jewish State, Buber had this to say many years later, "Just as where my existence *qua* human being is concerned, the State does not enter into it, so where my being a Jew is concerned, the Jewish State does not come into it either. And when Cohen talks about the urge to power in a people that can contrive to maintain its living identity, this means nothing to me. I have seen and heard too much of the effects of an unrestrained desire for power. The real issue is of a different kind. It is not a question of the Jewish State. If that should come into being now, it would be built, surely, on that same foundation that every modern State is built on. . . . What is really at issue is an 'establishment' that independently of what moves and activates nations . . . can make it a reality."—M. A. Beek and J. Sperna Weiland, *Martin Buber, Personalist and Prophet* (Westminster and New York: Newman Press, 1968), p. 3.

4. Buber, *Hasidism and Modern Man*, pp. 58-60, quoted in Bernard Martin, ed., *Great 20th Century Jewish Philosophers; Shestov, Rosenzweig, Buber* (New York: Macmillan Co., 1970), p. 242; cf. Beek and Weiland, *op. cit.*, pp. 42ff.

5. Cf. Ronald Gregor Smith, *Martin Buber* (Richmond: John Knox Press, 1967), p. 5.

6. *Die Schrift*, translation of the Old Testament from Hebrew into German: vols. I-X, Genesis-Isaiah (in the Jewish order of the books) translated by Martin Buber in collaboration with Franz Rosenzweig (Berlin: Verlag Lambert Schneider); vols. XI-XV, Ezekiel- Proverbs (in the Jewish order of the books) (Berlin: Schocken Verlag).

7. "His Zionism today is essentially a call to take up the task which Hasidism attempted and at which it failed under conditions appropriate to the task. The task is 'the unperformed task' that has hung over Jewry from the days of the Prophets, the task of building true community."—Will Herberg, *The Writings of Martin Buber* (New York: Meridian Books, 1956), p. 36; cf. Martin Buber, *Israel and the World: Essays in a Time of Crisis* (New York: Schocken Books, 1958), pp. 229-30; Will Herberg, *Four Existentialist Theologians*, Anchor Books (New York: Doubleday and Co., 1958), p. 157.

8. Martin Buber in a letter to Stefan Zweig (1918), quoted in Beek and Weiland, *op. cit.*, p. 5.

9. Cf. *Arab-Jewish Unity*. Testimony before the Anglo-American Inquiry Commission for the Ihud (Union) Association by Judah Magnes and Martin Buber (London: Victor Gollancz, 1947). "The test of 'this dream which has as yet found no fulfillment, the dream of Zion' [a spiritual goal founded on, but higher than, the purely material or physical goal] would be Israel's ability to form ties of cooperation and partnership with Arabs, who were also struggling for national liberation and a spiritual renaissance. It was typical of Buber's deep-rooted realism that he devoted so much of his time to the search for a practical Jewish-Arab understanding, while engaged in his constant quest for solutions to the deepest mysteries of man's existence."—Aubrey Hodes, *Martin Buber: An Intimate Portrait* (New York: Viking Press, 1971), p. 91.

10. Concerning Martin Buber's influence on Christian as well as Jewish writers, cf. Maurice Friedman, *Martin Buber: The Life of Dialogue* (New York: Harper and Row, 1960), pp. 258-60; Malcolm Diamond, *Martin Buber: Jewish Existentialist* (New York and Evanston: Harper and Row, 1968), pp. 138-206; Macquarrie, *op. cit.*, pp. 196-97; Smith, *op. cit.*, pp. 35-39.

11. The term appears variously in English as *Chasidism, Hasidism*, and *Chassidism*. The word *Chasid* (literally "benevolent" is to be found in the Bible (Dt. 33:8; 1 Sm. 2:9; 2 Sm. 22:26; Jr. 3:12 et al.) In the *Psalms*, where the term is found frequently, it is generally used in the sense of saintliness and piety. As applicable to a specific group, the term applied in Pre-Maccabean times to those who opposed the advocates of Hellenization in Palestine. The Hasidim were the forerunners of the Pharisees. (1 M. 1:59-68; 7:12-14; 2 M. 6:9-11.)

Cf. Pfuetze, *op. cit.*, p. 206; Buber, *Hasidism and Modern Man*, p. 47; ———, *Ten Rungs: Hasidic Sayings* (New York: Schocken Books, 1962), pp. 13ff; Friedman, *Martin Buber*, pp. 16-23; Lowell Streiker, *The Promise of Buber* (Philadelphia and New York: J. B. Lippincott, 1969), pp. 21-28; Victor Tcherikover, *Hellenistic Civilization and the Jews*, Philadelphia: JPS, 1959), pp. 196ff; S. W. Baron, *A Social and Religious History of the Jews* (Philadelphia: JPS, 1952), I, 237, quoted in Nissan Mindel, *Rabbi Schneur Zalman of Liadi* (Brooklyn: Kehot Publication Society, 1969), p. 271, note 1.

12. "The movement had its roots among rural Jews who found themselves ridiculed when they ventured into the synagogues of neighboring towns; but for all of their rude simplicity, they were a people intimately involved in an earthbound culture that was in direct contact with the elemental rhythms of nature."—Nathan Scott, *The Unquiet Vision: Mirrors of Man in Existentialism* (New York and

Cleveland: World Publishing Co., 1969), p. 159; cf. Beek and Weiland. *op. cit.,* pp. 43-51; Friedman, *Martin Buber,* pp. 16-21; Streiker, *op. cit.,* pp. 26-27.

On *Chabad Hasidism,* cf. Joseph Schneersohn, *Some Aspects of Chabad Chassidism* (Brooklyn: Machne Israel Publishing Co., 1961) pp. 5ff; Gershon Kranzler, *Rabbi Shneur Zalman of Liadi* (Brooklyn: Kehot Publication Society, 1967), pp. 6ff; A. C. Glitzenstein, *The Arrest and Liberation of Rabbi Shneur Zalman of Liadi* (Brooklyn: Kehot Publication Society, 1964), pp. 9ff.

13. Maurice Friedman sees Hasidism as a molding of three separate traditions, "Within the context of post-biblical Judaism, Hasidism may be considered as a union of three different currents. One of these is the Jewish law as expressed in the Talmudic *Halakhah;* the second in the Jewish legend and sayings as expressed in the Talmudic *Haggadah* and in later Jewish mythology; and the third in the *Kabbalah,* the Jewish mystical tradition."–Freidman, *op. cit.,* p. 17.

14. St. Bonaventure, *Breviloquium,* II, 12; cf. Étienne Gilson, *The Philosophy of St. Bonaventure,* trans. Dom Illtyd Trethowan and Frank Sheed (Paterson: St. Anthony Guild Press, 1965), pp. 191ff; ———, *History of Christian Philosophy in the Middle Ages,* pp. 333-34; Armand Maurer, *Medieval Philosophy* (New York: Random House, 1962), p. 146; Anton Pegis, "St. Bonaventure, St. Francis and Philosophy," *Medieval Studies,* XV (1953) 1-13; Martin Buber, *At the Turning: Three Addresses on Judaism* (New York: Farrar, Straus and Cudahy, 1952), p. 58; Smith, *op. cit.,* pp. 12-13.

15. "The first and foremost principle of Hasidic teaching, Buber believes is the concept of a life of fervor and exalted joy."–Arthur Cohen, *Martin Buber* (London: Bowes and Bowes, 1957), p. 81.

16. Zalman Aryeh Hilsenrad, *The Baal Shem Tov: His Birth and Early Manhood* (Brooklyn: Kehot Publication Society, 1967), p. 10.

17. Pfuetze, *op. cit.,* p. 208, note 19. Pfuetze further observes, "Buber saw something of this same ideal in the Society of Friends, a society living in unity and sanctity. Many parallels are also to be found in the Third Order of Franciscans which was an attempt to carry the Gospel of love and service into the domain of the home and marketplace. They were pledged only to penetrate their lives with a passion for Christ, to live with joy and enthusiasm and to make of life a radiant blessing."–p. 209, note 28.

18. Hodes, *op. cit.,* p. 53.

19. "The Chassidim were recognized as the pious representation of traditional Judaism. Within a half century, half of the world Jewish population belonged to the Chassidic movement. Today 200 years after the demise of the Baal Shem Tov, the Chassidic movement, in all its colorful ramifications, constitutes one of the most, if not *the* most, vigorous, dynamic, and creative forces of orthodox Jewry."–Nissan Mindel in J. I. Schneersohn, *Lubavitcher Rabbi's Memoirs* (Brooklyn: Kehot Publication Society, 1960), II, pp. xi-xiii; cf. Joseph Schneersohn, *"The 'Tzemach Tzedek' and the Haskala Movement* (Brooklyn: Kehot Publication Society, 1966), p. 32, note 37.

Buber, *Hasidism and Modern Man,* p. 180, quoted in Maurice Friedman, *To Deny Our Nothingness* (New York: Dell Publishers, 1967). p. 109; cf. Hilsenrad, *op. cit.,* pp. 10ff; Salomo Birnbaum, *The Life and Sayings of Baal Shem* (New York: Hebrew Publishing Co., 1933) pp. 4ff.

21. Diamond, *op. cit.,* pp. 125-26; cf. Martin Buber, *Hasidism* (New York: The Philosophical Library, 1948), pp. 34ff.

22. Mindel, *op. cit.,* pp. 14-15.

23. *Ibid.,* p. 16.

24. Martin Buber, *Tales of the Hasidim, The Early Masters* (New York: Schocken Books, 1948; London: Thomas and Hudson, 1955), pp. 6, 8, quoted in Pfuetze, *op. cit.,* p. 123.

25. Beek and Weiland, *op. cit.,* pp. 146-47. It is rather ironic that today Hasidism finds itself charged with the same legalism and rigidity against which its founders rebelled. As Beek and Weiland pointed out, "In the earliest period, the Zaddik owed this unsolicited function [as leader] to a charismatic gift recognized by those around him. In the period of decline, there appeared the dynasties of tsaddikim who maintained what was basically a royal court and allowed themselves to be venerated as priest-princes. They were the guardians of fixed traditions, but they imparted no further impetus to religious life."–*Ibid.,* p. 44; cf. Ronald Sanders, "Joyous Days for the 'Spark' of Judaism." *New York Times,* CXXII (Oct. 8, 1972), 6-8.

26. Martin Buber, *Between Man and Man* (New York: Macmillan Co., 1968); pp. 13-14. Henceforth BMM; cf. Streiker, *op. cit.,* pp. 21-22; Smith, *op. cit.,* pp. 14-15.

27. Hodes *op. cit.,* p. 10; cf. Cohen, *op. cit.,* p. 44; Friedman, *Martin Buber,* p. 50 note 3.

28. BMM, p. 14.

29. Pfuetze, *op. cit.,* p. 136.

30. Buber, *Ten Rungs,* p. 15. "In this dialogue God speaks to every man through the life which he gives him again and again. Therefore man can easily answer God with the whole of life–with the way he lives this given life. . . . There is no true human share of holiness without the hallowing of the every day."– Buber, *Israel and the World,* p. 33; cf. Diamond, *op. cit.,* pp. 110-37.

31. Buber, *Hasidism and Modern Man,* p. 172.

32. *Ibid.,* pp. 170-71.

33. Friedman *op. cit.,* p. 22. "What impressed Buber about Hasidism was not only the single and deep wisdom of its teachers, its emphasis on the mutuality

and directness of the relationship between the individual and God, and the unremitting concern with 'hallowing the everyday,' but also the fact as he saw it, that it made the most serious effort at the establishment of genuine community undertaken in Jewish quarters from the time of the Hebrew prophets to the pioneering settlement in Palestine in modern times."—Martin, *op. cit.*, p. 243.

34. Buber, *Hasidism and Modern Man*, pp. 49-50.
35. Pfuetze, *op. cit.*, p. 126.
36. BMM, pp. 200, 202.
37. *Ibid.*, p. 200.
38. *Ibid.*; cf. Pfuetze, *op. cit.*, pp. 186ff. "Modern individualism with its flat hedonism, its pursuit of sensual happiness, activates some aspects of man but never the whole I. The purely mechanical association of such predominantly egoistic individuals is in the eyes of Buber the real reason for modern man's sickness and malaise."—Breisach, *op. cit.*, p. 168.
39. BMM, p. 200; cf. Friedman, *op. cit.*, pp. 62-65.
40. BMM, p. 201.
41. *Ibid.* "The collective aims at holding in check the inclination to personal life. It is as though those who are bound together in groups should in the main be concerned only with the work of the group."—Martin Buber, *The Knowledge of Man*, Torchbook (New York: Harper and Row, 1965), p. 73.
42. BMM, pp. 31-32 (emphasis added). "Nor is socialism, at present the most popular form of collectivism, an answer to this predicament. Instead of building man into a person, every collectivism submerges him in an amorphous faceless mass."—Breisach, *op. cit.*, p. 168.
43. Cf. Herberg, *The Writings of Martin Buber*, p. 21: Cohen, *op. cit.*, pp. 92-93.
44. BMM, pp. 201-02. "Community is essential, for only in the unity of man, can a person become aware of and actualize his unique selfhood. A true community is a living *we*, an aggregate of *I's* and *You's* bound together in a cluster of interpersonal relations by a common concern."—Streiker, *op. cit.*, p. 40.
45. Friedman, *op. cit.*, p. 64; cf. Martin Buber, *I and Thou*, trans. Ronald Gregor Smith (New York: Charles Scribner's Sons, 1960), pp. 45ff; ———, *Paths in Utopia*, trans. R. F. C. Hull (Boston: Beacon Press, 1958), pp. 141-42.
46. Breisach, *op. cit.*, p. 168.
47. BMM, p. 203; cf. Pfuetze, *op. cit.*, pp. 202-03.
48. Friedman, *op. cit.*, p. 85.
49. BMM, 36-37; cf. Paul Roubiczek, *Existentialism For and Against* (Cambridge: University Press, 1964), pp. 142-43.
50. BMM, p. 204. *The Knowledge of Man*, pp. 80-85; cf. Nathan Rotenstreich, "Some Problems in Buber's Dialogical Philosophy," PT III (1959) 152-55.
51. Will Herberg, *Martin Buber: Personalist Philosopher in an Age of Depersonalization*, McAuley Lecture XV (West Hartford: McAuley Institute of Religious Studies, Saint Joseph College, 1972), p. 5.
52. Buber, *I and Thou*. Translator's Introduction, p. v. An example of the world-wide appeal of this book is the fact that just before his untimely death in an air crash, the late Secretary General of the United Nations Organization, Dag Hammarskjöld, was in the process of preparing a Swedish translation of *Ich und Du*. "It was no secret that, as a member of the Swedish Academy, Hammarskjöld was advocating the grant of the annual Nobel Prize in Literature to Buber. That is why he started on that translation [of *Ich und Du*] into Swedish. On two occasions, works translated by Hammarskjöld into Swedish—so that his fellow members in the Swedish Academy could read those works more easily—led to the award of the Nobel Prize to the writers thus pinpointed by Hammarskjöld."—Saul Carson, "Dag Hammarskjöld and Martin Buber," *The Connecticut Jewish Ledger*, December 10, 1964, 4.
53. Joseph Oldham, *Real Life Is Meeting* (Greenwich, Conn.: Seabury Press, 1953), p. 27, quoted in Herberg, *op. cit.*, p. 14; cf. Hodes, *op. cit.*, pp. 136-51.
54. Smith, *op. cit.*, p. 21. It is also interesting to note in this connection, the traditional Quaker form of address.
55. Martin Buber, *I and Thou*, ed. and trans. Walter Kaufmann (New York: Charles Scribner's Sons, 1970), pp. 14-15.
56. *Ibid.* "It is doubtful that Kaufmann's translation will replace the older and more elegant translation which so many readers have come to admire."—James Moran, *Review in the New Scholasticism*, XLVI, 2 (1972) 269.
57. Buber, *I and Thou* (Smith ed.) p. 3; cf. Herberg, *The Writings of Martin Buber*, p. 14; ———, *Four Existentialist Theologians*, pp. 8-9; Streiker, *op. cit.*, pp. 34-40; Beek and Weiland, *op. cit.*, pp. 55ff; Rem Edwards, *Reason and Religion* (New York: Harcourt Brace Jovanovich Inc., 1972) pp. 328-33.
58. Herberg, *op. cit.*, p. 14. "The life of dialogue, Buber insisted, is not an exalted activity to be indulged in by choice spirits at rare moments. 'It does not begin in the upper story of humanity.' It can be practiced not only in relationship between two persons directly encountering each other but even by the head of a large factory or business enterprise in his attitude to the thousands of employees who work in it."—Martin, *op. cit.*, p. 249.
59. Herberg, *op. cit.*, p. 14.
60. Friedman, *op. cit.*, p. 57; cf. Buber, *Eclipse of God*, pp. 4ff; Leslie Paul, *The Meaning of Human Existence* (London: Faber and Faber, 1949), p. 148.
61. Herberg, *Martin Buber: Personalist Philosopher*, p. 4.
62. Buber, *I and Thou* (Smith) p. 28; cf. ———, *Eclipse of God*, pp. 127-28.
63. Pfuetze, *op. cit.*, p. 140.

64. *Ibid.;* cf. Diamond, *op. cit.,* p. 52.
65. Buber, *I and Thou,* pp. 8, 78.
66. *Ibid.;* cf. Smith, *op. cit.,* pp. 32-34.
67. Pfuetze, *op. cit.,* pp. 153-56. "The self as such is not ultimately the essential, but the meaning of human existence given in creation again and again fulfills itself as self. The help that men give each other in becoming a self leads the life between men to its height. The dynamic glory of the being of man is first bodily present in the relation between two men, each of whom in meaning the other also means the highest to which this person is called, and serves the self-realization of this human life as one true to creation, without wishing to impose on the other anything of his own realization."—Buber, *The Knowledge of Man,* p. 84, quoted in Friedman, *To Deny Our Nothingness,* p. 301.
68. Buber, *I and Thou* pp. 16-17; cf. Friedman, *Martin Buber,* pp. 62ff.
69. Buber, *I and Thou,* pp. 33-34 (Emphasis added). "A man lives by dint of things; he alters, uses, regulates, *has* them, and even he or she is a thing for me, a 'person-thing,' whom I have at my disposal. . . . The person is no longer a person to me, but some sort of thing. He is mine to manipulate and I am as solitary as he." —Beek and Weiland, *op. cit.,* pp. 33-34.
70. Borowitz, *op. cit.,* p. 168; cf. Buber, *The Knowledge of Man,* p. 26; Breisach, *op. cit.,* pp. 164-65. "Buber saw man in the twentieth century coming increasingly under the sway of a 'pantechnical mania.' The unchecked growth of the I-It attitude, it seemed to him, would in the end completely dehumanize man. Hence, he was not content calmly to diagnose the situation but felt called passionately to urge the application of the remedy. Only a renewal of dialogical existence, he was convinced, could save man's inhumanity from progressive atrophy and ultimate disappearance."—Martin, *op. cit.,* p. 250.
71. Diamond, *op. cit.,* p. 22; cf. Gabriel Marcel, above, pp. 116-20; Sanborn, *op. cit.,* p. 59. "To survive, we must engage in depersonalizing and dehumanizing our fellow man, and therefore ourselves as well. Here we have the most poignant expression of the 'wrongness' of the 'broken character of existence.' "—Herberg, *Four Existentialist Theologians.* p. 21. "The 'I-It' relationship is not necessarily an evil relationship according to Buber. . . . It is only in terms of this relationship that we are able to manipulate and control our environment and therefore get anything at all done. The danger arises only when this 'I-It' relationship threatens to obscure the 'I-Thou' dimension."—Joseph Bettis in *Phenomenology of Religion,* Harper Forum Books (New York and Evanston: Harper and Row, 1969), p. 222.
72. Buber, *Eclipse of God,* p. 129; cf. Bettis, *op. cit.,* p. 220.
73. Gabriel Marcel, cf. above, pp. 98-101; ———, MB, I, 34-35; ———, *Existential Background of Human Dignity,* pp. 163-64.
74. Nikolai Berdyaev, *Spirit and Reality,* trans. George Reavey (London: Geoffrey Bles, 1939), p. 49. "Modern science, abused by a rampant industrial technology, has, for managerial purposes, reduced him to traits and ratings. A person is a personal item, the unique intersection of social and psychological patterns. The tests and diagrams tell what he is—as far as management or public relations are concerned. How many men are thought of and unconsciously think of themselves as a series of punches in a card."—Borowitz, *op. cit.,* p. 174.
75. Herberg, *Martin Buber: Personalist Philosopher,* p. 13.
76. Cf. Beek and Weiland, *op. cit.,* p. 60.
77. Herberg, *The Writings of Martin Buber,* p. 17.
78. BMM, p. 43.
79. Joseph Oldham, "Life as Dialogue," *The Christian News-Letter,* Supplement to #281 (March 19. 1947), p. 7, quoted in Friedman, *Martin Buber,* p. 270.
80. Buber, *I and Thou,* p. 75. In the *Eclipse of God,* Buber rejects both the postulatory atheism of Jean Paul Sartre and the Heideggerian posture of a rebirth of God. "Of the two who have taken up Nietzsche's expression of the death of God, one, Sartre, has brought it and himself, *ad absurdum,* through his postulate of the free invention of meaning and value. The other, Heidegger, creates a concept of rebirth of God out of the thought of truth which falls into the enticing net of historical time."—Buber, *Eclipse of God.* p. 103; cf. Hans Urs von Balthasar, *Martin Buber and Christianity* (New York: Macmillan Co., 1961), p. 113; Eugen Biser, "Martin Buber," PT VII (1963) 112.
81. BMM, p. 15, quoted in Smith, *op. cit.,* p. 11. Smith adds by way of explanation, "Buber was here making the specific point that it is only where men speak to one another, more precisely where they try, but only half succeed, in hearing one another, that God's speech may truly be heard."—*ibid.*
82. Herberg, *Martin Buber: Personalist Philosopher,* p. 7.
83. Buber, *I and Thou,* pp. 112, 75ff; cf. James Brown, *Kierkegaard, Heidegger, Buber, Barth* (New York: Collier Books, 1962), p. 120; Rotenstreich, *op. cit.,* pp. 157-59. "This encounter with the 'other' or the 'Thou' is man's encounter with God. The divine-human encounter, therefore, is not a form of mysticism in which man somehow is removed from his everyday world. . . . Religious activity for Buber is activity which takes place on the basis of an 'I-Thou' relationship. . . . This is why Buber can say that in the 'I-Thou' dialogue the 'larger Thou' leads and the conversants follow."— Bettis, *op. cit.,* pp. 221-22.
84. Buber, *I and Thou,* pp. 135ff.
85. Roubiczek, *op. cit.,* p. 152. "This attempt to reactivate the eternal, to bring back the awareness of the absolute which he felt we had lost in our century, was linked with the concept of God as the eternal Thou, in which the I-Thou found its highest conception. . . . Every I-Thou, every loving relationship with man and the world opens the window to the ultimate Thou. God has to be approached through

an I-Thou relationship with people, animals, trees. . . . Without these life-enhancing encounters, real relationship with God could not be achieved on earth. Similarly a real relationship with other human beings could be attained only if the link between the I and the Eternal Thou is also present."—Hodes, *op. cit.*, p. 31.

86. Buber, *Eclipse of God*, pp. 96-97.
87. *Ibid.*, p. 67.
88. Biser, *op. cit.*, p. 113.
89. Herberg, *op. cit.*, pp. 14-15.

CHAPTER V

1. Heidegger describes himself in a privately printed autobiography, *Der Feldweg*, as a little boy, the son of the sexton of St. Martin's of Messkirch "whose hands often rubbed themselves hot in ringing the church bell . . . which had its peculiar relationship to time and temporality."—Spiegelberg, *op. cit.*, I, 292.

2. *Ibid.*, William Richardson, in *Heidegger: Through Phenomonology to Thought* (The Hague: Martinus Nijhoff, 1963), p. 3, identifies the donor of the book as Dr. Conrad Gröber, pastor of Trinity Church in Constance, who gave it to Heidegger in the summer of 1907 while the latter was still a student in the Gymnasium. Richardson's source is Martin Heidegger, *Unterwege sur Sprache* (Pfullingen, Neske, 1950); cf. Franz Brentano *Von der mannigfachen Bedeutung des Seienden nach Aristoteles* (Freiburg im Breisgau, 1862).

3. Concerning his brief theological training, Heidegger has said, "Without this theological beginning, I would never have entered the path of philosophy. But the beginning always looks towards the future."—Martin Heidegger, "Aus einem Gespräch von der Sprache," a dialogue with Fezuka of the University of Tokyo, published in the collection, *Unterwege zur Sprache*, p. 96, quoted in Borzaga, *op. cit.*, p. 141 and note 3.

4. Joseph Kockelmans, *Martin Heidegger: A First Introduction to His Philosophy* (Pittsburgh: Duquesne University Press, 1965), p. 3; cf. Spiegelberg, *op. cit.*, I, 294 and note 2. "There is much to be said for treating Heidegger's philosophy as a secularized Scotism and the reader may find it valuable to compare Heidegger's vision with the Scotist vision of the poet Gerard Manley Hopkins."—I. M. Bocheński, *Contemporary European Thought* (Berkeley and Los Angeles: University of California, 1961), pp. 154-55, note 5.

5. Spiegelberg, *op. cit.*, I, 294, 297.
6. *Ibid.*, p. 281.
7. Cf. Alvin Diemer, *Edmund Husserl: Versuch einer systematischen Darstellung seiner Phänomenologie* (Meisenheim am Hain, 1956), pp. 29ff; Spiegelberg, *op. cit.*, I, 282 and note 1.

8. *Jahrbuch für Philosophie und phänomenologische Forschung*, XI, (1930), 551; also *Husserliana*, V, 140, quoted in Spiegelberg, *op. cit.*, I, 282.

9. Cf. Kaufmann, *From Shakespeare to Existentialism*, p. 340; Sidney Finkelstein, *Existentialism and Alienation in American Literature* (New York: International Publishers, 1965), p. 87.

10. Although born a Catholic and having studied, as we have seen, for the Catholic priesthood, Heidegger left the faith during his university days.

11. Martin Heidegger, *Die Selbstbehauptung der deutschen Universität* (Breslau: Verlag Korn, 1933); cf. Borzaga, *op. cit.*, p. 149; Collins, *The Existentialists*, pp. 168-69. Heidegger likewise had the following to say in his inaugural address concerning the question of academic freedom; "The highly touted 'academic freedom' is being banished from the German university; being merely negative, this freedom was spurious. It meant indifference, arbitrariness of goals and inclinations, actions without restraint."—*op. cit.*, p. 15, quoted in Richard Schmitt, *Martin Heidegger on Being Human* (New York: Random House, 1969), p. 251.

12. P. Hühnerfeld, *In Sachen Heideggers, Versuch über ein deutsches Genie* (Hamburg, 1959), quoted in Kockelmans, *op. cit.*, p. 5. For a similar reaction of another student, cf. Karl Löwith, "Les implications politiques de la philosophies de l'existence chez Heidegger," *Les Temps Modernes*, II (November 1946 and July 1947); cf. Thomas Langan, *The Meaning of Heidegger* (New York and London: Columbia University Press, 1961), p. 4. "It seems clear that much of Nazism did not appeal to Heidegger. But there is absolutely nothing to suggest that the Nazis' systematic inhumanity or their contempt for all nobility, freedom and honesty appalled him. Heidegger's disenchantment was not based on moral grounds."—Kaufmann, *op. cit.*, p. 343.

13. Editorial, *Der Alemanne*, May 3, 1933, quoted by Dagobert Runes in Martin Heidegger, *German Existentialism*, trans. Dagobert Runes (New York: The Philosophical Library, 1965), p. 13; cf. Guido Schneeberger, "Supplement to Heidegger: Documents of His Life and Thought," in Maurice Friedman, *The Worlds of Existentialism* (New York: Random House, 1965) p. 532; Finkelstein, *op. cit.*, pp. 92ff.

14. Martin Heidegger, "The University under the New Reich" in *Heidelberger Neueste Nachrichten*, July 1, 1933, p. 4; ———, "German Student," in *Freiburger Studentenzeitung*, November 3, 1933, p. 1, quoted in Heidegger, *German Existentialism*, pp. 24, 27. On October 1, 1933, the teaching licenses of Jewish professors of Freiburg University were revoked. Curiously, Arland Ussher, *Journey Through Dread* (London: Darwen Finlayson, 1955), writes, "This must be said [concerning Heidegger's acceptance of Nazism] with one important reserve. Though Heidegger could write 'Only the Führer himself is the German reality, present and past and the law' *he at no time would have anything to do with 'racism.'* During his rectorship of Marburg [in actuality, Heidegger was rector of Freiburg and not Marburg],

he refused to allow the names of Jews like Husserl and Bergson to be struck off the course."—p. 84, note 1 (italics added).

In spite of the above statement, Heidegger did assume office on May 27, 1933 and held it for a period of one year. The revocation of the teaching licenses of the Jewish professors was dated October 1, 1933. We read another curious statement in Macquarrie, *op. cit.*, "He [Heidegger] was suspended after the Second World War on account of his *alleged* [italics added] sympathies with the Nazi regime."—p. 353, note 1. This strikes us as a remarkable understatement in view of the testimony which has just been examined; cf. Finkelstein, *op. cit.*, pp. 94-96.

Nino Langiulli's extremely favorable treatment of Heidegger's Nazi period leaves many questions unanswered, Cf. Langiulli, *op. cit.*, pp. 188-92.

15. Cf. Borzaga, *op. cit.*, p. 150 and note 12. For some possible reasons why Heidegger espoused Nazi socialism, cf. Roberts, *op. cit.*, p. 149; William Kluback and Jean Wilde, "A Heideggerian Limitation," in Martin Heidegger, *The Question of Being*, trans. William Kluback and Jean Wilde (New York: Twayne Publishers, 1958), pp. 15-16; Schneeberger, *op. cit.*, p. 533.

16. "Heidegger thrives on the fascination of ambiguity; he loves mystery and he never tires of insisting that he is misunderstood. He claims that his interpreters, including old friends and students, have quite failed to get the point of *Being and Time*, the early work on which his reputation largely rests. Devoted former students who are now full professors . . . and those who pride themselves on being classical philologists as well as professors insist that his readings are based on outright mistakes. When such mistakes are pointed out to him in manuscript, he is said to respond gruffly, 'So it is all wrong'—and then the text appears in point without the least alteration."—Kaufmann, *op. cit.*, pp. 377-78; 339-69. ————, *Existentialism from Dostoevsky to Sartre*, pp. 33-39; John Macquarrie, *Martin Heidegger* (Richmond: John Knox Press, 1968), pp. 2-3 Collins, *op. cit.*, p. 169; Heinemann, *op. cit.*, p. 89.

17. Stefan Schimanski, "Foreword" in Martin Heidegger, *Existence and Being*, ed. Werner Brock (Chicago: Henry Regnery Co., 1949), pp. ix-x.

18. "Admittedly, in some of his writings, Heidegger appears to forget his own warning against 'word-mysticism.' For instance, he can speak of language as the 'domain of being' where one can listen to the 'dictation' of being."— John Macquarrie, *The Scope of Demythologizing: Bultmann and His Critics* (New York: Harper and Row, 1966), p. 195; cf. Schmitt, *op. cit.*, pp. 19-20; Roubiczek, *op. cit.*, pp. 130-31; Erich Dinkler, "Martin Heidegger" in Michalson, *op. cit.*, p. 98.

19. Spiegelberg, *op. cit.*, I, 273; cf. Collins, *op. cit.*, pp. 171-72; Kockelmans, *op. cit.*, pp. 9-10; Bocheński, *op. cit.*, pp. 161-62; Walter Kaufmann, *Critique of Religion and Philosophy* (New York: Doubleday and Co., 1961), pp. 29-30. Heidegger himself makes this interesting observation concerning the German language, "Along with the German, Greek language [in regard to its possibilities for thought] is the most powerful and most spiritual of all languages." (New York: Doubleday and Co., 1961), pp. 161-62; cf. J. L. Mehta, *The Philosophy of Martin Heidegger*, Torchbook (New York and Evanston: Harper and Row, 1971), pp. 65-80.

20. Quoted in Reinhardt, *op. cit.*, p. 132.

21. *Bulletin de la societé française de philosophie*, XXXVII, no. 5 (1937), p. 193, quoted in Kockelmans, *op. cit.*, p. 22. For an earlier repudiation of the label of existentialism, cf. Heinemann, *op. cit.*, p. 87.

22. Herbert Kohl, *The Age of Complexity*, Mentor Book (New York: The New American Library of World Literature, 1965), p. 129; cf. Macquarrie, *Martin Heidegger*, p. 8.

23. Blackman, *op. cit.*, pp. 86-87. On the other hand, "The belief that his [Heidegger's] is a philosophy of existence is actually the result of incompleteness of *Sein und Zeit*. For while Heidegger planned to use his existential studies only as an entering wedge for his major problem, the sense of Being in general, the nonappearance of the later parts meant that only his analytics of existence was available." —Spiegelberg, *op. cit.*, I, 289.

24. Charles Kegley and Robert Bretall, eds., *The Theology of Paul Tillich* (New York: Macmillan Co., 1952), p. 14. "Tillich's theology stresses, for instance, the distinction between Being and 'a being' very much as Heidegger did from *Sein und Zeit*. . . . Also, Tillich's whole conception of ontology, whose subject is described as *being*, as distinguished from the sciences which deal with *beings*, reflects Heidegger's thought. To be sure, thus far Heidegger has steadfastly refused to identify Being with God, as Tillich now does."—Spiegelberg, *op. cit.*, I, 272, note 3; cf. Macquarrie, *op. cit.*, p. 58.

25. Macquarrie, *Twentieth Century Religious Thought*, pp. 362-63; cf. ————, *Martin Heidegger*, p. 55; ————, *An Existentialist Theology: A Comparison of Heidegger and Bultmann*, Torchbook (New York and Evanston: Harper and Row, 1965); Erich Dinkler, "Existentialist Interpretation of the New Testament," *Journal of Religion*, XXXII (1952) 87-96; Brown, *ip. cit.*, p. 93; Thomas O'Meara and Donald Weisser, eds., *Rudolf Bultmann in Catholic Thought* (New York: Herder and Herder, 1968) esp. Helmut Peukert, "Bultmann and Heidegger," pp. 196-221. For a short but trenchant critique, cf. Bouillard, *op. cit.*, pp. 115-37.

26. *Sartre, Existentialism is a Humanism*, p. 26. Martin Heidegger rejects this claim in his *Letter on Humanism* (*Platons Lehre von der Wahrheit. Mit einem Brief über den "Humanismus"* (Bern: Francke, 1947), pp. 79ff. "In spite of such more or less outspoken dissents, [from Heidegger], it seems plain enough that Sartre's ontological enterprise leads him closer to Heidegger than to any other philosopher before him."—Spiegelberg, *op. cit.*, II, 454 and note 1. Fabro, *op. cit.*, p. 909.

27. Martin Heidegger, *Being and Time,* trans. John Macquarrie and Edward Robinson from the Seventh Edition, Neomarius Verlag, Tübingen (New York and Evanston: Harper and Row, 1962). Henceforth BT. All references will be to this English edition which conveniently carries in its margins the pagination of the original German text.

28. Cf. Sciacca, *op. cit.,* pp. 281-82; Kockelmans, *op. cit.,* p. 141; Heinz Moenkemeyer, "Martin Heidegger," in Patka, *op. cit.,* p. 94.

29. Cf. Kaufmann, *From Shakespeare to Existentialism,* pp. 344-69; ———, *Existentialism from Dostoevsky to Sartre,* p. 34.

30. BT, p. 19; Plato, *Sophist,* 244a.

31. BT, *ibid.*

32. *Ibid.,* p. 21; cf. Michael Wyschogrod, *Kierkegaard and Heidegger* (London: Routledge and Kegan Paul, 1954), pp. 51-52.

33. Martin Heidegger, *Einführung in die Metaphysik* (Tübingen: Niemeyer, 1953), p. 64; cf. Spiegelberg, *op. cit.,* I. 154-55, note 19.

34. Fabro, *op. cit.,* pp. 915-16; cf. Giles Driscoll, "Heidegger: A Response to Nihilism," PT, XI, 1 (1967), 17-19.

35. BT, p. 44; cf. William Barrett, *Irrational Man,* Anchor Book (New York: Doubleday and Co., 1962), pp. 210-11; ———, *What Is Existentialism?,* Evergreen Book (New York: Grove Press, 1965), pp. 140ff.

36. Macquarrie, *Scope of Demythologizing,* pp. 126-27.

37. Cf. St. Thomas Aquinas, *Summa Theologiae,* I, q. 3, art. 3, 4; Pegis, *Basic Writings,* I, pp. 28-31; Francis Lescoe, ed., *St. Thomas Aquinas: Treatise on Separate Substances* (West Hartford: Saint Joseph College, 1963), pp. 85-91; Gilson, *Christian Philosophy of St. Thomas Aquinas,* pp. 33-45, ———, *History of Christian Philosophy in the Middle Ages,* pp. 361-83; ———, *Elements of Christian Philosophy,* Mentor-Omega Book (New York: American Library of World Literature, 1960), pp. 123-24, 131, 138-40; ———, "Can the Existence of God Still Be Demonstrated?" in *St. Thomas Aquinas and Philosophy,* McAuley Lectures 1960 (West Hartford: Saint Joseph College, 1961), pp. 1-14; ———, *On the Art of Misunderstanding Thomism,* pp. 33-43; Pegis, *Thomism as a Philosophy,* pp. 15-29.

38. Cf. Heinemann, *op. cit.,* pp. 94-95. "Heidegger's analysis of Plato attempts to show that a transformation occurs in the nature of truth in Plato's philosophy, as a consequence of which, Being is subordinated to the correct perception of beings. This subordination, Heidegger maintains, characterizes the history of Western philosophy as metaphysics."—Bernd Magnus, *Heidegger's Metahistory of Philosophy: Amor Fati, Being and Truth* (The Hague: Martinus Nijhoff, 1970), p. 69.

39. Collins, *The Existentialists,* p. 177.

40. Cf. Barrett, *Irrational Man,* p. 212. "[According to Heidegger] failure to see that Being is not a thing (whether *Ideal, energeia* or God) nor the totality of things, but that *Sein* and *Seiende* are radically different, even though one cannot be without the other, is disastrous, both for the tradition as a whole, and for the existence of the individual DASEIN."—Gilson, Langan and Maurer, *op. cit.,* p. 147.

41. Gilson, *On the Art of Misunderstanding Thomism,* pp. 40ff.

42. Cf. Martin Heidegger, "On the Essence of Truth" in Brock, *op. cit.,* pp. 313-16; Joseph Owens, *The Doctrine of Being in the Aristotelian Metaphysics* (Toronto: Pontifical Institute of Mediaeval Studies, 1957).

43. Fabro, *op. cit.,* p. 811. For a critique of Heidegger's interpretation of Plato, cf. Magnus, *op. cit.,* 79ff.

44. Heidegger, *Brief über Humanismus,* p. 76, trans. and quoted by Richardson, *op. cit.,* p. 6 "In his quest for being, Heidegger supplements his phenomenological analysis of man's being with a religious or mystical experience of being itself. . . . Being takes the place of God in Heidegger's thought. He thinks that the biblical God is an entity rather than being itself."—Macquarrie, *op. cit.,* p. 219 and note 2.

45. James Collins, "The Religious Themes in Existentialism," in *Philosophy and the Modern World,* ed. Francis Canfield (Detroit: Sacred Heart Seminary, 1961), pp. 28-29, also found in ———, *Three Paths in Philosophy* (Chicago: Henry Regnery Co., 1962); cf. Frederick Copleston, *Existentialism and the Modern Man* (Oxford: Blackfriars, 1948), pp. 17-18.

46. Heinemann, *op. cit.,* pp. 104-05.

47. Kaufmann, *From Shakespeare to Existentialism,* pp. 363-65. Richard Kroner pointedly asks, "Is [Heidegger's] being not furnished with attributes which we can and should ascribe to the living God alone?"—"Heidegger's Private Religion," *Union Seminary Quarterly Review,* XI, 4, pp. 39ff; quoted in Macquarrie, *op. cit.,* pp. 218-19; cf. John Doyle, "Heidegger and Scholastic Metaphysics," *The Modern Schoolman,* XLIX, 3 (1972) 201-20.

48. Sciacca, *op. cit.,* pp. 192-93. Bernd Magnus has this comment to make concerning Heidegger's highly subjective interpretation of the history of philosophy: "When confronted with the history of criticism of his interpretation of Kant, Heidegger simply said, 'it may not be good Kant, but it is excellent Heidegger.' I think substantially the same comment can be made, substituting for the word 'Kant,' the words 'Plato,' 'Descartes,' or 'history of philosophy.' "—*op. cit.,* p. 80.

49. Blackham, *op. cit.,* p. 108.

50. Gilson, *op. cit.,* pp. 40-41.

51. Collins, *The Existentialists,* p. 180 and note 17; cf. BT, p. 126, for Heidegger's totally inadequate and superficial treatment of the doctrine of analogy.

52. Borzaga, *op. cit.,* pp. 154 and note 1; pp. 186, 202.

53. *Ibid.*

54. Cf. Martin Heidegger, *The Way Back into the Ground of Metaphysics*

in Kaufmann, *Existentialism from Dostoevsky to Sartre*, pp. 213-14; Kockelmans, *op. cit.*, pp. 14-15; Bocheński, *op. cit.*, 162-63; Richardson, *op. cit.*, pp. 34-35; Brock, *op. cit.*, pp. 14ff. "DASEIN denotes human beings but is not synonymous with 'human being' in the sense of 'person,' Heidegger wants to differentiate the sense in which DASEIN is, from the sense in which things, events, states, properties are said to be. The sense of 'to be' in which DASEIN is, therefore, will be called 'existence.' Possessing an understanding of being, including an understanding of human being, now called DASEIN is an essential feature of DASEIN."—Schmitt, *op. cit.*, p. 15.

55. BT, pp. 26, 27, 32; cf. Karl Löwith, *Nature, History and Existentialism* (Evanston: Northwestern University Press, 1966), p. 35; Dinkler, *Martin Heidegger*, pp. 103-04; Kaufmann, *op. cit.*, p. 213; Molina, *op. cit.*, pp. 54ff; J. Rodman Williams, *Contemporary Existentialism and Christian Faith* (Englewood Cliffs: Prentice-Hall, 1965), pp. 5ff.

56. Barrett, *op. cit.*, p. 218; cf. Heinemann, *op. cit.*, pp. 91-93; Langan, *op. cit.*, pp. 27ff; Magda King, *Heidegger's Philosophy. A Guide to His Basic Thought*, Delta Book (New York: Dell Publishing Co., 1966), pp. 44-45; Calvin Schrag, "Whitehead and Heidegger," PT, IV, 1 (1960), 30.

57. Cf. Thomas Prufer, "Dasein and the Ontological Status of the Speaker of Philosophical Discourse," in *Twentieth Century Thinkers*, ed. John Ryan (Staten Island: Alba House, 1965), pp. 159, 169; Ludwig Landgrebe, *Major Problems in Contemporary European Philosophy*, trans. Kurt Reinhardt (New York: Ungar Press, 1966), pp. 47-49; Richardson, *op. cit.*, p. 36; Kockelmans, *op. cit.*, p. 14, note 8; Loy Vail, "Heidegger's Conception of Philosophy," NS, XLII, 4 (1968), 488.

58. Heidegger, *The Way Back Into the Ground of Metaphysics*, p. 124. "Existence is the specifically human mode of being, the distinguishing characteristic of DASEIN. All other beings merely are; DASEIN alone exists. . . . DASEIN is not merely something there, not a pure object like a rock on the beach. Rather, it has responsibility for its own being and an obligation to be significant. DASEIN recognizes its own being as a task to be fulfilled; it must do something about its being."—James Demske, *Being, Man and Death* (Lexington: University of Kentucky Press, 1970), p. 16.

59. BT, pp. 67-69; cf. Arne Naess, *Four Modern Philosophers: Carnap, Wittgenstein, Heidegger, Sartre*, trans. Alastair Hannay (Chicago: University of Chicago Press, 1968), pp. 194-95; Vincent Vycinas, *Earth and Gods: An Introduction to the Philosophy of Martin Heidegger* (The Hague: Martinus Nijhoff, 1961), pp. 26-28; Karsten Harries, "Martin Heidegger: The Search for Meaning," in *Existential Philosophers: Kierkegaard to Merleau-Ponty*, ed. George Schrader (New York and London: McGraw Hill, 1967) pp. 188-89.

60. Macquarrie, *Martin Heidegger*, pp. 12-13; cf. George Seidel, *Martin Heidegger and the Pre-Socratics* (Lincoln: University of Nebraska Press, 1964), pp. 14-15; Moenkemeyer, *op. cit.*, pp. 102-03; Blackman, *op. cit.*, pp. 88-89; Sciacca, *op. cit.*, pp. 192-93; Vail, *op. cit.*, pp. 486-89.

61. The English translators of *Sein und Zeit* write, "The word 'Dasein' plays so important a role in this work and is already familiar to the English-speaking reader who has read about Heidegger, that it seems simpler to leave it untranslated, except in the relatively rare passages in which Heidegger himself breaks it up with a hyphen (Da-Sein) to show its etymological construction."—BT, p. 27, note 1; cf. Wyschogrod, *op. cit.*, p. 52, note 2.

62. BT, pp. 49-63; cf. above, pp. 19-21. Joseph Kockelmans, "What Is Phenomenology?" in *Phenomenology: The Philosophy of Edmund Husserl and Its Interpretation*, ed. Joseph Kockelmans, Anchor Book (Garden City: Doubleday and Co., 1967), pp. 24-36; Laszlo Versenyi, *Heidegger, Being and Truth* (New Haven and London: Yale University Press, 1965), pp. 74-77; King, *op. cit.*, pp. 150-63: H. J. Blackman, ed., *Reality, Man and Existence: Essential Works of Existentialism* (New York: Bantam Books, 1965), pp. 9-10.

63. BT, p. 38ff; cf. Versenyi, *op. cit.*, pp. 7-8; Dondeyne, *op. cit.*, pp. 33-35; Vycinas, *op. cit.*, pp. 28-30; Richard Palmer, *Hermeneutics* (Evanston: Northwestern University Press, 1969), pp. 127-30; James Watson, "Heidegger's Hermeneutic Phenomenology," *Philosophy Today*, XV, 1 (1971), 30ff; Martin Heidegger, "The Idea of Phenomenology," trans. John Deely, Joseph Novak and Eva Leo, NS, XLIV, 3 (1970), 340-44.

64. Kockelmans, *Martin Heidegger*, p. 19; cf. BT, p. 54; Calvin Schrag, "Phenomenology, Ontology and History in the Philosophy of Heidegger," in Kockelmans, *The Philosophy of Edmund Husserl*, pp. 279-81, reprinted from *Revue Internationale de Philosophie*, XII (1958) 117-32.

65. Cf. above, pp. 19-21; Richard Zaner, *The Way of Phenomenology*, Pegasus Book (New York: Western Publishing Co., 1970), pp. 129ff; Robert Sokolowski, *The Formation of Husserl's Concept of Constitution* (The Hague: Martinus Nijhoff, 1964); Spiegelberg, *op. cit.*; Quentin Lauer, *Phenomenology: Its Genesis and Prospect*, Torchbook, (New York and Evanston: Harper and Row, 1965), esp. pp. 20ff; Marvin Farber, *The Aims of Phenomenology*, Torchbook (New York and Evanston: Harper and Row, 1966); ———, *The Foundation of Phenomenology* (Albany: State University of New York Press 1943); Donald Vandenberg, *Being and Education: An Essay in Existential Phenomenology* (Englewood Cliffs: Prentice-Hall, 1971), pp. 18-33; William Luijpen and Henry Koren, *A First Introduction to Existential Phenomenology* (Pittsburgh: Duquesne University Press, 1969), pp. 18; Joseph Kockelmans, *A First Introduction to Husserl's Phenomenology* (Pittsburgh: Duquesne University Press, 1967); Maurice Natanson, ed., *Essays in Phenomenology* (The Hague: Martinus Nijhoff, 1966); Pierre Thévenaz, "What is Phenomenology?" in *Christianity and Existentialism*, ed. William Edie, James Edie and John Wild

416 EXISTENTIALISM

(Evanston: Northwestern University Press, 1963); Fernando Molina, "The Husserlian Ideal of a Pure Phenomenology," in *An Invitation to Phenomenology*, ed. James Edie (Chicago: Quadrangle Books, 1965), pp. 161-77; Thomas Langan, "The Future of Phenomenology," in *Phenomenology in Perspective*, ed. F. Joseph Smith (The Hague: Martinus Nijhoff, 1970), pp. 1-15.

66. Cf. BT, pp. 59-60; Naess, *op. cit.*, pp. 192-93; Richardson, *op. cit.*, pp. 46-47; Palmer, *op. cit.*, pp. 124-26; Schmitt, *op. cit.*, pp. 103-04.

67. Kockelmans, Martin Heidegger, p. 21; cf. Aaron Gurwitsch, "Husserl's Theory of Intentionality of Consciousness in Historical Perspective," in *Phenomenology and Existentialism*, ed. Edward Lee and Maurice Mandelbaum (Baltimore: Johns Hopkins Press, 1967), pp. 25ff; Helmut Kuhn, *Encounter With Nothingness* (London: Methuen and Co., 1951), pp. 129-39; Barrett, *What Is Existentialism?*, pp. 79-84; I. M. Bocheński, *The Methods of Contemporary Thought*, Torchbook (New York and Evanston: Harper and Row, 1968), pp. 15-29; Herbert Spiegelberg, "On Some Uses of Phenomenology," F. J. Smith, *op. cit.*, pp. 16-31.

68. Macquarrie, *op. cit.*, p. 11; cf. F. Joseph Smith, "Being and Subjectivity: Heidegger and Husserl," in Smith, *op. cit.*, pp. 122-56. Angel Medina, "Husserl on the Nature of the Subject," NS XLV. 4 (1971), 547-72, James Collins, *Interpreting Modern Philosophy* (Princeton: University Press, 1972), pp. 285-300.

69. Cf. Palmer, *op. cit.*, pp. 127-30.

70. Spiegelberg, *Phenomenological Movement*, I, 328; cf. BT, pp. 78ff; Breisach, *op. cit.*, pp. 84-85; Harries, *op. cit.*, pp. 170-72; Williams, *op. cit.*, pp. 109ff.

71. BT, p. 78. "We see then what 'being in the world' ultimately means for Heidegger: interrelatedness has taken on the expanded sense of the mutual involvement of all things earthly and heavenly, and man as mortal is but one corner of the totality in which he participates."—F. Christopher Smith, "Heidegger's Critique of Absolute Knowledge," NS XLV, i (1971), 77.

72. BT, Part I chaps. III-IV, pp. 91-224.

73. BT, p. 170; Wild, *op. cit.*, pp. 75-78.

74. BT, pp. 79-80. "As the being which understands being, DASEIN exists in the world as being consciously present to beings other than itself, as well as to itself and to the task of its own existence. It must relate to all things, persons, events and ideas which it encounters in experience as coming from the outside, as being somehow other than itself. in the constant context of its own responsibility to be."—Demske, *op. cit.*, p. 19; cf. Macquarrie, *op. cit.*, p. 15; Spiegelberg, *op. cit.*, I, 328, Richardson, *op. cit.*, pp. 58-59.

75. Richardson, *ibid.*, p. 52; cf. Kockelmans, *op. cit.*, pp. 24-25.

76. King, *op. cit.*, pp. 67-88; cf. BT, p. 79. "The world is not a spatial container in which *Dasein* is placed. The relationship of *Dasein* to the world is the relationship of practical preoccupation and personal involvement. To say that *Dasein* is in the world is to say that he lives, dwells and sojourns in the world. . . . Walter Biemel has aptly characterized Heidegger's concept of 'being-in-the-world' as an attitude of intimacy or familiarity—as 'being-with' in distinction from purely spatial relationship of 'being-beside.' "—Schrag, *op. cit.*, p. 282, note 8.

77. BT, p. 83; cf. Bocheński, *Contemporary European Thought*, pp. 164-65; Reinhardt, *op. cit.*, p. 134.

78. BT, p. 94. "World is not the whole of all beings but the whole in which the human being finds himself already immersed, surrounded by its manifestations as revealed through an always pregrasping, encompassing understanding."—Palmer, *op. cit.*, p. 132.

79. Versenyi, *op. cit.*, p. 14; cf. Richardson, *op. cit.*, pp. 52-58; King, *op. cit.*, p. 90; Julian Marias, *History of Philosophy*, trans. Stanley Applebaum and Clarence Strowbridge (New York: Dover Publications, 1967), pp. 432-33; Karl Rahner, "The Concept of Existential Philosophy in Heidegger," PT, XIII, 2 (1969), 132-33.

80. Cf. above, pp. 92ff.

81. BT, p. 73.

82. Cf. above, pp. 194-95.

83. Schrag, *op. cit.*, p. 288, note 19; cf. Reinhardt, *op. cit.*, p. 133; Molina, *Existentialism as Philosophy*, p. 56; Brock, *op. cit.*, p. 366, note 14; Löwith, *op. cit.*, p. 37.

84. BT, pp. 154-55; cf. Macquarrie, *op. cit.*, p. 18; Kockelmans, *op. cit.*, pp. 56-57.

85. Blackham, *op. cit.*, pp. 90-91.

86. Vycinas, *op. cit.*, p. 41; cf. Barrett, *What Is Existentialism?*, pp. 55-56; Richardson, *op. cit.*, p. 59.

87. Langan, *Meaning of Heidegger*, pp. 230ff. "Authentic life is also undermined by Heidegger's isolation of the individual. His 'facticity' is entirely subjective, so subjective that it does not even include personal relationships. . . . Man, however, does not live in isolation, so that Heidegger's representation must remain artificial and misleading. *Angst* and *Sorge*, by themselves, are no substitute for what he omits."—Roubiczek, *op. cit.*, pp. 136-37.

88. Marjorie Grene, *Martin Heidegger* (London: Bowes and Bowes, 1957), pp. 56, 58; cf. Karl Löwith, *Heidegger: Denker in dürftiger Zeit* (Frankfurt: S. Fischer Verlag, 1953), pp. 61ff; ———, *Nature, History, and Existentialism*, pp. 61-62; Roubiczek, *op. cit.*, pp. 136-37.

89. Renée Weber, "A Critique of Heidegger's Concept of 'Solicitude,' " NS, XLIII, 4 (1968) (Heidegger Issue). 558-59; 540, note 5. On the other hand, cf. John Caputo, "Heidegger's Original Ethics," NS, XLV, 1 (1971), 127-38; cf. Grene,

Introduction to Existentialism, pp. 68-70.
    90. Cf. BT, p. 172, note 1; Versenyi, *op. cit.*, p. 18; Molina, *op. cit.*, pp. 61ff; King, *op. cit.*, translates *Befindlichkeit* as "attunement," adding, "The ontic manifestations of *Befindlichkeit* are familiar to everyone as the feelings which constantly 'tune' man and 'tune him in' to other beings as a whole."—p. 77.
    91. BT, p. 174; cf. Manfred Frings, "Heidegger and Scheler," PT, XII, 1 (1968), 26.
    92. BT, *ibid.*; cf. Kuhn, *op. cit.*, pp. 33-34; King, *op. cit.*, pp. 77-78. "The burden of human existence as thus manifested according to Heidegger consists in the poignant fact that human being 'is and has to be,' 'whence and whither, however, remain in the dark.' . . . For this situation of facticity Heidegger coins the striking though ponderous word *'Geworfenheit,'* which would have to be rendered by a passive participle of verbs like to throw, to fling, or to cast. However, to Heidegger, 'thrownness' is not a mere brute fact, it represents an intimate part of our way of being, even though it is usually pushed into the background."—Spiegelberg, *op. cit.*, I, 330-31; cf. Molina, *op. cit.*, p. 61; Bocheński, *op. cit.*, p. 166; Vycinas, *op. cit.*, pp. 43-44.
    93. Macquarrie, *An Existentialist Theology*, p. 83; cf. Kuhn, *op. cit.*, p. 33; Robert Olson, *An Introduction to Existentialism* (New York: Dover Publications, 1962), pp. 135-36.
    94. BT, p. 174.
    95. BT, p. 82; Macquarrie, *op. cit.*, pp. 82-89.
    96. BT, *ibid.*
    97. BT, p. 174.
    98. Macquarrie, *Martin Heidegger*, p. 21; cf. ——, *An Existentialist Theology*, pp. 82-89.
    99. BT, p. 188; cf. Borzaga, *op. cit.*, p. 159; Schmitt, *op. cit.*, pp. 166-70.
    100. BT, pp. 184-85; cf. Langan, *op. cit.*, pp. 45-46.
    101. Molina, *op. cit.*, p. 64; cf. Schmitt, *op. cit.*, pp. 165-66, 176ff.
    102. Macquarrie, *Martin Heidegger*, p. 22; cf. Versenyi, *op. cit.*, pp. 20-25.
    103. King, *op. cit.*, p. 83; cf. Kockelmans, *op. cit.*, pp. 68-72; Richardson, *op. cit.*, pp. 59-63; Barrett, *Irrational Man*, pp. 221-22.
    104. BT, p. 172.
    105. BT, pp. 203-04; cf. Kockelmans, *op. cit.*, pp. 72-73; Langan, *op. cit.*, pp. 48-49; Vycinas, *op. cit.*, pp. 47-50.
    106. Cf. above, pp. 12-13.
    107. BT, pp. 164-66; cf. Barrett, *What Is Existentialism?*, pp. 56-57; Richardson, *op. cit.*, pp. 47-49; Reinhardt, *op. cit.*, pp. 134-35; Gilson, Langan and Maurer, *op. cit.*, p. 148.
    108. BT, p. 164; cf. William Luijpen, *Existential Phenomenology* (Pittsburgh: Duquesne University Press, 1962), pp. 331-32; Thomas Higgins, *Ethical Theories in Conflict* (Milwaukee: Bruce Publishing Co., 1967), pp. 127-28; Naess, *op. cit.*, pp. 200-05; Wild *op. cit.*, pp. 130-39.
    109. BT, p. 127; cf. Oswald Schrag, *Existence, Existenz and Transcendence* (Pittsburgh: Duquesne University Press, 1971), p. 54.
    110. Bocheński, *op. cit.*, p. 168; cf. BT, pp. 165-68; Kohl, *op. cit.*, pp. 165-68; *op. cit.*, pp. 138-39; MAMS, pp. 37ff; Brock, *op. cit.*, p. 41.
    111. BT, p. 220; cf. Luijpen, *op. cit.*, p. 331. "This absorption in the world Heidegger speaks of in terms of the quasi-Biblical metaphor of Fallenness, presumably suggesting that the Person tends to be content with an inauthentic existence because the uncompromising demand to take charge of shaping his own being is too great a task."—Fernando Molina, *The Sources of Existentialism As Philosophy* (Englewood Cliffs: Prentice-Hall, 1969), p. 125.
    112. BT, *ibid.*; cf. Richardson, *op. cit.*, pp. 70-71; Naess, *op. cit.*, pp. 204-05.
    113. BT, *ibid.*; cf. Langan, *op. cit.*, p. 48; Reinhardt, *op. cit.*, pp. 134-35.
    114. BT, *ibid.*
    115. Olson, *op. cit.*, p. 135.
    116. Cf. BT, pp. 211-19, 221-22; Langan, *op. cit.*, pp. 25-27, 48; Robert Morrison, *Primitive Existentialism* (New York: Philosophical Library, 1967), pp. 61-67.
    117. Richardson, *op. cit.*, p. 332; Olson, *op. cit.*, pp. 135-36.
    118. Cf. Molina, *Existentialism As Philosophy*, p. 67; Kockelmans, *op. cit.*, pp. 74-75; Langan, *op. cit.*, pp. 22-24.
    119. Although the more common rendering of *Angst* is *dread*, the English translators of *Sein und Zeit* have preferred to use the word *anxiety*.
    120. BT, p. 231; cf. Barrett, *Irrational Man*, pp. 225-27; Reinhardt, *op. cit.*, pp. 136-37; Richardson, *op. cit.*, pp. 72-74.
    121. William Richardson, "Heidegger's Critique of Science," NS, XLII, 4 (1968), 528-29; cf. Brock, *op. cit.*, pp. 61-64; Spiegelberg, *op. cit.*, I, p. 333; Gilson, Langan and Maurer, *op. cit.*, p. 149. "What makes me dread is wholly undeterminable, it cannot be pointed out. What threatens me does not approach me here or there; the dreadful is not really anywhere, but nevertheless it is so close that it takes my breath away."—Luijpen, *op. cit.*, p. 333.
    122. Cf. below, pp. 235-44.
    123. Macquarrie, *op. cit.*, p. 30; cf. Kockelmans, *op. cit.*, p. 82; Luijpen, *op. cit.*, pp. 334-40; Dinkler, *Martin Heidegger*, pp. 106-07; Langan, *op. cit.*, pp. 31ff.
    124. BT, p. 289. St. Augustine of Hippo, some 15 centuries ago, gave one of the most penetrating analyses of "being-toward-death" in his *De Civitate Dei*, when he said, "From the first moment that we find ourselves in a mortal body,

something happens within us which steadily leads us toward death. . . . Each one of us is nearer death a year hence than a year ago, nearer tomorrow than he was today. . . . Our entire lifetime is nothing but a racing toward death, in the course of which no one is permitted to stop for a little while or to slow down his walk; all are forced to keep in step, all are driven on to the same speed."—XIII, 10, quoted in Reinhardt, *op. cit.*, p. 137; cf. Blackham, *op. cit.*, 96-98; Harries, *op. cit.*, pp. 188-89.

125. BT, p. 232; cf. Spiegelberg, *op. cit.*, I, 331-32; Versenyi, *op. cit.*, pp. 18-20; Borzaga, *op. cit.*, pp. 158-59, Breisach, *op. cit.*, pp. 87-89; Demske, *op. cit.*, pp. 35-58, 192-96. "It is hard not to see in this transformation of death into a distinct modality of human being a final crowning of the voluntaristic effort to introduce an element of volition and of freedom into our relationship to what has always been regarded as the most unassimilable fact of human life."—Frederick Olafson, *Principles and Persons* (Baltimore and London: Johns Hopkins Press, 1970), p. 174.

126. Langan, *op. cit.*, p. 32; cf. Paul-Louis Landsberg, "The Experience of Death," in Natanson, *op. cit.*, pp. 205-07; Marias, *op. cit.*, pp. 433-34.

127. Kockelmans, *op. cit.*, p. 85; cf. Wyschogrod, *op. cit.*, pp. 103-06.

128. Luijpen, *op. cit.*, p. 341; cf. Brock, *op. cit.*, pp. 65-68.

129. BT, p. 354; cf. Wyschogrod, *op. cit.*, p. 107; Luijpen, *op. cit.*, pp. 340-41.

130. Bocheński, *op. cit.*, pp. 168-69; Macquarrie, *op. cit.*, pp. 32-33; Langan, *op. cit.*, pp. 35-38.

131. BT, p. 237; cf. Harries, *op. cit.*, pp. 183-87; Langan, *op. cit.*, pp. 28-31; Wyschogrod, *op. cit.*, pp. 61-67; Wild, *op. cit.*, pp. 100-03.

132. Copleston, *Contemporary Philosophy,* pp. 181-82; Barrett, *What is Existentialism?*, pp. 60-62; Naess, *op. cit.*, pp. 215-16; Landgrebe, *op. cit.*, pp. 46ff.

133. BT, p. 236; cf. Schmitt, *op. cit.*, 197ff. "The possible is what I can do; and Heidegger's point may be expressed as the view that the use of 'can' in statements of the form 'I can . . .' is unique and irreducible to any set of hypotheticals in which the causal relationship between certain types of events are set forth."—Olafson, *op. cit.*, p. 97. "The emphasis here is squarely put on the fact that it is possibilities that are definitive of the Person, these possibilities in turn being realizable or not realizable as the Person chooses."—Molina, *Sources of Existentialism as Philosophy*, p. 121.

134. Macquarrie, *Twentieth Century Religious Thought,* p. 353.

135. BT, p. 236.

136. Cf. above, pp. 211-12.

137. BT, pp. 236-237.

138. BT, p. 238; cf. Brock, *op. cit.*, pp. 49-51; King, *op. cit.*, pp. 136-39; Kockelmans, *op. cit.*, pp. 83-85; Macquarrie, *An Existentialist Theology,* pp. 112-16; Grene, *op. cit.*, pp. 26-27.

139. Cf. above, pp. 198-206.

140. Cf. above, pp. 202-06.

141. Cf. above, p. 210.

142. Cf. above, p. 214.

143. Cf. above, pp. 216-19.

144. Cf. above, p. 219.

145. Cf. above, p. 225.

146. Cf. above, p. 219.

147. Cf. BT, pp. 274-88; Borzaga, *op. cit.*, pp. 164-65; Vycinas, *op. cit.*, pp. 63-65; Bocheński, *op. cit.*, pp. 169-70; John Sallis. "World, Finitude. Temporality in the Philosophy of M. Heidegger," PT, IX, 2 (1965), 40-52.

148. Macquarrie, *Martin Heidegger,* p. 34.

149. *Ibid.*

150. Richardson, *Heidegger: Through Phenomenology to Thought,* p. 86.

151. BT, p. 376.

152. BT, p. 375; cf. Macquarrie, *An Existentialist Theology,* pp. 159-60; King, *op. cit.*, pp. 170-72.

153. BT, pp. 376-77; cf. Breisach, *op. cit.*, pp. 90-91; Roberts *op. cit.*, pp. 157-59; Blackham, *op. cit.*, pp. 99-101.

154. Claude Jeffré, "Bultmann on Kerygma and History," in O'Meara, *op. cit.*, p. 171.

155. Grene, *op. cit.*, p. 36; Kockelmans, *op. cit.*, p. 86; Langan, *op. cit.*, pp. 52-53.

156. BT, p. 374.

157. BT, p. 377; cf. Wyschogrod, *op. cit.*, pp. 63-64; Brock, *op. cit.*, pp. 77-81.

158. BT, p. 325; cf. Richardson, *op. cit.*, p. 86; Heinrich Rombach, "Reflections on Heidegger's Lecture 'Time and Being,'" PT, X, 1 (1966), 24-26.

159. Cf. Spiegelberg. *op. cit.*, I, 336. "The essence of Heidegger's conception of time, which may have been inspired by Plotinus, but has been extricated from Kant, can perhaps be summed up in this thesis: temporality is not something which can add to human existence; it is integral to human existing and to the acts, cognitions, and decisions which are elements of that existing and comprise its constituting 'moments.' "—Charles Sherover, *Heidegger, Kant and Time* (Bloomington and London: Indiana University Press, 1971), p. 212.

160. Cf. Spiegelberg, *ibid.*; Wild, *op. cit.*, pp. 103ff. "This temporality is very much intrinsic to him [DASEIN], *identical* with him: he it is who constitutes time in the first place."—Rahner, *op. cit.*, p. 134.

161. BT, pp. 375-76; cf. Brock, *op. cit.*, pp. 77-78. "As against the traditional conception, according to which the present, is itself something that is present in the present, i.e., as essent, it was suggested [*in Being and Time*] that time in the primordial sense is that in terms of which Being itself may be understood, in terms, that is, not of presence only but of the integral unity of future, past and present. . . . Time is the being of DASEIN and, as the ultimate horizon for the manifestation of anything as essent, identical with Being itself."— Mehta, *op. cit.*, pp. 235-36.

162. BT, pp. 378, 373; cf. Harries, *op. cit.*, pp. 187-88. "The future indeed plays a privileged part in constituting existential temporality."—Jeffré, *op. cit.*, p. 171.

163. BT, p. 373; cf. Grene, *op. cit.*, p. 37; Kockelmans, *op. cit.*, pp. 86-87; Harold Alderman, "Heidegger on Being Human," PT, XV, 1 (1971), 24-29.

164. Kockelmans, *ibid.*

165. BT, p. 374; cf. Sciacca, *op. cit.*, pp. 196-197; Schrag, *op. cit.*, p. 116.

166. BT, p. 428; cf. Bernard Rollin, "Heidegger's Philosophy of History in *Being and Time*," MS, XLIX, 2 (1972), 77-112. John Wild calls Heidegger's description of history and temporality "one of the most profound and original expressions of existentialist phenomenology."—*op. cit.*, p. 115.

167. BT, p. 430; cf. Martin Heidegger, *What Is A Thing?*, trans. W. B. Barton and Vera Deutsch, Gateway (Chicago: Henry Regnery Co., 1970), pp. 39ff; Spiegelberg, *op. cit.*, I, 337-38; Bocheński, *op. cit.*, 169-70; John Nota, *Phenomenology and History* (Chicago: Loyola University Press, 1967), pp. 18-20.

168. BT, p. 438; cf. Borzaga, *op. cit.*, pp. 166-67; Kohl, *op. cit.*, pp. 135-36; Macquarrie, *Existentialist Theology*, pp. 159-61.

169. Peukert, *op. cit.*, p. 209; cf. BT, p. 428. "History is possible for man because his temporality is not just a being within time (*Innerzeitigkeit*) but rather a being constituted by past, present and future in such a way that at any given moment, not only the present but the past and the future as well, are disclosed to him and are real to him."—Macquarrie, *op. cit.*, p. 160.

170. Wild, *op. cit.*, p. 114.

171. BT, p. 433; Macquarrie, *Martin Heidegger*, pp. 36-39; ———, *Existentialist Theology*, p. 160; Spiegelberg, *op. cit.*, I, 377-39. "The possibility of factual history or of historiological understanding, the very possibility of historiography as a science, depends for its basis upon the historicity of DASEIN, and not vice versa."—Seidel, *op. cit.*, p. 18.

172. Macquarrie, *op. cit.*, p. 162. "Men are not in a stream of history. . . . Possibility is the very heart of human history, as it is the guiding center of human care. The past that is the object of historical study is a past with a human future, and a future that we may share and repeat."—Wild, *op. cit.*, pp. 112-13.

173. Macquarrie, *Martin Heidegger*, p. 38; Richardson, *op. cit.*, pp. 89ff.

174. BT, p. 447; cf. Macquarrie, *The Scope of Demythologizing*, p. 89; ———, *Existentialist Theology*, p. 164; Vycinas, *op. cit.*, pp. 64-65.

175. Macquarrie, *Martin Heidegger*, pp. 39, 41; ———, *Existentialist Theology*, p. 163; John Anderson, "Truth, Process and Creature in Heidegger's Thought," in Frings, *op. cit.*, pp. 40-41.

176. Grene, *op. cit.*, pp. 120-21.

177. Cf. above, pp. 184ff.

178. Martin Heidegger, "What is Metaphysics?" in Brock, *op. cit.*, pp. 325-61. Henceforth WIM; cf. Brock's excellent introduction to the essay, "An Account of the Four Essays," pp. 202-31; John Walsh, "Heidegger's Understanding of Nothing-ness," *Cross Currents* (1963) 308ff; P. C. Smith, *op. cit.*, pp. 393ff.

179. WIM, p. 326.

180. WIM, p. 327.

181. WIM, p. 328; cf. Barrett, *What Is Existentialism?*, pp. 182-89.

182. WIM, p. 328; cf. Bocheński, *op. cit.*, pp. 171-72; Breisach, *op. cit.*, pp. 85-86; Naess, *op. cit.*, pp. 218-22.

183. WIM, *ibid.*

184. WIM, p. 329.

185. Cf. above, pp. 184-92.

186. Brock, *op. cit.*, p. 203. Brock claims that Heidegger's study of nothing-ness is another proof that Heidegger is genuinely meditating on Being. He further contends, "And not one of his [Heidegger's] readers who once grasps the meta-physical range of the problem of 'nothingness,' i.e., its preparatory character for the conceiving and unfolding of the problem of 'Being' could ever come to interpret Heidegger's approach as nihilistic."—p. 203.

187. WIM, p. 330.

188. *Ibid.*; cf. Richardson, *op. cit.*, pp. 196-97.

189. WIM, p. 331.

190. Brock, *op. cit.*, pp. 205-06.

191. Collins, *Existentialists*, p. 197. " 'Logical' negation (*Verneinung*), certain-ly an abiding characteristic of our normal thought processes, betokens some com-prehension of non-being. For it implies a pre-view of a 'not' that can become manifest."—Richardson, *op. cit.*, p. 199.

192. WIM, p. 333; Cf. Brock, *op. cit.*, p. 207.

193. Brock, *ibid.*; cf. Kockelmans, *op. cit.*, pp. 155-56.

194. Vycinas, *op. cit.*, p. 103.

195. Egon Vietta, *Die Seinsfrage bei Martin Heidegger* (Stuttgart: Curt Schwab, 1950), p. 84, trans, and quoted by Vycinas, *op. cit.*, *ibid.*

196. Richardson, *op. cit.*, pp. 200-01.

197. Sciacca, *op. cit.*, p. 201.

198. WIM, p. 334.

199. WIM, p. 335.
200. Cf. above, pp. 215-16.
201. WIM, p. 336. To use Werner Brock's example, dread can be likened to sense perception which makes it possible for us to grasp an object, i.e., Nothingness. —*op. cit.*, p. 211.
202. Cf. Vycinas, *op. cit.*, pp. 104-05.
203. Brock, *op. cit.*, pp. 213-15; cf. WIM, pp. 338-39.
204. WIM, p. 339; cf. Wyschogrod, *op. cit.*, p. 73.
205. WIM, p. 340; cf. Collins, *op. cit.*, pp. 198-99.
206. Richardson, *op. cit.*, p. 529. "It becomes swiftly apparent in the present essay [*What is Metaphysics*]—no matter what has been written about Heidegger's nihilism and independently of all his own intepretations—that he understands Being and Non-being to be one."—*Ibid.*, p. 200.
207. Martin Heidegger, *Zur Seinsfrage* (Frankfurt, 1950), pp. 220-23, trans. and quoted by Richardson, *op. cit.*, p. 530. "In the act of transcendence by which personal existence separates itself from what-is and even from its own brute existence and its solidified past, its freedom and its originative force lie in its nothingness, and it is then close to Being."—Blackham, *op. cit.*, p. 105; cf. Kockelmans, *op. cit.*, pp. 156-57.
208. Langan, *op. cit.*, pp. 92-93. Bocheński sees human existence related to nothingness in the following manner: "First, human existence has no ground; it originates in the abyss of nothingness; second, it culminates in death, which is another abyss of nothingness; third, the very being of human existence is an anticipation of death, of nothingness, it is intrinsically void."—*op. cit.*, p. 171.
209. WIM, p. 340.
210. Cf. above, pp. 192ff.
211. Spiegelberg, *op. cit.*, I, p. 288.
212. Macquarrie, *op. cit.*, pp. 41-42; Harries, *op. cit.*, pp. 194-95. "The turning in Heidegger's thought is a change of (a) perspective, in which the focus moves from the transcendence of DASEIN to being as the horizon of this transcendence, and (b) a change in the relation between being and DASEIN, in which being assumes the role of ontological primacy in the process of transcendence."—Demske, *op. cit.*, p. 179. On the other hand, cf. John Caputo, "The Rose is without the Why: the Later Heidegger," PT, XV, 1 (1971), 3-15.
213. Spiegelberg, *op. cit.*, I, 312. "The emphasis of the later Heidegger is not upon man as the active center of Being, but upon Being itself as that which perpetually claims man. Man is not only *ek-sistenz*—the creature who actively transcends himself—but also an *in-sistenz*—a being who, however he may stand beyond himself, must always stand within Being itself."—Barrett, *op. cit.*, p. 179; cf. Demske, *op. cit.*, pp. 92-117.
214. Heidegger, *Brief in Platons Lehre von der Wahrheit*, p. 72, trans. and quoted by Spiegelberg, *op. cit.*, I, 310. "There is evidence that a new formulation of 'Time and Being' exists and will eventually be published."—John Anderson in Martin Heidegger, *Discourse on Thinking*, trans. by John Anderson and E. Hans Freund (New York: Harper and Row, 1966), p. 18, note 3.
215. Cf. Borzaga, *op. cit.*, pp. 177ff; Harries, *op. cit.*, pp. 196ff. "Heidegger's aim is no longer to clear a path from anthropology to Being. Today he wants to comprehend human thought of the possibility of man's questioning about Being by an opposite approach: by beginning with Being (of the *Wahrheit des Seins*) which reveals itself, opens itself and speaks first. The problem of the foundation (*Grund*) which was originally posed from the side of Being. That is to say that '*it is no longer a problem.*' It is an 'advent' or a 'happening,' a sort of 'grace'; it is what renders human questioning in general possible."—Pierre Thévenaz, *What is Phenomenology?* (Chicago: Quadrangle Books, 1962), p. 156.
216. L. Glenn Gray, "Poets and Thinkers: Their Kindred Roles in the Philosophy of Martin Heidegger," in Lee and Mandelbaum, *op. cit.*, p. 101.
217. Cf. Kockelmans, *op. cit.*, pp. 167-69; Charles Scott, "Heidegger's Attempt to Communicate a Mystery," PT, X, 2 (1966), 135ff.
218. Cf. William Earle, James Edie and John Wild, *Christianity and Existentialism* (Evanston: Northwestern University, 1963), pp. 134-35; Rudolph Gerber, "Focal Points in Recent Heidegger Scholarship," NS, XLII, 4 (1968), 572-73; Donald Cress, "Heidegger's Criticism of 'Entitative Metaphysics' in His Later Works," IPQ, XII 1 (1972), 69-86.
219. Martin Heidegger, *Identity and Difference*, p. 52, trans. and quoted by Kockelmans, *op. cit.*, pp. 165-66; cf. Collins, *Religious Themes in Existentialism*, pp. 30-31.
220. Cf. above, pp. 184ff; Joseph Kockelmans, "Language, Meaning and Ek-Sistence," in F. J. Smith, *op. cit.*, pp. 94-121.
221. Heidegger, *op. cit.*, pp. 70-71; cf. Breisach, *op. cit.*, p. 93.
222. Kockelmans, *Martin Heidegger*, p. 167; cf. Spiegelberg, *op. cit.*, I, pp. 339-49.
223. "The voice of the holy calls the poet to speak. The poet can reveal its meaning because this meaning has revealed itself to him."—Harries, *op. cit.*, p. 196; cf. Seidel, *op. cit.*, pp. 144-52; Lambert van de Water, "The Work of Art, Man and Being: A Heideggerian Theme," IPQ, IX, 2 (1969), 214-35.
224. Martin Heidegger, "Hölderlin and the Essence of Poetry," in Brock, *op. cit.*, pp. 281-82. "Poetry not only finds truth, it even establishes it, says Heidegger . . . poetry is a parallel enterprise to thinking, in its highest achievements even superior to thinking."—Spiegelberg, *op. cit.*, I, 343; cf. Rouhiczek, *op. cit.*, pp. 132-33.

225.   Cf. Reinhardt, *op. cit.*, pp. 141-42, note 23; Borzaga, *op. cit.*, pp. 188-89; Langan, *op. cit.*, pp. 108-16; Barrett, *Irrational Man*, pp. 237-38. "After the disappointment in political involvement, Hölderlin becomes for Heidegger the guardian, exponent and prophet of the history of being. The similarity of Hölderlin's own situation helps to explain this alliance."—Karlfried Gründer, "Heidegger's Critique of Science in its Historical Background," PT, VII, 1 (1963), 23; cf. Stanley Hopper, "On the Naming of the Gods in Hölderlin and Rilke," in Michalson, *op. cit.*, pp. 148-90.

226.   Reinhardt, *op. cit.*, p. 142; cf. John Smith, "The Experience of the Holy and the Idea of God," in *Phenomenology in America*, ed. by James Edie (Chicago: Quadrangle Books, 1967), pp. 295-306.

227.   Heinemann, *op. cit.*, p. 107; cf. Gilson, Langan, and Maurer, *op. cit.*, pp. 150-52.

228.   Blackham, *op. cit.*, p. 103. "But if this is the case [that the obstacle of metaphysics must be surmounted], if Being is nothingness and foundation, if it speaks first and if man must efface himself before it, then human intelligence is no longer a problem. To this unquestioned intelligence there inescapably corresponds a sort of absolute thought: the effort of the thinker 'does not tend so much to think as to be silent' or 'to let itself be thought by Being,' so to speak. It is Being that founds thought: the only question is to open and to be opened. But is a philosophy of *openness* still philosophy or is it revelation? In any case, it is no longer metaphysics."—Thévenaz, *op. cit.*, pp. 157-58.

229.   Gerber, *op. cit.*, p. 571; cf. Hans Jonas, "Heidegger and Theology," *The Review of Metaphysics*, XVIII (1964) 207-33.

230.   Versenyi, *op. cit.*, pp. 172-73.

231.   Thévenaz, *op. cit.*, p. 158.

232.   Roubiczek, *op. cit.*, p. 132.

233.   Jean Paul Sartre, *Existentialism is a Humanism* in Kaufmann, *Existentialism from Dostoevsky to Sartre*, p. 287 (emphasis added).

234.   Heidegger, *Brief über Humanismus*, trans. and quoted by Langan, *op. cit.*, p. 207.

235.   Collins, *Religious Themes of Existentialism*, p. 28.

236.   Langan, *op. cit.*, p. 208.

237.   *Ibid.*

238.   *Ibid.*, pp. 208-09. "While theologians speak of our alienation from God, Heidegger suggests that our tragedy consists in the oblivion of Being. It is hard to give any precise meaning to this suggestion, and Heidegger does not exert himself in this direction, but even in the absence of any exact meaning, or perhaps owing to the absence of an exact meaning, his suggestion is evocative: it arouses associations with estrangement from God, without committing Heidegger to any particular belief."—Kaufmann, *From Shakespeare to Existentialism*, p. 363.

239.   Langan, *op. cit.*, p. 208.

240.   Kuhn, *op. cit.*, p. 144.

241.   Sciacca, *op. cit.*, p. 203.

242.   Löwith, *op. cit.*, pp. 68-69 (emphasis added).

243.   Versenyi, *op. cit.*, p. 164.

244.   Fabro, *op. cit.*, pp. 936-37.

245.   BMM, p. 168.

246.   Luijpen, *op. cit.*, pp. 349-50.

247.   Dietrich Bonhoeffer, *Akt und Sein*, Transzendentalphilosophie und Ontologie in der systematischen Theologie (Munich, 1964), p. 50, trans. and quoted by Fabro, *op. cit.*, p. 937.

248.   Marcel, *Problematic Man*, p. 115.

249.   Langan, *op. cit.*, p. 234.

250.   Versenyi, *op. cit.*, p. 195.

251.   Gerber, *op. cit.*, p. 574.

252.   Collins, *Existentialists*, p. 208.

253.   Wyschogrod, *op. cit.*, p. 140.

254.   Sciacca, *op. cit.*, p. 285.

255.   Heinemann, *op. cit.*, p. 108.

CHAPTER VI

1.   Of his maternal grandfather, Sartre wrote, "Charles chose to teach German. He defended a thesis on Hans Sachs, adopted the direct method, of which he later called himself the inventor, published in collaboration with M. Simonnot, a highly esteemed *Deutsches Lesebuch*, and was rapidly promoted: Mâcon, Lyons, Paris."—Jean Paul Sartre, *The Words*, trans. Bernard Frechtman (New York: Fawcett World Library, 1966), p. 6.

2.   *Ibid.*, p. 23.

3.   *Ibid.*, p. 14.

4.   *Ibid.*; cf. Germaine Brée, *Camus and Sartre*, Delta Book (New York: Dell Publishing Co., 1972). pp. 55, 59-61.

5.   *Words*, pp. 13, 15; cf. Philip Thody, *Sartre* (New York: Charles Scribner's Sons, 1971), pp. 8-9.

6.   *Words*, p. 62.

7.   *Ibid.*, pp. 16, 63; cf. Régis Jolivet, *Sartre: The Theology of the Absurd*, trans. Wesley Piersol (Westminster: Newman Press, 1967), pp. 33-34.

8.   *Words*, pp. 30-31. Martin Buber's childhood years were likewise greatly influenced by his grandfather, the scholarly Solomon Buber with, however, much more favorable results.

9. Marc Beigbeder, *L'Homme Sartre* (Paris, 1947), p. 14.

10. After having passed his "Licence," the equivalent of an M.A. degree, Sartre then applied for the "agrégation," which means admission to the group of French professors who are qualified to teach in the lycées and universities of France. Admission to the group is possible only through examination, and it is this examination which Sartre failed in 1928.

11. In his autobiography, *The Words*, Sartre admits that he was Antoine Roquentin. He writes, "At the age of thirty, I executed the masterstroke of writing in *Nausea*—quite sincerely, believe me—about the bitter and unjustified existence of my fellowmen and of exonerating my own. I *was* Roquentin; I used him to show without complacency, the texture of my life. At the same time, I was *I*, chronicler of Hell, a glass and steel photomicroscope peering at my own protoplasmic juices. Later, I gaily demonstrated that man is impossible: I was impossible myself and differed from the others only by the mandate to give expression to that impossibility, which was thereby transfigured and became my most personal possibility, the object of my mission, the springboard of my glory. I was a prisoner of that obvious contradiction, but I did not see it, I saw the world through it. Fake to the marrow of my bones and hoodwinked, I joyfully wrote about our unhappy state. Dogmatic though I was, I doubted everything except that I was the elect of doubt. I built with one hand and destroyed with the other, and I regarded anxiety as the guarantee of my security: I was happy."—pp. 157-58; cf. Thody, *op. cit.*, p. 41.

12. Henceforth BN.

13. Simone de Beauvoir, *La force de l'age* (Paris: Gallimard, 1960), p. 440, trans. and quoted by Maurice Cranston, *Jean Paul Sartre* (New York: Grove Press, 1962), p. 8.

14. Of this period of Nazi occupation, Sartre wrote, "We were never more free than under the Nazi occupation. We had lost all our rights, beginning with the right to speak. We were insulted daily and had to bear these insults with silence. On one pretext or another—as workers, Jews, political prisoners—Frenchmen were deported. . . . And because of all this we were free: precisely because the Nazi poison was seeping in our thoughts, every true thought was a victory. . . . Every instant we lived to the full meaning of that banal little phrase 'All men are mortal.' The choice that each of us made of his life and his being was a genuine choice because it was made in the presence of death."—*Situations*, 6 vols. (Paris: Gallimard, 1947-1965), III, II, trans. and quoted by Cranston, *op. cit.*, p. 6; cf. James Sheridan, *Sartre: The Radical Conversion* (Athens, Ohio: Ohio University Press, 1969), p. 15.

15. On the Sartre-Camus debate, cf. Wilfrid Desan, *The Marxism of Jean Paul Sartre*, Anchor Book (Garden City: Doubleday and Co., 1966), pp. 20-21. Sartre's attempts to effect a doctrinal liaison between atheistic existentialism and Marxism are too intricate and involved for an introductory volume such as ours. Interested students can consult with profit four excellent works on the subject, viz., Desan, *op. cit.*, Walter Odajnyk, *Marxism and Existentialism*, Anchor Book (Garden City: Doubleday and Co., 1965); George Novack, *Existentialism versus Marxism* (New York: Dell Publishing Co., 1966); Raymond Aron, *Marxism and the Existentialists*, Clarion Book (New York: Simon and Schuster, 1970).

Odajnyk's brief description of Sartre's failure is to the point. He writes, "Instead of adding a helpful dose of free and creative existentialism to deterministic and stultifying Marxism, Sartre has managed to do the opposite; he has buried existentialism in a Marxism of his own making, and in the process he has lost precisely those concepts that he believed Marxism required if it were to serve as a true and complete philosophy for modern times—the free subjective, creative and purposeful individual, moral responsibility, and personal humanism."—*op. cit.*, p. 170.

16. "Day after day and all day long I set myself up against Sartre, and in our discussions, I was simply not in his class. . . . In the end, I had to admit I was beaten; besides, I had realized, in the course of our discussions, that many of my opinions were based only in prejudice, dishonesty, or hastily formed concepts, that my reasoning was at fault, and that my ideas were in a muddle. 'I'm no longer sure *what* I think, nor whether I can be said to think at all,' I noted with a sense of anticlimax."—Simone de Beauvoir, *Memoirs of a Dutiful Daughter*, trans. James Kirup (New York: Popular Library, 1963), p. 336.

Curtis Cate writes of Simone in the following words: "And when at the age of 20, she finally entered France's foremost teaching college, the prestigious École Normale Supérieure, it was the madcap fantasy, the irrepressible wit, the inexhaustible inventiveness (everything from scabrous ditties to comic drawings of Leibnitz) ('bathing with the monads') which drew her to that superlative philosophical mountebank, that genius of intellectual juggling, the capricious, unpredictable, ebullient Jean Paul Sartre. . . . Sartre, who was twenty-three when they first met in 1929, felt that he had to expand his intimate acquaintance of womankind beyond the cramped horizons of monogamy if he was to be a great author he was burning to become. He thus insisted from the start that while their own love was necessary, it had to make room for other which (in a mischievous distortion of Leibnitz) he termed 'contingent' amours."—Curtis Cate, "Europe's First Feminist Has Changed the Second Sex," *New York Times Magazine*, CXXI (July 11, 1971) 37-38.

17. Cranston, *op. cit.*, p. 6.

18. Simone de Beauvoir, *Force of Circumstance*, trans. Richard Howard (New York: G. Putnam's Sons, 1965), p. 653. Some of Simone de Beauvoir's better known works include: *The Second Sex, She Came To Stay, The Mandarins, Memoirs of a Dutiful Daughter, Prime of Life, Force of Circumstance, Ethics of Ambiguity, Old Age*.

19. de Beauvoir, *Force of Circumstance*, p. 658.

20. "People," *Time*, January 15, 1965, p. 36.

21. "He regards God's non-existence as a postulate, a freely taken attitude that is not necessarily forced upon him by the actual situation of man. Atheism is the emotional a priori corresponding to the theoretical absolutizing of the phenomenological reduction."—Collins, *Existentialists*, p. 70; cf. Bourke, *op. cit.*, II, 194-95; Reinhardt, *op. cit.*, pp. 156-76; Joseph Kockelmans, *Contemporary European Ethics*, Anchor Book (Garden City: Doubleday and Co., 1972), pp. 265-66.

22. Cf. above, pp. 192-95.

23. Cf. above, pp. 198-202.

24. Cf. Spiegelberg, *op. cit.*, II, 472; Bocheński, *op. cit.*, p. 174. "*In Being and Nothingness*, Sartre's basic categories are Hegelian: they are taken mainly from *Phenomenology*, with important supplementation from the *Logic*; for-itself and in-itself, consciousness and self-consciousness, being and nothingness. . . . However, the use to which Sartre puts his Hegelian categories is un- and even anti-Hegelian. His is a truncated dialectic without synthesis, without reconciliation . . . the in-itself and the for-itself are irreconcilable; their opposite is unmediatable."—George Kline, "Existentialist Rediscovery of Hegel and Marx," in *Sartre: A Collection of Critical Essays*, ed. Mary Warnock, Anchor Book (Garden City: Doubleday and Co., 1971), pp. 297-99.

25. Cf. above, pp. 195-98; Samuel Stumpf, *Philosophy, History and Problems* (New York: McGraw Hill Book Co., 1971), pp. 466-67.

26. Cf. above, p. 89.

27. Jean Paul Sartre, *Existentialism Is a Humanism*, trans. Philip Mairet (London: Methuen and Co., 1960), p. 26. This translation is also available in Languilli, *op. cit.*, pp. 391-416 and in Kaufmann, *Existentialism from Dostoevsky to Sartre*, pp. 287-311. Sartre is in error concerning Karl Jasper's religious affiliation.

28. Cf. Heidegger, *Brief über dem Humanismus* and above, p. 253; Étienne Gilson, "The Idea of God and the Difficulties of Atheism," PT, XIII, 2 (1969), 174-205.

29. Sartre, *op. cit.*, p. 56. "Sartre is a convinced atheist. . . . His very philosophical conception is built upon the impossibility of the existence of God. His thought is intentionally and brutally opposed to God."—Spier, *op. cit.*, p. 64; cf. Morton White, *The Age of Analysis*, Mentor Book (New York: New American Library of World Literature, 1964), pp. 120-22.

30. Sartre, *op. cit.*, pp. 27-28; cf. Roger Shinn, *The Existentialist Posture* (New York: Associated Press, 1959), p. 75. "We here find ourselves in the presence of a man who not only explicitly declares himself an atheist, but who claims—very naively, one must admit,—to have furnished the proof of the non-existence of God. One could also show without difficulty that this pretension is incompatible with the profound exigency which is at the heart of the philosophies of existence." Marcel, *Problematic Man*, p. 115.

31. Spier, *op. cit.*, p. 27; Cranston, *op. cit.*, pp. 41ff.

32. Spier, *op. cit.*, p. 28. "By Sartre's well known definition 'existence precedes essence' is meant that we can never say what a person is, because he is always in the process of becoming. The term essence includes in its connotation, the notion that man is subject to laws, rules and fixed norms to which he more or less responds. Existentialism has radically broken with such a view. Man is nothing because he exists. His existence precedes his essence, because as free creating subjectivity, man is also the origin of his own law, rule and meaning."—*Ibid.*, pp. 69-70.

33. "Two kinds of being are distinguished by Sartre: *être en-soi*, to be in-itself, is the reality of a static *thing*, the being of anything inanimate, with no openness to be anything else; and *être pour-soi*, which is to be consciously, to be human in the sense that the subject is able to be separated from himself, to be pregnant with dynamic potentiality. It will be evident why 'ambiguity' is a constant theme in Sartre; he feels that there was always internal and contrary tension implicit in the human person."—Bourke, *op. cit.*, II, 204.

34. "I must admit to a particular dislike of the pair of Hegelian terms used by Sartre which can only be translated into English as 'in-itself' and 'for-itself.' I have been very tempted to translate them by 'things' and 'consciousness.' "—Anthony Manser, *Sartre: A Philosophic Study* (New York: Oxford University Press, 1967), p. 45; cf. Jean Wahl, *A Short History of Existentialism*, trans. Forrest Williams and Stanley Maron (New York: Philosophical Library, 1949), pp. 28-29; Colin Wilson, *Introduction to the New Existentialism* (Boston: Houghton Mifflin Co., 1960), pp. 58ff.

35. BN, pp. lx-lxii. "Thus consciousness and the self do not have an independent existence; it is the object of consciousness which defines it."—Thomas Molnar, *Sartre: Ideologue of Our Time* (New York: Funk and Wagnalls, 1968). p. 50; cf. Robert Cumming. *The Philosophy of Jean Paul Sartre*, Modern Library (New York: Random House, 1966), pp. 10ff; Stephen Dinan, "Intentionality in the Introduction to Being and Nothingness," in *Research in Phenomenology*, I (1971), 91-118.

36. Cf. Blackham, *op. cit.*, pp. 43ff; René Albérès, *Jean Paul Sartre: Philosopher Without Faith*, trans. Wade Baskin (New York: Philosophical Library, 1961), p. 51. "If everything is exterior to consciousness, *consciousness is not anything, it is nothingness*. It is more bare than a *tabula rasa*. . . . On the one side there is being, the fulness which is everything (being-in-itself); on the other is consciousness which breaks itself away from being, which becomes unstuck, which is nothingness or 'being-for-itself.' "—Pierre Thévenaz, *What Is Phenomenology?* (Chicago: Quadrangle Books, 1962), p. 70.

37. BN, p. lxii; cf. Justus Streller, *Jean Paul Sartre: To Freedom Condemned,* trans. Wade Baskin (New York: Philosophical Library, 1960), pp. 27-31; Wilde and Kimmel, *op. cit.,* pp. 218-19.

38. Norman Greene, *Jean Paul Sartre: The Existentialist Ethic* (Ann Arbor: University of Michigan Press, 1963), p. 17. "For Sartre, the *pour-soi,* or human mind, contains nothing. Indeed, in a way, it is nothing but a force, immediately conscious of itself and of the world, a force which knows its capacity for change and self-denial and wishes to escape from it. But it does not wish, in escaping, to lose its self-awareness and longs rather for that moment when it will coincide as absolutely with itself as the *en-soi* does, while still retaining that self-awareness which the *en-soi* lacks. This is, Sartre repeats throughout *L'Être et le Néant,* a self defeating and self-contradictory ambition."—Thody, *op. cit.,* p. 71; cf. Wesley Barnes, *The Philosophy and Literature of Existentialism* (Woodbury, N.Y.: Barrows Educational Series, 1968), p. 211; Molina, *Existentialism as Philosophy,* pp. 89ff.

39. Bocheński, *op. cit.,* p. 177. "Through crisis 'Being-for-itself' is continually active, trying to escape from itself. This 'Being-for-itself' expresses its life principle by carving out of the 'Being-in-itself' all the multiple living and non-living experience of the world."—Barnes, *op. cit.,* p. 72. "The human intellect is but a lacuna in the solid expanse of a meaningless, unconscious being that transcends it in all directions, a metaphysical fissure that yawns for a brief span of years and then is covered over by the mysterious event known as death."—Joseph Wieczynski, "A Note on Jean Paul Sartre: Monist or Dualist," PT, XII, 3 (1968), 186.

40. Greene, *op. cit.,* p. 26; cf. Reinhardt, *op. cit.,* pp. 160ff; Roubiczek, *op. cit.,* p. 131. "Sartre's argument is that 'man defines himself by his project.' In other words, we each make ourselves what we are by what we do. No one has any *essence.* A man's being is the history of his achievements."—Maurice Cranston, *The Quintessence of Sartrism,* Torchbook (New York and Evanston: Harper and Row, 1971), p. 19; cf. Douglas Greenlee, "Sartre: Presuppositions of Freedom," PT, XII, 3 (1968), 178-79.

41. Blackham, *op. cit.,* p. 112. "A man defines himself by his project. The true structure of a life is this immediate relation, beyond the given and the constituted with other-than-self. This ceaseless production of self by work and praxis . . . our needs, feelings, and even our most abstract thoughts . . . are in a perpetual state of being-beyond-themselves-towards. This is what we call existence, and by this term we clearly do not mean a stable substance reposing within itself but a perpetual disequilibrium."—R.D. Laing and D. G. Cooper, *Reason and Violence: A Decade of Sartre's Philosophy,* 1950-1960 (New York: Random House, 1971), p. 62; cf. Richard Beis, "Atheistic Existentialist Ethics: A Critique," MS, XLII, 2 (1965), 156-57.

42. Cranston, *Jean Paul Sartre,* p. 45. In answer to a journalist who was interviewing him on the subject of existentialism, Sartre had the following to say: "I do not believe that green peas spring up and grow round in accordance with the idea of green peas, and I think that man does not grow in accordance with a preconceived idea called *human nature.* He grows, that's all. It is in throwing himself into the world, in suffering and struggling there, that he defines himself bit by bit. And the definition always remains open. One can in no way say what *this* man is before his death, nor what humanity is before it has disappeared."—Jean Paul Sartre, *Figaro litteraire,* April 13, 1946, quoted in Roger Mehl, *Images of Man,* trans. James Farley (Richmond: John Knox Press, 1965), p. 28.

43. Collins, *Existentialism,* p. 66; cf. Stumpf, *op. cit,* pp. 466ff.

44. BH, pp. 106-07; cf. Beis, *op. cit.,* p. 174.

45. Alfred Stern, *Sartre: His Philosophy and Existential Psychoanalysis,* Delta Books (New York: Dell Publishing Co., 1967), p. 51.

46. Frederick Copleston, *Existentialism,* Public Lecture delivered at Saint Joseph College, West Hartford, April 22, 1967.

47. Paul Foulquié, *Existentialism,* trans. Kathleen Raine (London: Dennis Dobson, 1963), p. 64.

48. Jean Paul Sartre, *Reflexions sur la question juive* (Paris: Morihien, 1947), p. 76, trans. and quoted by Wilfrid Desan, *The Tragic Finale: An Essay on the Philosophy of Jean Paul Sartre,* Torchbook (New York: Harper and Bros., 1960), pp. 162-63.

49. Sartre, *Existentialism is a Humanism,* pp. 45-46.

50. Desan, *op. cit.,* pp. 163-64.

51. Régis Jolivet, *Les Doctrines Existentialistes de Kierkegaard à Sartre* (Paris, 1948), p. 23, trans. and quoted by Desan, *op. cit.,* p. 164.

52. Roberts, *op. cit.,* p. 218.

53. Desan, *op. cit.,* p. 162.

54. BN, p. 553.

55. Aimé Patri, *"Remarques sur une nouvelle doctrine de la Liberté,"* Deucalion, I: 79 (1946), quoted in Desan, *op. cit.,* p. 163.

56. Desan, *op. cit.,* p. 162.

57. Roubiczek, *op. cit.,* pp. 124-25.

58. René Lafarge, *Jean Paul Sartre: His Philosophy,* trans. Marina Smyth-Kok (Notre Dame: Notre Dame University Press, 1970), p. 178.

59. Paul Tillich, "Existentialism and Psychotherapy," *Review of Existential Psychology and Psychiatry,* I, no. 1, p. 9, quoted in Jean Paul Sartre, *Existential Psychoanalysis* (Chicago: Henry Regnery, 1962), pp. 6-7.

60. BH, p. 106.

61. BN, p. 74; cf. Bocheński, *op. cit.,* pp. 174-75; Foulquié, *op. cit.,* pp. 74-75.

62. Jean Paul Sartre, *Imagination* (Ann Arbor: University of Michigan Press,

1962), p. 1; cf. Desan, *op. cit.*, pp. 11ff; Lafarge, *op. cit.*, pp. 32-34, 89; Mihalich, *op. cit.*, pp. 14-15.

63.   Cf. Manser, *op. cit.*, pp. 45-48; Stern, *op. cit.*, pp. 30ff; Odajnyk, *op. cit.*, pp. 10ff.

64.   Sartre, *Nausea*, p. 180. "Allowing for dramatic license, these words contain Sartre's basic themes—viz., that existing is 'absurd' (*de trop*) in that it cannot be explained or justified; that existing itself is fraught with confusion and bad faith; and that death, too, is *de trop* and wholly beyond anticipation and preparation."—Mihalich, *op. cit.*, p. 14.

65.   Jolivet, *op. cit.*, p. 24; cf. Kuhn, *op. cit.*, pp. 144-45; Gallagher, *op. cit.*, pp. 128ff.

66.   Jean Paul Sartre, *The Age of Reason*, trans. Eric Sutton (New York: Bantam Books, 1959), p. 48. For a critique of Sartre's notion of the For-itself and the In-itself, cf. Luijpen and Koren, *op. cit.*, pp. 43-44.

67.   Barrett, *Irrational Man*, p. 246; cf. Jacques Salvan, *To Be and Not To Be: An Analysis of Jean Paul Sartre's Ontology* (Detroit: Wayne State University Press, 1962), p. 29; Jolivet, *op. cit.*, p. 37; Nathan Scott, *The Unquiet Vision: Mirrors of Man in Existentialism* (New York and Cleveland: World Publishing Co., 1969), p. 139.

68.   Joseph Mihalich, "Jean Paul Sartre," in Patka, *op. cit.*, p. 128.

69.   BN, pp. 89-90. "That which is sought (valued) is the firmness of thing-like being (*être-en-soi*) combined with the transparency of consciousness (*être-pour-soi*): a state of complete lucidity and complete changelessness. But this combination is patently unattainable. The self which is excluded by the opaque absurdity of matter on one side, falls short on the other of this magnetic totality, which is unattainable because it is self-contradictory. Such a condition, that of being en-soi-pour-soi, . . . is the condition of being God."—Iris Murdock, *Sartre: Romantic Rationalist* (New Haven: Yale University Press, 1961), pp. 57-58.

70.   BN, pp. 575-76.

71.   BN, p. 566. "Man's desire is therefore to be in-and-for-itself, to become the proof and foundation of his self (*an ens causa sui*); he wishes to free himself from contingency, that is, to become God."—Streller, *op. cit.*, p. 14. "For Sartre, God is a mere concept—that of a *pour-soi* which would simultaneously be *en-soi*, that of a self which would be a thing, of a subject-object, of emptiness-fulness, of activity-passivity. Manifestly, such a concept is contradictory and nothing corresponds to it in reality. But the human existent inevitably and inexorably fabricates it because of the absurd, frustrating unrest built into the very nature of consciousness and knowledge."—Leo Sweeney, *A Metaphysics of Authentic Existentialism* (Englewood Cliffs: Prentice-Hall, 1965) p. 25, note 20; cf. Wieczynski, *op. cit.*, pp. 187-88.

72.   BN, p. 615; cf. Breisach, *op. cit.*, pp. 105-06; Spier, *op. cit.*, pp. 64-65. "For Sartre, God is in the first place, the *'artisan supérieur,'* a sort of super *homo faber* who in the act of 'producing' man pre-empts him of all possibility toward freedom. God is in the second place 'absolute start' (*régard absolu*) under the impact of which all men turn into objects of the world. In the third place, God is the contradictory identification of 'in-itself' and 'for-itself'. . . . Certainly the God of Christian religion could not truthfully be defined in this way."—William Luijpen, *Phenomenology and Humanism* (Pittsburgh: Duquesne University Press, 1966), p. 92.

73.   Collins, *Existentialists*, p. 72; cf. Molnar, *op. cit.*, pp. 48-49. "Because Sartre depends uncritically upon Feuerbach and Marx for the principle of limiting the real to the active whole of man-working-in-nature, his remarks on God and religion have a somewhat fantastic quality about them. Within his system, the only valid significance for the term 'God' is that of designating the basic human project of identifying reflection and matter, history and matter. Since the merger of these components cannot be achieved without collapsing the structure of reality, at least as described by Sartre and Marx, the former judges that our religious tendency is self-destroying and that man himself is a useless passion, insofar as he continues to strive after transcendence and God."—Collins, *Crossroads in Philosophy*, p. 51.

74.   Stern, *op. cit.*, p. 150. "Sartre's literary productions, though interesting and brilliant, are anything but engaging. The air of decadence which pervades them and their preoccupation with diseased pleasures, lurid incidents and promiscuous love suggest cynicism rather than a constructive philosophy."—Kuhn, *op. cit.*, p. 10.

75.   Sartre, *Existentialism is a Humanism*, p. 45.

76.   Cumming, *op. cit.*, pp. 25-26.

77.   BN, p. 254.

78.   *Ibid.*, p. 255. "The decisive moment when he becomes a subject for me arrives when his gaze turns from our common world to me, and I experience the shock of being looked at, as it occurs especially in the shame that goes with the situation of being surprised in an embarrassing situation. This is the experience which establishes the existence of the other as definite, in fact as indubitable."—Spiegelberg, *op. cit.*, II, 506.

79.   Jean Paul Sartre, *The Reprieve*, trans. Eric Sutton (New York: Alfred Knopf, 1947), p. 135, quoted in La farge, *op. cit.*, p. 118 and Desan, *op. cit.*, p 67, note 10.

80.   BN, p. 288.

81.   *Ibid.*, p. 260-61.

82.   *Ibid.*, pp. 222, 261. "The pattern changes fundamentally when we see him and recognize him as a human being. For now we see him as a being with a gaze looking at the same objects we ourselves see. This means that these cease to be merely our private objects. He too is now a potential focus for them. To this extent, they 'escape' me, as though a leakage."—Spiegelberg, *op. cit.*, II, 506.

83.   BN, pp. 288-89.
84.   Mehl, op. cit., p. 30.
85.   Sartre, The Reprieve, p. 405-07.
86.   BN, p. 364. Robert Olson disagrees with Sartre's assumption that the look or glance is the basis for conflict between two human beings. He writes, "Clearly Sartre's 'the look' is not a basic ontological fact from which all conflict is derived and in terms of which conflict must be defined. A moment's reflection will reveal that we do not enter into conflict with one another because we look at one another. . . . 'The look' is not even a wholly apt metaphor or symbol for conflict. There is nothing particularly upsetting or conflict-generating in, say, the look of an adoring mother or the look of an admiring crowd."—Olson, op. cit., p. 187.
87.   Cf. above, pp. 12-13.
88.   Cf. above, pp. 203-06.
89.   "The distinctiveness of Sartre's position is that he regards conflict, not merely as a necessary element in human relations, but as the very foundation of human relations. . . . Sartre contends that the essence of the relations between consciousnesses is not the Mitsein; it is conflict."—Olson, op. cit., pp. 183-84.
90.   BN, p. 376. "He [Sartre] takes from Hegel the dialectic of master and serf . . . and uses it to construct a psychology in which love between people is always deformed into mastering and being mastered. He is able to do this because he sees an ultimate distinction between my being a subject (what I necessarily am for myself) and my being an object (what I necessarily am for others)."—Alisdair Macintyre, "Existentialism," in Sartre, ed. Mary Warnock, Anchor Book (Garden City: Doubleday and Co., 1971), p. 30.
91.   Vincent Miceli, The Gods of Atheism (New Rochelle: Arlington House, 1971), p. 229; cf. Cranston, Quintessence of Sartrism, pp. 42-43.
92.   BN, pp. 376-77.
93.   Jean Paul Sartre, No Exit, trans. Stuart Gilbert (New York: Alfred Knopf, 1948); cf. Francis Jeanson, "Pessimism and Optimism in Sartre's Thought," in Warnock, op. cit., pp. 176-85.
94.   BN, p. 377.
95.   Barrett, Irrational Man, p. 257.
96.   Sciacca, op. cit., p. 270. "If, therefore, I make someone else an object of my regard, I necessarily treat him as something that is now an object for me; in so doing, I impose myself on him. I manifest not love but sadism. If, to correct this, I try to make myself an object of the other's regard, I equally destroy the possibility of love, for now I substitute masochism. Imprisoned within the cycle of sadism and masochism, what way out can there be?"—Macintyre, op. cit., p. 31.
97.   BN, p. 377.
98.   Ibid., p. 378. "Since the subjectivity of one is exclusive of the objectivity of the other, the attempt to gain recognition as a free consciousness from another's consciousness is doomed to failure. In despair, one may decide to remain an object for the other. This is masochism."—Salvan, op. cit., p. 90.
99.   BN, 378-79. "But masochism is also doomed to fail, since that object that I wished to be, I will be only for another and never for myself. My conscience inexorably sends me back to the anguish of my subjectivity."—Jolivet, Sartre: Theology of the Absurd, p. 83.
100.   Friedman, To Deny Our Nothingness, p. 260.
101.   BN, p. 394. "Desire . . . seeks to compass the same object by merging; unable to overcome the opposite number, I try to drag him or her with me into fleshiness. . . . I seek to 'en-glue' his liberty in his flesh, to capture it like a wolf in the sheep pen, like the armed men in the Trojan horse."—Ussher, op. cit., pp. 116-17.
102.   BN, pp. 398-99. "But desire, too, contains its own frustration . . . the pleasure that accompanies such an act is irrelevant to, even destructive of, the profounder meaning of desire. For pleasure, at first immediate, produces a reflective consciousness of pleasure which becomes itself an end; and as I seek my own pleasure, I am distracted from . . . the other's incarnation, which is the proper function of desire."—Grene, op. cit., p. 85.
103.   BN, p. 403. "In sadism, consciousness is still seeking incarnation, but merely through the other. It wants to enjoy the incarnation of the other's consciousness in the lucidity of its own non-incarnation. It wants the other's consciousness to be entirely absorbed and fascinated by body-consciousness through pain. . . . Sadism contains the principle of its failure. As the sadist is about to reach his aim, i.e., when the victim's liberty capitulates, he faces a mere flesh object which, since his aim is to capture a liberty, he can no longer utilize."—Salvan, op. cit., pp. 95-96.
104.   "The explosion of the Other's look in the world of the sadist causes the meaning and goal of sadism to collapse."—BN, p. 406. "The look of the victim is something which the sadist cannot kill. It torments him with the realization that he has not only failed to catch the other's freedom qua freedom, but that he himself is not protected from being made an object before the Look of the victim who judges him."—Hazel Barnes, Humanistic Existentialism (Lincoln: University of Nebraska Press, 1959), p. 121.
105.   Cf. BN, pp. 410-11.
106.   Ibid., pp. 411-12.
107.   Ibid.
108.   Grene, op. cit., p. 87.
109.   Cf. BN, p. 377.
110.   Miceli, op. cit., p. 230.
111.   Jean Paul Sartre, The Devil and the Good Lord and Two Other Plays,

trans. Kitty Black (New York: Vintage Press, 1962), pp. 62-63; cf. Cranston, *op. cit.*, pp. 53-55.

112. Lafarge, *op. cit.*, p. 127.

113. Scott, *op. cit.*, pp. 142-43; cf. Robert Kreyche, *The Betrayal of Wisdom* (Staten Island: Alba House, 1972), pp. 82-83.

114. Jolivet, *op. cit.*, pp. 84-85.

115. PE, pp. 74, 76.

116. Sartre, *Existentialism is a Humanism* p. 34.

117. BN, p. 349. "Man's freedom is not a gift which a benevolent nature has placed in his cradle. It is nothing other than the battle which man takes up against the oppositions to his freedom. Therefore, precisely because these oppositions belong to his freedom, they are to a certain extent its material."—Hans Walz, "Man's Freedom in Existentialism and in Christianity," *Cross Currents*, II, i (1951) 59.

118. Sartre, *Age of Reason*, pp. 275-76.

119. Jean Paul Sartre, *The Flies*, trans. Stuart Gilbert (New York: Alfred Knopf, 1947), p. 158; cf. Greenlee, *op. cit.*, pp. 181-83.

120. Cf. Lafarge, *op. cit.*, p. 62. "Moreover without God and without stable natures which would ground norms of conduct, there can be no invariable, universal laws—rather, each man is a law to himself as he finds himself now in this, now in that actual situation. Without God, too, there is no divine providence and hence, the countless chance events constituting reality are totally meaningless and unintelligible. The career of each existent begins and ends in random absurdity."—Sweeney, *op. cit.*, p. 25.

121. BN, pp. 38-39. "His moral philosophy rests in perpetual creation, for the world offers situations that are forever new. There is no wisdom of the ages to serve as a guide, no past experience to compromise the future, no universal value."—Albérès, *op. cit.*, p. 115; cf. John Scanlon, "Intolerable Human Responsibility," *Research in Phenomenology*, I (1971) 75-90.

122. BN, pp. 553, 555-56. "Sartre in 'Existentialism' does say that the relation between my free choice and the free choice of other persons is one of humanitarian altruism and not one of egoistic conflict. In freely choosing, he says there, I am responsible for myself and in being responsible for myself, I am responsible for all men. . . . But such a position is not the one Sartre outlines in 'Being and Nothingness,' nor is it the one which ultimately guided Sartre to his conversion to Marxism. For it was the need of clarifying the concept of conflict which ultimately led Sartre to Marx."—Thomas Davitt, *Ethics in Situation* (New York: Appleton, Century, Crofts, 1970), p. 13, note 16.

123. BN, p. 38.

124. Spiegelberg, *op. cit.*, II, 486-87.

125. BN, p. 43.

126. Cf. *ibid.*, p. 70; Spiegelberg, *op. cit.*, II, 487-88; Copleston, *Contemporary Philosophy*, p. 192.

127. BN, p. 38.

128. Sartre, *Existentialism is a Humanism*, p. 52; cf. Stern, *op. cit.*, p. 74; Frederick Olafson, "Authenticity and Obligation," in Warnock, *op. cit.*, pp. 121-75.

129. Cf. below, pp. 374-75.

130. Stern, *op. cit.*, p. 75.

131. Copleston, *op. cit.*, pp. 192-93. "Nietzsche's idea of the man who has been raised to the stature of the Superman is here echoed and even surpassed. According to Sartre, it is only in the certitude of possessing boundless and groundless freedom that man can gain an attitude which makes it possible for him to form his world, an attitude which implies an obligation to act without asking for a 'why' of the action, simply because the action is itself the reason for every 'why.' "—Langrebe, *op. cit.*, p. 50.

132. Heinemann, *op. cit.*, pp. 127-28; cf. Davitt, *op. cit.*, p. 82, note 8, Thomas Anderson, "Is a Sartrian Ethics Possible?", PT, XIV (1970), 117-40; Francis Jeanson, "Moral Perspectives in Sartre's Thought," in *Contemporary European Ethics*, ed. Joseph Kockelmans (Garden City: Doubleday and Co., 1972), pp. 270-97.

133. Collins, *Existentialists*, pp. 82-84.

134. Wild, *op. cit.*, pp. 164-67.

135. Odajnyk, *op. cit.*, p. 13.

136. Copleston, *op. cit.*, pp. 194-95. "Camus came to believe that there is a university of human fraternity and of moral demand upon man. The Sartrean ethics, he concluded, encouraged too much arbitrariness and expediency—often for the sake of some distant good but at the cost of immediate compassion."—Roger Shinn, *Man: The New Humanism* (Philadelphia: Westminster Press, 1968), p. 134.

137. Kuhn, *op. cit.*, pp. 158-59.

138. "Thus Sartre is neither the whole nor the first of existentialism. In France, in particular, Gabriel Marcel, who was born in 1889, had developed the broad outlines of an existential philosophy long before Sartre had published anything at all."—Troisfontaines, *What Is Existentialism?*, p. 9.

139. Cf. above, pp. 277-90.

140. Sartre, *Words*, p. 158.

141. Novack, *op. cit.*, pp. 334-35.

142. Reinhardt, *op. cit.*, pp. 165-68.

143. Sciacca, *op. cit.*, pp. 313-14.

144. Manser, *op. cit.*, p. 164.

145. Fritz Pappenheim, *The Alienation of Modern Man* (New York and London: Monthly Review Press, 1968), p. 122.

146. Foulquié, *op. cit.*, pp. 94-95.
147. Mihalich, *op. cit.*, p. 136.
148. Miceli, *op. cit.*, pp. 245-46.
149. Heinemann, *op. cit.*, pp. 132-33.
150. Mary Warnock, *Existentialist Ethics* (New York: St. Martin's Press, 1967), p. 47.
151. Stern, *op. cit.*, p. 41.
152. Buber, *Eclipse of God*, pp. 69-70.
153. Murdock, *op. cit.*, pp. 76-77. "Existentialism—in its atheistic varieties—thus sinks back into a nature emptied of its metaphysical roots in being. It falls back into nothing at all. For these reasons, Auden and others have called our age the time of anxiety. This anxiety gives the lie to the proponents of the 'Secular City.' If man could live without God or if man could live as though God were dead, he would not be stretched upon the psychiatrist's couch from Berlin to San Francisco."—Frederick Wilhelmsen, *The Paradoxical Structure of Existence* (Irving, Texas: University of Dallas Press, 1970), p. 108.
154. Sartre, *Words*, pp. 158-59; (italics added).

CHAPTER VII

1. "There were five of them living together: the grandmother, her younger son, her elder daughter, and the daughter's two children. The son was almost dumb; the daughter an invalid, could only think with difficulty; and of the two children, one was already working for an insurance company, while the other was continuing his studies."—Albert Camus, "The Wrong Side and the Right Side," in *Lyrical and Critical Essays*, trans. Ellen Kennedy, ed. Philip Thody (New York: Alfred Knopf, 1968), p. 26; cf. Germaine Brée, *Camus* (Brunswick: Rutgers University Press, 1961), pp. 15ff; John Cruickshank, *Albert Camus and the Literature of Revolt* (New York: Oxford University Press, 1960), pp. 12ff.
2. Camus, *op. cit.*, p. 32; Cruickshank, *op. cit.*, p. 12.
3. Albert Camus, *Notebook, 1935-1942*, trans. Philip Thody (New York: Modern Library, 1965), pp. 3-4.
4. Camus, *Wrong Side and Right Side*, p. 32; cf. Brée, *op. cit.*, p. 16; Borzaga, *op. cit.*, observes, "Camus thought that only the poor are given the privilege of understanding the deep meaning of friendship and honesty."—p. 271; cf. Brée, *Camus and Sartre*, pp. 126-30.
5. Germaine Brée, "Introduction," in *Camus: A Collection of Critical Essays*, ed. Germaine Brée (Englewood Cliffs: Prentice-Hall, 1962), p. 5. On the other hand, Nathan Scott writes, "He and his widowed mother lived together, in poverty and silence, neither ever managing in any deep way to reach the other. . . . Though held together by the primitive power of the filial bond itself, each was a stranger to the other, and neither found in the other the comfort that might have reduced their sense of being strangers in the world."—*Albert Camus* (New York: Hillary House, 1962), pp. 14-15.
6. Cf. Brée, *Camus*, p. 24; Camus, *Lyrical and Critical Essays*, p. 350.
7. Albert Camus, "Preface," to the new edition of *Les Iles*, quoted by Robert de Luppé, *Albert Camus*, trans. John Cumming and J. Hargreaves (New York: Funk and Wagnalls, 1968), p. ix.
8. Camus, *Notebooks*, p. 17, note 9. "Suddenly, the dominant climate of enchantment dissolves completely into a bitter and pained obsession with the absurd. . . . The shock of physical sickness had a brutal effect upon his sensibilities. The note of death detected in his youthful essays swells to a loud protest against the treachery of life."—Bernard Murchland, "The Dark Night Before the Coming of Grace," in Brée, *Camus: Collection of Essays*, p. 60.
9. Camus, *op. cit.*, p. 44. "Twice, in order to take an examination for his degree in philosophy, he had to face a medical test and twice he was disqualified. This swept him off the path to what almost certainly otherwise lay in wait for him, being bogged down in teaching in Metropolitan France. . . . Camus found himself forced first to stay on in Algeria, his homeland, and then, to earn a living, to take on a job which, paradoxically, was more dangerous for his health than teaching but so much more rewarding—journalism."—Morvan Lebesque, *Portrait of Camus*, trans. T. C. Sharman (New York: Herder and Herder, 1971), p. 19.
10. Emmett Parker, *Albert Camus: The Artist in the Arena* (Madison: University of Wisconsin Press, 1966), p. 4.
11. Cf. *ibid.*, pp. 54-55; Adele King, *Albert Camus* (New York: Grove Press, 1964), pp. 6-7.
12. Brée, *Camus*, pp. 36-41. In the issue of August 25, 1944 of *Combat*, Camus wrote under the title "The Night of Truth," the following words: "While the bullets of freedom are still whistling throughout the city, the cannons of liberation are entering the gates of Paris amid shouts and flowers. In the most beautiful and hottest nights, the eternal stars over Paris mingle with the tracer bullets, the smoke of fires and the colored rockets of a mass celebration. This unparalleled night marks the end of four years of monstrous history and of an unspeakable struggle in which France came to grips with shame and wrath."—Albert Camus, *Resistance, Rebellion and Death*, trans. Justin O'Brien (New York: Alfred Knopf, 1966), p. 38; cf. Lebesque, *op. cit.*, pp. 62-68.
13. For an account of Camus' early political activity, cf. Parker, *op. cit.*, pp. 3-24.
14. Albert Camus, *The Rebel*, trans. Anthony Bower (New York: Alfred Knopf and Random House, 1956), p. 287. "His [Camus'] experience in the Resistance had not affected his dislike of the political and repressive machinery of the

Russian state. He thoroughly hated the maneuvers of the French Communist leaders intent on co-opting the whole heroic legend of the Resistance for their own political ends. . . . Although a man of the left, he considered Russia to be no longer in fact a socialist democracy. It had become a police state, a tyranny. . . . What exasperated him was the unwillingness of the leftist French intellectuals to face the Russian reality and their haste in labeling 'bourgeois' and 'reactionary' any attempt openly to confront the facts."—Brée, *Camus and Sartre*, pp. 206-07.

15. Albert Camus, *Actuelles I* (Paris: Gallimard, 1950), p. 111. "Camus seldom made use of the term 'engagement' (commitment) [Sartre's favorite] except, ten years after it was launched, to voice his distrust of the word, and of the connotation it had acquired." Brée, *op. cit.*, p. 34.

16. King, *op. cit.*, p. 9. Nicola Chiaromonte says that Sartre and his followers are "amateur Communists" who are satisfied with answers from the Communist catechism and "once they had declared themselves in favor of the Proletariat, the consistency of their ideas was a matter of automatic adjustment of which no account was due to 'others'. . . . The crudeness of the arguments used by Sartre against Camus cannot be explained if one does not assume that, having established an intellectual connection with the Marxist-Leninist-Stalinist mentality, he is intellectually dominated by it. . . . It remains that Jean Paul Sartre has not answered Albert Camus."—"Sartre Versus Camus: A Political Quarrel." in Brée, *Camus: Essays*, pp. 36-37.

In an interview, Camus stated, "No, I am not an existentialist. Sartre and I are always surprised to see our names linked. . . . Sartre is an existentialist and the only book of ideas that I have published, *The Myth of Sisyphus*, was directed against the so-called existentialist philosophers."—Camus, *Lyrical and Critical Essays*, p. 345; cf. Jean Paul Sartre, "Tribute to Albert Camus," in Brée, *op. cit.*, p. 173; Parker, *op. cit.*, pp. 136-43.

17. Thomas Hanna, "Albert Camus and the Christian Faith," in Brée, *op. cit.*, p. 49. "It appears to me that Camus' basic point of departure is quite sound. *L'Homme revolté* is in the final analysis an attempt to explain a posteriori the causes for a situation the existence of which had become evident in the light of Camus' own experience."—Parker, *op. cit.*, p. 141.

"The confrontation with *Les Temps modernes* was merely an epiphenomenon. It reveals the familiar human flaws in many intellectuals: the taunting tone and smug assumption of intellectual superiority on the part of Jeanson; his deliberate *reductio ad absurdum* of Camus' argument; the mocking parody and style. The need to refute was obviously overriding. Camus was incensed: Sartre, Camus felt, and to a certain extent, was right to feel, had betrayed the tacit code of friendship by delegating the hatchet job to an accomplice; and it is true that, involved in his own crisis, about to 'commit' himself in the opposite way, Sartre made short shrift of Camus' point of view—discussing it in terms of his own postulations."—Brée, *Camus and Sartre*, p. 247.

18. King, *op. cit.*, p. 10; cf. Breisach, *op. cit.*, p. 107. "This may explain the brittle tone and 'ad hominem' arguments both Sartre and de Beauvoir adopted at the time of their disagreement. Sartre asserted pompously that Camus had 'entered into History and by the same token into solid union with all those who bear the scars of historical injustice' only at the time of German occupation. He overlooked Camus' early and sustained advocacy of the cause of the Algerian Muslims to which Sartre in those years paid scant attention. Simone de Beauvoir, freely impugning his motives, cast Camus in the role of 'resolute champion of bourgeois values' (*The Force of Circumstance*, p. 259), a rather silly and typically erroneous judgment."—Brée, *op. cit.*, p. 85, note 22.

19. Cf. Brée, *Camus*, p. 31.

20. Camus wrote and staged a play, *The Revolt in the Asturies*. He also adapted André Malraux's *A Time of Contempt;* André Gide's *The Return of the Prodigal* and the *Prometheus* of Aeschylus. He also staged Charles Vildrac's *The Steamship of "Tenacity";* Ben Jonson's *The Silent Woman;* Pushkin's *Don Juan* and Jacques Copeau's adaptation of *The Brothers Karamazov*. Morvan Lebesque describes the group and its *modus operandi:* "There was little scenery; the actor and the text were everything. Camus, in very truth, had his finger in every pie. He was author, actor, producer, effects man and prompter. Performances were given in the open air or in little suburban halls."—*op. cit.*, p. 22.

21. Sartre, *op. cit.*, p. 175.

22. François Mauriac, in *New York Times*, January 5, 1960, quoted in Anthony Padovano, *The Estranged God* (New York: Sheed and Ward, 1966), p. 103.

23. L. A. Boyd, *André Gide* (1859-1951): *A Memorial Lecture* (Belfast: Boyd, for Queen's University, 1951), p. 12, quoted in Cruickshank, *op. cit.*, pp. 22-23. Thomas Hanna maintains, "This lack of an extended critique of Christianity is explained by the fact that although Camus is anti-Communist, he is not an anti-Christian—*he is simply a non-Christian*."—"Albert Camus and Christian Faith," in Brée, *Camus: Essays*, p. 49. On the other side, Jean Onimus contends, "Contrary to what he sometimes said, then, Camus was not raised entirely outside Christianity, but what he knew of it and the experiences that he had of it on the threshold of adolescence amounted to very little. Religion made up of absurd superstitions, designed to reassure, to console the sick and the aged. . . . Religion petrified by habit, without true faith or true love, the mania of the old, a kind of pitiful bauble. And Camus' mother . . . had long ceased to practise her faith."—*Albert Camus and Christianity*, trans. Emmett Parker (University, Alabama: University of Alabama Press, 1970), pp. 32-33. Germaine Brée gives the following interesting insight:

"Camus was in daily contact with Algerian Muslims. It is quite true that at the level of everyday life, the 'Mediterranean' way of life in southern Europe . . . was still in the early thirties as Camus observed closer to Islam than to what we call 'Western' rhythms of living. At that level he then thought 'North Africa is one of the only lands where Orient and Occident cohabit.' (*Essais*, 1325)."—*Camus and Sartre*, p. 80.

24. Cruickshank, *op. cit.*, p. 32; cf. Albert Camus, *A Happy Death*, trans. Richard Howard (New York: Alfred Knopf, 1972), pp. 86-87; 107-110; 140-41; Roger Quillot, "Albert Camus' Algeria" in Brée, *Camus: Essays*, pp. 38-39; Lebesque, *op. cit.*, pp. 24-25.

25. Camus, "The Nuptials" in *Lyrical and Critical Essays*, p. 90. "Camus was first of all—and remained essentially so all his life—a Mediterranean. That is to say his attention was first drawn and held by the beauty of sky and sea, physical pleasures, and the flowering of the simplest kind of happiness. . . . For Camus, born in Algiers, the authentic realities were, first of all, almond trees in bloom, swimming in the sea, the softness of summer evenings. His first gods were given him along with the beauty of the world; offering himself to the sun or contemplating the night radiant with stars sufficed to convince him that the world was replete."—Onimus, *op. cit.*, pp. 7-8.

26. Camus, op. cit., p. 91; cf. MAMS, pp. 116-18; MB, II, 182. Cf. above, p. 351. "Instinct and doctrine blend in Camus' pagan assertions . . . *Hic et nunc*: here and now Camus, the young Pagan, wants to savor the delights of life. The notion of hell appears but as a pleasant joke, conceived by the imagination of the most virtuous persons. Immortality and any ultimate rewards promised to those who elect the Pascalian wager, are spurned."—Henri Peyre, "Camus the Pagan," in Brée, *op. cit.*, p. 66.

27. Camus, *The Rebel*, p. 305.

28. Camus, *The Nuptials*, p. 76. "Each essay [of *Noces*] has its own resonances and mood but all are united in the persistent confrontation of the permanence of nature with what is sensual and mortal. Pervading all the muscular paganism and the insistence upon a 'common resonance between man and the earth' is the horror and rejection of death."—S. Beynon John. "Albert Camus: A British View," in Brée *op. cit.*, p. 87; cf. Peyre, *op. cit.*, pp. 65-70.

29. Albert Camus, *The Myth of Sisyphus*, trans. Justin O'Brien (New York: Random House, 1961), p. 1.

30. "A distinction must be made between the ideas expressed in *The Myth of Sisyphus* and those in *The Rebel*. Camus invites us to do this when he warns us in the preface that the description of an 'intellectual malady' is not a definitive statement of his ideas, for *The Myth* is provisional."—de Luppé, *op. cit.*, p. 1; cf. Thomas Hanna, *The Thought and Art of Albert Camus* (Chicago: Henry Regnery Co., 1958), pp. 20-21; Cruickshank, *op. cit.*, p. 42; Philip Thody, *Albert Camus: A Study of His Work*, (New York: Grove Press, 1957), p. 9.

31. Camus, *Myth*, p. 7; cf. Brée, *Camus*, pp. 200ff; Sanborn, *op. cit.*, p. 108.

32. *Myth*, p. 15; cf. Thody, *op. cit.*, pp. 3-5.

33. *Myth*, p. 10; cf. Cruickshank, *op. cit.*, pp. xi-xii; King, *op. cit.*, pp. 21-22; de Luppé, *op. cit.*, p. 3.

34. *Myth*, pp. 10-11.

35. *Ibid.* "Contact with nature itself reveals something materially different from human consciousness. The world appears dense and alien to us."—de Luppé, *op. cit.*, p. 3.

36. *Myth*, p. 11; cf. de Luppé, *op. cit.*, p. 51.

37. *Myth*, p. 12.

38. Albert Camus, *The Stranger*, trans. Stuart Gilbert (New York: Alfred Knopf, 1946), p. 152. "Camus alone among atheist existentialists offered a genuinely empirico-practical code of living, consistent and held in its precarious consistency by the supreme relativizing principle, death; not viewed with terror or hate or cynicism, but gently and with a kind of respect."—Arthur Gibson, *The Faith of the Atheist* (New York and Evanston: Harper and Row, 1968), p. 74; cf. Robert Champigny, *A Pagan Hero*, trans. Rowe Portis (Philadelphia: University of Pennsylvania Press, 1969), pp. 91-92, 102; E. Freeman, *The Theatre of Albert Camus* (London: Methuen and Co., 1971), pp. 35-75; Vincent Martin, *op. cit.*, pp. 22-24.

40. *Myth*, p. 16; cf. Thody, *op. cit.*, p. 4; Naomi Lebowitz, *Humanism and the Absurd in the Modern Novel* (Evanston: Northwestern University Press, 1971), p. 6.

41. *Myth*, p. 21. "In the strict sense of the word, the absurd is neither the world nor myself, but the *link* between the world and myself. The link is based on the confrontation: the opposition of my consciousness to the walls that hem it in. The absurd is implied in the very shock of conscious discovery that desires are meaningless; it is the shock itself which consists of a sudden separation."—de Luppé, *op. cit.*, p. 6. "Primary absurdity manifests a cleavage, the cleavage between man's aspirations to unity and the insurmountable dualism of mind and nature, between man's drive toward the eternal and the *finite* nature of his existence, between the concern which constitutes his very essence and the vanity of his efforts. Chance, death, the irreducible pluralism of life and truth, the unintelligibility of the real—all these are extremes of the absurd."—Jean Paul Sartre, "An Explication of 'The Stranger,'" in Brée, *op. cit.*, p. 109.

42. Hanna, *op. cit.*, p. 23.

43. *Myth*, pp. 22-23. Jean Paul Sartre in *Paru* (December 1945) distinguishes between the meaning which he and Camus give to the word "absurd."

He writes, "Camus' philosophy is a philosophy of the absurd. For him, the absurd arises from the relation between man and the world, between man's rational demands and the world's irrationality. The themes which he derives from it are those of classical pessimism. I do not recognize the absurd in the sense of scandal and disillusionment that Camus attributes to it. What I call the absurd is something very different; it is the universal contingency of being which is, but which is not the basis of its being; the absurd is the given, unjustifiable, primordial quality of existence."—quoted in Cruickshank, *op. cit.*, p. 45, note 1.

44. David Denton, *The Philosophy of Albert Camus* (Boston: Prime Publishers, 1967), p. 27.

45. *Myth*, p. 5.

46. *Ibid.*, p. 3; cf. Denton, *op. cit.*, p. 30; Cruickshank, *op. cit.*, pp. 46-47.

47. *Myth*, p. 5; cf. Thody, *op. cit.*, pp. 5-6.

48. *Myth*, p. 40.

49. *Ibid.*

50. *Ibid.*, p. 24. Camus complains that all existential philosophers without exception suggest escape; in this connection, cf. de Luppé *op. cit.*, p. 7.

51. *Myth*, p. 25. "Whatever the method, rational or irrational, the religious philosopher pursues a path leading to the 'leap' which solves all. For these men it is only a question of the will to arrive at this point. . . . Philosophical suicide 'neither meets nor solves the problem.'"—Hanna, *op. cit.*, p. 27.

52. *Myth*, p. 25.

53. *Ibid.* Camus concludes the passage, "To Chestov reason is useless but there is something beyond reason. To an absurd mind reason is useless and there is nothing beyond reason."—p. 27; cf. Cruickshank, *op. cit.*, pp. 58ff.

54. *Myth*, p. 29; cf. Lebesque, *op. cit.*, pp. 58-59.

55. *Myth*, pp. 33, 37.

56. NAMS, pp. 116ff; HV, p. 200; cf. above, 111-16.

57. *Myth*, p. 5.

58. *Ibid.*, p. 38; cf. Hanna, *op. cit.*, pp. 23-30; Scott, *Camus* pp. 21-22.

59. *Myth*, p. 40.

60. Friedman, *To Deny Our Nothingness*, p. 332.

61. *Myth*, p. 41; cf. Breisach, *op. cit.*, pp. 107-08.

62. Brée, *Camus*, p. 204; Fabro, *op. cit.*, p. 955.

63. *Myth*, p. 43. "In the absurd revelation, man realizes that he was conforming to given goals which seemed to be part of a non-existent larger meaning. To the measure that he had planned his life as if the world had meaning, to that extent had he lost his actual freedom."—Hanna, *op. cit.*, p. 32.

64. *Myth*, pp. 41-44.

65. *Ibid.*, p. 47; cf. King, *op. cit.*, p. 25; Scott, *op. cit.*, p. 23; de Luppé, *op. cit.*, pp. 10-11.

66. *Myth*, pp. 45-46.

67. Denton, *op. cit.*, p. 32; cf. *Myth*, p. 47; Hanna, *op. cit.*, p. 32.

68. *Myth*, pp. 45-47; cf. de Luppé, *op. cit.*, pp. 8-9.

69. *Myth*, p. 47.

70. *Ibid.*, p. 88.

71. *Ibid.*, pp. 89-90; cf. Cruickshank, *op. cit.*, p. 87; Denton, *op. cit.*, pp. 34-35. "Void of hope, he nevertheless finds life so fully satisfying that he is content to spend it in his eternal struggle to the heights."—Philip Rhein, *Albert Camus* (New York: Twayne Publishers, 1969), p. 31.

72. Scott, *op. cit.*, p. 28; cf. John Hayward, *Existentialism and Religious Liberalism* (Boston: Beacon Press, 1962), p. 32. "There is a silent joy, a tremendous affirmation in this image of the absurd man, whose fate belongs to him and who is the master of his days."—Friedman, *op. cit.*, p. 334.

73. *Myth*, p. 91; cf. Gaidenko, *op. cit.*, p. 276.

74. Camus, *Stranger*, pp. 1-46; cf. Denton, *op. cit.*, p. 33.

75. *Stranger*, pp. 151, 154; cf. Sidney Finkelstein, *Existentialism and Alienation in American Literature* (New York: International Publishers, 1965), p. 115. And yet, Nathan Scott sees in this passage a kind of repudiation of Camus' own philosophical position, for Meursault seems to achieve that 'leap' from absurdity to some kind of faithful affirmation. Scott writes, "He [Meursault] somehow moves from the sullen hopelessness and indifference in whose grip he is throughout most of the novel to the almost ecstatic affirmativeness of his final mood."—*op. cit.*, p. 37.

76. *Myth*, pp. 46-47; cf. George Thomas, *Religious Philosophies of the West* (New York: Charles Scribner's Sons, 1965), p. 435.

77. Cf. above, pp. 165-68.

78. Martin, *op. cit.*, p. 38.

79. *The Rebel*, p. 31.

80. Martin, *op. cit.*, p. 39. As David Denton observes, "Camus had to decide why he, a nihilist, was fighting on a side opposite that of the German nihilistic philosophers and writers."—*op. cit.*, p. 42.

81. Camus, "Letters to a German Friend" (Fourth Letter) in *Resistance, Rebellion and Death*, p. 27; cf. Friedman, *op. cit.*, p. 285; Denton, *op. cit.*, p. 42.

82. Albert Camus, *Fourth Letter, ibid.* "Camus' indignation was born not of the intellect but of an unusually acute, exacerbated sensitivity to human suffering and indignity. Right and wrong in this realm are things of the flesh. . . . The *Lettres à un ami allemand* are also a confession, the expression of a personal credo. . . . [They] demonstrate that Camus' truths were personal and passionate in nature, that they were arrived at intuitively, that they were reasoned only *a posteriori* and in the light of their evidence in his eyes. They are a record of an experience, they are

not a mental exercise."—Brée, *Camus*, pp. 45-46.

83. Martin, *op. cit.*, p. 39; cf. Onimus, *op. cit.*, p. 80.

84. *The Rebel*, p. 5. "Camus was here saying that though the Absurd must be resisted, our *method* of resistance must not be allowed to become something whose final effect is that of betraying man himself—which was the immense tragedy involved in the whole experiment of Nazism." Scott, *Unquiet Vision*, p. 108.

85. Cf. Cruickshank, *op. cit.*, pp. 92, 94.

86. Cf. Padovano, *op. cit.*, p. 108.

87. Albert Camus, *The Plague*, trans. Stuart Gilbert (New York: The Modern Library, 1948); cf. Scott, *op. cit.*, pp. 109-11. John Cruickshank prefers to describe *The Plague* as a symbolical novel (roman-mythe) because an allegorical novel calls for "two levels of interpretation continuously maintained throughout. But a reading of *La Peste* shows that its symbolism, though frequent, is of an intermittent kind."—*op. cit.*, p. 167.

88. Hanna, *op. cit.*, pp. 205-06. "By relying on the strength of the soul in adversity and exalting the purest values in man, Camus, in *La Peste*, invites us to put bets on hope."—Albert Maquet, *Albert Camus: The Invincible Summer* (London: John Calder, 1958), p. 108.

89. *The Plague*, p. 230.

90. *Ibid.*, p. 237.

91. *The Plague*, pp. 260-61. "That the fight against the plague is hopeless, led by the relative few who do this as existentialists, demonstrates that science is a broken crutch, that history is meaningless, that nobody can really know anything about the world."—Finkelstein, *op. cit.*, p. 123.

92. *The Plague, ibid.* "Camus believes that we can exist 'authentically' only if we stand up and out to life by agreeing that suicide is a possibility of man, that all life is absurd, that the world is totally absurd and that we should, individually, persist in being human in spite of these formidable obstacles. Our very 'seeking for' indicates that despite the meaninglessness of life, such meaning as there is must be that of the human being who experiences the absurdity."—Wesley Barnes, *Existentialism* (Woodbury, N.Y.; Barron's Educational Series, 1968), p. 119. "*The Plague* is a deeply personal novel and it makes a clear statement. The tactics used to counter a collective evil are determined by the character of the threat. They are not in themselves absolutes; they are temporary and relative, a therapy, not a cure. Dr. Rieux's task is to circumscribe the infection. He and his helpers are on the defensive; their efforts, the novel suggests, may have had little to do with the evolution of the situation."—Brée. *Camus and Sartre*. p. 220.

93. *The Rebel*, pp. 8, 10. As early as 1938, Camus criticized Jean Paul Sartre's position that absurdism is an end in itself and not only a beginning. In *Alger-Républicain*, 20-10-38, Camus wrote of Sartre's *Nausea* ". . . M. Sartre's hero has perhaps not supplied the meaning of his anguish when he insists on what he finds repugnant in man, instead of basing reasons for despair on certain aspects of man's grandeur. To assert the absurdity of life cannot be an end in itself, but only a beginning."—quoted in Parker, *op. cit.*, p. 110.

94. Camus, *Lyrical and Critical Essays*, p. 356; cf. Cruickshank, *op. cit.*, p. 92. "The following essential affirmations should be remembered:—the absurd, taken separately, does not give rise to any rule of action;—it is valid only as a starting point; —it is in fact only an auxiliary, because it is contradictory: it sets two conditions which must be overcome by a creative act. This ineluctable process through which the absurd is overcome, is the rebellion which sets the two elements of experience against one another. The experience of the absurd bears direct witness to one thing: my rebellion."—de Luppé, *op. cit.*, p. 15.

95. *The Rebel*, p. 4.

96. *Ibid.*

97. *Ibid.*

98. Herbert Read, "Foreword," in Albert Camus, *The Rebel*, p. ix; cf. Cruickshank, *op. cit.*, pp. 90ff.

99. *The Rebel*, p. 13.

100. *Ibid.*, pp. 14ff: cf. Hazel Barnes, *Humanistic Existentialism: The Literature of Possibility* (Lincoln: University of Nebraska Press, 1959), p. 218.

101. King, *op. cit.*, p. 29.

102. Camus adds, "When he rebels, a man identifies himself with other men and so surpasses himself, and from this point of view human solidarity is metaphysical."—*The Rebel*, p. 17.

103. Hanna, *op. cit.*, p. 98. "The rebellion conceived by Camus is informed with a purity capable of protecting love. It should not be confused, in fact, (and Camus emphasizes this), with the negative conception of *resentment* defined by Scheler; it is not hatred; neither is it envy, nor a desire of possession. It is a struggle against hatred; it is the source of sacrifice and unselfishness. Rebellion can therefore enter the service of love; or rather it can direct it towards those objects which are its only possible sources of nourishment."—de Luppé, *op. cit.*, pp. 32-33.

104. *The Rebel*, p. 16. "Solidarity implies a human nature that transcends particular, historical circumstances . . . solidarity implies communication among men."—King, *op. cit.*, p. 39.

105. Parker, *op. cit.*, p. 126. "The true ethic of rebellion is *concrete* and active; it is part of daily life and part of the life of the individual and that of the nation as a whole. It is an ethic of the continual effort to maintain moderation or balance in all things and it is accompanied by the wearying intransigence that this implies."—de Luppé, *op. cit.*, p. 26.

106. *The Rebel*, p. 294. "Camus in 1939 had viewed the Nazi experiment as

one of the cases in which justifiable revolt had gone beyond the limit. In giving form to their revolt, the German people and their leaders had reversed the master-slave relationship and thus violated the fundamental maxim of revolt: 'I rebel, therefore we are!' Human life had ceased to have any universal value to the Nazis." —Parker, *op. cit.*, p. 134.

107.   *Ibid.*, pp. 126-27. "In his great analytical essay, *The Rebel*, he warns that rebellion against the infinite transcendent God brings with it its own special dangers: chiefly that of the erecting by finite man of new tyrannies which Camus lumps together under the global designation of Caesarism. The rebellion itself, Camus holds, is vitally necessary to man's very existence; but it must respect its own limits."—Gibson, *op. cit.*, p. 74.

108.   Scott, *Camus*, p. 67.

109.   Hanna, *op. cit.*, p. 149.

110.   Breisach, op. cit., p. 108.

111.   Onimus, *op. cit.*, pp. 85-86; cf. Denton, *op. cit.*, pp. 48ff.

112.   Albert Camus, *The Fall*, trans. Justin O'Brien, Vintage Book (New York: Alfred Knopf and Random House, 1956). "*The Fall* . . . is the most ambiguous work which Camus has as yet published."—Thody, *op. cit.*, p. 75 (written in 1957). Robert de Luppé speaks of the work's ". . . sombre tone, moral irony and ambiguous effect."—*op. cit.*, p. 66.

113.   Hanna, *op. cit.*, p. 232; cf. Lebesque, *op. cit.*, pp. 124-32.

114.   Sartre, *The Words*, p. 158.

115.   Cf. Conor Cruise O'Brien, *Albert Camus of Europe and Africa* (New York: Viking Press, 1970), pp. 92-100. John Cruickshank states, "There are, admittedly, straightforward Christian parallels in *La Chute*."—*op. cit.*, p. 187; cf. Charles Moeller, *Man and Salvation in Literature*, trans. Charles Quinn (Notre Dame and London: University of Notre Dame Press, 1970), pp. 50ff.

116.   Onimus, *op. cit.*, pp. 100-101.

117.   Murchland, *op. cit.*, p. 63.

118.   Thody, *op. cit.*, p. 77. Several writers even considered the possibility of Camus' conversion to Catholicism, cf. Murchland, *op. cit.*, p. 63; Thody, *op. cit.*, pp. 77. Ignace Lepp wrote, "Camus' friends know that between the years 1947-1950, he was very close to Catholicism; several friends anticipated his immediate conversion. . . . Sartre in his polemic with Camus in 1952, was not far from the mark when he suspected that a certain nostalgia was concealed under the very vehemence with which Camus proclaimed absurdity."—*Atheism in Our Time* (New York: Macmillan Co., 1963), p. 185.

119.   O'Brien, *op. cit.*, p. 100.

120.   *Ibid.* For an opposite interpretation, cf. Scott, *Camus*, pp. 82-85, who refuses to discern any genuine movement toward religious values in *The Fall*. Albert Maquet feels that the work represents a return to the negative position of *The Stranger*. He writes. "After the optimism of *La Peste*, the impossible revolt of Clamence and his fallen-angel's acrimony seem to mark a volte-face of Camus' attitude which rather sharply drives his thought back towards the negative position of *L'Etranger*. Just as man's need of enlightenment and justice will make him come to grief against the absurd walls, so his demands for purity and his yearning for innocence will painfully exhaust him in his efforts to surmount the fatal inevitability of his faults.'—Maquet, *op. cit.*, pp. 165-66; cf. also Roger Quillot, "An Ambiguous World," in Brée, *Camus: Essays*, pp. 157-62; Hanna *op. cit.*, pp. 215-36; Gibson, *op. cit.*, p. 83; Parker, *op. cit.*, pp. 160ff. On the other hand, Robert de Luppé observes. "It is possible that Camus was writing [in *The Fall*] a subtle condemnation of the Christian conception of an all-merciful God; it is equally possible that he was moving towards a more Christian position."—de Luppé, *op. cit*,. p. 72.

121.   Cf. Parker, "Preface," in Onimus, *op. cit.*, p. ix.

122.   "In an interview given on this occasion [Nobel Prize Award], Camus sums up thus his position with regard to Christianity: 'I have only veneration and respect for the person of Christ and for his life. I do not believe in his resurrection." —Onimus, *op. cit.*, p. 148.

123.   Fabro, *op. cit.*, p. 957.

124.   *Ibid.*

125.   John Hayward, *Existentialism and Religious Liberalism* (Boston: Beacon Press; Toronto: S.J. Reginald Saunders Co., 1962), p. 62.

126.   Gibson, *op. cit.*, p. 88.

127.   Parker, "Preface," in Onimus, *op. cit.*, pp. xii-xiii.

Bibliography

Adams, Pedro. "Marcel: Metaphysician or Moralist." *Philosophy Today*, X (1966), 182-89.
Albérès, René. *Jean Paul Sartre: Philosopher Without Faith.* Trans. Wade Baskin. New York: Philosophical Library, 1960.
Alderman, Harold. "Heidegger on Being Human." *Philosophy Today*, XV (1971), 16-29.
Allison, Henry. "Christianity and Nonsense." *Essays on Kierkegaard.* Ed. Jerry Gill. Minneapolis: Burgess Publishing Co., 1969.
Anderson, John. "Truth, Process and Creature in Heidegger's Thought." *Heidegger and the Quest for Truth.* Ed. Manfred Frings. Chicago: Quadrangle Books, 1968.
Anderson, Thomas. "Is a Sartrian Ethics Possible?" *Philosophy Today*, XIV (1970), 117-40.
Aron, Raymond. *Marxism and the Existentialists.* Clarion Book. New York: Simon and Schuster, 1970.
Augustine, St. *Confessions.* Trans. Edward Pusey. New York: Modern Library, 1949.
————. *The City of God.* Trans. Marcus Dods. New York: Modern Library, 1950.

Ballard, Edward. "Gabriel Marcel: The Mystery of Being." *Existential Philosophers: Kierkegaard to Merleau-Ponty.* Ed. George Schrader. New York: McGraw-Hill Book Co., 1967.
von Balthasar, Hans Urs. *Martin Buber and Christianity.* New York: Macmillan Co., 1961.
Barnes, Hazel. *Humanistic Existentialism: The Literature of Possibility.* Lincoln: University of Nebraska Press, 1959.
Barnes, Wesley. *The Philosophy and Literature of Existentialism.* Woodbury, N.Y.: Barrows Educational Series, 1968.
Baron, S. W. *A Social and Religious History of the Jews.* Philadelphia: JPS, 1952.
Barrett, William. *Irrational Man.* Anchor Book. Garden City: Doubleday and Co., 1962.
————. *What Is Existentialism.* New York: Grove Press, 1965.
Beek, M. A. and Weiland, J. Sperna. *Martin Buber, Personalist and Prophet.* Westminster and New York: Newman Press, 1968.
Beigbeder, Marc. *L'Homme Sartre.* Paris, 1947.
Beis, Richard. "Atheistic Existentialist Ethics: A Critique." *The Modern Schoolman*, XLII (1965), 153-77.
Birnbaum, Salomo. *The Life and Sayings of the Baal Shem.* New York: Hebrew Publishing Co., 1953.
Biser, Eugen. "Martin Buber." *Philosophy Today*, VII (1963), 100-14.
Blackham, H. J., ed. *Reality, Man and Existence: Essential Works of Existentialism.* New York: Bantam Books, 1965.
————. *Six Existentialist Thinkers.* Torchbook. New York and Evanston: Harper and Row, 1959.
Blain, Lionel. "Marcel's Logic of Freedom in Proving the Existence of God." *International Philosophical Quarterly*, IX (1969), 177-204.
Blanshard, Brand. "Kierkegaard on Faith." *Essays on Kierkegaard.* Ed. Jerry Gill. Minneapolis: Burgess Publishing Co., 1969.
Bocheński, I. M. *Contemporary European Philosophy.* Trans. Donald Nicholl and Karl Aschenbrenner. Berkeley and Los Angeles University of California Press, 1961.
————. *The Methods of Contemporary Thought.* Torchbook. New York and Evanston: Harper and Row, 1968.
Borowitz, Eugene. *A Layman's Introduction to Religious Existentialism.* New York: Dell Publishing Co., 1966.
Borzaga, Reynold. *Contemporary Philosophy: Phenomenological and Existential Currents.* Milwaukee: Bruce Publishing Co., 1966.
Bouillard, Henri. *The Logic of the Faith.* New York: Sheed and Ward, 1967.
Bourke, Vernon. *History of Ethics.* Image Book. 2 vols. Garden City: Doubleday and Co., 1970.
Boyd, L. A. *André Gide (1869-1951): A Memorial Lecture.* Belfast: Boyd, for Queen's University, 1951.
Brée, Germaine. *Camus.* New Brunswick: Rutgers University Press, 1961.
————. *Camus: A Collection of Critical Essays.* Englewood Cliffs: Prentice-Hall, 1962.
————. *Camus and Sartre.* Delta Book. New York: Dell Publishing Co., 1972.
————. "Introduction." *Camus: A Collection of Critical Essays.* Ed. Germaine Brée. Englewood Cliffs: Prentice-Hall, 1962.
Breisach, Ernst. *Introduction to Modern Existentialism.* New York: Grove Press, 1962.

Brentano, Franz. *Von der mannigfachen Bedeutung des Seienden nach Aristoteles.* Freiburg in Breisgau, 1962.
Bretall, Robert, ed. *A Kierkegaard Anthology.* New York: Modern Library, 1946.
Brock, Werner, ed. *Existence and Being.* Chicago: Henry Regnery Co., 1949.
Brown, James. *Kierkegaard, Heidegger, Buber and Barth: Subject and Object in Modern Theology.* New York: Collier Books, 1962.
Buber, Martin. *At the Turning: Three Addresses on Judaism.* New York: Farrar, Straus and Cudahy, 1952.
————. *Between Man and Man.* Trans. Ronald Gregor Smith. New York: Macmillan Co., 1968.
————. *Eclipse of God.* Torchbook. New York and Evanston: Harper and Row, 1957.
————. *Hasidism.* New York: The Philosophical Library, 1948.
————. *Hasidism and Modern Man.* Trans. Maurice Friedman. Torchbook. New York: Harper and Bros., 1966.
————. *I and Thou.* Trans. Walter Kaufmann. New York: Charles Scribner's Sons, 1970.
————. *I and Thou.* Trans. Walter Kaufmann. New York: Charles Scribner's Sons, 1960.
————. *Israel and the World: Essays in a Time of Crisis.* New York: Schocken Books, 1948.
————. *The Knowledge of Man.* New York: Harper and Row, 1965.
————. *The Origin and Meaning of Hasidism.* Trans. Maurice Friedman. New York: Harper and Bros., 1966.
————. *Paths in Utopia.* Trans. R. F. C. Hull. Boston: Beacon Press, 1958.
————. *Die Schrift.* Trans. Martin Buber and Franz Rosenzweig. 15 vols. Berlin: Schocken Verlag.
————. *Tales of the Hasidism. The Early Masters.* New York: Schocken Books; London: Thames and Hudson, 1955.
————. *Ten Rungs: Hasidic Sayings.* New York: Schocken Books, 1962.

Cain, Seymour. *Gabriel Marcel.* New York: Hillary House, 1963.
Camus, Albert. *The Fall.* Trans. Justin O'Brien. Vintage Book. New York: Alfred Knopf and Random House, 1956.
————. *A Happy Death.* Trans. Richard Howard. New York: Alfred Knopf, 1972.
————. "Letters to a German Friend." *Resistance, Rebellion and Death.* Trans. Justin O'Brien. New York: Alfred Knopf, 1966.
————. *Lyrical and Critical Essays.* Trans. Ellen Kennedy. Ed. Philip Thody. New York: Alfred Knopf, 1968.
————. *The Myth of Sisyphus.* Trans. John Cumming and J. Hargreaves. New York: Funk and Wagnalls, 1966.
————. *Notebooks 1935-1942.* Trans. Philip Thody. New York: Modern Library, 1965.
————. "The Nuptials." *Lyrical and Critical Essays,* Trans. Ellen Kennedy. Ed. Philip Thody. New York: Alfred Knopf, 1968.
————. *The Plague.* Trans. Stuart Gilbert. New York: Modern Library, 1948.
————. *The Rebel.* Trans. Anthony Bouwer. New York: Alfred Knopf and Random House, 1956.
————. *Resistance, Rebellion and Death.* Trans. Justin O'Brien. New York: Alfred Knopf, 1966.
————. *La Révolte dans les Asturies. Essai de Création collective.* Algiers: Charlot, 1936.
————. "The Wrong Side and the Right Side." *Lyrical and Critical Essays.* Trans. Ellen Kennedy. Ed. Philip Thody. New York: Alfred Knopf, 1968.
Caputo, John. "Heidegger's Original Ethics." *The New Scholasticism,* XLV (1971), 127-38.
————. "The Rose is without Why: the later Heidegger." *Philosophy Today,* XV (1971), 3-15.
Carson, Saul. "Dag Hammarskjöld and Martin Buber." *The Connecticut Ledger,* Dec. 10, 1964.
Casalis, George. *Portrait of Karl Barth.* Anchor Book. Garden City: Doubleday and Co., 1964.
Casserley, Langmead. "Gabriel Marcel." *Christianity and the Existentialists.* Ed. Carl Michalson. New York: Charles Scribner's Sons, 1956.
Cate, Curtis. "Europe's First Feminist Has Changed the Second Sex." *New York Times,* CXXI (July 11, 1971).
Champigny, Robert. *A Pagan Hero.* Trans. Rowe Portis. Philadelphia: University of Pennsylvania Press, 1969.
Chiaromonte, Nicola. "Sartre versus Camus: A Political Quarrel." *Camus: A Collection of Critical Essays.* Ed. Germaine Brée. Englewood Cliffs: Prentice-Hall, 1962.
Cohen, Arthur. *Martin Buber.* London: Bowes and Bowes, 1957.
Colette, Jacques. *Kierkegaard, The Difficulty of Being Christian.* Trans. Ralph McInerney. Notre Dame: University of Notre Dame Press, 1968.
Collins, James. *The Existentialists.* Gateway Book. Chicago: Henry Regnery Co., 1964.
————. *The Mind of Kierkegaard.* Chicago: Henry Regnery Co., 1965.
————. "The Religious Themes in Existentialism." *Philosophy and the Modern World.* Ed. Francis Canfield. Detroit: Sacred Heart Seminary, 1961.
————. *Three Paths in Philosophy.* Chicago: Henry Regnery Co., 1962.

————. *Interpreting Modern Philosophy.* Princeton: University Press, 1972.
Copleston, Frederick. *Aquinas.* Baltimore: Penguin Books, 1970.
————. *Contemporary Philosophy.* Westminster: Newman Press, 1956.
————. *Existentialism and the Modern Man.* Oxford: Blackfriars, 1948.
————. *A History of Philosophy.* 8 vols. Westminster: Newman Press, 1953-1963.
Cranston, Maurice. *Jean Paul Sartre.* Evergreen Book. New York: Grove Press, 1962.
————. *The Quintessence of Sartrism.* Torchbook. New York and Evanston: Harper and Row, 1971.
Cress, Donald. "Heidegger's Criticism of 'Entitative' Metaphysics in His Later Works." *International Philosophical Quarterly,* XII (1972), 69-86.
Cruickshank, John. *Albert Camus and the Literature of Revolt.* New York: Oxford University Press, 1960.
Cumming, Robert. *The Philosophy of Jean Paul Sartre.* New York: Random House, 1966.

Davitt, Thomas. *Ethics in The Situation.* New York: Appleton Century Crofts, 1970.
de Beauvoir, Simone. *Force of Circumstance.* New York: Putnam Co., 1965.
————. *Memoirs of a Dutiful Daughter.* Trans. James Kirup. New York: Popular Library, 1963.
Demske, James. *Being, Man, and Death.* Lexington: University of Kentucky Press, 1970.
Denton, David. *The Philosophy of Albert Camus.* Boston: Prime Publishers, 1967.
Desan, Wilfrid. *The Marxism of Jean Paul Sartre.* Anchor Book. Garden City: Doubleday and Co., 1966.
————. *The Tragic Finale: An Essay on the Philosophy of Jean Paul Sartre.* Torchbook. New York: Harper and Bros., 1960.
Diem, Hermann. *Kierkegaard.* Trans. David Green. Richmond: John Knox Press, 1966.
————. *Kierkegarrd's Dialectic of Existence.* Trans. Harold Knight. New York: Frederick Ungar Co., 1965.
Diemer, Alwin. *Edmund Husserl: Versuch einer systematischen Darstellung seiner Phänomenologie.* Meisenheim am Glan: Hain, 1956.
Dinan, Stephen. "Intentionality to the Introduction to *Being and Nothingness.*" *Research in Phenomenology,* I (1971).
Dinkler, Erich. "Existentialist Interpretation of the New Testament." *Journal of Religion,* XXXII (1952), 87-96.
————. "Martin Heidegger." *Christianity and the Existentialists.* Ed. Carl Michalson. New York: Charles Scribner's Sons, 1956.
Dondeyne, Albert. *Contemporary European Thought and Christian Faith.* Trans. Ernan McMullin. Pittsburgh: Duquesne University Press, 1958.
Doyle, John. "Heidegger and Scholastic Metaphysics." *The Modern Schoolman,* XLIX (1972), 201-20.
Driscoll, Giles. "Heidegger: A Response to Nihilism." *Philosophy Today,* XI (1967), 17-37.
Dupré, Louis. *Kierkegaard as Theologian.* New York: Sheed and Ward, 1963.

Earle, William; Edie, James; and Wild, John. *Christianity and Existentialism.* Evanston: Northwestern University Press, 1963.
Ebner, Ferdinand. "Word and Personality." *Philosophy Today,* XI (1967), 233-37.
Edwards, Rem. *Reason and Religion.* New York: Harcourt Brace Jovanovich Inc., 1972.
van Ewijk, Thomas. *Gabriel Marcel.* Trans. Matthew van Velzen. Deus Book. Glen Rock: Paulist Press, 1965.

Fabro, Cornelio. "Faith and Reason in Kierkegaard." *A Kierkegaard Critique.* Ed. Howard Johnson and Niels Thulstrup. Chicago: Henry Regnery Co., 1967.
————. *God in Exile: Modern Atheism.* New York and Westminster: Newman Press, 1968.
Faber, Marvin. *The Aims of Phenomenology.* Torchbook. New York and Evanston: Harper and Row, 1966.
————. *The Foundation of Phenomenology.* Albany: State University of New York Press, 1943.
Finkelstein, Sidney. *Existentialism and Alienation in American Literature.* New York: International Publishers, 1965.
Fitzgerald, Eugene. "Gabriel Marcel." *Existentialist Thinkers and Thought.* Ed. Frederick Patka. New York: Citadel Press, 1964.
Foulquié, Paul. *Existentialism.* Trans. Kathleen Raine. London: Dennis Dobson, 1963.
Freeman, E. *The Theatre of Albert Camus.* London: Methuen and Co., 1971.
Friedman, Maurice. *To Deny Our Nothingness.* Delta Book. New York: Dell Publishers, 1967.
————. *Martin Buber: The Life of Dialogue.* New York: Harper and Row, 1960.
————, ed. *The Worlds of Existentialism: A Critical Reader.* New York: Random House, 1964.
Frings, Manfred, ed. *Heidegger and the Quest for Truth.* Chicago: Quadrangle Books, 1968

Gaidenko, Pyama. "Existentialism and the Individual." *Existentialism versus Marxism.* Ed. George Novack. Delta Book. Dell Publishing Co., 1966.
Gallagher, Kenneth. *The Philosophy of Gabriel Marcel.* New York: Fordham University Press, 1962.
Gallagher, Thomas. "Kierkegaard." *Existentialist Thinkers and Thought.* Ed. Frederick

Patka.. New York: Citadel Press, 1964.
Garelick, Herbert. *The Anti-Christianity of Kierkegaard.* The Hague: Martinus Nijhoff, 1965.
Garvey, Edwin. *Process Theology and Secularization.* Houston: Lumen Christi Press, 1972.
Gerber, Rudolph. "Focal Points in Recent Heideggerian Scholarship." *The New Scholasticism,* XLII (1968), 561-77.
————. "Marcel and the Experiential Road to Metaphysics." *Philosophy Today,* XII (1968), 262-81.
Gibson, Arthur. *The Faith of the Atheist.* New York and Evanston: Harper and Row, 1968.
Gill, Jerry, ed. *Essays on Kierkegaard.* Minneapolis: Burgess Publishing Co., 1969.
Gilson, Étienne. "On the Art of Misunderstanding Thomism." *In Search of Saint Thomas Aquinas, McAuley Lectures,* 1966. West Hartford: Saint Joseph College, 1966.
————. "On Behalf of the Handmaid." *Renewal of Religious Thought.* Ed. Lawrence Shook. 2 vols. Montreal: Palm Publishers, 1968.
————. "Can the Existence of God Still Be Demonstrated?" *Saint Thomas Aquinas and Philosophy, McAuley Lectures,* 1960. West Hartford: Saint Joseph College, 1961.
————. *The Christian Philosophy of Saint Thomas Aquinas.* New York: Random House, 1956.
————. *Elements of Christian Philosophy.* Mentor-Omega Book. New York: New American Library of World Literature, 1960.
————. *Existentialisme Chrétien.* Paris, 1947.
————. *A Gilson Reader.* Ed. Anton Pegis. Image Book. Garden City: Doubleday and Co., 1957.
————. *History of Christian Philosophy in the Middle Ages.* New York: Random House, 1955.
————. "The Idea of God and the Difficulties of Atheism." *Philosophy Today,* XIII (1969), 174-205.
————. *Spirit of Medieval Philosophy.* New York: Charles Scribner's Sons, 1940.
————. "A Unique Philosopher." *Philosophy Today,* IV (1960), 278-89.
Gilson, Étienne, Langan, Thomas; and Maurer, Armand. *Recent Philosophy: Hegel to the Present.* New York: Random House, 1962.
————. "What Is Christian Philosophy?" *A Gilson Reader.* Ed. Anton Pegis. Image Book. Garden City: Doubleday and Co., 1957.
Glitzenstein, A. C. *The Arrest and Liberation of Rabbi Shneur Zalman of Liadi.* Brooklyn: Kehot Publishing Society, 1964.
Gray, L. Glenn. "Poets and Thinkers: Their Kindred Roles in the Philosophy of Martin Heidegger." *Phenomenology and Existentialism.* Ed. Edward Lee and Maurice Mandelbaum. Baltimore: John's Hopkins Press, 1967.
Greene, Norman. *Jean Paul Sartre: The Existentialist Ethic.* Ann Arbor: University of Michigan Press, 1963.
Greenlee, Douglas. "Sartre: Presuppositions of Freedom." *Philosophy Today,* XII (1968), 176-83.
Grene, Marjorie. *Introduction to Existentialism.* Phoenix Book. Chicago and London: University of Chicago Press, 1962.
Gründer, Karlfried. "Heidegger's Critique of Science in its Historical Background." *Philosophy Today,* VII (1963), 15-32.
Gurwitsch, Aaron. "Husserl's Theory of Intentionality of Consciousness in Historical Perspective." *Phenomenology and Existentialism.* Ed. Edward Lee and Maurice Mandelbaum. Baltimore: Johns Hopkins Press, 1967.

Hamer, Jerome. *Karl Barth.* Trans. Dominic Maruca. Westminster: Newman Press, 1962.
Hamilton, Kenneth. *The Promise of Kierkegaard.* Philadelphia and New York: J. B. Lipincott Co., 1969.
Hanna, Thomas. "Albert Camus and the Christian Faith." *Camus: A Collection of Critical Essays.* Ed. Germaine Brée. Englewood Cliffs: Prentice-Hall, 1962.
————. *The Thought and Art of Albert Camus.* Chicago: Henry Regnery Co., 1958.
Harries, Karsten. "Martin Heidegger: The Search for Meaning." *Existential Philosophers: Kierkegaard to Merleau-Ponty.* Ed. George Schrader. New York: McGraw-Hill Book Co., 1967.
Hay, William; Singer, Marcus, eds. *Reason and the Common Good: Selected Essays of Arthur Murphy.* Englewood Cliffs: Prentice-Hall, 1963.
Hayward, John. *Existentialism and Religious Liberalism.* Boston: Beacon Press; Toronto: S.J. Reginald Saunders Co., 1962.
Heidegger, Martin. *Being and Time.* Trans. John Macquarrie and Edward Robinson. New York and Evanston: Harper and Row, 1962.
————. "Brief über dem Humanismus." *Platons Lehre von der Wahrheit.* Bern: A. Francke, 1947.
————. *Einführung in die Metaphysik.* Tübingen: Niemeyer, 1953.
————. "On the Essence of Truth." *Existence and Being.* Ed. Werner Brock. Chicago: Henry Regnery Co., 1949.
————. *German Existentialism.* Trans. Dagobert Runes. New York: Philosophical Library, 1965.
————. "German Students." *German Existentialism.* Trans. Dagobert Runes. New York: Philosophical Library, 1965.

————. "Aus einem Gespräch von der Sprache." *Unterwegs zur Sprache.* Pfullingen: Neske, 1933.
————. "The Idea of Phenomenology." Trans. John Deely, Joseph Novak and Eva Leo. *The New Scholasticism,* XLIV (1970), 325-344.
————. *An Introduction to Metaphysics.* Trans. Ralph Manheim. Anchor Book. New York: Doubleday and Co., 1961.
————. *Platons Lehre von der Wahrheit. Mit einem Brief über den "Humanismus."* Bern: Francke, 1947.
————. *The Question of Being.* Trans. William Kluback and Jean Wilde. New York: Twayne Publishers, 1958.
————. *Die Selbstbehauptung der deutschen Universität.* Breslau: Verlag Kirn, 1933.
————. "The University under the New Reich." *German Existentialism.* Trans. Dagobert Runes. New York: Philosophical Library, 1965.
————. *Unterwege zur Sprache.* Pfullingen: Neske, 1959.
————. "The Way Back into the Ground of Metaphysics." *Existentialism from Dostoevsky to Sartre.* Ed. Walter Kaufmann. New York: World Publishing Co., 1956.
————. "What Is Metaphysics?" *Existence and Being.* Ed. Werner Brock. Gateway Book. Chicago: Henry Regnery Co., 1949.
————. *What Is A Thing?* Trans. W. B. Barton and Vera Deutsch. Gateway Book. Chicago: Henry Regnery Co., 1970.
Heinemann, F. H. *Existentialism and the Modern Predicament.* Torchbook. New York: Harper and Bros., 1958.
Henriksen, Auge. *Methods and Results of Kierkegaard Studies in Scandinavia.* Copenhagen: Ejnar Munksgaard.
Herberg, Will. *Four Existentialist Theologians.* Anchor Book. New York: Doubleday and Co., 1958.
————. *Martin Buber: Personalist Philosopher in an Age of Depersonalization.* McAuley Lecture XV. West Hartford: McAuley Institute of Religious Studies Saint Joseph College, 1972.
————. *The Writings of Martin Buber.* New York: Meridian Books, 1956.
Higgins, Thomas. *Ethical Theories in Conflict.* Milwaukee: Bruce Publishing Co., 1967.
Hilsenrad, Zalman Aryeh. *The Baal Shem Tov.* Brooklyn: Kehot Publishing Society, 1969.
Hodes, Aubrey. *Martin Buber: An Intimate Portrait.* New York: Viking Press, 1971.
Hollander, Lee. *Selections from the Writings of Kierkegaard.* Garden City: Doubleday and Co., 1960.
Hopper, Stanley. "On the Naming of the Gods in Hölderlin and Rilke." *Christianity and the Existentialists.* Ed. Carl Michalson. New York: Charles Scribner's Sons, 1956.
Hubben, William. *Dostoevsky, Kierkegaard, Nietzsche and Kafka.* New York: Collier Books, 1962.
Hühnerfeld, P. *In Sachen Heideggers, Versuch über ein deutsches Genie.* Hamburg, 1959.

Jeanson, Francis. "Moral Perspectives in Sartre's Thought." *Contemporary European* Press, 1952.
Jeanson, Francis. "Moral Perspectices in Sartre's Thought." *Contemporary European Ethics.* Ed. Joseph Kockelmans. Anchor Book. Garden City: Doubleday and Co., 1972.
————. "Pessimism and Optimism in Sartre's Thought." *Sartre.* Ed. Mary Warnock. Anchor Book. Garden City: Doubleday and Co., 1971.
Jeffré, Claude. "Bultmann on Kerygma and History." *Rudolf Bultmann in Catholic Thought.* Ed. Thomas O'Meara and Donald Weisser. New York: Herder and Herder, 1968.
Johnson, Howard and Thulstrup, Niels, eds., *A Kierkegaard Critique.* Gateway Book. Chicago: Regnery Co., 1967.
Jolivet, Régis. *Les Doctrines Existentialistes de Kierkegaard à Sartre.* Paris, 1948.
————. *Introduction to Kierkegaard.* Trans. W. H. Barber. London: Frederick Muller, 1950.
————. *Sartre: The Theology of the Absurd.* Trans. Wesley Piersol. Westminster, New York: Newman Press, 1967.

Kaufmann, Walter. *Critique of Religion and Philosophy.* Anchor Book. New York: Doubleday and Co., 1961.
————. *Existentialism from Dostoevsky to Sartre.* New York: World Publishing 1956.
————. *From Shakespeare to Existentialism.* Anchor Book. Garden City: Doubleday and Co., 1960.
Keen, Sam. *Gabriel Marcel.* Richmond: John Knox Press, 1967.
Kegley, Charles and Bretall, Robert, eds. *The Theology of Paul Tillich.* New York: Macmillan Co., 1952.
Kierkegaard, Søren. *Armed Neutrality and An Open Letter.* Ed. trans. Howard Hong and Edna Hong. Clarion Book. New York: Simon and Schuster, 1969.
————. *Attack Upon Christendom.* Trans. Walter Lowrie. Boston: Beacon Press, 1966.
————. *Concluding Unscientific Postscript to the Philosophical Fragments.* Trans. David Swenson and Walter Lowrie. Princeton: University Press, 1960.

————. *Either/Or.* Trans. Walter Lowrie. Anchor Book. 2 vols. Garden City: Doubleday and Co., 1959.
————. *Fear and Trembling.* Trans. Walter Lowrie. Anchor Book. Garden City: Doubleday and Co., 1954.
————. "The Instant." *Attack Upon Christendom.* Trans. Walter Lowrie. Boston: Beacon Press, 1966.
————. *Journals.* Ed. Alexander Dru. Torchbook. New York and Evanston: Harper and Row, 1959.
————. *Point of View.* Trans. Walter Lowrie. Oxford: University Press, 1939.
————. *Samlede Veerker.* Ed. A. B. Drachmann; J. L. Heiberg; and H. O. Lange. 2nd edit. 15 vols. Copenhagen: Gyldendalske Boghandel, Nordisk Forlag, 1920-1936.
————. *Sickness Unto Death.* Trans. Walter Lowrie. Princeton: University Press, 1941.
————. *Stages on Life's Way.* Trans. Walter Lowrie. New York: Schocken Books, 1967.
————. *Training in Christianity.* Trans. Walter Lowrie. Princeton: University Press, 1944.
King, Adele. *Albert Camus.* New York: Grove Press, 1964.
King, Magda. *Heidegger's Philosophy. A Guide to His Basic Thought.* Delta Book. Dell Publishers, 1966.
Kline, George. "Existentialist Rediscovery of Hegel and Marx." *Sartre: A Collection of Critical Essays.* Ed. Mary Warnock. Anchor Book. Garden City: Doubleday and Co., 1971.
Kluback, William and Wilde, Jean, eds. *The Question of Being.* New York: Twayne Publishers, 1958.
Kockelmans, Joseph, ed. *Contemporary European Ethics.* Anchor Book. Garden City: Doubleday and Co., 1972.
————. *Edmund Husserl's Phenomenological Psychology.* Pittsburgh: Duquesne University Press, 1967.
————. *A First Introduction to Husserl's Phenomenology.* Pittsburgh: Duquesne University Press, 1967.
————. *Martin Heidegger: A First Introduction to His Philosophy.* Pittsburgh: Duquesne University Press, 1965.
————. "Language, Meaning and Ek-Sistence." *Phenomenology in Perspective.* Ed. Francis J. Smith. The Hague: Martinus Nijhoff, 1970.
————. ed. *The Philosophy of Edmund Husserl and its Interpretation.* Anchor Book. Garden City: Doubleday and Co., 1967.
————. "What Is Phenomenology?" *Phenomenology: The Philosophy of Edmund Husserl and Its Interpretation.* Ed. Joseph Kockelmans. Anchor Book. Garden City: Doubleday and Co., 1967.
Kohl, Herbert. *The Age of Complexity.* Mentor Book. New York and Toronto: The New American Library of World Literature, 1965.
Kranzler, Gershon, *Rabbi Shneur Zalman of Liadi.* Brooklyn: Kehot Publishing Society, 1967.
Kreyche, Robert. *The Betrayal of Wisdom.* Staten Island: Alba House, 1972.
Kroner, Richard. "Heidegger's Private Religion." *Union Seminary Quarterly Review.* XI, 4.
Kuhn, Helmut. *Encounter With Nothingness.* London: Methuen and Co., 1951.

Lafarge, René. *Jean Paul Sartre: His Philosophy.* Trans. Marina Smyth-Kok. Notre Dame: Notre Dame University Press, 1970.
Laing, R. D. and Cooper, D. G. *Reason and Violence: A Decade of Sartre's Philosophy, 1950-1960.* New York: Random House, 1971.
Landgrebe, Ludwig. *Major Problems in Contemporary European Philosophy.* Trans. Kurt Reinhardt. New York: Ungar Press, 1966.
Landsberg, Paul-Louis. "The Experience of Death." *Essays in Phenomenology.* Ed. Maurice Natanson. The Hague: Martinus Nijhoff, 1966.
Langan, Thomas. "The Future of Phenomenology." *Phenomenology in Perspective.* Ed. Francis J. Smith. The Hague: Martinus Nijhoff, 1970.
————. *The Meaning of Heidegger.* New York and London: Columbia University Press, 1961.
Langiulli, Nino, ed. *The Existentialist Tradition.* Garden City: Doubleday and Co., 1971.
Lapointe, François. "Bibliography on Gabriel Marcel." *The Modern Schoolman,* XLIX (1971), 23-49.
Lauer, Quentin. *Phenomenology: Its Genesis and Prospect.* Torchbook. New York and Evanston: Harper and Row, 1965.
Lawrence, Nathaniel and O'Connor, Daniel, eds. *Readings in Existential Phenomenology.* Englewood Cliffs: Prentice-Hall, 1967.
Lebesque, Morvan. *Portrait of Camus.* Trans. T. C. Sharman. New York: Herder and Herder, 1971.
Lebowitz, Naomi. *Humanism and the Absurd in the Modern Novel.* Evanston: Northwestern University Press, 1971.
Lee, Edward and Mandelbaum, Maurice, eds. *Phenomenology and Existentialism.* Baltimore: Johns Hopkins Press, 1967.
LeFevre, Perry. *The Prayers of Kierkegaard.* Chicago and London: University of Chicago Press, 1969.
Lepp, Ignace. *Atheism in Our Time.* New York: Macmillan Co., 1963.
Lescoe, Francis, ed. *St. Thomas Aquinas: Treatise on Separate Substances.* West

Hartford: Saint Joseph College, 1963.
Lindstrom, Valter. "The Problem of Objectivity and Subjectivity in Kierkegaard." *A Kierkegaard Critique*. Ed. Howard Johnson and Niels Thulstrup. Gateway Book. Chicago: Henry Regnery Co., 1962.
Löwith, Karl. *Heidegger: Denker in dürftiger Zeit*. Frankfurt: S. Fischer Verlag, 1953.
————. "Les implications politiques de la philosophie de l'existence chez Heidegger." *Les Temps Modernes*, II (1946-1947).
————. *Nature, History and Existentialism*. Evanston: Northwestern University Press, 1966.
Lowrie, Walter. *Kierkegaard*. 2 vols. New York: Harper and Bros., 1962.
————. *A Short Life of Kierkegaard*. Princeton: University Press, 1965.
Luijpen, William. *Existential Phenomenology*. Pittsburgh: Duquesne University Press, 1962.
————. *Phenomenology and Humanism*. Pittsburgh: Duquesne University Press, 1966.
Luijpen, William and Koren, Henry. *A First Introduction to Existential Phenomenology*. Pittsburgh: Duquesne University Press, 1967.

MacIntyre, Alisdair. "Existentialism." *Sartre*. Ed. Mary Warnock. Garden City: Doubleday and Co., 1971.
Mackey, Louis. *Kierkegaard: A Kind of Poet*. Philadelphia: University of Pennsylvania Press, 1971.
Macquarrie, John. *An Existentialist Theology: A Comparison of Heidegger and Bultmann*. Torchbook. New York and Evanston: Harper and Row, 1965.
————. *Martin Heidegger*. Richmond: John Knox Press, 1968.
————. *The Scope of Demythologizing: Bultmann and His Critics*. Torchbook. New York and Evanston: Harper and Row, 1966.
————. *Twentieth Century Religious Thought*. New York and Evanston: Harper and Row, 1963.
Magnes, Judah and Buber, Martin. *Arab-Jewish Unity*. London: Victor Gollancz, 1947.
Magnus, Bernd. *Heidegger's Metahistory of Philosophy: Amor Fati, Being and Truth*. The Hague: Martinus Nijhoff, 1970.
Malantschuk, Gregor. *Kierkegaard's Thought*. Trans. Howard Hong and Edna Hong. Princeton: University Press, 1971.
Manser, Anthony. *Sartre: A Philosophic Study*. New York: Oxford University Press, 1967.
Maquet, Albert. *Albert Camus: The Invincible Summer*. London: John Calder, 1958.
Marcel, Gabriel. "Authentic Humanness and its Existential Primordial Assumptions." Baldwin Schwarz, *The Human Person and the World of Values*. New York: Fordham University Press, 1960.
————. *Being and Having*. Torchbook. New York and Evanston: Harper and Row, 1965.
————. *Le Coeur des Autres*. Paris: Grasset, 1921.
————. "Contemporary Atheism and the Religious Mind." *Philosophy Today*, IV (1960), 252-62.
————. *Creative Fidelity*. Trans. Robert Rosthal. New York: Farrar, Straus and Giroux, 1964.
————. "Desire and Hope." Trans. Nathaniel Lawrence. *Existential Phenomenology*. Ed. Lawrence and Daniel O'Connor. Englewood Cliffs: Prentice-Hall, 1967.
————. "The Drama of the Soul." *Three Plays*. Mermaid Dramabook. New York: Hill and Wang, 1965.
————. *The Existential Background of Human Dignity*. Cambridge: Harvard University Press, 1963.
————. "Foreword." Vincent Miceli, *Ascent to Being*. New York: Desclée, 1965.
————. *Homo Viator: An Introduction to a Metaphysic of Hope*. Trans. Emma Craufurd. Torchbook. New York: Harper and Bros., 1962.
————. *Man Against Mass Society*. Trans. G. D. Fraser. Gateway Book. Chicago: Henry Regnery Co., 1962.
————. *Metaphysical Journal*. Trans. Bernard Wall. Chicago: Henry Regnery Co., 1962.
————. *Le Monde Cassé*. Paris: Desclée de Brouwer, 1933.
————. *The Mystery of Being*. Gateway Book. 2 vols. Chicago: Henry Regnery Co., 1960.
————. *Philosophical Fragments, 1909-1914 and The Philosopher and Peace*. Notre Dame: University of Notre Dame Press, 1965.
————. *The Philosophy of Existentialism*. Trans. Manya Harari. New York: Citadel Press, 1971.
————. *Presence and Immortality*. Pittsburgh: Duquesne University Press, 1967.
————. *Problematic Man*. Trans. Brian Thompson. New York: Herder and Herder, 1967.
————. *Du refus à l'invocation*. Paris: Gallimard, 1940.
————. *Searchings*. New York and Westminster: Newman Press, 1967.
————. "Some Reflections on Existentialism." *Philosophy Today*, VIII (1964), 248-57.
Marsak, Leonard, ed. *French Philosophers from Descartes to Sartre*. Meridian Book. Cleveland and New York: World Publishing Co., 1961.
Martin, Bernard, ed. *Great 20th Century Jewish Philosophers: Shestov, Rosenzweig, Buber*. New York: Macmillan Co., 1970.

Martin, Vincent. *Existentialism.* Washington: The Thomist Press, 1962.
McCarthy, Donald. "Marcel's Absolute Thou." *Philosophy Today* X (1966), 175-81.
McNeill, John. "Martin Buber's Philosophy of History." *International Philosophical Quarterly,* VI (1966), 90-100.
Medina, Angel. "Husserl on the Nature of the Subject." *The New Scholasticism,* XLV (1971), 547-72.
Mehl, Roger. *Images of Man.* Trans. James Farley. Richmond: John Knox Press, 1965.
Mehta, J. L. *The Philosophy of Martin Heidegger.* Torchbook. New York and Evanston: Harper and Row, 1971.
Miceli, Vincent. *Ascent to Being.* New York: Desclée, 1965.
—————. *The Gods of Atheism.* New Rochelle: Arlington House, 1971.
Michalson, Carl, ed. *Christianity and the Existentialists.* New York: Charles Scribner's Sons, 1956.
—————. *The Witness of Kierkegaard.* Reflection Book. New York: Associated Press, 1960.
Mihalich, Joseph. *Existentialism and Thomism.* New York: The Philosophical Library, 1960.
—————. "Jean Paul Sartre." *Existentialist Thinkers and Thought.* Ed. Frederick Patka. New York: Citadel Press, 1964.
Moenkemeyer, Heinz. "Martin Heidegger." *Existentialist Thinkers and Thought.* Ed. Frederick Patka. New York: Citadel Press, 1964.
Moeller, Charles. *Man and Salvation in Literature.* Trans. Charles Quinn. Notre Dame: University of Notre Dame Press, 1970.
Molina, Fernando. *Existentialism as Philosophy.* Englewood Cliffs: Prentice-Hall, 1962.
—————. "The Husserlian Ideal of a Pure Phenomenology." *An Invitation to Phenomenology.* Ed. James Edie. Chicago: Quadrangle Books, 1965.
—————. *The Sources of Existentialism As Philosophy.* Englewood Cliffs: Prentice-Hall, 1969.
Molnar, Thomas. *Sartre: Ideology of Our Time.* New York: Funk and Wagnalls, 1968.
Morrison, Robert. *Primitive Existentialism.* New York: The Philosophical Library, 1967.
Murchland, Bernard. "The Dark Night Before the Coming of Grace." *Camus: A Collection of Critical Essays.* Ed. Germaine Brée. Englewood Cliffs: Prentice-Hall, 1962.
Murdock, Iris. *Sartre: Romantic Rationalist.* New Haven: Yale University Press, 1961.
Murphy, Arthur. "On Kierkegaard's Claim that Truth is Subjectivity." *Essays on Kierkegaard.* Ed. Jerry Gill. Minneapolis: Burgess Publishing Co., 1969.

Naess, Arno. *Four Modern Philosophers: Carnap, Wittgenstein, Heidegger, Sartre.* Trans. Alastair Hannay. Chicago: University of Chicago Press, 1968.
Natanson, Maurice, ed. *Essays in Phenomenology.* The Hague: Martinus Nijhoff, 1966.
Nauman, St. Elmo. *The New Dictionary of Existentialism.* Secaucus, N.J.: Citadel Press, 1972.
Niebuhr, H. Richard. "Søren Kierkegaard." *Christianity and the Existentialists.* Ed. Carl Michalson. New York: Charles Scribner's Sons, 1956.
Nota, John. *Phenomenology and History.* Chicago: Loyola University Press, 1967.
Novack, George. *Existentialism versus Marxism.* New York: Dell Publishing Co., 1966.

O'Brien, Conor Cruise. *Albert Camus of Europe and Africa.* New York: Viking Press, 1970.
Odajnyk, Walter. *Marxism and Existentialism.* Anchor Book. Garden City: Doubleday and Co., 1965.
Olafson, Frederick. "Authenticity and Obligation." *Sartre.* Ed. Mary Warnock. Anchor Book. Garden City: Doubleday and Co., 1971.
—————. *Principles and Persons.* Baltimore and London: Johns Hopkins Press, 1970.
Olson, Robert. *An Introduction to Existentialism.* New York: Dover Publications, 1962.
O'Malley, John. *The Fellowship of Being.* The Hague: Martinus Nijhoff, 1966.
O'Meara, Thomas and Weisser, Donald, eds. *Rudolf Bultmann in Catholic Thought.* New York: Herder and Herder, 1968.
Onimus, Jean. *Albert Camus and Christianity.* Trans. Emmett Parker. University, Alabama: University of Alabama Press, 1970.
Owens, Joseph. *The Doctrine of Being in the Aristotelian Metaphysics.* Toronto: Pontifical Institute of Medieval Studies, 1957.

Padovano, Anthony. *The Estranged God.* New York: Sheed and Ward, 1966.
Palmer, Richard. *Hermeneutics.* Evanston: Northwestern University Press, 1969.
Pappenheim, Fritz. *The Alienation of Modern Man.* New York and London: Monthly Review Press, 1968.
Parain-Vial, Jeanne. "Notes on the Ontology of Gabriel Marcel." *Philosophy Today,* IV (1960), 271-77.
Parker, Emmett. *Albert Camus: The Artist in the Arena.* Milwaukee and London: University of Wisconsin Press, 1966.
—————. "Preface." Jean Onimus, *Albert Camus and Christianity.* Trans. Emmett Parker. University, Alabama: University of Alabama Press, 1970.
Patka, Frederick, ed. *Existentialist Thinkers and Thought.* New York: Citadel Press, 1964.
—————. "Five Existentialist Themes." *Existentialist Thinkers and Thought.* Ed. Frederick Patka. New York: Citadel Press, 1964.

Patri, Aimé. "Remarques sur une nouvelle doctrine de la liberté." Deucalion, I:79 (1946).
Paul, Leslie. The Meaning of Human Existence. London: Faber and Faber, 1949.
Pax, C. V. "Philosophical Reflection: Gabriel Marcel." The New Scholasticism, XXXVIII (1964), 159-77.
Pegis, Anton, ed. Basic Writings of St. Thomas Aquinas. 2 vols. New York: Random House, 1945.
————. "St. Bonaventure, St. Francis and Philosophy." Medieval Studies, XV (1953), 1-13.
————. ed. A Gilson Reader. Image Book. Garden City: Doubleday and Co., 1957.
————. St. Thomas and Philosophy. Milwaukee: Marquette University Press, 1964.
————. "Thomism as Philosophy." St. Thomas Aquinas and Philosophy. Mc-Auley Lectures, 1960. West Hartford: Saint Joseph College, 1961.
————. "Thomism 1966." In Search of St. Thomas Aquinas. McAuley Lectures 1966. West Hartford: Saint Joseph College, 1966.
Perkins, Robert. Soren Kierkegaard. Richmond: John Knox Press, 1969.
Peukert, Helmut. "Bultmann and Heidegger." Rudolf Bultmann in Catholic Thought. Ed. Thomas O'Meara and Donald Weisser. New York: Herder and Herder, 1968.
Peyre, Henri. "Camus the Pagan." Camus: A Collection of Critical Essays. Ed. Germaine Brée. Englewood Cliffs: Prentice-Hall, 1962.
Pfuetze, Paul. Self, Society, Existence. Torchbook, New York: Harper and Bros., 1961.
Plato, Sophistes. The Dialogues of Plato. Trans. B. Jowett. 2 vols. New York: Random House, 1937.
Price, George. The Narrow Pass. New York Toronto: McGraw-Hill Book Co., 1963.
Prufer, Thomas. "Dasein and the Ontological Status of the Speaker of Philosophical Discourse." Twentieth Century Thinkers. Ed. John Ryan. Staten Island: Alba House, 1965.

Rahner, Karl. "The Concept of Existential Philosophy in Heidegger." Philosophy Today, XIII (1969), 126-37.
Reinhardt, Kurt. The Existentialist Revolt. New York: Frederick Ungar, 1964.
Rhein, Philip. Albert Camus. New York: Twayne Publishing Co., 1969.
Richardson, William. "Heidegger's Critique of Science." The New Scholasticism, XLII (1968), 511-36.
————. Heidegger: Through Phenomenology to Thought. The Hague: Martinus Nijhoff, 1963.
Richter, Liselotte. "Kierkegaard's Position in his Religio-Sociological Situation." A Kierkegaard Critique. Ed. Howard Johnson and Niels Thulstrup. Chicago: Henry Regnery Co., 1967.
Roberts, David. Existentialism and Religious Belief. New York: Oxford University Press, 1959.
Rohde, Peter. Søren Kierkegaard. Trans. Alan Williams. New York: Humanities Press, 1963.
————. "Soren Kierkegaard: The Father of Existentialism." Essays in Kierkegaard. Ed. Jerry Gill. Minneapolis: Burgess Publishing Co., 1969.
Rollin, Bernard. "Heidegger's Philosophy of History in Being and Time." Modern Schoolman, XLIX (1972), 97-112.
Rombach, Heinrich. "Reflections on Heidegger's Lecture 'Time and Being.'" Philosophy Today, X (1966), 19-29.
Rotenstreich, Nathan. "Buber's Dialogical Philosophy: The Historical Dimension." Philosophy Today, III (1959), 168-75.
————. "Some Problems in Buber's Dialogical Philosophy." Philosophy Today, III (1959), 151-67.
Roubiczek, Paul. Existentialism For and Against. Cambridge: University Press, 1964.
Ryan, John, ed. Twentieth Century Thinkers. Staten Island: Alba House, 1965.

Sallis, John. "World, Finitude, Temporality in the Philosophy of Martin Heidegger." Philsophy Today, IX (1965), 40-52.
Philosophy Today, IX (1965), 40-52.
Salvan, Jacques. To Be and Not To Be: An Analysis of Jean Paul Sartre's Ontology. Detroit: Wayne State University Press, 1962.
Sanborn, Patricia. Existentialism. New York: Western Publishing Co., 1968.
Sanders, Ronald. "Joyous Days for the 'Spark' of Judaism." New York Times, CXXII (Oct. 8, 1972), 6-8.
Sartre, Jean Paul. The Age of Reason. Trans. Eric Sutton. New York: Bantam Books, 1959.
————. Being and Nothingness: An Essay of Phenomenological Ontology. Trans. Hazel Barnes. New York: The Philosophical Library, 1956.
————. The Devil and the Good Lord and Two Other Plays. Trans. Kitty Black. New York: Vintage, 1962.
————. Existentialism and Humanism. Trans. Philip Mairet. London: Methuen and Co., 1960.
————. Existential Psychoanalysis. Chicago: Henry Regnery Co., 1962.
————. "An Explication of The Stranger." Trans. Annette Michelson. Camus: A Collection of Critical Essays. Ed. Germaine Brée. Englewood Cliffs: Prentice-Hall, 1962.
————. Figaro littéraire., April 13, 1946.
————. The Flies. Trans. Stuart Gilbert. New York: Alfred Knopf, 1947.
————. Imagination. Trans. Forrest Williams. Ann Arbor: University of Michigan

Press, 1962.
————. *Nausea.* Trans. Lloyd Alexander. New York: New Directions Publishing Co., 1964.
————. *Réflexions sur la question juive.* Paris: Morihien, 1947.
————. *The Reprieve.* Trans. Eric Sutton. New York: Alfred Knopf, 1947.
————. "Tribute to Albert Camus." *Camus: A Collection of Critical Essays.* Ed. Germaine Brée. Englewood Cliffs: Prentice-Hall, 1962.
————. *The Words.* Trans. Bernard Frechtman. Crest Book. New York: Fawcett World Library, 1966.
Scanlon, John. "Intolerable Human Responsibility." *Research in Phenomenology,* I (1970), 75-90.
Schimanski, Stefan. "Foreword." *Existence and Being.* Ed. Werner Brock. Gateway Book. Chicago: Henry Regnery Co., 1949.
Schmitt, Richard. *Martin Heidegger on Being Human.* New York: Random House, 1969.
Schneeberger, Guido. "Supplement to Heidegger: Documents of His Life and Thought." *The Worlds of Existentialism.* Ed. Maurice Friedman. New York: Random House, 1964.
Schneersohn, J. I. *Lubavitcher Rabbi's Memoirs,* Brooklyn: Kehot Publication 1960.
————. *Some Aspects of Chabad Chassidim.* Brooklyn: Machne Israel Publishing Co., 1961.
————. *The 'Tzemach Tzedek' and the Haskala Movement.* Brooklyn: Kehot Publication Society, 1969.
Schrader, George, ed. *Existential Philosophers: Kierkegaard to Merleau-Ponty.* New York: McGraw-Hill Book Co., 1967.
Schrag, Calvin. "Phenomenology, Ontology and History in the Philosophy of Heidegger." *The Philosophy of Edmund Husserl and Its Interpretation.* Ed. Joseph Kockelmans. Anchor Book. Garden City: Doubleday and Co., 1967.
————. "Whitehead and Heidegger." *Philosophy Today,* IV (1960), 27-35.
Schrag, Oswald. *Existence, Existenz and Transcendence.* Pittsburgh: Duquesne University Press, 1971.
Schwarz, Balduin. *The Human Person and the World of Values.* New York: Fordham University Press, 1960.
Sciacca, Michele. *Philosophical Trends in the Contemporary World.* Trans. Attilio Salerno. Notre Dame: University of Notre Dame Press, 1964.
Scott, Charles. "Heidegger's Attempt to Communicate a Mystery," *Philosophy Today,* X (1966), 132-41.
Scott, Nathan. *Albert Camus.* New York: Hillary House, 1962.
————. *The Unquiet Vision: Mirrors of Man in Existentialism.* New York and Cleveland: World Publishing Co., 1969.
Seidel, George. *Martin Heidegger and the Pre-Socratics.* Lincoln: University of Nebraska Press, 1964.
Sheridan, James. *Sartre: The Radical Conversion.* Athens, Ohio: Ohio University Press, 1969.
Sherover, Charles. *Heidegger, Kant and Time.* Bloomington and London: Indiana University Press, 1971.
Shinn, Roger. *The Existentialist Posture.* New York: Association Press, 1959.
————. *Man: The New Humanism.* Philadelphia: Westminster Press, 1968.
Shmueli, Adi. *Kierkegaard and Consciousness.* Trans. Naomi Handelman. Princeton: University Press, 1971.
Smith, Colin. *Contemporary French Philosophy.* New York: Barnes and Noble, 1964.
Smith, Chistopher. "Heidegger and Hegel and the Problem of Das Nichts." *International Philosophical Quarterly,* VIII (1968), 379-405.
————. "Heidegger's Critique of Absolute Knowledge." *The New Scholasticism,* XLV (1971), 56-86.
Smith, Francis Joseph. "Being and Subjectivity: Heidegger and Husserl." *Phenomenology in Perspective.* Ed. Francis J. Smith. The Hague: Martinus Nijhoff, 1970.
————, ed. *Phenomenology in Perspective.* The Hague: Martinus Nijhoff, 1970.
————. "Phenomenology of Encounter." *Philosophy Today,* VII (1963), 194-208.
Smith, Ronald Gregor. *Martin Buber.* Richmond: John Knox Press, 1967.
Søe, N. H. "Kierkegaard's Doctrine of the Paradox." *A Kierkegaard Critique.* Ed. Howard Johnson and Niels Thulstrup. Chicago: Henry Regnery Co., 1967.
Sokolowski, Robert. *The Formation of Husserl's Concept of Constitution.* The Hague: Martinus Nijhoff, 1964.
Shook, Lawrence, ed. *Renewal of Religious Thought.* 2 vols. Montreal: Palm Publishers, 1968.
Spiegelberg, Herbert. "On Some Uses of Phenomenology." *Phenomenology in Perspective.* Ed. Francis J. Smith. The Hague: Martinus Nijhoff, 1970.
————. *The Phenomenological Movement,* 2nd edit. 2 vols. The Hague: Martinus Nijhoff, 1965.
Spier, J. M. *Christianity and Existentialism* Trans. David Freeman. Philadelphia: Presbyterian and Reformed Publishing Co., 1953.
Stack, George. "The Basis of Kierkegaard's Concept of Essential Possibility." *The New Scholasticism,* XLVI (1972), 139-72.
————. "Kierkegaard and Nihilism." *Philosophy Today,* XIV (1970), 274-92.
Stern, Alfred. *Sartre: His Philosophy and Existential Psychoanalysis.* Delta Book. New York: Dell Publishing Co., 1967.
Streiker, Lowell. *The Promise of Buber.* Philadelphia: J. B. Lippincott Co., 1969.

Streller, Justus. *Jean Paul Sartre: To Freedom Condemned*. Trans. Wade Baskin. New York: The Philosophical Library, 1960.
Stumpf, Samuel. *Philosophy: History and Problems*. New York: McGraw-Hill Book Co., 1971.
Sweeney, Leo. "Marcel's Position on God." *The New Scholasticism*, XLIV (1970), 101-24.
————. *A Metaphysics of Authentic Existentialism*. Englewood Cliffs: Prentice-Hall, 1965.

Tcherikover, Victor. *Hellenistic Civilization and the Jews*. Philadelphia: JPS, 1959.
Thévenaz, Pierre. "What Is Phenomenology?" *An Invitation to Phenomenology*. Ed. James Edie. Chicago: Quadrangle Books, 1965.
Thody, Philip. *Albert Camus: A Study of His Work*. New York: Grove Press, 1957.
————. *Sartre*. New York: Charles Scribner's Sons, 1971.
Thomas, Aquinas St. *On the Truth of the Catholic Faith*. Ed. Anton Pegis, Bk. I. Garden City: Doubleday and Co., 1955.
Thomas, George. *Religious Philosophies of the West*. New York: Charles Scribner's Sons, 1965.
Tillich, Paul. "Existentialism and Psychotherapy." *Review of Existential Psychology and Psychiatry*, I, 1.
Troisfontaines, Roger. *De l'Existence à l'Etre*. 2 vols. Louvain: Nauwelaerts, 1968.
————. *What Is Existentialism?* Overview Studies. Albany: Magi Books, 1968.

Ussher, Arland. *Journey Through Dread*. London: Darwen Finlayson, 1955.

Vail, Loy. "Heidegger's Conception of Philosophy." *The New Scholasticism*, XLII (1968), 470-96.
Vandenberg, Donald. *Being and Education: An Essay in Existential Phenomenology*. Englewood Cliffs: Prentice-Hall, 1971.
Versényi, Laszlo. *Heidegger, Being and Truth*. New Haven and London: Yale University Press, 1965.
Vietta, Egon. *Die Seinsfrage bei Martin Heidegger*. Stuttgart: Curt Schwab, 1950.
Vycinas, Vincent. *Earth and Gods: An Introduction to the Philosophy of Martin Heidegger*. The Hague: Martinus Nijhoff, 1961.

de Waelhens, Alphonse. "The Phenomenology of the Body." *Readings in Existential Phenomenology*. Ed. Nathaniel Lawrence and Daniel O'Connor. Englewood Cliffs: Prentice-Hall, 1967.
Wahl, Jean. *A Short History of Existentialism*. Trans. Forrest Williams and Stanley Maron. New York: The Philosophical Library, 1949.
Walz, Hans. "Man's Freedom in Existentialism and in Christianity." *Cross Currents*, II, 1 (1951).
Warnock, Mary, ed. *Sartre*. Anchor Book. Garden City: Doubleday and Co., 1971.
————. *Existentialist Ethics*. New York: St. Martin's Press, 1967.
van de Water, Lambert. "The Work of Art, Man and Being: A Heideggerian Theme." *International Philosophical Quarterly*, IX (1969), 214-35.
Watson, James. "Heidegger's Hermeneutic Phenomenology." *Philosophy Today*, XV (1971), 30-43.
Weber, Renée. "A Critique of Heidegger's Concept of 'Solicitude.'" *The New Scholasticism*, XLII (1968), 537-60.
Weiss, Raymond. "Kierkegaard's 'Return' to Socrates." *The New Scholasticism*, XLV (1971), 573-83.
White Morton. *The Age of Analysis*. Mentor Book. New York: The New American Library of World Literature, 1964.
Wieczynski, Joseph. "A Note on Jean Paul Sartre: Monist or Dualist." *Philosophy Today*, XII (1968), 184-89.
Wild, John. *The Challenge of Existentialism*. Bloomington: Indiana University Press, 1959.
Wilde, Jean and Kimmel, Wade, eds. *The Search for Being*. New York: Noonday Press, 1962.
Wilhelmsen, Frederick. *The Paradoxical Structure of Existence*. Irving, Texas: University of Dallas Press, 1970.
Williams, J. Rodman. *Contemporary Existentialism and Christian Faith*. Englewood Cliffs: Prentice-Hall, 1965.
Wilson, Colin. *Introduction to the New Existetnialism*. Boston: Houghton Mifflin Co., 1966.
Winter, Gibson. *Being Free: Reflections on America's Cultural Revolution*. New York: Macmillan Co., 1970.
Wyschogrod, Michael. *Kierkegaard and Heidegger*. London: Routledge and Kegan Paul Ltd., 1954.

Zaner, Richard. *The Way of Phenomenology*. Pegasus Book. New York: Western Publishing Co., 1970.
Zuidema, Sieste. *Kierkegaard*. Trans. David Freeman. Philadelphia: Presbyterian and Reformed Publishing Co., 1960.
————. "Gabriel Marcel: A Critique." *Philosophy Today*, IV (1960), 283-88.

Index